T0373192

MODI'S INDIA

Modi's India

HINDU NATIONALISM AND THE RISE OF ETHNIC DEMOCRACY

CHRISTOPHE JAFFRELOT

TRANSLATED BY CYNTHIA SCHOCH

PRINCETON UNIVERSITY PRESS

PRINCETON & OXFORD

Published by Princeton University Press
41 William Street, Princeton, New Jersey 08540
99 Banbury Road, Oxford OX2 6JX

press.princeton.edu

First paperback printing, 2023
Paperback ISBN 9780691247908

The Library of Congress has cataloged the cloth edition as follows:

Names: Jaffrelot, Christophe, author. | Schoch, Cynthia, translator.
Title: Modi's India : Hindu nationalism and the rise of ethnic democracy /
    Christophe Jaffrelot ; translated by Cynthia Schoch.
Other titles: lnde de Modi. English
Description: Princeton : Princeton University Press, [2021] |
    Includes bibliographical references and index.
Identifiers: LCCN 2021006332 (print) | LCCN 2021006333 (ebook) |
    ISBN 9780691206806 (hardback) | ISBN 9780691223094 (ebook)
Subjects: LCSH: Modī, Narendra, 1950– | India—Politics and Government—
    21st century. | Hindutva. | Democracy—India—History—21st century.
Classification: LCC DS480.853 .J32513 2021 (print) | LCC DS480.853 (ebook) |
    DDC 954.05/33—dc23
LC record available at https://lccn.loc.gov/2021006332
LC ebook record available at https://lccn.loc.gov/2021006333

British Library Cataloging-in-Publication Data is available

Editorial: Fred Appel, James Collier
Jacket/Cover Design: Karl Spurzem
Production: Erin Suydam
Publicity: Kate Hensley, Kathryn Stevens

Jacket/Cover image: Indian Prime Minister Narendra Modi delivers his address to more than 60,000 British Indians during a rally at Wembley Stadium hosted by the Europe India Forum, November 13, 2015, London, UK. Photo: PIB / Alamy Stock Photo

This book was prepared with the assistance of the French Ministry of Culture— Centre National du Livre (CNL).

This book has been composed in Arno

Printed in the United States of America

For Mushirul Hasan (1949–2018),
whose writings and conversation taught me so much.

CONTENTS

AUTHORITARIANISM**   253

8   Deinstitutionalizing India   255

    Who's Afraid of the Lokpal?   256
    The Slow Death of the Right to Information   260
    The Vain Resistance of the Central Bureau of Investigation   262
    The National Investigation Agency and the CBI:
        From "Caged Parrots" to Watchdogs on a Leash   270
    The Supreme Court, from Resistance to Surrender   276
    What Fourth Estate?   298

9   Toward "Electoral Authoritarianism": The 2019 Elections   310

    Chowkidar Modi   311
    A Well-Oiled Election Machine   323
    Caste Politics and Its Paradoxes   329
    An Uneven Electoral Playing Ground   332
    Modi's BJP: The Elitist Hegemon   342

10 The Making of an Authoritarian Vigilante State   349

    Fighting Political Opponents by Other Means—
        in and out of Parliament   351
    The Making of a Majoritarian State Fighting Dissent   359
    Policemen as Vigilantes and "Urban Naxals" as
        Political Prisoners   400

11 Indian Muslims: From Social Marginalization to
    Institutional Exclusion and Judicial Obliteration   406

    Invisible in the Republic: Long-Standing but Aggravated
        Institutional Marginality   408
    Muslims in Dealings with the Police and the Courts   421
    Judicial Majoritarianism: Preparing the Ground for a
        Ram Temple in Ayodhya   428

    Conclusion   445

ACKNOWLEDGMENTS

THIS BOOK WOULD NOT HAVE BEEN POSSIBLE without the patience and encouragement of my family, and especially Tara, Milan, and Vadim. It also owes much to my students, from whom I continue to learn so much.

The French version of this manuscript benefited from substantial improvements owing to the critical eye of Judith Burko and Didier Sandmann, whom I thank from the bottom of my heart. Any remaining errors are my own.

The French edition was the last in a long line of books I have authored for Fayard—on the initiative of one of its eminent elders, Olivier Bétourné. The English edition—for which I have written three new chapters—has been made possible by Fred Appel, from Princeton University Press, one of my old Princeton friends, thanks to whom I enjoyed some of my best academic moments on this wonderful campus. Last but not least, I am immensely grateful to Cynthia Schoch for a great translation and so many factual verifications! And to Hemal Thakker for his help in the last mile—the hardest one.

ABBREVIATIONS

ABVP Akhil Bharatiya Vidyarthi Parishad (RSS Indian Student Association)

BD Bajrang Dal (VHP youth movement)

BJP Bharatiya Janata Party

BJS Bharatiya Jana Sangh

CAA Citizenship Amendment Act

CAB Citizenship Amendment Bill

CAG Citizens for Accountable Governance

CAG Comptroller and Auditor General

CEC chief election commissioner

CIC Central Information Commission

CID Criminal Investigation Department

CJI chief justice of India

CPI(M) Communist Party of India (Marxist)

CVC Central Vigilance Commission

ECI Election Commission of India

FIR First Investigation Report

GRD Gau Raksha Dal (cow protection movement)

IIT Indian Institute of Technology

IM Indian Mujahideen

IAS Indian Administrative Service

IPS Indian Police Service

HYV Hindu Yuva Vahini (Hindu Youth Brigade)

JD(U) Janata Dal (United)

JNU Jawaharlal Nehru University

LET Lakshar-e-Taiba (Pakistani jihadi movement)

MLA member of legislative assembly

MP member of parliament

NDA National Democratic Alliance

NIA National Investigation Agency

NJAC National Judicial Appointments Commission

NRC National Register of Citizens

NSA National Security Act

OBC Other Backward Class

PMK Pattali Makkal Katchi (political party in Tamil Nadu)

POTA Prevention of Terrorism Act

RAW Research and Analysis Wing (Indian foreign intelligence agency)

RBI Reserve Bank of India

RSS Rashtriya Swayamsevak Sangh (National Volunteer Association)

SC Scheduled Caste

SEZ special economic zone

SIMI Students Islamic Movement of India

ST Scheduled Tribe

TDP Telugu Desam Party

UP Uttar Pradesh

UPA United Progressive Alliance

VHP Vishva Hindu Parishad (World Hindu Organization)

MODI'S INDIA

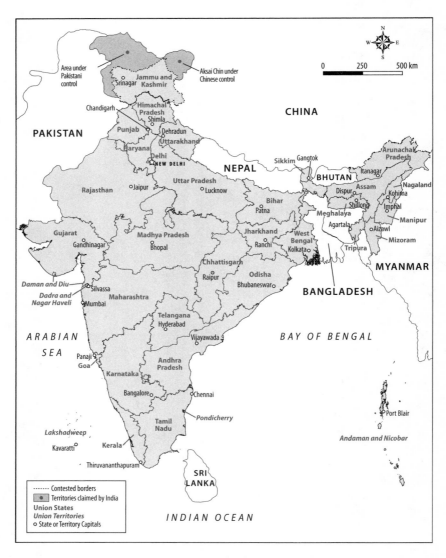

Map of India

Introduction

THE THREE AGES OF INDIA'S DEMOCRACY

THE COMPARATIVE STUDY OF DEMOCRACIES has long since deter-mined that this type of regime warrants qualification.[1] While liberal democracy remains an ideal form, many "hybrids" that blend this arche-type with other political genres have long existed, giving rise to such notions as "people's democracies," "guided democracies," "illiberal de-mocracies," or even "authoritarian democracies."[2] India, even though it claims to be "the world's largest democracy" due to the number of vot-ers it regularly calls to the polls, is not immune to this trend and has always been a "democracy with adjectives." However, the adjectives have changed over the years, with the country going from a "conserva-tive democracy" to experiencing a "democratization of democracy" and today inventing a variant of "ethnic democracy."

The form of democracy framed by the Constitution of 1950 in the 1950s and 1960s, and even the 1970s, can be described as conservative, despite the socialist rhetoric of its leaders, both Jawaharlal Nehru and Indira Gandhi. Nehru, who governed from independence in 1947 to his death in 1964, never managed to emancipate his party, the Indian Na-tional Congress (also known simply as "Congress"), from notables who were attached to their privileges and traditions. While he no doubt drew inspiration from ideologies he deemed "progressive" (an adjective his heirs still use today) to set up the Planning Commission and launch a

1

program of nationalization (however moderate) that asserted the state's role in the economy, when it came time to contest elections, the prime minister resigned himself to relying on local leaders and regional heavyweights, the only ones capable of handing him a victory owing to their patronage networks. These were based not only on classic economic motives (landholdings for large landowners, financial clout for the business community) but also on status, as all of these notables belonged to upper castes. This strategy of clientelism enabled Congress to win the elections in 1952, 1957, and 1962, but it forced the party in power to endorse conservative notables who in no way shared Nehru's socialist ideology, preventing him from carrying out the land reform that was one of the pillars of his election campaigns.[3]

Under Nehru, positive discrimination remained limited. To be sure, the Scheduled Castes (SCs)—a euphemism to which the ex-untouchables prefer the term *Dalits* (the oppressed)—continued to benefit from quotas introduced by the British in the public sector, universities, and elected assemblies. However, when non-Dalit lower castes—mostly known as Shudra in the traditional caste system—asked to benefit from positive discrimination as well, they hit a brick wall, despite the fact that their offspring often had no other prospect than going to work in the fields. In 1953, when the government appointed a commission to examine the condition of a social category that had been laid down in the Constitution as Other Backward Classes (OBCs), it concluded that this category in fact corresponded to the bulk of the Shudras and that caste, in their case, was the most decisive factor of social backwardness. To combat this backwardness, the commission recommended instituting quotas modeled after those in place for the Scheduled Castes. But, arguing that caste should not be institutionalized, the Nehru government rejected the report. The aim was to prevent further quotas from contributing to the rise of castes much more likely than Dalits to oust from power the upper castes who dominated the Congress Party.[4]

The fate of Indira Gandhi's progressive discourse was to some extent similar to her father's. After winning the 1971 elections on a populist platform of highly ambitious social promises—hadn't she sworn to

eradicate poverty?—Indira admitted that in light of the clientelist structure of Congress, she could not win elections without the support of
local notables who were as reluctant as ever toward any reform that
went against their interests. Backed into a corner by the opposition and
the judiciary, she suspended democracy between 1975 and 1977, declaring the Emergency—during which, no longer needing local notable
support since elections had been postponed sine die, she took the liberty of redistributing a little more land. But the Emergency was almost
as socially conservative as it was politically authoritarian.[5] The opposition, which came together to bring down Mrs. Gandhi's government,
was more keen on helping the OBCs and appointed the Second Backward Classes Commission to this end. But the ruling coalition proved
to be extremely disparate, and early elections, held in 1980, restored
Indira Gandhi to office. She then refrained from pursuing a true social
agenda, instead promoting a growth strategy with the backing of the
private sector, a policy that her son Rajiv would pursue on succeeding
her in 1984.

The democratization of Indian democracy did not come about until
the late 1980s when Rajiv Gandhi was beaten by a coalition of opposition parties in many respects similar to the one that had triumphed over
his mother in 1977. These two assemblages of heterogeneous forces had
one essential characteristic in common: they were determined to do
away with the hegemony exercised by the upper castes, those who stood
to gain the most from the conservative democracy. The expression
"upper castes" here refers not only to the three highest castes (Brahmins, Kshatriyas, and Vaishyas) but also the dominant castes. These
castes, which belong technically to the Shudras, were very powerful in
demographic terms and in economic terms, as they included many
farmers who, especially since the Green Revolution in the 1960s, were
in a position to sell off a surplus.

While Congress was ruled by representatives of these upper castes,
the Janata Party, in power from 1977 to 1980, and the Janata Dal, which
ruled from 1989 and 1991, were more representative of the lower castes,
especially the OBCs. In 1978, the Janata government had, as mentioned
above, appointed another Backward Classes Commission, named after

its chairman, B. P. Mandal. This commission was tasked with looking into the living conditions of OBCs and recommending avenues and means by which to improve them. The Mandal Commission concluded that the situation of the OBCs was dire enough—due to their poor access to landownership as tenant farmers or landless peasants and their poor education—that a program of positive discrimination needed to be designed for them. The commission recommended a 27 percent reservation for them in the civil service, in addition to the 15 percent and 7 percent in favor of the SCs and the Scheduled Tribes (STs), respectively. The project was shelved as soon as Congress was voted back in office in 1980, but the Janata Dal tabled it again, and Prime Minister V. P. Singh implemented it in 1990.[6] The upper castes instantly mobilized and even took to the streets to prevent a reform that would curb their public-sector job opportunities—which remained the most valuable ones before the 1991 economic liberalization. Their resistance aroused indignation among the lower castes, which formed a common front to challenge the old clientelist rationale. Now many OBCs stopped voting for upper-caste notables and instead sent representatives from their own social milieu to parliament. Thus, long kept on the margins of power, the uneducated, usually rural masses became a force to be reckoned with in the political arena. In the Lok Sabha (People's Assembly), the lower house of parliament, the proportion of OBC members of parliament (MPs) from the Hindi belt[7]—the most important battlefield, representing 45 percent of the Lok Sabha seats—doubled, reaching more than 20 percent, thanks to the Janata Dal and its regional offshoots. The Janata Dal fell apart in the early 1990s, but that did not affect the dynamics of democratization that it had set in motion. First, all parties, including Congress, now resigned themselves to fielding a number of OBC candidates, being unable to rely on former clientelist mechanisms: as OBCs made up over half of the population, the new "OBC vote" could not be ignored. Second, new public policies designed to defend the interests of lower castes were implemented not only by the parties representing them but also by Congress, which, when it returned to power in 2004, set a quota of 27 percent for OBCs in public universities—again provoking the ire of the upper castes.

This phase in the democratization of Indian democracy to the detriment of the former elites, which I have described as a "silent revolution,"[8] first resulted in a relative retreat of upper-caste, middle-class voters from the democratic arena—as evident from the low turnout of this category in the late 1990s through the early 2000s.[9] It then brought on a counterrevolution—a sequence of action/reaction that has been observed elsewhere in recent decades, as Michael Walzer has shown.[10] The Hindu nationalist party, the Bharatiya Janata Party (BJP—Indian People's Party), became the vanguard of this revenge of the elite—an Indian-style conservative revolution. This backlash took the path of an ideology dating back to the 1920s, Hindutva, the history of which will be overviewed in the first chapter and which at the turn of the twenty-first century had the advantage of transcending caste identities in the name of Hindu unity and its defense against Islam, increasingly perceived as a threat. But the backlash was not yet strong enough to do more than conquer a few states (in the 1990s) or win more than a relative majority and thus to form coalition governments (as in the years 1998–2004). The BJP was not truly in a position to govern on its own until 2014, when it interlaced Hindutva with populism, an alchemy achieved by Narendra Modi, a man his supporters viewed as providential, whose ascension in his home state of Gujarat in the first decade of the 2000s and then to head of state in 2014 will be traced in chapter 2.

The BJP victory in 2014 (chapter 3) ushered in a new era for India. This third age of Indian democracy marked the rise of populist politics, as promises made to the poor during election campaigns did not translate into policies (chapter 4). This stage also meets the criteria for two other "democracies with adjectives": "ethnic democracy" and "electoral democracy." The second part of this book will focus on the former aspect. The Indian variant of ethnic democracy—a notion that came to the social sciences out of the Israeli melting pot of the "Jewish state," as will be seen—is both informed by the promotion of a Hindu definition of the nation in opposition to the secularism enshrined in the 1950 Constitution and defended by its "progressive" champions (intellectuals, NGOs, etc.) (chapter 5) and by its opposition to the Christian and (more especially) Muslim minorities, the main victims of the rise of vigilante-group violence (chapter 6). These groups have played a key role in the making of a de facto majoritarian Hindu Rashtra (Hindu nation). The third part of the book argues that the Modi government has promoted a new form of authoritarianism: the government has weakened the institutions of the state (chapter 8), distorted the electoral process (chapter 9), and targeted minorities in a more official and direct way than the vigilante groups (chapter 10), making Muslims second-class citizens (chapter 11). India is, therefore, transitioning from a de facto Hindu Rashtra to an authoritarian Hindu Raj (Hindu nation-state).

PART I

The Hindu Nationalist Power Quest

HINDUTVA AND POPULISM

AS IN MANY COUNTRIES, including France and the United States, two ideas of the nation have been competing in India for more than a century, one universalist, the other more ethnic. The dominant idea following the country's independence in 1947, even shaping its Constitution, was democratic, federal, and "secularist" in nature.[1] Attention will be focused here solely on the latter term due to its multiple meanings, the other two being more immediately comprehensible. It does not imply *secularization* but—on the contrary—refers to equal recognition of all religions in the public sphere, in contrast to *laïcité*.[2] The Indian state not only does not recognize any official religion, but it also guarantees freedom of conscience and of worship, which were enshrined in the Constitution of 1950. Article 15 prohibits any discrimination on religious grounds; Article 16 applies this rule to civil service recruitment and Article 29 to admission to public school or those receiving state subsidies; Article 25 stipulates, "Subject to public order, morality and health . . . all persons are equally entitled . . . freely to profess, practice and propagate religion." The Indian secular Constitution, while it bans religious teaching in public schools, stipulates that "all minorities, whether based on religion or language, shall have the right to establish and administer educational institutions of their choice."

India thus fulfills the essential criteria of secularism that Charles Taylor laid out: (1) everyone can freely exercise his or her religion, (2) every religion—whether of the majority or the minority—is considered on equal footing in the public sphere, and (3) "all spiritual families must be heard."[3] Indian secularism reflects a conception of the nation that, rather than being based on a separation of the religious and the political sphere (or even on the secularization of society), is instead founded on the official recognition of religious communities that all enjoy the same rights. Jawaharlal Nehru, Indian prime minister from 1947 to 1964, stated as much in 1961: "We talk about a secular state in India. It is perhaps not very easy even to find a good word in Hindi for 'secular.' Some people think it means something opposed to religion. That obviously is not correct. What it means is that it is the state which honours all faiths equally and gives them equal opportunities."[4] Around the same time, the president of the Indian republic, Sarvepalli Radhakrishnan, further refined Nehru's thinking by pointing out that "when India is said to be a secular state, it does not mean we reject the reality of an unseen spirit or the relevance of religion to life or that we exalt irreligion. It does not mean that Secularism itself becomes a positive religion or that the state assumes divine prerogatives. Though faith in the Supreme is the basic principle of the Indian tradition, the Indian State will not identify itself with or be controlled by any particular religion."[5]

Indian secularism is in fact rooted in a centuries-old civilization in which a wide variety of religions have cohabited on Indian soil. Some of its political leaders have written fine chapters in the story of this civilization, including Ashoka, the first Buddhist emperor, and the Mughal emperor Akbar the Great, who established a dialogue between Islam, Hinduism, and Christianity. In contemporary history, the most prestigious political figure to have inherited this legacy is none other than Mahatma Gandhi. His first (and only) book, *Hind Swaraj*, published in 1909, championed a conception of the Indian nation that excluded any sort of identification with any particular religion but recognized all creeds on par: "If the Hindus believe that India should be peopled only by Hindus, they are living in dreamland. The Hindus, the Mahomedans, the Parsis and the Christians who have made India their country are fellow countrymen, and they will have to live in unity, if only for their own interest. In no part of the world are one nationality and one religion synonymous terms; nor has it ever been so in India."[6] This definition of the Indian nation—not individualist, but rather based on a pool of communities; that is, universalist—came into conflict early on with another approach that considered religious communities as potentially full-fledged nations. This approach gave birth to the notion of "communalism." Among Muslims, this perspective spawned a separatist movement that led to the formation of Pakistan.[7] Among Hindus, it gave rise to a form of ethnic nationalism that assimilates the Hindu majority to the Indian nation, putting forth the argument—like so many other xenophobic "sons of the soil" movements throughout the world—that it was first to occupy a territory that its ideologues even considered—and still consider—"sacred."

1

Hindu Nationalism

A DIFFERENT IDEA OF INDIA

HINDU NATIONALISM IS ROOTED in a vast array of allegedly apolitical movements whose sole mission is to reform society. These *socioreligious reform movements*, as they are known, came in reaction to the arrival of Europeans in India, especially missionaries. To resist their proselytism and denigration of Hinduism (accused of idolatry, superstition, and inhumanity due to its treatment of women and lower castes), Hindu reformers in the nineteenth century invented a golden age for their religion to which such criticism could not apply, as they attributed a sober (almost Protestant) mode of worship and egalitarian values to their ancestors. The reformers took this golden age back to the Vedas, Sanskrit texts the oldest of which probably date to 2000 B.C. and which, given their highly abstract nature, lend themselves to all sorts of interpretations. Arya Samaj, a movement that began in 1875, went so far as to present the Hindus as descending from the Aryans, the first people to appear on earth. This claim to fame helped Hindu reformers shift from a defensive attitude to a revivalist repertoire better able to combat Western arrogance. One of the figureheads of this transition, Swami Vivekananda, presented India as a land of spirituality, in contrast with the West, which was sinking into materialism. This was the gist of his address to the World Parliament of Religions in 1893, one of the first instances of Hinduism taking revenge on the West. But in the twentieth century, Hindu nationalism was to be, more than anything, structured in opposition to Islam.

Hindutva: What It Means to Be a Hindu

As an ideology, Hindu nationalism was largely born in reaction to the pan-Islamic inclinations of India's Muslims, real or imagined. This tendency culminated at the beginning of the twentieth century, especially when some Indian Muslims mobilized in 1919 to defend the Caliphate of Constantinople, which was being threatened by the dismantling of the Ottoman Empire during the peace talks following the First World War. The movement degenerated into anti-Hindu riots on a number of occasions.[1] Among some members of the Hindu intelligentsia, this bred a sense of vulnerability that paradoxically even took on a sort of inferiority complex, given that Hindus made up more than 70 percent of India's population according to the 1911 census. This "majoritarian inferiority complex"[2] was rooted in a lack of self-esteem that had been induced by a nineteenth-century colonial stereotype making Hindus out to be a "puny race."[3] It was also fostered by caste and sectarian divisions, two weaknesses that became obsessive in the Hindu nationalist discourse. This sentiment of vulnerability was sustained by the dread of a population decline, measured by decennial censuses showing the proportion of Hindus to have dropped from 74.3 percent in 1881 to 68.2 percent in 1931.[4] These figures prompted some Hindu nationalist ideologues to describe their community as a "dying race."[5]

It was in this context that V. D. Savarkar codified the Hindu nationalist ideology in a book published in 1923, *Hindutva: Who Is a Hindu?*, outlining the basic features of the identity to be defended. This ideological construction is based primarily on an ethnic myth defining the Hindus—in the wake of the Arya Samaj—as descendants of the first Aryans to have inhabited the subcontinent.[6] Savarkar even claimed that Hindus "have in their veins the blood of the mighty race incorporated with and descended from the Vedic fathers."[7] This ethnic nationalism is territorial as well, given that Vedic India is indissociable from the sacred land where the holy rivers flow (starting with the Ganges) and on which only the traditional rituals are effective.[8] In the prestige of this antiquity, Savarkar also found a common language, Sanskrit, established by Hindu nationalists as the "mother of all languages," an idea that British and German Orientalists were partly responsible for. Savarkar only cited Hindu culture as the fourth criterion of national belonging, after race, territory, and language. And he viewed religion only as a secondary attribute of culture, not having practiced Hinduism with any regularity and hardly observing Hindu rites. His thinking falls in line with a subset of ethnic nationalism that Anthony Smith defined as that of a "chosen people." Like Zionists, who are more interested in the Jewish people and their golden age (a blend of history and mythology), sacred land, and mission in the world than in Judaism as a religion, Hindu nationalists place more emphasis on ethnic historical-cultural traits than on spirituality and Hindu rites.[9] Savarkar himself makes the comparison when he writes: "No people in the world can more justly claim to be recognized as a racial unit than the Hindus and perhaps the Jews."[10] The fact that Hindu nationalism emphasizes ethnoracial traits and defines the Hindus as a people—and not only as a community of believers—is evident from the way Savarkar describes Muslims: they might be considered part of the nation not only if they looked at India as their *punyabhoomi* (sacred land) but also if they were to marry Hindus and have children.[11]

Savarkar considered Hindu civilization as embodying and epitomizing an Indian identity to which Muslims posed a threat. Not only was their contribution to Indian culture totally disregarded, but since the start of the Khilafat movement, they were perceived as swearing allegiance to the Middle Eastern holy places of Islam rather than the sacred Hindu territory. Savarkar's priority was to organize the vulnerable majority that formed the Hindus, against the Muslims.[12]

In this regard, his ideological contribution was supplemented in the 1930s by another book aiming to define the Hindu nation, *We, or Our Nationhood Defined*, which is attributed to another champion of Hindutva, M. S. Golwalkar.[13] His target was not only the Muslim or Christian Other but also the Gandhi-led Congress and its "amazing theory . . . that the Nation is composed of all those who, for one reason or the other happen to live, at the time in the country."[14] He uses Czechoslovakia's failure as a multinational state as an argument justifying the views "of many political scholars, regarding the wisdom of heaping together in one State, elements conflicting with the National life."[15] Golwalkar's model is Germany and its "political writers" who concocted an ethnic definition of nationhood. He believed Muslims had to either submit or leave: "[They] must either adopt the Hindu culture and language, must learn to respect and hold in reverence Hindu religion, must entertain no idea but those of the glorification of the Hindu race and culture . . . , or may stay in the country, wholly subordinated to the Hindu Nation, claiming nothing, deserving no privileges, far less any preferential treatment—not even citizen's rights."[16] The choice was thus between assimilation and a status not even worthy of second-class citizens. The first option meant that Muslims could continue to practice Islam as a faith, in private, but that they had to pay allegiance to Hinduism in society.

The RSS, or How to Build Up Hindus Physically and Mentally

To defend the Hindus and to ensure their domination over the Indian nation, one of Savarkar's followers, K. B. Hedgewar (soon assisted by Golwalkar), founded a movement in Nagpur, central India, called the Rashtriya Swayamsevak Sangh (RSS, National Volunteer Association) in 1925. The very structure of the RSS—which, like its ideology, has scarcely changed over the years—reflects its ambition to be the crucible of a new Hindu nation. Each day in its local units, *shakha* (lit. "branches"), children, adolescents, and adults gather for calisthenics and other physical exercises (or games for the younger ones) as well as ideological training sessions in which the same exemplary deeds and glorious feats dating back to the Vedic era—or at least to the kingdoms that predated the Muslim invasions and later resisted them—have been evoked for nearly a century now. Although the movement was initiated by Brahmins in Maharashtra, who have led it almost systematically ever since Hedgewar's day, the shakha have a mission to recruit new members without distinction of caste, as will be seen below. The shakha are the framework for social and psychological reform on which the Hindu nation is supposed to be built, in the form of a "brotherhood in saffron,"[17] the color of Hinduism. The RSS intends to drill into its members not only the physical strength Hindus supposedly lack, according to the British stereotype mentioned previously, but also a nationalist conscience and a sense of solidarity to overcome caste and sectarian divisions that Hindu nationalists have always viewed as a weakness compared to Muslims, whom they believe to be strongly united.

Founded to overcome this sense of vulnerability and lack of self-esteem so as to better resist the Muslim threat, the RSS was in fact supposed to enable Hindus to assimilate the qualities perceived as contributing to Muslim strength, starting with their intense sense of community. This process of assimilating the cultural traits that, allegedly, make the Other superior—which I have theorized as a form of "strategic syncretism" or "strategic emulation"[18]—was expressed in an attempt at socio-psychological reform, the main purpose of which was not only to abolish "nation-dividing castes" (for instance, by establishing "pan-Hindu temples") but also to increase the Hindus' physical strength. In the 1920s, K. B. Hedgewar's mentor, B. S. Moonje, urged the Hindus to imitate the way in which Muslims resorted to "organized violence." He claimed to appreciate "the Muslims for the virile vigilance with which they protect their racial interests . . . , which, alas, is visibly lacking in the present-day Hindu race."[19] Moonje even went as far as eating meat—thus transgressing the vegetarian diet his Brahmin caste adhered to—better to rival with the Muslims.[20] The majoritarian inferiority complex Hindu nationalists thus expressed toward Muslims does not only have to do with divisions within Hindu society itself and their physical weakness but also Hindu isolation compared to a Muslim minority perceived as being able to count on ties of pan-Islamic solidarity throughout Arab and Gulf countries.

The RSS leaders' aim to fashion the movement as the matrix of a homogeneous Hindu nation immediately made theirs a long-term project. Its mission was to cover the entire country with a network of shakha radiating out from the organization's birthplace in central India: Nagpur, Maharashtra. In 1947, the RSS already had 600,000 branches.[21] These shakha were usually led by RSS cadres who had followed a special training course. Hedgewar created the first Officers' Training Camps in 1927 that would train *pracharak* (full-time preachers and organizers). This elite corps was the spearhead for the RSS, which set out to form new shakha throughout all of India. They were—and still are—young activists who showed an aptitude for organization work and were willing to give up a career and family life for an itinerant lifestyle, even though they were often studying for a university degree or had already finished it. They worked as volunteers, the organization supporting them with the help of local notables. Their renunciation of life's pleasures and, more generally speaking, of anything that satisfies the ego (a cardinal value in Hinduism inherited from Buddhism) was a major source of their prestige among young Hindus they were tasked with recruiting into the shakha and initiating into Hindutva. These pracharak trained by the RSS to help develop the organization were sent throughout the country to expand the network of shakha or transferred to various branches of the RSS when these began to be established after 1947.

From the RSS to Sangh Parivar, or How to Cover the Social Space

The RSS mission of covering the social space took on a new dimension in the aftermath of independence, when the movement began setting up specialized affiliates. It began by combating the communists, who were increasingly active in the 1940s and 1950s, to the point of becoming the main parliamentary opposition force after the 1951–1952 general elections. The RSS first established a student union in 1948, the Akhil Bharatiya Vidyarthi Parishad (ABVP, Indian Student Association), and then in 1955 a trade union, the Bharatiya Mazdoor Sangh (BMS, Indian Workers' Association). Other more sector-based organizations also came into being in the 1950s, such as the Vanavasi Kalyan Ashram (VKA, Ashram for Tribal Welfare), instituted in 1952 primarily to counter the influence of Christian missions among India's aboriginals (or tribals), the conversion of whom was perceived as a process of "denationalization."[22] Hindu nationalists once again imitated a so-called threatening Other, all the better to resist him. In 1964, the conversion issue even justified the establishment of yet another affiliate, the Vishva Hindu Parishad (VHP, World Council of Hindus). This body was tasked with grouping as many heads of Hindu sects as possible to set up a sort of consistory. The founding of this new structure once again proceeded from strategic emulation: as the proselytizing practiced by the international Christian network was arousing an ever-greater sense of vulnerability, RSS leaders undertook to import its structure, perceived as a model of efficiency, and endow Hinduism with a church.[23] In 1979, a new organization, Seva Bharti (Indian Service), was added to the "RSS family." Its aim was to work against untouchability and provide aid to the most destitute populations. Seva Bharti sometimes provides health care but is mainly involved in education.[24] This line of action, however, overlaps with the Sarasvati Shishu Mandir (temples for students of Sarasvati—the goddess of knowledge), which since 1950 has built up a network of schools with a highly ideological and Sanskritized curriculum that was federated in the 1970s by an umbrella organization, Vidya Bharti (Indian Knowledge).

One of the newest of all these affiliates, the Bajrang Dal, is also among the largest of them. It came into being in the 1980s as a youth movement under the VHP, for which it handled security and provided shock troops on occasion, as will be discussed in greater detail further on.

These myriad affiliates prompted the network to describe itself as of the 1950s as a "family,"[25] the Sangh Parivar (the Sangh family), with the RSS forming its matrix.[26] Despite the diversity of backgrounds in which these subsidiaries moved, their unity was ensured by the origin of their cadres: all came from the RSS, the "parent organization," which rotated them from one organization to another and one region to another—as do some state bureaucracies—to prevent them from identifying too closely with specific issues and places.[27]

Sangh Parivar and Politics

The main reason that the RSS went into politics in the early 1950s is closely tied in with circumstances, as it was related to the assassination of Mahatma Gandhi. His murderer, Nathuram Godse, was a close associate of Savarkar's and allegedly an active RSS member.[28] During his trial, he moreover explained his act by echoing the organization's favorite themes, starting with the Mahatma's weak stance toward Muslims in general and partisans of Pakistan in particular.[29] In response to this act, which provoked widespread outrage throughout the entire nation of India, Nehru and Vallabhbhai Patel, deputy prime minister, who was also minister of home affairs, had 20,000 *swayamsevaks* arrested and decided to outlaw the RSS, forcing many of its cadres underground. Golwalkar thus gauged the extent of his isolation in a political system that was dominated, at least in the highest offices of the state, by Nehru's idea of India. Indeed, the prime minister viewed the RSS as the Indian embodiment of fascism. Despite his prejudice against the political sphere and politicians, Golwalkar thus approved the formation of a new party in 1951, the Bharatiya Jana Sangh (BJS, Indian People's Association), better known as the Jana Sangh.[30] Golwalkar seconded a number of pracharak to structure this new organization but established a clear dividing line between the two organizations, whose hierarchies were entirely separate.

For many years, the BJS was caught in a vice by the "Congress system":[31] on one hand, the party in power had a number of conservative notables within its ranks, "Hindu traditionalists"[32] who were, in practice if not outspokenly, against Nehru in the name of cow protection, the promotion of Hindi as the national language, and so on, thereby depriving the Jana Sangh of arguments in the public debate, at least at the local level; on the other hand, the country's leadership, embodied by Nehru and later by his daughter Indira Gandhi, championed strictly secularist positions and did not hesitate to wage campaigns against the Jana Sangh and the RSS, even to the point of banning some of its shakha.

In the late 1960s, the BJS resolved to conceal certain ideological aspects inherited from the RSS in attempt to gain more acceptance from other opposition parties, whether the socialists, peasant parties, or those born out of splits from Congress, such as the Congress (Organization) formed in 1969. The state of emergency declared by Indira Gandhi in 1975 precipitated this evolution, which ultimately led to the Jana Sangh's merging into the coalition of anti-Congress forces that came together in the Janata Party (People's Party). In 1977, the Jana Sangh provided this new party with the largest contingent of MPs, allowing it to win a majority in the elections. The underlying logic for this strategy of integration clearly consisted in shaping the political system from within.[33] The aim was to promote a political culture that combined a somewhat diluted version of Hindu nationalism with the Hindu "traditionalism" of former members of the Congress (Organization) whose leader, Morarji Desai, had become prime minister.

Hindu nationalist influence within the new government was reflected in three types of measures indicative of the resonance of ideological categories inherited from the RSS. The group of former Jana Sanghis first backed a bill aiming to ban cow slaughter, as minorities—primarily Muslims—were accused by champions of Hindutva of consuming beef and even of offering cows in sacrifice. Second, former Jana Sangh members introduced a bill aiming to curb religious conversions, which they viewed as often having been done in exchange for payment or the result of pressure from Christian churches. This determination to intervene "from on high," which mainly targeted missionaries in tribal areas, reflected a fear of Hindu demographic decline that is indissociable from the majoritarian inferiority complex mentioned previously. It was a largely irrational fear given that, according to the 1971 census, Hindus made up 82.7 percent of the population—compared to 84.1 percent in 1951 and 83.45 percent in 1961. The third Hindu nationalist measure involved a campaign to revise history textbooks, which they felt had been written by the Marxist-leaning intelligentsia and did not do enough to highlight the Hindu princes of yesteryear and their fight against the Muslim invaders.

These measures and projects, hardly compatible with the constitutional framework, helped to sideline the ex-Jana Sanghis within the Janata Party and then served as a pretense for ousting them in 1980. In March that year, they left the party to form the BJP (Indian People's Party). This setback prompted the RSS to change its strategy. Even before the split in 1980, the troubles that Hindu nationalists encountered in their relations with other components of the Janata Party had led Balasaheb Deoras, who had taken over for Golwalkar in 1973 as head of the RSS, to revisit the strategy of diluting its ideological discourse that was supposed to enable the Sangh Parivar to strike up alliances with other opposition forces. At a VHP conference in 1979, he argued, "Hindus must now awaken themselves to such an extent that even from the elections' point of view the politicians will have to respect the Hindu sentiments and change their policy accordingly."[34] As the BJP, now the RSS's political front organization, pursued a strategy of playing mainstream party politics by considerably moderating its Hindu nationalism, the VHP was tasked within the Sangh Parivar with spearheading the campaign that was to produce this "Hindu awakening."

The Ayodhya Movement and the BJP's Rise to Power

The VHP decided to focus its agitation on the demand to rebuild the temple that stood on the alleged birthplace of the god Ram, one of Vishnu's avatars, in Ayodhya, Uttar Pradesh. The building is said to have been replaced by a mosque in the sixteenth century after the Mughal dynasty came to power. It was these rulers who gave the mosque its name, Babri Masjid, after the first Mughal emperor, Babur. But in 1949, a Ram idol mysteriously appeared in the mosque—actually placed there by Hindu nationalists[35]—arousing such expressions of fervor that the authorities placed seals on the place of worship.[36] A few decades later, this issue, even though it had receded into the background, remained as compelling as ever, given the immense popularity of Ram, especially in northern India.[37]

In the mid-1980s, the VHP therefore reactivated the Ayodhya movement, which significantly came to a head in another election year, 1989. The BJP, finally convinced of the strategic relevance of the agitation, then became actively involved in it. The BJP's popularity increased as a result, and the party went from two seats in 1984 to eighty-five in 1989, as shown in table 1.1.

Immediately after the 1989 election, the BJP decided to back V. P. Singh, a Congress dissident who had caused a split in the party and campaigned against Rajiv Gandhi in the name of fighting corruption at the highest level of the state. (Rajiv was accused at the time of taking

TABLE 1.1. BJP performance in general elections, 1984–2009 (seats and % of the vote)

1984 BJP	1989 BJP	1991 BJP	1996 BJP	1998 BJP	1999 BJP	2004 BJP	2009 BJP
2 (7.4)	85 (11.4)	119 (20.1)	160 (20.29)	178 (25.59)	182 (23.75)	138 (22.16)	116 (18.84)

Source: Election Commission of India.

kickbacks from a Swedish arms manufacturer, Bofors.) V. P. Singh's party, the Janata Dal, had won the most votes but did not have a majority in parliament. To help it defeat Congress, the BJP had to take part in a very disparate parliamentary coalition (alongside communists from the Communist Party of India (Marxist) [CPI(M)]) that enabled V. P. Singh to become prime minister. But that did not induce it to dilute its ideology any more than in 1977–1979. In 1990, BJP president L. K. Advani even launched a huge "chariot procession" (Rath Yatra) throughout India that aimed to mobilize Hindus in support of the (re)construction of a temple in Ayodhya, despite a Supreme Court ruling that defended the status quo.[38] This Rath Yatra degenerated into communal rioting in several towns and cities. Advani was arrested before reaching Ayodhya, his final destination, but some of his supporters managed to storm the Babri Masjid. The police crackdown resulted in about a dozen deaths, giving the Hindu nationalist movement its first martyrs. Their ashes were paraded throughout India—provoking more riots. The BJP withdrew its support for the V. P. Singh government as soon as Advani was arrested, precipitating early elections in 1991 in which the party went from 85 to 119 seats.

This radical phase culminated with the demolition of the Babri Masjid by Hindu nationalist extremists on December 6, 1992. The BJP leadership claimed the episode was an instance of spontaneous activism, whereas the report by the commission of inquiry—the conclusions of which only became known owing to leaks—shows that the BJP, which governed Uttar Pradesh at the time, had taken part in orchestrating the destruction.[39]

Having made unprecedented gains on the strength of its radical stance, the BJP moderated its discourse as of 1996 for other reasons.

That year, the BJP won the general elections with 160 seats in the Lok Sabha, but A. B. Vajpayee, the most popular of its leaders, was unable to cobble together a majority coalition when called on to form a government. L. K. Advani would later recall that moment as a turning point: "Though we were the largest party, we failed to form a government. It was felt that on an ideological basis we couldn't go further. So we embarked on the course of alliance-based coalitions."[40] The BJP's partners within coalitions led by that party—in power and in the opposition as of 1998—were largely responsible for toning down its discourse.

The BJP's Forced Moderation (1998–2014)

The BJP clearly shifted toward a more moderate stance as of 1998 when the party, in the wake of early elections, again assumed first place with 178 seats. This time, its leaders took pains to reassure their potential partners in order to form the National Democratic Alliance (NDA), a coalition comprising about a dozen regional parties, some of which had no desire to alienate their Muslim voters. The BJP and its partners thus drew up a "National Agenda for Government" on the basis of which Vajpayee was able to form a government in March 1998. Mainstays of the BJP platform were deleted from this road map, foremost among them the idea of (re)building a temple in Ayodhya. It also abandoned the idea of abolishing article 370 of the Constitution, which granted a degree of autonomy to Jammu and Kashmir and which the BJP considered a cause of separatism, and of introducing a uniform civil code by which the shariat would cease to be a source of law. Keen to minimize the Hindu nationalist dimension of the BJP, Advani emphasized the aim of "good governance" that any ideology could adapt to: "A large area of governance has little to do with ideology—any ideology—except the overriding principle of national interests. Indeed, good governance in most spheres of national life becomes possible only when it is de-ideologized and de-politicized."[41]

In 1999, on the occasion of new early elections due to the defection of an NDA component, the BJP gave up the idea of having a separate election manifesto. The one established together with their NDA partners

contained none of the contentious issues mentioned above, and the Vajpayee government did not try to revisit them.[42] After the BJP's defeat at
the polls in 2004, the party strove to further its coalition policy and
thereby preserve the NDA's cohesion. But with the approach of the 2014
elections, the main issue facing the BJP was precisely that of alliances. On
one hand, Advani—who had shifted to the center after Vajpayee's retirement left a gap—continued to argue that the BJP needed allies and that
it had to dilute its ideology to secure them. On the other, the RSS and
most of the party cadres—who moreover came from this organization—
were prepared to lose partners for the sake of mobilizing the Hindu majority. This strategy ended up taking the fore and explains how Narendra
Modi came to be chosen as BJP candidate for prime minister, in particular
owing to the Sangh Parivar's desire to overcome the sociological limits of
the Hindu nationalist electoral base by playing the populist card.

The Social Profile of Hindu Nationalism

From the very start, the Hindu nationalist movement has been borne
by the upper castes due to the social conservatism it promotes. Indeed,
while in theory it aims to abolish the "nation-dividing" caste system,
such an ambition does not rule out a strong adherence to Brahminical
values and the Hindu traditional social order. Deendayal Upadhyaya,
the most prominent postindependence Hindu nationalist ideologue,
claimed that the original caste system, known as the *varna vyavastha*,
needed to be restored in its pristine form. In his book *Integral Humanism*,
published in 1965, he argues that "society is 'self-born'" and forms an
"organic unity" inherited from a caste-based antiquarian arrangement
that should not be disturbed: "In our concept of four castes, they are
thought of as an analogous to the different limbs of Virat-Purusha.[43] . . .
These limbs are not only complementary to one another, but even further, there is individuality, unity. There is a complete identity of interest,
identity of belonging."[44] This social harmony is necessarily hierarchical,
as evident from the metaphor of the body inherent in the Virat-Purusha
(where the Brahmin comes from the mouth whereas the Shudra was born
from the feet), but it should not be disturbed by outside forces—at least,

not by the state, a traditionally weak institution for Upadhyaya.[45] Attached as they are to the social status quo, Hindu nationalists could only be hostile to positive discrimination. They found these measures particularly irritating when such efforts set castes against one another, as during the mobilization brought about by the implementation of the Mandal Commission recommendations, thereby hampering the Sangh Parivar's efforts to unite the Hindu majority behind a common cause.

Resisting Positive Discrimination toward Lower Castes

When on August 7, 1990, Prime Minister V. P. Singh announced he would implement the recommendations of the Mandal Commission, the RSS reacted vehemently. Its English-language weekly magazine, *The Organiser*, called it a reactivation of the "caste war" that was a source of division in a nation that the Sangh was striving to unify over and above caste and class differences. One editorialist even wrote: "The havoc the politics of reservation is playing with the social fabric is unimaginable. It provides a premium for mediocrity, encourages brain drain[46] and sharpens caste-divide."[47] *The Organiser* then came to embrace the cause of the upper castes. Another columnist, for instance, wrote of "an urgent need to build up moral and spiritual forces to counter any fall-out from an expected Shudra revolution."[48] The RSS high command naturally followed the same line. In 1993, the secretary-general of the movement, H. V. Seshadri, in a blend of threats and paternalism, pronounced that

> in any confrontation with the rest of the society, the weaker sections always stand to lose. It is only with the goodwill and cooperation of the entire society that they can get the necessary opportunities to raise themselves up. . . . And this is possible only when the society becomes imbued with a spirit of oneness and harmony among all sections just as a weak limb can get strengthened only when the entire bodily life-force is quite active and ensures that the body goes out to continuously nurture that limb. This is exactly how the Hindutva works in the case of our society.[49]

As mentioned above, a social welfare mission aiming to defuse lower-caste demands had already been entrusted to one of the more recent Sangh Parivar branches, Seva Bharti, which gained momentum and exploited the desire for Sanskritization among certain low castes.[50] M. N. Srinivas has defined "Sanskritization" as "the process in which a 'low' Hindu caste, or tribal or other group, changes its customs, ritual, ideology and way of life in the direction of a high, and frequently, 'twice-born' caste that is the Brahmins, but also the Kshatriyas or even the Vaishyas."[51] But many Dalits and OBCs wanted more than to imitate Brahmins: in the late twentieth century, symbols were no longer enough. What they were more interested in were jobs and elected representatives defending their cause in parliament.

The BJP, which could no longer disregard OBCs, who made up 52 percent of the population and therefore of the electorate, was faced with a dilemma: if it did nothing for them, it was destined to remain in the opposition; if it defended quotas, it would lose a large portion of its traditional base made up of upper castes. Paralyzed, BJP leaders did not dare attack openly V. P. Singh's decision to implement the recommendations of the Mandal Commission so as not to alienate OBC voters. They instead discreetly backed students demonstrating against Mandal.[52] Then, the party experimented with three strategies, sometimes in succession, sometimes simultaneously. It first suggested replacing caste-based quotas by others based on income.[53] Second, in autumn 1990, the BJP attempted to divert lower-caste attention to quota policies by relaunching the Ayodhya movement. BJP president L. K. Advani himself led the Rath Yatra, mentioned previously, to unify Hindus of all castes behind the issue of Lord Ram's birthplace on which the Babri Masjid supposedly stood. The BJP thus hoped to put caste divisions aside and encourage the OBCs to view themselves as Hindus first and foremost. If the aim of the Rath Yatra was thus to defuse caste tensions, in practice it was also the moment that many upper-caste Hindus would choose to get behind the BJP—on the pretense of defending their religion but also because they saw it as a party that was against quotas for the lower castes. But upper-caste support was nowhere sufficient, not even in the North, where they were in greater numbers, to ensure the BJP a majority.

Hence the third strand of the party strategy, which was to orient its discourse to a more favorable stance on the quotas recommended by the Mandal Commission, after the 1993 regional elections, at which time the party's association with upper-caste Hindus proved to be crippling. In 1993, the BJP lost the elections in Uttar Pradesh and in Madhya Pradesh—which it had governed since the early 1990s—to an alliance of lower-caste parties (the Samajwadi Party and the Bahujan Samaj Party), in the first instance, and to the Congress, in the second instance. A debate immediately ensued between BJP leaders in favor of opening the party to the lower castes and those who remained true to the RSS organicist (and therefore hierarchical) ideal, a stance in which there was no room for positive discrimination. The chief advocate of the first strategy, K. N. Govindacharya, called the policy to which caste was to be the principal application "social engineering." He was instantly criticized by other BJP leaders who objected on principle to any artificial transformation of a social order that they described as potentially harmonious. According to them, Govindacharya's approach had the same "casteist" drift as the Mandal Report. A prominent figure of this group, Murli Manohar Joshi, a former BJP president, came out against "social engineering" in general—even for the SCs—viewing it as a factor of economic stagnation.[54] Lower-caste leaders were nevertheless co-opted into the party apparatus in the wake of the 1993 elections. Hukumdev Narain Yadav (an Ahir [OBC]) was thus appointed to the National Executive in January 1994, and Uma Bharti (a Lodhi [OBC]) was made head of the Bharatiya Janata Yuva Morcha (the BJP youth wing). The BJP nevertheless remained a party of upper castes from the standpoint of the social background of both its cadres and its elected officials. The proportion of BJP OBC MPs from the Hindi belt dropped back down from 20 percent in 1998 to 15 percent in 2004, whereas the proportion of upper-caste MPs remained high, at 41 percent. And while the portion of upper-caste BJP leaders in the National Executive dropped from 72 percent in 1991 to 55 percent in 1998, they remained a majority.[55] Similarly, although the BJP had become more responsive to OBC demands, it still was unable to attract large numbers of OBC voters, compared to upper-caste voters, as shown in table 1.2.

TABLE 1.2. Castes and tribes among BJS and BJP voters, 1971–2009

Castes and tribes	% of population*	1971	1980	1996**	1998**	1999	2004	2009
Upper castes	17.6	6.7	17.1	23.6	38.5	46	38	34
Intermediate castes		***	***	***	***	30	26	15
OBCs	52	3.5	10	23.6	34.6	Lower OBC 19 / Upper OBC 21	Lower OBC 24 / Upper OBC 22	Lower OBC 22 / Upper OBC 22
Scheduled Castes	15.05	2.1	14.3	14.4	20.9	12	13	12
Scheduled Tribes	7.51	4.1	5.4	19	25.6	19	28	23

Sources: For 1971–1998, "CSDS Data Unit" surveys cited in S. K. Mitra and V. B. Singh, *Democracy and Social Change in India: A Cross-Sectional Analysis of the National Electorate* (New Delhi: Sage, 1999), 135–37; for 1999, Y. Yadav, with S. Kumar and O. Heath, "The BJP's New Social Bloc," *Frontline*, November 19, 1999, 32 (https://frontline.thehindu.com/politics /article30159297.ece); for 2004 and 2009, Y. Yadav and S. Palshikar, "Between Fortuna and Virtu: Explaining the Congress' Ambiguous Victory in 2009," *Economic and Political Weekly* 44, no. 39 (September 26, 2009): 41.

* These figures are taken from the Mandal Commission Report.

** The BJP and its allies.

*** For 1971, 1980, 1996, and 1998, intermediate castes and upper castes are bracketed together.

While the BJP's electoral allies helped it top the symbolic mark of 30 percent of OBC voters in 1998, the percentage of OBCs who voted for the party fell back down to slightly over 20 percent in 1999 and remained at this level throughout the first decade of the 2000s. The proportion of SC voters hovered around 12–13 percent. With such scores, the party could not hope to rule alone. The defeats it suffered in 2004 and 2009 represented even greater challenges for the Sangh Parivar as the winning coalition, the United Progressive Alliance led by the Congress, conducted policies that tended to upset the social status quo. Thus in 2006, the Central Educational Institutions (Reservation in Admission) Act allocated a 27 percent reservation for OBCs in public institutions of higher education, including the Indian Institutes of Technology and Indian Institutes of Management. In June 2006, *The Organiser* vigorously opposed this plan, in vain:

In this competitive age, reservation cannot but be a retrograde step. Primary education is our right, but higher education cannot be so. It

has to be achieved. . . . The Congress-led-UPA government at the
Centre is bent upon destroying the last bastion of merit in the country
by introducing the extended reservation system to allow the students
of socially disadvantaged groups to get admission in our institutions of
excellence like the IITs, IIMs, etc., not on the basis of merit but on
the strength of quota.[56]

Upper-caste politicians opposed to positive discrimination have systematically argued that they were not against reservations but to the way
those reservations undermined the value of merit.[57]

The historical trajectory of Hindu nationalism over nearly a century that
has just been outlined leads to certain conclusions that will be but-
tressed in the following chapters. This introductory section has defined
Hindutva and its ideological underpinnings. It is a form of ethnoreligious nationalism that in the nineteenth and early twentieth centuries
came as a reaction to a perceived threat to the majority community, in
the eyes of certain Hindu elites, and which was embodied by Christian
missionaries and Muslims. Their majoritarian inferiority complex triggered an ideological construction process in which Hindus who felt
vulnerable sought to emulate the cultural features they saw as contributing to the Others' strength. This strategic emulation, combining stigmatization and mimicry, is typical of a variety of nationalism that is based
on resentment.[58] It confirms the malleability of identities when they
become politicized. Hindutva values certain aspects of Hinduism at the
expense of others, an indication that a political culture can harbor a
variety of repertoires: the nationalism propounded by Gandhi—which
also partly claimed to be an expression of Hinduism—thus puts value
on nonviolence, which Hindu nationalists condemn, and places all Indians on equal footing, whatever community they belong to, whereas
adherents of Hindutva have constantly tried to bring descendants of
converts to Christianity and Islam back into the fold of their religion.

Hence a first conclusion: the mechanisms at work in the crystallization phase of Hindu nationalism were repeated each time circumstances
enabled their champions to weaponize a sense of vulnerability, whether

it was Partition or the 1980s, a decade during which the Congress government yielded to Muslim pressures in the Shah Bano affair, when Rajiv Gandhi tried to pacify Muslim opinion leaders by reasserting the role of the shariat as the personal law of their community.[59] The idea—propagated by the BJP—that Congress's "pseudo-secularism" resulted in "minorityism" at the expense of Hindus, who were second-class citizens in their own country, helped the party to mobilize support in its Ayodhya campaigns.

Second, Hindutva is promoted by a tentacular organization that is exceptional for its longevity and its reach. The RSS came into being nearly a century ago and has developed continuously since then, both from an organic standpoint—by multiplying the number of shakha—and by establishing specialized affiliates. One of them, its political party, the BJS and later the BJP, is evidence of its interest in politics, even in the state, but the long-term endeavor that the RSS is attempting to accomplish pertains much more to society as a whole. Its aim is to reform minds to make each Hindu aware of his or her history, the threats to its civilization, and the need to shape a united social and political body—its hobbyhorse—the Hindu Rashtra, to resist the Other, principally the Muslim. The active ingredient of this unity can be found in the fundamental anti-individualism of RSS ideologues who have set out to make their organization a miniature Hindu Rashtra by disciplining the personality of its swayamsevak.

The third conclusion that can be drawn is that this anti-individualism has strong affinities with the caste system, a form of societal organization that the RSS wanted to rehabilitate in the 1950s and 1960s via a reform of the system of *varna*, viewed as the source for creating a potentially harmonious social whole. In the 1970s, Balasaheb Deoras challenged such references as being far too elitist. But the notion that the unity of the social body had to be achieved by spreading Brahminical values remained preponderant. To unite it beyond caste divisions and thus bring about a Hindu Rashtra, Sanskritization continued to be the preferred mechanism. The fact that the RSS does not acknowledge the various Hindu cultures, starting with that practiced by the Dalits, who have developed their specific identity, limits the appeal of Hindu nationalists for the lower castes. Not only have they generally spurned the Sangh Parivar, but they have also called for ever more quotas in the framework of positive discrimination policies perceived by Hindu nationalists as a divisive factor for the Hindus as a community and by voters as a danger. As of the 1990s, the BJP in fact became a haven for social elites in danger of losing their status owing to the rise of the OBCs and even the Dalits. While the party thus—in spite of some "social engineering"—strengthened its core of traditional support, it also took on an elitist image that cut it off from the majority of the electorate that alone could hand it a victory.

After the BJP was defeated in 2004, and even more in 2009, it became urgent to hone a strategy that would enable it to conquer power and prevent the deepening of social policies that went against the Hindu nationalist ideology and the interests of its base. It was in this context that Narendra Modi was picked as the man of the moment, owing to his ability to transcend caste barriers, wielding a variety of Hindu nationalist populism that he had already fine-tuned in Gujarat.

2

Modi in Gujarat

THE MAKING OF A
NATIONAL-POPULIST HERO

DRAWING SOME OF HIS INSPIRATION from his mentor, L. K. Advani, Narendra Modi gave the BJP a new dimension in the first decade of the 2000s: populism, and even more precisely, *national* populism.

Populism is, above all (to borrow Pierre-André Taguieff's description), a political style that throughout history has taken on the contours of various ideologies.[1] For Ernesto Laclau, it "is a necessary ingredient of politics *tout court*"[2] because those who are competing for power need to mobilize people against others in the name of a better world and, at the same time, to appear as unifiers of society. In this "populist logic," the "part which claims to be the whole" relies on "empty signifiers" for constructing "a global identity out of the equivalence of a plurality of social demands":[3] the more diverse the demands, the emptier the signifiers. Hence the intensive use of words like "unity," "justice," "freedom," and "nation" by leaders resorting to the populist repertoires.

Populists claim that they embody the people, that they *are* the people—not in a vacuum, but against elites.[4] They combat the *establishment* as an integral part of their repertoire, especially when they come from underprivileged backgrounds. Cas Mudde therefore defines populism as a "thin-centered ideology that considers society to be ultimately separated into two homogenous and antagonistic camps, 'the pure people' versus 'the corrupt elite,' and which argues that politics should be an expression of the *volonté générale* (general will) of the people."[5] In this sense, populism is based on a moral conception of politics: for its spokespersons, the people derive their purity from their authenticity.

As the populist claims that he embodies the people, this pretension leads him to also claim more legitimacy than any institution whatsoever. In the 1950s already, Edward Shils described populists as placing the will of the people above institutions and social groups (the existence of which they ignore); according to Shils, "populism identifies the will of the people with justice and morality"[6]—making the judiciary and other institutions in charge of law and order redundant.[7]

Populists also dismiss pluralism, because the people can only be one, as Jan-Werner Müller has recently pointed out—and they *are* the people.[8] Their tendency to disqualify their rivals as illegitimate explains their rejection of multiparty political competition and organizations that structure civil society. This ism moreover implies a high concentration of power, generally in conjunction with an extreme degree of personalization: populist leaders connect directly with their people, not hesitating to bypass even their own political parties in order to relate directly to their supporters.

The role of rhetoric is all the more important here as the populist has to convince his audience that he embodies the people in opposition to the "bigwigs." To relate to the masses, populists have to show that they share their culture, their manners, and their language, in opposition to the elites' "propriety."[9] Not only do populists "act like" ordinary people, but they enjoy transgressing the codes of good behavior, shocking the establishment in the name of an authenticity that the elites have betrayed by their cosmopolitanism or their bourgeois or even aristocratic ethos. From that standpoint, like the common people, populists readily claim to be victims. The repertoire of victimization is all the more powerful when the political establishment is perceived as betraying the people. But on the other hand, as Pierre Ostiguy aptly demonstrates, populists exhibit exceptional virtues through constantly staged performances (especially in the media), drawing on a performative repertoire. As a result, "the leader is both *like me . . . and* an ego *ideal*."[10] That is why body language often plays a key role in manufacturing the populists' image; the populist has to appear as a strongman to be the right conduit for expressing revenge: the revenge of "those on the bottom" against the elites and those they protect.

However, populism is plural. It can be of the Left as well as of the Right. When the people targeted by the populist leader are not only defined in social terms but in religious, racial, or linguistic terms as well, and when that leader speaks in the name of the majoritarian "sons of the soil," this idiom gives rise to what Gino Germani labeled "national populism,"[11] a term that bears obvious affinities with the nationalist Right. For while populism can be left or right, national populism calls up a clearly identifiable ideological repertoire. In that case, the national-populist claims that he defends the people not only against the elite groups but also against those who pose a threat to the ethnic majority and whom the establishment is accused of protecting: migrants, minorities, and so on. To mobilize "his" people, the populist will exploit the fear of the Other and the anger arising from the manner in which this Other is affecting the nation.[12] In the case of national populism, fear and anger are two sides of the same coin, as the ones who are feared (migrants, Muslims, and so on) are also the target of anger that does not spare the elites or the establishment, following the logic of "How can leaders let these people into our country and allow them to take up so much room in the public space?"

National-populists usually mobilize the people against the elites but do not intend to implement socioeconomic reforms in favor of the people: on the contrary, they resort to identity politics to replace social issues with more symbolic ones. They claim that class divisions are a mere illusion, as their nation needs to get united against the Other. It does not mean that populists do not promise economic prosperity and jobs: they do, but when they do not deliver, they make up for these limitations by emphasizing identity politics—this politics always prevails at the expense of redistribution policies (and policies at large). They are demagogues, in the sense that the ancient Greeks (who also invented democracy) use the word: expert manipulators who flatter the people and play on affects (here, mainly fear and anger).

To promote trust and a feeling of national unity and to instill the same proportion of fear and resentment, the populist leader not only projects himself as the savior of the nation but also employs sophisticated communication techniques that warrant particular attention, in both qualitative and quantitative terms.

India has experienced different forms of populism in its history, at the regional and national level—under Indira Gandhi in the 1970s, for instance.[13] In the 1990s, L. K. Advani, after his Rath Yatra, promoted the national-populist repertoire enthusiastically. But he failed to attract a large number of voters, partly because of the resilience of low-caste politics and partly because the politics of resentment was not easy to articulate: until the terrorist attacks in the 2000s, Islamism was not perceived as a major threat, despite the efforts of the Sangh Parivar to portray it as such. Narendra Modi, because of his personality and political acumen, has succeeded where Advani failed, in a context that lent itself to national populism. Gujarat was the laboratory of this new politics of Hindutva during the thirteen years Modi spent as chief minister there, from 2001 to 2014, when he invented a new style combining Hindu nationalism—his deep-rooted ideology—and populism.

A Pure Product of the RSS

Narendra Damodardas Modi was born on September 17, 1950, in a small town in northern Gujarat, Vadnagar (Mehsana District). He belongs to the Ghanchi caste, which produces and sells cooking oil, a caste that has been classified as part of the OBCs since the late 1990s. His father traded oil and ran a tea shop, where Narendra, as he has narrated, served customers as a child. He joined the local branch of the RSS at the age of eight, as it was the only extracurricular activity in town.[14] According to the biography penned by M. V. Kamath and K. Randeri, he aspired to renunciation very early on.[15] Ascetic vocations are not rare in the RSS. M. S. Golwalkar himself was a world renouncer for a time before becoming the organization's second in command. Like him, Narendra Modi first went to the Belur Math monastery run by the Ramakrishna

Mission in Calcutta—an organization started by Vivekananda—before going off to explore the Himalayas. Interestingly, he told Nilanjan Mukhopadhyay in an interview, "I went to the Vivekananda Ashram in Almora. I loitered a lot in the Himalayas. I had some influences of spiritualism at that time along with the sentiment of patriotism—it was all mixed. It is not possible to delineate the two ideas."[16] RSS members typically merge the Hindu religion and national culture in this way, viewing India as a sacred land (*punyabhoomi*) as much as a motherland (*matri bhoomi*).

Modi became a permanent member of the RSS in the late 1960s and went to live in the Hedgewar Bhawan (regional RSS headquarters) in Maninagar, an area of Ahmedabad. He worked there as assistant to the *prant pracharak* Lakshmanrao Inamdar, who was in charge of the Gujarat and Maharashtra branches.[17] This former lawyer considered Modi his *manas putra* (mind-born son),[18] and Modi viewed him as his mentor,[19] a rather typical relationship within the RSS in line with the *guru-shishya* (disciple) tradition. Modi was made a pracharak in 1972. The following year, he became involved in the Navnirman protest movement, a movement against corruption started by students in Gujarat. He took part in the movement after the RSS deputed him to the local branch of the ABVP, its student union. At the time, Modi was registered in the master's curriculum at the University of Gujarat after having allegedly completed his bachelor's degree by correspondence at the University of Delhi.[20] But already in 1975, he went underground to escape the Emergency declared by Indira Gandhi, which had landed a good number of RSS cadres in prison. His task, in addition to distributing antigovernment tracts under cover, involved looking after the families of RSS prisoners and soliciting aid from Gujaratis who had emigrated abroad.[21] After the Emergency, he was tasked with gathering testimony from victims of this dark episode in Indian history with a view to writing a book.[22] In this capacity, he ended up meeting a number of Jana Sangh politicians (who were among the first targets of the crackdown) and traveling throughout India.[23]

But it was in Gujarat that he pursued his career. In 1978, he was made *vibhag pracharak* (head of an RSS branch in a division [*vibhag*], made up of several districts) and subsequently became a *sambhag pracharak* (head of a branch of the RSS in a territory made up of more than one division) in charge of the RSS of Surat and Baroda—today's Vadodara—divisions. In 1981, he was made prant pracharak, with the mission of coordinating the various Sangh Parivar components present in Gujarat, from the farmer's organization (Bharatiya Kisan Sangh) to the ABVP and including the VHP.[24] As chief RSS organizer in Gujarat, Modi was the architect of a whole series of events known as *yatra* (lit. "pilgrimage"), a word designating demonstrations in forms of processions. For instance, he organized the Nyay Yatra (justice pilgrimage), designed to demand justice for the Hindu victims of the Hindu-Muslim riots in 1985[25]—even though the minority community suffered many more deaths.[26]

By the mid-1980s, Modi's talents as an organizer were widely recognized, and when L. K. Advani became president of the BJP in 1986, he decided to enlist Modi's services for the party. Modi was thus deputed to the BJP in 1987, taking up the key post of *sangathan mantri* (organization secretary) at the head of the party's Gujarati branch. The organization's secretaries have formed the party's backbone since the position was created for Deendayal Upadhyaya in the 1950s as the head of the Jana Sangh.

Modi was then responsible for the Gujarati segment of Advani's famous Rath Yatra in 1990 that left from Somnath temple on the state's western coast. The following yatra, the Ekta Yatra (unity pilgrimage), led by the new BJP president Murli Manohar Joshi, in 1991 signaled Modi's promotion to national organizer, in charge of a procession that departed from Kanyakumari (southern tip of India) to Srinagar in the north to demonstrate the unity of the Indian nation. His colleagues in the BJP complained on this occasion that Modi "did not function the way a full-time RSS pracharak should. He was seen as projecting himself and seeking the limelight."[27] In fact, during the Ekta Yatra, "not only was Modi accompanying Joshiji on his vehicle, but would, at every stop, address the crowds along with the BJP president."[28]

Modi was already attempting to combine the RSS's traditional sense of organization and the populist style of relating to the masses, even though he was not a politician yet. As the organizing secretary of the BJP in Gujarat, he strengthened the party's electoral base across the state. The BJP conquered municipal corporations and village councils, which Modi saw as the route to power,[29] in a state that Congress had practically never lost since 1947. The BJP won the municipal elections in Rajkot in 1983 and then four years later in Ahmedabad, following an election campaign for which Modi assumed full responsibility.[30] In 1995, the BJP won the six municipalities in the state, a sign of its increasing appeal among Gujarat's urban middle class, the party's traditional electorate. But it also made inroads in rural areas, winning eighteen of the nineteen *zilla parishad* (district councils).[31]

That same year, for the first time in its history, the BJP won the majority of seats in the Gujarat assembly. Modi was largely credited with the victory, and the veteran party member who became chief minister, Keshubhai Patel, had to take this into account: Modi, who soon came to be known as "super chief minister,"[32] took part in ministerial council meetings and even in meetings involving the chief minister and senior civil servants, contrary to common practice.[33]

But Modi was unable to preserve party unity and was even accused of dividing it. Keshubhai Patel's main rival within the BJP in Gujarat, Shankarsinh Vaghela, had resigned himself to not being picked to head the government, but he had hoped to get more than just the scraps for him and his followers. Modi, however, initiating a style of politics where there was no room for concessions, made sure that he got none. For instance, none of Vaghela's lieutenants was appointed to head any of the forty-two public agencies, sinecures offered in reward to the party's most loyal cadres.[34] In an editorial for the local press, Pravin Sheth, Modi's former political science professor at the University of Gujarat, explained this attitude in the following terms: he "has a Hubris complex. In this state, he tends to believe that his level of understanding is more than anyone else."[35]

Vaghela, as leader of a faction, engineered a split, taking with him forty-seven local BJP elected officials who were loyal to him. The government collapsed, and Vaghela became chief minister with Congress support. This fiasco induced the BJP high command to exfiltrate Modi from Gujarat.[36] He was posted to Delhi in November 1995, as national BJP secretary in charge of Himachal Pradesh, a (small) golden parachute. In 1998, owing to a change in BJP president, Modi was promoted to secretary-general of the party. The states of Punjab, Haryana, Jammu and Kashmir, and Chandigarh were added to his portfolio, and he was also put in charge of the BJP youth wing, the Bharatiya Janata Yuva Morcha.[37]

From Delhi, Modi connived to oust Keshubhai Patel from power. In his memoirs, Vinod Mehta, then editor in chief of *Outlook* magazine, recalls, "When he was working in the party office in Delhi, Narendra Modi came to see me in the office. He brought along some documents which indicated the chief minister, Keshubhai Patel, was up to no good."[38]

However, Modi continued to put forward his talent as an organizer more than a politician, and when Atal Bihari Vajpayee offered to have him replace Keshubhai Patel, whose popularity was on the wane, he answered, "That is not my work. I have been away from Gujarat for six long years. I am not familiar with the issues. What will I do there? *It is not a field of my liking.* I don't know anyone."[39] Even though he liked the contact with the people, Modi did not like politics—as is appropriate for many RSS cadres who consider politics dirty and politicians morally corrupt. While Modi did not see himself as a political figure, he nevertheless agreed to replace Patel as chief minister of Gujarat in the fall of 2001.

Modi knew that the BJP was in a bad position in Gujarat when he returned to his home state. The party had lost the 2000 municipal elections and was dreading the regional elections scheduled for February 2003. Upon taking office, he told his team, "We have only 500 days and 12,000 hours before the next election for the state assembly."[40] One year later, the BJP would win the election with an astounding majority for the party, thanks to Narendra Modi. Meanwhile, he had become the Hindu Hriday Samrat (the Emperor of Hindu Hearts) in the wake of the worst anti-Muslim pogrom that Gujarat had experienced since Partition in 1947.[41]

"The Emperor of Hindu Hearts"

To be sworn in as chief minister of Gujarat, Narendra Modi had to be elected to the state assembly within six months. He managed—not without difficulty—to get a BJP member of the legislative assembly (MLA) to resign so that he could contest a by-election and win a seat in the city of Rajkot. Three days later, on February 27, 2002, clashes broke out between Hindus and Muslims in Godhra, a district headquarters in eastern Gujarat.[42] Fifty-nine Hindus were killed, including twenty-five women and fourteen children, burned alive aboard the *Sabarmati Express*, the train bringing them back from Uttar Pradesh. The train had originated in Faizabad, the closest station to Ayodhya. It was carrying Hindu nationalist activists, known as *kar sevak* (lit. "service-action men"), who, on the VHP's instigation, had gone to Ayodhya to try to build a temple dedicated to Lord Ram on the ruins of the Babri Masjid. They were on their way home, frustrated that their undertaking had been postponed by central government and court mediation, parties that were seeking a legal solution for a compromise between Hindus and Muslims.

The kar sevak were singing Hindu nationalist songs and chanting slogans, some of which were offensive to Muslims. One Muslim family was forced off the moving train for refusing to utter the kar sevak's war cry: "Jai Shri Ram!" (Long live the god Ram!) At the stop in Godhra, the first city in Gujarat on the train's route, a Muslim shopkeeper was ordered to shout the same slogan and refused, and the kar sevak turned on a Muslim woman with her two daughters. One of them was forced to board the train.[43] They had hardly left the station when a passenger pulled the emergency chain. It was yanked several times, until the train came to a halt in the middle of a Muslim neighborhood inhabited by Ghanchis, a community from which many of the Godhra street vendors at the station hailed. Hundreds of Muslims then allegedly attacked with stones and torches, particularly the two wagons where the fifty-nine victims were found. The facts must be stated with caution here, because expert reports and counter reports have continued to contradict each other ever since.[44] The essential aspect for the present discussion is Narendra Modi's attitude following the episode.

He arrived in Godhra at 2:00 P.M. with several members of his cabinet and made a televised address that very evening. He presented the Godhra tragedy as a "pre-planned attack," contradicting statements by the local Godhra district magistrate a few hours earlier, who described it as an "accident."[45] In the meantime, the government had ordered the victims' bodies to be transferred to Ahmedabad. Their arrival was shown on television, shocking viewers all the more as they were merely covered with a sheet. The following day, Modi told the Gujarati press that what had happened in Godhra "was a one-sided collective violent act of terrorism from one community."[46] The reference to the notion of terrorism justified recourse by the government to enact a drastic ordinance, the Prevention of Terrorism Act (POTA), which became law in 2002, despite the National Human Rights Commission's opposition.[47]

Riot Politics: The Polarization-Elections Stratagem

On February 28, the VHP announced a *bandh* (shutdown) in Ahmedabad, a city known to be prone to communal violence.[48] As tension was mounting, the police were conspicuously absent. Some officers simply advised cars seeking to enter sensitive areas to turn back.[49] The rioters, wearing saffron headbands, by which the Bajrang Dal (the VHP youth movement described above) members recognize one another, stormed the Gulberg Society, a primarily Muslim residential complex in a Hindu neighborhood of Ahmedabad. This was "probably the first carnage to have been unleashed after the Godhra tragedy."[50] The complex was most likely a prime target due to its best-known resident, Ehsan Jafri. Jafri was a writer and trade unionist who had joined the Congress Party in the 1970s and who had been elected to parliament under that label in 1977. He had recently been campaigning against Modi in the abovementioned by-election.[51] The Gulberg Society was considered safe by the local Muslims due to Jafri's presence, but it was overrun by rioters, and sixty-nine people were killed, including Ehsan Jafri, three Jafri brothers, and two nephews.

Ahmedabad and Godhra were hardest hit by the clashes, with approximately 350 and 100 deaths, respectively, according to official figures established in early March. But 26 cities altogether were put under curfew, violence having claimed a heavy toll in some of them, such as Mehsana (about 50 deaths) and Sabarkantha (about 40 deaths). And beyond that, rural areas saw unprecedented hostilities. In all, 151 towns and cities and 993 villages were affected.[52] According to one official report, the clashes left 1,169 dead, but NGO estimates place the number of victims at more than 2,000,[53] based on family depositions and the number of disappeared.[54]

Narendra Modi submitted his resignation to the BJP National Executive Committee at its April 12, 2002 meeting, a few months after the rioting, which had continued sporadically throughout the spring. The decision, which he did not explain, may have been motivated by criticism coming at him in his own camp. Not only had Shanta Kumar, food minister in the Vajpayee government, attacked him directly, but Prime Minister Vajpayee himself had expressed his uneasiness, partly in tune with BJP partners within the NDA that got Muslim votes in the elections. When Vajpayee had visited Ahmedabad a week before the executive committee meeting, he had come around to the idea that the Godhra tragedy had been "pre-planned," but he also stated, "Gujarat is a puzzle for me because civilised society does not target and kill women and children."[55] At that time, Vajpayee—who two years later blamed the BJP's defeat in the 2004 general elections partly on the violence in Gujarat—was probably in favor of Modi's resignation. But the prime minister did not control the party. Its president, Jana Krishnamurthi, rejected Modi's offer to step down. In his speech, Krishnamurthi blamed the Gujarat riots on Pakistan's military intelligence agency, the Inter Services Intelligence.[56] In the end, Shanta Kumar was called before a disciplinary committee, and Vajpayee backed Modi. According to *India Today*, "There was absolutely no way he could go against the ferocity of the pro-Modi sentiment."[57] As Vinod Jose would write later, "For perhaps the first time, a prime minister fell in line behind a chief minister."[58]

In the past, when communal violence had polarized society along religious lines, it had generally heightened the sense of communal identity at election time.[59] The BJP could then count on greater support from the Hindu majority during the next state election. But they were scheduled for February 2003, so Narendra Modi sought to bring them forward to better capitalize on the polarization due to the pogrom.[60] He therefore dissolved the state assembly to "seek a fresh mandate from the people of Gujarat" on July 19, 2002.[61] At the same time, he resigned as chief minister, while remaining at the helm to handle routine proceedings. In an open letter addressed to the state's citizens, he wrote,

> In the pretext of [the] Godhra incident and its aftermath, efforts were made to pressurise Gujarat. Power-hungry forces stooped to the lowest possible level and made a united effort to devour the prestige of Gujarat. . . . [These elements] now try to portray Gujaratis as rapists to the rest of the world. Those who nurture such elements, insulted five crore [50 million] Gujaratis [the total population] by describing Gujarat as Godse's Gujarat. . . . The best spirit of democracy is to go to the people. So we again seek your blessings in the form of people's mandate. After the elections, we want to march forward with fresh air and new trust. . . . The people of Gujarat are awaiting an opportunity to teach a lesson to those who played with the pride of Gujarat. . . . And so, I submit my resignation of my Cabinet at the feet of the five crore [50 million] people of Gujarat.[62]

I will return later to the theatrical dimension of Modi's style revealed by this speech, his appeal to the Gujarati identity and his sense of unanimity that are pillars of his populism as chief minister of Gujarat. For the moment, suffice it to underscore his attempt to appear as the savior of the Gujarati people against those who, according to him, attacked them, including the English-speaking media that had exposed the failure of the state machinery to contain violence. Even though Modi does not mention NDTV, this TV channel had become the bête noire of the Sangh Parivar in general and Modi in particular.[63]

On September 8, Modi launched his statewide election campaign as a Gaurav Yatra (pride pilgrimage), reminiscent of Advani's Rath Yatra. Like the huge political "pilgrimage" that had left from the Somnath Temple in Gujarat, this yatra departed from the Bhathiji Maharaj Temple in Phagval (Kheda District). Throughout the tour, Modi was introduced as the Hindu Hriday Samrat (the Emperor of Hindu Hearts), much to the dismay of the Shiv Sena leader Bal Thackeray, to whom the title had been previously attached.[64] During the tour, Modi's speeches were peppered with anti-Muslim references. On September 9, in Bahucharji (Mehsana District), he claimed at a rally, "Muslim philosophy is: '*hum paanch, hamare pachchees*'"; that is, "We are five [an allusion to Muslim polygamy], we will have twenty-five children"—an open criticism of the high Muslim birth rate that Hindu nationalists have turned into a political argument.[65]

The BJP campaign focused on denouncing the Islamist threat. Already in June, Narendra Modi had stated that the madrassas in Gujarat had to be reformed after a cache of firearms, including AK-47s, and RDX explosives had been allegedly found in one of them (but which one was never specified).[66] Five days earlier, Modi had stated, "Besides the proxy war in Jammu and Kashmir, Pakistan has perpetrated semi-terrorism in Gujarat and the beginning was made by Godhra carnage."[67] During the campaign, one of the BJP television commercials began with the sound of a train pulling into the station followed by the clamor of riots and women's screams before the ringing of temple bells was covered by the din of automatic rifle fire. A few frames later, Modi's reassuring countenance appeared, hinting to voters that only he could protect Gujarat from such violence.

Pakistan played a significant role in Modi's repertoire in 2002 and would continue to do so in subsequent election campaigns. In a rally in Ahmedabad on October 1—a day he declared "Anti-Terrorism Day"—speaking about General Pervez Musharraf, then president of Pakistan, he said, "India will continue to refer to him as Mian Musharraf [Musharraf the Muslim]. If the pseudo-secularists don't like it, they can go and lick Musharraf's boots. I dare him to send more terrorists to Gujarat, we are prepared this time. *Arey mian, taari goli khuti jashe* [Mian, your bullets will run out]."[68]

Modi covered 4,200 kilometers during the Gaurav Yatra, which set the tone for what was to become his political style. He held 400 rallies in 146 of Gujarat's 182 constituencies. The BJP won 126 seats, compared to 117 in 1998, with approximately 50 percent of the votes cast. It won 42 of the 50 seats in three of the districts most heavily affected by the communal violence—Panchmahals, Dahod, and Vadodara (where it scooped up 13 seats)—a clear indication of how the riots benefited the BJP electorally.

Religious polarization had become so strong as to relegate caste identities to the background among Hindus, one of the BJP's main priorities,
having suffered from the rise of caste politics in Gujarat since the 1980s.
Many years later, a lower-caste informant thus told Ward Berenschot,
"After the riots there were elections. At that time Vankars and Chamars
[two Dalit castes] had become Hindu [*sic*: they already were], so they
voted for a Hindu. So the Hindu won."[69] A new equation had been established between "BJP" and "Hindu," despite the fact that other candidates were also Hindus.

An exit poll conducted by the Centre for the Study of Developing
Societies (CSDS) noted that while 76 percent of the upper castes and
82 percent of the Patels (a dominant caste) continued overwhelmingly
to vote for the BJP, OBC castes now supported the party as well—
between 54 and 61 percent according to their subcaste (*jati*).[70] Another
survey taken at the same time showed that 59 percent of the respondents throughout Gujarat did not wish to have someone from another
community as a neighbor.[71]

Moditva: Personalization of Power and Heroization

Like many other populist leaders, Modi has propagated his image to
such an extent that, as of the early 2000s, the iconographic material put
out by the state of Gujarat displayed his portrait and little else, during
the 2002 election campaign and after. As the BJP had won the elections
because of him, he naturally concentrated power in his hands even more
after this victory.[72]

Saturating the Public Space

A STATE OF QUASI-PERMANENT MOBILIZATION
AND SPECTACLE

While the 2002 election campaign was a high point in Modi-style populism, he managed to maintain Gujarat in a state of constant mobilization by saturating that province with his presence. Not an opportunity
was missed to parade and gather crowds in his wake, so they could be

at one with the leader. In 2007, an anonymous editorial in the *Times of India* noted, "Modi is not just a man or chief minister, but an 'event' in Indian politics after Indira Gandhi to present that sole authoritative model of leadership. With a wider vision of brand building and systematic strategies of image positioning than Indira. So, in a way Gujarat has seen non-stop round the clock election campaign by him in the past five years."[73] It would be painstaking to make a complete inventory of the events participating in this political marketing (even "branding") effort, but a selected list will suffice to give an impression of the various festivities. In 2003–2004, more than twenty Vibrant Gujarat (see below) events were held throughout the state to tout the local economy's potential and its achievements. In September 2003, for the first time, the government staged an event in Ahmedabad combining the Hindu Navratri celebrations (lasting "nine nights," as its name indicates) and the international Vibrant Gujarat business fair.[74] In 2004, Vibrant Navratri was held in the fall, and the Vibrant Gujarat Global Investors Summit was moved to the month of January 2005. In 2006, five ceremonies were organized to celebrate the Jyotigram initiative, which aimed to supply rural areas with electric power twenty-four hours a day. In this context, the most remarkable event took place in Sidhpur,

> where the mythical Saraswati [river, which exists only in ancient texts but which some archeologists claim to have found] was revived with Narmada water [diverted by canals from a new dam]. A government officer in-charge of the programme says the administration spent Rs 5 crore [about 667,000 USD] mobilising people from far-flung areas. Over 5,000 sadhus [ascetics] attended. 'Five crore is a one-time expenditure the government has incurred. But what remains hidden is the electricity bill the state would have to cough up for keeping river Saraswati flowing. The water flowing in Saraswati is pumped from 80 km away at a daily cost of Rs 3 lakh [about 4,000 USD]' the official said.[75]

In 2010, the fiftieth anniversary of Gujarat's founding was celebrated with pomp and circumstance in ceremonies called Swarnim Gujarat. Most of these events fused Hindu beliefs or rituals and a sense of Gujarati pride—a notion we will revisit below. All these initiatives were set out to establish a direct relationship between Modi and Gujaratis and to cultivate their identity. This intention is best exemplified by the Sadbhavana Mission (bona fide, or goodwill, mission).[76] Between his birthday in September 2011 and the start of the 2012 election campaign, Modi visited each of Gujarat's 26 districts and fasted in each of them for a whole day in public (and in silence) in the context of this program, which had been organized in the name of social cohesion. After the completion of his "mission," which ended in a Hindu temple and was of course interrupted numerous times, he sent out an open letter several pages long, which included the following highlights:

> I fall drastically short of words to explain the powerful experience of seeing the poor and the rich, the old and the young, the educated and the uneducated classes come together without any inhibitions during the Sadbhavana Mission. . . .
>
> Shaking hands and personally meeting over 15 lakh [1.5 million] people is perhaps a sort of record in the history of public life. But personally, to me it is a never-before kind of experience which deeply touched my heart.
>
> It had been my personal decision to observe fasts. But thousands of my fellow citizens voluntarily observed fast with me. . . . Friends, I don't wish to assess the success of Sadbhavana Mission in mere numbers. "[77]

Despite the many passages deleted from this several-pages-long letter, Modi's populist style remains intact: he is histrionic, even emphatic and personal, verging on the affectionate when he addresses his "friends"— the word Modi uses most often in his speeches.[78] More importantly, in terms of substance, as in any populist discourse, this piece of rhetorical bravura smooths over social divisions to better enable Modi to appear as an everyman. This explains the reference to 50 million Gujaratis (not a single one missing from roll call) and the accumulation of statistics, which demonstrate that—despite Modi's final sentence in the above-mentioned letter—it is important to quantify in order to convince, even if that means exaggerating the figures.

In addition to rallies, Modi began using television early on, a medium that enabled him to reach a much wider public. He started his own television channel in 2007, called Vande Gujarat! (Praise Gujarat!)—an adaptation of a patriotic anthem with Hindu overtones, "Vande Mataram!" (I bow to thee, Mother [India]!), which found its origin in a poem by Bankim Chandra Chatterjee (1838–1894). Five years later, in time for the 2012 elections, he started another channel, this time calling it NaMo, using the first syllables of his first name and surname. Conventional television no longer sufficing, he invested in holograms that same year that made it possible for him to appear in 3D in several locations at once and therefore to hold many rallies simultaneously. He thus "held" 125 holographic shows in the first two weeks of December 2012, in other words ten per day, for the tidy sum of Rs 15 million (about 200,000 USD).[79]

PERSONALIZING THE RELATIONSHIP TO THE LEADER

Modi has sought to establish a personal relationship with his supporters in such a way that they can identify with him, illustrating the mimetic dimension of Ostiguy's definition of populism. He, for instance, invented the "Modi kurta," or "Modi tunic." The only distinctive feature of this long tunic is its short sleeves, which Modi explained by the fact that as a busy RSS pracharak, he saved time washing his clothes by cutting the sleeves. By 2004, the "Modi kurta" had become so popular that a clothing firm in Ahmedabad, Jade Blue, asked for permission to market it with his name. He gave his assent and later told his biographer, "It was part of my simplicity and has become a fashion for the outside world today."[80]

This mimetic dimension was taken a step further in 2007 when the BJP handed out Narendra Modi masks. His supporters canvassed in this disguise that even women donned, to the great astonishment of passersby who saw hundreds of Modis in saris. It was a way for them to identify with their leader, as if to say publicly, "We are all Narendra Modi." There could be no finer success for a populist leader, who, by definition, seeks to embody the people.

To strike up a direct relationship with the populace, Modi did not simply enable everyone to look like him. He also established a personal connection or created the illusion that one existed. In 2007, he was said to read the 200–250 emails he received daily and answered 10 percent of them, leaving the administration to deal with the rest of the messages. That same year, his election campaign made use not only of the internet but of mobile phones as well, as the rate of mobile phone possession among Gujaratis was very high (14 out of 52 million inhabitants possessed such a device in 2007). Telephones enabled Modi to remain in constant contact with his party cadres and voters via SMS, MMS, and internet connections. In 2012, he added social media to his array of communications techniques, acting as a trailblazer within the Indian political class. In 2012, he already had more than a million followers on Twitter.

The mere innovativeness of Modi's communication strategy has made an impression on people: he was the first to make such extensive use of social media, the first to resort to holograms, and so on. With each election, he was a step ahead of his rivals, and this had an impact on Indian citizens. In the 2007 and 2012 election campaigns, the high-tech communications channels Modi used thus helped to give him an image of modernity due to their high degree of sophistication, while grounding him in Hindu traditions (such as pilgrimages and fasting): the messenger was the message, so to speak. His innovations were well received beyond Gujarat in a very young society enamored of new technology, where the elite are trying to shed the sordid stereotype associated with poverty in India by emphasizing the country's high-tech achievements. The appetite for the moving image moreover draws its sources in Hindu mythology, brought alive by the cinema and special effects.

Beyond that, this familiarity with Gujaratis—which Modi established not only through his tours and his television appearances but also through his "personal" messages—has enabled him to enter the private lives of his supporters and become their "friend." This explains how they hung on his every word in the 2007 and 2012 rallies that brought about his reelection. Anyone who has attended one of his rallies could sense to what extent the audience felt Modi was speaking directly to them. And in fact, his speeches, his intonation, his jokes, and his exchanges with the public all conveyed a sort of magnetism: he used an authoritative tone to address the masses that was also very matter-of-fact, exhorting them to reason when he doubted their support, practically scolding them. This style has led one of his biographers to conclude that much of Modi's political draw "comes from his performances on the stage."[81]

BUILDING A NETWORK TO BETTER BREAK FREE FROM THE SANGH PARIVAR

To improve his political communication, Modi was one of the first Indian politicians to use the services of a U.S. public relations firm, APCO Worldwide, which he hired in 2007. This company—which had already worked for Nigeria's former dictator (Sani Abacha), the president for life of Kazakhstan (Nursultan Nazarbaiev), and the Russian oligarch Mikhail Khodorkovsky—was then grooming Modi's image for a monthly fee of $25,000.[82] The contract binding the government of Gujarat and APCO Worldwide (which already handled the promotion of Vibrant Gujarat, an economic fair that will be discussed in greater detail further on) was renegotiated in 2010 so as to identify journalists who could be media ambassadors for Gujarat, in connection with the Friends of Gujarat association of Gujaratis living in the United States and the United Kingdom.[83] Modi has also surrounded himself with political communication consultants, such as Prashant Kishor,[84] a U.S.-educated Bihari who joined his staff in 2012 at the age of thirty-five and who quickly established himself as a close advisor.[85] Such an entourage illustrates Modi's ability to rely on a team of communications experts who do not necessarily have affinities with Hindu nationalism.[86]

In addition, Modi hired an army of young supporters to flood social media with messages, for as Sunil Khilnani writes, "the real masterminds of Modi's political campaigns are not shadowy figures wearing RSS uniform under their plainclothes. They are smart, cheery IIT-ians [alumni of Indian Institutes of Technology]: men like Rajesh Jain."[87] This young man in fact represents the typical profile of these digital propaganda experts. With an engineering degree from Columbia University, Jain was not only active on social media; he also founded a company, IndiaWorld Web, soon renamed Netcore, which became a pillar of Modi's propaganda. On social media, Modi supporters have been tasked with countering criticism against him, and they often resort to particularly aggressive methods to do so.[88]

Modi's approach is typical of populist leaders who seek to shake free of intermediaries—including the organization or party that launched them—to establish a direct line of communication with the people and be accountable to no one else. In fact, once in power, Modi did not hesitate to put erstwhile leaders in their place—starting with Keshubhai Patel, whom he prevented from taking over the party in Gujarat[89]—and those such as Praveen Togadia, a VHP leader who claimed to have contributed to the BJP's victory in 2002.[90] He also took on the RSS farmers' organization, the Bharatiya Kisan Sangh, when it criticized the rise in electricity tariffs and the effect this reform would have on farmers.[91] Beyond that, no longer bowing to RSS authority regarding his policies, he did not bother to submit the list of BJP candidates for local elections to RSS headquarters, departing from the usual practice.[92] This prompted RSS cadres in Gujarat, starting with the prant pracharak Manmohan Vaidya, to back BJP dissidents and Keshubhai Patel in particular.[93] In the 2007 election campaign, the RSS publicly disavowed Modi's "political style."[94] One of the RSS grandees in Gujarat, the man in charge of ideological training, the *prant prachar pramukh* (state-level official in charge of the ideological line and propaganda) Mukund Deobhankar, told the press that the RSS would not get involved in election work.[95] One of his colleagues, Pravin Maniar, explained in an interview the reasons for this approach, which was highly different from the strategy employed in 2002: "This time around, we have not asked our workers to get involved in any poll related work. . . . We have always extended our support for the cause of Hindutva. But we are wedded to an ideology, not any individual."[96] The RSS was clearly reproaching Modi for his personalization of power at the expense of the Sangh Parivar's tradition of collegiality and for not having repaid those who had contributed to his success in 2002, starting with the VHP. Modi burned no bridges but established the right balance of power to secure Vaidya's transfer to Chennai[97]—and he developed his own network of communication and communicators. This parallel power structure would be made of the ones who would organize the campaigns that would keep Modi in the limelight in Gujarat and somewhat emancipate him from the Sangh Parivar—including the BJP apparatus.

A single person can hold sway over an entire crowd by using all kinds of communication channels. But his discourse has to lend itself to the exercise. The question of content in Modi's discourse will now be examined.[98]

Modi's Repertoire

Modi's national populism found expression in several themes, which were often inherited from his Hindu nationalist legacy but which sometimes were his own. In contrast to most other leaders of the Sangh Parivar, he was indeed in a position to reshape the mainstays of Hindutva— hence the notion of "Moditva," which was coined by the media during his Gujarat years.

THE BANALIZATION OF HINDUTVA

After the 2002 pogrom, Modi refrained from encouraging an aggressive Hindu nationalist discourse—it was no longer necessary and would have been detrimental to his quest for respectability. Ten years later, he even launched the abovementioned Sadbhavana Mission. But his government remained closely associated with Hindutva.

As chief minister of Gujarat, Narendra Modi cultivated his peculiar equation with the majority religion, even making repeated public appearances with Hindu religious figures. For instance, he invited saffron-clad priests and sadhus to take part in a ceremony that could have been a secular one instead: the mixing of the waters of the Narmada and the Sabarmati in the city of Ahmedabad, where the two river courses now join since the 2001 opening of an enormous dam built on the border with Madhya Pradesh. To commemorate the event, Modi performed a Hindu ceremony, a puja, from a craft moored near Ellisbridge, along with Pramukhswami Maharaj, the then president of the BAPS (the main branch of the Swaminarayan movement), one of the most popular Hindu sects in Gujarat. To give the event even greater impact, the ritual was telecast live on four giant screens, a technique that would become increasingly common.[99]

Not content simply with promoting Hinduism, Modi has also sought to distance himself from Muslims, even during the Sadbhavana Mission,[100] despite the fact that the program was supposedly intended to prove that harmony reigned in Gujarat above and beyond social and religious cleavages. The first glitch occurred at the very start of the mission at the Convention Hall of Gujarat University (Ahmedabad), where Narendra Modi was launching it in September 2011. Maulvi Sayed Imam, a cleric from a small village *dargah* (mausoleum of a Sufi saint), came on stage to greet him. But when "he took out a skull cap from his pocket and offered it to Modi, the latter's expression changed in a flash and he refused to wear it."[101]

In the same vein, Narendra Modi discontinued the tradition of "Iftar parties" upheld by all his predecessors. These festivities celebrated the end of Ramadan and were hosted by the Gujarati chief minister. True, when the BJP first came to power in 1995, Keshubhai Patel hesitated to go through with the ritual, but he did so on two occasions, simply making sure only vegetarian dishes were served[102]—and A. B. Vajpayee, as India's first BJP prime minister, held Iftar parties.

Pointing out Muslims' deleterious role in India's history was one of Narendra Modi's hobbyhorses. As chief minister of Gujarat, he mentioned on many occasions the "1200 years of slavery" endured by Hindus—including the entire reign of the Mughal Empire.[103] Narendra Modi's government in Gujarat even conducted discriminatory policies toward Muslims. Unlike all other states of the union—including those governed by the BJP—Gujarat under Modi refused to implement a scholarship program for needy Muslim students that the central government had initiated and mostly funded.[104] The state government moreover refused to help the Muslims of Gujarat—financially or otherwise—to rebuild edifices and monuments that were destroyed during the events of 2002.[105]

IN DEFENSE OF GUJARATIS AND THEIR *ASMITA*

The Hinduism defended by Modi in Gujarat was embodied in the local culture. Modi cast himself as the herald of its culture and its identity, its *asmita*, a word he readily associates with another, *garv*, "pride" or "glory," as in the expression "Garavi Gujarat" (Glorious Gujarat), which he used on several occasions.[106] Universities were renamed after prestigious Gujarati men of letters, such as Narmad, one of the founding fathers of Gujarati literature in the nineteenth century.[107] But the Gujarati golden age was naturally associated with the "pre-Muslim" era. In 2003, Modi did his best to revive the state's past glory by celebrating Independence Day, August 15, in Patan, the ancient capital of the Chalukya dynasty— the last to have resisted the Muslims.

Modi also promoted Gujarati figures of Indian history that he claimed the Congress had neglected or even scorned. Sardar Patel was one of these most prestigious figures who Modi felt had been sidelined by the Nehru/Gandhi dynasty.[108] Appropriating this iconic Congress Party figure, in October 2010, Narendra Modi announced the construction of an iron statue of Patel (who went down in history as "the iron man") near the dam on the river Narmada (which was supposed to provide irrigation water for the farming communities Patel came from). This *Statue of Unity*, 182 meters high (a world record), was to be built from iron farming implements donated by Indian farmers throughout the country converging at this remarkable site. Modi laid the cornerstone on October 31, 2013, on the occasion of the 138th anniversary of Patel's birth.[109] It was inaugurated on October 31, 2018, for a total cost of Rs 2,989 crore (about 400 million USD).[110]

A PLEBEIAN OUTSIDER "VICTIMIZED" BY THE COSMOPOLITAN ESTABLISHMENT

In the years 2001 to 2014, Modi sought to position Gujarat *in opposition to* the central government in New Delhi. As head of a peripheral state, he cast himself as a victim.[111] "I have been facing negativism of the centre at every front. It often appears as if they are dealing with an enemy nation when it comes to Gujarat."[112] His victimhood rhetoric reached new heights during the 2012 election campaign, in which Modi claimed, "Of all the Chief Ministers that the country has seen in the last 60 years, I have suffered the maximum injustice at the hands of the centre."[113] Modi, for instance, accused New Delhi of refusing to raise the height of the dam on the Narmada, thereby penalizing Gujarati farmers and their potentially irrigable land.[114]

Modi systematically projected himself as the protector of Gujarat against a predatory central power. During the 2012 campaign, he claimed that New Delhi made Gujaratis pay more for natural gas than the inhabitants of Maharashtra.[115] Congress had to remind Narendra Modi that the Manmohan Singh government had funded Gujarat more generously than the Vajpayee government had,[116] and the New Delhi government had to explain that if gas prices were higher in Gujarat than elsewhere, it was due to taxes levied by the state government.

When in the opposition, populist leaders readily cast themselves not only as victims of the powers that be but also as *outsiders*, new figures with respect to the political establishment, and hence as men with clean hands fighting against a corrupt political class. Narendra Modi—partly because of his RSS background—is no exception to this rule. He portrayed himself not only as honest but also as the one who could protect Gujarat against the center's predacious instincts. He called himself the *chowkidar* (guardian) of the Gujarati treasury, guarding it from the greed of Congress.[117] According to him, "Earlier, this money used to get swallowed. *Maaru koi Vhalu-dahalu nathi* [I don't have near and dear ones]. The six crore [60 million] Gujaratis [according to the 2011 census] are my family and their happiness is mine."[118] His dedication to his task of chief ministership as a bachelor who had no relatives to take care of (and finance illegally), and the sacrifices it implied, was one of his favorite themes. In one 2012 electoral speech he said, "I am a labourer who has not taken a break for an hour in the past 11 years in order to work for the development of Gujarat."[119]

Comparing himself to Congress leaders, Modi also claimed he was a son of the soil. By contrast, Sonia Gandhi was a foreigner, and he wondered aloud, "What kind of people are these Congressmen? They can regard an Italian woman as their own but they find a son of the soil like me an outsider."[120] During the 2012 campaign, he associated this pedigree with his patriotic virtues: "I am the son of this soil. I was born and grew up there. I don't require your certificate of nationalism."[121] Sonia Gandhi, on the other hand, remained a foreigner because of her origins, even though she had been naturalized in 1985.

Modi argued that this political dynasty embodied the establishment, a political aristocracy in power from father to daughter, grandson, and daughter-in-law over the course of four generations, whereas he was an *aam admi*, a "common man." To underscore his modest background, Modi explained that he had to work as a child serving tea in his father's shop. The *chaiwalla* (tea boy) theme was highly successful among members of the middle class who swear by the virtues of hard work and merit. Not only did Modi present himself as a self-made man, but he also refused to defend positive discrimination—from which he had never benefited. But his social background also put him on equal footing with the OBC masses, as he was from the same milieu: for the first time in Gujarat, a BJP leader from a lower caste remained in power, and could make his peers swell with pride.

While Modi identifies with the people in his rhetoric, the message is sometimes also the messenger himself, as mentioned above: here the substance of the discourse cannot be divorced from its overtones, particularly when "being from the people" justifies provocative, even vulgar, speech, and his body language clearly distinguishes him from the refined elites. In 2005, Narendra Modi told Shekhar Gupta, who criticized him in an interview for not raising the level of public debate, that he "believe[d] in sarcasm"[122]—which mostly consisted of below-the-belt personal attacks against the elite he wanted to rid the country of. Sonia and Rahul Gandhi were his prime targets. He called Sonia "Pastaben" ("Sister pasta," in reference to her Italian origins) and "Shetangana" (lit. "the white woman"). As for Rahul, he nicknamed him "Jersey Cow"[123] and *shehzada* (crown prince of the Muslim dynasties, especially during the Mughal Empire), a means of emphasizing at once the adolescent aspect of a political heir subject to maternal authority and Congress's pro-Muslim bias. In 2007, Modi began to call the government in New Delhi "the Delhi Sultanate,"[124] in reference to the sultanate the Muslim invaders had established in the eleventh century.

It is worth noting here that very early on Modi paid little attention to his Gujarati opponents, focusing first and foremost on national Congress leaders, as if he was conscious of his political future—or he was working to shape it.

"VIKAS" AND CRONY CAPITALISM

The promise of sustained economic development that is intended to benefit the poorest is an inherent aspect of the populist discourse. It reflects the attempt by populists to equate the *plebs* with the *populus*— the part and the whole, to use Laclau's categories. As chief minister of Gujarat, Modi constantly referred to the working masses, even as his policies neglected social welfare and were primarily business friendly. After the 2002 elections, he sought to improve his image among the business community, which is a force to be reckoned with in the very industrial state of Gujarat. At the time, Modi had a poor reputation among them due to the communal violence that had disorganized the economy for months, causing them to lose a lot of money. He worked, therefore, to supplement his Hindu Hriday Samrat image with that of a Vikas Purush (Development Man) both to cater to business circles and to woo the masses of voters in a situation of poverty.

In 2003, Modi released a document outlining his new industrial policy. It made a number of concessions to the business community: not only were new investors no longer obliged to offer stable employment contracts to be eligible for state subsidies or even encouraged to set up in deprived areas,[125] but also Labor Ministry inspections were made less stringent, antipollution regulations were relaxed, and administrative procedures to convert agricultural land for industrial purposes were simplified.[126]

In 2004, the Special Economic Zones (SEZs) Act granted even more advantages to business at the expense of the labor laws in effect outside SEZs,[127] and in 2009 the government defined a new industrial policy designed explicitly to make Gujarat "the most attractive investment destination of not only in India, but also that of the world,"[128] in particular through the network of SEZs. The acquisition of land for industry was one of its main pillars,[129] along with subsidized loans, tax breaks, and other state subsidies.[130] In 2010, the government of India had already given "approval to 60 SEZs in Gujarat covering an area of 31,967 ha"[131]—a record.

Indian investors appreciated not only these policy measures but also the Modi method—rapid decision making, simplified procedures, and secret deals. Tata Motors thus decided to manufacture the Nano (a low-cost car) in Gujarat in 2008 in exchange for a host of concessions, and many other industrials, such as Larsen and Toubro, the Essar Group, Reliance, and the group run by Gautam Adani, with whom Narendra Modi developed a special relationship, also set up business—for the same reasons—in Gujarat, where they also developed their existing activities.[132] The Comptroller and Auditor General (CAG) of India discovered these "irregularities" years later[133]—too late to make the man who would become prime minister pay (literally and figuratively) as well as his industrial partners.

The industrials' appreciation for the Modi government was most obvious with each successive edition of Vibrant Gujarat. Modi conceived this biannual event in 2003 in conjunction with the Chambers of Commerce and Industry (CCI) to attract Indian investors. Hundreds of companies drawn to the event pledged a total of Rs 660 billion (about 8.8 billion USD) in investments during the first edition of the summit.[134] The rate of investments has gradually dropped over the years, but in the middle of the first decade of the 2000s, investment in Gujarat had risen significantly, and Modi had become one of Indian capitalists' favorite chief ministers. These businessmen made a point of attending the Vibrant Gujarat meetings and showering praise on him. Gujaratis were usually the first to appear on the rostrum, the most eminent of them including Mukesh and Anil Ambani, Shashi Ruia (Essar group), and, of course, Gautam Adani.

Such investments, particularly heavy in energy production and petrochemicals, boosted Gujarat's economic growth rate. In the 1990s, Gujarat was already ahead of all the other states of India, and it remained so under Modi, with industry recording an annual average growth rate of 10.64 percent in the years 2005–2006 to 2011–2012.[135] But for the most part, growth occurred without development. By focusing on "megaprojects," the Gujarat model was betting on large industry without creating many jobs, as such projects are more capital intensive than labor intensive.[136] Fixed capital increased 3.6 times over ten years, going from Rs 666 million (about 8.9 million USD) in 1999–2000 to 2.396 billion (about 31.95 million USD) in 2009–2010, but the annual rate of job growth slowed considerably, dropping from 2.4 percent to 0.1 percent during the 1999–2000 to 2004–2005 period and 2004–2005 to 2009–2010, respectively.

Not only did the job growth rate fail to increase proportionally with the state's GDP—as the Gujarat government admitted in 2009[137] and even more explicitly in 2016[138]—but the quality of jobs did not improve, a fact borne out by the informalization process underway in the labor market.[139] One of the reasons why industrialists invest in Gujarat is precisely low labor costs. According to the 2011 National Sample Survey report, Gujarat had one of the lowest average daily wage rates for casual laborers in urban areas—Rs 144 (about 1.92 USD). On this criterion it placed well below the national average—Rs 170 (about 2.27 USD)—on a par with Uttar Pradesh, one of the poorest states of the union (Rs 143—about 1.91 USD).[140]

The Modi government's lack of attention to social welfare is also evident in the low level of expenditure on education and health. During the period from 2001–2002 to 2012–2013, Gujarat's education budget was only 13.22 percent, compared to a national average of 15.02 percent.[141] Only four states, out of the twenty-one largest, spent less than Gujarat in terms of budget percentage. As for health expenditure, Gujarat came in seventh place among Indian states in 2010–2011, with 4.2 percent of the total budget for this item.[142] The state, partly for that reason, ranked poorly for infant mortality and malnutrition.[143]

Like most populists, Modi made many promises to the poor but did not deliver on socioeconomic matters. He found it more important to cozy up to industrialists who would be in a position to support him financially[144]—and therefore enable him to saturate the public space. There, Modi mobilized people by exploiting emotions[145] (including fear, anger, and pride)—the Hindu nationalist way, as evident from his successful election campaigns, to be examined in the next section.

A Charismatic Leader Sealing the Fate of the Moderation Thesis

Right from the start of the 2000s, despite his purely regional role as Gujarat chief minister, Modi imposed his presence on the national stage. To all, he appeared to be an exceptional figure, and even those who reproved his style and his ideology were held in awe. He shook up the political class, even in his own camp, by pursuing a new strategy of radicalization that contradicted the generally admitted theory that only a centrist political force could govern India and that the rules of democratic regimes forced extreme parties to moderation.[146]

A "Dark Hero" Is Still a Hero

Max Weber's canonic definition of charismatic authority does not have any moral connotation: charisma is neither good nor bad in terms of ethics; it is a "certain quality of an individual personality, by virtue of which he is set apart from ordinary men and treated as endowed with supernatural, superhuman, or at least specifically exceptional powers or qualities. These are not accessible to the ordinary person but regarded as of divine origin, or as exemplary."[147] Narendra Modi exerts charismatic authority because of the exceptional nature of his actions and lifestyle.

Narendra Modi's impact on India's public sphere is first of all rooted in the events of 2002: not only did his state witness levels of unprecedented violence not seen since Partition, but he never expressed any remorse, never uttered the slightest apology—unlike Manmohan Singh, a Sikh prime minister who apologized to his community for the 1984 pogrom. Modi invented another repertoire: that of the strongman who stands as a muscular defender of the Hindu majority. In Gujarat, such an attitude is readily associated with the notion of *marut*, a form of viril-ity that can be seen in the body language Modi uses when standing at the podium. Thrusting out his torso, he claimed that only his suppos-edly "56-inch chest" could "protect Gujarat."[148]

But Modi's reputation had already reached beyond Gujarat. In 2003, the magazine *India Today* named him "Newsmaker of the Year," explain-ing the decision—made on the basis of an opinion poll—in these evoc-ative terms: "The national script is rewritten: he against the Other. He divides and dominates. Such men are the frontbenchers of history. There are many synonyms for them. Dictator. Liberator. Redeemer. Revolutionary. . . . Narendra Damodardas Modi shook India. And how. Look at him, look at him up close. For so long, he was just another poli-tician. Then one day, he was just another chief minister. Today, he is just Modi."[149] Although the title of the article—"Narendra Modi, Master Divider"—suggests that Modi did not act responsibly during the 2002 pogrom, what sparked admiration was the nerve he demonstrated in the course of the event. A process of heroization was underway among the Hindu majority, a process that, like populism, knows no ideology—and no morals: the avid Bollywood film watchers that most Indians are know that a *kala nayak* (a dark hero) is still a hero because what matters most is how extraordinary the show is.

If the personality cult that has gradually come to surround Modi was due to the original "exploit" of 2002 that made him the Emperor of Hindu Hearts and that he subsequently cultivated, modern means of communication have also helped to build him up—as mentioned above. But beyond his instruments of propaganda, Modi has become a media idol, first because his ability to reinvent the rules of the po-litical game proved good for sales, even before newspaper and televi-sion station owners saw him as the next prime minister. His success at the polls in 2007 and in 2012 can be explained by the broad palette his national populism relies on, but one aspect in particular warrants special attention: his ability to polarize by raising fears of the Others (Muslims) and his spurning of those perceived to tolerate them (Congress).

The Politics of Fear and the Art of Winning Elections

Populists do not have a monopoly on utilizing the politics of fear, which can commonly be found in the repertoires of political strategists of all stripes. For a politician—whether in office or in the opposition—enacting such tactics involves exploiting the fears aroused by a mounting threat, at once by posing as a protector and stigmatizing the source of the danger. A polarization strategy can naturally take shape when the risk allegedly comes from the same Other whom a political leader had already stigmatized for cultural difference, as a demographic threat to the community, and so on. Media attention to such anxiety-inducing discourse, of course, plays a key role.[150] Fear of Islamist terrorism in the wake of the September 11, 2001 attacks amplified recourse to this tactic in the United States.[151] In Gujarat, during this period, a similar stock of techniques was available due to a series of attacks foiled by the police between 2002 and 2006. Each time, the terrorists—usually identified by the police as being linked to Islamist groups based in Pakistan—were arrested or killed before reaching their target, which according to the Gujarat police was often none other than Narendra Modi himself.[152] In December 2002, D. G. Vanzara, a police officer promised a bright future, accused three young Muslims who had just been arrested in Delhi of plotting to assassinate Modi and P. Togadia (then VHP leader). He alleged that they came to Ahmedabad to recruit thirty-three young men in refugee camps to send them to Pakistan for training.[153] Seven years later they were set free by the judge, who finally looked into the case, only to realize that it was entirely lacking in evidence. Less than a month after these first arrests, on January 13, 2003, Sadiq Jamal, who, according to the Gujarat police, had been sent by Lashkar-e-Taiba to assassinate Modi, was shot and killed in Ahmedabad before he could carry out the plan.[154] But the Central Bureau of Investigation "found there was no evidence suggesting Sadiq was working for any terror outfit"[155] and instead filed a charge sheet against eight policemen of Gujarat who were accused of extraconstitutional killing. The following year, four young Muslims, among them Ishrat Jahan, a nineteen-year-old female student, were gunned down by the police on the road between Ahmedabad and Gandhinagar. In a highly publicized press conference, the Gujarat police explained that, again, they were members of Lashkar-e-Taiba out to eliminate Narendra Modi. Five years later, a magistrate ruled against this interpretation, concluding that it was a case of extrajudicial murder and that the charges had been entirely fabricated by the authorities.[156] In the meantime, another similar case occurred in 2005, when on November 26, Sohrabuddin Sheikh, a known petty criminal, and his wife, Kauser Bi, were killed by the Gujarat and Rajasthan police near the border between the two states. Once again, D. G. Vanzara—who had become chief of Gujarat's Anti Terrorism Squad—gave a press conference to explain that Sohrabuddin had been sent by Lashkar-e-Taiba to assassinate Modi.[157] One of Sohrabuddin's underlings, Tulsiram Prajapati, was killed in December 2006. The same year, a journalist, Prashant Dayal, got information from the police officers involved in the 2005 operation suggesting that it was another fake case.[158] In 2012 the Supreme Court ordered a probe concerning some twenty other similar cases.[159] The investigation is still underway in some of the cases mentioned above and will be discussed further in the last part of this book.

In 2010, testimony from police officers who investigated Vanzara and his colleagues led to the arrest of several dozen police officers and the minister of state for home, Amit Shah (see chapter 8 for a more detailed account of the judicial procedure).[160] These judicial developments confirmed the hypothesis upheld by the Congress opposition, which from the start considered these "fake encounters" (the common expression in India referring to police–staged murders) part of the politics of fear meant to present Narendra Modi as the protector of Hindus and the target of Islamist terrorism.[161] In fact, between 2002 and 2006, these highly publicized events sustained an anxiety-filled atmosphere of religious polarization that Narendra Modi was able to use in his 2007 election campaign when he criticized Congress for being weak toward Islamist terrorism. He urged voters to trounce a "soft-on-terror Congress" and blamed the party for having put India at terrorists' mercy by abolishing the emergency laws that the BJP had passed when it was in power, particularly the Prevention of Terrorism Act (POTA), a law that extended the period of custody and provided for heavier sentences for people whose crimes were categorized as terrorism. In the city of Godhra, where the communal violence of 2002 began, he harangued the crowd as if the accusations levied against him were aimed at all Gujaratis, resorting to the Modi-equals-Gujarat equation mentioned above: "The Congress says you are terrorists. Are you terrorists? This is an insult to Gandhi's and Sardar Patel's Gujarat.[162] Teach the Congress a lesson for calling the people of Gujarat terrorists. . . . Sonia Behn [sister], it is your government that is protector of merchants of death. In Gujarat, we have eliminated the merchants of death [that is, the Muslims suspected of terrorism]."

In 2012, Narendra Modi traded this polarization strategy for a more consensual approach likely to give him the image of a responsible statesman as he was readying to don the trappings of a potential prime minister. This was the spirit in which he had launched the program known as the Sadbhavana Mission. He stressed his record regarding development and law and order. But he did not discard the politics of fear for all that. He claimed to have brought an end to the communal violence that reigned under Congress rule when "Ahmedabad's identity was curfew," suggesting that the riots in this city prone to communal violence[163] had been due to Congress's benevolence toward Muslim troublemakers, who were seen as the cause of the violence: "It has been 11 years. . . . Has the curfew gone or not?"[164]

However, in 2012, Modi once again used the "otherization" of the Muslims in the last days of his campaign, accusing the Congress of wanting to appoint Ahmed Patel, a close advisor to Sonia Gandhi, as chief minister of Gujarat if they won. Wielding sarcasm, Modi called Patel "Ahmedmian" (Ahmed the Muslim) and tried to make people believe that the Congress had decided to put him forward as the party's candidate to head the state if they won. Patel was not even contesting a seat in the assembly, without which he would not even be eligible to be part of the government. Still Modi hammered on, "Ahmedmian Patel says he does not want to be chief minister. But the Congress has already set the stage to make him the chief minister."[165]

In contradiction with the professed spirit of the Sadbhavana Mission, the BJP did not field a single Muslim candidate in the 2012 elections—as it had refrained from doing in 2007. A BJP party leader in Gujarat justified the decision in meaningful terms:

> It was too risky a gamble. This symbolic gesture may have confused the majority who see Modi as a saviour of the Hindus. More importantly, the conciliatory gesture toward the minorities could have alienated the party cadre. . . . If this election is a springboard for 2014 [the general elections], it is important to keep Gujarat's majority sentiment in mind. There will be enough time for symbolic gestures later. The party may think of nominating a Muslim to the Rajya Sabha when the time is right.[166]

Modi's national-populist bag of tricks, based on polarization and an impressive array of communication methods, helped ensure his electoral gains in 2007 and 2012.[167]

Religious polarization appears clearly in table 2.1, as only one-fifth of Muslims voted for the BJP in 2007 and in 2012.[168]

TABLE 2.1. Caste, tribe, and Muslim voting preferences in Gujarat in the regional elections of 2007 and 2012 (%)

Party	Congress		BJP		Others	
Caste and communities	2007	2012	2007	2012	2007	2012
Upper castes	26	22	69	60	13	18
Dominant castes (Patel)	21	10	71	61	9	30
OBCs (Kshatriya)	40	41	47	55	14	5
OBCs (Koli)	52	36	42	54	6	10
Other OBCs	38	28	54	56	8	16
Scheduled Castes	54	61	34	25	10	14
Scheduled Tribes	33	43	38	33	29	24
Muslims	67	69	22	21	11	10
Others	26	21	61	70	13	9

Source: Table adapted from the CSDS opinion poll for CNN-IBN. Christophe Jaffrelot, "Gujarat Elections: The Sub-Text of Modi's 'Hattrick'—High Tech Populism and the 'Neo-Middle Class,'" *Studies in Indian Politics* 1, no. 1 (June 2013): 79–96.

TABLE 2.2. Voting patterns by socioeconomic category in Gujarat, 2007 and 2012 state elections (%)

Party	Congress		BJP	
Class*	2007	2012	2007	2012
Upper*	31	28	60	57
Middle[†]	37	34	53	54
Lower[#]	40	45	39	41
Poor[§]	42	44	45	43

Source: "Gujarat Assembly Election 2012: Post Poll Survey by Lokniti, Centre for the Study of Developing Societies," 13, accessed March 18, 2013, http://www.lokniti.org/pdfs_dataunit/Questionairs /gujarat-postpoll-2012-survey-findings.pdf.

Note: In this table, column totals are under 100 percent because parties other than Congress and the BJP were not considered.

* Includes households (1) having a car or a tractor; (2) having a scooter plus a color television, a telephone, a refrigerator, air conditioning, or an irrigation pump if in a rural area; or (3) of which the monthly income is more than Rs 20,000.

[†] Includes households (1) having three of these four items: telephone, color television, a motorized two-wheeler, or a refrigerator; or (2) of which the monthly income is between Rs 5,000 and 20,000.

[#] Includes households (1) having three of the following items: a black-and-white television, an electric fan, a bicycle, or a gas bottle; or (2) of which the monthly income is between Rs 2,000 and 5,000.

[§] Includes households (1) having only two of the four items mentioned for the category above or (2) of which the monthly income is less than Rs 2,000.

Social polarization is obvious as well, but the intermediary categories tended to switch over to the BJP: wealthier voters cast their ballot for Modi's party more than for the Congress in 2007 and 2012 (table 2.2), but the middle class did so as well, and the BJP performed remarkably well among the lower social classes. In terms of caste, while the higher categories (upper castes and dominant castes) remained solid BJP backers and while the SCs and STs continued to throw their support behind Congress, Modi's party drew more OBCs. The conquest of the OBC vote was indeed the key to Modi's success. It was explained in part by his own social background, but even more by his national-populist strategy calling on all Hindus, whatever their caste, to unite behind him to face threats and benefit from development. It is worth pointing out that the lower castes, having experienced social ascension, tended to demonstrate considerable religious zeal in hopes of being more easily accepted by the upper-caste middle class they were attempting to join.

This phenomenon is perceptible throughout India,[169] but it has been particularly notable in Gujarat.[170]

Modi's appeal among certain OBCs can also be explained by the emergence of a class aspect. Internal differentiation by income was gradually affecting large OBC castes, as their members migrated from the villages to the city. This exodus was tied to the attraction of urban jobs, whether in industry or in the service professions. Even if such jobs were unstable and paid badly, they usually enabled these former villagers to improve their living conditions. New urban dwellers, whether they went to the city or the city came to them on the crest of a particularly dynamic urbanization process in Gujarat, made up a new form of semiurban class that Modi was the first to name: in the 2012 BJP election manifesto, he referred to them as the "neo-middle class," explaining the formation of this new category by double-figure industrial and services growth over the preceding ten years.[171] Local observers viewed this more as a gray area comprising those who had lifted themselves out of poverty but who were not yet part of the middle class.[172] They could afford a two-wheeler, but not a Nano; a few household appliances, but not any consumer electronics; hard-wall accommodation, but far from city centers. By leaving their rural environment, this young population's political culture tended to change: they became more entrepreneurial and believed that Modi, with his promises of development, would meet their aspirations. They were more susceptible to the political propaganda diffused through the media and social networks in cities, where, contrary to the village world, religious mixing had become rare due to the ghettoization of Muslims,[173] a phenomenon that was exacerbated by the pogrom in 2002. It is indeed all the easier to instill fear of Others when one has little contact with them. For all these reasons, OBCs who left the countryside and became part of the neo-middle class had tended to switch from the Congress to the BJP. The Koli, the largest OBC jati in Gujarat, was a case in point. Table 2.3 shows that the percentage of BJP voters rose from 44 percent in the villages to 65 percent in the semiurban areas.

Modi's strategy ended up paying off from an electoral standpoint: by polarizing Gujarati society along religious lines, and social lines to a

TABLE 2.3. The impact of urbanization on caste, tribe, and Muslim voting patterns in the 2012 Gujarat state elections (%)

Party	Congress			BJP		
Castes and communities	Rural*	Semiurban[†]	Urban[#]	Rural*	Semiurban[†]	Urban[#]
Upper Castes		16.1	22.5		64.5	60.5
Patel	12.4	16.1	10.7	62.8	71	72.9
Kshatriya	45	41.1	36.2	51.2	51.8	53.2
Koli	53.2	18.5	–	44	65.2	0.8
Other OBCs	40.7	26.6	17.9	50.9	51.6	65.5
Scheduled Castes	81.3	45	59.7	18.8	36.3	16.9
Scheduled Tribes	47.3	41.1	20	29.6	35.6	66.7
Muslims	70.2	81.4	68.5	20.7	7	29.6
Total	45.7	32.2	27.5	43.3	50.8	57.7

Source: Table adapted from the CSDS opinion poll for CNN-IBN. For further detail, see Christophe Jaffrelot, "Gujarat Elections: The Sub-text of Modi's 'Hattrick'—High Tech Populism and the 'Neo-middle Class,'" *Studies in Indian Politics* 1, no. 1 (June 2013): 79–96.

Note: In this table, column totals are under 100 percent because parties other than Congress and the BJP were not considered.

* Rural constituencies have 75 percent or more village-based voters.

[†] Semiurban constituencies have between 25 and 75 percent urban voters.

[#] Urban constituencies have 75 percent or more urban voters.

lesser extent, he managed to win between 48 and 50 percent of the vote from 2002 to 2012 and, due to the first-past-the-post system, thus had a majority in a state assembly made up of 182 members—despite a slight erosion, which saw the BJP go from 127 seats in 2002 to 117 in 2007 and to 115 in 2012. Never before had the BJP won three state elections in a row. Modi was clearly inventing a political repertoire that contradicted the moderation thesis that was taken for granted by most social scientists working on India up to that time.

In his thirteen years as chief minister of Gujarat, Narendra Modi added a new populist dimension to Hindu nationalism. Never before had a Hindutva-supporting leader been able to tick off as many boxes on the national-populist checklist.

He exemplifies Laclau's "populist reason" by presenting himself as the great unifier; hence, his intensive use of empty signifiers like "unity"— in the name of which he dedicated Patel's statue—and "harmony."

Moreover, he claimed to speak in the name of the 50 or 60 million Gujaratis whom he considered as his "friends" (this affective dimension being part of Laclau's model). Modi also initiated the Sadbhavana Mission to demonstrate that he stood above social and religious divisions. And in order to appear above political divisions as well, he cast himself as an outsider, a stranger to politics. In one interview he gave in 2006, he even declared, "I am an apolitical C[hief] M[inister]."[174] Some of his supporters indeed saw him as a man of action more concerned with efficiency than anything else.[175] Modi projected himself as a unifier *against* others, including the politicians who were part of the ruling establishment. To use Mudde's phrase, he represented "the pure people" against "the corrupt elite."[176]

He was in a position to play that role because of his social origins, which allowed him to claim that he came from a poor but honest family, in contrast to the political establishment dominated by corrupt dynastic heirs—the Nehrus/Gandhis—that "victimized" him. This sense of victimization also allowed Modi to relate even more effectively to the plebs who shared his social background. This victim status of the cosmopolitan elite attracted the sympathy of the plebeians even more effectively because it was combined with charismatic qualities (in the Weberian sense: Modi, indeed, was an exceptional character), as evident from the 2002 pogrom, the permanent state of mobilization that he orchestrated, his ability to attract big investors to the state, and his quasi-supernatural personal qualities. By the mid-2000s, Modi had indeed acquired some superhuman characteristics in the eyes of many Gujaratis. During the 2007 election campaign, the *Times of India* published a series of front-page articles narrating, for instance, (1) how Modi liked to swim in the lake near his house amid crocodiles as a child and supposedly even brought a baby crocodile home, immediately forced by his mother to release it back into the lake; (2) Modi's ability to digest any kind of poison (as he claimed on his website), like a sultan of Ahmedabad who had similar powers—another example of strategic emulation of the threatening Other; and (3) the fact that Modi, when he was ten, helped his father sell tea on the platform of a small railway station.[177] These accounts illustrate Ostiguy's theory that the populist is seen by the people as "like me" and "an ego ideal."[178] On one hand, he appears as "one of us"; on the other, he is "our hero." Modi's proximity to the plebs was also due to his disruptive style, including in terms of vulgarity and sarcasm.

As early as 2002, Modi's ability to connect with the Gujarati masses was especially remarkable. This contact went through various channels, traditional as well as high-tech, virtual as well as physical.[179] His presence at rallies was enough to electrify crowds after the 2002 pogrom, making him someone exceptional. But his rhetoric enabled him to mesmerize these crowds as well. This ability to relate directly to the people and to bypass—at least partly—his own party in order to stand above institutions, as emphasized by Shils, is another characteristic of populism.

But Modi's populism is somewhat specific and requires qualification. It belongs to the subcategory of *national*-populism defined by Germani. It means that those against whom the "Emperor of Hindu Hearts" mobilized supporters were not only members of the establishment but also adepts of secularism and its main beneficiaries, the religious minorities. This brand of populism is indissociable from the ideology of Hindu nationalism. Modi emphasized that he was a son of the soil, whereas Congress—led by an Italian—was cosmopolitan. He also appeared as determined to defend the Gujaratis against New Delhi and Pakistan, a theme that took on an ethnoreligious variant once he also committed to defending Hindus against Islamists, whom he felt the Congress was soft on.

Clearly the kind of unity that Modi tried to foster in Gujarat—despite his claim that he represented 50 or 60 million Gujaratis—pertained primarily to the majority community. His objective, inherited from his alma mater, the RSS, was precisely to unite the Hindus against the Muslims (hence *India Today's* title, "Master Divider"). This strategy was evident not only from the post-pogrom 2002 election campaign but also from the politics of fear that found expression in a long series of fake encounters in 2003–2006.

The strategy of Hindu majoritarianism was also intended to transcend caste divisions. Caste conflicts were very intense in the 1980s in Gujarat. In reaction to additional quotas introduced by the Congressional government, forward castes (including Patels) protested and ultimately went over to the BJP.[180] The party had used Hindutva to reunite the majority community, and Modi gave a new dimension to this repertoire as Hindus were invited to valorize not only their religious identity but also their Gujarati *asmita*, an identity that transcended castes and sects.

Additionally, Modi attempted to promote another social concept that was bound to dilute caste: the neo-middle class. OBCs' aspiring youth recognized themselves in this new category, which was supposed to be fed with migrants from the villages of Gujarat in proportion to the growth rate of the state economy. This double-digit rate was the symbol of what Narendra Modi presented as the "Gujrat model," a model of growth without development as, in fact, few good jobs were created and inequalities remained very pronounced. The characteristics of the "Gujarat model" showed that despite his pro-poor discourse, Modi's populism—like most populism of the Right—had been used to maintain the social status quo, not only by defusing lower castes' mobilization but also by maintaining or even restoring socioeconomic hierarchies. This state of affairs was not unrelated to the support Modi received from most Gujarati industrialists.

Like a Janus figure, Modi's populism exhibits two very different faces. On one hand, it is based on the promise of economic development for the plebeians and emphasizes unity. On the other, it exploits the fear of the Other in a cleverly orchestrated context of mounting threats. The two facets of this strategy have had a cumulative effect, giving the BJP the means to broaden its electorate along new avenues, by cashing in on two types of polarization. Social polarization has combined a neo-middle class with the traditional middle class within the BJP's electoral base. In so doing, Modi has relativized the weight of caste in favor of class, forging a society comprising two poles: the middle class (including the neo-middle class) and the poor. At the same time, religious polarization has made it possible to dilute caste identities and relativize social polarization, as some of the poor could also identify with Hindu nationalism and mobilize against Muslims. The superposition of these two lines of cleavage—one based on class, the other on religion—has enabled the BJP to mitigate the risk of a rise of the lower castes, a silent revolution driven by the plebeian mobilization so dreaded by the Sangh Parivar. Narendra Modi has thus given his camp the national-populist recipe the Hindu nationalists needed as an antidote to the politicization of the lower castes.

He achieved this tour de force by indulging in radical discourses and actions, in contrast to the BJP leaders, including L. K. Advani, who thought that the party should dilute its Hindu nationalism to retain its allies—in compliance with the moderation thesis. The political science literature supporting this thesis argues that inclusive regimes that incorporate radical parties in electoral games usually transform these parties into more moderate political actors.[181] This moderation process may result from four factors that are likely to have a cumulative impact. First, when an extremist party contests elections in a democratic framework, it accepts institutions that are based on liberal principles, including the rule of law. For instance, the extremist party is qua participation bound to commit itself to political diversity.[182] Second, when a radical party contests elections, it is bound to dilute its ideology to attract voters outside of its core constituency. Robert Michels and Joseph Schumpeter were the first party theoreticians to assume that extremist parties had to downplay their exclusivism once they enter the electoral arena.[183] Third, when radical parties are power driven and aspire to govern, those who fail to win an absolute majority are likely to rely on alliances with parties that do not share its extremism. Fourth, while extremist parties emerge in most cases from ideological movements displaying a deep sense of doctrinal purity, they gradually emancipate themselves from these movements in the process of transforming from niche into mass parties.[184]

In India, this theory applies to the Jama'at-e-Islami, a party that has gradually accepted the rules of democracy, as Irfan Ahmed has shown.[185] But the moderation thesis did not apply to Modi's BJP, nor probably to all the communal parties that claim to represent ethnic majorities. In their case, moderation makes sense only when they need allies who do not share their ideology. The alternative strategy that they can try to implement consists in polarizing the voters to their advantage along a racial, linguistic, or religious line. This is the strategy that Deoras suggested in 1979 when he realized that working in coalitions would not take the Hindu nationalists far enough. The Sangh Parivar prepared the ground for the making of a Hindu vote bank by using the Ayodhya issue. But senior leaders like L. K. Advani still thought that the BJP needed allies. Modi showed that an alternative strategy could work by resorting to polarization in what became, for thirteen years, the Gujarati laboratory.

Certainly, Modi's rhetoric resonated particularly well in Gujarat owing not only to the socioeconomic trajectory of the state but also to its history and political culture. The state has in fact traditionally had a complicated relationship with Islam. It was one of the first areas of India to be confronted with the Muslim invasions.[186] In the eleventh century, Mahmud Ghazni's sack of the Somnath Temple deeply traumatized Gujarati society, and it has since become a symbol for Hindus all over India.[187] This long history has contributed to making militant Hindus the champions of Gujarati identity. Their discourse became somewhat dominant in the twentieth century, as evidenced in the political subculture of Congress in Gujarat, where, through the influence of such leaders as Vallabhbhai Patel, the party was more inclined to defend Hinduism than any other of the party's regional branches.[188] Gujarat contains the characteristic features of a "majoritarianism" that is based not only on religious and ethnolinguistic ties, a shared historical narrative, and a fear of the Other (the Muslim), at the root of latent or explicit stigmatization. From this standpoint, many Hindus in Gujarat very early on regarded their state as a borderline area subject to pressure from its neighbors. This sentiment was magnified with the creation of Pakistan in 1947.[189] The fact that Gujarat has a common border with Pakistan reactivated ancestral fears in 1965 when the "Land of the Pure" declared war on India and used Gujarat as a battlefield. A certain brand of ordinary prejudice pervades in the state,[190] indicative of a dominant political culture characterized by hostility toward Muslims accompanied by communal violence that has made Ahmedabad the Indian city most affected in terms of casualties per inhabitant.[191]

But even if Gujarat is a special region whose culture had elective affinities with Hindu nationalism, Modi forged there a political style and repertoire that he managed to propagate, with variants, to the rest of India, using this state as his launchpad. Not only did he use his plebeian background and the growth-rate records of Gujarat to convince the plebeians that he would develop the country for them—as one of them—but he exploited the fear of the Other in the context of new Islamist attacks, which enabled the Sangh Parivar to reactivate the majority's inferiority complex and the Hindu sense of vulnerability mentioned previously.

3

Modi's Rise to Power, or How to Exploit Hope, Fear, and Anger

TO UNDERSTAND HOW NARENDRA MODI WAS PROPELLED to India's head of state in 2014, despite having never held national-level office—an achievement that only one of his predecessors as prime minister, H. D. Deve Gowda, had accomplished, in 1996—it is essential to revisit the circumstances in which the spring 2014 general elections were held. The political context played a significant role, as, for instance, the Congress Party was going through a delicate transition: after ten years as prime minister, the aging Manmohan Singh handed over the reins to an inexperienced Rahul Gandhi. The economic context was also important, as economic growth had taken a downturn in India, enabling Modi to tout the "Gujarat model" and its growth rate. But the social and psychological context warrant particular attention for, unlike the two preceding factors, they were less dependent on circumstances and even marked a turning point toward a new political culture that was destined to last.

The year 2014 in fact marked the height of a cycle that had begun at the start of the previous decade with the reactivation of the Hindu majoritarian inferiority complex in connection with a wave of Islamist attacks. In this context, Modi's unabashed Hindu nationalism found new resonance,[1] and his political style, which he had fine-tuned on the Gujarati scene, turned out to be relevant nationwide: fear of Pakistan and rejection of a threatening Other—the Indian Muslim, perceived as a potential Islamist with probable connections to Pakistan—formed the backdrop that seemed to legitimate a new political discourse.

But before voters could choose him, Modi first had to gain acceptance by his own family, not only his party, for which L. K. Advani was preparing to run for prime minister for the third time, but also—and especially—the RSS, whose leaders were not entirely pleased with Modi's manner of governing. And if Modi managed to impose himself on the Sangh Parivar in 2013, it was not only for a lack of rivals (Advani no longer seemed credible) but also due to an internal transformation of the Sangh Parivar—including its plebeianization—and the BJP's choice of polarization as an electoral strategy.

The 2014 elections thus involved the meeting of a man and an organization as well as a society undergoing transformation. Modi's success, however, was not a foregone conclusion. It relied on the national deployment of the populist "tool kit" he had used in Gujarat and the mobilization of an army of activists during one of the longest election campaigns in the history of India.

The Political Orchestration
of the Hindu Sense of Vulnerability

India was hit by an unprecedented wave of Islamist terrorism in the early 2000s, but the psychological impact of the attacks on the majoritarian community, in terms of its exacerbated sense of vulnerability, can only be explained by the Sangh Parivar's political exploitation of them.

Islamist Terrorism in the 2000s

Between 2001 and 2008, India was one of the countries in the world that witnessed the most terrorist attacks. For the first time since an episode in 1993, when attacks were limited to Mumbai, terrorists hit targets outside Kashmir, the usual epicenter of such violence. Listing them would be fastidious, but some of the incidents warrant mention.

In December 2000, the Red Fort bomb blast in Delhi, attributed to the Pakistan-based Lashkar-e-Taiba (LeT), marked the beginning of a series of violent attacks. On December 13, 2001, the attempt by a commando to infiltrate the Indian parliament was an even more striking turn in this trend: the fighting between the terrorist group and security forces claimed seven lives and sent a shockwave through India. Seven years later, on November 26, 2008, the shooting and bombing attacks in two luxury hotels, the main train station, a café patronized by foreigners, and a Jewish cultural center in Mumbai claimed 172 casualties; the shooting and hostage-taking went on for more than fifty hours. The commando, made up of twenty young Pakistani Laskar-e-Taiba members, was controlled from Pakistan. Although very well documented, these events were neither the deadliest nor the most significant in terms of domestic political implications in India.

The worst attack killed more than 200 people in Mumbai in July 2006 in a series of bomb blasts on suburban trains. The press, drawing from police sources, gave a detailed account of the attack.[2] According to the weekly magazine *India Today*, the plot was hatched in Bahawalpur (Pakistan) at the home of an LeT commander, with Indian LeT activists in attendance.[3] Some fifty people had received training in the manufacture of explosive devices in Bahawalpur. To conduct this operation, according to *India Today*, they split up into seven teams made up of a Pakistani and an Indian, each carrying a pressure cooker filled with between 2 and 2.5 kilograms of RDX explosive (coming from Pakistan) mixed with between 3.5 and 4 kilograms of ammonium nitrate (coming from Mumbai). A wide-circulation magazine, *India Today*, thus emphasized—on the basis of police sources—terrorist collaboration between Pakistani Islamists and Indian Muslims,[4] among whom were former members of a student organization, SIMI (Students Islamic Movement of India), that had been banned after September 11, 2001, for praising Osama bin Laden as "a true mujahid."[5]

SIMI had been founded in 1977 at the Aligarh Muslim University in Uttar Pradesh.[6] The campaign to build a temple in Ayodhya had accelerated the radicalization of the group, which called for a violent form of jihad in 1991.[7] The pogrom in Gujarat further amplified the phenomenon, while SIMI had already gone underground in 2001. A SIMI leader interviewed by Irfan Ahmad expressed the thirst for revenge that was driving the organization in the first decade of the 2000s:

> They [the RSS] are already killing Muslims on a daily basis. They rape our sisters, and we remain a mute spectator. What did we get in the past fifty years? Anti-Muslim riots! They visit tyranny upon Muslims, rape our sisters, and the government remains a spectator. If we do not take up swords and wage jihad, what will we do? Will we regain the lost chastity of our sisters? . . . It is our religious duty to protect their chastity and stop the genocide of Muslims. If we are killed in the course of jihad, we would become martyrs. This death is a thousand times better than the death of humiliation. In Gujarat we were slaughtered like carrots [*gajar muli ki tarah*].[8]

Former SIMI members allegedly founded the Indian Mujahideen (IM) movement that came together in 2006 or 2007. This group claimed four attacks in 2007–2008: the attack on Uttar Pradesh courts in 2007 and, in 2008, bombings in Jaipur in May, Ahmedabad in August, and New Delhi in September. Its messages claiming responsibility for these acts, all in English, presented IM as an organization acting in the name of India's Muslim community to avenge the violence perpetrated in Ayodhya and Gujarat.[9] The manifesto claiming the attack against the courts in Uttar Pradesh was a wholesale indictment against the judiciary system that had not delivered justice to Muslim victims of Hindu nationalist violence. It also insisted on the fact that IM was a "purely Indian" movement that had no connection with other foreign organizations and asked other movements based in Pakistan, such as LeT, not to claim these blasts.

Most of the suspects arrested in connection with the 2007–2008 attacks turned out to be Indian Muslims, including the ten defendants put behind bars after the violence in Ahmedabad. Many of them were members of SIMI. They often had attended university and belonged to the middle class. What appeared in the Indian media as an Indianization of jihadism was quite fragmentary, as evident in the 2008 Mumbai attacks, which were orchestrated from Pakistan. However, the fact that, according to press reports, Indian Muslims seemed to be increasingly taking part in terrorist acts on their own soil marked a turning point because it reactivated the Hindu sense of vulnerability.

From the Politics of Fear to the Politics of Anger—and Revenge

Long after the attacks in the early 2000s—and their near cessation in major cities—reliable opinion polls show that an Islamist threat was increasingly more keenly felt and that the fear of attacks remained omnipresent. In 2017, nearly ten years after the Mumbai bombings, a Pew Research Center survey revealed that 76 percent of Indians still considered terrorism the main problem facing India, just behind crime (84 percent).[10] Even more surprisingly, ISIS topped the list of threats facing the country for 66 percent of respondents—a record—even though the organization had never struck in the country.[11]

In the context of the wave of attacks in the first decades of the 2000s, Hindu nationalists tried to appear as defenders of their endangered community and conflated Islamism and Islam. In 2006, a veteran member of the movement, Subramanian Swamy, published a book titled *Hindus under Siege: The Way Out*. He wrote,

> *We Hindus are under siege today and we do not know it!!* That is what is truly alarming. Hindu society could be dismembered today without much protest since we have been lulled into complacency or have lost the capacity to think collectively as Hindus. . . . For example, recently, we had a near disaster in Ayodhya: Pakistan-trained foreign terrorists slipped into India and traveled to Ayodhya to blow up the Ram. Their attempt was foiled by courageous policemen. But did the representative government of 870 million Hindus of India react in a meaningful way—that is, did it retaliate to deter such attacks in the future? . . . No wonder terrorists have continued to target and disrupt India, and Hindus are their focus.[12]

Terrorism was not the only threat weighing on Hindus, according to Swamy: demographic trends were another, which also pertained to

Christians due to their proselytizing activities. He maintained that *"Hindus are facing a terrible pincer; Islamic fast population growth and illegal migration, in conjunction with Christian money-induced conversion activities."*[13] He viewed northeast India as a particularly critical area due to the strong Christian presence there, immigration from Bangladesh, and a high Muslim birth rate, which he claimed would make Muslims a majority in fourteen Assam districts by 2031. He wrote, "We see what Muslim majority will mean to Hindus when we look at the situation in Kashmir."[14]

This discourse, repeated at every possible turn by all Hindu nationalist press organs and leaders in keeping with a well-oiled politics of fear, heightened the majoritarian community's sense of vulnerability. This repertoire illustrates how, according to Arjun Appadurai, "predatory identities" exploit "the fear of small numbers" that comes from the demographic delusion mentioned above, as well as from the "anxiety of incompleteness" that afflicts ethnic communities when these communities do not coincide with the nation-state. In such cases, "the existence of even the smallest minority within national boundaries is seen as an intolerable deficit in the purity of the national whole."[15] This desire for purity (and therefore the elimination of minorities) has always driven the proponents of Hindutva aspiring to build a Hindu Rashtra, but it became even more pressing with the intensification of fear of external and internal threats, because national unity then became a categorical imperative.

The Sangh Parivar's goal, however, was first to bring Hindus from fear to outrage and anger, a theme that all populists exploiting social frustration have developed in the early twenty-first century.[16] But this is not a new phenomenon.[17] Ethnic nationalism always draws from a wellspring of resentment—the gap between an ideal to which one aspires and one's actual condition.[18] This mechanism, which was discussed in chapter 1 when explaining the birth of Hindu nationalism and which was reactivated in the 1980s, as mentioned above, had found expression in anti-Muslim anger. During the Ayodhya movement, the Sangh Parivar had promoted a new image of Ram as an angry god.[19] Today, they more frequently use the image of "angry Hanuman," the commander of Ram's armies, to represent an equally muscular and more savage form of outrage.[20]

Anger was simmering already among a large swath of Indian youth who felt increasingly frustrated in the early 2010s in the face of an obvious contradiction. On one hand, India had experienced two-digit economic growth for years, ushering the country into a new era whose ideal self-image increasingly overlapped with that of Western consumer society—hence the making of the aspiring neo-middle class mentioned in chapter 2, a social category living on hope. On the other hand, inequalities were increasing,[21] as the country was not creating enough jobs for its youth, at once due to a population growth rate that put 10 million newcomers on the labor market each year and a cyclical slump that considerably lowered India's growth rate at the end of the last decade. One of the social categories that suffered most from this contradiction was none other than the neo-middle class. However, many middle-class, upper-caste young people who already believed they were victims of positive discrimination felt similar frustration in cities and in rural areas alike, since the urban/rural divide was tending to blur as it did in Gujarat. Hindu nationalists began to focus on these "angry young men," seeking to channel their anger by devising a new polarization strategy targeting Muslims.[22]

This strategy emerges clearly from the analysis and fieldwork done by Prashant Jha in Uttar Pradesh in 2017. His conclusions highlight practices initiated ten years previously. One local BJP leader, in fact, explained to him how the party sought to portray Hindus as the victims of Muslims and those who protected them politically, especially because Muslim butchers continued to slaughter cows: "The point is to show we are the victims. This will get Hindus angry. They will then realize they have to unite against the Muslims."[23] The same BJP leader thus justified the "pink revolution" theme Modi introduced in the 2012 Gujarat election campaign to denounce the slaughtering of bovines: "When you think of these slaughterhouses, what images come to your mind? I think of Muslim butchers, cow slaughter and blood on the streets. I think of how the Muslims have taken over our public life, how they are destroying our culture and lifestyle, of how there are chicken and meat shops everywhere, and how they have become rich doing this. By raising it, we want to wake up the Hindu, get him angry."[24] Making Hindus angry by presenting Muslims as hostile to their values and enjoying privileges (granted to them in exchange for their electoral support for certain parties) is a BJP strategy that dates to the 1980s in connection with the aforementioned Shah Bano case. Circumstances in the 2000s have breathed new life into the tactic, however, by making the Muslim the ideal scapegoat in a context of extreme frustration among the youth.

A New Polarization Strategy for a New Culture of Rioting

As of 2004, this manufacturing of anger was combined with the polarization strategy that had proven successful in Gujarat in the 2002 balloting. In 2004, to everyone's surprise, the BJP lost the general elections, despite the strong economic performance that had led the BJP to adopt "India Shining" as its campaign slogan. Sangh Parivar opponents to the outgoing prime minister A. B. Vajpayee—who blamed the violence in Gujarat for the party's defeat—believed that in politics, economic achievements clearly did not guarantee victory and recommended reverting to the polarization strategy in a context that was propitious. The idea was not, of course, to orchestrate a pogrom but to step up low-intensity riots. Uttar Pradesh (UP), a key state due to its number of seats, was the testing ground for this strategy, which combined the mobilization of frustrated youth, victimization, outrage, and polarization. In UP, the 2004 defeat was particularly bitter for the BJP, as it went from twenty-two to ten seats, and proponents of the new strategy there were proportionally more numerous. Sudha Pai and Sajjan Kumar, two social scientists specializing in the region, see this as a "model": "The defining feature of this model is that rather than instigating major and violent state-wide riots as in the earlier phase, the BJP-RSS have attempted to create and sustain constant, low-key communal tension together with frequent, small, low-intensity incidents out of petty everyday issues that institutionalize communalism at the grass roots, to keep the pot boiling."[25] This approach was not solely motivated by political intentions, which is why the authors also mention the RSS: the aim was no longer only to polarize society prior to elections to gain immediate benefit in the polling; the goal was to promote social and even "civilizational" majoritarianism in such a way as to permanently Hinduize the country by delegitimizing minority cultures and secularism—to create what I call in the second part of this book a de facto Hindu Rashtra.

A distinctive feature of this model has to do with the actors involved. To instill Hindutva ideology deep into society, the Hindu nationalist leaders had to further integrate the masses and promote what Pai and Kumar call the "non Brahmanical Hindutva."[26] The best way to achieve this was to proceed by concentric circles, in such a way that local Sangh Parivar leaders recruited peripheral support for recurrent mobilization: "This group often trains a larger fuzzier group, often the educated, unemployed youth in backward states such as UP who are treated as a reservoir of support during agitations and lie dormant during lean times."[27] These men, in keeping with the state of virtually constant mobilization that Modi had initiated in Gujarat, were invited to take part in frequent and regular campaigns: against cow slaughter, conversions to a religion other than Hinduism, interreligious marriages, and so on. These mobilizations created an atmosphere of tension between Hindus and Muslims, making it possible to provoke a riot at the first available opportunity, as in Mau in 2005 and in Gorakhpur in 2007. The persistence of tension and the frequency of clashes were intended to prevent any return to normal—hostility between communities was supposed to become the rule, the new normal under which Hindus and Muslims were supposed to avoid interacting.[28] Implementation of this plan translated into a recrudescence of low-intensity riots (see table 3.1), enabling the Sangh Parivar to polarize society while staying "under the radar."

The strategy Pai and Kumar describe went together with a transformation of the Hindu nationalist movement affecting not only its mode of action but its social profile as well.

The Rise of the Bajrang Dal
and the Plebeianization of Hindu Nationalism

As mentioned above, from the 1980s onward, and even more clearly in the wake of the agitation against implementation of the Mandal Commission report in 1990, the ascension of lower castes and the increasing preponderance of caste politics in general had presented the RSS with a major challenge. Using religious populism to encourage the lower castes to think of themselves as Hindus first and foremost, in opposition to the Muslim Other, had become one of its priorities. The RSS spawned the Bajrang Dal precisely to reach out to these plebeians, who did not mix easily with the upper-caste-dominated ethos of the RSS.[29] The culture of the movement was intended to differ from its parent organization—it was even founded to avoid "mixing apples and oranges," according to Subramanian Swamy. Swamy put it even more bluntly: "The RSS may be Brahmin-dominated at the leadership level, but its front organizations like the Bajrang Dal are mostly the Hindu proletariats."[30]

The Bajrang Dal was founded in the spring of 1984 not by the RSS but under the auspices of the VHP, adding an additional layer of mediation that enabled the parent organization to work undercover. The Bajrang Dal was tasked with helping the VHP build up Hindu mobilization in the Ayodhya affair (see chapter 2), and it was also the organization expected to carry out the Sangh Parivar's dirty work. The name of this organization proved that the VHP was seeking to form shock troops: the word *Bajrang*, meaning "strong," is associated with Hanuman and refers to the club that he is always depicted as brandishing. In fact, the Bajrang Dal's first mission, in September 1984, was to ensure security for the Ram Janaki Yatra, a procession that set out from Sitarmahi in Bihar for Ayodhya, carrying effigies of Ram and Sita that the "pilgrims" claimed to want to "liberate."[31]

The first Bajrang Dal leader, Vinay Katiyar, was, as one might expect, an RSS pracharak who, after having embraced this career in 1972, had been organizing secretary of the ABVP. But his profile contrasted with the Brahminical archetype typical of this position due to his caste: he was not a

TABLE 3.1. Ten years of communal riots in India

Year	2007			2008			2009			2011		
States	N	D	W	N	D	W	N	D	W	N	D	W
Assam	7	0	29	10	2	34	20	10	83	9	3	2
Bihar	26	4	139	25	6	118	40	4	146	26	4	9
Gujarat	57	8	126	79	5	228	63	4	151	47	3	14
Jharkhand	18	2	60	29	8	105	20	1	53	12	5	6
Karnataka	64	4	207	108	4	163	110	13	292	70	4	18
Madhya Pradesh	180	22	459	131	32	323	106	14	316	81	15	18
Maharashtra	140	9	435	109	26	513	128	22	389	88	15	34
Rajasthan	30	1	89	39	4	139	52	10	140	42	16	20
Uttar Pradesh	138	37	397	114	18	408	159	32	525	84	12	34
West Bengal	18	1	73	10	0	73	17	5	83	15	3	3
Total, including figures from other states	761	99	2227	943	167	2354	849	125	2461	580	91	189

Sources: Statements in reply to Lok Sabha questions: Government of India, Ministry of Home Affairs, "Lok Sabha, Unstarred Question no. 590, to Be Answered on the 6th February 2018," accessed on March 18, 2018, http://164.100.47.190/lok-sabhaquestions/annex/14/AU590.pdf; Government of India, Ministry of Home Affairs, "Lok Sabha, Unstarred Question no. 3586, to Be Answered on the 8th August 2017," accessed March 18, 2018, https://mha.gov.in/MHA1/Par2017/pdfs/par2017-pdfs/ls-08082017-en-glish/3586.pdf ; Government of India, Ministry of Home Affairs, "Lok Sabha, Unstarred Question no. 1606 to Be Answered on the 2nd December, 2014," Ministry of Home Affairs, accessed December 10, 2020, https://mha.gov.in/MHA1/Par2017/pdfs/par2014-pdfs/ls-021214/1606.pdf; and "Annexure in Reply to Parts (a) & (b) of the Lok Sabha Unstarred Question no. 2545 for 10.08.2010 Regarding 'Communal Violence' Statement Showing Number of Communal Incidents, Person Killed and Injured therein in the Country during the Last Three Years, i.e. 2007, 2008 and 2009," accessed December 10, 2020, http://164.100.47.193/Annexure_new/lsq15/5/au2545.htm.

Note: N = number of riots; D = number killed; W = number injured.

"twice born" like nearly all of the pracharak at that time but a Kurmi (OBC). His origins are an indication of the plebeian nature of the Bajrang Dal, an organization that was not meant to cultivate the RSS ethos. Moreover, the Bajrang Dal did not claim to have the same degree of discipline. Its members were not required to meet daily like the swayamsevak in the RSS shakha but simply to take part in training camps where they were supposed to learn "how to be bold."[32] Up until 1993, the Bajrang Dal did not even have a uniform. Such attire does not seem to have particularly caught on since then: the Bajrang Dalis still recognize one another by one sign only, the saffron-colored headband marked "Ram." Those I interviewed in Madhya Pradesh in the early 1990s were for the most part unemployed and involved in semilegal activities, such as gambling and especially lotteries.

2012			2013			2014			2015			2016			2017		
N	D	W	N	D	W	N	D	W	N	D	W	N	D	W	N	D	W
0	0	0	0	0	0	1	0	23	3	0	10	12	3	19	16	4	45
21	3	172	63	7	283	61	5	294	71	20	282	65	4	230	85	3	321
57	5	5	68	10	184	74	7	215	55	8	163	53	6	116	50	8	125
11	1	35	12	2	35	10	1	102	28	3	118	24	5	110	49	2	204
69	3	221	73	1	235	73	6	177	105	8	337	101	12	248	100	9	229
92	9	245	84	11	256	56	12	167	92	9	177	57	3	191	60	9	191
94	15	280	88	12	352	97	12	198	105	14	323	68	6	234	46	2	136
37	6	117	52	2	194	72	14	139	65	5	150	63	5	117	91	12	175
118	39	500	247	77	360	133	26	374	155	22	419	162	29	488	195	44	542
23	9	66	24	1	80	16	6	32	27	5	84	32	4	252	58	9	230
568	94	2117	823	133	2269	644	95	1921	751	97	2264	703	86	2321	822	111	2384

Katiyar, moreover, said in an interview with the press, "Might is the only law I understand. Nothing else matters to me. In India it is a war-like situation as between Rama and Ravana."[33] According to one of Manjari Katju's informers, routine Bajrang Dal activities at the local level ranged from the surveillance (and protection) of Hindu girls in the neighborhood to preventing cows from being slaughtered in abattoirs and included systematic spying on local Muslims, especially when they were Bangladeshis.[34] But the biggest case involving the Bajrang Dal was of course the Ayodhya movement, in which its operatives were con-stantly on the front lines of the agitation. In 1990, many of them were among the kar sevak who stormed the Babri Masjid and were the first to face the Uttar Pradesh government crackdown. On December 6, 1992, they were again in the lead and actively took part in the demolition of the mosque in Ayodhya and the building of a makeshift temple (Ram Mandir) on its ruins. At the same time, the Bajrang Dal was also in-volved in countless riots pitting Hindus against Muslims all over India. For instance, in Bhopal, where rioting following the demolition of the Babri Masjid left 161 dead—most of them Muslims—Bajrang Dalis played a key role. One of the protagonists in the riot told me shortly afterward: "We received the order from the Sangh Parivar not to go to Ayodhya [on December 6, 1992] because there was the premonition [*purvabhas*] that a fight might happen here [in Bhopal]. Therefore, a few people stayed here on alert. . . . We took part in the riot. Muslim people killed policemen and looted the people. Therefore, we took part [in the riot] and then scared the Muslims away."[35] The Bajrang Dal was banned by Narasimha Rao's government, as was the VHP and the RSS after the demolition of the Babri Masjid. The group was legalized again the following year, but it was not in a position simply to revert to its prior activities, because the RSS and the rest of the Sangh Parivar—starting with the BJP—wanted to have a better grip on an organization that had resisted any form of discipline during the Ayodhya movement. While there is no doubt that the demolition of the Babri Masjid was part of the Sangh Parivar's plan, the sequence of events made its leaders fear they would be outflanked in the long run by elements determined to do things their own way. Seeing that some operatives who had taken part in tearing down the mosque went so far as to pose for the cameras with a knife between their teeth, it became particularly necessary to set the Bajrang Dal straight.

The RSS therefore drew up statutes to frame its activity. On July 11, 1993, the Bajrang Dal—which existed legally only in a few states— became a nationwide organization and was officially designated as the youth wing of the VHP.[36] It acquired a uniform—blue shorts, a white shirt, and an ochre-colored scarf—and a handbook for the trainers for the 350-odd camps the Bajrang Dal ran all over India.[37] In the preface to this little book written in highly Sanskritized Hindi, Acharya Giriraj Kishore, then VHP second in command, urged the Bajrang Dal to show greater discipline: "Whether it is an individual or a nation, the entire society or an organization, only one who knows discipline can achieve success, awareness and excellence. Without discipline, there can be no success."[38]

Despite having an emphasis on discipline reminiscent of the RSS, the Bajrang Dal differed from the parent organization with respect to its attitude toward violence. It was as if the RSS had outsourced violence to the Bajrang Dal, an organization that proved useful to reach out to young, plebeian Hindus.

A New Social Profile: The Sangh Parivar
and Its "Angry Young Men"

At the start of the 2010s, the Sangh Parivar appeared transformed by twenty-five years of activism and militancy in the framework of the Ayodhya movement and other campaigns. While the RSS sought to preserve its quietist, Sanskritized image, it had set in motion important changes regarding its social profile and modus operandi. The objective remained the same: in the name of Hindutva, the movement continued to mobilize Hindus against Muslims over and above caste and sectarian divisions. The strategy of emulating the Other was also omnipresent: that was the guiding rationale behind the Sangh Parivar's decision to arm these same Hindus to resist the Islamists by imitating them. Electoral tactics also continued to inform the Hindu nationalist approach in that polarization of society by resorting to communal riots had become a method to win elections. But gradually, new actors have gained momentum, starting with the Bajrang Dal and its "angry young men." These three words form the title of chapter 4 of Snigdha Poonam's book on India's youth, based on fieldwork done in the mid-2010s. This chapter shows the strong affinities this angry youth has with Narendra Modi's political repertoire.

One such figure that Poonam analyzes in detail is Vikas Thakur. A Rajput (upper caste) from Uttar Pradesh, he voices his resentment related to his family's social decline. This was typical of the cash-strapped petty aristocracy that found itself on the losing end of the rise of the lower castes. Thakur blamed Congress policies that had brought about social change detrimental to his milieu and himself personally: "'subsidies' to the poor, 'appeasement' of minorities, employment and education 'quotas' for the backward castes."[39] The alternative identity he found came to him from Hindu nationalism, through the Bajrang Dal, which he joined at age thirteen. He renewed his self-esteem through militant defense of his religion: the organization laid down the law in his neighborhood of Meerut, and, he remembers, in return, "People give you *izzat* (respect)."[40] At university, Thakur signed up to join the ABVP, the

RSS student organization, another of its branches that readily snatched up angry young men from upper castes who felt increasingly threatened by their loss of social status. In 2012, he was exasperated by the electoral gains of the Samajwadi Party (Socialist Party) in the state elections of Uttar Pradesh, where the party supporters were mainly composed of OBCs and Muslims. He devoted himself all the more to Sangh Parivar actions, such as the fight against "love jihad" (see chapter 6). In 2013, he placed himself in the service of Narendra Modi and was assigned to one of the teams in charge of social media. Thousands of others did the same.

Moyukh Chatterjee paints a similar portrait, though even more complex, of a Bajrang Dali from Ahmedabad, Kunal. Like Thakur, Kunal is a resentful Rajput: practically illiterate, this young man is obliged to live in a Dalit neighborhood whose inhabitants he despises. Having no stable job, he and the group of Bajrang Dalis he leads live from hand to mouth. To make up for his lack of status, he posts pictures of himself on Facebook in warrior-like poses, clutching a *trishul* (Shiva's trident). Kunal describes himself as a "fanatic" (*kattar*), because he is a "tough guy." He proved this during the 2002 pogrom when he took part in the violence by burning down a mosque with police complicity and continues to flex his muscle by preventing Muslims by force from going out with young Hindu women—and this is how he compensates: "In Ahmedabad—where everyone has finer clothes, smarter phones, and better paying jobs—Kunal and his boys are proud of saving Hinduism from effete Hindus and treacherous Muslims."[41] For those with no social capital, muscular devotion to the cause of the majority religion is their only claim to fame.

For all these young men, even more than for others, Modi is a hero. Like them, he started out with nothing, has remained single, and defends Hindus using force—without ever apologizing for it. Modi's popularity among these plebeian youth mattered to the RSS in 2013, when the BJP had to select its candidate for prime ministership. While the party could rely confidently on the support of the middle class, Modi could bring the plus vote not only of the neo-middle class in the making but of plebeians as well. One of the reasons the Sangh Parivar ultimately decided to make Modi its candidate in 2013 lies in his popularity with the movement's youth, not only among the swayamsevak meeting daily in the shakha but also among affiliates like the Bajrang Dal and the ABVP, which had gained in importance since the Ayodhya movement.[42] This transformation of the Sangh Parivar reflected deeper social evolutions: the emergence of the neo-middle class that Modi had already won over in Gujarat, mounting Islamophobia (in the context of terrorist attacks) among Hindus that tended to blur caste divisions, and unabashed Hindu nationalism for which the 2002 pogrom had cleared the way. Compared to Modi, L. K. Advani was no longer equal to the situation, due not only to his age but also to his generation: his style, although it had signaled a qualitative leap in Hindu nationalism in the early 1990s, was too moderate.

Modi, on the other hand, promised to win an absolute majority without smoothing over the ridges of this ideology. He started campaigning within his party, the BJP, to earn its nomination as soon as he was re-elected chief minister of Gujarat in December 2012, basking in his third electoral success in his home state. First, he was appointed to the BJP Parliamentary Board in March 2013 and then as president of the Central Election Campaign Committee in June, over objections from L. K. Advani, his former mentor, who immediately resigned from all the offices he held within the BJP—before changing his mind, swayed by benevolent pressure from both the party and the RSS. But Narendra Modi's conquest of the party did not only irk members of its old guard. Some of its partners within the NDA, the coalition forged by Advani and Vajpayee in the 1990s, severed their ties, starting with the JD(U), the leader of which, Nitish Kumar, was chief minister of Bihar.

The 2014 Election Campaign

Modi's election campaign for the prime ministership in 2014 was unique and indeed opened a new chapter in Indian history, an era Sanjaya Baru, a former media advisor to Prime Minister Manmohan Singh, has called the "second republic"[43]—it will be seen why in the second part of this book. For the first time, a state chief minister who had never held office at the national level (ministerial or other) was leading the polls, promising to replicate at the national level the economic achievements he boasted of in his state. While previous BJP campaigns had been fairly collegial, true to long-standing party practices,[44] this time Modi was its only face, its only leader, and even its only program. This aspect of the 2014 campaign thus ticked off one of the boxes on the populist checklist mentioned above—the direct relation of the leader to "his" people. But others would follow.

Modi, One-Man Band and Orchestra Conductor

In 2014, Modi's national-populist panoply was based in promises of development à la "Gujarat model," his hostility to the establishment (and to Congress leaders in particular), the subordination of state institutions to the people's will, an ethnoreligious definition of this people, and the exploitation of the supposed threats facing it.

Regarding promises, Modi's campaign watchword was *development* at a time when an economic slump—and the correlative drop in job offers—was causing anxiety in public opinion. A Carnegie Endowment survey, moreover, showed that growth was the main campaign issue for voters, who clearly saw jobs behind this stated objective.[45] In such a context, Narendra Modi could all the more easily pose as Vikas Purush, or "Development Man," since his state showed remarkable growth rates. The snappy slogan Modi imposed on the campaign boiled down to two words: the "Gujarat model." Although no one really knew what it meant, it conveyed hopes of a better life.

Throughout the entire campaign, Modi repeatedly contrasted the mediocre performance of the rest of India with that of his state, systematically claiming that the Congress Party was to blame. He even campaigned in the Nehru/Gandhi historic constituency, Amethi, posing as Vikas Purush, and affirmed, "In so many years they have ruined the dreams of three generations. I am here to sow seeds of hope among the youth. I have come here to share your sadness and make your problems mine."[46] And then Modi rattled off his accomplishments in Gujarat.

The BJP election manifesto was written in a similar vein. It promised to modernize rural areas by dangling hopes of exporting to villages certain urban characteristics so as to diminish the most striking disparities and bring about a "rurban" India: "Through the idea of Rurban, we will bring urban amenities to our rural areas, while retaining the soul of the village." As for urban areas, the BJP promised to build 100 "smart cities" "enabled with the latest in technology and infrastructure—adhering to concepts like sustainability, walk to work etc."[47] The style of these promises shows the emphasis placed on "ideas" and "concepts" rather than on public policy, an indication of the preponderance of rhetoric typical of any election campaign, especially when in the populist vein.

At the same time, Modi's dismissal of the Congress made the party out to be more than an opponent: it was an enemy. The rejection of this party—a part of India's political pluralism—that Modi had already evidenced in the past reached new heights on December 22, 2013, when he declared at a rally in Mumbai, "This is the same land, the same Mumbai from where the call of Quit India was made [in 1942, by Gandhi, addressing the British] and the British had to finally leave India. From the same land, let the call of a Congress Free India come. Let the land that said Quit India say Congress Free India. . . . [The Congress is] immersed in vote bank politics and a party that has learnt the art of divide and rule very well from the British."[48] Modi did not only reject Congress (in a rather ironic manner here, as this party was at the forefront of the freedom movement against the Raj); he also spurned party politics in the name of national unity that he purported to represent. He moreover cried out, "In 2014, let us not vote for any party or person but let us vote for India!" To establish a direct relationship with the people, populists systematically relegate parties—and many institutions, as will be seen in part III—to the background.

In the same manner, Modi left it to the ballot box to judge the crimes he had been accused of in 2002 and that Congress repeatedly emphasized during the 2014 campaign. Talking about himself in the third-person singular, in April 2014 he resorted to the idioms of victimization and heroization: "I am convinced that if there is even a grain of truth in the allegations, I feel for India's bright future and traditions, Modi should be hanged in the street square. . . . There is a small coterie who think they have worked hard and created a storm. But Modi does not lose, does not die. . . . Now, I am in the people's court and I am waiting to hear from them, and their verdict."[49] These remarks tick off another box on the populism checklist, the rejection of institutions (in this case, the judiciary) in favor of the people's voice, the only legitimate one, as if voting for a person amounted to giving him a clean chit.[50]

In 2014, Modi made copious use of his lowly social background, a theme that he had not highlighted to such an extent in Gujarat. This was because in some parts of India, such as Bihar, the lower castes were more conscious of their identity.[51] Modi resorted to this register to distinguish himself from the Nehru/Gandhis, whom he continued to depict as monarchical heirs who held the underprivileged in contempt. He now called Rahul Gandhi "Mr. Golden Spoon."[52] He laid into Priyanka Gandhi, Rajiv and Sonia's daughter, whose popularity—partly due to her resemblance to Indira—was a source of concern for the BJP. Modi explained in a rally that the only reason she was in politics was out of filial piety. Priyanka retorted that the level of such a remark was "low," a word Modi immediately—and tactically—interpreted as a reference to his caste. In a television interview with Arnab Goswami, he went on the defensive: "Don't I have the right to at least state the truth? Is it because I come from a humble background, from a humble family? Has this country become like that? Has my democracy submitted itself to one family? And when a poor man says something, there is uproar."[53] Goswami, whose complacency will be dealt with in part III,[54] did not object that there were no insinuations about social hierarchy in Priyanka Gandhi's remark. Casting himself as the standard-bearer for India's downtrodden—for the people against the patricians—in an election rally in Muzaffarpur, Bihar, Modi added that the next decade would belong to Dalits and OBCs.[55]

Along with these innovations, Modi continued to use the Hindu nationalist themes that had contributed so much to his success in Gujarat. There was no need to overdo it, as the memory of his actions in the 2002 pogrom persisted enough for a few discreet remarks to rekindle the aura of the Emperor of Hindu Hearts. Mindful of showing Muslims a token of interest while not treating them as ordinary citizens, Modi invited them to attend his rallies, reserving space for them in the audience. No one could ignore their presence as skullcaps and burqas were handed out at the entrance before they were directed to a corner.[56]

Modi's campaign took on an increasingly Hindu nationalist turn in the final days, as it had done in the elections in Gujarat. He made a point of visiting temples and holy places—all Hindu—at stops on the campaign trail. He thus paid obeisance at a Vaishno Devi shrine prior to a rally in Jammu and Kashmir.[57] He appeared with many religious figures, generally dressed in saffron clothing. He shared, for instance, the stage with Baba Ramdev on many occasions, thereby enjoying the popularity of this yogi who teaches yoga every morning to millions of people over television channels that he owns.[58] In the same vein, Modi decided to contest elections in the constituency of Varanasi, the spiritual capital of Hinduism—and not only in his native state, in Vadodara, where he also ran. (He won both seats but kept only the former.) He explained that he was merely answering the "call" of the sacred river Ganges.[59] The speech he gave in December 2013 in Varanasi was peppered with Hindu references, along with mentions of his visits to Kashi Vishwanath and Sankat Mochan Temples. To the sound of conch shells being blown (the call to Shiva devotees), he declared that he had "come from the land of Somnath to seek the blessing of Baba Vishwanath," spoke of the need to resurrect the Ganges, a dying river, and "exhorted the voters of UP to help usher in *Ram Rajya*." After him, Kalyan Singh, former BJP chief minister of UP, began his speech with ideological-religious slogans, such as "Jai Shri Ram" and "Har Har Mahadev," and bellowed, "I do not say that every Muslim is a terrorist. But I ask why every terrorist is a Muslim."[60] While he did not go to Ayodhya, Narendra Modi held one meeting in the neighboring town of Faizabad in May 2014, with a huge portrait of Lord Ram hung as a backdrop. At the same time, the closing lines of the BJP election manifesto simply mentioned that the party was committed to exploring "all possibilities within the framework of the Constitution to facilitate the construction of the Ram Temple in Ayodhya."[61]

As was his custom in Gujarat, toward the end of his campaign, Modi harped on the threat of Pakistan, not only to promote Hindu nationalism but also to disqualify his opponents. While campaigning in Jammu and Kashmir, he tweeted, "3 AKs are very popular in Pakistan: AK 47, AK Antony & AK-49." The first term of this three-part alliteration (one of Modi's favorite stylistic devices) referred to Islamic terrorism from Pakistan; the second pointed to A. K. Antony, the UPA defense minister under Manmohan Singh; and last, Modi made fun of Arvind Kejriwal by dubbing him "AK 49" in reference to his brief forty-nine-day stint as chief minister of New Delhi in 2013–2014. In a rally in Hiranagar, Modi said that these three AKs were helping Pakistan (a way of presenting Antony as a traitor to the nation out of weakness). In the case of Kejriwal, the accusation stemmed from the fact that his website showed half of Kashmir as belonging to Pakistan—a geopolitical reality India continues to challenge, as it claims the entire state.[62] One month later, a former BJP minister of the Bihar government known for his provocative statements, Giriraj Singh, said in a rally in Mohanpur, "Those opposing Narendra Modi are looking at Pakistan, and such people will have a place in Pakistan and not in India."[63]

The BJP's polarization strategy relied more, however, on the exploitation of local conflicts, such as the Muzaffarnagar riots and their aftermath. In August 2013, this outbreak of violence caused the death of 55 people—most of them Muslim—and the displacement of 51,000 others—a record in UP.[64] BJP MLAs who had been formally implicated by the police, in particular due to anti-Muslim provocations they had posted on social media, were "felicitated by the BJP at an Agra rally addressed by Narendra Modi, where they were hailed as 'heroes' who had 'ensured the safety of Hindus' at the time of riots."[65] When it came time to distribute tickets, the party nominated three of these MLAs who were under investigation for their role in the Muzaffarnagar riots.[66]

In an election speech in a riot-hit village near Muzaffarnagar, Amit Shah, who had been appointed by Modi in charge of the election campaign in Uttar Pradesh (a promotion to which we will return), called on voters to take "revenge," as if Muslims had been guilty of some crime: "Justice is not being done to the people and it's time to take revenge. It was during the Mughal rule that swords and arrows were used to take revenge. But now you have to vote to take revenge. Press the right button [on the voting machine] to show them their right place."[67] Such a speech provided the third logical term to the sequence mentioned above, moving from fear, to anger, and, in the end, to revenge. A BJP spokesman said that, in this speech, Shah had "captured the mood of the nation."[68] The Election Commission of India objected to such rhetoric, saying that it amounted to using religion to electoral ends and therefore contravened section 123(3) of the Representation of the People Act. But Amit Shah merely apologized, only to behave in a similar fashion one month later when he described Azamgarh—a city where several Islamic institutions are located—as "the base of terrorists."[69]

The Tsunamodi: High-Tech Communication and "Vote Mobilizers"

A number of observers called Modi's campaign—which swept up every district in its path in north and west India—a tsunami, giving rise to the neologism "Tsunamodi."[70] But the term applies as much to the election results—a "Modi wave," as will be seen below—as to his canvassing manner since, beyond the themes Modi stressed in his campaign, once again his style was the most impressive feature. Over the course of a campaign of exceptional duration (eight months), Modi traveled 186,411 miles to hold 475 regular rallies. (By contrast, Indira Gandhi had held only 252 such rallies over the two months of her 1971 campaign.)[71] Modi related to an unprecedentedly large number of people directly, sometimes scolding them, sometimes taking them into his confidence, addressing them as he might a "friend." ("My friends" continued to be his favorite expression.) The effect of these public gatherings was amplified by the use of holograms. While he sometimes spoke at three or four venues in a single day, his words—and his image—were broadcast to some 100 locations at the same time. According to his website, 3D holographic projections delivered twelve speeches across 1,350 venues during the months of April and May 2014.[72] Rajdeep Sardesai gives additional figures: "A crew of 2500 members handling 125 3D projector units were involved and more than 7 million people reportedly witnessed the 3D shows over twelve days" at the height of the hologram campaign.[73] An activist who coordinated the hologram operation in Uttarakhand explained, "In rural areas, the 3D projection is like magic. People came from faraway villages to watch this."[74] Modi continued to be seen by some people as endowed with supernatural powers.

Holograms, however, were intended to reach out mainly to urban dwellers. For villagers, Modi primarily used vans fitted with a big screen that broadcast propaganda videos. In Uttar Pradesh, for instance, 200 NaMo Rath (Maximos, a model made by Mahindra & Mahindra, equipped with giant screens) visited 19,000 villages in the 403 constituencies (out of 443 in all) to show a ten-minute recorded speech.[75] In addition, Modi made a direct connection with voters through thousands of tea stalls, where he held "Chai pe Charcha" (informal chats over tea) with Indian citizens who wished to interact with him via the internet.[76] In 4,000 tea stalls scattered across twenty-four states, he thus chatted with them using such technologies as videoconferencing and mobile broadband. A veteran RSS member who spent considerable time with Modi in the BJP—before finally abandoning politics—K. N. Govindacharya, told an investigative reporter, "Narendra's forte is political marketing. His mental matrix is simple. Politics is equal to power. Power stems to elections. Elections are battles of images. And therefore, politics revolves around images, messages, and signaling."[77]

Modi's connection with the people relied on an activist network that, as it had been in Gujarat, was far more extensive than even the Sangh Parivar. The techniques described above could only function thanks to a substantial body of "vote mobilizers," as Pradeep Chhibber and Susan Ostermann call them.[78] These individuals did more than install mics in tea stalls, canvass door-to-door, and hand out leaflets at markets as in the "good old days." They also mobilized voters over social media and the internet. These foot soldiers of Indian politics have played an especially important role in a country like India, where politicians cannot rely solely on media exposure to win elections. And Modi was particularly effective in recruiting vote mobilizers beyond the pool of BJP activists. A CSDS opinion poll found that only 19 percent of the mobilizers working for Modi were party members.[79] And 32 percent of them would have voted for another party had he not been the BJP candidate for prime ministership.[80] Chhibber and Ostermann have found a similar correlation between the number of vote mobilizers and BJP electoral performance in such key states as Uttar Pradesh and Rajasthan.

These vote mobilizers were part of a broader scheme that confirms Modi's ability to build a support network of people personally devoted to him, in that he reaped the fruit of a strategy already tried and tested in Gujarat when the RSS had withdrawn its backing, requiring him to design an alternative support structure. In 2012, he had professionalized this system, as mentioned above, by putting together a team of IT experts, many of whom were trained in the United States. Their leader, Prashant Kishore, officialized the organization in June 2013 by founding Citizens for Accountable Governance (CAG), headquartered in Gandhinagar—but officially apolitical, as Amogh Sharma explains:[81] "In the first few months after its inception, CAG cultivated an image of being an independent, non-partisan organisation unaffiliated with any political party, and its events were pitched with the purported aim of engaging citizens, especially young voters, in a conversation around participation in democratic politics in the lead up to the 2014 general elections. At the same time, however, these events were carefully designed to bolster Narendra Modi's image as a national leader—a fact that becomes clear only after analysing these events retrospectively."[82] This tactic, in the beginning, allowed Modi to be invited by the CAG to events organized with professionals or other nonpolitical groups. In 2014, CAG continued to deny any affiliation to any party and "claimed to be driven solely by their belief in Narendra Modi's leadership."[83] CAG was "associated with nearly every part of the campaign, ranging from door-to-door canvassing to social media management," and "by the virtue of Modi's fiat, CAG also had access to the support of all the BJP workers, all the *swayamsevak* from the Sangh Parivar who had been deputed to serve as foot soldiers for the BJP campaign, and was working with a number of other ad professionals that Narendra Modi had roped in for the campaign."[84] In other words, the Sangh Parivar was not on the forefront; Modi's team of professional campaigners and individual supporters was.

The 200–400 members of CAG were more than vote mobilizers, not only because, instead of being volunteers, they were paid, as were some 800 interns, but also because one of their missions was precisely to identify potential vote mobilizers and train them, so they could saturate the public space in their local area—and cyberspace—with their propaganda. Eventually, altogether, there were as many as 100,000 volunteer vote mobilizers campaigning for Modi in 2013–2014.[85] These supporters were grouped mostly into two networks: Modi 4 PM and Mission 272. (The latter name referred to the number of seats needed to give the BJP the majority in the Lok Sabha.)[86]

The vote mobilizers' motivations emerge clearly from the interview one of them gave Sheela Bhatt and which was reminiscent of Snigdha Poonam's portrait of Vikas Thakur. Pramod Singh, who runs a small travel agency in Bilaspur (a city in Chhattisgarh), first explains, "I was never interested in politics. I'm only interested in Modi. You can say I am a *Hinduvaadi* person [Hindutva activist]. But I have no interest in politics."[87] Pramod Singh joined the ranks of Modi supporters by registering on the India272.com website that the Gujarat chief minister launched in August 2013. He was tasked with posting propaganda messages on the website and then putting them out on Facebook and Twitter. All of Modi's support networks used social media. One such mobilizer told the press at the end of the campaign: "Every touch point with voters was critical for us. We aimed to connect with them wherever they were, and hence the use of TV, print, radio, hoardings, Facebook, Twitter, YouTube, WhatsApp, DTH, cable TV services, on-ground and offline people-connect initiatives."[88] While the communication teams handling Modi's campaign depended on CAG, a "nonpolitical" organization, the BJP's IT cell played a major role in Modi's 2014 campaign. Again, professionals instead of politicians had been at its helm since 2010, when it had been completely relaunched by the then–BJP president Nitin Gadkari. Its chief, Arvind Gupta, was another U.S.-trained IT expert who had worked in Silicon Valley before starting his own company in India.[89] After joining the BJP, he started the National Digital Operations Center in July 2013 at party headquarters with "a single point agenda—how to use digital technology to help win the 2014 election."[90] He was instrumental in recruiting a large number of vote mobilizers by calling on anyone who wanted to help out with Modi's campaign: one could simply call a toll-free number that would call back and assign a task. According to Gupta, the "BJP got 1.3 million volunteers through this."

If Gupta was based at BJP headquarters, this was not the case for another key figure in Modi's digital army, also an IT person returning from the United States, Rajesh Jain, whose role was mentioned above. His team had over 5,000 officers scrutinizing the attitude of the people in 155 key urban constituencies identified as "digital seats," as they had above-average internet penetration and greater social media use. The IT cells working for Modi fed them a constant stream of content. They broadcast Modi rallies live on a dedicated television channel, YuvaiTV, and the content was "simultaneously being edited into small clips for YouTube," while another team "live-tweeted most of Modi's key statements."[91] Up to 40,000 tweets were sent every day during the campaign. Gupta described some of the IT team's tactics as "multimedia carpet-bombing."[92] Many TV channels whose owners were already beholden to Modi or were laying the groundwork for the future contributed eagerly to this saturation of the public space by a candidate for the prime ministership,[93] taking advantage of the lack of legislation governing access to airwaves. A study by the CMS Media Lab showed that Modi received coverage on 33.21 percent of the prime-time news telecasts during the campaign from March 1 to April 30 (and more than 40 percent in the days before polling took place), compared to 10.31 percent for Arvind Kejriwal and 4.33 percent for Rahul Gandhi.[94]

The great communication steamroller was only possible owing to the financial resources the BJP could mobilize. In its May 24, 2014 edition, *The Economist* estimated that the party spent $1 billion out of a total of $4 billion during the 2014 election campaign, making the Indian elections the second most costly in the history of democracies after Barack Obama's first campaign for president of the United States.[95] This assessment tallies with the Center for Media Studies, which put the total figure closer to $5 billion.[96]

But what was the rhetoric of the campaign about? It was highly personalized, with slogans having the sole purpose of impressing Modi's name on people's minds, such as "Abki bar, Modi sarkar!" (This time, a Modi government!) In fact, the whole campaign focused on the candidate's qualities. In one ad taken out in newspapers and posted on walls, he was described as "Initiator, Innovator, Implementer." Another slogan spread like wildfire: "Acchhe din!"—referring to the "happy days" that awaited India.

The distribution of tickets reflected the new balance of power within the BJP. It was the handiwork of both Modi and Amit Shah, his trusted lieutenant for fifteen years in Gujarat. Born in 1964 into a wealthy merchant family from Mansa, near Ahmedabad, Shah had joined the RSS as a child. A VHP activist turned BJP politician, he was known for the handling of L. K. Advani's electoral campaigns in Gandhinagar in 1989.[97] Elected MLA in 1997 for the first time and subsequently reelected, he was not only the youngest member of Modi's government in 2002 but also the minister with the largest number of portfolios (up to ten[98]), including home. In addition, he "advised Modi on almost all matters related to party management and political strategy."[99] When Modi became the number one leader of the BJP in 2014, Shah automatically became the number two, and both of them prepared the list of candidates together.[100] They sidelined such BJP veterans as Jaswant Singh, minister for external affairs under Vajpayee. M. M. Joshi was persuaded to change constituencies to let Modi contest the seat he held in Varanasi.

The impression of a renewing of the political class that Modi wanted to give, like any populist leader battling an establishment accused of all manner of corruption, was enhanced by co-opting personalities from civil society—or, in any event, from outside the political sphere. Thus, a former chief of army staff, V. K. Singh, who had retired barely a year before, was given the BJP ticket to contest in Ghaziabad (Uttar Pradesh). The Mumbai police commissioner, Satyapal Singh, resigned from his post to be nominated by the party in Baghpat, another constituency of Uttar Pradesh. M. J. Akbar, whose journalistic career had taken him from *The Telegraph* to *India Today*, followed a similar trajectory, contesting in his home state of Bihar.

Modi played a central role in handing out tickets for seats in the Lok Sabha, after having explained to voters during his campaign tours that by voting for BJP candidates, they would be voting for him, further presidentializing the Indian parliamentary system. A full-page ad in English-language newspapers gave expression to this with a caption under Modi's portrait reading: "Your vote for the BJP candidate is a vote for me." Such personalization of the election worked to perfection. According to a CSDS exit poll, 27 percent of BJP voters backed its candidate only because of Modi.[101] The fact that BJP MPs owed him more or less everything was likely to induce them to obey Modi docilely if he became prime minister.

The personalization of the 2014 campaign thus undermined the collegial nature of decision making within the BJP. But Narendra Modi also wanted to emancipate himself from party allies in the NDA that had forced the Vajpayee government to water down the Hindu nationalist program in 1998–2004. Modi thus was not sorry to see the departure of the JD(U), which he found to be a particularly cumbersome partner. But to win an absolute majority for the BJP in the Lok Sabha, he had to avoid three-way contests that might have benefited the Congress. In some constituencies, he thus made a seat-sharing agreement not only with such long-standing allies as Shiv Sena in Maharashtra and Akali Dal in Punjab but also with other regional parties, such as the Telugu Desam Party in Andhra Pradesh and the Lok Janshakti Party in Bihar, both of which, hoping to ride the wave of Modi's popularity, returned to the NDA—having left it in protest over the pogrom in Gujarat in 2002.

New Wine in Old Bottles: The Sangh Parivar's Resilient Role

Concerning activist networks, one of Narendra Modi's major assets resided in his ability to combine new vote mobilizers and older networks. RSS backing was a significant factor in Modi's success in 2014, even if he had sought to break free from his old school by creating his own support network and making direct contact with certain RSS members. The organization's leadership did not take kindly to this show of independence typical of a populist approach, but it ended up backing Modi for reasons previously mentioned—and also because in 2014 the RSS was afraid that if the Congress remained in power, its leaders would step up its prosecution of RSS members accused of terrorism (an issue which will be further examined below).[102] As Modi was the most popular BJP leader within the Sangh Parivar and outside, the RSS leaders decided that he had to be supported by the whole "family."

During a meeting of the Akhil Bharatiya Pratinidhi Sabha, the top policy-making body of the RSS, held in March 2014 in Bangalore, the movement's joint general secretary, Dattatreya Hosabale, stated, "Modi is a strong leader. He is a swayamsevak himself and we are proud of it. The country wants a change. He has proved his worth in Gujarat."[103] But four days later, RSS chief Mohan Bhagwat, probably fearing the Modi mania that was taking over his organization—which was unaccustomed to personality cults—moved to rise above and even keep his distance from the rising star of Hindu nationalism: "We are not in politics. Our work is not to chant 'Namo, Namo.' We must work towards our own target."[104] In other words, the election notwithstanding, the RSS mission was to reform society through and through. Yet the RSS was already at work on the ground. Smita Gupta pointed out that "far from the TV cameras, it is the RSS that is working overtime, in the old fashioned way it knows best, door-to-door, its role extending well beyond managing the ubiquitous Namoraths that are penetrating the remotest villages."[105] In states where the BJP was still weak, such as West Bengal, the party's campaign relied even more heavily on the RSS.[106]

In Uttar Pradesh, India's largest state, where the stakes of the election were highest—it represented 80 seats out of 544—Modi preferred not to depend on the existing Sangh Parivar structure, though, partly because the BJP had been decaying and had even become ossified in that state. As mentioned above, he deputed Amit Shah,[107] who combined time-tested practices and unusual approaches. Shah reformed the BJP's organizational structure with the help of a young RSS cadre, Sunil Bansal.[108] They prioritized the booth level, forming "booth committees" with a mission of raising awareness among local voters of the importance of going to the polls—accompanying them if need be—and casting the right vote.[109] Shah also developed his own network of informers so as not to depend solely on components of the Sangh Parivar that might be somewhat biased. He hired specialized polling firms to help him monitor local opinion trends. He also adopted a tactic never before used by the Sangh Parivar on such a large scale: while until now, being proud of its ideology and the values it purported to convey, the movement was reluctant to co-opt external elements, Shah made it part of his doctrine to recruit turncoats, luring MLAs and cadres from other political parties in order to destabilize them. Even if Shah and Modi had used this technique in Gujarat to little consequence, due to the ideological proximity between the BJP and many members of the only other party of any significance, the Congress,[110] Shah applied this to members of the BSP and the SP in Uttar Pradesh. Last, Shah paid particular attention to the sociological makeup of the constituencies. Not content merely to resort to religious polarization strategy to unite Hindus against Muslims, he put candidates on the BJP ticket that had a useful social profile in terms of local class and especially caste arithmetic. In particular, he targeted the Dalit jatis and OBC jatis, which had not benefited from the rise to power of the BSP and the SP over the last two decades. As a result, he gave tickets to a large number of non-Jatavs SC politicians and non-Yadavs politicians. These candidates were in a position to attract voters who resented the dominant position that Jatavs and Yadavs had acquired in the state politics among Dalits and OBCs—a strategy that will be scrutinized in detail in the context of the 2019 election.

An (Almost) Unprecedented—and Unexpected— Electoral Success: Majoritarianism vs. Bahujanism

Never since 1984 had a political party managed to win an absolute majority in the Lok Sabha. Thanks to Modi, the BJP pulled off this feat, just barely—taking 282 out of the 543 seats with 31 percent of the vote—but it remained a remarkable score nonetheless, and unexpected, as no credible poll had anticipated it. The Congress Party, on the other hand, suffered the worst defeat in its history, winning only 44 seats with 19 percent of the vote, by 60 seats fewer than its first defeat by the BJP in 1998.

The BJP victory must nevertheless be qualified, as it reflects a high geographic concentration and hides the urban nature of its electoral base. The party fully benefited from the distortions inherent in the first-past-the-post system: less than one-third of the ballot enabled it to take 52 percent of the seats in the Lok Sabha. This "performance" was unique in the history of India. Up until then, no party—except the Congress in 1952—had managed to take half the seats with less than 40 percent of the vote. The amplification of the BJP's victory in terms of seats can be explained by the geographic concentration of its forces. While it is true that the BJP made headway in areas it set out to conquer, such as West Bengal, where it nearly tripled its 2009 score (from 6.1 to 16.8 percent of the vote), and Assam, where it progressed from 17.2 to 36.5 percent of the vote, it also advanced in Jammu and Kashmir, where it leaped from 18.6 to 32.4 percent. But these inroads did not translate into many seats (two in West Bengal and three in Jammu and Kashmir). On the other hand, the party won 190 out of the 225 seats in the Hindi belt, including 71 of the 80 seats in Uttar Pradesh, a decisive breakthrough. That figure rose to 216 when Gujarat was added (or 76 percent of the party's seats) and to 239 (nearly 85 percent) when Maharashtra was factored in. The BJP remained largely absent in the south—with the exception of Karnataka—and the eastern coastal states and northeastern states, with the exception of Assam and Arunachal Pradesh. If the BJP was thus kept out of entire regions, it was because regional parties put up strong resistance. Their stability was in fact remarkable, as they took exactly the same number of seats (212) with the same percentage of votes (46.6 percent) as in 2009.[111]

The BJP's performance was also particularly strong in urban areas. It had increased its appeal among voters in urban constituencies (those in which urbanites made up more than 75 percent of the total) as it garnered there 42 percent of the vote (or 11 percentage points more than its average score), while in semiurban constituencies (where urbanites make up between 25 and 74 percent of the total), it arrived at a score of 32 percent, and in rural constituencies (where urbanites make up less than 25 percent of the total), it was "only" 30 percent.

Even if it must be seen as nuanced, the BJP's success was remarkable. It was mainly explained by Modi's ability, already demonstrated in Gujarat in 2012, to mobilize traditional BJP supporters in larger numbers and to woo groups that until then did not vote for his party. While the BJP could count on the support of the upper-caste middle class, this category of voters tended to vote less than the plebeians since Mandal and the "silent revolution" of the 1990s: they thought that their vote made no difference because of the demographic strength of the Bahujans, the OBCs and the Dalits, who had acquired some power—at least at the state level.[112] In 2009, according to the CSDS, the turnout of the "Rich" was equal to that of the "Poor" at 57 percent—a parity that was not found in any other democracy. In 2014, it jumped by 10 percentage points—whereas that of the poor increased only by 3 percentage points.[113] This dramatic transformation, which accounts for the fact that the 2014 turnout exceeded all past records at 66.4 percent, was due to Modi's capacity to persuade the urban middle class that another majority, based on ethnoreligious criteria, was possible: majoritarianism was prevailing over Bahujanism.

Correlatively, this kind of identity politics and the other facets of Modi's populism reviewed above enabled him to attract lower and intermediary segments of Indian society as well, and especially, within it, the neo-middle class, which had previously shown little inclination to back the BJP. Modi won them over, as can be seen in table 3.2, which shows that the BJP gained between 9 and 12 percentage points in the lower and middle social categories that make up the majority of Indian society.

The BJP did not expand its support base in class terms only: it did the same in terms of castes (castes and class naturally overlapping somewhat). Table 3.3 shows that the percentage of BJP voters among the OBCs (the largest category, demographically) jumped from 22 to 34 percent, whereas the proportion of the SCs who supported the party doubled.

What factors made Narendra Modi so attractive for these plebeian voters? As there are no available opinion polls or surveys to elucidate his appeal, we can only rely on individual testimonies. Snigdha Poonam's interviews with angry young men and Sheela Bhatt's vote mobilizers are highly instructive in this regard. Their respondents say they were

TABLE 3.2. Vote by social class for the Congress and the BJP in the 2009 and 2014 Lok Sabha elections (%)

Class	INC 2014	INC 2009	BJP 2014	BJP 2009
Lower	20	27	24 (+9)	16
Lower middle	19	29	31 (+12)	19
Middle	20	29	32.3 (+10)	22
Upper	17	29	38 (+13)	25
Total	19	29	31 (+12)	19

Source: Lokniti-CSDS, National Election Survey (NES), 2014. Adapted from Christophe Jaffrelot, "The Class Element in the 2014 Indian Election and the BJP's Success with Special Reference to the Hindi Belt," in "Understanding India's 2014 Elections," special issue, *Studies in Indian Politics* 3, no. 1 (June 2015): 19–38.

Note: In this table, column totals are under 100 percent because parties other than Congress and the BJP were not considered.

TABLE 3.3. The 2009, 2014, and 2019 LS elections: Votes by caste, tribe, and religion (%)

Parties	Congress 2019	2014	2009	Cong. allies 2019	2014	2009	BJP 2019	2014	2009	BJP allies 2019	2014	2009
Upper castes	12	13	25	5.5	3	9	52	48	28	7	9	7
OBCs	15	15	24.5	7	4	7	44	34	22	10	8	6
Scheduled Castes	20	19	27	5.5	1	6.5	33.5	24	12	7	6	3
Scheduled Tribes	31	28	39	6	3	8	44	38	24.5	2	3	2
Muslims	33	38	38	12	8	9	8	8.5	4	1	1	2
Others	39	23	35	4	4	8	11	20	11	12	15.5	12.5

Source: CSDS-Lokniti, NES for 2009, 2014, and 2019, cited in Christophe Jaffrelot, "Class and Caste in the 2019 Indian Election—Why Have So Many Poor Started Voting for Modi?," *Studies in Indian Politics* 7, no. 2 (November 2019): 1–12.

drawn to Modi not only because he, too, came from lowly origins and was fighting against the establishment but also because he was a *victim* of it. Sheela Bhatt's informant Pramod Singh, an avid television watcher, found out about Modi through television, in a very peculiar fashion: "After the 2002 riots when the media and other political parties started blaming Modiji, thousands of people like us—now it must be crores of us—started becoming staunch supporters of Modiji. The more you blamed him, the more of our support he gained."[114] (A founding inci-

dent, from this standpoint, occurred in 2010 on NDTV[115] when Kiran
Thapar began an interview with Modi by talking about the violence in
2002, and a defensive Modi could not come up with a retort and even
walked off the set.)[116] To be sure, Singh subscribed to Hindu nationalism, but what brought him even closer to Modi was the way the people
from Delhi (where the television studios are located), all English speak-
ers belonging to the secularist, modern elite, denounced the pogrom.
Many angry young men who also perceived themselves as victims of
society and, hence, the elite, could identify with Modi. Added to that
was the fact that the journalists reporting on the events in Gujarat were
sometimes women dressed in the Western style (with short hair and
wearing pants), who lectured them on secularism, or so the claim went.
For the angry young men whom Poonam interviewed, they were "exactly
the kind of woman he loved to hate: urban, independent, opiniated."[117]
Not only did these men see themselves as victims, but the feeling arose
from a modernization process for which they did not have the codes,
lacking as they were the necessary education and sociability networks:
they did not speak English (or not well) and did not know how to deal
with female assertiveness in the public sphere. This prompted them all
the more to take refuge (and find self-esteem) in a staunch defense of
traditions.

While the BJP already had the support of the urban, upper-caste
middle class, Modi brought to the party voters who resented their sociocultural marginalization by the establishment—be they affected by
reservations or by the domination of the English-speaking elite. They
felt victimized like him. Those who experienced some decline were
upper castes; those who aspired to rise thanks to him came mostly from
the OBCs—the "plus vote" brought by Modi to the BJP.

Modi's sway over the neo-middle class opened a new sequence in the
social and political trajectory that had begun with the Mandal affair in
the 1990s: the mobilization that was set in motion at that time precipitated the emancipation of the OBCs, who were still living in the shadow
of the dominant castes. Starting in the 1990s, these groups formed their
own political parties and began to dream of climbing the social ladder,
not only because they benefited from quotas in the civil service but also

because of the promise of growth contained in the economic liberalization of 1991. Twenty-five years later, not only were the jobs not there, but the neo-middle-class OBCs, not having a command of English, were still in a position of inferiority vis-à-vis the middle class. On the rise but frustrated—like their upper-caste counterparts who had been disadvantaged by quotas (or believed they had been)—they found an alternative identity in Hindutva by identifying with Modi, in whom they had high hopes. For many "angry Hindus," be they upper-caste people experiencing some decline or neo-middle-class OBCs, Modi was "like me" and the "ego ideal," to use the words of Ostiguy. This alchemy convincingly defines here the way the populist relates to "his" people.

The decade from the mid-2000s to the mid-2010s saw a new cycle in the history of the Hindu nationalist movement. While features of the past subsisted, new elements appeared. What was reminiscent of an old pattern was the Sangh Parivar's ability to exploit the feeling of vulnerability among the Hindu community when it was struck by Islamist terrorism. Hindu nationalists were all the more eager to weaponize this fear when they were in the opposition, after 2004. They would often manage to transform fear into anger in a context that was all the more conducive when the terrorist threat no longer came only from Pakistan but was seen as also coming from Indian Muslims, and when anger was already a widespread feeling among a large segment of the youth plagued by countless frustrations.[118] One such frustration lay in the mass unemployment affecting Indian youth just when economic liberalization was transforming the country into the consumer society.

These angry young men, condemned to idleness, came both from a low-caste neo-middle class without enough education to find a good job and an upper-caste lower middle class that was quick to blame its decline on positive discrimination. These were the types of profiles the Sangh Parivar sought to recruit, in particular through the Bajrang Dal, with the dual aim of broadening its social base, deemed still too elitist, and going after Muslims to sustain the polarization of society by stepping up low-intensity riots.

The Bajrang Dal was the preferred instrument of this strategy. Its development evinces a dual transformation in the Sangh Parivar, first because it brought commoners into the organization whose manners contrasted with the RSS ethos, and second, being tasked with the movement's dirty work, it openly resorted to violence. The Bajrang Dal's growing influence within the Sangh Parivar fostered the emergence of a new political culture that had considerable affinities with Narendra Modi's background and style.

Even though Modi had never held office at the national level and BJP veterans, such as Advani, already occupied the field, he was the one whom the RSS and the coalition parties (except the JD[U]) ultimately chose as their candidate for prime minister in 2013. He could thus instantly count not only on RSS mobilization but also on the support of angry young men who saw in him someone like themselves who could defend them: not only did he promise these angry young men jobs, but like them, he also came from the underclasses and claimed to be a victim of the "liberal establishment," an epithet that took on highly negative connotations at that time.

Once on the campaign trail, Modi would use this human force, especially as vote mobilizers, together with a formidable propaganda machine that enabled him to saturate the public space as never before. The themes he used were national-populist ones that he had already honed in Gujarat and that he simply transposed to the national scene: promises of development along the lines of what Gujarat had become in the collective imaginary, rejection of the Congress (even the multiparty system) and the establishment at its head (legitimated by Modi's plebeian background), subordination of the republic's institutions to the will of the people, an ethnoreligious definition of this people, and exploitation of the supposed threats hanging over it, whether from Islamists or Pakistan. Modi did not only exploit fear and anger; he also aroused hope and even made people dream and feel proud, in difficult circumstances: not only were security and safety under attack, but aspirations were frustrated. Hence, probably, the very low position of India in the index of the UN Sustainable Development Solutions Network whose World

Happiness Report has been ranking India fairly low year after year, so much so that in 2013 it occupied the 111th slot, out of 156.[119]

In competition with a very weak opposition, this national-populist panoply and the electoral war machine set in motion by the Sangh Parivar and the Narendra Modi networks coordinated by Amit Shah—with funding from the business community, including Gujarati industrialists mentioned above[120]—enabled the BJP, for the first time in its history, to win a majority in the Lok Sabha with less than a third of the vote. It pulled this off by managing to transcend certain social red lines, particularly by attracting low-caste voters, who joined in with the party's traditional base, out of ethnoreligious sentiment and/or hope for a brighter future.

The same mechanism would be brought to bear on each state election after 2014, with Modi determined to win every single state, each time using the same method with RSS support. One of the movement's leaders even stated in 2015, "We would want the BJP to win all the state elections because only then can significant social, political and cultural changes take place in this country. . . . The 2014 election victory should be seen as the starting point of a long-term mission."[121]

This approach at once reflected the millenarian spirit of the RSS and demonstrated clear understanding of the increasing weight of states in the framework of Indian federalism. Between 2014 and 2018, the BJP came to control a record number of states of the Indian union, thus, with twenty states out of twenty-nine under its belt (which it governed alone or as part of a coalition), becoming a hegemonic party like the Congress was under Indira Gandhi in the 1970s and 1980s.

Between 2014 and mid-2018, Narendra Modi's BJP lost seven elections—in Bihar, Pondicherry, Delhi, West Bengal, Kerala, Tamil Nadu, Punjab, and Karnataka[122]—but won twice that many. In four years, the BJP was reelected to head Goa (despite an electoral setback; see chapter 8) and Gujarat (by a slim margin, with a lead of only 9 seats out of 182) and, most important of all, won Haryana, Maharashtra, Assam, Himachal Pradesh, Manipur, Uttarakhand, Uttar Pradesh, and Tripura.

The energy Modi invested in regional elections following his 2014 victory is exceptional. It demonstrated his desire to win it all, at once in order to control the entire country and to demonstrate his superior status as an invincible leader out to destroy his enemies, thus his stated goal in 2013 for a "Congress mukt Bharat" (an India free of Congress) and his definition of what an election is: by his own admission in 2017 at the end of the Uttar Pradesh regional campaign, "an election is a war, and I am the commander."[123]

Having become a hegemonic party, how would Narendra Modi's BJP wield its power? The following chapter focuses on the populist dimension of its social and economic agendas, and the second part of the book, on its attempt to establish India as an ethnic democracy.

4

Welfare or Well-Being?

NARENDRA MODI'S VICTORY IN 2014 was largely due to his ability to bring together the traditional support base of the BJP, the so-called neo-middle class, and poorer elements of India's society, as evident from table 3.3: even though a higher percentage of affluent voters supported the BJP than the percentage of poor who did, the poor contributed vastly to Modi's success because of their sheer number. Those who supported him did so partly for the elements of identity politics mentioned above and partly for socioeconomic reasons, since, during his election campaign, Modi had promised to help the poor get jobs and benefit from economic growth. He continued to do so immediately after being elected.

Such promises did not translate into concrete policies. This disconnect between discourse and practice is inherent in any demagogue, but in the case of Narendra Modi, it has reached extreme dimensions, unprecedented since Indira Gandhi's first term. The fact that they both spoke profusely and emotionally in the name of the poor but hardly delivered on their promises, instead allowing inequalities to increase, reflects their populist style. Populists often do little for the poor but claim to belong to them because they "are" the people, and the poor epitomize "the people." As mentioned previously, Laclau convincingly points out that populists need "a *plebs* who claims to be the only legitimate *populus*."[1]

The paradox of Modi's first term—typical of this populist repertoire—lies in the fact that once he became prime minister, he sought to portray himself as champion of the poor while enacting policies that in the stereotypical language of Indian politics can be described as anti-poor. Instead of prioritizing the financial needs of the poor, he continued to rely on one of the dimensions of his repertoire, identity politics, by emphasizing his action in favor of the dignity of the poor. The initiatives he took in this domain were all widely publicized and systematically associated with his *persona*.

Antipoverty Policies or Politics of Dignity?

Once in office, Narendra Modi and his right-hand man, Amit Shah—who was handed the BJP presidency right after the party's victory—continued to claim that they were working for the people, especially the poorest segment, which represented approximately 300 million Indians.[2] The cause of the poor was already at the heart of Indira Gandhi's populist rhetoric in the 1970s, when in answer to those who were chanting "Indira hatao!" (Banish Indira!), she came back with the slogan "Garibi hatao!" (Banish poverty!). Amit Shah would practically copy the theme verbatim,[3] and Modi sought to exploit this repertoire with his very first address to the Lok Sabha, pledging "to serve the poorest of the poor."[4] This rhetoric has been used repeatedly in the radio program he began hosting every month, called *Mann Ki Baat* (*Words from the Heart*), during which he addresses the nation at great length in the tone of a friendly chat.

Mann Ki Baat: *Communicating Self-Esteem to the People*

Like Indira Gandhi in the 1970s, Narendra Modi has used the radio as his favorite medium for communicating with Indians, especially with the poor, who, as he has said, may not have a TV set but most of whom own at least a small radio. In August 2014, he decided to hold a monthly program on Sundays at 11:00 A.M. called *Mann Ki Baat* "to communicate with people through the medium of radio."[5] The intention was twofold. First, it had to be "as interactive as possible,"[6] and, to that end, Indians were invited, by Modi himself via social media, to suggest topics for his talks. As a result, he could claim that *Mann Ki Baat* "did something unheard of—give the poor a voice and a medium to reach out to the government."[7] Second, his style of communication had to be father-like, even compassionate: "It is a voice of caring, from within the heart of governance that bridges distance. It is a warm conversation with citizens, rather than a cold diktat from authority. It is a gentle persuasion anchored in the popular interest shaped by the ethical impetus of shared introspection."[8]

Mann Ki Baat illustrates one variant of the populist repertoire: radio broadcasts aim to create an intimate, trust-based relationship between the leader and his people, a relationship that is no longer—allegedly—a one-way street. Modi insists on the fact that he keeps "getting many new suggestions and new ideas, and also good and bad information about our government. And, sometimes, it so happens, that a small comment from an individual in some remote village in India conveys something that just touches our hearts."[9] This style is typically populist in the sense that the leader, by establishing a direct relationship with the people, can claim that he strengthens democracy and justify the way he neglects the institutions of representative democracy, including the parliament (see chapter 8).[10] More importantly, Modi, by creating a trust-based relationship, gives the people the impression that he cares for them personally, that he even listens to them—a process that improves their sense of self-esteem and dignity.

Mann Ki Baat, moreover, is part of Modi's politics of dignity, a sentiment with which he wants to endow the poor. During one of his *Mann Ki Baat* shows, on May 31, 2015, he thus declared: "My heart is always yearning to do something for the poor people in our country. I always think of novel ideas and welcome suggestions from others in order to help the poor. Last month, we launched three key polices. . . . These schemes are aimed at giving our poor the dignity and security that they deserve."[11] The words that Narendra Modi uses the most in *Mann Ki Baat* are very revealing of his intention: "poor" comes in second place but, unsurprisingly, only after "nation"; then come "dream(s)" and, vying for fourth place, "tradition(s)" and "pride."[12] This lexicon reflects Modi's approach to the poor, to whom he wants to speak directly of their identity, to give them a better sense of their dignity—a synonym of "pride" and "self-respect"—and, of course, hope, a feeling that is, revealingly, translated here as "dream."

The Swachh Bharat Abhiyan, Pradhan Mantri Jan-Dhan Yojana, and Pradhan Mantri Ujjwala Yojana

The claim to be working for the poor was translated into three initiatives: the Swachh Bharat Abhiyan (Clean India Mission), Jan-Dhan Yojana (People's Wealth Scheme)—both launched in 2014—and Ujjwala Yojana (Brightness Scheme), which started in 2016. All of them were launched personally by the prime minister and remain closely associated with him, as evident from the way they have been marketed.

Narendra Modi announced what was to become the Swachh Bharat Abhiyan (SBA) in his first Independence Day speech on August 15, 2014—immediately bracketing the issues of poverty with cleanliness and connecting himself personally to both. It is useful to quote him at length to appreciate the rhetorical quality of his pro-poor discourse:

> Brothers and sisters, we want to promote tourism. Tourism provides employment to the poorest of the poor. Gram seller earns something, auto-rickshaw driver earns something, pakoda seller earns something and tea seller also earns something. When there is talk of tea seller, I feel a sense of belongingness. Tourism provides employment to the poorest of the poor. But there is a big obstacle in promoting tourism and in our national character and that is—the filthiness all around us. Whether after independence, after so many years of independence, when we stand at the threshold of one and half decade of 21st century, we still want to live in filthiness? The first work I started here after formation of government is of cleanliness. People wondered whether it is a work of a prime minister? People may feel that it is a trivial work for a prime minister but for me this big work. Cleanliness is very big work. Whether our country cannot be clean?

If 125 crore [1.25 billion] countrymen decide that they will never spread filthiness, which power in the world has ability to spread filthiness in our cities and villages? Can't we resolve this much? Brothers and sisters it will be the 150th birth anniversary of Mahatma Gandhi in 2019. How do we celebrate 150th birth anniversary of Mahatma Gandhi? Mahatma Gandhi, who gave us freedom, who brought so much honour to such a big country in the world, what do we give to Mahatma Gandhi? Brothers and Sisters, Mahatma Gandhi had cleanliness and sanitation closest to his heart. Whether we resolve not to leave a speck of dirt in our village, city, street, area, school, temple, hospital, and what have you, by 2019 when we celebrate 150th anniversary of Mahatma Gandhi? This happens not just with the Government, but with public participation. That's why we have to do it together.

Brother and Sisters, we are living in 21st century. Has it ever pained us that our mothers and sisters have to defecate in open? Whether dignity of women is not our collective responsibility? The poor womenfolk of the village wait for the night; until darkness descends, they can't go out to defecate. What bodily torture they must be feeling, how many diseases that act might engender. Can't we just make arrangements for toilets for the dignity of our mothers and sisters? Brothers and Sisters, somebody might feel that a big festival like 15th August is an occasion to talk big. Brothers and Sisters, talking big has its importance, making announcements too has importance, but sometimes announcements raise hopes and when the hopes are not fulfilled, the society sinks into a state of despondency. That's why [one word missing] are in favor of telling those things, which we can fulfill just within our sight. Brothers and sisters, you must be shocked to hear the Prime Minister speaking of cleanliness and the need to build toilets from the ramparts of the Red Fort.

Brothers and sisters, I do not know how my speech is going to be criticized and how will people take it. But this is my heartfelt conviction. I come from a poor family, I have seen poverty. The poor need respect and it begins with cleanliness. I, therefore, have to launch a "Clean India" campaign from 2nd October this year and carry it forward in 4 years. I want to make a beginning today itself and that is—

all schools in the country should have toilets with separate toilets for girls. Only then our daughters will not be compelled to leave schools midway.[13]

Modi speaks here, first, to "his" people, his "Brothers and Sisters," about very simple, trivial things—things that are part of their daily life and which, he says, have never been talked about from the ramparts of Delhi's Red Fort. But this is precisely the change he is bringing, as someone from the plebeian ranks himself—as he suggests in reference to his poor background. Second, he uses this opportunity to co-opt the legacy of Mahatma Gandhi—who was indeed keen on cleanliness.[14] Third, the Swachh Bharat Abhiyan is presented as an antipoverty campaign not so much because of the money it will bring to the poor—even if he mentions the jobs the poor would get if cleanliness made India more attractive for tourists—but because of the *dignity* the poor would enjoy if they had access to latrines, especially women, who are forced to defecate in the open and ashamed of it, and girls, who do not go to school because there are no toilets for them. Modi thinks that he is striking a very emotional chord here: while his antipoverty scheme relies more on symbols than material benefits, he assumes that it fulfills clear expectations. Fourth, cleanliness is not for the poor only but for all the people—a formula that populists often utilize. Beyond the poor, Indian society at large (including elite groups, as evident from the middle class's quest for "sanitized" politics[15]) is concerned with cleanliness, an issue that is amplified by the general sensitivity to purity (the main building block of the caste system) and to hygiene (as many diseases are linked to poor sanitation).[16]

On October 2, 2014—Gandhi's birthday—Modi "characteristically launched the scheme with a television flourish, personally sweeping up rubbish with a long broom in Valmiki [ex-untouchable sweepers] Basti [locality], a Delhi neighborhood where Gandhi once stayed."[17] And in the first monthly *Mann Ki Baat* radio broadcasts to the nation, he asked people to pledge to remove dirt from their lives.

Modi invested considerable money and energy in the SBA. He imposed a cess (tax) of 0.5 percent on all taxable services to help finance the campaign, on which the government spent up to Rs 15,373 crore (about 20.5 million USD) in 2018–2019. The objective that Modi assigned to the mission in 2014 was to build 120 million toilets to make India open-defecation-free (ODF) by October 2019. The campaign was publicized systematically: its logo—Mahatma Gandhi's spectacles—was every-where, including on the currency notes that replaced those which were demonetized in 2016. That same year, a few months before, Modi took some of the BJP's top leaders to Porbandar, Mahatma Gandhi's birthplace, to celebrate not only his anniversary—and that of the SBA—but also the fact that Gujarat "had eradicated open defecation in all urban areas."[18]

By October 2019, the Modi government declared that the SBA was "Mission accomplished": 66.42 lakh (6,642,000) household toilets in urban India and 924 lakh (92,400,000) in rural India had been built by 2019, making the country defecation-free. The 2019–2020 post-election budget dropped by 49 percent.[19] Several surveys questioned the impor-tance of this achievement because, among other reasons, many households equipped with toilets did not use them—sometimes because they had been very poorly built.[20] Furthermore, a large number of these toilets (60 percent in 2017) did not have a proper water supply.[21] The success of the scheme, however, needs to be qualified for other reasons too: it gained momentum at the expense of solid waste management in finan-cial terms and at the expense of manual scavengers in practical terms.

The SBA was not supposed to pertain solely to toilet construction. This component was supposed to receive only one-third of the total budgetary allocation for cleanliness so far as the urban component of the scheme was concerned in 2017–2018—for instance, one-half was earmarked for solid waste management activities. In reality, the former got 51 percent and the latter 38 percent.[22] Why? Because toilets were visible, concrete achievements that people could be proud of. But im-proving solid waste management would have been even more helpful to the manual scavengers because the new toilets needed more people for one of the most repugnant jobs.

The direct handling of human excreta by sanitation workers has been banned in India since 1993 under the Employment of Manual Scaveng-ing and Construction of Dry Latrines (Prohibition) Act, which also prohibited the construction and maintenance of dry latrines. But a majority of the toilets built in the framework of the SBA "have been constructed using technologies that would require periodic emptying and offsite treatment of fecal matter."[23] Indeed, the number of manual scavengers, almost systematically Dalits, has not declined—about 5 million in India—and the government has done little to help them. On the contrary, there has been a significant decline in the central budget allocations under the Self-Employment Scheme for Rehabilitation of Manual Scavengers between 2013–2014 and 2018–2019, from Rs 70 crore (9.33 million USD) to only Rs 5 crore (0.67 million USD—a 93 percent decrease), whereas the number of victims of toxic gas, infections, and, of course, stigma have remained very high.[24]

While manual scavengers—the poorest of the poor—numbered only 5 million, the rest of the poor appreciated the Swachh Bharat Abhiyan to a great extent because of the kind of recognition by the state it epitomized. The rest of society, including elite groups, appreciated it as well, not only due to its contribution to cleanliness in India but also because of its potential impact in terms of hygiene and international image. Press reports bear testimony to this sentiment:

> Call it the result of a strong political will or a multipronged assault on a nagging problem, what India is witnessing now is no less than a civilizational leap forward. Till five years ago, open defecation was a way of life for most in the country. The government was over and again pulled up at international platforms for hosting 60 per cent of the global population that defecates in the open. But at the last count on September 23, villages and cities in all the 37 states and union territories had declared themselves ODF. With verification pending for just 22 per cent of the districts, the country was on track to attain ODF on October 2.
>
> There is a sense of triumph among officials and community leaders who have been part of this sanitation program, dubbed the largest in the world.[25]

The general view of the SBA as a successful endeavor shows that Narendra Modi, as early as 2014, was able to initiate vast programs in the name of the poor that would increase his popularity across social milieus without distributing money to the poor in question. Two other *yojanas* (schemes) would fit the same pattern.

In his 2014 Independence Day speech, Modi not only announced what was to be known as the Swachh Bharat Abhiyan but also the Pradhan Mantri Jan-Dhan Yojana (PMJDY—Prime Minister People's Wealth Scheme), presented as another pro-poor program and named after the prime minister himself:

> Brothers and sisters, I have come here with a pledge to launch a scheme on this festival of Freedom. It will be called Pradhan Mantri Jan-Dhan Yojana. I wish to connect the poorest citizens of the country with the facility of bank accounts through this *yojana*. There are millions of families who have mobile phones but no bank accounts. We have to change this scenario. Economic resources of the country should be utilized for the well-being of the poor. The change will commence from this point. This yojana will open the window. Therefore, an account holder under Pradhan Mantri Jan-Dhan Yojana will be given a debit card. An insurance of Rs 1 lakh [1,333 USD] will be guaranteed with that debit card for each poor family, so that such families are covered with the insurance of Rs 1 lakh [1,330 USD] in case of any crisis in their lives.[26]

While Modi's reference to "an insurance of Rs 1 lakh [1,330 USD]" suggested that the poor were to receive some concrete benefit, in fact the PMJDY, like the SBA, was again a way to endow the poor with a sense of dignity and recognition—not to give them money. In that regard, the debit card was important because it attested to ownership of something—a bank account. As these accounts gradually multiplied, some of them received more money, partly because that was the route used by the Direct Benefit Transfer (DBT) program for an increasing number of subsidies—a route the government wanted to promote to save money, eliminate intermediaries, and centralize the whole process, as evident from the fact that the scheme was named after the prime minister.[27]

In 2017, a comprehensive World Bank report estimated that 48 percent of these accounts were "inactive."[28] But the accounts gradually gained momentum for the reason mentioned above. According to official sources, out of 371.1 million PMJDY accounts, zero-balance accounts made up around 48.8 million (about 13.15 percent) as of September 2019 and dormant or inactive ones, 66 million, or 17.8 percent.[29] DBTs of different subsidies had contributed to making PMJDY accounts popular as, by 2019, 75 million of these accounts were receiving one or more such DBTs. But many Indians had obviously opened such accounts for other reasons, including the pride of owning one, and among them, the rural poor were overrepresented. According to the 2017 World Bank report, bank account penetration among adults in the poorest 40 percent of households had risen by 30 percentage points, from 44 percent in 2014 to 77 percent in 2017.[30] Among the poor gaining access to bank accounts thanks to the PMJDY, women were overrepresented according to the World Bank survey, which noted, "In India in 2014 men were 20 percentage points more likely than women to have an account. That gap has shrunk to 6 percentage points."[31]

Narendra Modi could claim that program was a success for another reason too: the scheme saw a gradual increase in the average deposit per account from Rs 1,000 (13.33 USD) in March 2015 to Rs 2,853 (38.04 USD) in October 2019. Hence the comment of a close observer about what would seem to be a paradox: "Surprisingly, there has been a consistent rise in the PMJDY account balances despite a slowdown in rural consumption and falling rural income."[32] The only possible explanation is that while the rural poor did not earn more—on the contrary, in fact—the little money they got (at least most of it) was now in PMJDY accounts.

Indeed, the PMJDY was not a redistribution scheme. Nor did it address a key issue for the rural poor: access to formal credit. The 2016 Household Survey on India's Citizen Environment and Consumer Economy showed that two-thirds of the poor had to take credit from informal sources. Banks were prepared to open accounts for them but not to lend them money. As a result, they still had to depend on moneylenders. In 2017, in one of its reports, the Reserve Bank of India stated, "We document high levels of unsecured debt, and perhaps more importantly, debt taken from non-institutional sources such as moneylenders.

Such debt generates high costs for Indian households, and . . . is likely to lead to households becoming trapped in a long cycle of interest repayments."[33] To help the poor to emancipate themselves from the money-lenders would have been a substantial achievement, but the Modi government was not interested in such action, which would have implied an additional expenditure.

Modi's third initiative for the poor—the Pradhan Mantri Ujjwala Yojana (PMUY)—was launched in 2016, again in his name. It granted a Rs 1,600 subsidy to 80 million families living below the poverty line to provide them with natural gas. Modi inaugurated this scheme in Ballia, a poor town in Uttar Pradesh, on May 1, with another very telling speech:

> This cooking gas connection will not only help reduce cost for each family, but will also help better the health of women. The subsidy transfer will take place in the Jan Dhan account of the family's woman head. . . . I had appealed to people [who are not poor] to give up LPG [Liquefied Petroleum Gas] subsidy; it was a heartfelt plea. I hadn't thought of a scheme or follow-up campaign, but the people of this country were great enough to give up their subsidies. I want to laud the over 1 crore [10 millions] families who gave up their LPG subsidies. Those subsidies that were given up have reached the households of poor people through the Pradhan Mantri Ujjwala Yojana scheme. . . . Today is Labour Day, and I bow to all labourers in the country. Labourers of the world unite used to be the mantra. Now, I want that labourers should unite the world. . . . In the past, governments have destroyed the will of poor people to fight against poverty. Fruits of development have to reach the eastern part of India and then we will gain strength in the fight against poverty. . . . This is a Government for the poor. Whatever we will do will be for the poor. . . . In this century our Mantra should be "All Shramiks [laborers] of the world, let's make the world one." Unite the world.[34]

This speech is again revealing of several facets of Modi's style. First, it well illustrates the way he tries to appear as pro-poor—a constant since 2014, yet which takes on an unexpected twist here because of the way he tries to appropriate May 1, May Day, a day traditionally associated with the Left. Second, this speech reflects his craze for unity and even unanimity given how the people of India are presented as one, as evidenced from the fact that the rich gave to the poor—indirectly—when he asked them to give up their LPG subsidy. Third, he suggests that to assist the poor—as his predecessors have done—is not the best way to fight poverty as it destroys "the will of poor people to fight against poverty." This is exactly why Narendra Modi has always expressed reservations vis-à-vis positive discrimination and preferred to promote a sense of entrepreneurship among the poor (a point that will be returned to below).

The PMUY has been particularly popular among poor women, who have otherwise had to cook surrounded in wood smoke (from firewood they gather themselves). Modi designed and publicized the program with this huge category in mind, seizing this opportunity to remind the people—for instance, those with whom he was interacting via the NaMo app in 2018—of his plebeian origins with emotional overtones:

> Ujjwala Yojana has strengthened the lives of the poor, marginalised, Dalits, Tribal communities. This initiative is playing a central role in social empowerment. Till 2014, only 13 crore [130 million] families had Liquefied Petroleum Gas (LPG) connection, which mostly consists of rich people. In last four years 10 crore [100 million] new connections have been added for the benefit of the poor. When I was young and my mother would be cooking, we remember the smoke. I also remember the pains she took so that us, her little children to inhale the smoke [sic].[35]

The figure he gives in this speech is inflated, even by his own government's standards. The official PMUY website itself said, "Under this scheme, 5 Cr [50 million] LPG connections will be provided to BPL families with a support of Rs 1,600 (21.33 USD) per connection in the next 3 years." Indeed, the Ministry of Petroleum and Natural Gas claims that between 2016 and 2018, 4.48 crore (44.8 million) connections were provided under the PMUY. In fact, according to the seventy-sixth round of the National Sample Survey (NSS), only 31.7 million households received subsidized LPG connections through the PMUY during this period.[36] However, in 2018, the government expanded the scope of the PMUY from 50 million households to 80 million, and in late 2019 a report by the comptroller auditor general (CAG) mentioned that 71.9 million connections had taken place in the framework of the PMUY.[37]

Such figures, even the more modest ones, already represent quite an achievement, which should be qualified, however, because the annual average refill consumption dropped to 3.08 cylinders in the twelve months before September 2019, down from 3.21 refills in December 2018 and 3.66 refills in March 2018. This trend sent a clear message to the government:[38] the poor who had benefited from the scheme by receiving a gas cylinder could less and less often afford to refill it at market price—as they were supposed to do.[39] The 2019 CAG report is even more alarming: around 5.6 million beneficiaries (17.61 percent) who completed one year or more by December 31, 2018, never came back for a second refilling, and around 10.5 million (33.02 percent) beneficiaries consumed just one to three refills.[40] By 2018, more than 35 percent of those who had shifted to LPG thanks to the PMUY had reverted to traditional, unclean fuel.[41] As a result, the state-owned oil marketing companies had to announce deferment of loan recovery on up to six refills in 2019.[42]

The initial budget of the PMUY was Rs 8,000 crore (1.07 billion USD), but this amount was partly compensated for by the fact that 11.3 million beneficiaries of cooking gas subsidies were supposed to give them up, as they had been requested to do so by Modi. It seems that the numbers of those who did so were never made public, but the money spent on the scheme declined nevertheless. Furthermore, the proportion of actual spending on this scheme as a percentage of budgeted allocations kept declining from 58 percent in 2016–2017 to 49 percent in 2017–2018 and 13 percent in 2018–2019.[43]

To sum up, like most populist leaders, Modi has projected himself as the defender of the poor while to generally shifting pro-poor policies from redistribution to dignity-oriented schemes. This shift is well illustrated by the Swachh Bharat Abhiyan, Pradhan Mantri Jan-Dhan Yojana, and—to a lesser extent—Pradhan Mantri Ujjwal Yojana. Modi has made a point to associate all these schemes with his office, as their names themselves show.

In contrast with redistributive schemes, this *abhiyan* (mission) and these yojanas (schemes) do not seek to alter social balances or even to combat inequality, but they send the people an identity-oriented message. That is precisely how one local BJP cadre sums it up: "Ujjwala, toilets, Jan Dhan are so popular because they offer the poor dignity. And they give credit to Modiji for these schemes."[44] In the case of the three programs reviewed above, women's dignity has been especially highlighted. The Swachh Bharat Abhiyan has allowed them to have access to toilets—something women prioritize more than men. The Pradhan Mantri Jan-Dhan Yojana gives some priority to women, who, at long last, can emancipate themselves financially from their husbands, and the Pradhan Mantri Ujjwala Yojana has been explicitly designed for women.

Demonetization for the Poor

The populist quality of Modi's pro-poor rhetoric reached new heights during the course of demonetization, undertaken in November 2016.[45] The operation, which involved the withdrawal of 500- and 1,000-rupee banknotes, or 86 percent of the cash in circulation, brought the economy to its knees, taking a heavy toll on the poor, the workers of the informal sector—80 percent of the Indian economy—whose wages are paid in cash and who often have no bank account, checkbook, or credit card. Unpaid migrant workers returned to their villages, suppliers went bankrupt, peasants whose products could no longer be bought had to sell by bartering, and so on.

Modi claimed it was a measure against the rich intended to purge the economy of all dirty money. The speeches he made on the topic during the campaign for the 2017 state elections in Uttar Pradesh reveal his talent for turning the perspective around in this way and even reversing roles. At one rally after another, he explained that the measure was intended to fight corruption by withdrawing black money from circulation and that the rich would be much harder hit than the poor.[46] The address he gave on the theme in Moradabad is worth quoting at length. In the space of fifty minutes, he used the words "poor" and "poverty" dozens of times, delivering a speech in which his ability to interact with the crowd illustrates his oratory skills.[47] Modi declared himself a champion of the poor, at once as an agent of economic development and as protector of victims of rich class's corruption, who he claimed, again and again, were the main targets of demonetization. In the speech, he describes how corrupt rich people, who were allowed to deposit a limited sum of money in old bank notes in exchange for new notes—to prevent money laundering—turned to the poor, who had a bank account thanks to the Jan-Dhan Yojana and who did not reach this ceiling:

> Brothers and sisters, if we want poverty in India to be eradicated, you tell me, would it be possible to eliminate it only by eradication of poverty from a small region of India, population of 1, 1.2, 1.5 million? No! but if the poverty of a big state is lessened, will it not lessen the poverty of the country? For this reason if poverty is to be eradicated from India, then it should be eradicated first from the big states, be it Uttar Pradesh, Bihar, Maharashtra or West Bengal. As soon as we remove poverty from these places, the country will be free from poverty.
>
> Brothers and sisters, I ran for the parliamentary election from Uttar Pradesh, the people of Varanasi gave me immense blessings. But I have not contested the election from Uttar Pradesh only to become a Member of Parliament, I have contested in Uttar Pradesh because it is the largest state of India. Poverty is prevalent here. I want to go among the poor and fight poverty. To liberate it from poverty, I have accepted to serve Uttar Pradesh.
>
> My brothers and sisters . . .
>
> Crowd: Modi, Modi! [shouting]
>
> The governments which made announcements have been many, but this is the first government which gives an account of each rupee to the public. Our owners are the people. These are the government's owners, the 1.25 billion people of India. These people own the Prime Minister, the 1.25 billion people of the country. That's my high com-

mand, the divine people. I do not have any other leader, I do not have any one to call my own. You, the people, are the only ones I have to call my own. . . .

You tell me, has this country been destroyed by corruption or not? Has corruption looted the country or not? Has corruption done the most damage to the poor or not? Has corruption stolen the right of people or not? Corruption is the root of all our problems. Now tell me, should corruption remain or should it be eliminated? Should corruption remain or should it go? Should corruption be eliminated or not? Tell me if it will go automatically. Will it go on its own? Will corruption say, "Now that you have come, Modiji, I am scared. I'll leave?" No, it will not go on its own. We will have to take a stick and chase it away, won't we? We will have to use the law, won't we? Dishonest people will have to be straightened or not? Corrupt people will have to be put away or not? Shall we do this work or not? If someone does so, is he a criminal? If someone fights corruption, is he a criminal? Brothers and sisters, I am surprised nowadays, some people are calling me a criminal in my own country. I am surprised, brothers, what is the reason? Is my crime, the fact that the days of dishonest people are numbered? Is my crime the fact that I am working to give rights to the poor? Is this my crime? That those who have stolen the rights of poor people are now being held accountable.

Brothers and sisters, we hear news, that there was a raid in someone's house. Millions of rupees were found from under the bed. Whose money was this? Whose money is this? If there is anybody who has a right over the money of Hindustan, it is its 1.25 billion people. I'm fighting for you. Brothers and sisters, what is the most they can do to me? Tell me, after all I am a simple ascetic man [*fakir*]. I will take my small bag and move on.

Crowd: Modi, Modi!

Brothers and sisters, it is this asceticism [*fakiri*] which has given me the strength to fight for the poor. . . .

Brothers and sisters, dishonest people who have hoarded black money are queuing up in front of the houses of poor people. They do not have the power to queue up in front of the bank. The people standing in a line at the bank are those who have the fabric of honesty in them. People who have strength and honesty stand outside the bank. Dishonest people are slyly lining up outside the houses of poor. I tell the poor, when I had opened the Jan Dhan accounts, even the poor did not know how money will come, how it will work. Is it working, or not? But there is one thing I want to tell all the poor people who have the Jan Dhan accounts in the country. Whomsoever has given you money, whatever money you have placed in the bank at someone else's behest, do not withdraw that amount. That's the way. Do not withdraw a single rupee he's given you, you will see, he will visit your house every day. He will hold your feet, but do not say anything to him. Say "Don't act smart, or else I will write a letter to Modi" and if he still tries to harass you, tell him "Bring evidence that you have given money, bring evidence." They have been trapped in the box finally. Dishonest and corrupt people have been thoroughly caught in the box. However, we will only get success, when those who have put money in someone else's account do not see it again and the money remains in the account it was put in. I had asked for fifty days to handle the situation. Had I asked or not? I had said that there will be difficulty in the first 50 days. The trouble is slowly receding, isn't it? Work is progressing, slowly, slowly.

But I salute the nation's citizens. I want to ask the leaders discussing these "queues-queues" adversely that when we had had to stand in a queue even for sugar, had to stand in queue to bring kerosene oil, had to stay in the queue to buy wheat, where were you? You have made the country stand in queue for 70 years. To finish all queues, I have made this last queue, brothers and sisters.

Crowd: Modi, Modi, Modi!

Tell me, those people who have a Jan Dhan account, when you receive money from other people in your account, will you keep it there or not? No matter how much pressure is put on you, you will not succumb to the pressure, right? If you keep it safe, then I will find a way out, I'm still thinking, I'm searching for a solution. A solution in which those who illegally put money in the accounts of the poor, go to jail and their money goes to the house of that poor person. This is no handout, no kindness. This money belongs to the poor, and they had been robbed of it. Brothers and sisters, I am amazed, you must have seen, the faces of big people have lost their sheen. They are chanting "Modi, Modi" all day. Before, they used to say, "Money, money, money," all day. Now they are saying, "Modi, Modi, Modi." Brothers and sisters, I speak to all my citizens again, that the pain you are suffering, you have been suffering for the country. . . .

The problems of my farmers are my problems and I want to pay special respects to the farmers. Even after the discomfort [of demonetization], sowing has not come down. In fact, sowing has increased since last year. . . .

Come, brothers and sisters, let's all walk this path together. We have to stop this 70 year old disease. The country has to escape from the disease of the last 70 years. Come, shout with me. Close both fists and shout, "Bharat Mata Ki!"

The voice should be such that every dishonest person gets goosebumps, their hair stands up, every dishonest person should shiver and tremble.

Bharat Mata Ki, Bharat Mata Ki, Bharat Mata Ki!

Here Modi dons the guise at once of a fakir who has renounced life's pleasures and whose asceticism is placed in the service of the masses and of Robin Hood, who plots with the poor to deal the rich a nasty blow. By claiming that he is an ascetic, Modi tries to match a very prestigious repertoire of Indian politics that W. H. Morris-Jones has called "saintly politics,"[48] a repertoire epitomized by Mahatma Gandhi and emulated, after independence, by Jaya Prakash Narayan and even V. P. Singh.[49] This repertoire of "this-worldly asceticism," as Lloyd I. Rudolph and Susanne Hoeber Rudolph have suggested, was extremely popular in India because of the value traditionally attached to sacrifice.[50]

But Modi is also a Robin Hood, a man of the people, coming from the people and working for the people. This, in the truest populist style, he has demonstrated through complicity against the establishment (the likes of "we people at the bottom understand each other and will make the rich pay") and by establishing a direct line of communication when he invites the poor to write a letter to him if the rich bother them. Prashant Jha, a journalist with the *Hindustan Times* who attended the speech, was struck by its effectiveness. One of the women in the audience whom he interviewed afterward about the effects of demonetization told him, "If big people are troubled, how does it matter if I am troubled?"[51] Modi very effectively exploited the theme of sacrifice, a highly emotional one in India: not only did he impose asceticism on himself, but also he invited others to suffer to purify the nation, suggesting that while demonetization involved some "discomfort" (as he called it), the nation would be all the stronger for it. It was thus a test of patriotism that his victims were urged to heroically submit to. These rhetorical tricks worked in Uttar Pradesh, where Modi's tour was an immense success despite the economic disaster that demonetization proved to be.

The speech in Moradabad is also indicative of three other dimensions of Modi's style, in addition to its demagogic and beguiling aspect. First, he establishes an emotional relationship with his audience, which is none other than the 1.25 billion Indians, his people, whose instrument he claims to be. This affectivity is apparent in the systematic use of the expression "brothers and sisters," as is clear above and in many other speeches, including those previously cited.[52] Second, Modi, acting as a good father (or as an Indian-style "father of the people"), lectures in a gently commanding tone when he urges the poor who gripe about demonetization to move into the modern era and use "plastic money" by requesting a bank card or another dematerialized payment method, since mobile phones can now serve as online payment terminals. His manner in this regard is reminiscent of Mahatma Gandhi,[53] the only Indian leader, according to Modi, to have created a "brand"[54]—a feat he is attempting to match. Modi's natural authority, which shows in his ability to give orders without having to raise his voice (on the contrary, in fact, he simply takes on a more sanctimonious tone), elicits respect (blended with a degree of fear) as well as a type of submission that resembles obedience to a guru or a fakir. Third, Modi does not shy away from using any manner of untruth. Dealing out lies with total self-assurance is not rare in politics, and other populists have made it their trademark, but Modi uses and abuses this rhetorical device; for instance, when stating that demonetization has had no effect on crop sowing. Farmers in fact had to cut back their planting for lack of cash with which to purchase seed.

Despite all that, as Modi never takes part in debates or even press conferences, his rhetoric on poverty, like on other subjects, has the force of gospel. According to Prashant Jha, the 2017 elections even raised him from the status of Vikas Purush (Development Man) to Garibon ka neta (Leader of the Poor).[55] The Jan-Dhan Yojana did much to forge this image, because even if the program didn't give its beneficiaries more money to put in their accounts, at least they had an account, and sometimes even a bank card, a source of self-esteem! A young Dalit auto rickshaw driver told Jha, "We have to earn the money,"[56] espousing Modi's invitation to cultivate the spirit of enterprise rather than to expect everything to come from the state, a point to which we now turn.

Villagers as Losers

The Modi government tended to dislike the pro-poor programs it had inherited from the Congress-led government of Manmohan Singh for different reasons. First, the programs were costly, and the BJP was keen to contain the fiscal deficit. Second, Narendra Modi wanted to shrink the state, as evident from one of the slogans in his 2014 campaign: "Minimum government, maximum governance." This stand reflected the belief that economic liberalization was a prerequisite for growth. But it also harked back to the traditional worldview of the Hindu nationalist movement. As mentioned previously, its key ideologues—including Deendayal Upadhyaya—believed that the essence of Hindu civilization rested in society, and this supreme institution was supposed to self-regulate (an oblique reference to the caste system): social order prevailed over the state, which was accused of deforming society's natural harmony. In this context, the poor should not be assisted by the state but should instead develop a sense of self-help. For all these reasons, a number of existing pro-poor policies were compromised.

Targeting the MGNREGA

The vast program initiated by Manmohan Singh in 2005 under the Mahatma Gandhi National Rural Employment Guarantee Act (MG-NREGA) was the main victim of this approach at the start of Modi's first term. It was one of the most ambitious programs to help the rural poor that India (and therefore the world) had ever known.[57] The method was a novel one that aimed to minimize dependence on government aid, as the state committed to providing 100 days of actual *work* paid at minimum wage for any rural family suffering from chronic underemployment.[58] The amount that the Singh government earmarked for the program represented up to 0.6 percent of India's GDP, providing work to 50 million households and bringing 14 million people out of poverty, not only by giving them an income but also by revising the minimum wage in rural areas (which rose from Rs 65 [0.9 USD] per day in 2005 to Rs 162 [2.16 USD] in 2013).[59] Partly for this reason, the growth of per capita rural income went from 2.7 percent per year between 1999 and 2004 to 9.7 percent between 2006 and 2011.[60]

Yet Modi and the BJP considered the program a disaster, because it penalized farmers (who had to pay their workers higher wages) and because it involved welfare payments, as the wages, they claimed (quite plausibly), were disbursed even when no work was available, for instance, during periods of drought. In the first BJP government parliamentary budget session in February 2015, after an hour-long speech in which he presented himself as "pro-poor" and "pro-farmer," Modi concluded that the MGNREGA was nothing but a "monument" to the "failures" of previous governments. Speaking to Congress MPs, he exclaimed, "I will keep MGNREGA alive. I may not have your experience, but all of you will grant me political skills and that acumen has told me to keep it alive as a monument to your failures since Independence. After 60 years, you are still making people dig holes."[61] These words betrayed his thinking: to get rid of a program as popular as the MGNRGEA would have been politically very costly, but the prime minister did not believe in its virtues. As a result, he stifled it by cutting funds allocated to it, without saying so. It is worth citing a few figures to illustrate this budgetary hocus-pocus. As the budget sessions proceeded, enormous amounts continued to be allocated to the program.[62] Finance Minister Arun Jaitley even said in 2015, "Our government is committed to supporting employment through MGNREGA. We will ensure that no one who is poor is left without employment."[63] But during the fiscal year, either the funds were not distributed, or else drastic cuts were made, reducing the size of the envelope. The Supreme Court was obliged to intervene in May 2016 to compel the government to disburse the funds earmarked for the MGNREGA. But local government officials in charge of the program, grouped by state into a WhatsApp group, received instructions via the social network not to disburse the funds, with little concern for administrative transparency.[64] Year after year, most of the MGNREGA funds had already vanished midway through the fiscal year.[65] As a result, the number of people who worked 100 days per year fell from 470,000 in 2013–2014 to 250,000 in 2014–2015 and to 170,000 in 2015–2016.[66] The aggregate number of days worked dropped from 221.15 crore (22.1 million) in 2013–2014 to 166.32 crore (16.6 million) in 2014–2015.[67] The average number of days worked by beneficiary in the framework of the program fell from 46 in 2013–2014 to 39 in 2014–2015.[68] Last but not least, the average real MGNREGA wage rate declined from Rs 142 (1.95 USD) a day to Rs 136 (1.89 USD) between 2014–2015 and 2016–2017.[69] As a result, many states had a minimum wage higher than the MGNREGA wage.

Those who did work had to endure delays in their wage payments. In 2014–2015, only 28 percent of the beneficiaries were paid 15 days after they had worked, whereas the law stipulated that these people, who live from hand to mouth, should not have to wait longer than that for their money.[70] This proportion rose to 40 percent after the Supreme Court's intervention.[71] But it fell back down to 28 percent in 2017.[72] The scheme's decline especially penalized laborers who lived in states declared to be in a situation of natural disaster due to drought. While by law these people were entitled to 150 work days, the clause benefited only 7 percent of them in 2015–2016, a particularly harsh year during which a third of the country was officially affected by drought.[73] At the same time, the minister of communication and information technology announced a year-end bonus of Rs 14,724 crore (1.96 billion USD) for government employees.[74]

While the MGNREGA has been the main victim of Modi's policies toward rural dwellers, it is not the only one.

Rural Socioeconomic Decline

While antipoverty programs, including the MGNREGA, were not sustained by the first Modi government (also known as NDA II), other policies have pushed other groups back into poverty, mostly in rural India.[75] Indeed, rural development programs have had their budgets cut drastically, starting with those designed to develop irrigation, despite rural areas being in dire need.[76] The assessment made by Himanshu, an expert in this matter, captures the essence of the problem:

> Excluding the interest subsidy component, the overall budget for agriculture increased by 26% per annum during the UPA years but by only 8.7% per annum under the NDA-II government. It is also important to note that except in 2016–17, in none of the years has the actual expenditure been close to the budget allocation. The marginal increase in the agricultural budget in recent years has largely been on subsidy on interest and on insurance premium. But this increase has come at the cost of a decline in investment in agriculture. Real investment in agriculture declined by one percentage point per annum during the first four years of the Modi government.[77]

The BJP did not even come to the aid of farmers, those who—unlike farmworkers—owned parcels of land and sold their surplus. When measures to help them were announced, beneficial effects did not follow. The crop insurance scheme against natural disasters suffered from excessive bureaucratic centralism—related to the fact that Modi was seeking to take personal credit for it.[78] Its management was handed over to a private firm, Anil Ambani's company, which profited more from it than farmers did.[79]

The issue of farm prices proved even more problematic.[80] In his campaign platform, Modi had promised farmers that the state would buy their products on agriculture markets at 1.5 times production cost. But the means of calculating such costs were never specified, and in fact, minimum support prices proved to be not high enough.[81] Worse still, when market prices rose, the government tried to bring them back down by importing more of the commodity in question and/or by preventing farmers from exporting so as to maintain an abundant supply.[82] As a result, the Wholesale Price Index declined and even became negative in 2018,[83] while the inflation rate remained at 4.8 percent. This policy, very detrimental to the terms of trade between urban and rural India, infuriated farmers, who stepped up protest actions in 2017. In some areas, demonstrations were crushed with violence, ratcheting up the tension.[84]

In response to the farmers' distress, the BJP governments waived loans in states they governed, such as Uttar Pradesh and Maharashtra. However, the majority of farmers had no access to the banking system (the only way to waive loans) but instead were beholden to local moneylenders,[85] and the loan waivers were sometimes ridiculously small.[86]

Farmers asked only to be given a fair price for their produce and nothing more.[87] But that is exactly what Modi's BJP refused to do. Why? Because the "people" it represented were primarily urban. In 2014, the BJP's success was clearest in the cities, as mentioned above. It is worthwhile to repeat here that its appeal with voters in urban constituencies increased, as it won 42 percent of the vote in such areas (11 percentage points more than its average score), while in semiurban constituencies, its score reached 32 percent, and in rural constituencies, it fell to 30 percent.[88] It is certainly due to its relative lack of dependence on the rural electorate and its goal to prevent its urban voters from having to pay more for their food that the BJP decided not to raise farm commodity prices and ceased combating poverty in rural areas by cutting funds for the MGNREGA (which otherwise would have led to an increase in farmworkers' wages). Ashok Gulati, an agricultural economist, described this approach as "urban consumer bias."[89]

The impoverishment of rural India explains the rise of poverty that was revealed in 2019 when a National Statistical Office (NSO) survey titled *Key Indicators: Household Consumer Expenditure in India* showed that the average amount of money spent by an Indian in a month fell by 3.7 percent to Rs 1,446 (19.28 USD) in 2017–2018 from Rs 1,501 (20 USD) in 2011–2012, whereas it had risen 13 percent between 2009–2010 and 2004–2005.[90] Such a drop in consumption in real terms had not been seen since 1972–1973. This contraction was primarily due to rural India. While consumer spending had increased by 2 percent in towns and cities, it had decreased by 8.8 percent in villages: while rural Indians spent on average Rs 580 (7.73 USD) monthly on food in 2017–2018, they had spent Rs 643 (8.6 USD) in 2011–2012 (in both cases in real terms). Analyzing these trends on the basis of other NSO surveys, Himanshu has shown that the decline started in 2015–2016 and that until 2019–2020 it was affecting rural as well as urban dwellers to almost the same extent: −4.4 percent per annum in rural areas and −4.8 percent per annum in urban areas.[91]

The return of mass poverty largely explains India's drop in rank in the World Bank's Human Capital Index (115 out of 157 in 2018)[92] and in the Global Hunger Index (103 out of 119 in 2018—against 100 in 2017 and 97 in 2016).[93] In 2016, already India's National Nutrition Monitoring Bureau had concluded that 35 percent of rural men and women were undernourished and 42 percent of the children underweight, with malnutrition being worse than in the 1970s.[94] In 2017, the International Food Policy Research Institute (IFPRI) ranked India 100 out of the 119 countries studied.[95]

Diluting Reservations

Among the traditionally aided social categories, Dalits have been especially penalized by the Modi government, despite his rhetoric. His speeches and campaign promises attempted to present him as an advocate of the Dalits. And so, at the beginning of his term, he professed that he drew his inspiration from their historic leader, B. R. Ambedkar, who, he claimed, had not been given the respect he deserved by the Congress and Nehru in particular (who, however, had appointed him Law Minister).[96] In terms of promises, the BJP electoral platform in 2014 included a section entitled "SCs, STs and other Weaker Sections: Social

Justice and Empowerment," which read, "The BJP is committed to bridge the gap, following the principle of *Samajik Nyaya* (social justice) and *Samajik Samrasata* (social harmony). The social justice must be further complemented with economic justice and political empowerment—we will focus upon empowering the deprived sections of society. Steps will be taken to create an enabling ecosystem of equal opportunity—for education, health and livelihood. We will accord highest priority to ensuring their security especially the prevention of atrocities against SCs and STs."[97] As for SCs, or Dalits, the aim at the top of the list of BJP campaign pledges was to form an "ecosystem" conducive to furthering education and the sense of enterprise. In practical terms, however, the funds earmarked for Dalit education in the Indian budget have been reduced. While this budget item, within the Special Component Plan (a subcategory of the annual budget), is supposed to be proportional to the demographic weight of the Dalits, 16.6 percent, it fluctuated between 9 and 6.5 percent during Modi's first term.[98] As a result, scholarship funds were cut drastically. Nearly 5 million Dalit students have been affected by this reduction and—once again—by delays in payment.

In parallel, the Modi government and BJP state governments have undermined the system of positive discrimination that had been a large factor in helping the Dalits emancipate themselves from the legacy of centuries of caste oppression. First, the erosion of the public sector has resulted in a steady decrease in the number of jobs occupied by Dalits in the reservations framework. For instance, the number of civil service candidates short-listed by the Union Public Service Commission (UPSC) dropped by almost 40 percent between 2014 and 2018, from 1,236 to 759.[99] This evolution was not only due to old trends (like the rise of vacancies and the privatization of Public Sector Undertakings) that have continued but also to new policies. The creation of a lateral entry in the Indian administration is a case in point. This reform was intended to "to draw expertise from the industry, academia and society into the services."[100] In February 2019, 89 applicants were short-listed (out of 6,000 candidates from the private sector) to fill ten posts of joint secretary.[101] This new procedure diluted the reservations system because the quotas did not apply.

Second, the introduction of a 10 percent quota in 2019 for the economically weaker sections (EWS) has altered the standard definition of backwardness; that is, by foregrounding economic backwardness but, at the same time, restricting such a quota to upper castes alone, who are neither socially nor educationally backward. By setting an income limit of Rs 800,000 (10,667 USD) per annum, below which households are classified as EWS, the government made this quota accessible to about 99 percent of the upper castes—not to the poor only. According to Ashwini Deshpande and Rajesh Ramachandran, it "completely overturn[ed] the original logic of reservations on its head."[102] They continued:

> By stipulating a quota for non-SC–ST–OBC (Other Backward Class) families earning Rs. 800,000 or less, the government is effectively creating a quota exclusively for Hindu upper castes who are not in the top 1% of the income distribution. This means that despite being presented as a quota on economic criteria and not caste, the reality is that this is very much a caste based quota, targeted towards castes that do not suffer any social discrimination; on the contrary, these rank the highest on the social scale of ritual purity.[103]

By introducing this quota, the Modi government sent a twofold message: one, the Mandal moment was over, as caste-based quotas were no longer the only reservation technique; two, the upper castes would be in a position to get jobs that would have been taken by OBCs or SCs otherwise. Indeed, the SCs/STs/OBCs who, thanks to their marks, would have made it through the general category would not do so anymore because the 10 percent quota in this general category would decrease the number of seats available.[104]

The decline of the traditional reservation system in favor of SCs, STs, and OBCs and the introduction of a new quota were well in tune with the old Sangh Parivar's approach to positive discrimination. As mentioned above, the RSS and its offshoots claimed that caste-based quotas were dividing the Hindu community and did not reward individual merit sufficiently. In both cases, Hindu nationalist ideologues tended to minimize the relevance of caste as a factor of inequality in India's society—a clear reflection of their irenic view of the social system and a clear indication of their attempt to protect the upper castes, which have also benefited from the Modi government for reasons other than the EWS quota.

Modi, Champion of the Elite

Not only has the Modi government not honored its promises in terms of combating poverty, but it has also enabled the upper castes to make an impressive comeback in Indian politics, widened inequality, and promoted crony capitalism.

The Resurgence of Upper Castes in Indian Politics

The EWS quota coincided with the return of the upper castes to the public scene: these were the two sides of the post-Mandal coin, as the so-called saffron wave that brought Modi to power was largely a reaction of the upper castes, a counterrevolution as hypothesized in the introduction of this book.

This evolution is evidenced in the sociological profile of BJP MPs. While in the Hindi belt—a region that represents almost half of the seats of the lower house—the proportion of Lok Sabha MPs from the upper castes had already started to increase in 2009 at the expense of OBCs and Muslims, this trend continued in 2014, largely due to the BJP's unprecedented win. Indeed, 47.6 percent of BJP MPs came from the upper castes in 2014.[105] As a result, as shown in figure 4.1 and table 4.1, the percentage of MPs from the upper castes took an upward turn, with 44.5 percent, on par with its representation in the 1980s, whereas the share of OBCs dropped to 20 percent.[106] Among the BJP upper-caste MPs, Brahmins and Rajputs were especially overrepresented.

This overrepresentation of forward castes among the BJP MPs was nothing compared to the makeup of the Modi government, where they represented 79.4 percent of the ministers and ministers of state. As Katharine Adeney and Wilfried Swenden have shown, such an overrepresentation had never prevailed since the Mandal moment.[107]

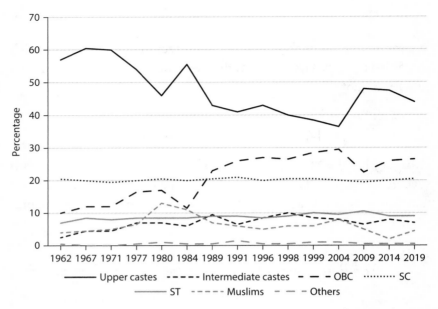

FIGURE 4.1. Caste and community representation in the Hindi belt (1962–2019)
Source: Christophe Jaffrelot and Gilles Verniers, "The Reconfiguration of India's Political
Elite: Profiling the 17th Lok Sabha," *Contemporary South Asia* 28, no. 2 (May 18, 2020): 245,
https://doi.org/10.1080/09584935.2020.1765984

TABLE 4.1. The caste profile of the Lok Sabha BJP MPs in the Hindi belt

In numbers	1989	1991	1996	1998	1999	2004	2009	2014	2019
Upper castes	32	49	56	58	45	32	30	87	80
Intermediate castes	2	4	8	9	9	7	2	14	14
OBCs	10	13	21	24	21	13	11	38	35
SCs	10	16	26	21	22	14	8	36	33
STs	7	3	7	9	13	11	11	16	15
Muslims	1	1	0	0	1	0	0	0	1
Others	1	1	1	1	0	1	0	0	0
Total	63	87	119	122	111	78	62	191	178
In percentage	**1989**	**1991**	**1996**	**1998**	**1999**	**2004**	**2009**	**2014**	**2019**
Upper castes	50.8	56.3	47.1	47.2	40.2	41	47.6	45.5	44.9
Intermediate castes	3.2	4.6	6.7	7.3	8	9	3.2	7.3	7.9
OBCs	15.9	14.9	17.6	19.5	18.8	16.7	17.5	19.9	19.7
SCs	15.9	18.4	21.8	17.1	19.6	17.9	12.7	18.8	18.5
STs	11.1	3.4	5.9	7.3	11.6	14.1	17.5	8.4	8.4
Muslims	1.6	1.1	0	0	0.9	0	0	0	0.6
Others	1.6	1.1	0.8	0.8	0	1.3	0	0	0

Source: SPINPER—The Social Profile of the Indian National and Provincial Elected Representatives,
a CNRS-supported international virtual lab associating Ashoka University and Sciences Po.

The BJP certainly did not ignore the lower castes. For instance, many were given new responsibilities in the party machine.[108] But these promotions were usually limited and very sophisticated so as not to alienate the upper castes: rather than putting newcomers in places occupied by existing cadres, they were appointed to additional posts created especially for them. As a result, out of seventy-five district president jobs in Uttar Pradesh, fifty-four were now occupied by OBCs and three by Dalits.[109]

Not only upper castes were back in larger numbers at the helm of the Indian state(s), but BJP leaders eulogized their moral superiority without any inhibition. Inaugurating the Brahmin Business Summit in Ahmedabad, the BJP Speaker of the Gujarat assembly, Rajendra Trivedi, himself a Brahmin, seized this opportunity to valorize his caste fellows: "After studying Constitutions of 60 countries in detail, do you know who made a draft Constitution and handed it over to Dr Babasaheb Ambedkar? It was B N Rau. . . . Benegal Narsing Rau means Brahmin,"[110] an oblique attack on Dalits, who are usually proud of the fact that one of them, Ambedkar, had been the architect of the Indian Constitution. Trivedi also said, "Of eight Nobel prize winners in India, seven have gone to Brahmins. Does anyone remember the name of the ninth Nobel Prize recipient? Abhijit Banerjee got it. Abhijit Banerjee means a Brahmin." During the same meeting, the chief minister of Gujarat, Vijay Rupani, emphasized the Brahminical roots of the Sangh Parivar, something the organization, till then, had avoided. He declared, "The Brahmin community has always spoken about national interest, and because of that, the community has joined with the BJP and the RSS"—as evident from the fact, he said, that the Jana Sangh had been created by three Brahmins in Gujarat.

The BJP Speaker of the Lok Sabha itself, Om Birla, went one step further; the way he eulogized the Brahmins came as a defense of the caste system: "Brahmin community always works towards guiding all other communities, and the community has always held a guiding role in this nation. It has always played a role in spreading education and values in the society. And even today if just one Brahmin family lives in a village or a hutment, then that Brahmin family always holds a high position due to its dedication and service. . . . Hence, Brahmins are held in high regard in society by the virtue of their birth."[111] Until then, Sangh Parivar ideologues had been reluctant to attribute the superiority of Brahmins to their birth. They usually claimed—using the vocabulary they had inherited from reformists and revivalists like Swami Dayananda— that if Brahmins were at the top of society, it was because of their qualities (*gun*). Birla was saying something different, and in the same vein, he also defended caste endogamy as the best way to sustain social order and unity. Speaking on the occasion of a Brahmin *parichay sammelan*, a meeting of Brahmins meant to help them to choose Brahmin spouses for their sons and daughters, he added: "If we want to bind the society together, then there is only one arrangement today; like our ancestors used to forge alliances for marriage, we today have parichay sammelan, and if we want to save the society, then this is the lone alternative." For Birla, the unity of society could only come from caste order. It had, therefore, to be hierarchical.

Indeed, BJP leaders have made caste-based observances that reflected their belief in the Dalits' impurity. For instance, after Yogi Adityanath was elected chief minister of Uttar Pradesh, Hindu priests "made elaborate arrangements for sacred purifying rituals at the sprawling chief minister's bungalow,"[112] which had been previously occupied by Akhilesh Yadav, Mayawati, and Mulayam Singh Yadav. Similar rituals were also organized in Udipi, by a Sangh Parivar-affiliated group in the surroundings of the Sree Krishna Temple, "alleging that it was rendered 'impure' due to the presence of Dalits" demonstrators.[113] Incidentally, the Information and Broadcasting Ministry and the Ministry of Social Justice and Empowerment issued orders stating that the word *Dalit* should no longer be used in official communication. Only the term *Scheduled Caste* was permissible.[114]

The BJP is not elitist only in terms of caste; it is also so in terms of class. In this regard, it has mainly attracted people from the business community, whether wealthy magnates or local businessmen. The sociological profile of its MPs again sheds light on this fact. While the share of business occupations among Lok Sabha representatives rose from 14.20 percent in 1991 to 26.33 percent in 2014 along a virtually linear progression,[115] the BJP contributed more than any other party to this proportion in 2014, as 86 of its 282 MPs, or 30.5 percent of them, came from the business community. These 86 MPs accounted for more than half of the 144 businessmen in the Lok Sabha.

The sociological profile of BJP MPs is not only an indication of the party's elitist nature; it also reflects its practice of crony capitalism. While Congress policies fostered a similar osmosis between politics and business in the wake of the 1990s economic liberalization, the BJP brought it to new heights by giving free rein to wholesale collusion. First, some BJP leaders were blatant wheeler-dealers, mindless of the conflicts of interest that might be involved. Nitin Gadkari, transportation minister in the first Modi government, owned businesses tied in with his portfolio. His colleague, Piyush Goyal—son of a former BJP treasurer—was also a businessman, who, *after* having been appointed minister in 2014 (with a whole range of portfolios, including power and coal), sold his company for a grossly overvalued price to Piramal, a firm that has interests in infrastructure and energy.[116] Second, businessmen got themselves elected to parliament under the BJP label— such as Rajeev Chandrashekhar, a venture capitalist who founded a television channel called Republic TV (to which we will return in chapter 8)—and could thus influence laws that regulated their sector, enjoy preferential treatment, and even take advantage of insider dealings.[117]

The Rich Get Richer

Under Narendra Modi, the rich have become richer, and inequalities have increased. A 2018 Oxfam report revealed that 10 percent of the richest Indians garnered 77.4 percent of the nation's wealth (against 73 percent the year before)[118] and that 58 percent of it was in the hands of India's "1 percent" (while the world average is 50 percent). The earnings made by this handful of people in 2017 were equal to India's budget for that year. Also in 2017, the fortune of India's 100 richest tycoons leaped by 26 percent. The richest of them all, Mukesh Ambani, increased his wealth by 67 percent, according to *Forbes India*[119]—a publication, moreover, that belongs to this billionaire. Ambani's fortune again rose by 24 percent in 2018.[120]

Going slightly beyond the 100 richest, the IIFL Wealth Hurun India Rich List identified the 953 richest Indian families and gave figures showing that their fortune represented more than 26 percent of the country's GDP[121]—which meant that if a tax rate of 4 percent was applied to the nation's 953 richest families, it would give the government the equivalent of 1 percent of India's GDP.[122] According to Crédit Suisse, the number of dollar millionaires in India jumped from 34,000 in 2000 to 759,000 in 2019,[123] which means that the country has one of "the world's fastest-growing population of millionaires."[124] The average wealth level of these millionaires increased by 74 percent over this period.

THE UNFAIRNESS OF THE TAXATION POLICY

While the rich became richer, the taxation policy of the government, instead of correcting this trend, actively strengthened it. One of the first decisions of the first Modi government was to abolish the wealth tax that had been introduced in 1957. While the fiscal resources generated by this tax were never significant, the decision was more than a symbolic one.[125] The wealth tax was replaced with an income tax increase of 2 percent for households that earned more than Rs 10 million (133,333 USD) annually.[126]

Few people pay income tax in India anyway: only 14.6 million people (2 percent of the population) did in 2019. As a result, the income-tax-to-GDP ratio remained below 11 percent. Not only has the Modi government not tried to introduce any reforms to change this, but it has instead increased indirect taxes (such as excise taxes), which are the most unfair as they affect everyone, irrespective of income. Taxes on alcohol and petroleum products are a case in point. As some state governments have also imposed their own taxes, this strategy means that India has one of the highest taxation rates on fuel in the world. The share of indirect taxes in the state's fiscal resources has increased under the Modi government to reach 50 percent of the total taxes—compared to 39 percent under UPA I and 44 percent under UPA II.[127]

Modi's taxation policy, a supply-side economics approach, is in keeping with the managerial rhetoric of promoting the spirit of enterprise that the prime minister, who readily presents himself as an efficiency-conscious "apolitical CEO," relishes. One of the neoliberal measures the Modi government enacted in the name of economic rationality, right from his very first budget in 2015, was to lower the corporate tax.[128] For existing companies it was reduced from 30 to 22 percent, and for manufacturing firms incorporated after October 1, 2019 that started operations before March 31, 2023, it was reduced from 25 to 15 percent—the biggest reduction in twenty-eight years. In addition to these tax reductions, the government withdrew the enhanced surcharge on long- and short-term capital gains for foreign portfolio investors as well as domestic portfolio investors.[129]

As the 2019 elections were approaching, the Modi government felt the need to appear less pro-rich and more pro-poor again. But the union budget passed in February was somewhat a missed opportunity so far as the peasants were concerned. No loan waivers were announced in their favor, simply an enhanced interest subvention on loans and an annual income support of Rs 6,000 (80 USD)—6 percent of a small farmer's yearly income—to all farmers' households owning two hectares or fewer.[130] In fact, the union budget was once again more geared to pleasing the middle class. The income tax exemption limit jumped from Rs 200,000 (2,667 USD) to 250,000 (3,333 USD), and the income tax rate up to Rs 5 lakh (6,667 USD) was reduced from 10 to 5 percent. The income tax on an income of Rs 10 lakh (13,333 USD) dropped from Rs 110,210 (1,470 USD) to Rs 75,000 (1,000 USD).[131]

The poor were doubly affected by the fiscal policy of the Modi government in 2014–2019: not only did the tax cuts in favor of the middle class, the abolition of the wealth tax, and, more importantly, the reduction of the corporate tax rates have to be offset by increased indirect taxes, but the stagnation of fiscal resources did not allow the government of India to spend more on public education and public health—all the more so as Narendra Modi wanted to reduce the fiscal deficit. First of all, tax collection diminished. The exchequer "lost" Rs 1.45 lakh crore (1.933 billion USD) in the reduction of the corporate tax, for instance. That was the main reason

why gross direct tax collection dipped 4.92 percent[132] in 2019–2020, a
fiscal year during which gross tax collections were less than those in
2018–2019. Tax collections had never declined on a year-on-year basis
since 1961–1962.[133] Second, government expenditures diminished. The
central government reduced its spending on education from 0.63 percent
of GDP in 2013–2014 to 0.47 percent in 2017–2018. The trend was mar-
ginally better on the public health front, where the Center's spending
declined from 0.37 percent of GDP in 2013–2014 to 0.34 percent in
2015–2016, before rising again to reach 0.38 percent in 2016–2017.[134]

This strategy, together with the partial dismantling of measures to
fight poverty, partly explains the continuous rise of inequalities in India.
However, some of the rich have become richer for other reasons as well,
including the close relationship between the Modi government and
industrialists.

FROM CRONY CAPITALISM TO COLLUSIVE CAPITALISM

While the Modi government is not responsible for the enrichment of
Indian tycoons, which began in most cases prior to the BJP victory in
2014, it continued to help them. In Gujarat, the Modi government had
granted unwarranted advantages to industrialists, including the sale of
land below market prices, dispensations from environmental standards,
unjustified tax rebates, interest-free loans, and so on.[135] After forming
the central government, the NDA government shielded Indian industrialists from banks to which these men owed billions. Such collusion
has contributed to destabilizing a banking system undermined by dubious debts—particularly those held by these big investors, who do not
pay back their loans.[136] Even if the problem began under the previous
government, it has persisted in part owing to collusion between businessmen and the ruling class. The government's cronies continued to
receive huge loans from public-sector banks (whose heads have trouble
disobeying the government),[137] which they proved unable to pay back.
In May 2018, nonperforming assets (NPAs) vested in public banks—in
other words, loans for which the borrower had not made payment on

either the interest or the principal in at least ninety days—accounted for 12.65 billion dollars, or about 14 percent of their total loans (compared to 12.5 percent in March the previous year[138] and only 3 percent in March 2012).[139] A small number of borrowers were largely responsible for this evolution, among whom were prominent large industrialists.[140] In 2015, in a fifty-seven-page document, Credit Suisse gave a detailed analysis of the astounding level of debt of ten Indian corporations that continued to borrow even though all the red flags had gone up.[141] In 2018, 84 percent of the dubious loans were owed by major corporations, and twelve of them accounted for 25 percent of the outstanding NPAs.[142] Among them is the group owned by Gautam Adani, a supporter of Prime Minister Narendra Modi since 2002.[143] In 2015, the group increased its debt level by 16 percent to acquire a seaport and two power plants. Consequently, its debt soared to 840 billion rupees (11.2 billion USD), compared to only 331 billion rupees (4.41 billion dollars) in 2011.[144] If banks kept lending it money, it was on account of Gautam Adani's association with Narendra Modi.

The banking crisis prompted the Reserve Bank of India (RBI) to prohibit several banks from granting loans, thereby penalizing farmers and, even more so, small- and medium-sized enterprises (SMEs), whose access to credit had already started to shrink due to the decline in bank resources. A number of these SMEs—some of them very small—have gone bust. And yet these are the largest providers of jobs in industry, handicrafts, and services in India. The crisis this sector is experiencing partly explains the crunch in the labor market, where the first victims of unemployment are the poorest.

Why are indebted industrialists not obliged to sell all or some of their assets to pay back the banks by applying the 2016 law known as the Insolvency and Bankruptcy Code? Partly because of the courts, where cases have dragged on for years (the liquidation of some of Essar's assets took 841 days, against the 270 days that the law had fixed as a time limit),[145] and partly because some of the companies in question have been close to power—so much so that the list of the largest defaulters has remained secret.

Conclusion to Part I

IN THE FIRST DECADE OF THE 2000s, Narendra Modi's ascension to power, by virtue of his populist stance, marked a turning point in the Sangh Parivar's history. Certainly, he did not break with the core ideology of the movement: a pure product of the RSS, he cultivated all the facets of Hindu nationalism, including the otherization of Muslims, which was exacerbated in words and in actions, especially during the 2002 pogrom, when Modi became the Emperor of the Hindu Hearts, following the old BJP strategy of polarization. Subsequently, he was able to exploit the feeling of vulnerability among the majority community vis-à-vis Muslims and Pakistan, which was especially pervasive in Gujarat, a border state, in the context of a wave of Islamist attacks.

But Modi brought something new to Hindutva because of his populist style. In fact, he already fulfilled most of the criteria of populism, as defined by theoreticians of this ism, during his Gujarat years. He cast himself as an embodiment of the people in their entirety. As chief minister, he always spoke in the name of 50 or 60 million Gujaratis and, as prime minister, he systematically expressed himself on behalf of 1.2 or 1.3 billion Indians, using "unity" as a recurrent "empty signifier," along with emotionally charged terms like "friends" and "brothers and sisters." Laclau's theory can be refined here, or adapted to the Indian context, as Modi tried to epitomize this unifying figure by adopting features of the "fakir" who sacrifices everything for others, and this repertoire reso-nated culturally.

To cast himself as the great unifier and the people's man, Modi estab-lished a unique, direct relation with the people, another touchstone of the populist style and something L. K. Advani had initiated with his Rath Yatra but not sustained. (In the end, he could never prevail over A. B. Vajpayee for long.) What Modi achieved was unprecedented because it went against the RSS ethos, which constantly resisted the personalization of power—within the organization and in the Sangh Parivar generally. Considering that the cause it championed was beyond the human scale and that allowing a single personality to embody the movement would make it vulnerable, the RSS, in the training it im-poses on the swayamsevak in the shakha, crushes egos and inhibits individualism—to such an extent that the strong personalities required to enter politics, particularly for public debate, are rarely found in the organization. Modi is atypical from this standpoint: he went from the RSS to the BJP in the 1990s, where he rose above the organization, dominated it, and to some degree freed himself from it while remaining loyal to its ideology. Populism, through the personalization of power, indeed implies some institutional decline: the leader who relates di-rectly to the people does not rely as much as his predecessors on a po-litical party; he uses his own network of activists and social media in-stead, as populists are disruptive politicians who emancipate themselves from institutions (including their own parties) in order to change the rules of the game, as Shils has suggested. Certainly, Modi related effec-tively to the people owing to his energy and oratorical skills, but it took the huge financial resources available to him to saturate the public space.

However, like all populists, this great unifier à la Laclau mobilizes supporters in the most simplistic way: against enemies, "the corrupt elite" Mudde describes, which Congress and the Nehru/Gandhis pri-marily represent. In contrast to the way this family occupied power for decades, like a dynasty, Modi presented himself as a self-made man, coming from a poor background. This social profile not only helped him vis-à-vis the Congress party; it also contributed to his rise within the Sangh Parivar in the post-Mandal context, when the organization needed to project a more plebeian face and was, in fact, undergoing a process of plebeianization. Here, Modi neutralized a contradiction that the Sangh Parivar has long suffered from: the opposition between the movement's elitist identity and its desire to appeal to the masses. The RSS was founded by Brahmins, and for a long time its cadres were solely from the upper castes. While it wanted to recruit among the common people, the only lower-caste elements who came to the shakha were those seeking the company of the local elite to improve their status by emulating them, according to the logic of Sanskritization. With Modi, this social line of cleavage was blurred because he was at once a pure product of the RSS *and* a man of lower caste. Beyond this pedigree, he symbolized the rise of a new social category—which he himself dubbed the neo-middle class. This class came into being in the first decade of the 2000s owing to the rise of lower-caste elements that benefited from the post-Mandal quotas and two-digit economic growth in the wake of economic liberalization. While Vajpayee's BJP attracted upper-caste voters who saw the BJP as protection against positive discrimination, Modi's BJP lured voters of the same profile *as well as* those who benefited from positive discrimination and growth but were frustrated because it could not continue its rise in the context of the economic slowdown of the 2010s. This category (mostly OBCs), which the RSS had tried to co-opt after Mandal, had become increasingly influential within the Sangh Parivar, as evidenced by the assertiveness of the Bajrang Dal. But this plebeianization of the Hindu nationalist movement did not rely on caste only: many upper-caste "angry young men" sought Modi's help in resisting socioeconomic decline and losing self-esteem by creating jobs and endowing them with new pride. All these youth identified with him, a victim of the English-speaking liberal elite and a strongman who never apologized after the 2002 pogrom. They made a significant impact in the 2014 election. The eighteen- to twenty-five-year-olds who represented about one-fourth of the voters had a record turnout of 68 percent (2 percentage points above the national average). And according to the CSDS survey, 34.4 percent of them supported Modi's BJP, more than 3 percentage points above the party's overall performance.[1]

Modi related very effectively to these youths, and to the people in general, because he could appear as both a victim like them and a superhero at the same time, to paraphrase Ostiguy. Modi claimed that he had been victimized by the establishment because of his social background. This background helped people identify with him but also made his achievements even more exceptional—and it is precisely in exceptional qualities that Weber's charismatic legitimacy is rooted. This canonic concept also can be refined—and Indianized—here. Modi's charisma is more easily understandable if the analysis factors in the permeability of society to supernatural phenomena that endows heroes with superhuman powers.

Modi was able to use the populist repertoire by claiming that he belonged to the social periphery, but he could also argue that he was from the geographical periphery as well, a periphery that is more "authentic": he had never been part of the cosmopolitan Delhi circuit and had never been a national leader before 2013–2014. This position helped him to appear as an outsider and a clean man rooted in the Indian soil, whereas the Congress leaders appeared as corrupt in material terms (something the Anna Hazare movement had allegedly demonstrated) and in cultural terms: Sonia Gandhi was a foreigner, and Rahul Gandhi had her blood in his veins.

This is an essential point, because Modi's populism belongs to the subcategory of *national* populism theorized by Germani. He therefore attacked the Congress leaders more aggressively and sarcastically than any other BJP leaders before him. He dared to insult and humiliate them in the most vulgar way, claiming that they were not legitimate adversaries but enemies of the nation he embodied. Here, his style illustrates the antipluralism dimension of populism. But his main targets are of course minorities. While his predecessors at the head of the BJP all found ways of coping with minorities, at least symbolically Modi has made no concessions. Hence, he invented a Hindu variety of national populism in which the majoritarian community came together against the Muslim Other, who was forced to submit, in the face of violent means, or leave. As I show in the second part of the book, this gave birth to a de facto ethnic democracy after the resounding victory of 2014, which was largely due to the unprecedented combination by Modi of Hindu nationalism and populism.

Before turning to the ethnic democracy question, we need to review the last dimension of Modi's populism: its socioeconomic character on the basis of some of the discourses and policies he implemented after taking power. While he insisted that he was the champion of the poor— as evidenced by dozens of speeches and the way he presented the SBA, PMJDY, and PMUY—in contrast to socialists or social democrats who redistribute some of the national wealth to the poor, Modi has decreased state spending for the poor, including the MGNREGA scheme. This approach fit within the BJP's traditional aspirations of reducing the size of the state to prevent the government from interfering with the social order—a hierarchical concept inherited from the caste system. Instead of redistributing wealth, the Modi government has provided the poor with nonfinancial resources, endowing them with a new sense of dignity and a feeling of taking revenge against the rich, a sentiment he exploited in particular in the wake of demonetization. Such an exploitation of social emotions is part the populist style, all the more so as all the schemes analyzed in chapter 4 were aggressively marketed, associating his image on each and every advertisement published in newspapers or on bills.

Political scientists have tried to understand why poor voters supported the BJP, a party clearly associated with the Indian elite.[2] This is not too difficult to explain in the case of the upper-caste poor, who try to defend their status by identifying themselves with a political force that is hostile to caste-based positive discrimination and appear as the custodians of the Hindu high tradition.[3] It also makes sense where the BJP is doing social work among the poor.[4] But with Modi, another variable has to be factored in: the attractivity of the national-populist leader over everyone belonging to his community, including the poor, who felt considered, even respected, by the new leader supremo, a leader who, on top of it, could be seen as one of them by the plebeians.

While in India, the word *populist* is often used to designate the lavish public spending done by demagogic rulers,[5] populism, here, appears as a form of counterrevolution, an antidote to politics of equality—and *national* populism even more so because this repertoire allows its architects to blur identities based on caste and class and to defuse social conflicts, not only by mobilizing the community against an Other but also by giving a new, immaterial sense of dignity to the poor. The subtext of national populism, indeed, is elite revenge, and upper-caste politicians have continued to stage a political comeback since 2014: reservations have been diluted, and inequalities have flourished after pro-poor programs like the MGNREGA were cut back. Instead of correcting these trends, tax policies have accentuated them, as the rich and middle class have benefited from fiscal reforms whereas the poor have been adversely affected by indirect taxes. Last but not least, cronies of the government have been allowed to strengthen their position as the super-rich, generally speaking, prospered. In this general assessment, rural India is clearly at the receiving end in spite of official discourses, with mass poverty rising again in villages.

These features of Modi's politics conform to the canons of populism: Modi has delivered pro-poor rhetoric in the full range of tones (literally speaking: from compassion to confidence to commandment), without this rhetoric being acted on. To the contrary, Modi has mobilized the poor against the establishment while, at the same time, some of his policies have made the rich even richer. The two facets of national populism are at work here: on one hand, elite groups and middle-class elements fearing for their status have used identity and religion to mobilize the plebeians against the Other by manipulating emotions; on the other, the only promises in terms of economic development that have been fulfilled are mostly nonfinancial, as inequality has been allowed to increase.

Populists pose as champions of the people, but they do very little for the people, except in the realm of identity politics, accusing the Other of all ills while making minor concessions to the most destitute. In Modi's case, while the Muslim scapegoat has been thoroughly exploited, the common masses have hardly seen their lives improve from an economic standpoint, and the rich have benefited immensely from his policies. This method can be explained, first, by the nature of the BJP electorate: Modi's "people," in 2014, were primarily made up of upper-caste, middle-class urbans and the neo-middle class to whom the rural poor have been sacrificed—as evidenced by the government's decision to connect Ahmedabad and Mumbai by a "bullet train" that only the rich and the middle class will find affordable.[6] Second, Modi's BJP depended to a great extent on the business community for election campaign funding.

Modi therefore differs from many populists who win elections owing to support from populations that feel abandoned by the political establishment. He was perceived as the man for the task particularly by the upper castes, who felt threatened by the rise of the OBCs and the neo-middle class among these same OBCs, who wanted to continue their climb up the social ladder by moving from reservations in the public sector to private enterprise, as they believed Modi had done in Gujarat.

PART II

The World's Largest De Facto Ethnic Democracy

SAMMY SMOOHA, WHO DEVELOPED THE THEORY of ethnic democracy, defines this political system on the basis of a broad set of criteria. Ethnic democracy is the product of ethnic nationalism—the ideology of a group that considers itself bound by racial, linguistic, religious, or other cultural characteristics and derives from these bonds a strong sense of belonging and often of superiority. Its sense of identity goes along with a rejection of the Other, generally perceived as a threat to the survival and integrity of the ethnic nation. For Smooha, one of the conditions for the emergence and persistence of an ethnic democracy is "the existence of a threat (real or perceived) to the ethnic nation that requires mobilization of the majority in order to preserve the ethnic nation."[1] While this internal condition is the most important of all (together with the ethnic majority's relative size, which must necessarily be significant), two external conditions must be fulfilled: the lack of protection for the minority in one or more states governed by the same ethnic group, and the neutrality (or even support) of the international community toward the ethnic nation-state.[2]

Smooha claims that many countries have gone down the road of ethnic democracy but that the archetype of this political system remains Israel, a state that endeavors to combine an ethnic (Jewish) identity and a parliamentary system drawing its inspiration from Western Europe.

The two sides of this coin are the Jewish nature of the nation-state and the restriction it imposes on the rights of minorities, primarily the Palestinians, also known as Israeli Arabs. The ethnic aspect of the nation can be seen in the Judaization of identity symbols that inform everyday life: "Israel's titular name, calendar, days and sites of commemoration, heroes, flag, emblem, national anthem, names of places, ceremonies and the like are all Jewish."[3] Not only does the state promote the Jewish community in terms of identity references; it also helps it in financial terms, as seen in the action of the Jewish Agency and the Jewish National Fund, semipublic institutions that provide aid only to Jews. Smooha adds that most discrimination is unofficial but exists in practice, such as making military service a criterion of eligibility for benefits, which rules out most members of minorities.

The discriminatory practices visited on Israeli Arabs were explicitly recognized by the Or Commission—named for Theodore Or, the former Supreme Court justice who presided over it. Appointed by the government to investigate police repression, which in October 2000 claimed thirteen Arab lives at the start of the al-Aqsa Intifada, the commission found that "Israeli democracy is not democratic towards the Arabs to the same extent that it is democratic towards the Jews."[4]

The notion of ethnic democracy, indeed, is a contradiction in terms because it divides the demos into two categories: some citizens do not have the same rights as others simply because of their religious identity. But Israeli Jews claim to support the principles of democracy, as the Supreme Court moreover stated in a 1988 decision denying the right of the Progressive List for Peace to participate in elections because the party refused to recognize Israel as a Jewish state in essence: "There is no contradiction whatsoever between these two things: The state is the state of the Jews, while its regime is an enlightened democratic regime that accords rights to all citizens, Jews and non-Jews."[5] The judges even went so far as to consider that "the existence of the State of Israel as a Jewish state does not negate its democratic nature, any more than the Frenchness of France contradicts its democratic nature."[6]

While the Supreme Court of Israel seems to assume that all the country's citizens have the same rights, according to Smooha, "Jewish public opinion not only condones constraints imposed on Arabs, but also endorses preferential treatment of Jews."[7] An opinion poll taken in 1995 among Israeli Jews showed that 74.1 percent of them expected the state to give Jews preferential treatment over Arabs—who, for 30.9 percent of the respondents, should not even have the right to vote or be hired in civil service jobs, according to 32.2 percent.[8] Smooha adds, underscoring the scope of the problem, "Most Jews do not even perceive the above differential practices as discriminatory against Arabs, but consider them rather as preferences rightfully accorded to them as Jews in a Jewish state."[9]

Paradoxically, Smooha concludes, "The Israeli case demonstrates the viability of an ethnic democracy as a distinct type of democracy in deeply divided societies."[10] He considers on the whole that, "as a mode of conflict regulation, it is superior to genocide, ethnic cleansing, involuntary population transfer and systems of non-democratic domination."[11] It certainly is, but ethnicizing democracy does not save minorities from violence either.

Part II of this book deals with the exercise of power by Hindu nationalists from the specific angle of the ethnicization of India's democracy.[12] During Narendra Modi's first term, 2014–2019, this process involved few judicial alterations: not only was the Constitution not amended (the BJP did not have the majority needed to do so anyway), but also few new laws were passed, even at the state level. That is why Modi's India, during NDA II, can be said to have invented a de facto ethnic democracy, a political system in which the state remained relatively in the background, leaving the field open to vigilante groups, which, with the tacit or explicit support of law enforcement bodies, went after "deviants," whether they were champions of secularism or members of minorities. This brand of moral policing, reminiscent of the orthopraxy—or social control—characteristic of patriarchal traditions and the caste system, was coupled with promotion of the Hindu culture, defined as Indian culture and equated with it, in which the state, for a change, played a key role. This last aspect will first be studied before turning to the targeting of secularists and attacks on minorities by vigilantes.

5

Hindu Majoritarianism against Secularism

FROM THE MOMENT NARENDRA MODI TOOK OFFICE, Hinduism started being promoted in the public arena. In fact, the move was set in motion even before he was appointed prime minister. As soon as the election results were announced, the BJP candidate decided to celebrate in his constituency of Varanasi—which he chose to keep before resigning from the other seat he had won, in Gujarat. It was in Varanasi, in fact, that Modi's first inauguration took place, the one that would ratify his cultural legitimacy, while his official inauguration was simply a matter of institutional formality. In Varanasi, a Shivaite *tilak* (symbol of Shivaite Hindus) adorning his forehead, Modi performed a Hindu ritual known as Ganga Aarti (an offering made on the banks of the holy river) in the presence of other BJP dignitaries, including Amit Shah.[1]

The following week, on May 26, after his official swearing in, during a ceremony with RSS officials in attendance, he formed a government that included several Hindu nationalist figures. One of them, Uma Bharti—who wears the saffron-colored clothing typical of Hindu religious figures[2]—was appointed minister of water resources, river development, and Ganges rejuvenation. The other portfolios were not as directly linked to the promotion of Hinduism—except of course the so-called AYUSH minister, an acronym covering yoga and Ayurvedic medicine[3]—but cabinet members (most of whom belonged to the

RSS) have all gone to great lengths to defend the Hindutva articles of faith, both in their discourse and in their decisions. The RSS moreover penetrated the state apparatus in new ways and had access to the bureaucracy in an unprecedented manner. Secularism and its champions, starting with academics and some NGOs, were the first targets of India's new masters, who also devoted themselves to rewriting the country's history, all the better to spread their ideology. At the same time, the new government went about surreptitiously tweaking the legislative apparatus.

Hinduizing the Public Space

Defending the Cow and Fighting Conversion

While Modi's India during his first term could be described as a de facto but not a de jure ethnic democracy because the Hinduization of the public sphere had mostly followed informal channels, there is one area in which the BJP passed laws to that end (and even then, not at the national level): that of cow protection. Protection of cows, that most sacred animal in Hinduism, is an article of faith for defenders of Hindutva—and even for their nineteenth-century predecessors.[4] Modi had made it one of his pet themes during his 2012 election campaign in Gujarat, when he railed against the "pink revolution," which he blamed on the Congress Party.[5] In 2014, he only mentioned this baneful revolution in two public speeches, in Bihar and in Assam, but he posted a most significant message on his blog: "It saddens me that present UPA government led by Congress is promoting slaughtering cows and exporting beef to bring 'Pink Revolution.'"[6] Naturally, he was fully aware that the meat in question[7] was not beef but instead buffalo—a totally different species, of which India had become the world's biggest exporter, ahead of Australia.[8]

Hindu nationalists were fighting against cow slaughter not only because they considered it sacrilege but also because they considered cow products, including urine and milk, to have special virtues. One of them thus explained that milk from Indian cows, unlike milk from Jersey cows, chased away evil thoughts and even kept children from a life of crime.[9] The BJP chief minister of Uttarakhand similarly argued that "living in close proximity with the animal can cure one of tuberculosis."[10] But others, including the chief ideologue and leader of the RSS, Manmohan Vaidya, advanced additional arguments. Vaidya claimed, "The question isn't religious only. Research shows cow-based agriculture is environmentally better while chemical fertilizers harm the soil. Dung and urine of cows of Indian breed also have medicinal value, just as tulsi [holy basil] plant."[11]

For all these reasons, after 2014, the BJP took advantage of its success at the polls in some states to pass laws that had long been part of the Hindu nationalist program or to amend existing laws. In Maharashtra, where the BJP took the reins of government in October 2014, the new coalition government formed by the BJP and the Shiv Sena in 2015 toughened a law that dated from 1995 (thus passed by the first BJP-Shiv Sena coalition government): not only was cow slaughter now prohibited, but it became forbidden to slaughter other bovines (except for water buffalos) and to be in possession of cow meat.[12] This crime was now punishable by up to five years in prison and a heavy fine.

A "beef ban" was also passed in 2015 in Haryana, a state that the BJP won alone in 2014. There, the penalty could be as much as ten years in prison and a fine of up to Rs 100,000 (1,330 USD). Soon after, Gujarat toughened its legislation: in 2017, the legislative assembly of that state, which has been governed by the BJP for longer than any other, amended the Gujarat Animal Preservation Act of 1954, making the slaughter of any bovine now punishable by a prison term of up to seven years and a fine of Rs 500,000 (6,667 USD), and convicted offenders are not eligible for bail.[13]

But tightening up legislation was not a necessary prerequisite for cow protection. In Uttar Pradesh, for instance, the BJP did not deem it necessary to alter legislation to combat cattle slaughter after its victory in 2017. The new chief minister, Yogi Adityanath, using the argument that many slaughterhouses were "illegal" or "mechanized," had them shut down less than two days after taking office. It turned out that the supposedly illegal slaughterhouses were in fact municipal abattoirs for which the licenses were not renewed by the local authorities due to inadequate hygiene and sanitary maintenance.[14] The state court based its decision against the government order on this fact and on the Constitution,[15] stating, "To provide an immediate check on unlawful activity should be simultaneous with facilitating the carrying of lawful activity, particularly that relating to food, food habits and vending thereof that is undisputedly connected with the right to life and livelihood."[16] The "right to life" mentioned here is based on article 21 of the Constitution in accordance with which the court added that with the "beef ban," "it is the private life of an individual that is also affected who may desire to have such foodstuffs as his private choice of consumption."

Despite this ruling—which the government appealed—the central authorities decided to issue a notification regarding the transport of cattle, which could no longer be hauled to cattle markets when they were suspected of being the last stop before the slaughterhouse. This decision, which instantly paralyzed this economic sector and which four states—West Bengal, Karnataka, Kerala, and Tripura—refused to comply with, was immediately brought before the Supreme Court, which demanded an explanation.[17] Justice Minister Ravishankar Prasad then made a candid statement that well illustrates the majoritarian philosophy characteristic of ethnic democracies: "This government does not want to control people's food habits but it is a reality that a large section of the Indian population reveres the cow."[18]

In addition to the multiplication of rules and public policies aimed at protecting cows, the BJP has also adopted and enforced a large number of new procedures to stem religious conversions. Maharashtra thus passed a law making religious conversion very difficult. Hindu nationalists point to the demographic downturn of the majority community to justify this measure: according to the 2011 census, Hindus now made up slightly less than 80 percent of its population, for the first time in India's post-1947 history. In so doing, Maharashtra followed the example of other states already controlled by the BJP, such as Gujarat and Madhya Pradesh. In each of these states, such laws aimed to curb the activity of Christian missionaries and, to a lesser extent, to prevent certain groups (tribes or lower castes) from converting to Islam.

Bharat vs. India

The nature of new legislation to promote Hinduism, the extent of which remained very limited, indicates that it was not through lawmaking that the BJP primarily intended to operate: discourse and practices were the preferred means of action in their repertoire, as can be seen in debates about the respect owed to India's very name.

The country's Constitution baptized it both India and Bharat in article 1, which states, "India, that is Bharat, shall be a Union of states." This duality, at the root of a fundamental ambiguity, refers to debates in the Constituent Assembly from 1946 to 1950 in which two ideas of India were competing. The idea of India promoted by Nehru and Ambedkar was embodied in the English word *India*, whereas Hindu traditionalists in the Congress had opted for the Sanskrit *Bharat*,[19] the name of the tutelary figure who, in Hindu mythology, presided over the creation of the territory bearing the same name. Their demand reflected a very Hindu conception of the nation. One of the champions of this idea of India, Hargovind Pant, made no secret of it: "The word 'Bharat' or 'Bharat Varsha' is used by us in our daily religious duties while reciting the Sankalpa. Even at the time of taking our bath we say in Sanskrit: Jamboo Dwipay, Bharata Varshe, Bharat Khande, Aryavartay, etc."[20] Bharat Mata has moreover been depicted as a mother goddess in the popular imagination ever since the famous novel by Bankim Chandra Chatterjee, *Anandamath* (*The Abbey of Bliss*) (1882),[21] and then, in the early years of the twentieth century, in the nationalist discourse to the tune of "Bande Mataram!" (Hail to the Mother!), before she came to be associated more with Hindutva iconography in the years 1920–1930.[22]

The 1946–1950 debate was rekindled in 2014. While the BJP was not asking to rebaptize India officially (unlike Buddhist Sinhalese Sri Lankans in 1976), the party wanted to spread the use of the name Bharat, in keeping with its strategy of operating through practices rather than the law. The party thus made promotion of the expression "Bharat Mata ki Jai!" (Hail Mother India!) its hobbyhorse and in March 2016 passed a resolution stating, "Our Constitution guarantees Freedom of Expression to every citizen; but that freedom is enjoyable only within its framework. Talking of destruction of Bharat can't be supported in the name of freedom of expression. Similarly, refusal to hail Bharat—say Bharat Mata ki Jai—in the name of freedom is also unacceptable."[23] The RSS chief, Mohan Bhagwat, went so far as to conclude that, in view of the universal nature of Hinduism, the whole world should chant "Bharat Mata ki Jai!"[24] But the objective was indeed a domestic one: the aim was to advance the Indian-Hindu equation by stigmatizing minorities that were reluctant to embrace a symbol of the majority community. The BJP chief minister of Maharashtra applied this approach to the letter by asserting that those who refused to chant "Bharat Mata ki Jai!" did not belong in India. And he concluded: "We are open to criticism against the BJP. But not against country."[25]

At the same time, Modi government ministers and RSS leaders continued to make statements aiming to assert the Hindu essence of Indian identity to the detriment of secularism, although the latter is enshrined in the Constitution. Nitin Gadkari, a former BJP president who became transport minister in 2014, said of the Modi government upon inaugurating the stretch of highway linking Ayodhya and Sultanpur, Uttar Pradesh: "This is government of Ram bhakts [devotees of the god Ram] . . . a government of those who gave the slogan Jai Shri Ram"[26]—which enjoyed great success during the Ayodhya movement. The usually more moderate foreign affairs minister, Sushma Swaraj, came out in favor of the Indian state recognizing the Bhagavad Gita (the jewel of the Mahabharata epic) as "National Scripture" (Rashtriya Granth), in the religious sense of the term, basing her recommendation on the fact that Narendra Modi had just given a copy of the book to President Barack Obama. M. L. Khattar, the BJP chief minister of Haryana, followed suit, claiming that the Gita was "above the Constitution."[27]

Opposition parties rose up against such challenges to secularism. Sharad Pawar, the leader of the National Congress Party, protested, "I am a Hindu and proud of my religion's rich heritage. But does that mean I have the right to hurt the sentiments of other religions? All religions should be treated equally."[28] One of the Tamil Nadu-based NDA parties, the Pattali Makkal Katchi (PMK), also reacted in eloquent terms through the voice of its founder, S. Ramadoss: "There is no denying that

Gita has noble values. The same values are in Holy Quran and Holy Bible. While, [sic] this attempt only strengthens the argument that the Modi government is making efforts to make India a Hindu nation."[29]

Six months after the Modi government was formed, two visions of Indian identity were thus at odds, and the question of secularism—and thus a possible revision of the 1950 Constitution—was subject to debate. Discussion often took on an extrareligious or ethnoreligious dimension, proving that what was at stake was the identity of a people that supposedly descended from the "sons of the soil." In December 2017, Anantkumar Hegde, union minister of state for skill development and entrepreneurship in the Modi government, said, "Those claiming to be secular and progressive do not have an identity of their parents and their blood. One will get self-respect through such identity. . . . A few people say the Constitution mentions the word secular, so you have to agree. Because it's there in the Constitution, we will respect it, but this will change in the near future. The Constitution has changed many times before. We are here and have come to change the Constitution. We will change it."[30] The following day, the opposition boycotted the parliamentary session and demanded Hegde's resignation. The minister reasserted his party's respect for the Constitution and said no revision was on the agenda. In any event, the BJP did not have the two-thirds majority in parliament needed to revise the Constitution without proceeding by referendum. But it was clear that one of the new government's objectives was to challenge the secularism enshrined in the Constitution.[31]

Advocates of Hindutva set out to delegitimize secularists (which Hindu nationalists call "sickularists" in the social media) by attacking present and past Congress leaders. Nehru remained a prime target, accused by the BJP of marginalizing Hinduism in Indian political life and of conducting policies in favor of Muslims. But Gandhi was not spared, either. A BJP member of the Lok Sabha, Sakshi Maharaj, a cleric who had developed a chain of ashrams and schools in Uttar Pradesh, glorified Nathuram Godse, the man who assassinated Gandhi. Maharaj, who had also been investigated by the police for two cases of rape and murder,[32] called Godse a "patriot," unleashing a profusion of praise on social media.[33] The Mahatma's grandson, Tushar Gandhi, made a much-noted comment on this outburst: "Sakshi Maharaj is at least honest enough to come out and say what's in his heart. . . . The government should endorse what Sakshi Maharaj has said, they shouldn't be double faced."[34]

The challenge to secularism was not merely a matter of speech, and it is not because the BJP was not in a position to reform the Constitution that their policy was without impact. Among their significant acts was the access it gave the RSS to the state apparatus.

The State Apparatus Opens Up to RSS Influence

While promoting a given personality within the BJP—and even acceptance of a certain personality cult—was new for the RSS,[35] another novelty was the interest this organization showed in the state apparatus as soon as Narendra Modi was elected. Within the RSS, appetites for *political* power were traditionally frowned upon, as the organization preferred to work on changing society from within, as noted previously. At least two reasons can explain this new attention turned to the state. First, the RSS could expand even more rapidly if it enjoyed state protection. Second, the RSS could envisage using the state apparatus to accelerate reforms it felt strongly about without diverting it from its traditional missions. And indeed, the organization sought to influence key ministers via, for instance, the new BJP president, Amit Shah, who went to the RSS headquarters in Nagpur even before his appointment was ratified by the BJP's National Council. There, he was told "not to allow [*sic*] Modi government to overshadow the party" and reminded about the "Sangh's Hindutva agenda," which included the building of the Ram temple in Ayodhya, the abolition of article 370 and the making of a Uniform Civil Code.[36] To tighten its grip on the BJP, the RSS took part in the formation of the National Executive of the BJP.[37] As a result of these negotiations, Ram Madhav, a member of the RSS executive committee who had been spokesman of the RSS since 2003, was appointed to the BJP National Executive, as well as Shiv Prakash, another RSS cadre.

The RSS also set up coordination mechanisms that enabled it to influence ministers whose portfolios it was most interested in. In October 2014, the Agriculture, Labor, Energy, and Information Ministries held a meeting with specialized branches of the RSS, including the Bharatiya Mazdoor Sangh, Bharatiya Kisan Union, and Vanvasi Kalyan Ashram. One of the participants explained at the end of this work session, "With today's meeting, the process of coordination between the government and the RSS has been initiated. Today, the meeting was with the ministries related to economic activities. It was a general meeting and will be followed by consultations between the individual organisations and the concerned ministries. The ministers will take suggestions and feedback from the Sangh leaders and, in the process, confrontation on policy matters can be avoided."[38] Similar meetings took place with other ministries, including the Ministry of Human Resource Development, in charge of education. To better ensure liaison with this key ministry, the RSS set up a consultative body, the Bharatiya Shiksha Niti Ayog (BSNA), in which representatives of different components of the Sangh Parivar took part.

Beyond the ministers themselves, the RSS gained special access to their administrations. A government order issued in 1966 had made civil servants who joined the RSS and the Jama'at-e-Islami liable to disciplinary action. This red line had never yet been crossed. Even A. B. Vajpayee, while he was prime minister, had repealed in 2000 a decision made in the state of Gujarat, given that this decision authorized the state civil servants to participate in RSS activities. Things changed in 2014. In 2016, the movement spokesperson, Manmohan Vaidya, protested, "Banning RSS members from joining government service is unjust, unlawful and undemocratic."[39] Without officially reconsidering the rule, the central state and states governed by the BJP started ceasing to comply with it. Even if senior civil servants did not formally join the RSS, members of the organization were admitted into the state apparatus, particularly through ministerial staff (the interface between politicians and the administration), and were allowed to engage with high-ranking state officials, whether civil or military. The RSS general secretary, Bhaiyyaji Joshi, thus met with an officer of the Border Security Force who invited him to visit Tinbigha Corridor in Cooch Behar (West Bengal), a highly strategic strip of land, also known as the "chicken's neck," that connects the Northeast to the rest of India. The RSS weekly magazine, *The Organiser*, candidly admitted, "Walking in the corridor along with BSF officer, Bhaiyaji had information about the corridor since 1992 and also the present security system."[40]

The RSS also penetrated the state apparatus, as under Vajpayee, by having some of its leaders, many of whom had never engaged in any political activity, appointed to the post of governor. This is how Kaptan Singh Solanki, a former prant pracharak in Madhya Pradesh, became governor of Haryana; P. B. Acharya, governor of Nagaland; and O. P. Kohli, governor of Gujarat, in the two months following the BJP victory in 2014.[41]

The RSS penetration of the state also found expression in the growing presence of the RSS on Doordarshan, the public television station. In 2014 the RSS chief's annual address to his troops during a Hindu festival, Vijayadashami, was broadcast on television for the first time. The information minister justified the initiative, saying that Mohan Bhagwat "talked about important national issues in his speech."[42]

On public television or not, Bhagwat loosened his tongue after the BJP came into power, making his presence felt in the public sphere in unprecedented proportions. His favorite claim was to assert that all Indians were Hindus, denying religious differences and thereby refusing the multiculturalism inherent in the secularism set out in the Constitution.[43] Six months after Modi's victory, he stated, "The cultural identity of all Indians is Hindutva and the present inhabitants of the country are descendants of this great culture."[44] In 2017, he went so far as to say, "The Muslims in India are also Hindus,"[45] suggesting or implying that they descended from converts whose blood was "Hindu"—a reconfirmation of the racial dimension of the Hindu nationalist ideology. Along with these sweeping generalizations, Bhagwat also held forth on more precise topics, among them Sangh Parivar campaigns and public policy. He thus defended the movement to reconvert Hindus, known as Ghar Wapsi, in eloquent terms: "We will bring back our brothers who have lost their way. They did not go on their own. They were robbed, tempted into leaving. . . . Now the thief has been caught and the world knows my belongings are with the thief. I will retrieve my belongings, so why is this such a big issue? . . . We should not be scared. Why should we be afraid? We are not infiltrators. We are not foreigners. This is our moth-erland. This is our country. This is a Hindu Rashtra."[46] Along the same lines, he declared—shortly before the Supreme Court examined the case—that only one religious edifice could be built at Ayodhya, a temple devoted to Ram, whereas a compromise was emerging that planned for a mosque to be rebuilt as well.[47] He also argued in favor of abolishing article 35A of the Constitution, added to article 370, excluding nonper-manent residents of Jammu and Kashmir from holding public office in that state and from purchasing property.[48]

Even if the RSS leader was accustomed to making public statements, never had he done so with such frequency and with such a radical stance. In 2018, Mohan Bhagwat held a series of three-day conferences at Vigyan Bhawan, a prestigious Government of India convention cen-ter in New Delhi. He thereby asserted his will to appear as the nation's mentor, or, to use the RSS's expression, as India's "Raj guru."

Educating and Reeducating: Hindutva, History, and Science

One of the government spheres in which the RSS has always shown great interest is education. This interest is determined over and above everything else by the RSS's desire to reshape India's collective psyche through the classroom so as to expand the work accomplished in its shakha and in its publications.[49] It feels particularly strongly about the teaching of history, not only because it contributes to defining the na-tional identity but also because it believes that the version of the past portrayed by secularists does not reflect reality.[50]

Shortly after Modi's rise to power, in August 2014 the RSS formed a committee, the Bharatiya Shiksha Niti Ayog, intended to "Indianize" the education system[51] by orienting the policies of the Ministry of Human Resource Development, in charge of education. The committee was headed by none other than Dinanath Batra, a long-standing mem-ber of the RSS who had specialized in rewriting Indian history accord-ing to the canons of Hindu nationalism. Thus, in 2010, he filed a civil suit to ban Wendy Doniger's book *The Hindus*, which he felt gave Hin-duism a bad image. Penguin India, fearing reprisal, pulped the book even before a court decision was handed down. Batra also pressured the University of Delhi to remove from its syllabus an essay by the well-known Indian anthropologist A. K. Ramanujan, "Three Hundred Ramayanas," which contradicted the Hindu nationalist idea that there was a single version of the epic poem.[52]

At the same time, Batra, longtime general secretary of the Sangh Parivar network of religious schools, Vidya Bharti, devoted most of his energy to combating perceived errors in history textbooks written by secularist authors. In his book published in 2001, *The Enemies of Indianisation: The Children of Marx, Macaulay and Madrasa*, he listed forty-one major flaws that all reflected the historic tropisms of the Hindu nationalists.[53] Most of these flaws fell under four tenets held by this school of thought. First, it discards the idea that the Aryans came from another part of the world in ancient times because the Hindus could only be sons of the soil.[54] Second, it attributes to India all the glory of its epic poems, which are presented as an accurate reflection of historical reality. Third, it considers that the Muslim invasions opened the darkest chapter in Indian history, starting with the destruction of Nalanda University in the twelfth century[55] up until the end of the Mughal Empire.[56] And fourth, it criticizes the standard account of the national liberation movement as ascribing too much importance to Gandhi and Nehru to the detriment of Hindu nationalist heroes. For Hindu nationalist ideologues, these serious flaws come from the secularist or Westernized nature of history textbook authors.[57]

This point was particularly emphasized by the Hindu nationalist historian Y. Sudershan Rao, who was appointed by the Modi government in summer 2014 to head the Indian Council of Historical Research. A former faculty member of Kakatiya University, Rao is a forceful advocate of the "Indianization" of the writing of history and the social sciences. In an interview with *The Organiser*, he declared:

I honestly feel that Indian social science research in general and history research in particular is dominated by Western perspectives, in the name of liberal or left perspectives. Most of us see India through western prism—may be because under British rule we began considering and understanding Indian history from there [*sic*] point of view.... Every nation has the right to write its own history from its own perspective, with certain national objectives. I call this process as "Indianisation." At best you can call it a patriotic approach.[58]

Rao, viewing history and mythology as being the same thing, believes that historiographic research should focus on identifying the locations where the "events" described in the epics took place.[59] This conflation of history and mythology has become common since 2014.

In March 2018, investigative reporters revealed the existence of a committee tasked by the culture minister, Mahesh Sharma, to revise India's history. This fourteen-member committee (including archaeologists, bureaucrats, and ideologues) was commissioned by the minister to produce a "holistic study of origin and evolution of Indian culture since 12,000 years before present and its interface with other cultures of the world."[60] The idea that the age of Hindu civilization is three or four times greater than what has been established by contemporary historiography aimed to achieve two explicit goals. First, it was coupled with the persistent effort by Hindu nationalists to present their mythology as history. Mahesh Sharma himself told Reuters: "I worship Ramayana and I think it is a historical document." And he added, in keeping with the tried-and-true method of strategic emulation, "If the Koran and Bible are considered as part of history, then what is the problem in accepting our Hindu religious texts as the history of India?"[61] Second, uncovering evidence from ancient history aimed "to prove that today's Hindus are directly descended from the land's first inhabitants many thousands of years ago"[62] and thereby give Hindu nationalists arguments to claim a sort of superiority.

While Mahesh Sharma's task concerned his culture ministry, similar plans also affected public education. The government made its intentions clear. The former minister of state for human resource development Ram Shankar Katheria had said two years before, "There will be saffronisation of education and of the country. Whatever is good for the country will certainly happen, be it saffronisation or *sanghwaad* (propagation of the RSS ideology)."[63] Unlike the Vajpayee government, which tailored the National Council for Education Research and Training (NCERT) to suit its wishes[64] and published guidelines for writing new textbooks,[65] the Modi government has preferred to proceed with stealth and allow states to make changes to textbooks, even postponing the idea of publicizing the New Educational Policy promised by Modi, not because it had given up on the idea[66] but because it valued undercover efficiency over open public debate.[67]

The textbooks put out by the NCERT, which can be used in schools affiliated with the Central Board of Secondary Education (CBSE), have been extensively rewritten. According to the *Indian Express*, repeated interventions from the minister of human resource development (Prakash Javadekar, another RSS member) resulted in 1,334 changes in 182 textbooks originally put out by the NCERT,[68] without following the procedures that should have involved the NCERT and its experts.[69] These changes once again enhanced ancient Indian history (in terms of medicine, astronomy, yoga, etc.) and major Hindu figures from the past (Maharana Pratap, Shivaji, Aurobindo, Vivekananda, etc.) at the expense of "the Muslim era."[70] Such alterations were not only made to history textbooks. The class 10 science textbook included two hymns of the Arthavaveda, and for class 8, it cited "what Indian mythology says about the constellation Ursa Major."[71] Many textbooks also showcased key Modi government policies, starting with the Swachh Bharat Abhiyan and Beti Bachao, Beti Padhao (Protect Girls, Educate Girls).

The scale at which Hindu nationalists are rewriting history can be most clearly gauged on the state government level, where they have been extremely active on that front in BJP-ruled states. As primary and secondary education come under the responsibility of the states, such an approach made sense, especially since the nationwide influence of its ideologues could be felt at this level as well. Batra was thus tasked with writing several textbooks used in Gujarat and in Haryana.[72] In Haryana, he was appointed to head the committee in charge of renovating the education system as soon as the BJP won in 2014. He immediately brought in the moral education textbooks he had written for the schools in Gujarat. Six of them were introduced in autumn of 2015 for classes

7 to 12 (ages thirteen to eighteen). They all begin with praise to the goddess Saraswati, but Batra argued that it was not a form of Hinduization: "Saraswati is not a religious figure. Each part of the goddess is a symbol of qualities that every student should emulate. . . . Which right-thinking Muslim student will not want to have these qualities?"[73] The textbooks also include a poem by Batra: "I have a dream, of building a school on the foundations of Hindutva and patriotism."[74]

The state most spotlighted in the media, however, was Rajasthan, where considerable changes to history textbooks were made: in the class 10 social science textbook, the Rajput king was thus presented as victorious in the battle of Haldighati against Emperor Akbar (contrary to researchers' conclusions).[75] The new social science textbook purely and simply failed to mention Jawaharlal Nehru and the assassination of Mahatma Gandhi, contrary to the textbook used when the Congress was in government.[76] The education minister, Vasudev Devnani, explained these changes by stating his desire to teach children about Rajasthani heroes, to make them proud of Indian culture and create patriots as much as citizens.[77]

Other states also reoriented their telling of regional and national history. In Maharashtra, in the rewriting of history textbooks, a drastic cut was made in the book for class 7: the chapter on the Mughal Empire under Akbar was cut down to three lines.[78] Uttar Pradesh simply deleted the Mughal Empire from some of its history textbooks,[79] while the University of Delhi drastically reduced the study of this period in its history curriculum.[80] In the syllabus of Nagpur University, a chapter that discussed the roles of the RSS, the Hindu Mahasabha, and the Muslim League in the making of communalism has been replaced by another one titled "Rashtriya Swayamsevak Sangh (RSS) Role in Nation Building."[81] Alongside official examinations in Uttar Pradesh, the Sangh Parivar organized a test of general culture open to all schools in the state. According to the brochure designed to help students prepare for this test, which Amit Shah released in Lucknow in August 2017, India was a Hindu Rashtra, and Swami Vivekananda had defended Hindutva in Chicago in 1893.[82] In Karnataka, after canceling Tipu Sultan Jayanti, the festival that the state used to organize to celebrate the birth of this eighteenth-century Muslim ruler, the BJP government also dropped the chapter dealing with this historical figure from the class 7 textbook in 2019.[83] This decision was made in the context of the COVID-19 pandemic that had led the government of India to ask all states to reduce syllabi for students in classes 1 through 10 by 30 percent, in light of the learning challenges brought about by the lockdown.[84] The decision of the Karnataka government, in fact, fit in with a larger picture. Under cover of the pandemic, the Central Board of Secondary Education (CBSE), India's largest education board, decided that all over India "government-run schools no longer have to teach chapters on democratic rights, secularism, federalism, and citizenship, among other topics."[85]

To foster assimilation of knowledge that amounted to propaganda, final exams have increasingly focused on the heroic deeds of Hindu icons and reforms initiated by the Modi government, even on the person of the prime minister. The economics exam at Lucknow University for the bachelor of commerce (BCom) asked students to evaluate schemes launched by Modi, such as Digital India (to develop digitization throughout the country) and Startup India, or to describe job-creation schemes.[86] The civil service exam went even further. In Madhya Pradesh, candidates to join the state administration were thus asked in 2016: "The Swachh Bharat campaign led by the honorable Prime Minister has a great impact on the society because 1) People understood the importance of cleanliness, and 2) People across the country like the campaign."[87] The trap was obviously only discernible to Modi supporters: both answers were correct!

The nationalist tone of textbook rewriting deliberately extols ancient Indian knowledge systems over contemporary science.[88] For instance, the minister of state for human resource development responsible for higher education, Satya Pal Singh, denied the validity of the theory of evolution[89] and in one of his speeches claimed that it was an Indian who invented the airplane.[90] The deputy chief minister of Uttar Pradesh maintained that the test-tube baby procedure had existed in ancient India because Ram's wife, Sita, was born in an earthen pot, while the chief minister of Tripura, Biplab Kumar Deb, explained that the technologies of satellites and the internet existed in ancient India.[91] In the same vein, the education minister of Rajasthan claimed that the law of gravity had been discovered in India in the seventh century.[92] And along the same lines, another BJP minister—health, education, and finance minister in Assam—claimed that cancer patients were paying for their "sins."[93] The Uttarakhand BJP president declared similarly that pregnant women could avoid caesarean deliveries if they drank water from a river in the state.[94] Prime Minister Narendra Modi himself claimed that India invented reproductive genetics and plastic surgery. In October 2014, he told a gathering of doctors and other professionals at a hospital in Mumbai: "We all read about Karna in the Mahabharata. If we think a little more, we realize that the Mahabharata says Karna was not born from his mother's womb. This means that genetic science was present at that time. That is why Karna could be born outside his mother's womb. . . . We worship Lord Ganesha. There must have been some plastic surgeon at that time who got an elephant's head on the body of a human being and began the practice of plastic surgery."[95] Remarks such as these were met each time with protestation from "rationalists," a category of intellectuals often affiliated with the communist Left. Three of them, known for their criticism of Hindu nationalist sectarianism and obscurantism, were murdered between 2013 and 2015: Narendra Dabholkar, the founder of the Maharashtra Blind Faith Eradication Committee; Govind Pansare, a long-standing member of the Indian Communist Party; and M. M. Kalburgi, former vice-chancellor of Kannada University in Hampi[96] (see chapter 7). For obscurantists (whether they belong to a religious sect or an ethnonationalist movement), rationalists are key targets because they are viewed as blasphemers and pose a threat to their belief system by exposing the myths in which they believe.

The Crusade against "Liberals"

Promotion of Hinduism went hand in hand with an incessant fight against "liberals," a highly derogatory term in the mouths of Hindu nationalists, which they use to refer to academics, NGOs, and journalists that do not adhere to their ideology.

Bringing Universities to Heel—the Case of Jawaharlal Nehru University

Universities with a "progressive" reputation have long been a Hindu nationalist target, but tensions further intensified after 2014. They have been subjected to two types of interference. First, the government appointed men from the Sangh Parivar or fellow travelers to head them with the task of reforming them. Second, the RSS student wing, the ABVP, could finally try to call the shots on university campuses with the government's blessing.

This dual strategy is most clearly apparent in the treatment inflicted on Jawaharlal Nehru University (JNU). This institution, known for the excellence of its teachers—especially in the social sciences—had drawn bitter Hindu nationalist criticism as soon as it was founded in the 1960s due to the leftist leanings of many teachers and some of its main student organizations.[97]

In 2016, the Modi government appointed Mamidala Jagadesh Kumar vice-chancellor of JNU. This electrical engineering professor had been teaching at the nearby Indian Institute of Technology until then, and he had allegedly played an active role in Vijana Bharati, an organization under the Sangh Parivar umbrella that aims to promote indigenous Indian science.[98] He brought about drastic budget cuts—academic spending was almost halved over three years[99]—and a decline in student recruitment, while systematically hampering the activities of student unions and faculty opposed to the RSS. The political disciplining of the campus took various routes, such as the harassment of professors who were openly hostile to the Sangh Parivar.[100]

A research university that primarily awards master's degrees and PhDs, JNU saw the number of seats offered to students wishing to enroll in a master's or a doctoral program plummet by 84 percent, from 1,234 to 194 in one year.[101] Furthermore, admissions committees were made up solely of experts appointed by the JNU vice-chancellor, flouting university statutes and guidelines followed by the University Grants Commission (UGC), which stipulate that academics should be involved.[102] This made it possible to hire teachers from Hindu nationalist circles,[103] with few qualifications,[104] and some facing charges of plagiarism.[105] In particular, several former ABVP student activists from JNU have been appointed as assistant professors even after being disqualified by the committee in charge of short-listing applicants.[106] The vice-chancellor replaced deans in the School of Social Sciences without following appointment procedures, cutting the number of researchers by 80 percent and ceasing to apply rules JNU had set to ensure diversity through a mechanism taking into account the social background and geographic origin of its applicants.[107] The new recruitment procedure strongly disadvantaged Dalits, Adivasis, and OBCs, who used to make up nearly 50 percent of the student intake and who now accounted for a mere 7 percent. The vice-chancellor also issued ad hoc promotions, nominating recently appointed faculty members to the post of full professor. Conversely, the freeze on promotions for "antigovernment" teachers who should have been promoted on the basis of seniority prompted some of the diktat's victims to take the matter to court.[108] However, even after the court—taking note of the illegality of the rejection procedure—ordered a reexamination of the claimants' promotions, the latter were once again denied.[109] By exerting administrative obstruction against dissenting faculty and students, judicial litigation has become nearly systematic in the conduct of JNU affairs.[110] A major controversy arose from the fact that forty-eight teachers were "issued charge-sheets by the JNU administration on the basis of Central Civil Service (Conduct) Rules (CSS Rules), for raising their voices against its anti-teaching-learning policies."[111] The unions argued that the CCS Rules "should not be applicable to autonomous institutions like universities as it would come in the way of academic freedom."[112]

Among JNU alumni, Sanjaya Baru, a nonpartisan media person, bemoaned in an opinion piece that "the systematic attempt by JNU's administrative leadership to harass, humiliate and demoralise the faculty has given the impression that this is a good-for-nothing institution."[113] In reaction, after a number of demonstrations that came to naught, the Jawaharlal Nehru University Teachers' Association (JNUTA) held a referendum demanding the vice-chancellor's resignation—279 of the 300 voters called for him to step down.[114]

In addition to these tensions, which did not make the Modi government budge an inch, the JNU campus became a battleground for a fight among student organizations. The nature and scope of the clashes were reflected in a particularly revealing episode in 2016. On February 9, elected members of the JNUSU (in which leftist unions were a majority) held a ceremony to commemorate the execution of Afzal Guru.[115] Speeches made during the event, in particular by Umar Khalid and the president of the JNUSU, Kanhaiya Kumar, criticized central government policy in Jammu and Kashmir, the home state of Afzal Guru, where uprisings had intensified at the cost of several lives. The ABVP protested the rally, terming it "antinational."[116]

Over the years, the ABVP has become the largest student organization in India, with an official membership of 3.2 million and chapters in 20,000 of the 35,000 institutions of higher learning registered in India.[117] However, its influence is not only measured in figures but also stems from its political role. The organization has served as a launching pad for many BJP political leaders, who learned to debate and/or do battle in the ideological arena during their time in the ABVP. The organization has also been involved in Sangh Parivar movements outside of university campuses. The ABVP thus claims to have mobilized 2 million demonstrators against UPA government corruption in the context of the Anna Hazare movement between 2011 and 2013.[118] But its activities are mainly deployed on university campuses. In these places, the student organization has been acting as a sort of moral police since 2014, laying down the law every time a political issue arose. In 2015, it managed to prevent a film on the Muzaffarnagar (UP) riots from being shown at Delhi University.[119] But JNU was a more important focal point, a land of conquest where the ABVP's aim was to crush leftists.

The event organized by the JNUSU over the Afzal Guru issue provided an excellent opportunity to go to battle, as it involved questions of Islamist terrorism and Kashmiri separatism, Guru having hailed from that province. The ABVP wielded its power of intimidation to get the JNU administration to ban the event, but the organizers refused to comply. After Home Minister Rajnath Singh used the occasion to denounce the organizers' "anti-India slogans,"[120] the police raided the campus and arrested students, including Kanhaiya Kumar and a few fellow students, who were accused of sedition and brought before the Delhi district courts located at Patiala House on February 14. Students and faculty who wished to attend the proceedings[121] were assaulted by some forty lawyers chanting "Bharat Mata ki Jai" and "Vande Mataram," along with Hindu nationalist leaders, including a BJP MLA, O. P. Sharma, who did not hesitate to use his fists. In addition to JNU students and faculty, journalists on the scene were also targets of violence.[122] At the same time, the ABVP marched through Delhi University, shouting, "JNU bandh karo, deshdrohi vapas jao" (Close down JNU, traitors go back) and "Kashmir hamara hai, hamara rahega" (Kashmir is ours and will stay ours).[123] The following day, sixty-three intellectuals from all over the world signed a petition demanding Kumar's release, arguing that the accusation of sedition was baseless.[124] One piece of "evidence" the police referred to was an allegedly live report from a February 9 meeting that ZeeTV kept running over and over in which pro-Pakistani slogans could be heard, such as "Pakistan zindabad!" (Long live Pakistan!) When the police finally asked the channel to hand over the original recording, more than ten days after the fact,[125] the police were forced to admit that the clip broadcast had been tampered with and that no pro-Pakistani slogan had been chanted on February 9. In fact, the demonstrators were praising the Indian judicial system, shouting, "Bharatiya court zindabad" (Long live Indian courts).[126] Even before the findings of the forensic analysis were revealed, a ZeeTV journalist, Vishwa Deepak, resigned and made public a long letter that read:

> The video that never had a slogan of "Pakistan Zindabad" we ran again and again to stoke passions. How could we convince ourselves so easily that the voices in the darkness belonged to Kanhaiya or his friends? Blinded by prejudice we heard "Bharatiya court zindabad" as "Pakistan zindabad." . . . Ever since Mr Modi became the prime minister of India, every newsroom in the country more or less has witnessed a communalization but the conditions in this organization [ZeeTV] are far more grim. . . . An agenda behind every news, an attempt to deify the Modi government as great in every news show,

an attempt in every debate to "shoot" down all of Modi's opponents—
no lesser word than attack is acceptable to us. What is all this? Sometimes when I pause and think about it I feel as if I have gone mad.[127]

While the third part of the book will return to the role of the media in
Modi's India, it is important to complete the present analysis of the 2016
crisis in JNU. This episode prompted three ABVP officials at JNU to
quit the organization, because, according to one of them, Pradeep Narwal,
the government "was legitimising this mob culture."[128] But the government neither condemned the attacks launched against JNU nor lodged a
complaint against ZeeTV.[129] Smriti Irani, the minister of human resource
development, at the helm of the ministry that oversees all universities, including JNU, added that "the nation can never tolerate any insult to Mother
India."[130] Other ministers in the Modi government seized this opportunity
to accuse the demonstrators of being "anti-national."[131]

The Hindu nationalist movement continued to denigrate JNU as
being at once antinational and immoral after this crisis. Campaigns followed in succession, attacking the university for its so-called rampant
debauchery. A BJP MLA from Rajasthan claimed in a public statement
on February 22: "2,000 Indian and foreign liquor bottles are found daily
in JNU. More than 10,000 butts of cigarettes and 4,000 pieces of beedis
are found. 50,000 big and small pieces of bones are found. 2,000 wrap-
pers of chips and namkeen are found, and so are 3,000 used condoms—
the misdeeds they commit with our sisters and daughters there. And
500 used abortion injections are also found."[132] At the same time, a police report, based on close surveillance of people living on the JNU
campus since 2015, stated that in addition to their antinational activities,
students worshipped Mahishasur, a demon in Hindu mythology, and
ate beef—which was in no way illegal but signaled their rejection of
Hindu orthodoxy.[133] This is a sign of the tendency of the police to indulge in cultural policing, the primary mission of the vigilante groups
(see chapter 7). In early March, Smriti Irani spoke at a workshop attended by RSS and ABVP members for an exchange of views on JNU.
During the event, a booklet was distributed headlined "Communists
and Jehadists at Work in JNU."[134]

At the same time, to hush up news of the crackdown, police officers telephoned or called on journalists covering it, recommending restraint—recommendations that were sometimes accompanied by thinly veiled threats.[135] Two students close to Kanhaiya Kumar, Umar Khalid and Anirban Bhattacharya, who had gone into hiding before finally turning themselves in, remained in preventive detention for several days, during which they were interrogated with the aim of giving up the names of the organizers and participants in the February 9 meeting.[136]

Subsequently, tension became virtually permanent at JNU, and clashes never failed to turn violent, whether for a film screening (as for the so-called documentary on "love jihad" that the ABVP wanted to show; see chapter 6)[137] or for demonstrations against the vice-chancellor's policies.[138] Yet another petition defending JNU garnered widespread international support once again in the spring of 2018, in vain.[139] Two years later, the confrontation took an extreme turn when about "100 masked persons had gone on a rampage with sticks and rods inside the university for around four hours on January 5 [2020], leaving 36 students, teachers and staff injured."[140] An FIR was registered, but one year later, at the time of writing, no action had been initiated, either against the assailants or against the police forces that were supposed to protect the university.

A student, Najeeb Ahmed, after an altercation with ABVP activists has been missing since October 2016.[141]

The traitorous, antipatriotic, and anti-Hindu shadow the authorities attempted to cast over JNU resulted in turning other universities and academics away from it. For instance, the vice-chancellor of the Central University of Jharkhand in Ranchi suspended a professor for having invited a colleague from JNU, N. M. Panini, whom he described as "mentor of the group of students of JNU, who were involved in antinational activities in JNU campus recently."[142] A similar occurrence took place in Jodhpur, where this time the incriminated guest was Nivedita Menon, one of JNU's political science professors.[143]

In fact, while JNU was at the epicenter of such conflicts, the ABVP was tending to lay down the law at many other university campuses. At Delhi University, one of the organization's historical bastions, it already wielded considerable influence. In 2016, the organization once again

convinced the university's ruling body to cancel the invitation a philo-
sophical society at Ramjas College had extended to several JNUSU
leaders, including Umar Khalid.[144] In reaction to this diktat, students
sympathetic to the JNUSU marched on the campus where the ABVP
was cracking down. Clashes left thirty wounded, including journalists who had come to cover the event. Eyewitnesses to the scenes of
violence—reporters in particular—pointed out how the police had
come to the aid of ABVP activists. The union minister of state for home
affairs, Kiren Rijiu, justified the repression with these words: "No anti-
India slogans will be allowed in the name of freedom of speech. Freedom of expression in the country does not give anyone the right to
make college campuses hub of anti-national activity."[145] In reaction, a
student at Delhi University, Gurmehar Kaur, daughter of an officer who
died in combat in 1999 during the Kargil war, launched a social media
campaign with the hashtag #StudentsAgainstABVP.

Aside from Delhi, turmoil was on the rise in other states, in particular
at Hyderabad University, pitting the ABVP against left-leaning and Dalit
student organizations, such as the Ambedkar Students' Association.
Rohit Vemula was one of the students who suffered the most directly
from persecution orchestrated by the ABVP and the university board.
He was subject to ill treatment for having protested against the impos-
sibility of showing the film about the Muzaffarnagar riots and the execution of Yakub Memon, one of those accused of perpetrating the Bombay
bombings in 1993, the charges against whom were disputed. He took his
own life, causing immense grief in student circles and beyond, after his
fellowship—on which his entire family depended—was suspended for
several months.[146]

The list of incidents that have tarnished university campus life due to
the ABVP is too long to examine here. Some of them are appended to
Nandini Sundar's article "Academic Freedom and Indian Universities"[147] and her very comprehensive 2020 report.[148] Snigdha Poonam
offers as a case study a detailed account of the organizations actions on
the campus of Allahabad University through the portrait of a female
student who put up resistance against the ABVP.[149]

Hindu nationalist efforts to bring Indian universities,[150] especially JNU, to heel provide apt illustrations of two structuring principles of the regime set up in 2014. First, the state outsourced its moral policing to violent vigilante groups, such as the ABVP (a topic that is discussed in further detail in chapter 7). Second, the government's attitude toward universities is revealing of the liberticidal implications of national populism, which are also evidenced in its attacks against NGOs.

NGOs under Pressure

NGOs that defend secularism or religious minorities have also been prime targets of the Indian government since 2014. Starting in August, the Intelligence Bureau sent Narendra Modi a memo stating the several Indian NGOs were "negatively impacting economic development."[151]

To neutralize the dissenting NGOs, the Modi government resurrected a law introduced by Indira Gandhi in 1976, in the dark days of the Emergency. The government at the time, to insulate India from democratic influences from abroad, subjected foreign contributions to NGOs to prior authorization: the Foreign Contributions (Regulation) Act (FCRA). In 2015, the Indian state used the FCRA to prevent thousands of NGOs from receiving funds from abroad, without which they could no longer operate.[152] The official reason given for revoking their FCRA license was almost always the same: the incriminated organizations had not previously reported what the funds had been used for, raising suspicions that they might have gone to illicit activities, such as laundering money or financing terrorism.[153] Between 2013–2014 and 2014–2015, the measure resulted in a 30 percent drop in foreign contributions made to NGOs in India—but this was only the beginning of a policy that would become systematic.[154] In March–April 2015, 10,117 NGOs had their FCRA licenses revoked.[155] A similar number of organizations were affected the following year, reducing the number of Indian NGOs from 33,000 to approximately 13,000, most of them being unable to meet their financial needs without foreign help.[156] This trend continued, so much so that by 2019, the central government had canceled the FCRA licenses of more than 19,000 recipient NGOs.[157] Still, it had an amendment to the FCRA passed in parliament just after the 2019 Lok Sabha election, to make it tougher for NGOs to get foreign funds and use them freely. Public servants were not eligible to receive foreign donations anymore; no more than 20 percent of the total foreign funds received could be defrayed for administrative expenses (against 50 percent previously); and no FCRA grant could be transferred to another organization.[158]

Among the NGOs targeted were not only such major organizations as Greenpeace India, which was fighting against environmentally unfriendly industrial and mining projects,[159] but also organizations known for their defense of secularism, including ANHAD (Act Now for Harmony and Democracy),[160] the Lawyers Collective, and Citizens for Justice and Peace. The reason for the government's perseverance against these three NGOs lies in their commitment to defending the victims of the riots in Gujarat when Narendra Modi was chief minister there. Shabnam Hashmi had founded ANHAD in 2003 to work toward reconciling Hindus and Muslims and rehabilitating riot survivors. The Lawyers Collective,[161] founded in 1981 by Indira Jaising and her husband, Anand Grover, was a prime target,[162] given these two lawyers' unwavering engagement in the service of secularism and human rights.[163] Relying on a January 2016 investigation of the Ministry of Home Affairs, the Central Bureau of Investigation filed a criminal case against the Lawyers Collective in June 2019.[164] In particular, Jaising and Grover defended Testa Setalvad, the founder—together with her husband, Javed Anand—of Citizens for Justice and Peace (CJP), the NGO the government has gone after with the fiercest determination. Setalvad and Anand, along with other human rights activists, had founded the CJP in April 2002, again in the wake of the pogrom in Gujarat. These journalists by training had already started a magazine in 1993, *Communalism Combat*, to fight against all manner of fundamentalism. Among other campaigns, Setalvad supported Ehsan Jafri's widow throughout the entire court case she filed against the government in Gujarat when Narendra Modi was at its head.[165] In her petition, Zakia Jafri accused him directly, along with other politicians and senior police officers in the state.[166] As of 2014, in addition to freezing the assets of Sabrang Trust, the institution that publishes *Communalism Combat* and administers the CJP, and dogged criminal proceedings against Testa Setalvad, accusing her of "hatred-filled, disharmony-spreading, ill-will generating, enmity-creating explosive writings,"[167] her trust lost its FCRA license in August 2016.

For having funded the CJP, the Ford Foundation in India also saw its FCRA license revoked. This action prompted the organization, which has been established in India since 1952 and contributed in particular to the success of the Green Revolution, to freeze 4 million USD it was preparing to distribute to various projects throughout the country. U.S. ambassador Richard Verma lamented the "chilling effect" of such a decision on Indian civil society and the country's democratic traditions.[168] A few months earlier, the United Nations special rapporteur on the rights to freedom of peaceful assembly and of association, Maina Kiai, submitted a report in which he concluded that the Indian government's use of the FCRA was not "in conformity with international law, principles and standards."[169]

These international reactions did not impress the Modi government. While 1,300 more NGOs had lost FCRA licenses in 2019,[170] in 2020, the FCRA was amended, as mentioned previously, in such a way that not more than 20 percent of the foreign funds received by NGOs could be spent on administrative expenditures, compared to 50 percent until then—forcing some NGOs to reduce their staff.[171] In parallel, the Modi government froze the bank account of Amnesty International India in 2018. It was unfrozen by the High Court. Then the Ministry of Home Affairs initiated an inspection. In 2019, the Central Bureau of Investigation raided the NGO's office. And finally, in 2020, its bank accounts were frozen again, a move that the NGO described as the "latest in the incessant witch-hunt of human rights organisations by the Government of India."[172] Amnesty International, whose reports on the police role in anti-Muslim violence during the Delhi riots and the use of torture in Jammu and Kashmir (see chapter 10) had been rejected by the government as "far from truth,"[173] decided to halt its India operations soon after.

The ethnicization of India's democracy that took place during Narendra Modi's first term lies particularly in the government's active promotion of Hinduism at the expense of secularism. This process found expression not only in the daily rhetoric of the new leaders, who kept eulogizing the culture of the majority community—occasionally alluding to the need to give a constitutional translation to this new discourse—but also in five different concrete ways. First, new laws were passed, and new rules were applied, both at the national and state level, to protect Hinduism and its symbols: if India during Modi's first term was not a de jure ethnic democracy, official decisions against cow slaughter, transport of cattle, and conversions gave it some institutional flavor. Second, the Modi government made decisions affecting secularists, including the appointment of vice-chancellors in universities (like JNU) that were the last bastions of the Left and the use of laws (like the FCRA) against NGOs. Third, the Modi government legitimized the RSS in the public sphere (as evident from the new visibility of its chief on Doordarshan, among others) and opened up the state apparatus to the organization. Fourth, the government and the Sangh Parivar jointly reshaped aspects of the education system, including the teaching of history by rewriting textbooks. Last but not least, this kind of joint venture restructured the public sphere to some extent as state actors (ranging from the government to the police) protected nonstate actors; that is, offshoots of the Sangh Parivar (including the ABVP) that impose their own cultural policing in the public space: ministers and vigilantes joined hands to delegitimize the "antinationals" who did not sing "Vande Mataram." I return in detail in chapter 7 to this new dispensation where even officials defend illegal actions in the name of their legitimacy.

Narendra Modi is not the sole embodiment of a different idea of India than the one described in the introduction to this book, but his election as prime minister of India has enabled him to promote the Hindutva agenda at the expense of secularism on an unprecedented scale and not only at home but also abroad. Since his unofficial inauguration ceremony in Varanasi, recounted at the start of this chapter, he has indeed taken the stance of champion of Hinduism in his travels abroad. He has visited holy places all dressed in saffron, as in Nepal, or negotiated the construction of Hindu temples, as in Abu Dhabi. The international dimension of Hinduism's promotion was indeed one of

Modi's priorities. He wanted Hindu civilization to be recognized globally—hence his attempt at persuading the United Nations to introduce an International Yoga Day, which bore fruit. As Jyoti Puri points out, "By successfully lobbying the United Nations (UN) to adopt an international yoga day, Prime Minister Modi recuperated yoga as an invaluable gift to the world."[174] But of course, Modi has celebrated this International Yoga Day every June 21, from 2016 onward in India and seized this opportunity to relate to the Indian people on a massive scale: on the occasion of the first celebration, 50,000 people performed yoga with him, and millions watched the show on TV. This festival was part on the strategy of quasi-permanent mobilization that he had initiated as chief minister of Gujarat and which made some of his critics say that he was an "event manager." Indeed, the national-populist conquest of power and the transformation of India into an ethnic democracy formed a continuum: once in office, Modi could take the majoritarian discourse to its logical conclusion through actions and, at the same time, prepare the ground for the next elections. This is also why he made a point to further polarize society along religious lines, as evidenced by his treatment of minorities, another pillar of the ethnic democracy in the making.

6

Targeting Minorities

HISTORICALLY, HINDU REVIVALISM WAS FOUNDED on opposition to the Other, embodied successively and then simultaneously in the West (or the "sickuralists" viewed as representing it), in Christians (described as a subclass of the former), and in Muslims. Hindu nationalists perceive these three groups—which in some instances overlap—as threats, whether they are viewed as hostile to Hinduism or as cultural invaders inclined to proselytize.

All three groups, along with the communists, were targeted by M. S. Golwalkar in his book *Bunch of Thoughts*, published in the 1960s.[1] They were once again the focus forty years later in the book by Subramanian Swamy *Hindus under Siege*, which accuses the British, such as T. B. Macaulay, of having denigrated Hindu culture in the early nineteenth century and stripping the author's co-religionaries of their "self-esteem by disparaging their tradition."[2] Swamy also presents Christians and Muslims as threats, not only due to demographic evolutions and terrorism, as discussed previously, but also because of historic legacies. For him, "today, every Muslim and Christian in India is a living example of that despicable violence against the Hindus"[3] that came in the wake of the Muslim invasions and the British conquest. The Hindu nationalist propensity to live in the past, not only to extol the grandeur of their civilization but also to emphasize the violence suffered hundreds of years ago by sons of the soil, is evident in the list of temples destroyed that Swamy enumerates, calling for revenge against the perpetrators' descendants.[4]

Swamy concludes that specific legislation is needed to protect Hindus from Christians and Muslims,[5] a Hindu nationalist accomplishment that can be seen in the passing of laws against cow slaughter and conversions in the BJP-ruled states. But the party could hardly go any further and ban conversion and cow slaughter nationally without a majority in the upper house of parliament (Rajya Sabha) and with a judiciary ensuring compliance with the Constitution. It is through practices rather than through legislation that they have therefore targeted Christians and Muslims over these two issues as well as others, including mixed marriages.

Anti-Christian Xenophobia

Stigmatization and Sidelining

Christians had already been the object of all sorts of attacks in a number of states, whether governed by the BJP or not,[6] but they became prime targets under the post-2014 dispensation.[7] As the RSS readily perceived Christian schools—in particular the Jesuit network—as loci of socialization in contradiction with the Sangh Parivar's plan to mold minds, the government required some Christian schools to perform Hindu ceremonies, such as Aarti,[8] and associated chants.[9]

However, the main grievance Hindu nationalists have toward Christians relates to missionary proselytism. The rejection of conversion activities—which are constitutionally legal—is rooted in the age-old demographic obsession, the "dying race" syndrome, which remains strong even if no statistical data corroborate it. Certainly, the population of the majority community has eroded slightly, but the Christian minority as a percentage of the Indian population, in parallel, has dropped below the threshold of 2 percent.

Yet the RSS chief, Mohan Bhagwat, added a dimension to the usual Hindu nationalist anti-Christian indictment by directly criticizing

Mother Teresa in 2015, opining, "Mother Teresa's service would have been good. But it used to have one objective, to convert the person, who was being served, into a Christian."[10] Yogi Adityanath—who would become chief minister of Uttar Pradesh in 2017—echoed this rhetoric, reviving an old Hindu nationalist trope that the separatist ambitions of Christian ethnic groups in the Northeast were due to their religion:[11] "Teresa was part of a conspiracy for Christianization of India. Incidents of Christianization had led to separatist movements in parts of North-East, including Arunachal Pradesh, Tripura, Meghalaya and Nagaland."[12] Indresh Kumar, the man in charge of minority relations within the RSS leadership, wrote an open letter to Pope Benedict XVI in 2016, complaining about the immoral aspect of Catholic proselytism: "Conversion to Christianity in the pretext of service, health, education and cooperation is an insult and devaluation to the service itself and a crime against humanity. It proves that your services are selfish motivated and expansionist as well as intolerant. Wherever the Christian missionaries are active and powerful, the hatred, crime, social unrest, separatism, addiction are on the increase and the environment of peace, harmony, brotherhood and happiness are fading away."[13] This view contains a kernel of truth in the sense that Christian missions—whether run by foreigners or Indians—have contributed to what they call "consciousness raising" and empowerment, which in fact has resulted in challenges to the social hierarchy and the submission of peripheral ethnic groups in which Hindu nationalists see a harmonious order.

It is also therefore in the name of combating Christian proselytism that the government rescinded the right of some Christian NGOs to receive funds from abroad. This was the case, for instance, of Compassion International, an American NGO working to help poor children that has been operating in India since 1968. In 2017, 145,000 children benefited from Compassion's aid, owing to external funds amounting to 45 million USD per year. This flow of cash dried up when its Foreign Contribution (Regulation) Act (FCRA) license was not renewed in 2017.[14] Colorado Republican senator Cory Gardner expressed his indignation regarding the decision to Secretary of State Rex Tillerson in terms that roused Hindu nationalists to respond. The RSS weekly magazine, *The Organiser*, justified the revocation of Compassion's license, arguing that children had been victims of sexual abuse on the part of pastors and priests in India as well as attempts at forced conversion—while admitting that no such case had involved the NGO.[15]

Compassion International, which claimed that it had experienced "an unprecedented, highly coordinated, deliberate and systematic attack intended to drive us out,"[16] argued that only 23 percent of the children served by its programs were Christians and that 73 percent of them were Hindus.[17] Media outlets in the United States—including the *New York Times*—took an interest in the case, with the *Los Angeles Times* placing the case of Compassion in the broader framework of a "crackdown against civil society organizations" targeting many other NGOs, such as those defending Dalits.[18] Due in part to this mobilization, the U.S. embassy voiced its dismay, and U.S. secretary of state John Kerry himself took up the issue[19] with the Indian authorities, which finally allowed Compassion to fund 10 NGOs (out of the 250 that the organization previously helped)—a small consolation indeed.[20]

Physical Abuse

Ostensibly to combat Christian proselytism, churches have been vandalized and clerics physically attacked by anonymous individuals. In 2014–2016, around 250 Christian places of worship suffered attacks (profanation, partial or entire destruction, pillage) each year,[21] in Delhi,[22] Haryana (where assailants replaced a cross with a statue of Hanuman),[23] Chhattisgarh,[24] Mangalore,[25] Jharkhand,[26] Uttar Pradesh,[27] Orissa,[28] Tamil Nadu,[29] and so on. Cases of physical abuse ranged from the brutal arrest of members of a Christmas choir in Madhya Pradesh, suspected of forcibly converting villagers,[30] to the murder of Pastor Sultan Masih in front of his church in Ludhiana on July 15, 2017,[31] not to mention several instances of assault on priests. The Evangelical Fellowship of India and the All-India Christian Council enumerated "incidents" of this nature, counting 147 of them in 2014, 177 in 2015, 441 in 2016, and 410 in the first six months of 2017.[32] An Irish NGO, Church in Chains, examined 57 "incidents" that took place in the following six months. Its report directly accused Hindu nationalist groups, including the RSS, on the basis of detailed eyewitness accounts, and regretted the authorities' complacency, first and foremost the police's attitude.[33] For instance, the kin of Pastor Masih claimed that the police were not dealing with the case seriously.[34] The 2019 annual report of the Evangelical Fellowship of India (EFI) listed 366 incidents where Christians were targeted, against 325 in 2018 (an increase of 12.5 percent). According to the report, "Most incidents are physical violence, threats, harassment and the disruption of church services by religious radicals or the police."[35] In the first six months of 2020, 293 cases of hate crimes against Christians, including six murders and five rapes, were recorded according to the half-yearly report of the organization Persecution Relief (founded in 2016)—a more than 40 percent increase comparted to the previous year.[36]

This state of affairs has prompted the creation of new Christian organizations such as Persecution Relief and repeated démarches on the part of Christian clerical dignitaries. In December 2017, Cardinal Baselios Cleemis, then president of the Catholic Bishops Conference in India, stated, "The country is being divided on the basis of religious belief. It is bad in a democratic country. I want my country to be united in a secular fabric.[37] But now, this country is being polarised due to religious affiliations. We should fight against it. . . . I agree such incidents can happen in a big country. . . . But how do you evaluate the strength and stand of the government? It is [sic] the subsequent action and the legal protection are what matter."[38] The last sentence, despite its grammatical awkwardness, is key: while no one is immune from the actions of extremist groups, the way the state resists them or, on the contrary, plays along with them or even outsources its dirty work to them is a clear indication of what sort of regime we are dealing with. The impunity that Hindu nationalist militias enjoyed led Christian figures to surmise that India had slid into "majoritarianism." In 2015, Julio Ribeiro, a long-serving official in the Indian police force and widely respected for his integrity, penned an editorial entitled "As a Christian, Suddenly I Am a Stranger in My Own Country." He lamented the fact that Hindu extremists were never called to account by those who are supposed to safeguard the rule of law: "It is tragic that these extremists have been emboldened beyond permissible limits by an atmosphere of hate and distrust. The Christian population, a mere 2 per cent of the total populace, has been subjected to a series of well-directed body blows."[39] As the situation still had not improved, the archbishop of Goa, Filipe Neri Ferrao, stated in April 2018 before an assembly organized by the Catholic Bishops Conference of India, "The idea of India with its strongest pillars of diversity and pluralism is being threatened by several emerging trends," starting with "the emergence of both majoritarian hegemony and the growth of terror and extremism engendered by the growth of exclusivist religious fundamentalism."[40] The archbishop of Delhi, Anil Couo, wrote to all the parish priests in his diocese, calling on them to pray with the approach of the 2019 elections: "We are witnessing a turbulent political atmosphere which poses a threat to the democratic principles enshrined in our Constitution and the secular fabric of our nation. It is our hallowed practice to pray for our country and its political leaders all the time, but all the more when we approach the general elections." He added that the nation "looks forward towards 2019 when we will have a new government" and then concluded: "May the ethos of true democracy envelop our elections with dignity and the flames of honest patriotism enkindle our political leaders."[41] The letter sparked heated reactions from Amit Shah and members of the government, starting with Home Minister Rajnath Singh. The president of the Catholic Bishops Conference of India, Cardinal Oswald Gracias, was called in by the home minister—who claimed that the government did not discriminate against religious communities.[42] Julio Ribeiro reacted with an even more scathing editorial than the preceding one, a sign that the situation was worsening. In fact, Ribeiro saw the advent of a Hindu Rashtra that reduced minorities to second-class citizens: "I, for one, am preparing for the Hindu Rashtra! . . . I should be prepared for second-class citizenship that denies top jobs like that of a judge in the Supreme Court, a governor of a state, the chief of defence staff or the intelligence bureau. What I will not accept is being accused falsely of being anti-national and pilloried on that count."[43]

Recurrent Mobilizations against Muslims

While Christians have been the butt of stigmatization and repressive policies, the situation for Muslims is even more fragile from these two perspectives,[44] for Hindu nationalists disqualify them even more systematically as Indian citizens. For adherents of Hindutva, Muslims are the epitome of the Other.[45] During the 2017 election campaign in Uttar Pradesh, Parvesh Verma, an MP representing the West Delhi Lok Sabha constituency, less sophisticated than his leaders and therefore less guarded about his language, demonstrated during a rally why the BJP, far from seeking the Muslim vote, wanted to ostracize this minority using already tried-and-true tactics of polarization: "Muslims have never voted for us and they never will. It is a very simple matter. . . . Why is every terrorist in the country a Muslim and why do Muslims not vote for BJP[?] . . . Because the BJP is a patriotic party, that's why Muslims don't vote for us."[46] Answering Congress's criticism of his rhetoric, he added that the Muslim problem came from relations "between India and Pakistan. Why are terrorists only Muslims? From where do they get all the funding and from where do they get all the weapons?" As seen in the first part of the book, this is the main leitmotif of Modi's national populism, a claim he diffused in Gujarat before distilling it at the national level. It holds Muslims to be potential traitors due to their alleged connection with Pakistan and the Islam-equals-terrorism equation.

The other motive for stigmatizing Muslims pertains to the ravages done by the Mughals—which in this case justifies the BJP's disregard for this minority at election time and its attempt to obliterate it from the public sphere. After winning the elections in Uttar Pradesh in 2017, the BJP tackled this task by removing the Taj Mahal—the most visited monument in India—from the state's tourist brochures. Sangeet Som, a BJP MLA from Sardhana, in the district of Muzaffarnagar, western Uttar Pradesh, justified the decision by saying the Taj Mahal was "a blot on Indian culture."[47] Venting his wrath at the alleged anti-Hindu practices of the Mughal emperors, he added, "It is quite sad and unfortunate that such tyrants are still part of our history."[48] This statement foreshadowed the rewriting of school textbooks[49] and the renaming of the "Moghol museum" after Shivaji.[50]

Hindu nationalists would make even more radical attempts to exclude Muslims from the public sphere through unrelenting campaigns against them. Again, the practice is reminiscent of Narendra Modi's tactics in Gujarat as chief minister there, in that it relied on militias with close ties to the RSS. This plan of action has a number of advantages. First, it offers symbolic satisfaction for the Hindu nationalist rank and file who might otherwise be disappointed in the Modi government's performance in the economic and social realm (in terms of job creation, for instance) and even fulfills their yearning for a good brawl. Second, by multiplying the number of small militant groups and changing their names, it throws up a smokescreen to conceal BJP, and even RSS, responsibility[51] for repeated anti-Muslim violence triggered by one issue or another.

Between 2014 and 2019, the Sangh Parivar launched at least four types of campaigns: against the movement dubbed "love jihad," against conversions to Islam and Christianity, against "land jihad," and against cow slaughter. Muslims were always the primary targets. And each time, ad hoc vigilante groups in the Sangh Parivar nexus were found in the front lines.

Resisting "Love Jihad"

The notion of love jihad—an expression intended to shock—dates back to the 2000s. It allegedly first appeared in Gujarat in 2007, prior to resurfacing in 2009 in Kerala and in Karnataka under the auspices of Pramod Muttalik, a former swayamsevak who founded his own movement, Ram Sena (see chapter 7), and who defined the notion as follows: "In love jihad, fanatic boys are encouraged to attract young Hindu girls outside icecream [sic] parlours, schools, colleges and theatres. . . . There is an organised effort to demoralise the Hindu community."[52] The idea of love jihad calls up two typical obsessions that have plagued Hindu nationalism since its inception: a physical inferiority complex regarding Muslims, thought to be better built and more virile (and therefore more appealing),[53] and the dread of a demographic decline, given that

Muslims who have seduced Hindu women supposedly convince them to convert to Islam (and then produce Muslim offspring).

This rhetoric, which Hindu nationalists had often rehashed discreetly until then, became explicit in public in 2014. In September of that year, a few months after Modi was voted into office, two weekly magazines put out by the RSS—in English, *The Organiser*, and in Hindi, *Panchjanya*—devoted their cover stories to love jihad, one showing the photo of a Hindu "victim," the other an Arab wearing a keffiyeh and dark glasses beneath which read the title, "Pyar andha ya dhanda?" (Is love blind, or is it a business?).[54] *The Organiser* explained, "There are examples of feigning love, followed by devastating tales of pain, suffering, blackmailing and torture for conversion."[55]

A few months later, Subramanian Swamy, who would be elected to the Rajya Sabha in 2016, took part in a meeting of Hindu religious leaders aiming to draw "attention of the Hindu society to the growing menace of jihadi terrorism and stressed the need to act tough against the larger conspiracy of 'Love Jihad.'"[56] According to him, the threat was mainly demographic, given "the huge population growth of Muslims i.e. 22 per cent, whereas the growth of Hindus population is hardly 1.5 per cent." These figures—which are entirely false, as the annual growth rates of the Hindu and Muslim community were 1.4 and 2.2 percent, respectively, between 2001 and 2011[57]—were an indication, according to Swamy, that "love jihad is also part of a larger conspiracy to increase Muslim population." The only available statistics—contained in the report of a Criminal Investigation Department (CID) police investigation between 2005 and 2009 into cases of "missing" girls, 229 of whom were found to be married to a man of a different religion than theirs—show that only 63 had converted to another religion, not all of them from Hinduism. In fact, 38 of them were Muslim and 20 were Christians married to Hindus.[58]

In reaction to what the Hindu nationalists presented as a dire threat to the survival of their community, they launched a counteroffensive to prevent young Hindu women from being wooed by Muslim men. They formed special groups, such as the Hindu Behen Beti Bachao Sangharsh Samiti (Save Hindu Sisters and Daughters Committees). Activists offered to help parents who lamented their daughter's marriage to a Muslim and developed a network of informers in police stations and courts where parents might go to report a missing daughter (if she runs away to marry), to file a complaint for abduction, or to keep abreast of a case.[59] This network of informers indicates the degree of osmosis that exists between the state apparatus and the Sangh Parivar.[60] In Rajasthan, for instance, Bajrang Dal activists who spied on their neighbors (partly via social media) also relied "on an informal intelligence network [that the local BD chief has] cultivated in courts, tehsil offices and marriage registration offices"—largely made up of clerks and lawyers—to tip off the organization about interfaith marriages.[61]

Once on a case, warriors against love jihad resorted to all sorts of tactics, ranging from disinformation to intimidation to coercion. Their methods were revealed by journalists working for two investigative news websites, Cobrapost and Gulail.com. Posing as students sympathetic to the Hindu nationalist cause, they used hidden cameras to record their conversations with activists. They discovered that the first task of the Hindu nationalists was to convince young Hindu women—whom they systematically claimed were "vulnerable"—to go back on their decision to marry a Muslim. Lalit Maheshwari, district president of the VHP in Muzaffarnagar explained, "We talk about her future. We tell her the importance of women in our Hindu society. We tell her how we see a woman and how those Muslims look like [sic]. How we respect our women and how they only use women as a form of enjoyment and treat her nothing more than a baby-making machine and also generally have a target of keeping three–four wives."[62] A UP MLA from the district of Muzaffarnagar, Sangeet Som, chimed in again to emphasize the importance of moral pressure:

> We make her see the reason that this is not good for her. We tell her that they are Muslims, they never settle for one woman, whereas a Hindu boy will be automatically sent to jail if he does so. On the other hand, a Muslim can marry up to four women and those women can adjust among themselves. You tell me which Hindu girl will adjust like that? There are, of course, some exceptions. Such cases are

rare. . . . Most importantly we exert on her emotionally that her mother will die, her father will die and brother might even commit suicide as he would not be able to face the society.[63]

If persuasion failed, other techniques were brought to bear. An RSS leader from Muzaffarnagar, Omkar Singh, who "rescued 125 girls 'from the clutches of Muslims' and remarried them to Hindu men," explains, "Usually, a rape and kidnapping case is filed against the Muslim youth with whom she has eloped."[64] This is an often-used stratagem that Singh speaks openly about: "After the girl has fallen for Sonu Monu . . . they [Muslim boys] use such names . . . the girls realize that their lives have been ruined, [they think] it is better to stay with them. Then we make them understand and if they still disagree, we file false cases against their men."[65] Sanjay Agarwal, a Hindu activist who ran in the Muzaffarnagar municipal elections under the BJP banner in 2014, admitted to having forced false testimony out of Hindu girls going out with a Muslim boy—in general so as to file fake rape and kidnapping charges against him and reconvert her to Hinduism if she has left her community, and this in the name of what he views as a sacred cause: "We have to work towards ensuring every citizen of India is a Hindu."[66] And Agarwal adds: "If she doesn't listen to us, we hit her. We get her beaten up. We misbehave [Poori badtameeze karte hain]." If a girl persisted in refusing to give false testimony, Agarwal explains, his crew didn't let her appear in court for days, with the authorities' tacit approval:

> We say that the girl is not listening. They [police] say it's alright, we will see her tomorrow. If she isn't listening even tomorrow, they say it's alright. They help us a lot. They send her mother to us to talk. We are not allowed to do that. They help us a lot. Judges help us, so does the SSP [Senior Superintendent of Police]. . . . The judge gives the girl to us in his judgment. He hands her over to her parents. Once she is under her parents' control, we can get her married in three days.[67]

I return to the role of the police and the judges in chapters 7 and 8. For the moment I would simply like to focus on what this special report tells us about the methods used by Hindu nationalist groups combating love jihad. The accounts mentioned thus far illuminate the role of persuasion, intimidation, and coercion. To better understand these different facets, it is worth looking at other cases. The journalists for Cobrapost and Gulail.com also took their investigation to Karnataka and Kerala, where love jihad is allegedly coupled with "love gospel," in other words, attempts by Christians to woo young Hindu women. These investigations also demonstrate how fear factors in.

In Kerala, Hindu nationalists created a "Hindu Helpline" and counseling centers, particularly in Ernakulam. The head of one of these centers admitted that her team sometimes resorts to duress when the girl does not want to mend "her ways" and even wants to convert to Islam:

> When she is adamant on Islam, we will send her to a religious counselling centre so that she can have a debate with our experts on the Quran. Even with that if she is not convinced, we send her to a medical hospital where she will be kept in a cell, she will be under some medication if she is aggressive. . . . [If she doesn't relent even then], we will send her somewhere [else] where she can be kept for some days. . . . There are a lot of classes, a lot of Hindu organisations are working on that. I don't know how to say it, we are successful in creating fear. "Why should I bother?" That was the question earlier. "Because jihad will come to your doorstep today or tomorrow. It may be as your sister, wife or mother. So be careful yourself." We have to create a true fear in the society, about Muslims.[68]

The fight against love jihad thus relies at once on means of intimidation and the politics of fear, methods that are obviously implemented by a vast network of organizations across the country, the existence of which the state is necessarily aware. However, other even more violent methods to prevent an interfaith marriage exist as well, as evident from the way Bajrang Dal militants sometimes interfere with wedding ceremonies or physically attack Muslims who wish to marry a Hindu woman— or already have.[69]

In Shamli (western Uttar Pradesh), the team of Premi, the local Bajrang Dal leader, was in a position to "micromanage the dating scene in a town of 100,000," not only because of the way it had "infiltrated hundreds of [WhatsApp] groups" and thanks to a dense network of lawyers from the local court but also because of its physical strike force—as gathered from the testimony of one of the lawyers involved:

> If any Muslim man approaches the courts to register his marriage to a Hindu woman, he said, other workers in his office tell him when the couple has arranged to visit the court. Then all he has to do is call or send a quick WhatsApp text to Premi's entourage. "On the day the couple comes to the court, the workers of Bajrang Dal take care of them at the gate," which means that they "told him to strip so they could see whether he was circumcised, a sure sign that he wasn't Hindu" and then "the group handed the man over to police."[70]

The impact of the campaign against love jihad has been all the more influential as, since marriages are still often arranged by the parents, parents of girls who dare choose to make a love marriage with a Muslim do not hesitate, sometimes, to turn to Hindu nationalist networks to bring their progeny back into the fold.[71] But organizations in the Sangh Parivar orbit have also sought to prevent interfaith marriages even when parents were not opposed.[72] Hindu nationalist groups then turned to the police, whose anti-Muslim bias (to be discussed in the third part of the book) provides another explanation for the scale anti–love jihad operations have taken. Not only have the police sometimes annulled marriages (in total disregard for the law when bride and groom were both of age),[73] but they have also let Sangh Parivar (or affiliated) brigades stalk interfaith marriages in which the bride was a Hindu. This indicates the degree of influence such groups have over the police, from the outside as well as from within. In 2014, at the start of the movement, *The Hindu* published conversations about love jihad that certain police officers engaged in on the internet—one of them qualifying the love jihad phenomenon as "organized crime"—forcing a discussion forum called TopCop to be shut down.[74]

In addition to the police, the judiciary apparatus has also aided anti-love-jihad Hindu nationalist militants not only by informing them of new cases brought before the courts but also by joining in on strong-arm operations, an indication of strong ideological affinities between both milieus.[75] These Hindu nationalist sympathies came to light in an emblematic case concerning a young woman from Kerala named Hadiya. She had converted to Islam in 2015 and had married a Muslim man in 2016. Her parents immediately petitioned the court, claiming she had been forcibly married and converted, despite her insistence that she had acted of her own free will. The state's high court sided with the parents, invalidated the marriage in May 2017, and placed Hadiya under their guardianship, arguing that this "vulnerable girl" had probably been the victim of Islamist groups.[76] Her husband appealed the decision in the Supreme Court, which, highly exceptionally in such a case, ordered the National Investigation Agency (NIA), created by the Manmohan Singh government to combat terrorism, to investigate a possible Islamist conspiracy.[77] The NIA, while it was starting its probe, pointed out that such a ploy could not be ruled out and that Hadiya's case was not an isolated one. But even before waiting for the probe's findings, the judges released her into parental custody. And when they saw the investigation results, they ruled in March 2018 that her marriage was valid.

The BJP considered overtly exploiting the notion of love jihad with the approach of by-elections in Uttar Pradesh in 2014. The party's state unit included the fight against love jihad in its program before deciding against it.[78] But the party made it a campaign issue without using the words[79] and fully utilized it during the 2017 elections only. Shortly after forming his cabinet, Yogi Adityanath established "anti-Romeo squads" to "protect" women—especially from Muslims.[80] These entities officialized the osmosis that already existed on the ground between Sangh Parivar activists (starting with the Bajrang Dal) and government employees (starting with the police)—a question scrutinized in the next chapter.

Sangh Parivar involvement in the fight against love jihad came out in the open after the lynching of a Muslim accused of having seduced a Hindu woman in Rajasthan. The murderer received moral and financial support (to cover court costs) from several Sangh Parivar cadres, including BJP elected representatives.[81] Such a development is even more significant as it was prompted by the posting on social media of a particularly gruesome crime scene filmed by the killer's young nephew.[82]

At the same time, the Sangh Parivar engaged in what it called a "reverse love jihad," which involved marrying Muslim women to Hindu men. The Hindu Jagran Manch, the Sangh affiliate in charge of this campaign, labeled "Beti bachao, balu lao" ("Bring a daughter-in-law, save a daughter"), announced 2,100 such unions in 2017.[83] The other idea that one BJP MLA put forward to prevent Muslim men from marrying Hindu women was to encourage child marriages.[84]

Ghar Wapsi (or Homecoming): A Reconversion Campaign

The anti-love-jihad combat aiming to prevent Hindu women from converting to Islam was followed by a campaign to bring Hindus converted to Islam or Christianity back into the fold of their native community. The initiative for this campaign lies directly with the RSS, which gathered 1,200 of its members and sympathizers in Nagpur on November 7 and 9, 2014 (a few weeks after the campaign against love jihad was launched). The Sangh branch responsible for carrying out the conversion operations was the Dharm Jagran Samiti (Religious Awakening Committee). The RSS assigned 58 pracharak to the task, a considerable number for such a campaign,[85] all the more so as the VHP, traditionally in charge of this type of action, also remained involved.

The VHP's leader, Praveen Togadia, claimed during a convention in Bhopal, as soon as the Ghar Wapsi campaign was launched in 2014, that there once was a time when the entire world was inhabited with Hindus but that instead of totaling 7 billion as they should, there were only 1 billion left, a downward trend that had to be stopped: "We want to protect Hindus today and 1,000 years from now. We won't let their population decline from 82 per cent to 42 per cent because then their property and women will not remain safe."[86] Making the connection between the campaigns against love jihad and for Ghar Wapsi, Togadia added, "When Sayeed marries Savita she becomes Salma. In 100 marriages involving Hindus and Muslims 50 Savitris become Salmas, why can't 50 Salmans become Ram?"[87]

In practical terms, campaigns to bring Hindus back into the fold took on the same ritual forms as in the past. The subjects concerned were purified during a ceremony around a sacred hearth fire called a *havan* and/or through ablutions using water from holy rivers. They "reverted" to a Hindu name and vowed no longer to perform Muslim or Christian rites[88] and then could be brought back into a caste.[89] These rituals have a religious dimension, with men in Sangh Parivar saffron robes playing a key role. Among them, Yogi Adityanath was particularly active. In December 2014, he gave a major speech in Bihar (one of the states, along with Uttar Pradesh, selected for Ghar Wapsi) before 2,200 clerics from all over India that the Sangh Parivar had brought together to prepare the campaign: "If 15 lakh [1.5 million] saints start visiting 6.23 lakh [623,000] villages of the country, the handful of Christian priests and maulvis will not be able to convert Hindus."[90] Yogi Adityanath then gave the mantra of "mala ke saath bhala" ("pray and fight").[91] The idea that Hindus who had gone over to Islam or Christianity had "lost their way" or had been coerced and/or lured by material benefits was central to the long address delivered by RSS chief Mohan Bhagwat in Calcutta on December 20, 2014, in support of the Ghar Wapsi movement.[92]

It is difficult to gauge the impact of reconversion to Hinduism operations given that their effect is hardly verifiable. But the Sangh Parivar raised money to set up "conversion camps,"[93] and these certainly contributed to the Ghar Wapsi movement in the two main states targeted, Bihar and Uttar Pradesh. The movement experienced a serious setback, however, when the press revealed that fifty-seven families in Agra had agreed to convert when they were promised "ration cards" or "Below Poverty Line cards" to access state-sponsored low-cost food shops.[94] This strategy caused an uproar in parliament, where the BJP offered to put an end to the controversy by passing a law against involuntary conversion. But the proposal—backed by Mohan Bhagwat[95]—fell flat given that according to the 1950 Constitution the matter falls under the states' jurisdiction. The party in power thus settled for simply passing anticonversion laws in states it ruled or tightening existing laws and preventing some faith-based NGOs from receiving funds from abroad—as discussed earlier—perceived by Hindu nationalists as one reason for their successful proselytizing.[96]

While converts to Islam were the Hindu nationalists' prime target, Christians were also the focus of these policies. In a village in Jammu District, after the (re)conversion of forty-five Christian families, the four Christian families that resisted were subjected to such pressure that the state assigned seventeen police officers to protect them.[97]

As is often the case, caste issues intertwine with the conversion question. Thus, in 2018, Bajrang Dal activists in Uttar Pradesh forcibly reconverted (and shaved) a young Dalit who had become a Muslim, he said, "because upper caste people don't allow a decent life for Dalits."[98]

Like what has been described in the fight against love jihad, the police in the northern Hindi-speaking states have often remained passive in the face of such reconversion activities or even been complicit in them. The police in Uttar Pradesh, for instance, arrested a twenty-one-year-old man who had converted to Islam on the pretext that he had acted under duress, whereas this was not at all the case.[99]

Ghettoization, "Land Jihad," and Forced Privatization of the Religious Space

Reconversion is only one means of making Muslims invisible. Not mingling with them in mixed neighborhoods is another. To achieve segregation, a process of ghettoization was set in motion in riot-prone cities. In Ahmedabad, for instance, the recurrent violence minorities have been subjected to has prompted them to group together in outlying settlements, such as Juhapura.[100] In this city, municipal decrees prevent them from buying or renting property in Hindu-majority areas, ostensibly due to local communal tensions.[101]

Another practice used since the 1990s consists in preventing Muslims from renting or buying property in a Hindu-dominated area. In the press, this attitude—first noted in Mumbai, including in the fancier neighborhoods, after the riots in 1992–1993—has been described as resistance to "land jihad," a phenomenon for which, again, Hindu nationalists are in large part responsible. Like the schemes discussed previously to prevent marriages between Hindus and Muslims, Sangh Parivar activists sometimes arrive on the premises of a real estate transaction they want to block. Meerut, in Uttar Pradesh, for instance, witnessed the incursion of a youth wing of a local BJP chapter, the BJP Yuva Morcha (BJPYM), in 2017. The BJPYM general secretary justified the group's action in terms that expressed beyond any doubt the refusal to cohabit: while Hindus are "continuously selling properties . . . Muslims are buying them. Their culture, thoughts and way of life are different from ours. It starts with one house and slowly, the whole area will become Muslim-dominated. We cannot allow this to happen."[102]

While the fight against land jihad has not taken on the proportions of the campaign against love jihad, it has morphed sometimes into a more general attempt to exclude Muslims from mixed neighborhoods. In Gurgaon, for instance, Hindu nationalist brigades managed to oust Muslims from public spaces where they were accustomed to gathering for Friday prayers. On April 20, 2018, members of a mysterious organization called Samyukt Hindu Sangharsh Samiti (SHSS) (United Hindu Combat Commission) forcefully dispersed Muslims gathered in a vacant lot for Friday prayers. The following week, the same thing happened in six different locations in the city. Although the police watched on without intervening,[103] they nevertheless subsequently interrogated six activists. The SHSS leader asked for their release on bail and justified his request in an edifying letter. The praying Muslims were allegedly repeating such slogans as "Long live Pakistan!" and "Death to India!" using their *namaz* (prayer) as an excuse to annex a piece of land that did not belong to them.[104] The letter concluded: "Rohingyas and Bangladeshis residing in Gurgaon should also be identified and marked. Permission should not be given to read *namaz* [prayers] in Hindu colonies, sectors and neighborhoods. Permission should only be given in those places where the strength of this population is more than 50 per cent, otherwise there will continue to be a possibility of peace being obstructed."[105] These remarks define Islam's new relationship with the public sphere. Observance of this religion is now only tolerated in Muslim areas, which amounts to introducing a new factor of ghettoization. Haryana chief minister M. L. Khattar went even further. Failing to criticize the way in which the Friday prayer had been disrupted, he indicated that "there has been an increase in offering namaz in the open." And to maintain law and order, "Namaz should be read in mosques or *idgahs* rather than in public spaces," stating that "if there is shortage of places for offering namaz, it should be done in personal spaces, inside homes."[106] This discourse amounts to expressing aloud something Hindu nationalists up until then had merely suggested, out of fear of coming directly into conflict with the Constitution: minorities should worship privately, and Hinduism is the only legitimate religion in the public sphere, as evident from the way state leaders patronized huge gatherings with extensive media coverage, one example being the staging of Narendra Modi's participation in the Khumbh Mela in 2019. This development is, of course, a pillar of everyday ethnic democracy. The fact that Gurgaon, the city with the highest average income in all of India, has served as a testing ground to radically challenge the Indian tradition of cultural coexistence and even hybridization is evidence of the affinity middle-class culture has with Hindu nationalism.[107]

Lynching in the Name of Cow Protection—or Not

The last campaign to be examined, the cow protection movement, has already been referred to in part I of this book. But here it will be studied from a different angle, the perspective of its Muslim victims. In the name of this so-called protection, not only have Muslim cattle breeders frequently been prevented from buying and selling livestock at the usual markets, but they have also been subject to abuse by Hindu nationalists watching their every move.

Between 2015 and 2018, in India a series of Muslim lynchings followed a nearly identical scenario each time: Muslims accused of cattle smuggling or consuming beef were attacked and, in dozens of cases, died of their wounds. The series began with the murder of Mohammad Akhlaq on September 28, 2015, in Dadri, a village in Gautam Buddha Nagar District, located in Uttar Pradesh but adjacent to the state of Delhi. That day, a group of young Hindus gathered near Akhlaq's house at 10:00 P.M. Among them was the son of the local BJP leader and his cousin. The mob persuaded the temple priest to announce over his loudspeaker that

Akhlaq ate beef. They then stormed his house and exhibited meat taken from his refrigerator, claiming it was beef. Akhlaq was savagely beaten and later died of his injuries in the hospital in Noida, while his son, Danish, who had intervened, was grievously wounded.[108]

The lynching of Pehlu Khan is sadly even more typical. Khan, a breeder specializing in dairy cows, was on his way home to Haryana after having purchased cattle in Rajasthan, when his truck was intercepted on National Highway 8. Some fifty Hindu youths forcibly searched it, accusing him of taking his animals to slaughter. He produced proof that his activity was perfectly legal, including the sales receipt showing he had paid Rs 50,000 (667 USD) for the cow and was therefore unlikely to sell it for Rs 6,000 (80 USD) for butcher meat. He was nevertheless brutally beaten, as were his sons. He died shortly thereafter, though not before giving the police the name of his assailants—who were from the neighborhood—when they arrived on the scene.[109]

While Muslim cattle transporters (who sometimes raise cattle as well) have become favorite targets for self-appointed Hindu nationalist cow protectors, other Muslims have been lynched as well, for different reasons and in different parts of the country, including Rajasthan,[110] West Bengal,[111] Assam,[112] Haryana,[113] Gurgaon,[114] Jharkhand,[115] Madhya Pradesh,[116] and so on. In many of these cases, a typical scenario gradually emerged in which the victim was asked by vigilantes to chant "Jai Shri Ram" (Victory to Lord Ram) repeatedly.[117] In Jharkhand, twenty-four-year old Tabrez Ansari was tied to a pole, beaten for hours, and forced to chant Lord Shri Ram.[118] The chant did not save him, as he died four days later from his injuries. The video that his tormentors made went viral, like many others. To film these scenes of torture also became part of the typical scenario.

The phenomenon took on such proportions that it ended up no longer making headlines.[119] Some publications, however, began to compile databases. IndiaSpend[120] estimates that in 2017 there were thirty-four bovine-related incidents, compared to twenty-five in 2016, thirteen in 2015, three in 2014, one in 2013, and one in 2012. Twenty-four out of

TABLE 6.1. Cow-related violence in India, 2012–2018

Year	2012	2013	2014	2015	2016	2017	2018
Incidents	1	2	3	13	30	43	31
Victims	2	0	11	49	67	108	57
Deaths	0	0	0	11	9	13	13

Source: IndiaSpend, "Hate Crime: Cow-Related Violence in India," accessed March 26, 2018, http://lynch.factchecker.in.

the twenty-eight yearly victims during the period ending in June 2017 were Muslim.[121] In 2018, this online publication started up another website with the specific purpose of logging cow-related lynchings, from which table 6.1—slightly different from the figures mentioned above—has been drawn. The website had to be discontinued shortly after.

The scale of the phenomenon prompted the Supreme Court—petitioned by Mahatma Gandhi's grandson Tushar Gandhi and Congress Party leader Tehseen Poonawala—to hand down a very vehement and highly detailed ruling. In it the magistrates stated, "Lynching and mob violence are creeping threats that may gradually take the shape of a Typhon-like monster as evidenced in the wake of the rising wave of incidents of recurring patterns by frenzied mobs across the country, instigated by intolerance and misinformed by circulation of fake news and false stories."[122]

The judges blamed mobs and social media (first and foremost WhatsApp), through which false information was spread to provoke and coordinate assaults. By doing so, the Supreme Court shunned its responsibilities by not seeking the guilty parties, as Raheel Dhattiwala has pointed out,[123] and played the game of the Hindu nationalists, who systematically legitimate anti-Muslim violence by referring to emotions and, more specifically, the "religious sentiment" that fuels champions of the faith who can quickly whip themselves up into a fury for a sacred cause. Crowds can have a rationality that is generally inspired by their leaders.[124] In fact, the perpetrators of lynchings are not spontaneous righters of wrongs but well-trained and ideologized activists. Most lynching cases have been committed by vigilante militias or were the result of the mood they fomented, a topic to be explored in the follow-ing chapter.

Since 2014, Christian and Muslim minorities have been subjected to forms of stigmatization and violence in India that are transforming them into de facto second-class citizens who are no longer in a position to assert their rights. Many of them are being obliterated from the public arena, forced to submit or resign themselves or even convert and swear allegiance to the majority culture or else withdraw into ghettos and no longer maintain any sort of relationship with Hindus, be it matrimonial, economic, or social.

Lynchings of Muslim breeders and butchers have not only penalized the whole community in financial terms,[125] but they have also some-times severed ties with Hindus to whom the Muslims sold milk, for instance. This was indeed one of the nationalists' goals. Vinay Katiyar, leader of the Bajrang Dal, moreover stated in 2018 that Muslims should "abstain from touching cows,"[126] an assertion that clearly goes beyond the fight against slaughter. The destruction of everyday relations be-tween communities is part of a bigger plan to establish an ethnic democ-racy in which the majority no longer has anything to do with the mi-norities and relegates them beyond the cognitive horizon of the masses. That was already the subtext of the new kind of communal riots that Sudha Pai and Sajjan Kumar have studied in UP.[127]

Responsibility for this ethnoreligious polarization has been attrib-uted to the masses or "mobs" by the Supreme Court and many social media actors (such as those who started the hashtag #lynchmobs), but in fact, the initiative for the entire process lies with Hindu nationalists and the state apparatus they control. This was evident from the fact that the campaigns mentioned above took place in sequence, in the order they have been presented here, a clear indication of some coordination. The masses have no doubt played a role, but because they were mobilized by vigilante groups whose ideological orientation was obvious. They often insisted, for instance, that their victims shout "Jai Shri Ram," "Gau Mata ki Jai" (Hail the Cow-mother!), or "Jai Hanuman!" (Hail Hanuman!)[128]

while beating them up.[129] Crowd mobilization via the exploitation of identity symbols by experienced activists is a phenomenon that has been noted in past riots between Hindus and Muslims, particularly during religious processions—the very epitome of a crowd—that expert provocateurs can easily turn into hordes of attackers.[130]

While the responsibility for anti-Muslim violence related to the cow protection as well as the anti-love-jihad and Ghar Wapsi campaigns lay with Hindu nationalist groups, collusion between vigilantes and the state apparatus, especially the police, was obvious in most of these movements—an all-pervasive phenomenon to which we now turn.

7

A De Facto Hindu Rashtra

INDIAN-STYLE VIGILANTISM

GILLES FAVAREL-GARRIGUES and Laurent Gayer define vigilantism as "a range of collective coercive practices, which are often violent and usually illegal, that aim to keep order and/or mete out justice, in order to enforce legal or moral norms."[1] Vigilantes, therefore, act as "outlaw law enforcers," whether in self-defense groups or ideological militias, setting up people's courts or handing their victims over to the police. Although this repertoire covers a variety of modi operandi, two ideal types stand out: first, vigilantes attack individuals or groups whose customs are perceived as deviant and/or who arouse fear among the local majority;[2] second, these same groups (and others) go after members of their own community on the pretense that they are betraying the said community and its traditions (be they religious, cultural, social, or other). In both cases, the method used involves a degree of physical and symbolic violence.

Vigilantism is inherent in the mission that the RSS assigned itself from its inception. After all, Hedgewar's aim was to defend and promote Hindus' interests, by force if necessary, over other groups seen as posing a threat to them, starting with Muslims. But the RSS only very rarely resorted to the use of force itself, preferring to rely on persuasion and to outsource its coercion through violence to some of its affiliates.[3] In addition to the Bajrang Dal (BD), other vigilante organizations, especially those specializing in cow protection, have developed since 2014. These vigilante groups—which do not systematically have ties with the Sangh Parivar, as will be seen in this chapter—could not have blossomed and flourished without the tacit consent of the state and, in particular, its armed wing: the police. The osmosis between the state's repressive apparatus and these private armies has been conducive to the emergence of a de facto Hindu Rashtra. Furthermore, the violence has not only affected minorities and has not only been physical, as digital vigilantism has emerged on social media.

The Bajrang Dal, the Sangh Parivar's Armed Wing

In previous chapters, the Bajrang Dal was most often described as one of the RSS branches best capable of broadening the Sangh Parivar's social base. But more than an instrument of plebeianization, the BD has become the RSS's armed wing. As early as the 1990s, the BD set up training camps at which its activists were put through grueling physical exercises. In 2004, the organization's president justified the activities at these camps by pointing to the Muslim threat, claiming they were "to defend society and the social fabric against abductors and molesters of women, thieves, Pakistan's Inter-Services Intelligence agents and Bangladeshi infiltrators."[4] The leader of the camp in Ahmedabad, in fact, explained in one of the rare interviews published on the topic: "The jehadis have no fear of death. They learn this at an early age in the madarassas. We must also end our fear of death."[5]

This rhetoric clearly indicates that the Bajrang Dal camps still follow a logic of strategic emulation that involves imitating the Other in order to resist him. This process also brings in new references to Zionism and a mental transposition of the situation prevailing in Israel to India. One BD leader thus explained in 2000 that, in fact, Hindu nationalists draw their inspiration from Israel, as that country trains its citizens in the art of war to enable them to defend themselves in a hostile environment. And the man goes on: "India's [situation is] even worse. Israel has threat only from outsiders while India faces threat from even those inhabiting it."[6] Another BD member at the camp added an equally telling remark:

"I am of the secret service of Bajrang Dal. Israel's Mossad is my inspiration."

Some thirty Bajrang Dal camps were established throughout India in the 1990s, along with others going by the name of Durga Vahini. These Durga Brigades (named after the Hindu goddess better known as Kali), which appeared in the 1990s to band together Hindu nationalism's female "youth," adopted *modi operandi* entirely copied from the BD, even if they stressed the defense—especially self-defense—of young Hindu women. Female Hindu nationalists would undergo the same rigorous calisthenics and paramilitary exercises as Bajrang Dalis, including training in the use of firearms.[7] The BD has continued to organize training camps of that kind on a yearly basis. In 2017, it held seven-day camps in six regions of Uttar Pradesh. That year, the number of the youngsters who signed up increased from 240 in 2016 to almost 400. The training module at the camps includes martial arts, hurdle jumping, air gun firing, rope climbing, and use of lathi (sticks) in combat situations.[8]

Although guns made their first appearance in the Bajrang Dal in the mid-1980s, the outfit places greater attention on bladed and other melee weapons. The movement's preferred instrument is the trishul (trident), a weapon associated with Shiva, which, as a result, is exempt from the provisions of the Indian Arms Act. The organization likes to describe the object as a harmless religious symbol, but in fact its blades are more than ten centimeters long, and many of the victims of riots in which BD activists were involved were wounded by them. Altogether, the movement estimated that it had handed out more than 500,000 of these weapons between 1986 and 2004.[9] And in fact, by the early 2000s, the BD claimed at least twice as many activists, with a membership of 1,250,000 in 2001, according to its president.

What does the Bajrang Dal use this strike force against? The organization has sent some of its troops to Jammu and Kashmir to protect Hindu victims from attacks by jihadists; it has fought against Christian missionaries, particularly in Gujarat and Odisha;[10] and it has assigned itself the mission of moral policing. Among the BD's primary targets have been artists who, according to the group, do not show Hindu culture

sufficient respect. Its initial target was the celebrated painter M. F. Husain.[11] In 1996, BD activists attacked the gallery selling the artist's work
in Ahmedabad. They destroyed canvases and wall hangings representing
the Buddha, Hanuman, and Ganesh worth Rs 15 million (200,000
USD). But the official cause of their fury was a canvas dating from 1976
that depicted the goddess Saraswati too scantily clad for their taste.[12]
Hussain again fell prey to the BD's vigilantism on May 2, 1998, when
activists ransacked the painter's apartment in Bombay in protest against
his painting *Sita Rescued*, which depicted the famous scene in the Ramayana where Sita is freed from Ravana's clutches.[13]

The Bajrang Dal does not direct its moral policing solely at the supposedly blasphemous nature of certain works. They also take issue with
artwork that, according to them, attacks Hindu social traditions. The
BD has used strong-arm tactics in relation to depictions of the status of
women in society, for instance, as exemplified in the controversies surrounding the films of Deepa Mehta. In 2000, the Canadian Indian director made a film on the life of Hindu widows in Varanasi in the 1930s,
when these women were condemned to celibacy and begging. The VHP
president immediately declared that the film insulted "ancient Indian
culture and traditions"[14] and threatened "more violent protest" if Deepa
Mehta tried to shoot in India. She did so nevertheless after having se-
cured all the necessary authorizations from the central government and
the authorities of Uttar Pradesh. A set that was built on the banks of the
Ganges was totally ransacked by BD militants.

The movement has also protested celebrations perceived as Western.
The event that receives the most attention is Valentine's Day, described
as a symbol of Western depravity, giving BD activists the opportunity
to indulge in brutal physical attacks: young people who celebrate the
day together have been beaten up, and shops selling Valentine's Day
iconography or decorated with it have been plundered.

In Gujarat, while the Bajrang Dal was only one actor among many in
the 2002 pogrom, in the aftermath it made sure that victims of the violence did not lodge complaints and that witnesses kept quiet. Babu Bajrangi, a BD leader who has since been sentenced for his participation in

the Ahmedabad riots, deployed intimidation tactics on a vast scale. In 2006, he notified the owners of movie theaters in Gujarat that he was opposed to the screening of the film *Parzania*, which recounts the 2002 riots through the true story of a family whose child has been missing ever since. All of the theaters yielded under pressure, and as a result, the film has not been distributed in the state in which it was set.[15] A retired civil servant from Mehsana District, N. K. Acharya, petitioned the court to make the screening of the film possible.[16] He in turn was subject to acts of intimidation, kidnapped, and confined for two weeks in March 2007.[17]

While the Bajrang Dal thus got its start many years ago, it very naturally gained ground in the context spawned by the Hindu nationalists' power grab. Since 2014, the BD has taken part in every agitation campaign launched by the Sangh Parivar, from the fight against love jihad to Ghar Wapsi to the cow protection movement. It draws the same idle, angry young men as it did in the 1990s–2000s, helping them recover their self-esteem. One twenty-three-year-old member told Annie Gowen, a *Washington Post* correspondent in India, that after having taken part in a training camp run by the VHP (the BD's parent organization), "I have a strange sense of confidence now. The group has taught us what is right, what we need to do for society." Such confidence attests to the ability of the Sangh Parivar to instill meaning in the lives of youth in search of self-esteem or even simply a goal in life. But the same person also admitted that he had been trained to exert a form of violence that left no mark: "We have been taught to not hit the head and chest— that can be fatal. We beat them in such a way so they get these serious, silent injuries—on the backs, on the legs—so they do not die. Otherwise, there will be a case against us."[18]

These remarks confirm that this brand of violent vigilantism is anything but spontaneous. Not only that: they imply an undercover relationship with the state. In the preceding discussion of the campaigns against love jihad, for Ghar Wapsi, and in the name of cow protection, forms of collusion with state institutions, whether the police or the judiciary, were brought to light.[19] I will now examine the implications of this attitude in terms of osmosis or state capture by the Sangh Parivar since 2014, especially in states governed by the BJP, such as Haryana and Uttar Pradesh.[20]

Vigilantes and State Administrations

In the social science literature on vigilantism, the relationship between the state and vigilante groups is subject to intense discussion.[21] Some authors, such as Les Johnston, define vigilantism as a citizens' movement whose actions are spontaneous and undertaken without the state's authority or support.[22] Others, such as R. M. Brown[23] and R. Abrahams,[24] do not rule out the existence of ties between such groups and state institutions, starting with the police. The motivations behind these relationships can vary in nature: ideological affinities, convergence of interests, compliance with a political diktat when rulers impose biased behavior on law enforcement, and so on. Such dynamics can lead to establishing a continuum (the police outsource their dirty work to vigilantes) or overlapping functions (men in uniform assist vigilantes in the field or join them when their workday is finished). The variety of interpretations partly reflects the diversity of practices, as some vigilantes take the law into their own hands (historically, this is the case especially in the United States), whereas others simply turn their prey over to the police. Moreover, not only is the state not a monolith, but within an institution such as the police, the lower echelons sometimes act with considerable autonomy.

The variety of social science researcher interpretations of the phenomenon thus partly mirrors the diversity of methods. I offer my own interpretation in the present case, drawing on studies of more specialized movements than the Bajrang Dal. Indeed, since 2014—and even prior to then—the BD is no longer the sole agent for Hindu vigilantism, either because the Sangh Parivar has founded similar movements to confuse matters or because Bajrang Dalis themselves have joined these new movements or started others. Among the groups affiliated with the Sangh Parivar, the Gau Raksha Dal and Yuva Hindu Vahini warrant special attention due to their relations with the state.

The Police and Militias in Haryana in
Osmosis for Cow Protection

Although the Bajrang Dal has traditionally taken part in cow protection operations,[25] the most visible Hindu nationalist organization involved in this activity during Modi's first term was the Gau Raksha Dal (GRD—the Cow Protection Association), which had chapters in Punjab, Uttar Pradesh, Rajasthan, Himachal Pradesh, Gujarat, Madhya Pradesh, Maharashtra, Goa, Delhi, and Haryana. In Haryana, one of the movement's strongholds, the GRD emblem was none other than a cow's head flanked by two AK-47s (see figure 7.1). Elsewhere, daggers sometimes replace firearms on the movement's coat of arms. In practice, its members use cruder instruments: cricket and baseball bats, field hockey sticks, lathis, and so on.

As is the case in the Bajrang Dal, GRD activists are mostly young, unemployed men who are glad to be paid for their task and to recover a sort of self-esteem. An interview recorded on hidden camera by NDTV journalists thus showed that lynchings that took place in Hapur (Uttar Pradesh) and Alwar (Rajasthan) were perpetrated by a handful of young gau rakshak (and not a vengeful mob), who demonstrated extraordinary cruelty. (The victim in Alwar was beaten to death for over an hour—as evident from the videos posted on social media.) One of the assailants in Hapur who was arrested and then released—a typical scenario—told NDTV reporters that when he came out of prison, "people welcomed me with open arms, I felt very proud"—and added that he was prepared to do the same thing again.[26] The fact that a quest for self-esteem is one of the gau rakshak's motivations moreover explains why they film their exploits or have them filmed to post them on social media.

The organization's modus operandi is terribly brutal and involves relations with the police, as a body of investigative reporting has revealed. In 2016, Ishan Marvel, in The Caravan, recounted how he managed to be accepted into a GRD group in Haryana patrolling the highway linking Chandigarh and Delhi. Armed with field hockey sticks, gau rakshak searched trucks likely to be transporting cows and beat up the drivers

गो रक्षा दल

हरियाणा

FIGURE 7.1. Emblem of the Gau Raksha Dal in the state of Haryana

when they were Muslim. (Hindus merely received a reprimand.) The GRD existed before the BJP came to power in Haryana in 2014,[27] but the situation changed in 2015 with the passing of a law prohibiting cow slaughter and the sale of beef. The GRD's schemes were no longer considered illegal—and even if they were, the authorities did not find fault with them. On the contrary, in practice, the GRD and the police have arrived at a division of labor. Ishan Marvel explains that the night he joined the gau rakshak for their nocturnal highway patrol—on the pretense of helping them—their SUV was already parked near police vehicles. One of the policemen (who preferred not to be named) told Marvel, "'We put up checkpoints and wait. The volunteers [the GRD vigilantes] keep driving around, and call us when they find something. See, we have a hundred other things to think of beside cows. These guys do the job. It's good, right? Prashasan bhi poora saath de raha hai ab'— now, the administration is also supporting them fully."[28] During their patrol, one of the "volunteers" described how the "beef ban" law passed by the new BJP government of Haryana in 2015 had changed their activity: "Before the BJP brought in the new law against cow-slaughter, the vehicles [cattle trucks] were returned to the owners. So we used to get angry and burn the trucks. Now, we don't have to. The vehicles become government property. So we just hand them over to the police."[29] One of the leaders even stated, "The C[hief] M[inister] is happy with our work, and we have his blessings and full support."[30]

In Haryana, the gau rakshak have organic ties with the state. The president of the Haryana branch of the GRD, Yogendra Arya, who is also national vice president of the GRD, sits on the board of the Gau Seva Ayog, a cow welfare institution established by the Haryana government. Arya himself outlined the terms of GRD collaboration with the authorities: "'We have a huge network of volunteers and informants. As soon as someone sees something fishy, they call us up, and we then inform the volunteers of the relevant district, and the local police, who then set up joint *nakas* [checkpoints] to catch the smugglers.' He added that GRD activists usually reach the spot before the police. 'Police can't do what we do, they have to follow the laws. They don't have the resources and network we have,' he said. 'Besides, our boys work with great religious zeal.'"[31] The GRD thus acts as a community moral police, with its members closely monitoring every move of those they deem deserving of not only being reported but also receiving punishment that the group itself metes out.[32]

Nine other long-standing Sangh Parivar members also sit with Arya on the Gau Seva Ayog board.[33] The president is none other than Bhaniram Mangla, an RSS veteran who presided over the BJP in Gurgaon District for many years. Mangla has long touted the virtues of five cow-based products. He is, for instance, convinced that cow urine is effective in the treatment of cancer.[34] More prosaically, Mangla oversaw the convergence of two kinds of policing—unofficial (by the GRD) and official—with the establishment of the Haryana Cow Protection Task Force within the state police apparatus. A female police officer from the Indian Police Service, Bharati Arora,[35] was appointed to head this network, which now has specialized police officers in each district with brigades composed of seventeen persons, including two police subinspectors. But Mangla maintains that the police "cannot do all the work by itself" and thus rely on "support from gau rakshak."[36] The task force, therefore, works hand in hand with the GRD, to which it subcontracts the most thankless tasks. One local policeman thus told Marvel: "There are uncountable trucks. Who can check them all? So, we provide supervision while the GRD boys use their fervour to do the job."[37]

Haryana is known for being the state with the most vigorous cow protection operations[38] and for having the most Sangh Parivar members included in the government at the decision-making level, to the point of raising concerns among its civil servants. Its chief minister, Manohar Lal Khattar, created a specific status for these advisors with whom he meets at the start and the end of the day. These so-called officers on special duties all come from the RSS.[39] But while Haryana has gone further than other BJP-governed states, its case is not unique.

BJP-led Maharashtra made beef consumption a criminal offense in 2015, taking even one more radical step: the state government appointed honorary animal welfare officers to implement this new law, hiring former gau rakshak for the job.[40] They took pride in now having an official status with which to undertake their activities.[41] Never had the lack of distinction between nonstate actors and government authorities been so obvious.

Enjoying state protection, the GRD has gone beyond its stated agenda in many ways. Some of its members do not merely attack Muslims transporting poultry and sheep; they also seek to impose vegetarianism on the whole society[42] in defiance of the law.[43] Beyond that, they sometimes prefer extortion to the purity propounded by their leaders. Instead of confiscating the transporter's cargo, they exact payment of often large sums of money to buy their silence. And the police themselves began to practice similar acts of extortion.[44] They, for instance, demanded bribes to turn a blind eye on cow smuggling or on the sale of dishes prepared with cow meat by Muslim restaurants and shops.[45] Such practices were denounced not only by investigative journalists but also by some recruits, such as the former Dacoit Renu Yadav[46] and even one of the 114 GRD squad leaders in Haryana, who complained to Pragya Tiwari, another investigative journalist: "I did so much for Hindu society. I broke the back of Muslim cow smugglers. But Hindu traitors and some rakshak take bribes from Muslim smugglers and let cows get slaughtered."[47]

Such incidents prompted Narendra Modi himself to come out of the silence he had observed regarding love jihad and Ghar Wapsi. Two days after a report on Times Now (a channel that generally supports the government) described some of the gau rakshak's practices, he stated, "I urge the state governments to prepare a dossier of such self-proclaimed volunteers and big cow protectors. It will be found that 70 to 80 per cent are such people who commit such bad deeds which society does not accept. To hide their bad activities, they don the mantle of cow protectors."[48] Shortly afterward, on August 20, 2016, the GRD chief in Punjab, Satish Kumar, was arrested on three charges: rioting, extortion, and sodomy.[49] At the same time, two states governed by the BJP, Haryana and Uttarakhand, decided to draw up a list of officially recognized gau rakshak after having checked their service records.[50] Modi drew the wrath of the most radical Sangh Parivar elements, including an RSS spokesman who pointed out that such a remark should have been "avoided."[51] In a new speech, Modi replaced the figures of "70–80%" by a very different approximation ("a handful"), to the RSS's great satisfaction.[52] Then, RSS chief Mohan Bhagwat, in his annual speech given during the autumn Vijaydashami celebration, took the opportunity to praise the gau rakshak.[53]

It has already been shown how the RSS has penetrated the state with the BJP's rise to power, putting it in a position to influence the administration, particularly in matters of education. The preceding pages have illustrated an additional case, this one pertaining to the sphere of law and order. There, the Sangh Parivar is playing both sides of the board. On one hand, it is involved in direct action through its specialized militias, in particular the Gau Raksha Dal, dedicated to cow protection. On the other, it exercises indirect authority on the police through such government bodies as the Gau Seva Ayog, in Haryana, or even the office of the chief minister. This indirect authority primarily aims to enable the militias to implement the Sangh Parivar agenda without hindrance, as outlaw law enforcers. The RSS, in this regard, displays features not only of a shadow government dictating its law to elected officials but also of a parallel power structure, its pyramid connecting the top leaders to a dense network of activists. The way in which Bhagwat contradicted Modi's remarks about gau rakshak accused of criminal activity, and the role of RSS members in the administration of Haryana, reflect the RSS's long-standing aspiration to take on the role of the prince's advisor, the Raj Guru, in addition to its traditional activities aiming at reforming societies at the grassroots level.

A Priest and Militia Chief Captures the State: Yogi Adityanath in Uttar Pradesh

The situation described above—and which can be observed in Haryana in its purest form—is not the only possible scenario. In Uttar Pradesh, Yogi Adityanath's rise to power has created an atypical situation in which the head of the executive is also a religious leader and a militia chief.

Yogi Adityanath is primarily the *mahant* (chief priest) of the Nath Hindu sect, whose base is established at one of the most prestigious Hindu complexes (both temple and monastery) in northern India, Gorakhnath, located in the city of Gorakhpur (Uttar Pradesh). In this regard, he is also the heir of a long line of Hindu nationalists. His two predecessors were Digvijaynath, who joined the Hindu Mahasabha in 1937 and was elected MP of Gorakhpur thirty years later (in 1967), and Avaidyanath, who succeeded him as the head of the temple and as a Hindu Mahasabha MP, before going over to the BJP.[54] Both these men (from the Rajput caste, like Adityanath, an aspect revisited further on) were embodiments of Savarkarism, an ideology that is less interested in reforming Hinduism over the long term—a clear goal of the RSS—than by immediate action (through political channels and/or violence).[55] Yogi Adityanath has remained true to this radical activism even as he was promoted within the BJP.

Yogi Adityanath—initiated into the Nath sect by Swami Avaidyanath in 1993—first attracted attention when he elbowed his way into politics in the late 1990s. Although he was not made chief priest until 2014, upon the death of Swami Avaidyanath, in 1998, he was elected at the age of twenty-six to the MP seat previously held by Avaidyanath in Gorakhpur. He immediately established the Gau Raksha Manch (Cow Protection Front), which recruited and trained young Hindu nationalists. A year later, in 1999, the police filed a case against him—along with twenty-four of his supporters—for having launched an assault on a Muslim village in Uttar Pradesh, with the aim of desecrating its cemetery. The ensuing clashes, during which Yogi Adityanath's men made use of firearms, left one person dead.[56]

Following the BJP's defeat in the Uttar Pradesh state elections in 2002, Yogi Adityanath converted his Gau Raksha Manch into a militia, the Hindu Yuva Vahini (HYV—Hindu Youth Brigade), with the purpose of promoting his political career beyond Gorakhpur. While cow protection remained an important article of faith, the primary goal of the HYV, as set out in its constitution, was to "reorganize the Hindus" to strengthen Hindu society and religion.[57] On the pretext of better organizing Hindus, Yogi Adityanath assigned the HYV activists a road map to promote his interests in some dozen districts of eastern UP: in January–February, they were supposed to reach out to Dalits and share at least one meal with them; in February–March, their mission was to recruit new members; in April–May, they went door-to-door soliciting volunteers to attend rallies; and the rest of the year they were instructed to consolidate the organization.[58] The HYV soon mushroomed.[59] As a militia devoted to one man, the HYV is thus also at the confluence of religious and criminal dynamics, all the while bearing out the definition of vigilantism as outlaw law enforcement. On June 19, 2002, for instance, HYV activists raided Mohan Mundera village, where a young Dalit woman had allegedly been raped and killed by Muslims. They torched forty-two Muslim homes in retaliation.[60]

The movement became specialized in fomenting the kind of low intensity communal riots that Sudha Pai and Sajjan Kumar have analyzed in *Everyday Communalism* (see chapter 3). The clashes, which numbered in the dozens as of 2002, aimed to polarize the electorate along religious lines.[61] During Ramadan in 2005, for instance, the HYV stepped up its provocation in the little city of Mau by using loudspeakers to recite the Ramayana in the vicinity of mosques at prayer time. A riot broke out, leaving nine people dead.[62] Two years later, rioting again occurred in Gorakhpur when the HYV intervened following clashes between the Moharram procession and a Hindu wedding procession in which one of the members was grievously injured. The violence left five dead. The police ended up putting Yogi Adityanath in prison for the duration of the Moharram celebration during which he vowed to destroy the *tazias* (replicas of Hussain's tomb carried in the procession).[63]

This sudden surge of the rule of law was short-lived, and Yogi Adityanath continued to groom his image with increasingly provocative speeches. He, for instance, instructed his followers attending a rally in 2013: "Shout 'Jai Shri Ram' whenever you hear the Azaan [call to prayer]. . . . Workers of the Hindu Yuva Vahini will not allow Muslims to live in Hindustan."[64]

Yogi Adityanath is one of the Hindu nationalist leaders who has expressed his anti-Muslim xenophobia in the most forthright manner since 2014. In 2015, for instance, he declared in a speech in Varanasi: "When the Hindu *samaj* goes for *darshan* of Vishwanath then Gyanvapi mosque taunts us. If that's how it is, give us permission, we will install Gauri, Ganesh and Nandi in every mosque. . . . Everyone can come to Kashi [Varanasi] but only Muslims are allowed in Mecca and Medina."[65]

Due to the controversies surrounding the HYV, Yogi Adityanath was forced to dissolve the organization. In its place he started the Yogi Adityanath Hindu Yuva Vahini (YAHYV), explaining on its website that the movement's leaders

don't want any kind of mafia or criminal elements to join this group. If any member of the group is found doing offensive activity then such candidates will be eliminated from the group. As the Hindu Yuva Vahini has a constitution and the membership of the candidates can be canceled if the candidate is convicted in any kind of offense by the court. Before providing the membership the candidates' background will be checked in details and all the activities of the candidates will be over looked for 6 months. If in these 6 months the candidates is [*sic*] found doing any kind of activity against the terms of the group, such candidates will not be provided the membership for the group. So all the candidates who want to become the member of the Yogi Hindu Yuva Vahini group must not go against the terms of the group and must not be indulge [*sic*] in any kind of criminal activity.[66]

The raft of precautions Yogi Adityanath took in this case attests to the presence of criminal elements in the former HYV that he was clearly seeking to exclude.

Even more than Yogi Adityanath's scandalous image, it is his independence that made the BJP and even the RSS chafe, the latter fearing that it could no longer control a man hailing from a tradition that had never been entirely in step with the Sangh Parivar. In fact, Yogi Adityanath recurrently tried to twist the arm of the BJP leaders, threatening to withdraw his support if the party did not field some of his protégés in local or national elections. When, in 2002, the BJP rejected the candidacy of one of Adityanath's aides, Radha Mohan Das Agrawal, he ran under the Hindu Mahasabha banner with Yogi Adityanath's backing— and defeated the BJP candidate. Five years later, Yogi Adityanath threatened the BJP that he would field seventy candidates if the party did not nominate one of his lieutenants.[67] The BJP gave in. As the 2017 election to renew the Uttar Pradesh assembly approached, the BJP attempted to neutralize Yogi Adityanath by making him a minister in the Modi government,[68] but he resisted the pressure and retained his freedom, emancipated from the HYV as well,[69] and ended up establishing himself as the party's leader in the most populous state of India—even when, according to CSDS exit polls, only 7.4 percent of respondents wanted him to become Uttar Pradesh's chief minister.[70]

The Yogi Adityanath Regime

In 2017, the BJP made Yogi Adityanath the first chief minister in India able to lay claim at once to a religious status and a private army, which reflected both the balance of power he had established and an admission within the party, which no longer ruled out collaboration with a group of violent vigilantes and a form of theocracy. In fact, one of Yogi Adityanath's deputy chief ministers, Keshav Prasad Maurya, was himself a former Bajrang Dal cadre who had been active in the Ramjanmabhoomi movement as well as in cow protection campaigns and who faced charges in ten criminal cases, including a murder case in which he is the primary accused.[71] Before joining the state government, he had been appointed BJP state president, again confirming that the BD could serve as a launchpad for a political career. While Maurya was the OBC face of the BJP in the Yogi Adityanath government, most of the ministers belonged to upper castes, yet another example of the sociological profile of the Hindu nationalist ruling class and core constituency: in a council of ministers thirty-seven strong, twenty-eight belonged to upper castes.[72]

The regime Yogi Adityanath installed reserved a role for his militia. Some militants relished in his taking office in extremely blunt terms. One of them, comparing Yogi Adityanath and Modi, told the *New York Times*: "All of us in our colony felt that Modi would allow us to kill Muslims. Muslims were scared. But nothing happened. When Yogi became chief minister, they [the Muslims] were scared again."[73] The YAHYV went about threatening Muslims in the same vein.[74] And they carried out their threats on numerous occasions, beating to death Muslims accused of love jihad,[75] storming the dome of a mosque to raise the Indian flag above it[76] and increasing operations to combat land jihad.[77] But after becoming chief minister, Yogi Adityanath disbanded the YAHYV to promote a form of state-sponsored vigilantism.[78]

Two of his initial decisions involved shutting down all slaughterhouses that did not have proper licenses—thereby depriving many Muslims of their livelihood—and setting up brigades within the police force called anti-Romeo squads, which carried out moral policing on the pretense of protecting women:

Out in full force, the newly-formed squads at all the 1,500 police stations of UP appear to have set the cat among the pigeons and panicked everyone. The anti-Romeo squads can strike with lightning speed, putting over 2,000 young men through the wringer in just the first three days: some, for sporting long hair; some, for standing near

girls' schools and colleges; and, some, for doing nothing. They haul
up, chastise, upbraid, frisk, humiliate, shame—one man was made to
do sit-ups in public, holding his ears—forced to take good-conduct
pledge, whisked off to police stations, detained, interrogated, let off
or arrested. Young girls and couples (so what if some have been sib-
lings or married?) usually get morality lectures. Across markets,
malls, schools, colleges, coaching centres, crowded places-the UP
police are very, very busy.[79]

In this case the police were doing the work of a "soft" vigilante militia,
but soon they were asked to work hand in hand with armed groups
previously associated with Yogi Adityanath. Ex-members of the YAHYV
and the Hindu Samaj Party (an offshoot of the Hindu Mahasabha) thus
devoted their energies to provoking clashes between Hindus and Muslims, with the aim of destroying Muslim homes, shops, restaurants, and
small businesses. If the police intervened, it was more often to appre-
hend the victims rather than the instigators of violence. Once the victims were released on bail by the local courts, the police arrested them
again, detaining them according to a stringent law passed in 1980, the
National Security Act (NSA), intended for criminals posing a threat to
state security, under which individuals can be held without charge for
up to twelve months. The riots of 2017—during the first year of Yogi
Adityanath's government—saw not only a rise in the number of deaths
(forty-four, compared to twenty-nine in 2016 and twenty-two in 2015)
but 160 arrests in the framework of the NSA as well.[80] Recourse to the
NSA has devastated entire families, and the fear of being subjected to it
has instilled mute apprehension among Muslims.[81] A former police officer, S. R. Darapuri, noted in this regard, "Chief minister Yogi has
turned Uttar Pradesh into a police state. . . . For the first time in Indian
history, this law is being misused so much. This is part of the BJP policy
to rule through terror. They are using the police as their power arm to
overawe the Dalits and minorities."[82]

Not only have the police been allowed to resort to the NSA in new
ways, but they have also been encouraged to open fire, in the name of
law and order, on those suspected of a crime in the framework of Opera-

tion Clean.[83] Explaining the modus operandi of this operation, Yogi Adityanath informed the Uttar Pradesh assembly that forty criminals had thus been killed within a year in shootouts with the police. There were reportedly 1,200 shootings of this kind—which are supposed to be preceded by a warning shot—between February 2017 and February 2018, a record.[84] Victims of such shootings were mainly Muslims, some of whom their families claim were killed in cold blood. One of the most respected lawyers in India, Prashant Bhushan, an advocate at the Supreme Court, after having investigated the subject with support from the NGO Citizens Against Hate, concluded, "People are being murdered in an organised manner and on a large scale on the orders of the Uttar Pradesh chief minister."[85] The National Human Rights Commission launched an inquiry to determine the facts in seventeen cases concerning Muslims in which the victims were abducted and then killed. The commission, even before undertaking its investigation, issued a statement saying, "The police personnel in the state of Uttar Pradesh appears to be feeling free, misusing their powers in the light of an undeclared endorsement given by the higher-ups. It further appears that they are using their privileges/legal authority to settle scores with the people which in a civilized society, where rule of law is fundamental edifies [sic] cannot be accepted. The police force is to protect the people and this kind of alleged encounter killings would send a wrong message to the society by creating an atmosphere of fear."[86] The sense of police impunity in Uttar Pradesh was further reinforced by the fact that as soon as Yogi Adityanath came into office, he proceeded to withdraw all the complaints that state had filed against him and his associates since the 1990s and that had remained on hold.[87] Some pertaining to him dated back to 1995;[88] others concerned VHP and BJP members implicated in the Muzaffarnagar riots[89] (including 13 charges—out of a total of 131—for murder).[90] At the request of human rights organizations, in the summer of 2018 the Supreme Court reacted to Yogi Adityanath's activities on two fronts: first, it asked him to explain the rise in the number of victims of police violence (which totaled fifty-eight between his swearing in and the month of August 2018);[91] second, it refused to dismiss the case over his 2007 hate speech, for which he had been briefly imprisoned.[92] This intervention did not significantly alter Yogi Adityanath's policies.[93] First, the petitioner in the 2007 hate-speech case was implicated in a rape case and sentenced to life imprisonment.[94] Second, Yogi Adityanath's conduct vis-à-vis minorities remained the same. The UP police were asked to make sure that there would be no animal sacrifices during the Eid celebration in August 2018 "in public or in areas which have mixed population."[95] This measure—which resulted in forms of harassment preventing Muslims from celebrating Bakrid in several places[96] and in some Muslims refraining from taking part in the festival[97]—was consistent with Yogi Adityanath's attempts to suppress Islam from the public sphere. In 2017, this approach had already resulted in the removal of the Taj Mahal from tourist brochures in Uttar Pradesh,[98] as the chief minister claimed it did not reflect Indian culture.[99] The "Mughal Museum" that was under construction in Agra was also renamed after Shivaji in 2020.[100]

Yogi Adityanath also presided over the militiaization of the police in his state by saffronizing it. This evolution occurred with the chief minister extending an invitation in 2017 to police stations throughout Uttar Pradesh to partake in Hindu Janmasthani celebrations and decorate the premises appropriately. Whereas "for most Indians, the thana [police station] is the site of their most basic—and often most important—interactions with the state," an informed observer commented, "The police station is no longer, even symbolically, a secular entity."[101] This evolution of the police could already be detected in the religious devotion some officers showed the chief minister. In 2018, during Guru Purnima (a religious celebration in which disciples pay tribute to their guru), one of the police officers responsible for security at the Gorakhnath Temple had himself photographed in uniform kneeling before the chief priest and receiving his blessing. Guru Purnima, together with Vijaydashami, is one of the two ritual occasions when Yogi Adityanath trades his role as head of government for that of mahant (high priest) of Goraknath and therefore resides at the temple. During the Navratri celebration, he is also expected to perform the Kanya Puja by washing the feet of nine young girls, pasting a devotional symbol (*tika*) on their forehead, and giving them a garland called a *chunri*.[102] But Yogi

Adityanath is not perceived as a priest only during these rituals. All manner of actors in the public sphere—including journalists[103]—routinely bow at his feet.

The Rise of a Parallel State: Law and Order as Moral Order

BJP governments have traditionally protected Hindu nationalist vigilantes. The interpenetration of militias and Haryana police departments, for instance, mirrors BJP practices in Gujarat, where, when the BJP came to power in the state, Hindu nationalists were able to appoint trusted associates leagued with such controversial organizations as the Bajrang Dal to jobs in the administration and especially in the police.[104] In fact, the boundary between law enforcement and these movements became so blurred in Gujarat that it contributed to Bajrang Dali members entering the police and vice versa. The paramilitary Home Guards—a civilian force used by the authorities to maintain law and order at the local level—have recruited vast numbers of RSS members and Bajrang Dalis.[105] In the 1990s, Digvijay Singh, then the Madhya Pradesh chief minister who had BD militants arrested when they came to demonstrate in his state, noted that among the people brought in were four police officers from Gujarat.[106]

Between 1998 and 2004, the Vajpayee government resisted pressing demands from Congress-governed states—Madhya Pradesh and Rajasthan—to dissolve the Bajrang Dal. At the time of the Vajpayee government, a certain restraint nevertheless prevailed. When Dara Singh, the man who murdered the Christian missionary Graham Staines and his sons in 1999, was jailed in January 2000 after a year on the run and a BJP MP, Dilip Singh Judeo, offered to take on his defense, he had to recuse himself after being reprimanded by the BJP president.

Such inhibitions have melted away since 2014, as illustrated in the cases of Haryana and Uttar Pradesh. Several factors account for this change. First, the RSS, as a modern Raj Guru, exerts a strong influence over the government of certain states, such as Haryana, thus shaping public policies—some of which pertain to law and order—from within. This enables its militias to act with total impunity. In Uttar Pradesh, as mentioned above, the functions of head of government, spiritual leader, and militia chief are all wrapped up in one person.

The Weight of Political Protection

Beyond these two cases in point—Haryana and Uttar Pradesh—the significance of the trend can be perceived by enlarging the focus. In every state governed by the BJP, members of Sangh Parivar militias enjoy political protection. In Gujarat, the Bajrang Dal member Kunal, as portrayed by Moyukh Chatterjee, said that in the event of trouble with the police, he calls the Bajrang Dal office in Ahmedabad and "make[s] [his leaders] speak to the police." And Chatterjee concludes, "For Kunal and his boys, the police are a malleable force that can be molded to fit their agenda of Hindu supremacy. This happens through persuasion and appeals to policemen to help protect shared Hindu interests or through connections with politicians."[107]

Such political protection exists at the national level in a diluted form. In its ruling against the banalization of lynching cited in chapter 6, the Supreme Court recommended that the government pass a law creating "a separate offence for lynching." Instead of doing so, the government stated that responsibility for the matter fell to the states. Some ministers even defended lynchers who were wanted by the police. Jayant Sinha, the minister of state for civil aviation, for instance, took up the defense of seven gau rakshak indicted by the court in the state of Jharkhand— where Sinha was elected MP in 2014—before they were released on bail. Sinha even feted them upon their release from prison by placing garlands around their necks.[108] The ensuing controversy took on still greater proportions when another member of the government, Nitin Gadkari, justified these actions in the name of "free speech."[109] The government eventually set up a high-level committee headed by Home Secretary Rajiv Gauba to examine how best to stem "mob violence and lynchings," of which it still claimed to be unable to gauge the scale for lack of reliable statistics.[110]

Alongside this, Hindu nationalist leaders justified lynchings in multiple ways. A BJP MLA from Hyderabad explained that they would continue as long as the cow was not recognized by law as Rashtra Mata (Mother of the Nation),[111] and another MLA, from Uttar Pradesh, claimed that the lynchings were due to Muslim population growth.[112] Indresh Kumar, a senior RSS leader, said that the condition for lynchings to cease was for people to stop eating beef.[113] Vasundhara Raje Scindia, BJP chief minister of Rajasthan, ascribed the lynchings to the underemployment affecting Indian youth: "This is the problem that stems out of population explosions. People wanting jobs, people are frustrated that they are not being able to get jobs. There is frustration which is spreading across communities and people. . . . It's not something that is coming out of the state. It's coming out of the people's angry reaction to their circumstances."[114] These Sangh Parivar leaders, who held responsibilities at the national and state levels, justified the lynchings in the name of cow protection instead of trying to control them.

Militias as Interface and Police Porosity

While the political protection of vigilantes defending cows renders the police powerless to stop them, the same police can also be complicit with Sangh Parivar militia groups, such as the Gau Raksha Dal and Bajrang Dal. Some police officers adopt this attitude because they participate in an extortion racket linked to cow protection, as mentioned above. Additionally, in BJP-ruled states, they sometimes help Hindu nationalist armed wings out of a sort of zeal, particularly those hoping for a promotion.[115] Last, ideological sympathies and anti-Muslim bias are not rare among them. Such affinities sometimes reflect the strategy of entryism deployed by Hindu nationalists. Captain Ganesh Karnik, a BJP Member of the Legislative Council (the upper house of the state legislature) in Karnataka, interviewed by journalists from Cobrapost and Gulail.com at party headquarters in Mangalore (Karnataka), briefly explained the techniques used by the Sangh Parivar to infiltrate the police: "We have tried to send some of our boys into police. When I talk to students I tell them to join the police. So when we need help there are a lot of karyakartas [activists], RSS. Sixty percent of the young constables are our students."[116]

The role played by the militias as an interface between state and society on the ground is worth noting. Once again, Kunal's case is highly instructive: on one hand, he acts as a police informer, used by them to keep abreast of all manner of trafficking; on the other, he aids citizens in their dealings with the police or to dispense summary (or "the people's") justice through a "civil defense committee." This is a source of pride for these young, idle "muscle men." Chatterjee points out, in this regard, that militias "give many young men a chance to be part of something bigger and grander than their precarious everyday lives. It gives them influence with powerful state officials and institutions like the police."[117]

In this respect, Kunal is one of those local intermediaries that were the focus of Ward Berenschot's ethnographic study of Ahmedabad—Kunal's native city. Like Berenschot's intermediaries (*dalal*, in the vernacular, or "brokers"), he is at the nexus of a local patronage network based on the exchange of favors among Hindus. These intermediaries help the inhabitants of their "constituencies" to gain access to state resources (from food rations for those living below the poverty line to reserved jobs); in riot situations, these men are opinion leaders and gang leaders for whom "their" neighborhood provides foot soldiers and protection.[118]

The Making of an Unofficial Hindu State

For all the reasons listed above, Sangh Parivar militias are participating in a process of state formation, as defined by Bruce Berman and John Lonsdale. These authors aptly distinguish the formation of the state as a social institution and state building as an administrative process.[119] Reasoning solely in terms of state building tends to reduce the history of states to their foundational period and the actions of official agents. Berman and Lonsdale's analysis, on the other hand, has the merit of considering state trajectories over the long term, while factoring in the

role of private actors as well. As the authors point out regarding the
experience of Kenya, social groups systematically work their way into
the process of state formation through the "vulgarization of power,"
which involves commandeering public authority to further private
ends.[120] This approach has obvious heuristic advantages for the analysis
of Hindu vigilante groups and the Sangh Parivar in general. It helps to
put the prima facie antistate aspect of these private armies in perspective in that, to some extent, they are the state and they form the state,
whether they actually exercise authority or influence the bureaucracy
(including the police).

State formation has, in fact, been the RSS's aim from the very start.
Since 1925, the organization has aspired to bring about a Hindu Rashtra,
which is based on the culture of a society defined as a nation and which
is self-regulating rather than being established on constitutional or
legal-rational foundations, to use Max Weber's terms. The RSS counters
the legality of the Weberian state with the legitimacy of an identity it
holds to be sacred—and it embodies "the Hindu Rashtra in miniature"
(according to Hedgewar[121]). Hindu militias in charge of moral policing
help to bring about a Hindu nation based on social structures drawing
from the sources of Hindu traditions. Vigilantes do not merely disqualify the law; they replace it by the social norms—the orthopraxy—of the
upper castes. The RSS may well be defending the state as it never has
before but only in that, by taking control of it, it can influence minds
through education and giving free rein to Sangh Parivar affiliates, the
only ones in a position to create a Hindu nation.

The Hindu Rashtra is therefore indeed underway. This label perfectly
describes the ambivalence of the process at stake, as Hindu Rashtra
refers as much to a people united by blood ties, a culture, and community codes as to a political framework; it is at once a society, a culture, a
nation, and—last—a political construct. In this way, the Sangh Parivar's
work partakes of a new formation of the state, the formation of a de
facto Hindu Rashtra on the basis of parastate societal regulations. The
Indian state was built up around a bureaucracy handed down from the
British, but there remained the task of *forming* a Hindu state, and vigilantes are working to that end. Bhagwat makes no secret about it, as evi-

denced in *The Organiser*'s account of the solemn address he gave, as
every year, at the yearly Dusshera (or Vijayadashami) rally in 2014—a
few months after the BJP victory: "Sounding the warning bell that 'mere
political power cannot bring about the desired change in society,' Shri
Bhagwat laid more emphasis on creating a class of active and vigilant
[*sic*] individuals and organisations engaged in giving direction to the
society and solving various problems. This class could help the government through its activism, awareness and maturity in national interests
and protecting the nation from possible detraction in the game of power
politics."[122] These words implicitly demonstrate that taking control of
the state matters especially in that it allows the RSS to pursue its work
on the ground without hindrance. The state is not valued in and of itself,
unlike in other ideologies that carry a certain mystique about the state.
It is merely a "facilitator," the essential role falling to social organizations
that are "vigilant" enough to guide the nation, the Hindu Rashtra. There
is no better definition of the RSS as a parallel power structure embed-
ded in the country's polity and society. It is at once the Raj Guru guiding its rulers behind the scenes and the semi-informal coordinating
body at the interface between government people and vigilante networks, those activists who are constantly on the alert and in direct contact with the society that they are out to reform and control. This arrangement may not be legal—after all, RSS leaders are influencing
governments without being accountable to the voters—but it enjoys an
increasingly strong *legitimacy* in the majority community.

The Gau Raksha Dal moreover claims to have greater legitimacy than
even the law of the Indian state. Dinesh Arya, the chief of the GRD in
Haryana in 2017, in answering Reuters journalists, does not claim to be
acting within the law but instead in accordance with a sacred cause:
"Seizing cattle is not legal and we know that well. We are not authorized
to do this, it's the police department's work," Arya said. But he claims a
higher calling: "Our religion has given us the right to stop our mother
being butchered," he said, referring to *gau mata*, or "mother cow." "We
have forcefully taken that right."[123]

This is where the Hindu Rashtra, Modi's populism, and ethnic democracy have elective affinities. The Hindu Rashtra draws its legitimacy

from the defense of the majority community's sacred culture; the prime minister embodies this majority that equates with the nation; and if the Hindu majority is equivalent to the people, democracy is the Sangh Parivar's preferred regime because, as a result, the legitimacy of its actions can appear democratic. Consequently, vigilantes even further relativize the role of the state and the partisan hue of those in power. In his interview with Cobrapost and Gulail.com, Sardhana Sangeet Som thus gives the best definition of majoritarianism in the militia state: "This is Hindustan and it does not matter which party is running the government. In a democratic country like this, there are many other ways to get things done. The police knows it well that we will do picketing, hold demonstration and all this will lead to rioting. So, they perforce cooperate with us."[124] These statements illustrate a fundamental dimension of a de facto ethnic democracy, a regime in which the majority lays down the law owing to its legitimacy and the fact that the law of the state can no longer do very much to counter this dynamic.

Digital Vigilantism and Physical Violence against "Sickularists"

In addition to minorities, secularists—called "sickularists" by Hindu nationalists, as mentioned in chapter 5—have also been targeted by vigilantes. Here, the main victims of harassment have been journalists, intellectuals, figures in the arts—filmmakers in particular[125]—such minority advocates as Harsh Mander,[126] and even religious figures fighting communalism. These men and women have been targeted physically as well as online.

Trolls and the Online Harassment of Journalists

Harassment waged via social media has given rise to veritable digital vigilantism. The 2014 election campaign described in chapter 3 offered an opportunity to measure the importance of social media for the BJP—and Narendra Modi in particular. Beyond that, the RSS, which quickly got on the digital media bandwagon—especially to spread its influence among the Hindu diaspora in the West[127]—invested very early on in this means of propagating its message, under the guidance of Ram Madhav. As of 2001, he set up "IT shakha" in Bangalore to bring together computer science engineers.[128] He then developed applications enabling him to remain in contact with the movement's cadres. Ultimately, he became involved in popular social media, such as Facebook. In an interview with Swati Chaturvedi, he explained that such channels enabled him to "connect with the masses directly" or, when the goal had a more precise focus, "[to reach] out to my target group."[129]

The entire Sangh Parivar—including the BJP—gradually started directing its army of social media correspondents away from the task of promoting its ideas and its heroes (first and foremost Narendra Modi) toward a new form of moral policing.[130] Even if the violence became verbal rather than physical, it could be almost equally damaging. Swati Chaturvedi, in her investigation into this post-2014 phenomenon, calls these so-called trolls "the goons of the online world."[131] Herself a victim of this new brand of Hindu nationalist militant, she sought them out to understand their motivations. She started with a reformed troll, Sadhavi Khosla, an enterprising young woman who, in 2014, after having spent six years in the United States, volunteered to further Modi's cause, believing in his promises of development. She became a foot soldier in the BJP's army of trolls, taking her orders from Arvind Gupta, head of the well-known National Digital Operations Centre and the person who designed Modi's social media campaign in 2014. For two years, she took part in a sort of cyberwar as a good little soldier. (The military metaphor is used by Arvind Gupta himself, who compares trolls to *yodha*, in other words "warriors.") As Khosla recalled, "It was a never-ending drip feed of hate and bigotry against minorities, the Gandhi family, the journalists on the hit list, liberals . . . anyone perceived as anti-Modi."[132] She went on:

> The mails, some of which ran into a hundred pages, made startling claims against the Congress. They said that Sonia Gandhi had conspired against Rajiv Gandhi as part of her anti Hindu stance, that Priyanka Gandhi was bipolar and had separated from her husband

Robert Vadra, that Rahul was a drug addict and married to a non-Hindu and had children but this was kept hidden. Over the years they also had reams on the corrupt deals of P. Chidambaram [former Congress finance minister] and on Barka [sic] Dutt [see below] and her "Muslim husbands."[133]

Insults took on a particularly obscene turn when they were directed at women. Among the minorities, Muslims were of course preferred targets and, among them, such Bollywood stars as Salman Khan, Shah Rukh Khan,[134] and Amir Khan, who were the victims of ferocious attacks. In 2016, Khosla sent Gupta a letter of resignation in which she wrote,

> I am a believer of Hinduism and my Hinduism has no room for such hate. If they [the trolls] go on like this they will destroy Hinduism. Even after winning they are only focused on polarizing and hate. I can't understand why we need to keep demonising Muslims and photoshop incendiary pictures. I have a young son. I don't want him to grow up in an India which is a mirror of Pakistan. I have dreams for him and I really want him to be a good person and not be infected with the virus of bigotry. My son is an American citizen. For the first time ever I am so scared at how we are turning on each other that I may move to the USA.[135]

Chaturvedi interviewed some thirty Hindu nationalist trolls, all based at BJP headquarters. These men, who, for the most part, belonged to the upper-caste lower middle class, made no secret about their disagreement with positive discrimination, which they blamed for their trouble finding jobs.[136] Above all, they were systematically critical of Islam. Chaturvedi concluded with the following point: "Every troll I met was clear about two things: Muslims are very violent and they are violent because they are non-vegetarian."[137] These trolls also exhibited an adulation for Modi that stemmed from a dual motivation, the ambivalence and potency of which was analyzed in chapter 2 when dissecting the characteristic features of his brand of populism by using Ostiguy's thesis: "Modi is seen by his bhakt as both an avenger who will persecute

those who have committed historical wrongs against them and simultaneously a man persecuted and victimized by the 'sickular' establishment."[138] Chaturvedi was perceived by her interviewees as an example
of this cosmopolitan anglophone elite, educated in "Christian colleges"
and cut off from India's realities. They said to her face what the BJP
distills with more discretion, one of them claiming,

> See, I could make out those nuns have brainwashed you. People like
> you have no idea of the reality of India. You don't know these Mus-
> lims and nuns just want to rule us again. Well, at least the nuns are
> not doing love jihad. Muslim men only want to corrupt Hindu
> women and have mixed breed with them. . . . These Muslims are
> oversexed and their own women don't satisfy them so they go after
> ours. It's all the beef they eat. . . . People like you are not really Indian
> so you don't care how much we suffer. You people are all funded by
> the West so you have to do their propaganda. You know we got real
> independence only when Modiji became PM.[139]

This quote contains a condensation of Islamophobic stereotypes, rejection of Westernized liberals, and idolatry of Modi, the only one who can
understand the people in whose name the trolls—excluded from the
anglophone elite—speak. It also illustrates the inferiority complex of
the usually poorly educated trolls, which overdetermines their rage
against knowledge and logic—especially when these qualities are displayed by assertive women.[140]

Trolling Journalists

Journalists are among the persons most often targeted by digital vigilantism. An overwhelming proportion of women are in this group, and
the threats proffered are often sexual in nature, for instance, the menace
of gang rapes. Rana Ayyub, who used to write for *Tehelka* and is the
author of *The Gujarat Files*, about the 2002 pogrom, fell prey to trolls
seeking to silence her not only by increasing their online threats but also
by posting fake messages in her name—such as one making excuses for
child rapists.[141]

Barkha Dutt, a committed Indian television journalist who spent twenty-one years at NDTV before going independent in 2017, was a victim of similar intimidation, which she alleged came from within the Indian government. She denounced it publicly when threats also targeted members of her family.[142]

The journalist who has described in greatest detail the digital vigilantism he has been subjected to is Ravish Kumar, a prominent journalist on NDTV's Hindi news channel.[143] Among the trolls harassing him is a man that Modi follows on Twitter. In his autobiographical account, *The Free Voice*—in which the word "fear" appears very often—he confides, "I make that journey from fear to courage every day. My days start with the trolls' abuses and threats and end with the thought that I should be careful for the sake of my job."[144] Like academics who refrain from inviting JNU colleagues out of fear of reprisal, local newspapers no longer commission editorials from Ravish Kumar, and parents forbid their children from following him on Twitter and Facebook.[145]

Social media has become the trolls' preferred means of spreading fake news to denigrate "liberals" and "libtards" (a combination of "liberal" and "retard" imported from Trump supporters in the United States). Arundhati Roy, for instance, was accused of giving an interview to a Pakistani journalist in which she allegedly said that "the 700,000 strong Indian Army cannot defeat the azadi gang of Kashmir."[146] This interview, which went viral on social media, never took place.

It would be extremely tedious to compile a list of all the fake news with which Hindu nationalists inundate social media. (We return to this issue in the context of the 2019 election campaign.) A number of websites have specialized in this field. One of them, AltNews, regularly provides a sampling. Such fake news presents Muslims as child rapists, women oppressors, bloodthirsty criminals, and so on, using Photoshop software or captioning illustrations in a way intended to mislead (either because the event shown took place elsewhere or years before).[147]

Modi has established direct relations with numerous trolls. In 2016, when Chaturvedi published her book, Modi had 21.6 million followers on Twitter and followed 1,375 himself. Among these carefully selected "happy few" were known trolls: "Among the handles followed by Modi,

26 accounts routinely sexually harass, make death threats and abuse politicians from other parties and journalists with special attention given to women, minorities and Dalits."[148] Modi even invited 150 of those he followed on social media to a meeting dubbed Digital Sampark, during which some of the most combative yodha took a number of selfies with him.[149] One of them, Priti Gandhi, presents himself on social media as "a huge fan of Nathuram Godse," Mahatma Gandhi's murderer.[150] Modi follows other Godse admirers on Twitter as well.[151] Among the trolls he has followed are even some who applauded the murder of the journalist Gauri Lankesh (see below),[152] "trolls" that Information and Technology Minister Ravi Shankar Prasad fiercely criticized at the time, in 2017.[153]

Arun Shourie, a former minister in the Vajpayee government sidelined by Modi like so many other BJP leaders of his generation, reckons, "By following them Modi is giving the message: I am following it. . . . It's now a party operation, one of the many operations being used to silence voices in the whole country."[154] These ruthless attacks have in fact fulfilled their mission with some victims.

It is also noteworthy that some trolls have gone after Hindu nationalist leaders deemed too moderate. Sushma Swaraj, minister of external affairs during Modi's first term, was the object of vicious attacks after she helped a Hindu-Muslim couple obtain their passports and took punitive action against the civil servant who unlawfully refused to issue their travel documents. The official also berated the wife for marrying a Muslim and asked the husband to convert to Hinduism.[155]

Criminals as Fringe Elements?
The Banalization of Savarkarism

In parallel with online harassment, traditional forms of violence have also been unleashed against "sickularists" by vigilantes—as their admiration for Nathuram Godse foretold. Godse, indeed, has become a symbol for those who claim that resorting to violence against secularists is legitimate. These characters traditionally belonged to the Savarkarite school of thought: in contrast to the RSS strategy based on discretion and long-term agendas, the Savarkarites ask for immediate, radical action and have no inhibitions. Considering that the RSS was focused on a long-term psychological and social transformation of Hindus, which implied a certain immobilism, Savarkar opted for political action through the Hindu Mahasabha, and some of his followers left the RSS to form their own militias, such as the Ram Sena and the Hindu Rashtra Dal (Hindu Nation Group), which advocated direct violent action. Nathuram Godse allegedly came from within the latter's ranks.[156] A similar itinerary was followed by Bal Thackeray, a man trained by the RSS before he broke away to form the Shiv Sena, Shivaji's Army.[157]

The Hindu Mahasabha has remained true to this political culture in the twenty-first century. In Meerut (western Uttar Pradesh), where a statue and a temple had been dedicated to Godse,[158] the local chief of the Hindu Mahasabha, Pooja Shakun Pandey, reenacted Gandhi's murder on a video that went viral. She declared: "I say with pride that if Godse did not kill Gandhi, then I would have killed him"[159]—and that the Hindu Mahasabha was about to set up Hindu courts on the lines of shariat courts to deal with "property and marriage issues."[160] Like any Hindu vigilante group, the Hindu Mahasabha combined cultural policing and the cult of violence against secular Indians.

The latter became all-pervasive during Modi's first term as new private armies started to mushroom[161] and individuals took the law into their own hands. In 2018, as mentioned in the previous chapter, two members of a Haryana-based cow vigilante group tried to kill with a pistol the student leader Umar Khalid to silence the "mad dogs" of the "JNU gang."[162] But vigilantes attacked Hindus too, including religious figures like Swami Agnivesh. The latter, even though he was a prominent member of Arya Samaj and used to wear the saffron robe, was brutally assaulted in Jharkhand (a state then governed by the BJP) in 2018 on his way to attend a rally in support of local tribes threatened with expropriation on account of an industrial construction project. Swami Agnivesh was beaten, stripped of his turban, and had his clothing torn before he could attend the function. This incident showed that the line between the Savarkarite culture and the RSS ethos was becoming increasingly blurred, as the rise of the Bajrang Dal had already shown. Even though the Sangh Parivar claimed to have had nothing to do with the incident, the eight people named in the complaint lodged with the police belonged to either the BD, the BJP, its youth wing (the BJYM), or the RSS. Local Sangh Parivar officials moreover explained the attack against Swami Agnivesh by his tolerance for meat eaters and his work in favor of tribals, which they believed indicated his affinities with the Maoists (who were active among indigenous communities), and his contacts with Christian missionaries.[163] One month later, Swami Agnivesh was again attacked by BJP supporters as he was coming to pay homage to A. B. Vajpayee, who had just died.[164]

Others were victims of killers who belonged to organizations that were either not affiliated with the Sangh Parivar or that had been founded by former RSS members who retained some relation with mainstream Hindutva. The Sanatan Sanstha (Eternal Organization) offers a good illustration of the former. It was founded by Jayant Balaji Athavale, a hypnotherapist seeking to reconcile spirituality and science. Little is known about the organization's history other than it was established in 1995, that the ashram it uses as its headquarters is located in Goa, and that it wanted to establish a Hindu Rashtra, as evident from its mouthpiece *Sanatan Prabhat*.[165] Athavale's book, *Kshatradharma* (Religion of Khastriyas), explicitly justifies violence in politics.[166] The group came to public attention in the wake of investigations by the police into two types of violent actions. First, the Sanstha set out to bomb celebrations it considered blasphemous (such as Narkasura, celebrated in Goa on the eve of Diwali)[167] and plays showing Hindu gods in a poor light.[168] Second, Sanstha *sadhak* (seekers [of truth]) used an improvised explosive device in 2008 at Cineraj Cinema at Panvel (near Mumbai) during the screening of the movie *Jodha Akbar*, which showed the Mughal emperor in a positive light. Five sadhak were arrested.[169]

Then, the Sanstha was apparently[170] implicated in the murder of four "liberals" between 2013 and 2017: Narendra Dabholkar, founder of the Maharashtra Blind Faith Eradication Committee; Govind Pansare, a veteran Indian Communist Party member; M. M. Kalburgi, former vice-chancellor of Kannada University in Hampi; and Gauri Lankesh, a Bangalore journalist who had become the Hindu nationalists' bête noire due to her courage and the stance she took against Hindutva.[171] The first three were known as "rationalists," and, as P. Sainath has pointed out, "the focus of the fundamentalists is on killing rationalists. They attack the secular spectrum as a whole, but save their worst for rationalist activists. Those, after all, are the people who attack superstition and strike at the core of fundamentalist mythologies."[172]

The Sanstha had begun campaigning against Dabholkar when he sought to convince the Maharashtra government to pass an antisuperstition bill.[173] Pansare is also believed to have been murdered by Sanstha activists for having claimed in his book on Shivaji that the ruler had Muslims in his entourage, even among his bodyguards.[174] Police have evidence that these two murders and Kalburgi's were perpetrated with the same weapon.[175]

In the case of Gauri Lankesh, the confession of one of the accused, K. T. Naveen Kumar, is revealing of the psychology and sociology of the nebula of activists at the interface of the Sangh Parivar and fringe organizations. Kumar, who had begun his Hindu nationalist career as a Bajrang Dal cadre near Mangalore—the oldest RSS bastion in Karnataka[176]—started his own organization and then met Sanatan Sanstha leaders, including Praveen, a man who told him about Gauri Lankesh and who said that he had decided "to kill her for her anti-Hindu ideology."[177] Lankesh was indeed an uncompromising secular journalist who expressed her views freely in her weekly Kannada tabloid. As a result, defamation cases had been filed by Hindu nationalist leaders, including a BJP MP.[178] Another BJP leader, an ex-Karnataka minister, commented on her murder by referring to her writings: "If Gauri Lankesh had refrained from writing articles like that, she would have probably been alive today. Gauri is like a sister to me but the way she has written against us, it is unacceptable."[179]

Such statements carried a clear message: others could meet the same fate if they said something "unacceptable." The fact that such a warning was expressed by a former minister and a sitting BJP MLA blurred the boundary between the Sangh Parivar and the fringe groups of the other Hindutva tradition herein described as Savarkarite.

After the murder of Lankesh, the boundary became even fuzzier for two reasons. First, despite the fact that the police recovered a massive cache of weapons, which included twelve crude bombs, gelatin sticks, and detonators,[180] and "details of plans to target 36 others"[181] in the course of their investigation, the government refrained from banning the Sanatan Sanstha—something the Anti Terrorist Squad of Maharashtra had sought in 2015 after the murders of Dabholkar and Pansare.[182] Furthermore, the investigation and the framing of charges have both been remarkably slow.[183] Second, some of those who posted the most indecent comments regarding Lankesh's murder were followed on social media by top BJP leaders. In reaction to a tweet by Pramod Muthalik, the founder of the Ram Sene, C. T. Ravi, the BJP MLA of Chikmagalur (Karnataka), declared online: "I condemn Muthalik's statement comparing Dogs to Gauri Lankesh. He has insulted the Dogs." Narendra Modi was among Ravi's 117,000 followers on Twitter at that time. Roop Darak, who published a similar tweet was followed by then BJP president Amit Shah. His tweet was forwarded by @NikunSahu, who was followed by both Prime Minister Narendra Modi's official handles.[184] Modi was already following several Twitter accounts that trolled Gauri Lankesh.[185]

The porosity between so-called fringe elements who had inherited the legacy of the Savarkarite modus operandi and mainstream Hindutva embodied by the RSS is largely due to the role of the Bajrang Dal, a vigilante group at the interface of both. This state of things is well illustrated by the Ram Sene (Ram's Army). The founder of this Karnataka-based organization, Pramod Muthalik, began his activist career in the RSS, which he had joined as a child, like so many other swayamsevak. And like many others, he was imprisoned for being an RSS member during the Emergency in 1975–1977. He was made a pracharak and in 1993 was seconded to the VHP, whose leader at the time, Ashok Singhal, tasked him the following year with setting up the regional branch of the Bajrang Dal.[186] In 2001, he became head of the BD for the four southernmost states of India. But for some reason, he broke away from the Sangh Parivar in 2005 to set up the Ram Sene.[187] In September 2008, in the wake of attacks in Bangalore ascribed to Islamists, he announced that 700 members of his organization had now received training in suicide bombings, adding: "We have no more patience. Tit for tat is the only mantra left to save Hinduism. If centres of religious importance for Hindus are targeted, twice the same number of religious centers of the opposite party will be smashed."[188]

The Ram Sene, like the Sanatan Sanstha, began planting bombs. The police attributed the Hubli bombing in 2008 to one of Muthalik's close associates. But the movement did not make headlines until the following year when some of its members went after women in a pub in Mangalore, deeming that they were violating Hindu tradition by drinking alcohol in public: amateur videos showing activists in the process of molesting the "guilty parties" made the rounds on social media. Unlike the Sangh Parivar, which preferred to act behind the scenes, the Ram Sene uses force openly in conducting its moral policing

Nevertheless, the Sangh Parivar and Ram Sene came closer together in the 2010s, to such an extent that in March 2014 Muthalik joined the Karnataka section of the BJP with great fanfare. However, he remained a member only for a few hours, as national headquarters rejected the decision made by its regional branch to accept him.[189]

A few months later, Modi's election having given the Hindu nationalists wings, the Sangh Parivar showed much less reserve toward figures having Muthalik's characteristics. This is an important sign that the two Hindu nationalist traditions discussed above had converged, a fact further confirmed in 2017 by the appointment of Yogi Adityanath as chief minister of Uttar Pradesh. Not only did BJP leaders endorse extremist actions by vigilante groups, but their party opened itself to radical characters. The Bajrang Dal was the main avenue for this form of upward mobility. At the local, state, and national levels, BD activists have been shifted to the party—with the RSS's blessing or active intervention, as the Nagpur-based organization in charge of allocating human resources across the Sangh Parivar. At the local level, Premi, the BD activist, became district secretary of the BJP, for instance.[190] At the national level, Pratap Chandra Sarangi, who was appointed in 2019 minister of state in the Modi government, had been the state president of the BD in Orissa in 1999 when Graham Staines and his sons were killed and when he and his followers vandalized the Orissa state assembly during a protest for the building of a Ram temple in Ayodhya.[191] Sarangi was arrested by the police along with sixty-six other demonstrators on charges that included rioting, arson, and assault.[192] As a Lok Sabha member and a first-time MP, he displayed his militancy by claiming that those who did not say "Vande Mataram" had no "right to live in India."[193] The growing influence of the Bajrang Dal-like vigilante mindset within the Sangh Parivar largely explains the Sangh Parivar's rapprochement with heirs of the Savarkarite tradition, for which violence is explicitly a legitimate mode of action.

Conclusion to Part II

THE SECOND PART OF THE PRESENT BOOK has shown that ethnic democracy has found expression in three different ways in India. First, BJP governments at the center and at the state level have promoted their definition of Hindu culture by enhancing the legal protections of cows, by opening up the state to the RSS, by rewriting the history of the country, by harassing secularists (including academics and students), and by reducing the number of NGOs operating in the country, as well as their ability to function.

Second, under the first Modi government, minorities—mostly Christians and Muslims—were stigmatized and made victims of repeated campaigns led by the Sangh Parivar in its fight against conversions, love jihad, and land jihad and in its cow protection operations. These campaigns translated into intimidation as well as violence, and even the lynchings of Muslims.

Third, these campaigns were spearheaded by vigilante groups that were often related to the Sangh Parivar. The most prominent of these groups, the Bajrang Dal, was already on the rise not only as the strike force of the Sangh Parivar in the Ayodhya movement but also as its instrument to reach out to plebeians—who had become more aspirational in the context of the implementation of the Mandal Commission report. The plebeianization-cum-lumpenization of the Sangh Parivar

248

endowed it with the necessary network of activists for the kind of cultural policing that was unleashed after 2014.

Although Hindu nationalist vigilantism was not new in India—especially in BJP-ruled states—the BJP's rise to power has brought about a difference in degree, even in essence, that has altered the country's political regime. Hindu vigilantism has become more systematic by expanding into new areas of moral policing, such as the disruption of Muslim prayers in public places, and left minorities no respite. The launching of campaigns at regular intervals has created a state of permanent mobilization—subjecting minorities to an equally permanent state of fear. Before the BJP came to power, Hindu vigilantes might fear police reprisals for their actions. Since 2014, these groups have been protected—even sponsored and guided—by Sangh Parivar leaders elected to office on the BJP ticket or who have become part of the state apparatus as special advisors and thus in a position to influence the government from within.

Officially, the state does not break the law or transgress the spirit of the Constitution—it even constantly claims to uphold it. But officials and their actions are merely the tip of the iceberg. Moreover, when Modi accused certain gau rakshak of behaving in a criminal manner, even he was upbraided by RSS leaders and forced to back down. For it was the RSS itself, deep inside the iceberg, that was orchestrating the formation of a de facto Hindu Rashtra.

This parallel power structure also lurks behind the anonymous computer screens of an army of trolls that intimidate, slander, and disinform as systematically as vigilantes in the street. The Sangh Parivar is thus forging a de facto ethnic democracy that matters more to the group than does controlling the state apparatus, which it seeks to neutralize and prevent from interfering in the name of the law—the purpose Modi served by conquering the highest office. The RSS's main task is different in nature: the goal is to conquer not state power but minds and to impose cultural and social practices rather than laws. The vigilantes' moral and social policing is intended to put India on this road, gradually. This modus operandi does not necessarily imply a transformation of the legal framework built up around the state. Changing the law would have aroused suspicion[1] and might have forced the BJP to compromise with other political forces in the Rajya Sabha, where the party was still a minority.

In that sense, the Parivar's strategy differs from the Savarkarites' traditional approaches. The former is using vigilantes for conquering and converting society in the long term. Working at the grassroots level, the Parivar tries to propagate and impose its views through persuasion (the RSS way) and coercion (the Bajrang Dal way). The core values that are diffused in these ways derive from conservative values inherited from patriarchy and the caste system. Whereas the RSS prioritizes reforming society and the collective psyche, the Savarkarites believe in direct political action, including violent means. They are more interested in the state—to conquer it or to destabilize it—than in society, and they almost systematically resort to violence. This culture of violence has been reactivated by fringe groups, including the Sanatan Sanstha, which engaged in targeted killings after 2014.

Under the first Modi government, the rise of vigilantism blurred this contrast between the two groups, whose schools of thought started to converge as the Bajrang Dal, an offshoot of the Sangh Parivar, shared an increasingly large number of Savarkarite features. Certainly, by outsourcing their dirty work to the BD, the BJP and the RSS continued to try to maintain a facade of respectability, but the BD's style gradually permeated the Sangh Parivar and the state—as evident from the fact that Bajrang Dalis became BJP cadres and even ministers or deputy-chief ministers. Online vigilantes have also transitioned to politics, as evident from the way a famous Hindu nationalist troll, Tajinder Pal Singh Bagga, was elevated to the post of BJP's spokesperson.[2] Such developments have resulted in the making of a vigilante state whose ideal type has taken shape in Yogi Adityanath's Uttar Pradesh.

If the iceberg is a useful metaphor to describe the parallel power structure model, the floating ice cap is a helpful image to better understand this variant of state vigilantism. For nothing is truly hidden in Yogi Adityanath's Uttar Pradesh: the chief minister is not only a faith leader who cannot claim to honor the (secular) Constitution but also a militia chief subject to judicial proceedings. Yogi Adityanath makes no mystery of his desire to establish a regime in which minorities are merely second-class citizens and in which the police, even more than vigilante groups (the so-called faceless mob), use strong-arm tactics to bring minorities to heel. The third part of this book will show that state vigilantism is only one of the facets of the form of authoritarianism that crystallized during Modi's first term and asserted itself during his second term, after the 2019 elections.

PART III

The Indian Version of Competitive Authoritarianism

POPULISM OFTEN LEADS TO AUTHORITARIANISM, as theoreticians of this ism have shown. Jan-Werner Müller, as mentioned in chapter 2, argues that populists are against pluralism because they claim that they represent all the people, making political opposition not only redundant but also illegitimate and even antinational. Edward Shils, whose thesis was also reviewed in chapter 2, adds that the populist, since he *is* the people, stands above institutions; his legitimacy prevails over other power centers—even when they embody legality because legality cannot compete with his legitimacy.

National-populists are even more dangerous for democracy because they exclude minorities from the people they claim to embody. Their modus operandi often results in a form of ethnic democracy where these minorities are reduced to second-class citizens, which is in itself antidemocratic, especially in India, as in this process the ruling party has relied on vigilante groups for keeping minorities in their place. These vigilante groups have resorted to violence with the blessing of the state and at the expense of the rule of law—a factor in the movement toward authoritarianism. In *How Democracies Die*, Steven Levitsky and Daniel Ziblatt consider one of the indicators of authoritarian behavior the fact that rulers "endorse violence by their supporters by refusing to unambiguously condemn it and punish it."[1]

But an authoritarian state may exert coercion more directly, by distorting electoral competition, changing the law or the Constitution, and using its security apparatus (including police forces) to suppress all opposition and to repress minorities. In parallel, the state exerts its influence over society by resorting to propaganda, spreading disinformation, and controlling the media. All these processes document Juan Linz's definition of authoritarianism in terms of "limited pluralism": "The limitation of pluralism may be legal or de facto, implemented more or less effectively, confined to strictly political groups or extended to interest groups, as long as there remain groups not created by or dependent on the state which influence the political process one way or another."[2] (When such groups no longer exist, a country is on the path to totalitarianism.)

The four chapters of part III are devoted to the Indian version of these different facets of authoritarianism under Narendra Modi.

8

Deinstitutionalizing India

AUTHORITARIANISM FINDS EXPRESSION in neutralizing not only political opposition but any institutional power center. In the cases of institutions whose officeholders are not freely appointed by the executive, this neutralization policy can follow contrasting routes, ranging from co-optation to intimidation. The former is a corrupt practice that may imply financial transactions or sinecures, including postretirement appointments. The latter implies the use of state agencies, including those in charge of law and order—whose capture, therefore, is one of the rulers' priorities.

The institutions whose officeholders are appointed by the executive are easier to control or hobble: they can be rendered nonfunctioning (or dysfunctional) due to unfilled vacancies or populated with the ruler's "friends." The latter technique is naturally the most effective one for a ruler who is eager to concentrate state power by relying on a network of trusted lieutenants. Narendra Modi has used a large palette of such practices, including the appointment in key positions of bureaucrats and policemen who had started to work with him during his Gujarat years. The chronological approach that will be adopted in this chapter will demonstrate that he resorted to increasingly drastic methods over time, a trend that culminated in arguably unconstitutional maneuvers in his second term.

To understand the decline or malfunctioning of the institutions that had contributed to the making of the world's largest democracy since 1947, it is necessary to review and scrutinize them one by one. This method is somewhat repetitive, but for a good reason: it allows the close observer to identify a pattern of authoritarianism in the making.

Who's Afraid of the Lokpal?

During Modi's first term, his desire to minimize interference from custodians of the rule of law became clear in his attempt to reform the judiciary (as will be seen below) and in delaying the appointment of the Lokpal. As chief minister of Gujarat, Narendra Modi had supported the movement initiated by the social activist Anna Hazare against corruption in 2011.[1] Hazare was demanding the creation of a Lokpal, an ombudsman who would have been entitled to investigate irregularities committed by bureaucrats and politicians, including the prime minister. In an open letter to Hazare, Modi then wrote:

> Respected Annaji, my respect for you is decades old. Before I entered politics, I was full time RSS pracharak. At those times, national leaders of the RSS who came to attend our meetings invariably discussed your rural development activities so that it could be emulated. It has tremendous impact on me. In the past, I also had the good fortune of meeting you.
>
> I and my state of Gujarat are indebted to you for the courage and conviction you showed in saying good words for me and my state. In this show of courage, you exhibited commitment to truth and a soldier-like conviction. And because of this, your opinion has been universally accepted.
>
> I request you to also bless me that your praise shall not make me complacent and commit mistakes.
>
> Your blessings have given me the strength to do what is right and it is good. At the same time, my responsibility has also gone high. Because of your statement, crores of youth would be having great expectations and therefore even a small mistake on my part will dis-

appoint them. Therefore, I have to remain vigilant and seek your blessings for the same.[2]

This rhetoric raised expectations among those who were seeking the improvement of law and order in India: the changing of the guard that had taken place in 2014 was supposed to make India clean again. In 2013, the Congress-led UPA coalition—under the Anna Hazare movement's pressure—had passed an act creating the Lokpal—the Lokpal and Lokayuktas Act—but had not been able to appoint a Lokpal partly because of BJP opposition.[3] In 2014, many Modi voters expected him to make this law a reality—all the more so as the BJP's election manifesto promised that the government would appoint a Lokpal if it was in a position to form the government. But the Modi government, soon after it was constituted, objected that according to the act, the Lokpal had to be chosen by a selecting committee comprising the prime minister, the Speaker of the Lok Sabha, the Leader of the Opposition, the chief justice of India (or his nominee), and an "eminent jurist" appointed by those mentioned above. In this case, the Speaker refused to recognize a Leader of the Opposition in the Sixteenth Lok Sabha—despite the fact that it is a statutory post—because, he said, the largest opposition party, the Congress, had not gotten 10 percent of the seats. The Speaker claimed that he was following a ruling by the first Speaker according to which the largest opposition party needed to represent one-tenth of the assembly for its leader to be recognized as the Leader of the Opposition.[4] But such practice had never been enshrined in a ruling.

And this argument was also flawed because when a new chief information commissioner and a new Central Bureau of Investigation director had to be selected during Modi's first term, the provisions relating to their appointment had been amended to recognize the leader of the largest party as Leader of the Opposition—as required by official procedures. The Lokpal and Lokayuktas Act could have been amended as well. In fact, it was amended, in 2016, but in a different way: the provisions regarding the appointment procedure remained the same, but those pertaining to the anticorruption fight were diluted. According to the Lokpal and Lokayuktas Act, by July 31, 2016, even if no Lokpal had been appointed, section 44 of the act had to be operationalized—which meant that the assets of public servants (including bureaucrats, MPs, the prime minister, ministers, and officials of the government or of any organization, trust, or NGO that receives Rs 10 lakhs [13,330 USD] in foreign aid or Rs 1 crore [133,330 USD] in government aid) had to be disclosed. To minimize the risk of personal enrichment cases being exposed, the BJP government resorted to an emergency procedure[5] to pass the Lokpal Amendment Act, 2016—which (a) eliminated the statutory requirement of public servants to disclose the assets of their spouses and children, (b) did away with the need for *public* disclosure their assets, and (c) empowered the union government "to prescribe the form and manner of asset disclosure."[6] As a result, "the deadline for declaring assets and liabilities was extended indefinitely, and declarations will now have to be made only after the government comes up with fresh amendments to the Act."[7]

As Anjali Bhardwaj and Amrita Johri point out, this amendment "was a critical blow as the Lokpal was established to act on complaints under the Prevention of Corruption Act (PCA) [and] one of the grounds of criminal misconduct under the PCA relates to a public servant or any person on his/her behalf being in possession of pecuniary resources or property disproportionate to known sources of income."[8] But the government tried to amend the PCA itself to render the Lokpal toothless: according to the amendment introduced by the ruling party, the Lokpal had to request government permission before he could prosecute officials suspected of corruption![9]

Even though the Lokpal had become a much less powerful institution, the Modi government continued to argue that no one could be appointed in this capacity because there was no Leader of the Opposition in the Lok Sabha. In 2017, Anna Hazare wrote to Modi, saying that he had "reneged on the promise made to the people" and that the time had "come to relaunch a campaign against corruption"[10]—something he did not do, for unknown reasons. The Supreme Court became more vocal soon after. Already in November 2016, after the amendment mentioned above, a bench headed by Chief Justice T. S. Thakur had asked the attorney general, Mukul Rohatgi, why the government was so slow in appointing a Lokpal if it was "so committed to cleansing corruption."[11] Rohatgi continued to argue that no Lokpal could be appointed because there was no Leader of the Opposition.[12] In 2017, in response to petitions filed by Common Cause and other NGOs, the Supreme Court replied that the act itself empowered "a truncated Selection Committee to make recommendations for appointment of the Chairperson or members of the Lokpal."[13] In early 2018, while NGOs mobilized in favor of the Lokpal in the framework of the National Campaign for People's Right to Information (NCPRI),[14] the Modi government decided to include Mallikarjun Kharge, leader of the Congress in the Lok Sabha, as a "special invitee" to a meeting of the Lokpal Selection Committee, without specifying what kind of power he would have in this capacity. Incidentally, Jitendra Singh, a minister of state in the Prime Minister's Office, was also supposed to be part of the meeting as a "special invitee."[15] Finally, Kharge was to boycott the key meetings of the committee, considering that the 2013 act had no provision defining the role of "special invitees."

On January 17, 2019, the Supreme Court set the end of February as the deadline for the appointment of the Lokpal and his team. Finally, Pinaki Chandra Ghose, former Supreme Court judge, was appointed on March 15, less than one month before the Lok Sabha elections,[16] along with eight other people forming the first Indian Lokpal—after they had all been selected by a committee where government representatives were a majority.[17] Not only had the Lokpal and Lokayuktas Act been diluted, but three months after the appointment of Justice Ghose and his colleagues, no public information officer had been named, and the Lokpal was not endowed with a prosecution wing either—which meant that the institution would have to rely on the Central Bureau of Investigation, a police force whose independence had significantly eroded (as seen below).

The fact that it took five years for the BJP government to appoint a Lokpal and that it diluted the 2013 act it had backed, along with Anna Hazare, was "an indication of how the party [was] reneging with impunity on its poll promise of a corruption-free India,"[18] something that was also to be illustrated by the way many corruption cases were dealt with. But the fight against corruption was not the only matter at stake here: Narendra Modi was eager not to let an alternative power center crystallize in the form of the Lokpal—an attitude of his that had already gained notice when he was chief minister in Gujarat, a state that remained without a Lokayukta for ten years, while Modi tried to dilute the role of this office by introducing the Lokayukta Aayog Bill.[19] To create vacancies by delaying appointments is sometimes an easy way to weaken checks and balances—and Narendra Modi resorted to this strategy on many other occasions during his first term as prime minister.

The Slow Death of the Right to Information

The Central Information Commission (CIC)—the highest appeal body under the Right to Information (RTI) Act of 2005, to date one of the most effective laws for ensuring transparency in the public domain—is exemplary of such delay tactics. First, the government did not appoint a chief information commissioner for one year after the incumbent retired in August 2014[20] and did not fill any vacant information commissioner posts in the CIC between 2016 and 2018, a year when, consequently, only seven commissioners out of the sanctioned eleven were in place.[21] The Supreme Court intervened. Some appointments were made in January 2019, but four posts remained vacant in mid-2019,[22] a clear indication of the government's lack of interest in the CIC and of its attempt to weaken it.[23] The backlog of pending appeals reached 28,442 cases in July 2019[24] as the CIC has become a dysfunctional body. Second, the Modi government refused—often without giving any reason—to disclose information that had been previously available under the RTI Act.[25] As of 2016, queries about the number of wiretappings were no longer answered.[26] The Home and Finance Ministries rejected 15 percent of the applications they received each year under the Modi government. In 2016–2017, the Reserve Bank of India (RBI) and the public banks represented 33 percent of the rejections of requests.[27] The RBI, for instance, refused to give any information about demonetization.[28] Third, during the 2019 monsoon session of parliament—just after the Lok Sabha elections—the Modi government amended the RTI

Act so as to limit the power of the CIC. The fixed tenure of five years for the CIC and the information commissioners was abolished. Additionally, their salaries would not be set as they had been in the past—like those of other similar institutions, including the ECI—but decided and notified individually by the government, on a case-by-case basis. In other words, "the government can threaten or lure the chief information commissioner and information commissioners with arbitrary removal or extension and curtailment or increase in salary depending upon their suitability for the ruling dispensation."[29] The same new rules applied at the state level, where "even State Chief Information Commissioner and Information Commission would be chosen by the Centre."[30] The Modi government thereby limited the CIC's autonomy after the RTI Act had caused the ruling party serious embarrassment. In 2017, acting on an RTI application, Information Commissioner Sridhar Acharyulu ordered Delhi University to allow the inspection of records of students who had passed a BA course in 1978, the year in which Prime Minister Narendra Modi had allegedly passed the examination. Acharyulu was stripped of the human resource development portfolio immediately, and the application became a dead letter, as no inspection of the student records took place after Tushar Mehta, the additional solicitor general of India, asked the High Court for a stay order in 2018. The matter is still pending before the Delhi High Court.[31] Not long before, the Reserve Bank of India had been directed on an RTI application to provide details of the nonperforming assets in public-sector banks and the details of big loan defaulters. As mentioned in chapter 4, the RBI refused to reveal the information sought, citing its confidential nature. As a petition was subsequently filed, the Supreme Court directed the RBI to make the information available in April 2019. These two incidents showed that the CIC could prove to be a nuisance for the Modi government.

In addition to weakening institutions like the CIC, the Modi government diluted other laws, besides the RTI Act, that were intended to ensure transparency. The Whistleblower's Protection Act was one of them. In May 2015, the Modi government moved an amendment bill that sweetened the act: whistleblowers could now be prosecuted for possessing documents on which a complaint had been made and the list of eligibility restrictions was long: the matters raised by whistleblowers had to be in "the public interest" and should not be "affecting the 'sovereignty and integrity of India' or related to 'commercial confidence' or 'information received in confidence from a foreign government.'"[32]

The Vain Resistance
of the Central Bureau of Investigation

The Central Vigilance Commission (CVC) was established in 2003 to inquire into alleged offenses under the Prevention of Corruption (PC) Act. As a result, it also supervises the Central Bureau of Investigation (CBI) in investigations it conducts under the PC Act. Its chief, the central vigilance commissioner, takes part, along with the prime minister and the Leader of the Opposition in the Lok Sabha, in the committee in charge of selecting the CBI. E. Sridharan points out that the power of the commission may "depend upon the personality of the CVC,"[33] a conclusion one can draw from all the institutions under review in this chapter and which makes the selection process of their heads so important. The focus here will be on the CBI, the most important investigative agency in India.

The "politicization of the police"[34] has for decades been affecting the CBI, "the premier investigating agency of the Government of India in anti-corruption cases,"[35] which deals with all types of offenses, including murder, abduction, and economic crimes. The Delhi Special Police Establishment Act that set up the CBI vests this body's power of superintendence in the union government, making political interference possible at the investigation stage itself. In 1997, the Supreme Court—after the government of India had removed a CBI director who conducted investigations against its interests[36]—changed the rules in order to make the CBI more independent: its Director, who was now appointed for a two-year term, was to be selected by a committee consisting of the central vigilance commissioner, the secretary of the Home Ministry, and the secretary of the Department of Personnel. Last but not least, the CBI was now supposed to report to the CVC.

Some historical background harking back to Modi's and Shah's Gujarat years is useful here for understanding the way they targeted the CBI. While chief minister in Gujarat, Narendra Modi considered that these changes made no difference. He even declared that the CBI actually stood for the "Congress Bureau of Investigation"[37] during the two Manmohan Singh governments. In 2013, during a speech in Bhopal, he argued that "Congress will not fight the next Lok Sabha elections but will field the CBI instead."[38] This critique resulted mostly from the investigations that the CBI conducted into extrajudicial killings—better known in India as "fake encounters"—which had taken place in Gujarat between 2002 and 2006. In 2012, the Supreme Court itself even instructed the CBI to investigate such incidents.[39] Two of these cases, briefly mentioned in chapter 2, were particularly important, the Ishrat Jahan case and the Sohrabuddin case.

The Ishrat Jahan case refers to an encounter that took place on June 15, 2004, on the road between Ahmedabad and Gandhinagar. Four people were allegedly killed by a team from the Ahmedabad City Police Detection of Crime Branch, including Ishrat Jahan, a nineteen-year-old college girl preparing to complete her BS degree in Mumbai. After the encounter, the Gujarat police claimed that the group were Pakistanis from the jihadist movement Lashkar-e-Taiba (LeT) who had come to Gujarat to assassinate Narendra Modi. But in 2009, the metropolitan magistrate, S. P. Tamang, submitted a report to the metropolitan court of Ahmedabad indicating that the Pakistani IDs found on the corpses had been forged and that the four people had, in fact, been killed in police custody by policemen who were seeking promotions and rewards. Tamang gave the names of several senior policemen as being implicated in the fake encounter, including D. G. Vanzara, the chief of the Detection of Crime Branch.[40] The government of Gujarat objected that the policemen accused of fake encounters had not been able to advocate their case. The matter went to the High Court, which formed a special investigation team (SIT). On November 21, 2011, the SIT reported to the High Court that the encounter was not genuine. The court ordered that a complaint for murder should be filed against twenty policemen. In January 2012, the High Court asked the CBI to take charge of the case.

Sohrabuddin Sheikh was part of the underworld when he was killed in an allegedly fake encounter on November 26, 2005. He was particularly known for extorting protection money from marble factories in Gujarat and Rajasthan. He was traveling by bus with his wife, Kauser Bi, on November 23, 2005, between Hyderabad (Andhra Pradesh) and Sangli (Maharashtra) when the bus was stopped by the Gujarat Police Anti-Terrorist Squad. His wife was allegedly taken to a farmhouse outside of Ahmedabad in Vanzara's native village, where she was killed and her body burned. Sohrabuddin Sheikh was killed a few days later on a highway at Vishala Circle near Ahmedabad.[41] He was immediately presented as a terrorist by Vanzara, who, by then, had been promoted to Gujarat Anti-Terrorist Squad chief. He gave a press conference to explain that Sohrabuddin was an LeT jihadist who wanted to assassinate Narendra Modi.[42] But Sohrabuddin's younger brother, Rubabuddin, petitioned the Supreme Court in December 2005, despite intimidation,[43] claiming that his brother had been killed in a fake encounter. A journalist investigating the case, Prashant Dayal, gathered significant revelations from policemen who had taken part in the fake encounter—which he published in a Gujarati newspaper in 2006.[44] Allegedly, the Gujarat government thought that it would get rid of an extortionist and could exploit the politics of fear examined earlier in the book.

In March 2007, the Supreme Court ordered the Criminal Investigation Department (CID) to probe the case. The CID gathered enough evidence to enable the deputy inspector general (DIG) of police, Rajnish Rai, to arrest the three accused on April 24, 2007, including D. G. Vanzara, who had become DIG Border Range not long before.[45] The Supreme Court directed the CBI to take over the investigation in 2010 again, citing reasons for this decision similar to previous ones: "We feel that police authorities of the state of Gujarat failed to carry out a fair and impartial investigation as we initially wanted them to do. It cannot be questioned that the offenses the high police officials have committed was of grave nature which needs to be strictly dealt with."[46] In July 2010, the CBI filed a 30,000-page charge sheet that resulted in the arrest of several additional policemen and Amit Shah. Shah was accused of being implicated not only in the fake encounter targeting Sohrabuddin but also in an extortion racket.[47]

Shah was granted bail in October 2010, but the judges requested that he leave Gujarat for two years, as they feared he would interfere with the judicial process. Everything changed after Modi was reelected chief minister in 2012 and elected prime minister in 2014: the CBI had to be taken care of. The Modi government immediately tried to appoint at its helm policemen who had worked with Narendra Modi in Gujarat. In 2015, Y. C. Modi was appointed additional CBI director.[48] As a CBI officer, he had been part of the SIT that had probed Narendra Modi's role in the Gujarat pogrom and investigated the murder of Haren Pandya.[49] He was part of the team of investigators that announced that Pandya had been assassinated in a joint operation between Pakistan's Inter Services Intelligence, Lashkar-e-Taiba, and the Dubai-based underworld don Dawood Ibrahim. Twelve Muslim men had been arrested and charged with Pandya's murder, but eight years later, in September 2011, the Gujarat High Court had to acquit every single one and throw out the entire case. "The investigation has all throughout been botched up and blinkered," the judge said. "The investigating officers concerned ought to be held accountable for their ineptitude resulting into injustice, huge harassment of many persons concerned and enormous waste of public resources and public time of the courts."[50]

Also in 2015, Arun Kumar Sharma, another Indian Police Service officer of the Gujarat cadre, was transferred to the CBI as joint director. According to "highly placed officials" of the CBI, Narendra Modi wanted to give him the key charge of the Policy Division (known as JPC), making him the number two of the CBI. A CBI official told *Scroll.in*: "For a Prime Minister who has established his own direct link in different ministries through the secretary and joint secretary level officials bypassing ministers, it is only natural to try opening up a direct channel with the CBI bypassing its director."[51] Sharma, however, had a controversial past. He was one of the Gujarat police officers who had been accused of derailing the investigations into the killing of Ishrat Jahan. The post of special commissioner of the Ahmedabad Detection of Crime Branch had been created for him. The then CBI director, Anil Sinha, refused to appoint him JPC.

But in 2016, another IPS Gujarat cadre, Rakesh Asthana, was appointed additional director of the CBI a few months before Sinha's retirement. He had been inspector general of police in Vadodara, joint commissioner of police of Ahmedabad city, and commissioner of police in Surat and Vadodara. He had also been part of the SIT appointed by the Gujarat government to inquire into the 2002 Godhra tragedy. A few months after becoming additional CBI director, Asthana was appointed acting/interim CBI director, after R. K. Dutta, the man who was supposed to replace Sinha (who was retiring), was transferred to the Ministry of Home Affairs as special secretary (a post specially upgraded for him) two days before Sinha retired.[52] This transfer, which made Asthana's appointment possible, was ordered without following the rule by which the government must secure the CVC's approval before reducing the tenure of any CBI officer. The NGO Common Cause filed a case against the government for steps that it called "mala fide, arbitrary and illegal." For Prashant Bhushan, the Supreme Court lawyer who filed the Public Interest Litigation petition, the objective was to ensure that Asthana was given the charge of CBI director.[53]

The Supreme Court concluded that Dutta's transfer was all the more illegal as he was supervising sensitive cases for which he was reporting to the court—whose approval should have been sought before any transfer.[54] Additionally, Solicitor General Tushar Mehta said, at a meeting of the selection committee to appoint the CBI director, that the Supreme Court had forced the government to follow the right procedure, but surprisingly, it did not reverse Dutta's illegal transfer. However, the CBI resisted as an institution, and Asthana did not become CBI director. Instead, Alok Verma, the then Delhi police chief, was appointed to the post.

But Asthana's rise to power did not end there. A few months later, in 2017, he was appointed special director of the CBI despite opposition from the CBI director, Alok Verma, himself,[55] who argued that his appointment should be suspended until all the charges against him had been cleared. Indeed, Asthana's name had been mentioned in a First Investigation Report (FIR) registered by the CBI against a company accused of gratifying him and other civil servants in a money-laundering scam.[56] The Supreme Court dismissed the plea challenging Asthana's appointment as CBI special director after the central government defended him by referring to his "outstanding career."[57] Then, the CBI director, Alok Verma, accused Asthana of corruption[58]—and the latter did the same vis-à-vis the former. The government sent both on indefinite leave in late October 2018.[59]

The central government then appointed an interim CBI chief. This man, Nageshwar Rao, an Odisha cadre, was a controversial police officer in his state. As a young superintendent of police in Nabrangpur District, in 1994 he had "circulated a letter among the headmasters of government schools urging them to discourage the students against religious conversion."[60] Four years later, he gave a public lecture that was reported in an Odiya paper in which he said that Muslims, Christians, and Marxists were posing a threat to India: "These forces believe in violence and are intolerant of others. Christians and Muslims do not respect any sacred text other than the Bible and the Quran. They give primacy to their religion over the nation. They lure and convert people by offering incentives."[61] As these words—which violated the Indian Service (Conduct) Rules—were reported to the DIG of police, Rao was transferred. In 2008, Rao was serving as inspector general of the Central Reserve Police Force (CRPF)—the largest paramilitary institution in India—when the anti-Christian Kandhamal riots occurred. He allegedly restricted the movement of the CRPF platoons while the Christian minority was at the receiving end of communal violence. Gradually, Rao had become close to Ram Madhav and Sangh Parivar think tanks. He was a contributor to the Charter of Key Hindu Demands that such think tanks spelled out in 2018. Among these demands was the need to "change the anti-Hindu and anti-national narrative of the leftist-Marxist historians by telling Indian history from point of view of Indians."[62] Subsequently, Rao even wrote in the RSS mouthpiece, *The Organiser*.[63]

In October 2018, the government asked Verma to go on leave on the basis of a CVC report citing several grounds, including Asthana's accusations regarding the fact that Verma was obstructing the investigation against Laloo Prasad Yadav, the former chief minister of Bihar and the prime accused in the "fodder scam."[64] But Verma and Common Cause filed a petition before the Supreme Court. The court allowed the process of inquiry initiated by the CVC to continue with one major change, however: a former judge, Justice A. K. Patnaik, was appointed to supervise the inquiry—as if the court preferred not to rely on the CVC head to conduct it. The late October interim order of the Supreme Court also said that the CVC report should be completed in fifteen days and that, as an interim director, Rao should not do more than routine work. But one of his first decisions, on the contrary, consisted in transferring the thirteen CBI officers probing allegations of corruption against Asthana.

The CVC submitted its preliminary inquiry report into allegations against Verma in a sealed envelope. Incidentally, when the National Campaign for People's Right to Information coconvenor Anjali Bhardwaj filed RTI requests to gain access to the relevant documents of this case, which were not public, her request was denied by the CVC.[65] Not only had the CVC report remained secret, but retired justice Patnaik, who was supposed to supervise the inquiry, pointed out that the correct procedure had not been followed. During the hearings at the Supreme Court regarding the petition that Verma and Common Cause had filed, the union government justified its decision to force Verma and Asthana to step down because of the feud between the two men: "If the government had not stepped in, God knows where this spat between the top officials at CBI may have ended,"[66] said the attorney general. Such arguments presenting the central government as a pacifying force above the fray obliterates the fact that the Modi government had prepared the ground for such a crisis by appointing a second in command that his superior did not want. The CBI was destabilized because of this decision and, subsequently, by attempts to discredit its head, who turned out to have a mind of his own.

The final episode of this saga is the most revealing one. On January 7, 2019, the Supreme Court reinstated Alok Verma as CBI director, considering that the government and the CVC should have obtained prior consent of the committee set up under section 4A (1) of the Delhi Special Police Establishment (DSPE) Act, before divesting him as CBI director. But his authority was confined to "ongoing routine functions" until a meeting of this committee, henceforth called "the PM committee," could decide.

The Supreme Court's ambivalent ruling is highly indicative of the new balance of power: on one hand, the Supreme Court considered that the way Verma had been sent on leave was illegal; on the other, instead of sticking to the law, it let the PM committee decide in fine.[67] The PM committee was formed immediately to decide the fate of Alok Verma. Chief Justice Ranjan Gogoi nominated Justice Sikri to represent the Supreme Court there.[68] Two days later, the committee headed by Prime Minister Narendra Modi removed Verma from the post of CBI director on January 10 "on charges of corruption and dereliction of duty."[69] Alok Verma took early retirement immediately afterward and wrote a letter whose second paragraph is worth citing: "Institutions are one of the strongest and most visible symbols of our democracy and it is no exaggeration that the CBI is one of the most important organisations in India today. The decisions made yesterday will not just be a reflection on my functioning but will become a testimony on how the CBI as an institution will be treated by any government through the CVC, who is appointed by majority members of the ruling government. This is a moment for collective introspection, to state the least."[70] In his letter, Verma also said retired justice Patnaik considered that "the findings/conclusions of the [CVC] report are not his." In fact, Patnaik went one step further in an interview with the *Indian Express*: "There was no evidence against Verma regarding corruption. The entire enquiry was held on [CBI Special Director Rakesh] Asthana's complaint. I have said in my report that none of the findings in the CVC's report are mine. . . . Even if the Supreme Court said that the high-power committee must decide, the decision was very, very hasty. We are dealing with an institution here. They should have applied their mind thoroughly, especially as a Supreme Court judge was there. What the CVC says cannot be the final word."[71] Although retired justice Patnaik reported to the Supreme Court, the representative of the court in the PM committee that met on January 10, 2019, Justice Sikri, voted with Narendra Modi against Karge, who wrote a note of dissent—the only one. Why did the Supreme Court abstain from objecting that this modus operandi did not comply with its order? The matter of the court's complacency will be revisited below.

Verma was right: the CBI was bound to bow to the central government after his removal. The decline of the CBI's independence—which in any case had never been complete; far from it—found expression in several decisions.

First, the investigation regarding Asthana reached an impasse. In May 2019, the Delhi High Court gave the CBI four months to complete its probe. In August, the investigating officer in charge of the inquiry sought voluntary retirement from service. The rest of the CBI team probing the case was dismantled as well.[72] Finally, many months after the High Court deadline, in February 2020, the CBI told the High Court that it had found no involvement of Asthana and his deputy Kumar in the alleged bribery case filed in October 2018—and the court accepted this conclusion.[73]

Second, the CBI was used against dissenting voices, including media people, and its officers who were investigating cases in which Sangh Parivar leaders were probed were even more systematically sidelined. These dimensions of the deinstitutionalization process that started in 2014 and which has affected other agencies, including the National Investigation Agency (NIA), will now be explored.

To sum up, the detailed case study conducted above about the take-over of the CBI suggests that for Modi and Shah, who had suffered at the hand of this investigation agency, the best way to clip its wings was to appoint Gujarat police cadres who had been comrades in crime. The CBI, as an institution, resisted as much as it could but was finally defeated, largely because of the attitude of the Supreme Court. The NIA met a very similar fate.

The National Investigation Agency and the CBI: From "Caged Parrots" to Watchdogs on a Leash

If the CBI[74] was targeted by the Modi government because of what it had done in Gujarat, the NIA was in the eye of the storm after 2014 because of the famous "Hindu terror" cases. The notion of Hindu terror emerged in the late 2000s. The expression was coined by P. Chidambaram, the then home minister who attributed certain bombings investigated by police to Hindu nationalists. Some of these were suspected members of Abhinav Bharat, an organization named after the movement V. D. Savarkar had started in 1905 in Poona. According to the Indian police, and in particular to Hemant Karkare, the IPS officer at the helm of the Anti-Terrorist Squad (ATS) of Maharashtra, the organization was responsible for at least one terrorist attack in Malegaon, which had killed six people in front of a mosque in the town in September 2008, just after Ramadan. The report drafted by Karkare is exceptionally rich because it includes the transcripts of secret Abhinav Bharat meetings that the organizers recorded on a laptop in 2007 and 2008.[75]

Among the leaders of Abhinav Bharat at that time was Himani Savarkar, the then Hindu Mahasabha president and the daughter of Gopal Godse (the brother of Nathuram Godse); Sadhvi Pragya Singh Thakur, who was an ABVP student leader in Madhya Pradesh until 1997 before becoming a member of the national executive of the ABVP and becoming a *sadhvi* (world renouncer); B. L. Sharma, an RSS worker since 1940 who won the Lok Sabha seat of East Delhi in the 1990s; retired major Ramesh Upadhyaya, who once headed the BJP's Mumbai unit of the party's ex-servicemen cell; and Lieutenant Colonel Prasad Purohit, an army officer who was the main driving force behind the organization, according to Karkare.

While the Malegaon case attracted considerable attention—especially after Karkare was killed during the jihadi attack in Mumbai in November 2008—other blasts were allegedly attributed to Hindu nationalists. Three terrorist attacks were singled out by the police: the Samjhauta Express (February 2007), Mecca Masjid (May 2007), and Ajmer Dargah (October 2007) attacks, where sixty-eight, nine, and three people died, respectively. One of the accused named in the Ajmer Dargah charge sheet, Swami Aseemanand, made confessions in prison before a magistrate, in which he mentioned the role of RSS men in several cases. He named Indresh Kumar—a member of the RSS executive body—who appeared already in the Ajmer Dargah FIR, and an RSS pracharak, Sunil Joshi, whom he presented as a protégé of the former. According to Aseemanand, Joshi, who was murdered mysteriously in December 2007, was involved, along with other RSS pracharak, in the Samjhauta Express blast.

In this context, RSS chief Mohan Bhagwat declared in November 2010:

> For the first time in the history of the organisation, a Sarsanghchalak has not only attended a dharna but also addressed the meeting as a conspiracy was being hatched to tag terrorism with the RSS. . . . Those who are involved in blasts were either not members of the Sangh or they were ousted from the organisation long back due to their violent nature. . . . But taking advantage of the situation, some people started talking about Hindu terrorism. . . . An effort is being made to prove that the Sangh is a terrorist outfit. People against whom allegations are being made have an open character. They are the people who serve the country and teach others how to become a good citizen.[76]

When the BJP came to power in 2014, at least half a dozen Hindu nationalists were in jail because the police had named them as accused in one of the terrorist attacks mentioned above. Others were awaiting trial, including Indresh Kumar, who immediately declared: "The new government should review [our] cases."[77] The investigating agencies that had filed a case against them were either the CBI or the NIA, which was immediately targeted.

The National Investigation Agency, the Malegaon Cases, and Others

The NIA was founded after the 2008 Mumbai jihadi attacks to deal with terror-related crimes across India, including those attributed to Hindu terrorists. Government interference in the NIA's work came to light when, in June 2014, Rohini Salian, the special public prosecutor working for the NIA in the case related to the 2008 Malegaon blasts, was asked to "go soft" on the accused. In a 2015 interview with the *Indian Express*, Salian said: "Last year I got a call from one of the officers of the NIA, asking to come over to speak to me. He didn't want to talk over the phone. He came and said there is a message that I should go soft. . . . Again on June 12 this year, the same officer met me and conveyed orally that I was to be replaced by some other lawyer in this case."[78] Three months later, Salian filed an affidavit before the Bombay High Court to name the police officer who had talked to her and who had tried, she said, "to interfere with the delivery of the administration of justice, as a messenger."[79] Indeed, NIA policy had completely changed after the BJP's rise to power. In the case of Malegaon, Salian declared that the agency "filed the chargesheet behind my back."[80] The agency, instead of using the confessions of the accused and testimonies of witness, started to interrogate them again.[81] Many retracted and/or turned hostile.[82] Finally, the NIA argued that the ATS had "coerced"[83] some of the accused and had even "planted"[84] the explosives in order to accuse Lt. Col. Purohit. The NIA's U-turn resulted in a succession of acquittals, partly because, even when its local officers wanted to,[85] it *never* appealed verdicts, which often meant years of investigation were wasted. Regarding the Malegaon case, the NIA itself declared that evidence was weak, despite, for instance, the detailed charge sheet written by Karkare.[86] The cases of the Mecca Masjid and Ajmer followed a similar trajectory. In the former, it turned out that key documents implicating "senior RSS leaders" had disappeared.[87] Then the judge resigned the day after he gave his verdict.[88] In the Ajmer case, the judge, seeing the large number of witnesses turning hostile, listed all the basic steps the NIA should have taken to conduct the investigation properly. But "the lack of interest shown by the NIA during the trial" was such that the investigating officer did not make a single appearance at the hearing.[89]

As early as 2015, many accused, including Aseemanand, were granted bail. In 2016, the NIA decided not to name Pragya Singh Thakur in its charge sheet regarding the Malegaon case.[90] Instead, it insisted, despite a lack of evidence, on accusing a group of Muslims.[91] In 2017, all the accused in the Ajmer Dargah case were acquitted, and Purohit was granted bail. All five accused in the Mecca Masjid case were acquitted in April 2018.

The CBI, from the Sohrabuddin Case to the Loya Case

In the Sohrabuddin case,[92] in which the prime accused was Amit Shah, the CBI changed its modus operandi even before the 2014 elections, when it became clear that Narendra Modi would be the next prime minister. In April—one month before the elections—CBI chief Ranjit

Sinha removed a very effective officer, Sandeep Tamgadge, from the case. Tamgadge, who had interrogated Shah on two occasions in 2012 and 2013, was subsequently punished for this by the CBI, which indicted him for failing to perform his duty in two separate cases.[93]

Shah was supposed to appear before the judge of the CBI court in charge of the trial, Justice Utpat, on June 6, 2014—but he did not show up. The judge reprimanded him and fixed a new date for his appearance. The judge before whom Shah was supposed to appear was transferred one day before Shah's appearance in court. This judge had been posted for less than one year, whereas the average duration of such tenure is three years. He was replaced by Justice Loya, who died in Nagpur on December 1, 2014. While the hospital where he died attributed his demise to a heart attack, journalists from *The Caravan* who investigated the case persistently discovered that the postmortem had not been performed in accordance with standard practice[94] and learned from interviews with one of Justice Loya's sisters that he had "confided to her that Mohit Shah, then the chief justice of the Bombay High Court, had offered him a bribe of Rs 100 crore [about 13,333,330 USD] in return for a favorable judgment."[95] Lawyers immediately decided that the "suspicious death" of Judge Loya needed to be investigated[96]—to no avail.

Loya's successor in the CBI court disposed of the case in less than a month. On December 30, 2014, he discharged Amit Shah on the basis of the charge sheet alone, without the evidence being heard, and concluded that Amit Shah had been framed for "political reasons."[97] Among the accused, eleven others, including six police officers from Gujarat, were discharged in 2015–2016, including Vanzara, either for lack of evidence or for lack of sanction to prosecute.[98] What was rather exceptional was the fact that the CBI did not appeal the discharge of persons it had charged in a criminal matter.[99] In the case of Vanzara, the CBI even made its stance clear before the court that it was not opposing his discharge even though the organization, originally, had framed the charges and conducted the investigation![100]

There were only 22 accused left, but the CBI abstained from protecting the witnesses who turned hostile one after the other. By April 2018,

45 of them had turned hostile,[101] and the trend continued.[102] The High Court judge in charge of the case arraigned the CBI for not providing adequate protection for witnesses who might be subjected to intimidation or inducement by the accused or their party[103] and for failing "to put all evidence on record including the prima facie evidence." The judge was transferred.[104] Finally, 92 out of the 210 witnesses who were examined during the trial turned hostile—and the most important ones were among them.[105] The witnesses who had resisted such pressure "only partially supported the prosecution's claims,"[106] and others were not allowed to testify.[107] Rajnish Rai, Sandeep Tamgadge,[108] and V. L. Solanki (the police officers who had first investigated the case, and the former two of whom had already been punished by the CBI for their professionalism) were not examined.

Finally, in December 2018, Justice Sharma came to the same conclusion in the case of Amit Shah as his predecessor, Justice Gosavi: the investigation that the CBI had pursued in the Sohrabuddin case was politically motivated.[109] The twenty-two accused were acquitted, including fourteen policemen from Gujarat and six policemen from Rajasthan.[110] Once again, in a very unusual manner, the CBI did not file any appeal, despite the humiliating way its investigations had been castigated by the judges. The organization had fallen in line.

After asserting its control over the CBI and the NIA, the Modi government, logically enough, gave these agencies more power. In 2019, the NIA Act was amended to allow the agency to investigate offenses related to human trafficking, counterfeit currency or bank notes, manufacture and sale of prohibited arms, cyberterrorism, and offenses under the Explosive Substances Act.[111] These matters could now be investigated by the NIA and not by state police, an important change at a time when many states governed by the opposition refused to let centrally ruled police forces investigate on their territory. At the time of writing, seven states of the Indian Union—Mizoram, West Bengal, Rajasthan, Maharashtra, Chhattisgarh, Kerala, and Jharkhand—have withdrawn their general consent to let the CBI conduct investigations on their territory. This means that the CBI must ask for authorization from these states' governments for each investigation it wants to conduct.

The Supreme Court, from Resistance to Surrender

While a robust judiciary is a condition of democracy, besides the elite investigation agencies of the Indian police, the Supreme Court also abdicated some of its independence in the course of Modi's first term, under pressure as well as for other reasons.

The 2014 Blitzkrieg

After the Modi government was formed in 2014, the first incident regarding its relationship with the judiciary pertained to the appointment of a judge to the Supreme Court. In June 2014, the central government was asked to appoint four judges to the Supreme Court selected by the Collegium (a group made of the five senior-most judges, including the chief justice of India). The Modi government appointed all of them except Gopal Subramanium. The chief justice of India protested against this "unilateral segregation"—to no avail.[112] In the past, governments had returned files to the Collegium for clarification or reconsideration, but the objections were not as serious as this time.[113] In this instance, the government's rejection of Subramanium was based on Intelligence Bureau and CBI reports questioning his integrity. Subramanium wrote a nine-page letter to the chief justice in which he pointed out that he had been considered as "unsuitable" because he would not "toe the line of the government." He pointed out, as a sign of the Supreme Court's trust, that the court had appointed him amicus curiae in the Sohrabuddin case and added that he bore "no personal vengeance or any kind of grudge" against the then prime accused, Amit Shah[114]—but the reverse was probably not true. According to the Supreme Court advocate Sanjay Hegde, "the unstated reason for the government's opposition" to Gopal Subramanium was precisely his role in the Sohrabuddin case—including the fact that it was "on Subramanium's suggestion" that the Supreme Court "barred Shah from entering Gujarat in 2010."[115] Indeed, a couple of weeks after the CBI had questioned his integrity, it "did a U-turn to say that it [was] now eager to have him as its Special Prosecutor in the coal blocks allocation scam trial."[116] In his letter, through which he withdrew his candidacy for the Supreme Court, Subramanium wrote, rather prophetically, "The events of past few weeks have raised serious doubts in my mind as to the ability of the Executive Government to appreciate and respect the independence, integrity and glory of the judicial institution. I do not expect this attitude to change with time."[117]

As early as July 2014, the Modi government announced its intention to reform the way judges were appointed, in compliance with the BJP's election manifesto, which had pledged to "set up a National Judicial Commission for the appointment of judges in higher judiciary." The need to reform the Collegium system, which, since the late 1990s, meant that judges of the higher judiciary were co-opted by their peers, was felt beyond the BJP. The system was not only opaque, but it was suspected of generating corruption and criticized for lacking in accountability.[118] The Congress-led UPA had already tried to change the system by introducing the Judicial Appointments Commission Bill in 2013—which the BJP opposed and which lapsed.[119] In 2014, the Congress supported the constitutional bill tabled by the BJP, which was eventually passed unanimously by both assemblies of parliament as early as August 2014. As sixteen of the twenty-nine states of the Indian union ratified it also rather quickly, the bill was promulgated by the president of the republic of India in December 2014.

The chief justice of India criticized this reform the very day the bill was introduced in parliament in August 2014.[120] Many lawyers posited that the composition of the National Judicial Appointments Commission (NJAC) to be set up by the bill was bound to affect the independence of the judiciary.[121] The commission would consist of the chief justice of India (CJI), two senior judges, and two "eminent personalities" selected by a committee comprising the CJI, the prime minister, and the Leader of the Opposition in the Lok Sabha.

The same month the acts came into force, the Supreme Court admitted petitions challenging the reform's constitutional validity, and in October 2015, in a rare verdict,[122] it quashed the 99th Constitutional Amendment Act and the NJAC Act:[123] four of the five judges of the bench that delivered this verdict concluded that these acts would affect the independence of the judiciary, which was part of the basic structure of the Constitution of India.[124] They found two provisions especially problematic: the role of the "two eminent personalities"—who appeared as endowed with too much power given the fact that they were "unconnected with the administration of justice"[125]—and the presence of the law minister in the NJAC, which would create a conflict of interest.

The verdict arraigned the ruling party that had replaced almost all the governors immediately after its electoral victory in a manner illustrative of the spoils system—something the reform would have extended to the judiciary: "[It is] of utmost importance therefore, to shield judicial appointments, from any political-executive interference, to preserve the independence of the judiciary, from the regime of the spoils system."[126] In the following months and years, the appointment of judges would remain a bone of contention between the judiciary and the executive.

The 2015–2016 War of Attrition

After the judgment, the same bench headed by Justice Khehar, which had conceded that the Collegium system needed to be improved, in mid-December 2015 directed the government to propose a new memorandum of procedure (MoP) for appointments to the higher judiciary. A committee of ministers headed by External Affairs Minister Sushma Swaraj was designated to frame procedures (including eligibility criteria) that would make the appointment procedure more transparent. It submitted a draft of the MoP to the Collegium in March 2016. In May, the CJI returned the draft with the views of the Collegium, which found several provisions unacceptable, including the clause that would allow the government to reject any name recommended by the Collegium on grounds of national security. The government refused these objections.[127] Other bones of contention—besides the national security argument—pertained to the importance of seniority in the appointment process (something judges valued highly), the need for the Collegium to justify its choices (especially when the government asked for clarifications about a candidate),[128] and the Collegium's objection with respect "to the executive having the final say in rejecting names."[129] The tug-of-war was so fierce that initiatives unrelated to the issue of judges' appointments, such as the involvement of the private sector in e-courts, brought other reforms to a standstill.[130]

After the blitzkrieg of 2014—when the Modi government changed the appointment system for judges in six months—the years 2015–2016 were marked by a war of attrition during which the government not only refused to incorporate the Collegium's proposals into the MoP but also refused to appoint judges. In 2015, no new judge was appointed by the government for at least eight months.[131] And whereas in January 2015 35 percent of the High Court judges' posts were vacant,[132] almost 42 percent[133] were so in December of the same year and 45 percent in July 2016.[134] Chief Justice Lodha had already raised this issue in 2014.[135] His successor, Chief Justice T. S. Thakur, further highlighted it. In April, addressing the annual Conference of Chief Justices and Chief Ministers in the presence of Prime Minister Narendra Modi, he broke down, saying that the Indian judiciary was too understaffed to fulfill its obligation.[136] In May 2016—when about 170 proposals for appointment of High Court judges were pending with the government—the CJI pointed out that the country needed 70,000 judges (instead of the existing 21,000)[137] to clear millions of pending cases,[138] and in August, while hearing a public interest litigation petition on the shortage of judges, he told Attorney General Mukul Rohatgi: "Don't try to bring this institution to a grinding halt. We won't tolerate a logjam in judges' appointment. It is stifling judicial work. We will fasten accountability now. Why is there mistrust?"[139] In fact, the Modi government was in bargaining mode: it wanted the Supreme Court to succumb to the executive's pressure regarding the MoP. In October, once again, CJI Thakur slammed the Modi government for its inaction on the judges' appointment question: "Today we have a situation where court rooms are locked because there are no judges. It's happening in Karnataka. Why not have the whole institution locked up and lock out justice to people. . . . There should not be any deadlock. You have committed to process the files for appointment of judges without finalisation of the MoP. Finalisation of MoP has nothing to do with the appointment process in the judiciary."[140]

The CJI also said: "You cannot scuttle the working of the institution like this. Are you waiting for some revolutionary changes in the system?"[141] A "revolutionary change" was indeed what the Modi government was contemplating. As no change could be achieved by the government by creating the NJAC, it was trying to twist the Supreme Court's arm by framing a new MoP. In this context, "the court warned that it may summon the secretaries of the Prime Minister's Office and the ministry of law and justice to ascertain the factual position."[142] And the chief justice admonished, "If you go on like this, we will reconvene a five-judge bench and say that the government will not be allowed to scuttle judicial appointments till it frames a new MoP. . . . Do you want that?"[143]

But the Modi government denied that there was anything abnormal about the increase in High Court vacancies and did not succumb to such threats.[144] The gridlock continued, and the tension mounted when, on November 11, 2016, the government returned forty-three out of seventy-seven names recommended by the Collegium for the appointment of judges in high courts—where there were 500 posts lying vacant at the time.[145] The Supreme Court Collegium immediately reiterated these forty-three names.[146] A few days later, the Parliamentary Standing Committee on Law and Personnel stated that the "appointment of judges to the higher judiciary is essentially the function of executive."[147] More than one year after the Supreme Court's rejection of the NJAC, the legislative branch and the executive were still in league against the judiciary. Thakur was to retire one month later. When he did, in January 2017, the senior advocate Dushyant Dave hailed his "unwillingness to compromise."[148]

From Truce to Surrender, 2017–2020

Under T. S. Thakur's successor, Chief Justice Khehar, relations between the Supreme Court and the government improved dramatically: "By February 2017, a different tone prevailed. Modi, at a public gathering, complimented Khehar's 'quick decisions,' and said he wished Khehar could remain the CJI beyond the six months remaining until his retirement. Khehar assured the prime minister 'that we [would] keep within our boundary.' With Khehar in office, the government had started to clear judicial appointments."[149] What did it get in return?

Soon after becoming chief justice, Khehar resigned himself to including in the MoP provisions that had been a major bone of contention for one full year: the MoP now allowed the government to reject a judge's appointment on the grounds of national security. This clause was seen as a major concession to the Modi government, which had recurrently returned names to the Collegium on the basis of Intelligence Bureau or CBI reports—in the name of "national security," a remarkably vague formula that gave the executive considerable leeway. Sanjay Hegde pointed out that "what it provides for is that even if a good lawyer, who has a background in activism, is being considered for appointment in either the high court or the supreme court, the government can invoke the national security clause to block that appointment." What was even more worrying, he said, "is that the existence of such a clause will deter many able people from even trying to become a judge—no one wants that label of being anti-national on their name."[150]

The MoP was not yet finalized,[151] but relations between the government and the judiciary improved, largely because the latter ceased to resist the former as systematically as before.[152] On January 13, 2017, the court "refused to examine a petition alleging dilution in the Whistleblower Protection Act and seeking interim measures to protect whistleblowers who expose corruption in public administration and governance." The bench headed by Chief Justice Khehar explained that the law was discussed in parliament and that the petitioner should approach the court after it was passed if he was still not satisfied. The Hindu emphasized that "the tone of the court hearing was in complete contrast to the earlier hearing in January 2016, when the apex court had pressed the Centre to put in place a fool-proof interim mechanism to receive complaints and protect the lives of whistleblowers till the law was enacted."[153] That paled in comparison to what was to come after Arun Jaitley introduced the finance bill in March: "The bill made changes to 40 existing laws. It also made changes to a number of the country's tribunals—quasi-judicial bodies, such as the National Green Tribunal, that adjudicate cases requiring technical expertise and specialisation. Jaitley axed eight tribunals, whose functions were absorbed by other tribunals, and empowered the government to set the rules regarding the appointment and removal of the judges and members of these tribunals."[154] All the amendments proposed by Jaitley were passed as a money bill,[155] despite the fact that they fell well outside the limits set by the Constitution for money bills. Congress leader Jairam Ramesh filed a petition, but the Supreme Court reserved its verdict. That was to become its standard attitude in matters likely to result in conflicts with the government.

The same method was followed in the case of the Aadhaar Act (2016), which was also passed as a money bill and whose constitutionality had also been challenged by several petitions, because this system of biometric identification of 1.3 billion Indians was not sufficiently respectful of privacy and could not be passed as a money bill.[156] Here again, the Supreme Court, which had told the government in several interim orders since 2013 to wait for its verdict before making Aadhaar more systematic, opted not to decide for months and finally fell in line. In July 2017, a few weeks before Chief Justice Khehar retired, the Supreme Court finally ruled on Aadhaar in a 1,448-page convoluted judgment.[157] On one hand, the judges reaffirmed Indians' right to privacy, contradicting government assertions by defining it as a fundamental right protected by several articles of the Constitution. On the other, the judges declared Aadhaar legal regarding the various links the government had set up with social schemes and the PAN card (the one taxpayers use to pay their income tax). Even more surprisingly, a majority of judges, following circuitous reasoning, agreed to consider the Aadhaar Act a money bill. Supreme Court advocate Karuna Nundy sheds precious light on the issue:

> A lot of the criticism of the Supreme Court in the context of Aadhar is that either it is unable or unwilling to act in time. So you have a Government policy that is sometimes contrary to interim orders. In the case of Aadhar, it was in contempt and in violation of the court's orders. In theory, people should go to jail for that. This will not hap-

pen and instead Government said that, well, we have done it now and we spent a lot of money and most people have it so it is working fine, we might as well keep it. The Supreme Court then says okay, we will not make it compulsory for XYZ but we will make it compulsory for, say, income tax filings.[158]

Chief Justice Khehar's successor, Dipak Misra, also decided against confronting the government. His attitude was so noncollegial and submissive that the four senior-most members of the Supreme Court after the CJI—Justices Kurian Joseph, Jasti Chelameswar, Madan Lokur, and Ranjan Gogoi—held a press conference to denounce his modus operandi on January 12, 2018. This press conference, an unprecedented move that was intended to alert the public regarding things that were "not in order" in the Supreme Court, together with a letter the four judges sent to the CJI, suggested that there were three issues at stake: the Loya case that was still being investigated (but not properly according to them), the finalization of the MoP (which was still stuck), and the way Chief Justice Misra, as "master of the roster," constituted benches and, more importantly, assigned cases to benches. The fact that the Loya case had been assigned to a bench headed by Arun Mishra, a judge who, according to the senior advocate Dushyant Dave, had "close relations with BJP and top politicians"[159] (a point that will be discussed below), was a clear bone of contention. Mishra led the hearing in that case on January 12—before recusing himself—and the four judges decided to hold their press conference the same day after the CJI refused to assign the case to another bench.[160]

Retrospectively, retired justice Kurian Joseph explained the press conference in the following terms:

There were several instances of external influences on the working of the Supreme Court relating to allocation of cases to benches headed by select judges and appointment of judges to the Supreme Court and high courts. . . . Someone from outside was controlling the CJI, that is what we felt. So we met him, asked him, wrote to him to maintain independence and majesty of the Supreme Court. When all attempts failed, we decided to hold a press conference. . . . Starkly perceptible signs of influence with regard to allocation of cases to different benches selectively, to select judges who were perceived to be politically biased.[161]

This episode possibly led Justice Mishra to recuse himself and Chief Justice Misra to transfer the Loya case to a bench headed by himself—in which none of the four senior judges who had given the press conference took part. Still, the Loya case was disposed of in a nonconfrontational manner with the government. In January 2018, the Bombay Lawyers Association filed a petition with the Bombay High Court asking for an independent inquiry to probe the circumstances of Justice Loya's death.[162] The Supreme Court examined the issue in April 2018 to dismiss the petitions. Unexpectedly, Gautam Bhatia points out, the court acted as "the Supreme Magistrate, the Supreme Investigating Officer, and the Supreme Additional Sessions Judge, the Court of First and Last Instance": "It delivered a 114-page long judgment that went into great factual detail, drew almost-definitive conclusions about what had happened, effectively closed the case for all time, and did it all on the basis of its interpretation of the documents before it, untethered from the existing rules of evidence. The judgment, therefore, reads less like a verdict on a plea for an investigation, and more like a criminal appeal that results in an acquittal, but without the benefit of a trial court judgment."[163] The chief justice did not confront the government on the judges' appointment issue either. On January 11, 2018, the Collegium had recommended the elevation of Justice Indu Malhotra and Justice K. M. Joseph to the Supreme Court. The government waited three months before getting back to the Collegium: Justice Malhotra was approved, but not Justice Joseph because of his alleged lack of seniority and the fact that there was already a judge from Kerala in the court—two criteria that did not stand scrutiny, as the last appointments had not complied with the seniority rule and the sitting justice from Kerala was retiring in six months. Several lawyers explained that the government wanted to punish Justice Joseph for his role as chief justice of the Uttarakhand High Court in quashing president's rule, which the Modi government had imposed in the state in 2016, and enabling the Congress government to return.[164] Justice Kurian Joseph—the Keralite justice of the Supreme Court—in a letter to the chief justice that he had sent a few days before, made it very clear: by not implementing the Collegium's recommendations, the government was sending a "strong message [to] all judges down the line not to cause any displeasure to the executive lest they should suffer. . . . Is this not a threat to the independence of the judiciary?"[165] Other lawyers denounced the procedure. In a separate letter (examined below), Justice Chelameswar wrote an open letter to the CJI that "for some time, our unhappy experience has been that the government's accepting our recommendations is an exception and sitting on them is the norm."[166] A petition signed by more than 100 lawyers asked the CJI to hold the appointment of Justice Malhotra until both judges were appointed together. Chief Justice Misra preferred to temper his response to the government. He rejected the 100 lawyers' petition and declared, "If the centre has segregated the recommendation and sent one of the names for reconsideration then they are within their rights."[167] Many Supreme Court members disagreed, and some of them asked for a plenary meeting. The CJI did not call one, and when the Collegium met in May, instead of reiterating its recommendation on Justice Joseph, it deferred its decision, apparently because CJI Misra disagreed with the other members of the Collegium who wanted to resubmit Justice Joseph's name.[168] Finally, on July 16, 2018, the Collegium reiterated its recommendation of Justice Joseph, who was finally appointed. But this episode, by showing how divided the Supreme Court was and how suspicious of the CJI other justices had become, further damaged the reputation of the apex court. More importantly, the court appeared more and more at the mercy of the executive—and that was one of the reasons why CJIs were adopting a nonconfrontational attitude. They were now begging for judges' appointments, as Justice Joseph said in his letter to the CJI: "The dignity, honour and respect of this institution is going down day by day since we are not able to take the recommendations for appointment to this court to their logical conclusion within the normally expected times."[169] Not only did the Supreme Court have to wait an inordinate amount of time for the government's decisions, but these were more and more often contrary to the Collegium's recommendations. Justice Joseph finally made it to the Supreme Court, but others at the High Court level were never appointed despite having been selected by the Collegium. In April 2018, instead of making Justice Ramendra Jain a permanent judge of the Punjab and Haryana High Court (where he was an additional judge), the government gave him a six-month extension: for "possibly the first time since the collegium system was introduced, the Centre has unilaterally amended the recommendation of the judicial appointments body to apply its own writ."[170] Such "violation of settled law and procedure" became common practice under Dipak Misra.

Four lawyers—Harnaresh Singh Gill, Basharat Ali Khan, Mohammad Mansoor, and Mohammad Nizamuddin—who had been selected by the Supreme Court Collegium to become High Court judges in 2016, waited two years for the government's decision.[171] Finally, in June 2018, the government rejected the names of Khan and Mansoor in spite of the fact that the Collegium had already reiterated them, finding the objections of the government "frivolous."[172] Such an arbitrary attitude is illegal, as the recommendation of the Collegium is binding on the government if it has been reiterated.[173] While the reasons why the procedure was distorted in most of the cases mentioned remained mysterious, in other cases, lawyers have been sidelined and/or transferred for their past deeds. Justices Jayant Patel is a case in point, and others will be encountered in the following pages.

Justice Patel, as the acting chief justice of the Gujarat High Court, had ordered the CBI to investigate the murder of Ishrat Jahan in 2004. He "should have become Gujarat Chief Justice," as the senior-most lawyer Rajeev Dhavan pointed out,[174] but was transferred to Karnataka in 2016 and again, in 2017, to the Allahabad High Court—snatching away the opportunity for him to become chief justice of the Karnataka High Court when the senior-most judge retired a few weeks later. Instead of accepting this transfer, he preferred to resign. The Karnataka State Bar Association and Gujarat lawyers abstained from work for one day in protest.[175] But the Supreme Court did not intervene, even though the chief justice of India had not been consulted, as he should have been according to article 222 of the Constitution. Dhavan concluded, "If the collegiums cannot stand up to the government, the rule of law is at peril." Close observers of the Indian judiciary were struck by the fact that "while previous CJIs like Justice Lodha, Justice Thakur, and Justice Khehar have been very active in voicing concerns about delay and interferences in judicial appointments, the present CJI, Justice Misra, is not perceived as forthcoming in addressing exceeding executive interference."[176]

The conciliatory attitude of the CJI vis-à-vis the government continued to irk members of the Supreme Court, including Justice Chelameswar, who wrote an open letter to Chief Justice Misra in March 2018, as mentioned above. He had been prompted to do so because of another deviation from standard practices by the government, which had directly contacted the chief justice of the High Court of Karnataka to inquire about a judge recommended by the Collegium. Never before had the executive bypassed the Supreme Court in that manner. But Justice Chelameswar was especially worried about the attitude of the CJI, who was "more loyal than the King" by obliging the government. He warned Chief Justice Misra that "bonhomie between the Judiciary and the Government in any State sounds the death knell to Democracy."[177]

The image of the CJI was so tarnished that the Congress (along with the CPI, Communist Party of India [Marxist], NCP, SP, BSP, and IUML), initiated a procedure to impeach Dipak Misra in April 2018, one day after the Supreme Court decided to dismiss the petitions seeking an inquiry into the death of Special Judge Loya. That was a first in the history of India. The impeachment notice that was handed over by seventy-one Rajya Sabha MPs to the chairman of this assembly, Vice President Venkaiah Naidu, mentioned five grounds of behavior—including the corruption cases discussed below.[178] Naidu rejected this motion, and the MPs therefore turned to the Supreme Court. Kapil Sibal, the Congress MP who appeared before the court, asked who had constituted the bench he was addressing. As he got no response, he withdrew the impeachment notice.[179]

This incident took place under CJI Misra, but other similar ones occurred under his successor, Chief Justice Gogoi, who handled sensitive cases and the judges' appointment/transfers issues the same way. One of the sensitive cases that the Supreme Court kept postponing concerned electoral bonds. These bonds were introduced in February 2017 by the Modi government supposedly in the name of transparency, because they allowed anonymous donations to be made to political parties and thereby protected the privacy of the donors. The Election Commission of India immediately criticized the opacity of this financial mechanism and told the government: "This is a retrograde step as far as transparency of donations is concerned and this proviso needs to be withdrawn."[180] Petitions challenging the provisions of the Finance Act 2017, which made the electoral bonds possible, were filed by the CPI(M) and two NGOs (Common Cause and the Association for Democratic Reforms). But the Supreme Court sat on this highly sensitive issue until March 2019, by which time most of the electoral bonds had been purchased—in favor of the BJP (see chapter 9). And the only thing the three-judge bench headed by Chief Justice Gogoi did was to direct political parties to submit the details of donations received to the ECI in sealed envelopes by May 30; that is, after the elections.[181] Like the Aadhaar Act before, the electoral bonds had become a fait accompli due to lack of will on the part of the Supreme Court to control a highly controversial policy of the Modi government.

Under Chief Justice Gogoi, the Supreme Court did no more than the previous CJI to oppose the government's policy regarding the appointment and transfer of judges. Justice Kureshi, as a member of the Gujarat High Court, had remitted Amit Shah to police custody in 2010 for two days in the Sohrabuddin case. The Collegium recommended him for the post of chief justice of the Gujarat High Court, but the government preferred to transfer him to the Bombay High Court. The Collegium then recommended him for the post of chief justice of Madhya Pradesh. The law minister objected that he was "unfit" to be appointed chief justice of any high court because of his past "communal" records.[182] Instead, it appointed the senior-most justice of the Madhya Pradesh High Court as acting chief justice. The Gujarat High Court Advocates' Association described this decision as a "clearly uncalled for interference by the executive."[183] When the ministry said that it would have no objection if Justice Kureshi was appointed to a smaller court, the Collegium, instead of reiterating its recommendation, modified it and suggested that he be appointed chief justice of the Tripura High Court.

To sum up, under Chief Justices Misra and Gogoi, the Collegium stopped defending the independence of the judiciary and resisting, in particular, Law Ministry decisions regarding appointments and transfers of judges.[184] Retired Supreme Court Justice M. B. Lokur pointed out that "the unconstitutional NJAC is rearing its head and is now Frankenstein's monster. The advice of the two eminent persons postulated by the NJAC is no longer required. Actually, there is now no need to amend the Constitution to bring back the NJAC—it is already in existence with a vengeance."[185]

But the CJI's surrender did not pertain only to judge appointments and transfers: from 2017 onward, the Supreme Court has ceased to be at cross-purposes with the government, either because it has dismissed potentially embarrassing petitions (removal of Alok Verma, the Loya case) or because it has abstained from taking up a case for months or years (Electoral Bonds Act)—or both, in cases where the court took so much time before addressing an issue that a controversial law became a fait accompli, as in the Aadhaar case.

Why has the Supreme Court stopped opposing the executive since 2016?

Government Pressure, Self-Inflicted Wounds, and Judicial "National-Authoritarianism"

The nonconfrontational attitude of the Supreme Court may be explained from three points of view: government pressure, ideological affinities, and blackmailing.

GOVERNMENT PRESSURE

Supreme Court judges have inevitably been destabilized by the series of offensives that the Modi government launched after 2014, from blitzkrieg to a long war of attrition, a tug-of-war that was similar to previous battles Modi had fought since 2001 when he laboriously conquered the BJP in Gujarat against Keshubhai Patel and several Sangh Parivar leaders. As prime minister, he aimed to prevail over the judiciary, which had dared to resist him by quashing the NJAC, largely because he had experienced the power of an independent judiciary to stand in his way since his Gujarat years. After all, he had been forced to appear in court in the wake of the Gujarat pogrom.[186]

Modi attacked the independence of the judiciary as any populist leader would: in the name of the sovereignty of the people who had brought the BJP to power. Arun Jaitley, the law minister and a lawyer himself, maligned "the tyranny of the unelected"[187] after the NJAC was struck down. He also denounced the "encroachment of legislative authority by India's judiciary." He even claimed that "step by step, brick by brick, the edifice of India's legislature is being destroyed."[188] The nature of relations between the judiciary and the executive in 2014–2016 was reminiscent of the 1990s, when the judiciary initiated a phase of "judicial activism."[189] But in the 1990s, the Supreme Court—as well as the Election Commission of India under T. N. Seshan—was proactive, whereas in the mid-2010s, the executive was on the offensive and ultimately won.

But did the Supreme Court surrender in 2017–2018 simply because it could no longer bear the war of attrition waged by the government? Certainly, this fight had debilitating effects on the judiciary, as in any country where populists-turned-authoritarian rulers try to destabilize existing institutions. Supreme Court justices became divided and started to exhibit their differences in public, as in January 2018, when (only) four of them gave a press conference. The prestige of the judiciary has been tarnished by such moves, and that is precisely what the Modi government was trying to achieve: to discredit the last institution likely to counter its plans. However, the executive won the battle for other reasons, including growing ideological affinities and the alleged corruption of judges.

IDEOLOGICAL AFFINITIES: MAN-MADE AND SPONTANEOUS

Hindu nationalists have tried to infiltrate the judiciary as they have other institutions, including the police. That is why the Sangh Parivar has chosen law schools where the best Indian lawyers are trained as one of its favorite recruitment grounds and why it created a lawyers' branch, the All India Adhivakta Parishad (AIAP), founded in 1992 by D. P. Thengadi—who had already started the Sangh Parivar's labor union in 1955.[190] Among the founders of the AIAP were Rama Jois and Guman Lal Lodha, the former chief justices of the Punjab and Haryana High Court and of the Gauhati High Court. But the presence of lawyers connected with the Sangh Parivar in the High Courts and the Supreme Court gained momentum under the NDA governments. The career of A. K. Goel, which Atul Dev has studied closely, offers a fascinating illustration of the impact on the judiciary of the BJP's rise to power in the late 1990s to early 2000s:

AK Goel [was appointed] as a judge of the Punjab and Haryana High Court, in 2001. A couple of years after the fact, it was reported that the Intelligence Bureau's background check on Goel had noted that he was the general secretary of the All India Adhivakta Parishad, the lawyers' wing of the RSS. Under a field titled "Reputation/Integrity," the report had noted, "Corrupt person." The law ministry, then headed by the BJP's Arun Jaitley, approved Goel's nomination anyway. The president, KR Narayanan, refused to sign Goel's warrant of appointment, and sent his file back to the ministry. Instead of then returning the file to the collegium, Jaitley defended Goel's nomination himself, and dismissed the IB's findings as a "slur." Goel's file was sent to the president again, this time with the signature of the prime minister, Atal Bihari Vajpayee, attached. Narayanan, now that Goel's file had come before him a second time, reluctantly signed the warrant of appointment. "I feel that a more desirable course of action would have been to follow the same procedure . . . where the advice of the Chief Justice, which is integral to the selection process, was sought again and duly received," Narayanan wrote to the ministry. "I would also appreciate if my instant observations are shared with the Chief Justice of India along with my earlier observation." Goel went on to serve as the chief justice of two high courts. Shortly after Modi became the prime minister, Goel was appointed to the Supreme Court. Last year, just before he retired, he headed a bench that diluted the provisions of the Scheduled Castes and Tribes (Prevention of Atrocities) Act, a long-standing irritant in Hindutva eyes. Goel was elevated to the Supreme Court alongside Arun Mishra.[191]

Arun Mishra's profile is even more revealing of the way the judiciary has been infiltrated by sympathizers or members of the Sangh Parivar. He was appointed to the Supreme Court despite the fact that his name had been overlooked three times by the Collegium because his background check was not satisfactory.[192] A student of the Indian judiciary explained this promotion by his "proximity or otherwise to a right-wing NGO that treats the Bharatiya Janata Party (BJP) as its political wing [the RSS]."[193] This "proximity" became clear in 2016 when Justice Mishra held wedding receptions for his nephew in New Delhi and Gwalior because among the guests were the Madhya Pradesh BJP chief minister Shivraj Singh Chouhan, the union home minister Rajnath Singh, the union finance minister Arun Jaitley, and the Rajasthan chief minister Vasundhara Raje.[194]

Under the last three CJIs he worked with, Arun Mishra was the judge to whom the largest number of politically sensitive cases were assigned, including the Haren Pandya case (see note 55) and the case of the Sahara-Birla diaries, where one of the entries suggested payment by the companies of Rs 25 crore to Modi when he was chief minister and so on.[195] Analyzing these cases as well as many others, V. Venkatesan comes to the conclusion that "as the biggest litigant before the court, the Centre always stood to gain in cases listed before him."[196] In 2020, Arun Mishra praised the prime minister in a eulogizing manner surprising in a country observing the separation of powers. Delivering the vote of thanks at the inaugural function of the International Judicial Conference, he "thank[ed] the versatile genius, who thinks globally and acts locally, Shri Narendra Modi, for his inspiring speech" and added that "India is a responsible and most friendly member of the international community under the stewardship of internationally acclaimed visionary Prime Minister Shri Narendra Modi."[197]

Other Supreme Court judges have indirect links with the Sangh Parivar.[198] U. U. Lalit, for instance, is the son of a lawyer, U. R. Lalit, a founding member of the Akhil Bharatiya Adhivakta Parishad and one of its officeholders still today.[199] Note also that retired Supreme Court Justice K. T. Thomas was invited to address an RSS instructors' camp in Kottayam.[200]

But political affinities between judges and Hindu nationalism may not necessarily be due to connections with the Sangh Parivar and its members. In fact, many judges who were not part of this network shared the BJP's views on many issues, including Ayodhya (to be discussed in chapter 11), secularism, the need for a uniform civil code,[201] nationalism, and illegal migrants.[202]

Chief justices themselves have expressed views similar to those of the ruling party. The sense of ethnonationalism that Chief Justice Gogoi has shown is a case in point. Even before the BJP took power, Justice Gogoi, as a Supreme Court judge, supported one of the party's main objectives: to fight against illegal migrants coming from Bangladesh, in particular to Assam, his home state. In 2013, he heard a petition of the NGO Assam Public Works asking for the National Register of Citizens (NRC) to be updated in the state in order to identify illegal migrants. This move had been in the pipeline for years. He determined that the state government and the central government were acting too slowly, and in 2014, he "directed Prateek Hajela, the state coordinator of the NRC in Assam, to file an undertaking on whether the update could be completed by December 2016."[203] Subsequently, for five years, until Rajan Gogoi retired from the court, "throughout the hearings, the court exerted incredible pressure on government officials, monitoring every detail of the operation." The judge was in fact doing the work of the government by micromanaging a policy that was dear to the BJP. As the court had declared in 2014 that many more "foreigners tribunals" were necessary to ascertain the nationality of "doubtful citizens," the BJP government provided the necessary budget and human resources: half of the bureaucracy was mobilized to meet the deadline spelled out by Justice Gogoi, at the expense of other policies. Haleja had to show his progress by submitting reports to Justice Gogoi in sealed envelopes. As chief justice, he wanted larger numbers of those who had been declared illegal migrants to be deported. During one of the hearings, in April 2019, he told the Assam chief secretary: "Out of 4,600 declared foreigners only 4 have been deported? Is it not your constitutional duty? . . . It is your solemn duty by the Constitution to deport all those who are so declared by a court or a quasi-judicial body."[204] On May 30, 2019, the bench headed by the CJI ordered 200 more foreigners tribunals to be set up by September 1. This policy was well in tune with the Hindu nationalists' plans and ideology, as evident from the fact that on the very same day, the Home Ministry amended the Foreigners (Tribunals) Order, 1964: while foreigners tribunals had been limited to Assam until then, state governments and union territories were now authorized to create such tribunals anywhere in the country.[205]

On November 3, 2019, fifteen days before retiring, CJI Rajan Gogoi defended the NRC exercise, one of the BJP's main political planks, by adopting the party's discourse: "The Assamese people have displayed great magnanimity and large heartedness in accepting various cut-off dates for the purposes of preparation of the NRC that are at a considerable distance from the time when the first onslaught of forced migration hit them or their ancestors."[206] This quote substantiates the claim of close observers of Rajan Gogoi's career who explain his ideological affinities with Hindu nationalism on the basis of his ethnic roots. Not only does he hail from Ahom, the community claiming that they are the sons of the soil of Assam who have been overrun by migrants, but his "ancestors on his mother's side can be traced to the Ahom dynasty," and, as a student in Guwahati, he was trained by teachers who cultivated a strong sense of Assamese nationalism.[207]

FACETS OF CORRUPTION: FROM LOSS OF MORAL AUTHORITY TO BLACKMAIL—AND POSTRETIREMENT JOBS

In addition to ideological affinities, the nonconfrontational attitude of Supreme Court judges, including the chief justices, can be attributed to different forms of corruption.

The integrity of the last three chief justices has been questioned on many occasions over the past few years, compared to their predecessors' records. Two of them were mentioned in the Pul case. In 2016, Kalikho

Pul, before committing suicide, had written in a detailed diary-like notebook that Supreme Court judges were asking him for money in exchange for a favorable verdict in a particular case: he had become chief minister of Arunachal Pradesh with the support of Congress MLAs who, by defecting, had caused the fall of the previous chief minister, Nabam Tuki. But Tuki had turned to the judiciary, and the President's Rule had been imposed. Pul wrote:

> I received phone calls asking for 86 crore [11,466,660 USD] to give a judgment in my favour. But my conscience did not permit this. I didn't want to hurl the state into a well. . . . The MLAs of Arunachal Pradesh can be bought. The Congress party is also up for sale. But I never thought that the judges of the Supreme Court can also be bought. They contacted my associates and I several times to discuss a judgment in my favour. They asked for a bribe of 86 crore [11,466,660 USD]. . . . Virender Khehar, the younger son of Justice Khehar, contacted my associates and asked for 49 crore [6,533,330 USD]. And Aditya Misra, the brother of Justice Dipak Misra, asked me [for] 37 crore [4,933,330 USD]. . . . Until today, 25 July 2016, Ram Avtar Sharma has been contacting me on behalf of Justice Khehar. He is talking of how to get the judgment changed. . . . People must learn to recognise these brokers and traders in law and these corrupt traitors.[208]

Pul did not pay; he committed suicide. On July 13, 2016, a five-judge bench headed by Justice Khehar restored Nabam Tuki's government. Pul's notebook was released six months after his death, but "the administration had it all the while. How much did Prime Minister Modi know of it when he signed the order appointing Justice Khehar as chief justice?" asks Vijay Simha, suggesting that the government could now easily blackmail the new chief justice[209]—and his successor too. But in the case of Dipak Misra, other cases have been mentioned as well, including the Prasad Education Trust case[210] and the accusation of acquisition of government land by fraudulent means.[211]

Chief Justice Gogoi was accused of other things. In 2019, a former Supreme Court employee accused him of sexual harassment. He immediately formed a "special bench" for a "special sitting." The bench consisting of the CJI himself, Arun Mishra, and Sanjiv Khanna met the same day.[212] The CJI spoke first and for a long time about attacks against the independence of the judiciary, as "he did not think he should stoop so low as to even deny the charges."[213] The case was then handed over to another panel that followed ad hoc rules: "It did not tell the complainant what procedure it followed, did not give her any record of its proceedings, did not even allow her a lawyer when she appeared before it. She withdrew from the proceedings in protest."[214] One of the first people to express his support for Gogoi was Arun Jaitley, the then finance minister, in a blog post titled "It's Time to Stand Up with the Judiciary."[215] Finally, the panel found "no substance in the allegations," on the basis of a report it had received in a sealed envelope that was not even disclosed to the complainant.

These cases follow a pattern: in many of them, the CJI did not apply the basic principle of natural justice, as they were judges in their own cause,[216] and in many of them, as a result, the complainant often preferred to withdraw from the proceedings (like Kapil Sibal in the impeachment case), as if the dice were loaded. Whether the charges of corruption were justified or not, the absence of investigation gave rise to suspicion: the judiciary suffered from an unprecedented trust deficit and loss of moral authority. This feeling has been exacerbated by the systematization of a new practice, the use of sealed envelopes to hand over documents to judges—who will make judgments on the basis of documents no one else is allowed to see: "secrecy is the name of the game," to the great displeasure of Retired Justice Lokur.[217] According to him, this "new normal" tends to put the judiciary on the wrong side of public opinion—if only it cared—and is conducive to opaque transactions with the government.

The executive has benefited almost mechanically from this weakening of checks and balances. But it has exploited it actively, too: when a judge is accused of corruption, a case can be built, and a file can be used to blackmail him. Many close observers of the relations between the Modi government and the Supreme Court have come to the conclusion that the former had a file on the last three CJIs. Prashant Bhushan said it explicitly in the case of Dipak Misra: "The executive is blackmailing the chief justice through a CBI investigation into the alleged bribing of judges by medical colleges"[218]—one more reason for the government to control the CBI![219]

Along with sticks, the government used carrots as well. The Modi government not only came to the rescue of Chief Justice Gogoi when he was accused of sexual harassment; it also nominated him to the Rajya Sabha just four months after he retired. Reactions to this unprecedented move have been exceptionally strong. Dushyant Dave, senior advocate and president of the Supreme Court Bar Association, said, "This is totally disgusting, a clear reward in quid pro quo. The semblance of independence of the judiciary is totally destroyed."[220] Dave here suggests that some of the decisions Gogoi made as chief justice were overdetermined by the possibility of a postretirement sinecure. Indeed, to ensure the judiciary's independence, such appointments were not supposed to take place before a two-year cooling-off period. That was the stand Arun Jaitley himself took in 2012 when he declared that "pre-retirement judgements are influenced by a desire for a post-retirement job," and that a "cooling period" of two years should therefore be observed. He assumed that "clamour for post-retirement jobs is adversely affecting impartiality of the judiciary."[221]

But Rajan Gogoi was not the first ex–chief justice to get an important postretirement job. As early as 2014, former CJI P. Sathasivam had been appointed governor of Kerala. Analysts have speculated that he was rewarded for two things: First, as a Supreme Court justice, he "had quashed an FIR against BJP leader Amit Shah in an alleged fake encounter case [the Prajapati case]. Second, and more significantly, he was one of the two judges who upheld the Odisha High Court's verdict to sentence Bajrang Dal leader Dara Singh to life imprisonment for killing Australian missionary Graham Staines and his two children. This case had come to the apex court in an appeal seeking more severe punishment for Dara."[222]

Such postretirement rewards[223] showed lawyers that they could enjoy payback after retirement if they behaved. Retired Justice Lokur, interestingly, was not so surprised by Ranjan Gogoi's nomination but drew a grave conclusion from it: "There has been speculation for some time now about what honorific would Justice Gogoi get. So, in that sense the nomination is not surprising, but what is surprising is that it came so soon. This redefines the independence, impartiality and integrity of the judiciary. Has the last bastion fallen?"[224]

The evolution of the Supreme Court has indeed paved the way for a more authoritarian regime in India. This is the result of the executive's blitzkrieg and war of attrition and of ideological affinities that do not result only from the infiltration of RSS-affiliated judges but also from the personal inclinations of others who believed in ethnic nationalism and authoritarianism, a combination that has resulted in a form of national authoritarianism. The judges' rejection of dissent became evident in 2020 when a Supreme Court bench headed by Justice Arun Mishra condemned Advocate Prashant Bhushan for contempt of court because he was accusing the judiciary of corruption—including discretion and favoritism.[225] The Supreme Court of India, nolens volens, has invented what Pratap Bhanu Mehta has termed "judicial barbarism,"[226] an expression that refers, according to him, to "creeping hues of a Weimar judiciary."[227] The idea that the apex court, in charge of enforcing the rule of law, could indulge in authoritarianism may sound like a contradiction in terms, but it has been observed elsewhere, including in the United States, where in the early 1990s Supreme Court jurisprudence appeared "to manifest inflexibility, lack of compassion, and approval of oppression."[228] But in the case of India today, authoritarianism needs to be qualified due to its ethnonationalist overtones—hence the notion of judicial *national* authoritarianism. The propensity of the judiciary to support Hindu nationalism at the expense of secularism will be dealt with in detail in the last chapter of the book.

What Fourth Estate?

In a liberal democracy, the press is supposed to be the fourth pillar of democracy, provided it enjoys true independence—something it has lost to a great extent in Modi's India.

The government's efforts to muzzle dissent in the media reflect Narendra Modi's complex relation with the media since his Gujarat years.

Modi, who had been seriously affected by the media's critical coverage of the 2002 pogrom and its aftermath in Gujarat, did not trust the mainstream channels. As early as the summer of 2014, he chose to ignore them; as Sevanti Ninan points out, only official media would accompany him on his trips abroad, and he would not give any press conferences.[229] Instead, he decided to communicate "directly" with Indians via Twitter and the monthly radio program *Mann Ki Baat* (discussed in chapter 4), creating what can be described as a "one-way" style of communication in which the mainstream media were redundant.[230] As prime minister, he has never held a press conference and has given few interviews—almost never to newspapers or TV channels that have been critical of his policies or politics.

His government has shown palpable discomfort with the notion of free press. As early as 2014, the minister for information and broadcasting, Prakash Javadekar, declared that the media should observe the "Lakshman *rekha*" (Rubicon or red line) and should help the officials of India "to do good work" instead of frightening them "in the name of transparency."[231] Arun Jaitley, the then finance minister, went further when he declared in 2017 that he "personally believe[d] that free speech in India and in any society ha[d] to be debated."[232]

As mentioned in chapter 7, to begin with, the intimidation of journalists was left to trolls, who kept denigrating "presstitutes" and harassing them on social media or even physically.[233] But gradually the state itself became proactive. Five types of intervention can be identified here.

First, the government used ads as a tool. In June 2019, just after the Lok Sabha elections, it decided to cut off or reduce advertisements it had previously placed in three major newspaper groups: the *Times of India*, *The Hindu*, and *Amrita Bazar Patrika*, which also published *The Telegraph*. For the first and the last of these, this move represented a drop of 15 percent in these newspapers' ads.[234] It has been attributed, in each case, as a retaliation for unfavorable reports.[235]

Second, media outlets have been intimidated by "raids." The CBI raid at the residence of Prannoy Roy, cofounder and executive chairperson of NDTV, is a case in point. While the raid was "justified" by an "alleged loss to a bank" in relation to an ICICI loan—a loan that had already been reimbursed, said Roy—this police action was widely attributed to critical reporting by NDTV. Indeed, the raid took place one day after an on-air altercation between an NDTV anchor and Sambit Patra, a BJP spokesperson. In a press conference at the Press Club of India organized by Roy after the raid, the eminent lawyer Fali S. Nariman described it as "an unjustified attack on press and media."[236] Other kinds of raids have affected other media persons too. For instance, the Income Tax Department conducted a search at the residence of Raghav Bhal, the founder of *The Quint.* The Editors Guild of India immediately issued a communiqué regretting that this kind of "motivated income-tax searches and surveys will seriously undermine media freedom."[237]

Third, TV channels have been banned temporarily. In 2020, two Malayalam channels were banned for forty-eight hours by the Ministry of Information and Broadcasting because of their coverage of the Delhi riots (which will be further discussed in chapter 10). They were accused, among other things, of being "critical towards Delhi Police and RSS,"[238] a new red line. NDTV itself was banned for twenty-four hours because its coverage of the 2016 terrorist attack on the Pathankot Air Force Station "revealed strategically sensitive details." The Editors Guild objected that other channels had given the same information and were not sanctioned.[239]

Fourth, the government occasionally puts pressure on the owners of media outlets to get rid of committed journalists. While many journalists who were critical of the Modi government have resigned, including Faye D'Souza, who used to be the star anchor of Mirror Now, there is evidence of such pressure in only a few cases. Punya Prasun Bajpai is one of them. While his show, *Masterstroke,* was increasingly popular and critical of Modi, he was asked by the proprietor on ABP News to "refrain from mentioning the name of Prime Minister Modi" and then not to show his image on his program. But Bajpai remained critical of the government's policies and of some of the businessmen in Modi's entourage, including Gautam Adani. As a result, some of them—including Baba Ramdev—pulled their ads, the Sangh Parivar boycotted the channel's talk shows, and, even worse, ABP's satellite link became unstable during prime time, which resulted in even fewer ads. The moment Bajpai resigned at the proprietor's suggestion, the satellite glitches ceased and advertising returned.[240] The Foundation for Media Professionals said that it "deplores the manner in which pressure has apparently been brought on the management of ABP News by an influential section of the ruling establishment to do away with the services of Punya Prasun Bajpai."[241] A similar process was observed when Bobby Ghosh was allegedly invited to leave the post of editor in chief at the *Hindustan Times*. Ghosh, who had joined in 2016 after running *Quartz* and *Time* magazine, had started a special series on the lynchings of Muslims, "Let's Talk about Hate." This initiative was ill received by BJP leaders. He returned to New York less than a year and a half after joining the *Hindustan Times*, and the newspaper discontinued the "Hate Tracker" it had begun.[242]

Fifth, dissenting voices in the media have been harassed more and more systematically. Aakar Patel, a journalist and human rights activist, was booked by the police because he had retweeted a video showing people gathering near Colorado's capitol building to protest the killing of George Floyd, with this comment: "We need protests like these from Dalits, Muslims, Adivasis, poor and women. World will notice. Protest is a craft."[243] The police filed an FIR under three sections of the Indian Penal Code: section 505 (1) (b) ("with intent to cause, or which is likely to cause fear or alarm to the public, or to any section of the public whereby any person may be induced to commit an offence against the State or the public tranquility"), section 153 ("wantonly giving provocation with intent to cause riot"), and section 117 ("abetting commission of an offence by the public or by more than ten persons"). A BJP leader filed a sedition case against another senior journalist, Vinod Dua, accusing him of alleging that Narendra Modi was using terror attacks to get votes. The Supreme Court did not stay the investigation but asked Dua to join the probe.[244] The executive editor of *Scroll.in*, Supriya Sharma, was booked because of a report she did in villages of the constituency of Narendra Modi near Varanasi, where, she said, Dalits have been particularly affected by the COVID-19 lockdown. One of them, a Dalit woman, filed an FIR claiming that she had been defamed. When journalists of *The Wire* called her number, they were told that they should speak to the district magistrate to get more information.[245] Indeed, the state of Uttar Pradesh has taken a particularly aggressive stance against journalists during the COVID crisis.

According to the NGO Rights and Risks Analysis Group, across India, "at least 55 journalists faced arrest, registration of FIRs, summons or show causes notices, physical assaults, alleged destruction of properties and threats for reportage on COVID-19 or exercising freedom of opinion and expression during the national lockdown from 25 March to 31 May 2020."[246] Among them, the largest number—eleven[247]—were in Uttar Pradesh, where journalists were under attack even before the COVID crisis. In 2019 Prashant Kanojia, a freelancer, was jailed because of comments "maligning the image of the chief minister" on social media. He was only released after the Supreme Court intervened. In 2020 he was arrested again because of his sharing of a morphed post of the Ram Temple to be built in Ayodhya.[248] Another local journalist was booked because he showed the video of a minor girl cleaning the floor of a public hospital—something the police saw as an attempt at "maligning" the government.[249] Two other journalists from a local daily, the *Janadesh Times*, were sent show cause notices by the Varanasi district magistrate because of their report on a viral video that showed starving Dalit children eating grass in a village of the prime minister's constituency.[250] Kappan Siddique, a reporter with a Kerala-based news portal, was arrested by the Uttar Pradesh police on October 5, 2020 while on his way to cover a Dalit teenager's gang rape and murder in Hatras. He was charged under the Unlawful Activities (Prevention) Act for "conspiring" against the state government.[251] The UP authorities also filed a criminal complaint against Siddharth Vadarajan, one of the co-founders of *The Wire*, because of the outlet's reporting on a UP government minister violating the country's COVID-19 lockdown.[252]

Other local journalists met a similar fate in other states. In Chhattisgarh, a journalist was charged with sedition for sharing on social media a cartoon commenting on the Supreme Court's decision to reject petitions calling for an investigation into the death of Justice Loya. Another spent seventeen months in jail because he was covering an encounter with a Maoist guerilla and was accused of "complicity."[253] To list other cases would be tedious, given their number.[254]

In this context, fear has become all-pervasive. Josy Joseph, an expert in investigative journalism, who left "the mainstream media to practice journalism with full freedom," pointed out that "fear is the companion with which many puppeteers or editors in the mainstream newsrooms are getting up in the morning. I think they also go to sleep shrouded in sheets of fear and it is an amazing thing to watch people who acknowledge themselves as editors being so petrified by new facts and proof."[255] While in small towns in the countryside local journalists are mostly vulnerable to the local administration (including the police), in the big cities' mainstream newsrooms, editors in chief fear phone calls from ministers or BJP leaders. In 2017, the Vice India CEO told her journalists, "We cannot get a call from Amit Shah," which meant that self-censorship had to apply.[256]

Beyond self-censorship, the mainstream media has been taken over—at least in the realm of electronic media—by pro-government channels that have "sold out" (to use Josy Joseph's words), either because of ideological affinities or economic dependence. Pratap Bhanu Mehta emphasized in 2018 that "the Modi government added an insidious dimension to state-capital relations. Indian capital usually does not take on the government of the day for prudential reasons. But now private capital has been enlisted in a project of unprecedented alignment with the ideological purposes of the state. . . . There are some exceptions. But a shockingly large section of the private media are now the ideological vanguard of the state, its rhetorical stormtroopers in a politics of communalism, polarisation, distraction, anti-intellectualism, mendacity and hate."[257]

This dimension of the Indian brand of crony capitalism described in previous chapters found expression in many TV programs, not only during election campaigns, as in 2019, but routinely. Several mainstream channels funded by the corporate sector, while they claim to offer impartial information, have indeed echoed the government's line—after benefiting from its support. Republic TV, once again, is a case in point. First, the channel became available in 2017 on the government-owned Doordarshan Free Dish and Doordarshan DTH "without paying a dime" (like Zee TV).[258] Second, Republic TV's star anchor, Arnab

Goswami (who is also the managing director and editor-in-chief of Republic Media Network), has been so complacent with the Modi government[259] and so aggressive against the opposition that complaints were lodged against him for communal bias and defamation.[260] In addition to Goswami's shows, Republic TV and Republic Bharat (a Hindi channel) have dealt with the news in a most imbalanced way. From May 1, 2017, to April 1, 2020, the channel aired 1,136 political debates that totaled 63.8 percent of all its debates. Anti-opposition debates amounted to 33.4 percent politically neutral, to 16.2 percent pro-BJP, to 11.47 percent anti-BJP to 2.8 percent, and pro-opposition to 0 percent of all its debates.[261] When Arnab Goswami was arrested by the Maharashtra Police in November 2020 in connection with businessman Anvay Naik's death by suicide, every senior minister in Narendra Modi's cabinet came out openly in his support."[262] The Supreme Court of India, which dealt with his case at record speed, directed that he be released on interim bail.[263] One month later, the UK communications regulator fined Republic Bharat for a program, "Poochta Hai Bharat," that contained "uncontextualized hate speech" seen as "potentially highly offensive."[264]

Other news channels and anchors have indulged in the same kinds of practices, including Sudhir Chaudhary, who, on Zee TV—the channel that had allegedly aired doctored videos of JNU students (see chapter 5)—*routinely* accused intellectuals and artists of being "anti-national"[265] (something Arnab Goswami initiated as early as 2015 when he worked for Times Now).[266] Chaudhary was booked by the Kerala police for his segment called "Jihad" on his TV show, *Daily News and Analysis*. The senior BJP leader Syed Shahnawaz Hussain immediately called the case against him an "attack on press freedom."[267] Similarly, Amish Devgan, anchor of News18 TV, was booked by the Mumbai police for his communal overtones. Other TV anchors have been accused of similar bias, including Rajat Sharma (India TV).[268] Because of what it perceived as the anti-Muslim bias of so many Indian TV channels, *Gulf News*, the UAE-based newspaper, sought to have Republic TV, Zee News, India TV, Aaj Tak, ABP, and Times Now banned in the Gulf region.[269] But external pressure and FIRs have made no difference: the government continues to protect controversial anchors, who clearly represent its key asset for shaping public opinion.[270]

Why has mainstream "journalism become the new propaganda," to cite Ravish Kumar, the NDTV anchor?[271] This trend has been partly explained by the growing role of Sangh Parivar–affiliated journalists and owners of media outlets. Cobrapost tried to make this point in 2018 through a sting operation. One of its undercover reporters, who pretended that he was a pracharak working for a Hindu organization, Srimad Bhagwat Gita Prachar Samiti, offered to managing editors and marketing executives of big media houses millions (and even sometimes billions) of rupees for sponsoring advertisements, events, and advertorials to promote Hindutva. The campaign he wanted to launch, just before the 2019 elections, was supposed to be in two parts: after a phase of "soft Hindutva" relying on the broadcasting of mythological and religious programs, there would have been a sequence of systematic attacks on opponents, including Rahul Gandhi, Mayawati, and Akhilesh Yadav. The media outlets who were prepared to receive the money would then publicize the speeches of Sangh Parivar leaders, such as the RSS chief Mohan Bhagwat, Vinay Katiyar, and Uma Bharti.[272]

Some of the most influential executives of the top media outlets of India, including Vineet Jain, the managing director of the *Times of India*, who was offered Rs 500 crores (about 67 million USD) but asked for double that amount,[273] were shown on videos interacting with the Cobrapost reporter. Except two media houses, all the others were prepared to play the communal game in order to polarize voters—the official objective of the undercover reporter—including (besides the *Times of India*) the *Hindustan Times, New Indian Express, DNA*, Zee Group, ABP News, TV 18, India TV, ABN Andhra Jyothi, Dinamalar, Jagran Group, *Open* magazine, Lokmat, Sun Group, and Big FM. Some of the Cobrapost reporter's contacts were even willing to explain how the money could be routed to their accounts.[274]

The name of this operation by Cobrapost, "Operation 136," derived from the rank of India in the 2017 World Press Freedom Index. Indeed, India has been losing ground in terms of press freedom since 2014. India's ranking in the annual World Press Freedom of Reporters without

Borders slipped by nine spots between 2016 and 2020, when it was ranked 142 out of 180 countries.[275] One minor factor of this decline lies in the fact that visas for foreign journalists—who do not have easy access to Kashmir and the Northeast—"have been tightened."[276] Freedom House justified its own ranking of India—which is only partly based on press freedom—by emphasizing that "authorities have used security, defamation, sedition, and hate speech laws, as well as contempt-of-court charges, to curb critical voices in the media. Hindu nationalist campaigns aimed at discouraging forms of expression deemed 'antinational' have exacerbated self-censorship."[277]

What is at stake here is freedom of expression at large. In this regard, besides the independence of the media, access to the internet is a major issue in Modi's India. In 2016, the country registered more internet shutdowns than any other country.[278] In 2017, the government amended the Indian Telegraph Act of 1885 to specify that the law now allowed "the temporary suspension of telecom services."[279] The data compiled by the Software Freedom Law Center (SFLC), a Delhi-based digital rights group, show that the number of internet shutdowns has jumped from 3 in 2012, to 5 in 2013, 6 in 2014, 14 in 2015, 31 in 2016, 79 in 2017, and 134 in 2018, before decreasing to 106 in 2019 and 132 in 2020.[280] The rise of the number of internet shutdowns after 2014 reflects the BJP's policy: between Modi's election in 2014 and the fall of 2017, out of 89 internet shutdowns, 74 were due to the BJP and its allies at the national, state, or district levels.[281] Since 2016, every year India has resorted to internet shutdowns more than any other country worldwide, for two official reasons: public safety and public order. For instance, in 2019, internet shutdowns were used to complicate communications among protesters against the Citizenship Amendment Bill—even though their demonstrations were legal and peaceful (see chapter 10).[282] Similarly, the Facebook page of the peasants protesting against the laws meant to liberalize India's agriculture was blocked at the peak of the December 2020 demonstrations.[283]

In Modi's India, national populism has increasingly followed a course akin to authoritarianism. The government has tried to prevail over the country's institutions, either by constraining their power or by limiting their independence. A key strategy, in this respect, pertains to appointment procedures. The ruling party has gradually put itself in a position to nominate its people at the helm of major power centers or to reduce their margin for maneuver. Such a process has been achieved especially in the cases of the CBI and NIA, two "institutions of internal accountability," of great importance to the BJP given the number of sensitive cases against prominent leaders—including Amit Shah and Indresh Kumar[284]—that they were investigating and given the role these investigative bodies could play for intimidating opponents or blackmailing those who had something (even minor things) to hide.

However, the most important player in the traditional Indian system of checks and balances was the Supreme Court.[285] Here again the question of appointments is key, but it is more difficult to have "dependable" men named as justices and chief justices than as CBI or NIA directors. When the Supreme Court declared the NJAC unconstitutional, the Modi government initiated a war of attrition on judicial appointments and started forcing through a number of judge transfers. From 2017 onward, it no longer met any significant resistance from the chief justices. This change is difficult to explain. Had the chief justices resigned themselves to a new power balance? Were they blackmailed? While these variables (impossible to ascertain) need to be factored in, another one should be emphasized: some justices and chief justices demonstrated ideological affinities with the ruling party, either because they were connected to the Sangh Parivar network or because they shared some of its ideas—as evident from the way Chief Justice Gogoi supervised the NRC in Assam. In that case, a major institution of the Indian republic appears to have espoused values that are at odds with constitutional values, *irrespective* of the identity of the ruling party.

This state of things can also be detected in the institutions mentioned above. The NIA, for instance, was somewhat biased *even before* the BJP formed the government in May 2014. Rohini Salian gave revealing details in this respect: "It was difficult to trust everyone and I had worked with a committed team who were in sync with each other. Although I sensed infiltration had already begun into the NIA and not everyone in the newly formed team was in favour of building a strong case. But still, we had some very efficient officers. They stood by me and diligently investigated the case. But they too were shunted out when I was asked to hand over the case in June 2014."[286] It is probably because "infiltration had already begun into the NIA" that the agency had not filed an appeal against the bail granted to Swami Aseemanand in April 2014—before the BJP's victory—in the Samjhauta Express case.[287] Incidentally, the NIA director to whom the Modi government granted two extensions, Sharad Kumar, had been appointed in 2013, under the UPA government. Similarly, Ajit K. Doval, Modi's national security advisor, had been appointed Intelligence Bureau director in July 2004 by J. N. Dixit, Manmohan Singh's NSA, whereas, according to Praveen Donthi, "During his IB years, he had close links to the Bharatiya Janata Party and the Rashtriya Swayamsevak Sangh."[288] After retiring, the "overlapping of ideas" between Doval and the Sangh Parivar became obvious. Considering, as did the BJP, that the "infiltration of Bangladeshis" was "the biggest internal security problem," he said in a 2006 interview, "India's internal vulnerabilities are much higher than its external vulnerabilities."[289] In 2013, in a speech at a BJP event, he pointed out that the party was the only one that did not view identity as plural: "We cannot base our nation-building on diversity."[290] In between, as the founding director of a think tank, the Vivekananda Foundation, he played a key role behind the scenes in the Anna Hazare movement, which was also supported by the Sangh Parivar.[291] The editor of a leading newspaper who had been approached by Doval for his help emphasizes that "some of the senior bureaucrats from home ministry and intelligence officials were also clandestinely part of it."[292] So, in the early 2010s, some civil servants joined hands with forces fighting the government of India in connection with the Sangh Parivar—and unsurprisingly, these undercover officials belonged to the security apparatus.

The fact that key institutions of India's democracy appear to have become partly dominated by people who do not fully observe constitutional values but share, at least in part, the worldview of the Sangh Parivar—and in some cases are even connected to them—suggests the existence of a "deep state" before 2014. In South Asia, this notion has been primarily applied to Pakistan to qualify the way the army (and the security establishment at large) have influenced the polity behind the scenes. In the present book, so far, the notion of a parallel state has been used to describe Hindu nationalist vigilante groups that regulate social life at the grassroots level and RSS men—to whom the former report—who have no official government position but nevertheless advise BJP ministers or chief ministers. The notion of a deep state is different: here, the actors are not outside the state; they are part of the state. But they tend to hijack state institutions by implementing principles having ethnonationalist and authoritarian dimensions at odds with constitutional values. The parallel state and the deep state are the two legs on which an ethnic and illiberal democracy walks in India today. Since 2014, however, the notion of a deep state has lost most of its value, because those who were operating behind the scenes can now do so in the open.

The way the government has weakened (and somewhat politicized)[293] key institutions and/or intensified its control over them—including the mainstream media—has mechanically worked toward establishing an authoritarian regime.[294] Justice A. P. Shah, former chief justice of Delhi High Court, in the opening lecture of the Janta Parliament (People's Parliament)[295] on August 16, 2020, concluded that "since 2014, every effort has been made to systematically destroy these institutions, not necessarily in the blatantly destructive way that the Indira Gandhi government did in the past, but certainly, in ways that have rendered the Indian democratic state practically comatose, and given the executive the upper hand in most matters."[296] This strategy has made possible the transition from a Hindu Rashtra to an authoritarian Hindu Raj. But there are different forms of authoritarianism. India's variant under Modi fits the model that grants an important role to elections—be it called electoral authoritarianism or competitive authoritarianism. The crucial part of electoral competition—and, therefore, of the populist repertoire—was evidenced by the Lok Sabha elections in 2019.

9

Toward
"Electoral Authoritarianism"

THE 2019 ELECTIONS

THE EMASCULATION OF INSTITUTIONS likely to resist the executive is only one facet of the rise of authoritarianism in India. The distortion of the electoral process is another, which has given birth to a form of "electoral authoritarianism," a concept invented by Andreas Schedler. Schedler explains that, while, formally, electoral authoritarian regimes hold multiparty elections, "they deprive them of their democratic substance"[1] because they "distort . . . the formation of popular preference as well as the expression of popular preferences."[2] How? Not only by interfering with institutions in charge of organizing elections (like the Electoral Commission of India) but also by making competition unequal in terms of money and by restricting freedom of expression, including media independence.

India's transition from national populism to electoral authoritarianism became obvious during the 2019 election campaign, which took place in a rather difficult context for Modi, as the BJP had not been able to win a majority in any major state election since the 2017 Uttar Pradesh polls. In December 2018, a few months before the seventeenth general elections, it even lost Madhya Pradesh, Rajasthan, and Chhattisgarh. In July 2018, the CSDS-Lokniti Mood of the Nation Survey (MOTN) showed that the ruling party's popularity was on the wane to such an extent that the analysts confidently concluded, "One of the biggest takeaways from MOTN July 2018 poll is that the Bharatiya Janata Party cannot hope to maintain its Lok Sabha supremacy."[3]

These experts were to be proved wrong, as they had been in 2014, when none of the poll pundits had anticipated that the BJP would win a clear-cut majority. In 2014, Narendra Modi's election campaign had a major impact on the national-populist mode, and in 2019, too, Modi's campaign largely explained his success. It is therefore very tempting to look at the 2019 elections as a repeat performance of what had happened five years previously—especially as the BJP, like in 2014, had a one-point agenda (Modi) and even obtained a similar number of seats from almost the same states.[4]

But the 2019 elections were different. They were bound to be so because in 2014 Modi was an outsider, whereas in 2019 he was the incumbent. He could not repeat the development-oriented promises he had made five years before. Instead, he emphasized another facet of his populist repertoire: national security. While the message had shifted somewhat, the technique remained the same: Modi saturated the public space, with the BJP election campaign unfurling at a mind-boggling magnitude due to the money spent by the party. This unprecedented characteristic of the 2019 BJP election campaign partly resulted from the introduction of electoral bonds.

The 2019 election campaign marks a transition in India toward electoral authoritarianism precisely because electoral competition was no longer a level playing field, not only due to the ruling party's financial resources but also because of the role of the media and the bias of the institution in charge of the election process: the Election Commission of India.[5]

Chowkidar Modi

Modi's campaign style in 2019 repeated several populist features already displayed in 2014. Once again, Modi claimed to represent the people against elite groups made up of liberals, including the "Khan Market gang," a phrase he used in an interview to describe the habitués of this Delhi market geared to the affluent, where intellectuals, rich Indians, and expatriates shop and socialize in upmarket cafés.[6] Modi's followers, however, usually preferred to designate these "libtards" as "the Lutyens people," referring to the poshest part of New Delhi, designed by the British architect Edwin Lutyens. The establishment Modi was fighting continued to be epitomized by Congress leaders, including the Nehru-Gandhi family—as Rahul Gandhi was once again, as in 2014, his main opponent.

Emphasizing his plebeian background, Modi reiterated that his family belonged to a "most backward caste,"[7] and to align himself with the vulnerability of the subalterns, he projected himself as a potential victim of the former rulers. In a meeting in Madhya Pradesh, he claimed, "The Congress people have so much hatred for your Modi that they are even dreaming of killing Modi. But they are forgetting that people from Madhya Pradesh and India are batting for me."[8] Eager to appear close to the people, and even to be part of them, Modi chose to speak in the way he thought they spoke. Modi, despite his somewhat Sanskritized Hindi, had adopted a sarcastic and simple oratorical style since his Gujarat days, especially when attacking members of the Nehru-Gandhi family. He targeted Rahul Gandhi's deceased father, Rajiv Gandhi, saying, "Your father was termed 'Mr Clean' by his courtiers, but his life ended as 'Bhrashtachari No 1' (corrupt man number 1)."[9]

Like in 2014, Modi also cultivated the heroic mode that he had used since his Gujarat days. However, his brand of heroism relied as much on his muscular physique (the "fifty-six-inch" claim) as on his wisdom—something his age partly explained. He used this repertoire during the Kumbh Mela that began in Prayag in early 2019. Photographs of the prime minister praying and bathing in the Ganges were widely publicized.[10] The day after the polls concluded, he even "climbed" a Himalayan mountain to spend two days meditating in a cave just large enough for him and his photographer.[11] This is very well in tune with the "this-worldly asceticism" idiom of politics described by Susan Hoeber Rudolph and Lloyd Rudolph and W. H. Morris-Jones's notion of "saintly politics"[12] (see chapter 2). But it has also something to do with the "Bollywoodization" of the public scene, for in the populist era, politics is more than ever a spectacle. The combination of commonality and heroism is typical of the populist repertoire, which is why body language often plays a key role in manufacturing the populists' image.[13]

National-Security Populism

RESISTING PAKISTAN—AND DELEGITIMIZING CONGRESS

In 2019, Modi's heroic status was nurtured by his image as a strongman in the context of security threats. The Pakistani threat has always figured prominently in Modi's election campaigns—right from the first in 2002 in Gujarat. But he had never been in a position to exploit this factor as extensively and as successfully as in 2019.

On February 14, 2019, barely a few weeks before the beginning of the official campaign, a deadly attack in Pulwama (Jammu and Kashmir) led by a jihadi group based in Pakistan claimed the lives of forty-one Indian Central Reserve Police Force personnel. By way of response, Modi ordered air strikes to be conducted on Pakistani territory. A Jaish-e-Mohammed training camp was allegedly destroyed in Balakot. In the operation, the Indian Air Force lost a plane and a pilot, Wing Commander Abhinandan Varthaman (who would eventually be returned to India and came back as a hero), and mistakenly shot down one of its own helicopters, killing six airmen.[14] Despite the mixed results of these air strikes, Modi managed to portray himself as India's protector in a campaign dominated by nationalist and even warmongering rhetoric—largely because the fact that six airmen had died was hardly reported by the media. Ahead of the enforcement of the Election Commission's Model Code of Conduct (MCC), which prohibits involving the army in electoral campaigns, the BJP campaigned massively, through all channels, using visuals associating Modi with the air strikes and the military—especially Wing Commander Abhinandan Varthaman. Modi himself used martial rhetoric aimed at disqualifying Congress leaders as antinational because, "guided by their Modi hatred[, they] have started hating India:"[15] not only had they never dared to attack Pakistan the same way, but now they also even sought more detailed information about the Balakot operation—"demoralizing jawans [soldiers]."[16] In a rally he held in Maharashtra, Modi told first-time voters: "Dedicate your first vote to the Air Force which undertook the air strike at Balakot, to those jawans who were martyred in Pulwama. . . . Congress manifesto is full of anti-national thoughts. Whatever Congress says, Pakistan repeats. Congress wants talks with separatists, wants to lessen the presence of armed forces in Kashmir, wants to remove sedition law. Pakistan wants exactly the same. . . . Voters should teach a fitting lesson to such parties who do not trust the armed forces."[17] The so-called mainstream media, ably backing this cultivated patriotic hysteria, also helped propagate a militaristic image of the prime minister, something BJP leaders emulated on the ground. The Delhi BJP chief, for instance, campaigned dressed in army fatigues and recited poems about Wing Commander Varthaman onstage.[18] The BJP chief minister of Karnataka, B. S. Yeddyurappa, claimed that the Balakot air strike would help the BJP to win twenty-two Lok Sabha seats in his state.[19]

On March 17, Modi added the prefix "Chowkidar" (watchman or sentinel) to his Twitter handle and made that label—also adopted by a large number of his followers, including union ministers—a symbol of the BJP campaign. The #MainBhiChowkidar (I am a Chowkidar too) hashtag was quickly popularized by an army of digital activists. In his first campaign tweet, he wrote, "Your Chowkidar is standing firm & serving the nation. But I am not alone . . . today, every Indian is saying #MainBhiChowkidar."[20] This motto echoed similar communication techniques used previously to achieve a fusion of the masses with their leader. In 2007, in Gujarat, Modi's supporters wore Modi masks. Twelve years later, emulation had taken an immaterial turn in the age of digital communication.

However, Modi's campaign was not only digital. He also toured India, taking the country by storm as he had in 2014,[21] but this time as the nation's militarized "Chowkidar." Canvassing in Balod District (Chhattisgarh), he declared, "When there is a strong government, there is surgical strike and air strike and the world listens."[22] In Khargone (Madhya Pradesh) he urged voters to press the lotus button (the BJP's symbol, which appears on Indian voting machines), as if they were "pressing the trigger to shoot terrorists in their chest."[23] In Bihar he went even further:

After the Pulwama terror attack, the brave sons of India displayed their valour. . . . For the first time in Indian history, they entered the home of the terrorists to teach them a lesson. . . . The whole world is discussing the attack, but these mahamilavati [lit. "these contaminated," in reference to the opposition] are asking for proof [that the Balakot training camp had been destroyed] from Modi. . . . These people should tell the country whether they have faith in the brave sons of India or Pakistan's kupoot (bad son). . . . Are you people happy with what the "chowkidar" has done for the country? Whatever remains to be done too will be completed by this chowkidar.[24]

The BJP election manifesto, which was released just before the first day of polling, elaborated on the same theme, as "the natural culmination of the last few years, the sabre rattling and the politicization of the armed forces that gained ground first with the so-called surgical strikes along the Line of Control in 2016, then with the Pulwama attack and the airstrike on Balakot in Pakistan."[25] During the election campaign, the politicization of the army found expression in electoral ads featuring army men. Modi himself posted a video showing soldiers carrying out an operation in a jungle with the following lyrics sung in the background: "I will now no longer tolerate terror / I will no longer be quiet / I am a son of India, how long will I remain silent? / My war cry joins the courageous soldiers along the border."[26] The Pulwama factor played a major role in the 2019 election, which may well have put India on the path to a security state.

FIGHTING "INFILTRATORS"

While Pakistan figured prominently in the BJP's election campaign,[27] other external threats were mentioned in the first section of the party's manifesto, titled "Nation First," a formula echoing Donald Trump's slogan, "America first." The subheadings of this section form a very interesting list indeed, as external threats and internal threats are amalgamated: a zero-tolerance approach to terrorism, national security, soldiers' welfare, combating infiltration, coastal safety, implementing the Citizenship (Amendment) Bill, combating left-wing extremism, repeal of article 370. Three of these items refer to domestic issues: the Maoist movement, the autonomy of Jammu and Kashmir presented as a security problem, and the Citizenship (Amendment) Bill, which was used more than the other two during the campaign, mostly by Amit Shah, the BJP president. Shah was to connect the dots between two commitments that the BJP made in its manifesto under two different subheadings, "Combating Infiltration" and "Citizenship (Amendment) Bill," two points scrutinized below. The manifesto read:

1. There has been a huge change in the cultural and linguistic identity of some areas due to illegal immigration, resulting in an adverse impact on local people's livelihood and employment. We will expeditiously complete the National Register of Citizens process in these areas on priority. In future we will implement the NRC in a phased manner in other parts of the country [other than Assam].

2. We are committed to the enactment of the Citizenship Amendment Bill for the protection of individuals of religious minority communities from neighbouring countries escaping persecution. We will make all efforts to clarify the issues to the sections of population from the Northeastern states who have expressed apprehensions regarding the legislation. We reiterate our commitment to protect the linguistic, cultural and social identity of the people of Northeast. Hindus, Jains, Buddhists and Sikhs escaping persecution from India's neighbouring countries will be given citizenship in India.[28]

Amit Shah explained during the campaign that the NRC would enable the government to deport illegal immigrants, except those who had found refuge in India and belonged to one of the communities listed above in the context of the Citizenship (Amendment) Bill, which had been rejected by the Rajya Sabha in February 2019 but which the BJP promised to introduce again in parliament. Touring West Bengal, a state where the BJP was eager to make inroads, Shah promised to apply the NRC next to the state where Muslims (including some of those coming from Bangladesh) supported Mamata Banerjee's party. He said: "Mamata*ji* thinks that infiltrators will see her through in the polls. . . . We will bring NRC and oust every infiltrator from the State. . . . I want to assure all the refugees that the Citizenship (Amendment) Bill is our commitment and Hindu, Buddhist and Sikh refugees will not be required to leave the country. They can live here with respect."[29] These words, which echo an ethnoreligious definition of the nation at odds with the Constitution, were aimed at polarizing the Bengali voters along religious lines.[30] In fact, the communal overtones of the BJP's 2019 campaign were more pronounced than in 2014.

POLARIZING DISCOURSES AND PRACTICES

While Narendra Modi had left the polarization strategy in the hands of surrogates and local actors during his first term, things changed during the reelection campaign. In western Uttar Pradesh, he tried to mobilize Hindu voters by invoking again the 2013 Muzaffarnagar riots that had been fostered (if not instigated) by Hindu nationalists against Muslims, whom he presented as being responsible for atrocities against the majority:

> Recall, when there was Mahamilavati [massively adulterated][31] government in Delhi, and the SP's government here, they conducted an experiment in Muzaffarnagar. Atrocities were committed on the basis of caste and community. What crimes were committed, what atrocities happened against daughters, do you remember, will you remember? . . . Ajit Singh [the leader of a state opposition party, the Rashtriya Lok Dal] did not raise his voice against those who shelter rioters and today he is visiting every street to abuse this chowkidar. . . . Remember, they are people who threaten to chop others and we are people who ensure the security and honour of daughters.[32]

However, the most dramatic use of communal rhetoric pertained to the question of "Hindu terrorism." In April, the BJP nominated Pragya Singh Thakur in the Bhopal constituency, despite the fact that she was accused of domestic terrorism in a case of multiple blasts targeting

Muslims, including the Malegaon case.[33] Released on bail on grounds of health, Thakur campaigned fiercely, and Narendra Modi vindicated her nomination in the name of what she endured in jail and the honor of Hindus. In an interview with *Times Now*, he said, "A woman, a *sadhvi* was tortured like this, no one raised a finger. . . . They defamed a 5,000-year-old culture that believes in *Vasudhaiva Kutumbakam* (The world is one family). They called them terrorists. To answer them all, this is a symbol and it will cost Congress."[34] Narendra Modi used the same argument onstage during election rallies. In Wardha, during his first campaign day in Maharashtra, he gave an impassioned speech decrying what he described as Congress's treasonous mention of "Hindu terror" to refer to bombers who come from the majority community. The prime minister apparently believed that Hindus were incapable of resorting to this sort of violence, which was the preserve, he suggested, of Islamists: "How can the Congress be forgiven for insulting the Hindus in front of the world," he cried.[35]

Modi also accused Rahul Gandhi of contesting elections not only in his traditional seat, Amethi, but also in a Kerala constituency, Wayanad, seeking to find cover in a district with a Muslim majority (which is factually false). The party president, Amit Shah, went further by equating this district with Pakistan.[36] A government minister even accused Rahul Gandhi of being a Muslim (by his father) and a Christian (by his mother), backed by a Photoshopped image.[37] Yogi Adityanath was equally vehement when he accused the Congress of being infected by the "Muslim League virus" and of serving biryani to jihadis in jail, whereas Modi gave them "bullets and bombs."[38] Pragya Singh Thakur went further when she hailed Mahatma Gandhi's killer, Nathuram Godse, as a true "patriot." Narendra Modi said that he would not forgive her but did nothing to sanction her.

Welfare Populism

While fear and anger, the two emotions that were analyzed in part I as the main foundations of national populism, continued to play a major role in Modi's national-security populism, he also referred to socioeconomic issues in order to cash in on other emotions, including the craze for dignity that was mentioned in chapter 4. Indeed, the Chowkidar tag was not directed against aggressors and threats alone. It also pertained to the protection of the poor by Modi.

In 2014, Modi had essentially campaigned on the theme of economic development. But as prime minister, he had failed to deliver on his promises of job creation—something most people realized even if the government withheld some of the data documenting this setback. In early 2019, the Periodic Labour Force Survey of the National Sample Survey Office (NSSO) showed that India had the highest unemployment rate recorded in forty-five years. The authorities prevented the release of these findings—which led to the resignation of two National Statistical Commission's statisticians[39]—but they leaked to the press. The unemployment rate calculated by the NSSO was especially high among India's youth: 34 percent for those between twenty and twenty-four years old, even up to 37.5 percent among urban dwellers of this age group. These figures were consistent with those of the Centre for Monitoring Indian Economy, according to which the unemployment rate for twenty- to twenty-four-year-olds was 37 percent, against 17 percent in 2017,[40] and that of twenty- to twenty-nine-year-olds was around 28 percent. For the latter age group, this meant that 30.7 million young people were unemployed, compared to only 17.8 million in 2017. In two years, the number of unemployed young people had thus increased by 73 percent.[41] Other indicators, including rates of growth and investment, were slowing down as well.[42]

As Modi could not capitalize on the development agenda he had announced in 2014, he shifted the socioeconomic focus of his campaign to welfare policies to flagship centrally sponsored schemes that his government had launched for the poor, notably Swachh Bharat Abhiyan, Pradhan Mantri Jan Dhan Yojana, and Pradhan Mantri Ujjwal Yojana, which were promoted not only as socioeconomic schemes but also as programs that would give the poor some sense of dignity.

Surveys do not suggest any clear correlation between welfare schemes and electoral support, but the Lokniti-CSDS National Election Post-Poll Survey (NES) showed that among women beneficiaries of the

PMUY "more women voted for the BJP compared to those who did not benefit from it (41% and 33%, respectively). Among women beneficiaries of Jan Dhan Yojana, 42% of women beneficiaries opted for the BJP compared to 34% of non-beneficiaries."[43] These results can be attributed to a new form of welfare populism associating the personality of Modi with pro-poor programs, as mentioned in chapter 4—where it was shown that most of these schemes were implemented by and in the name of the prime minister. Yamini Aiyar makes this point in the context of the 2019 election campaign:

> The BJP's welfare schemes reflected Modi's persona. They featured loud, grand announcements, ambitious targets, and tightly centralized monitoring. And here lay their genius. Many schemes that are now identified with the Modi-led BJP government's welfare agenda were already part of the broad basket of programs that make up the welfare state in India, and many had been launched in the UPA years. . . . But more than the policies themselves, what distinguished Modi's approach to welfare was the presentation and handling of them in ways that enhanced the Modi persona. Policies that the government said had priority had the initials PM (for "Prime Minister" [or Pradhan Mantri]) added as a prefix before their names, suggesting the idea of a connection between Modi himself and the beneficiaries. Most flagship schemes directly provided private goods (housing, toilets, cooking-gas cylinders, pensions, cash income) rather than diffuse public goods such as education. Whether this was part of a grand vision for welfare or careful political strategy will remain a matter of speculation, but this choice of schemes allowed for the establishment of a convenient, direct relationship between "Modi" and the voter. Reporting from the 2019 campaign recounted many citizens describing how they had received benefits from "Modi" rather than from the government or even the ruling party.[44]

This analysis illustrates the point made by R. Deshpande, L. Tillin, and K. K. Kailash about the way the BJP "attempted a re-positioning of the PM as a leader of the poor rather than mere *Vikas Purush* of the 2014 version" during the 2019 election campaign.[45] This strategy was partly successful owing to the *vishwas* politics analyzed by Neelanjan Sircar, who rightly emphasizes that the change in one of Modi's slogans reflected a tactical shift:

> In 2014, Prime Minister Modi came to power with the simple slogan "sabka saath, sabka vikaas" (Supporting everyone, everyone's development). After bettering the BJP's impressive 2014 performance in 2019, Prime Minister Modi quipped, "sabka saath, sabka vikaas, aur ab sabka vishwas" (Supporting everyone, everyone's development, and now everyone's trust). The explicit inclusion of vishwas (trust/ belief) in the slogan is telling. It is an understanding of politics that is based on the personal popularity of Narendra Modi, and the trust that voters have placed in him. One can juxtapose this trust-based conception of politics against one of "democratic accountability," wherein voters place well-defined demands on the elected representative and support him/her based on the fulfillment of these demands.[46]

These slogans, including "Supporting everyone, everyone's development, and now everyone's trust," are typically empty signifiers intended to present Modi as the great unifier of the nation. The direct relationship that he established with "his" people through such an emotional charge emancipated him from accountability in the eyes of his supporters. As a tutelary figure combining the heroic features of strongman, sage, and father figure, he did not appear responsible for policy failures. If any failure was admitted, it was not attributed to him but to others—including the bureaucrats or the opposition. Modi could only do his best for his people. Indeed, some nonbeneficiaries were confident that he would deliver and that they would benefit from his policies if he was reelected. One of them, a poor tractor driver from Rajasthan, said: "Our name is there in the Pradhan Mantri Awas Yojana [a scheme launched in 2015 for providing housing for all in urban areas by 2022]. We openly defecate as we have not got money for building toilets yet. But we have full faith in Modi*ji* that if he comes back to power we will get our house and toilet."[47]

The "PM" schemes for the poor made Modi popular among many of them despite their diminishing financial resources, not only because the prime minister himself was seen as the schemes' initiator but also because they involved tangible (even material) benefits[48] addressing the issue of poor Indians' dignity. And the way the schemes were promoted further increased Modi's impact: on Swachh Bharat Abhiyan alone, the government spent Rs 4000 crore (533.3 million USD) on just publicity in 2014–2019.[49]

To sum up, Modi's 2019 election campaign retained core populist elements that were already evident in 2014 (including his plebeian background vis-à-vis the establishment and his targeting of Others posing a threat to Hindus). But there was a noticeable shift toward security-oriented, martial postures in the aftermath of the Pulwama attacks against Pakistan, and the vikas dimension of the 2014 campaign morphed into what Sircar calls vishwas politics. A last-minute decision somewhat justified this trust: the union budget that was announced in February granted an annual income support of Rs 6,000 (80 USD) to all farmer households owning two hectares or less—that is, 6 percent of a small farmer's yearly income.[50] But still, poor peasants who were in a rather desperate situation greatly appreciated this relief awarded to them in the framework of a program called PM-KISAN Yojana (Prime Minister Peasants' Scheme). This scheme, under which Rs 2,000 (26.7 USD) is transferred to the bank accounts of farmers with small landholdings every four months, seems to have made some of them swing in the BJP's favor. According to the Lokniti-CSDS National Election Post-Poll Survey (NES), among farmers who had benefited from the PM-KISAN Yojana and credited the central government for the same, 56 percent voted for the BJP (NDA 65 percent), and only 8 percent chose the Congress (UPA 11 percent). On the other hand, among those who credited the state government, the figures were almost the same for both (UPA 30 percent, NDA 29 percent). Interestingly, two-fifths of those who credited the state government voted for parties other than the UPA and the NDA.

Reinventing himself once again, Modi therefore combined multiple dimensions of the populist repertoire (and more precisely of national populism) and used them according to the time and context of the campaign.[51] And like in 2014, he was his party's one-point agenda,[52] to such an extent that, once again, a large proportion of BJP supporters chose the party because of him. The NES found in 2019 that 32 percent of those who had voted BJP declared that "their voting preference would have changed if Modi [had not been] the prime ministerial candidate," against 27 percent in 2014.[53] Without this, the BJP's electoral performance would have been very similar to that in the 1990s. And again, like in the 1990s, it would have needed the support of coalition partners to govern. But the BJP's NDA partners would also have been weaker in 2019 if Modi had not been in the fray. Indeed, 25 percent of the non-BJP NDA supporters would have voted for another party if Modi had not been the NDA candidate for prime ministership (against 21 percent in 2014). In this context, the party hardly needed a program—unsurprisingly, it released its election manifesto at the very last minute.

A Well-Oiled Election Machine

In 2019, Modi relied less on separate vote mobilizers and agencies like Prashant Kishor's Citizens for Accountable Governance and more on the Sangh Parivar and its party than in 2014. Since 2014, he and Amit Shah had taken over the latter and established a productive modus vivendi with the RSS. However, these traditional networks had modernized to a large extent and, in addition to foot soldiers, they provided an army of digital warriors.

A Dense Network of Foot Soldiers

The Sangh Parivar's traditional technique of door-to-door canvassing remained its strong point in 2019 due to its dense network of activists. In Madhya Pradesh, where the BJP lost the state election in late 2018, the RSS came to its rescue. The RSS chief himself, Mohan Bhagwat, stayed in Indore to oversee the deployment of swayamsevak in key districts, including Bhopal, where the Hindutva forces wanted to ensure the defeat of former chief minister Digvijay Singh, against whom Pragya Singh Thakur was nominated.[54]

The BJP relied more on the modus operandi that had been initiated by Amit Shah in 2014 with the creation of booth-monitoring teams, each in charge of only a few pages voter lists. In 2019, the party had activists "working in the position of *panna pramukh* (page chief), who were responsible for the voters listed on a single page of the published voter list (a single contain [*sic*] approximately 30 voters although in practice *panna pramukh* may have handled up to 60 voters)."[55] As part of the BJP's "Mera Booth Sabse Mazboot" (my polling booth, the strongest), 92,000 booth-monitoring teams were set up in Maharashtra alone.[56]

Regarding those who had been identified as undecided voters during the campaign, the modus operandi of the volunteers—whether they worked for the RSS or the BJP—was always the same: they claimed to be approaching Indian citizens as neutral voter mobilizers in order to increase voter turnout, and then gradually tried to persuade them to vote for the BJP. A district-level booth manager confided: "We would send our local workers to have tea at every neutral household for four days. In these four days, we would not discuss anything to do with politics. On the fifth day, we would make an appeal to them to vote for the BJP."[57] One of the points the volunteers emphasized pertained to the social welfare programs associated with the prime minister.[58]

Social Media and War Rooms

While traditional techniques of canvassing remained some of the Sangh Parivar's assets, the organization used social media to a greater extent in 2019. Shivam Shankar Singh, a former data analyst with the BJP who had joined Prashant Kishor's Citizens for Accountable Governance in 2013 and who left the BJP in 2018, explains that, to use social media more effectively, the BJP IT cells first "create[d] constituency profiles broken down to the booth level, and collated and analysed field survey data for actionable insights."[59]

To identify voters' socioeconomic profiles, the IT cells used electricity bills, which are not supposed to be publicly available but which can easily be obtained illegally. These helped them to classify voters by class (lower middle, middle middle, and upper middle). Voter lists offer a good source for identifying class and religion, because they give not only the name but also the address of the voters. The "insights gathered from the exercise identified talking points for leaders at specific election meetings." This strategy is reminiscent of the one Cambridge Analytica used during the Trump 2016 election campaign. But it was even more systematic, as the data collected included the phone numbers of the voters of each booth. To collect the relevant data, the Sangh Parivar used its traditional network—largely based on its 45,000–50,000 shakha—as well as new recruits who decided to support the BJP because of Modi even prior to 2014, when they first played the role of "vote mobilizers," to use the phrase coined by P. Chhibber and S. Ostermann after the 2014 elections.[60]

In September 2018, BJP president Amit Shah launched a "booth action plan" that aimed at recruiting and training 900,000 "cell phone *pramukh*"—one for each polling booth. These people were appointed not so much for collecting data as for disseminating propaganda. Shah "asked state units to compile the list of smartphone carrying voters in every polling station" and to send it to the BJP headquarters, where they were processed, classified according to their categories, and communicated to the "cell phone pramukhs"—who were provided with a cell phone and asked to first create WhatsApp groups.[61] The BJP IT cell boss, Amit Malviya, undertook the expansion and densification of this network. According to the *Economic Times*, before the 2019 elections he "travel[ed] extensively, including remote villages, to train volunteers in spreading information about the government's development initiatives and prepare for social media campaigns. He says he now has an army of over 1.2 million volunteers constantly spreading BJP's message."[62]

The digital organization of the BJP therefore came as a supplement to more traditional forms of mobilization. As in 2014, the BJP benefited from a formidable ground operation, from the polling booth to the top. Six months ahead of the campaign, it opened campaign offices in each Lok Sabha constituency, overseeing local activities.[63] The party recruited hundreds of *pravasi karyakarta* (outsider activists) to oversee these offices, usually superseding regular local party officeholders.

Among these activists, 452 were appointed "Lok Sabha in charge" and were flanked by a full-time RSS liaison activist. Again, the BJP hired hundreds of thousands (the BJP claims 800,000) of *panna pramukh*, local mobilizers whose essential task consisted in engaging with targeted voters on polling day to enjoin them to go vote. This kind of last-minute door-to-door campaign activity reaped great dividends.

The two facets of this modus operandi are obvious: many of the "geeks" who collected and processed data turned into "trolls" the moment they had messages to send in the context of the election campaign. They wore two hats, but the differing aspects of their roles had one thing in common: the very local nature of both jobs, as the trolls sent different kinds of message to the different categories of voters whom they had identified. The digital BJP had become as dense as the shakha network, and both worked in tandem.

This twofold strategy was largely the brainchild of Amit Shah, who personally presided over the making of an army of "IT yodha" (warriors) for the 2019 election campaign. One of them, Dipak Das, who was trained by the BJP state IT cell in Calcutta, declared that he handled 1,114 WhatsApp groups.[64] He belonged to a category of Modi followers who may not have been BJP party workers but acted as vote mobilizers or as "influencers" (to use Shivam Shankar Singh's expression).[65] The core group of this digital brigade was made up of the 10 million people who had taken the "Main Bhi Chowkidar Hun" pledge and who had often added "Chowkidar" to their social media handle. Modi interacted with them via videoconferencing on March 31.[66]

For these voter mobilizers / influencers, WhatsApp was the most relevant instrument, even more than Twitter and Facebook,[67] for three reasons. First, it is remarkably popular in India, where this messaging service had 300 million active monthly users in April 2019.[68] Second, it enabled the BJP to maximize its slicing of the electorate: WhatsApp groups could target sections and subsections of local voters that the BJP IT engineers had previously categorized. Third, WhatsApp groups, like Facebook pages, could appear as nonpolitical, and existing nonpolitical WhatsApp groups could be infiltrated as well. Many of the Facebook pages and WhatsApp groups created by parties propagated political views without presenting themselves as being related to any organization. Dipak Das explains that covert propaganda is part of his strategy on WhatsApp—and is standard practice: "No one will follow you or become your friend on Facebook if you post only party messages. I share important news, too, and engage in debates on various issues. This attracts people. Then I post a few party messages."

In 2019, the BJP was thought to have around 200,000–300,000 WhatsApp groups, against 80,000–100,000 for the Congress.[69] Among them were the highly specialized groups (professionals, students, shopkeepers, etc.) that entrepreneurs in WhatsApp groups had created and sold to parties, including the BJP, the richest of them all.[70]

In April, Facebook—the owner of WhatsApp since 2014—took down hundreds of pages that reflected what the company calls "coordinated inauthentic behavior"[71]—as they used fake accounts and propagated controversial news. BJP-related pages made up an overwhelming number of these. As Pooja Chaudhuri explains:

> The BJP's participation in "coordinated inauthentic behaviour" was veiled behind the accounts linked to the IT firm, Silver Touch, the company behind Prime Minister Narendra Modi's "NaMo App." Facebook said that it removed one page, 13 accounts and a group associated with this company. The page in question was The India Eye, a pro-BJP propaganda outlet that used to host its corresponding website on the servers of Silver Touch. The India Eye is also one of the 15 accounts promoted on the NaMo App, where users do not enjoy the discretion to unfollow its posts. The follower count of The India Eye was more than 10 times the follower count of all Congress pages combined.[72]

The Indian Eye was one of BJP's covert assets, which it used to propagate fake news.[73] There were many others. Shivam Shankar Singh told *The Caravan* in January 2019:

> The funding ecosystem of social media is outside the ambit of what the Election Commission tracks. But it should be tracked—a major part of their social media campaign is being outsourced to groups

which do not have anything to do with the BJP officially. It is equivalent to advertisements on TV or radio. I know of groups that work
out of Madhya Pradesh and Uttar Pradesh which control 20–30 pro-
BJP Facebook pages. "We support Indian Army," "We support
NaMo"—pages with names such as these have 1–1.5 million followers.
A group like "Nation with NaMo," which claims to have 1.5 million
followers, continuously advertises on Facebook, recruits graphic de-
signers and video editors. The only way to become so huge is if you
pay Facebook to boost your posts. So, someone is funding them, but
it is not clear who. Parties claim the pages are not theirs, but created
by some supporter, which is not a valid defence for a page that spends
Rs 1.5 crore [USD 200,000] to Rs 2 [USD 266,667] crore a month on
promotions.[74]

However, Facebook's records in India are very ambivalent. In 2020, the
Wall Street Journal convincingly argued that the company has kept allowing hate speech by BJP politicians on its platform in order to please
the ruling party—allegedly because India was the largest market for
Facebook and WhatsApp.[75] Facebook, like others, let the army of
trolls in charge of the BJP's social media very effectively bombard
users with their messages, including those of applications Narendra
Modi had launched in 2015. They could engineer the viral spread of
these messages, regardless of their veracity. Most such "news" portrayed Congressmen (the Nehru-Gandhi family in particular) negatively and demonized minorities. Like Donald Trump's tweets in
2016, the BJP IT cell tried to demolish the image of Modi's main political rival, Rahul Gandhi. To substantiate the rumor spread by BJP
leaders that Rahul Gandhi was Muslim, a photograph showing him
and his father offering prayers in a posture used by Muslims at what
was presented as Indira Gandhi's funeral went viral on social media
in January–February 2019. The photograph—which had been
retweeted by the BJP MP Subramanian Swamy, among others—had
been taken in 1988 at the funeral of Abdul Ghaffar Khan, also known
as "Frontier Gandhi."[76] Rahul was also accused of supporting the idea
of granting a Rs 50 billion (0.67 billion USD) loan to Pakistan on the

strength of a Photoshopped screenshot from a mainstream TV channel.[77] Priyanka Gandhi was attacked the same way. A Photoshopped image of her "showed" her wearing a Christian cross.[78] Other Congressmen were also targeted. In Rajasthan, Ashok Gehlot was shown ostensibly waving what was presented as the Pakistani flag (which it was not) at supporters.[79] In March, a video showing Congressmen singing "Pakistan Zindabad" was publicized and denounced as "an insult not just to our Armed Forces but to each one of us." It turned out that this old video, already posted by Madhu Kishwar in 2018, had been doctored: it showed Congress workers hailing a party candidate before the Rajasthan state elections.[80]

The use of fake news was part of the BJP's strategy. In September 2018, when Amit Shah was launching the booth action plan, he organized a party meeting in Rajasthan, at which he explained how the BJP IT cell had influenced (and intimidated) the media during the 2017 UP elections and went on to declare: "We should be capable of delivering any message to the public, whether sweet or sour, true or fake."[81]

Caste Politics and Its Paradoxes

In parallel to its pioneering use of social media, the BJP relied on one of the oldest electoral tactics of Indian politics by selecting some candidates on the basis of their caste background. This tactic was facilitated by the fact that reservations have not evenly benefited all the Scheduled Castes and Other Backward Classes: some subcastes—*jatis*—have gradually cornered a larger proportion of the quotas in the education system and the public sector. These socially mobile jatis have become more politically alert and mobilized—to such an extent that they have created their own parties. In Maharashtra, the Mahars, who supported the parties created by Ambedkar (including the Republican Party of India), are a case in point. In Uttar Pradesh, the Jatavs, who started supporting the Bahujan Samaj Party in the 1980s, illustrates the same process so far as Dalits are concerned, and the Yadavs, who have backed the Samajwadi Party since as early as the 1990s, represent the same trend for the OBCs. The Yadavs has similarly rallied around the Rashtriya

TABLE 9.1. The 2009, 2014, and 2019 Lok Sabha elections: Classwise support for BJP among SCs and OBCs

Class	OBCs			SCs		
	2019	2014	2009	2019	2014	2009
Poor	39	28	19	34	22	10
Lower	35.5	37	23	32	22	13
Middle	37	33	23	27	22	16
Rich	44	37	27	30.5	27	19

Source: Lokniti-CSDS, National Election Survey, 2009, 2014, and 2019.

Janata Dal in Bihar. In Uttar Pradesh and Bihar these jatis have benefited from their political affiliations when the BSP, the Samajwadi Party, and the RJD were in office from the 1990s onward.[82] They were the clients of new patrons and got jobs in the state administrations accordingly. Their growing power and affluence have fostered resentment among other SC and OBC jatis, which were smaller, less educated, and lagged behind, having limited access to reservations.[83]

In 2019, the BJP capitalized on this resentment. Despite the overrepresentation of the upper castes in the party apparatus, some of the nondominant SC and OBC jatis switched to the BJP to more effectively fight parties like the BSP and the SP (which had formed an alliance in Uttar Pradesh) as well as the RJD. This is one of the reasons why many more SCs and OBCs voted for the BJP. The percentage of the former who did jumped from 12 percent in 2009 to 24 percent in 2014 and to 33.5 percent in 2019; the proportion of OBCs voting for the BJP followed a similar evolution, from 22 percent to 34 percent and to 44 percent in 2019. Interestingly, the poor SCs and the poor OBCs tended to vote more for the BJP than the middle-class SCs and OBCs, as is evident in table 9.1.

The pattern reflected in table 9.1 is very clear in Uttar Pradesh, where the BJP had to perform well to retain a majority in the Lok Sabha—and where the two parties claiming to represent the SCs and the OBCs (the BSP and the SP) had formed a coalition. In UP, as table 9.2 shows, poor OBCs have voted more for the BJP than for the BSP-SP alliance, despite the BJP's elitist image: 59 percent of "poor" OBCs supported the BJP, against 33.5 percent who turned to the alliance. The fact that OBCs from

TABLE 9.2. The 2009, 2014, and 2019 LS Elections: OBC vote by class in Uttar Pradesh

Class	INC			BJP		
	2019	2014	2009	2019	2014	2009
Poor	17	20	27	36	24	16
Lower	21	19	29	36	31	19
Middle	21	20	29	38	32	22
Rich	20	17	29	44	38	25
All	19.5	19	29	37.5	31	19

Source: Lokniti-CSDS, National Election Survey, 2009, 2014, and 2019.

the "rich" and "middle" classes voted more for the BSP-SP alliance and that "poor" OBCs supported the BJP more is understandable when jatis are factored in: the SP remains a Yadav party to a large extent, and Yadavs tend to be richer than the average OBC.[84] The BJP has successfully wooed non-Yadavs OBCs—who often belong to poorer strata of society and usually resent Yadav domination, especially the way they have cornered some of the reservations—by nominating many candidates from this milieu. Whereas 27 percent of the SP candidates were Yadavs in 2019, Yadavs represented only 1.3 percent of the candidates of the BJP, which, on the contrary, gave tickets to 7.7 percent Kurmis and 16.7 percent other OBCs, who often came from small caste groups.[85] This strategy translated into votes: while 60 percent of the Yadavs voted for the SP-BSP alliance, 72 percent of the other OBCs supported the BJP,[86] showing that the OBC milieu was now polarized along jati lines, irrespective of class. Indeed, "poor" Yadavs and "rich" Yadavs voted for the SP-BSP alliance in the same proportions.

The same way the BJP consolidated the non-Yadav voters against the SP, the party has also become the rallying point of the non-Jatav voters against the BSP: once again, the BJP has cashed in on the resentment of small Dalit groups accusing the Jatavs—who are indeed better off than other Dalits[87]—of monopolizing access to reservations. In Uttar Pradesh, the BSP has given more than 20 percent of its tickets to Jatavs, whereas the BJP has nominated 5 percent of Jatavs, 7.7 percent of Pasis, and 9 percent of other SCs.[88] Certainly, the BSP-SP got 75 percent of the Jatav vote, but it received only 42 percent of the other SCs vote, against 48 percent, which went to the BJP.

TABLE 9.3. The 2009, 2014, and 2019 Lok Sabha elections: Classwise support for main parties—all India (%)

Class	Congress+			BJP+			BSP+SP	BSP		SP	
	2019	2014	2009	2019	2014	2009	2019	2014	2009	2014	2009
Poor	4	4	17	59	44	15	33.5	10	15	37	41
Lower	7	8.4	15	46.5	53	25	41	8	11	23	44
Middle	8	11.6	20	42	47	18	47	7	19	24	32
Rich	7	14	21	46.5	46	15	40.5	2	8	26	45

Source: Lokniti-CSDS, National Election Survey (NES), 2009, 2014, and 2019.

As a result of this caste politics, as well as the other mainstays of Modi's populist repertoire mentioned above, the percentage of poor voting for the BJP was only 1.5 percentage points below the overall performance of the party (37.5 percent), whereas the gap had been 7 percentage points in 2014 (see table 9.3).

To sum up, during the 2019 election campaign, the BJP combined a populist repertoire, its traditionally strong network of activists, its digital army, and a sophisticated brand of caste politics. While Modi was, by definition, the main actor of the populist repertoire, Amit Shah was the chief architect of the last two components of this multifaceted strategy, and the network of activists was the domain of the Sangh Parivar, which still held significant sway.[89] All these factors had already been at work in 2014. But the 2019 elections were different because, after five years in office, the BJP had transformed the political ground into a much less even playing field.

An Uneven Electoral Playing Ground

Liberal democracies begin to morph into competitive authoritarianism when elections are no longer fair, and from this point of view, the 2019 elections marked a turning point. Factors conducive to the de-democratization process included biased media, unequal access to financial resources at the expense of the opposition, and a lack of impartiality among the institution in charge of organizing the polls, the Election Commission of India.

TV Channels: Self-Censorship and Sycophancy

The coverage of the election campaign by TV channels did not offset the impact of social media studied above. In fact, they reinforced each other.

During the 2019 election campaign, anchors and editors were clearly under pressure from their respective media outlet owners, who did not wish to jeopardize their business by incurring the government's displeasure. After receiving chilling signals, newsrooms that could have been neutral actors indulged in self-censorship. Those TV channels that had always been pro-Modi (Republic TV, Times Now, and ZeeTV) regularly spread pieces of (dis)information that echoed to a large extent the social media handled by the BJP IT cell. They fostered nationalistic hysteria after the Balakot strike—accusing those who asked questions about this military operation of being "antinational." [90] The few interviews Modi gave on these channels were largely sympathetic and complacent affairs conducted by biddable anchors.[91]

Other channels did not lag behind. One month after the announcement of the Lok Sabha elections, the BJP had 100 percent more airtime coverage than the Congress on the state-run Doordarshan News and its regional channels—including the 84-minute live broadcast of Modi's "Main Bhi Chowkidar Hun" address on March 31.[92] The Hindi channels showed the greatest imbalance: the Broadcast Audience Research Council (BARC) analyzed the airtime of the top eleven Hindi channels between April 2 and 28 and found that they gave nearly 850 hours to Modi (722) and Shah (123) against 335 to Rahul Gandhi (251) and his sister Priyanka Vadra (84).[93] It seems, however, that the Indian public does not consider such anomalies to be problematic. It was only in India—among the countries surveyed by the Pew Institute in 2017— that political bias in the media was regarded as "acceptable."[94]

Beyond quantitative statistical data, some qualitative assessment is needed here. While Republic TV claims to be a news channel and remained number one among news channels in terms of viewership according to the BARC's 2019 ratings,[95] anti-opposition debates on Republic TV peaked in April (Lok Sabha elections were due in May) at 33

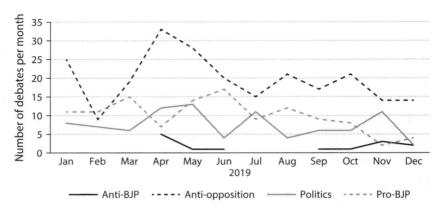

FIGURE 9.1. Republic TV 2019 debates by political topics, segregated monthly
Source: Christophe Jaffrelot and Vihang Jumle, "One Man Show," *The Caravan,*
December 15, 2020, https://caravanmagazine.in/media/republic-debates-study-shows
-channel-promotoes-modi-ndtv

debates (approximately one anti-opposition debate each day). While the number of anti-opposition debates dropped by 5 to 28 in May 2019, pro-BJP debates eventually picked up to compensate. Republic TV's anti-BJP debates remained at the bottom throughout, as shown in figure 9.1. In the whole year 2019, Republic TV organized 236 anti-opposition debates and 119 pro-BJP debates.[96] The title of some of them are very telling: "Will Congress' plan of a 'new government' represent threats and intimidation?" "Rahul Gandhi admits to secret China meeting. Should he disclose full details now?" "Congress exposes itself on 'fake Hindutva." "Massive Congress attack on Hindus." "Is Congress spooked with populism?" "Why does nationalism make the opposition nervous?" "Wanted proof on Balakot, silent on Jammu terror attack. Hypocrisy?" "Is the Opposition toeing Pakistan line by not calling out terror?" "Congress President Rahul Gandhi honouring terrorists?" "Congress 'likes' Pakistan Army strategy?" "Will #RahulWayanadEscape work?" "Rahul Gandhi links with 2G accused." "Rahul Gandhi wants to muzzle media?" "Is he Rahul Gandhi or Raul Vinci?" "Congress unites to praise Pakistan Prime Minister Imran Khan." "Has the Gandhi family reduced itself to a joke?" "Congress absolving Jinnah role in partition?"[97] This small sample offers a good illustration of the systematic targeting of Congress and Rahul Gandhi—to say nothing about the wrong information supporting the arguments and the vulgar style of the debates—whereas Republic TV never criticized the ruling party and its chief.

The BJP thus did not use social media as a substitute for traditional communication channels. Rather, it treated social media as a supplement. The party appointed three to five spokespersons for each state and around forty media panelists who were tasked with appearing daily in talk shows. The BJP thus had about 100 official spokespersons representing it on various channels, far outstripping each of its opponents.

Money Power: The World's Most Expensive Campaign

The BJP's saturation of the public sphere during the election campaign was largely due to vast financial resources spent on the party's propaganda. India's seventeenth general elections were the costliest ever in the history of any democracy to date,[98] with the parties spending 7.2 billion dollars according to a reliable estimate[99] (more than double what had been spent ten years before). The BJP spent between 45 and 55 percent of this total—or approximately 3.6 billion dollars, as compared to 15 to 20 percent for Congress. Moreover, never before had so much cash and other "prohibited substances" been seized during an election campaign, be they confiscated from the homes of parliamentary candidates or from political party headquarters: "Law enforcement agencies between March 10 and May 19 seized Rs 839.03 crore [111.8 million USD] in cash, liquor worth Rs 294.41 crore [39.2 million USD], drugs worth Rs 1,270.37 crore [169.4 million USD], precious metals, including gold, worth Rs 986.76 crore [13.16 million USD] and 'freebies,' including sarees, wrist watches, aimed at inducing voters, worth Rs 58.56 crore [7.81 million USD]."[100] The total amount—Rs 3,449.12 crore (459.9 million USD)—represented three times what had been seized five years previously, with the BJP beating all records in this regard.[101]

Political parties were able to amass some of this money due to a law the Modi government pushed through in 2016, authorizing businesses and individuals to make contributions to political parties through electoral bonds that were undisclosed to the public. The BJP reaped 95 percent of the contributions paid through this instrument.

Electoral bonds, however, were only one source of income. According to the Association for Democratic Reforms (ADR), in the financial year 2017–2018, India's seven largest political parties declared a combined income of Rs 1,397.90 crore (186.387 million USD), of which the BJP alone received 73.5 percent; that is, Rs 1,027.339 crore (136,979 million USD).[102] This rose to 80.12 percent in 2019 (against 13.64 percent for the Congress).[103] The sources of more than 50 percent of this money remained unknown, as political parties are not required to reveal the names of individuals or organizations that donated via electoral bonds (31 percent of the total according to the ADR) and contributed less than Rs 20,000 (267 USD). The ADR emphasizes the particularly significant role of opacity in the case of BJP: "During F[iscal] Y[ear] 2017–18, BJP declared Rs 553.38 crore [73.784 million USD] as income from unknown sources which is 80% of the total income of National Parties from unknown sources (Rs 689.44 crore [91.925 million USD]). This income of BJP forms more than four times the aggregate of income from unknown sources declared by the other five National Parties."[104] The former chief election commissioner S. Y. Quraishi has called electoral bonds a "legalization of crony capitalism."[105] Indeed, those who have given massive financial support to the ruling party expected something in return: the businessmen-politicians nexus deepened. While the Election Commission of India had expressed reservations vis-à-vis electoral bonds, the Supreme Court, in an April 2019 order, declined to grant a stay and merely asked the parties to disclose to the ECI, in sealed envelopes, the details of the donations they had received.

Between 20 and 25 percent of the 7.2 billion dollars mentioned above were handed out directly to voters in small bills or in kind, while 30 to 35 percent went to campaign expenses, particularly for communication.[106] A large part of the money collected by the BJP was spent on advertising, particularly—but not only—ahead of the campaign.[107] Between February 7 and March 2, AltNews, scrutinizing Facebook's Ad Library Report, discovered that pro-BJP and pro-central government pages accounted for 70 percent of the total ad revenue made public by Facebook.[108] Of the top ten political advertisers, eight were related to the BJP and spent Rs 2.3 crore (306,660 USD) on Facebook ads[109]—with Congress coming in a distant third, behind the Biju Janata Dal, a regional party. But many pages supported the BJP without declaring their links with the party. The total amount of money spent on Facebook ads by the BJP and supporting pages was over Rs 2.7 crore (360,000 USD) in one month. But much more money was to be spent in the following weeks and months. Between February 20 and April 24, 2019, the BJP spent about Rs 6 crore (800,000 USD) on political ads on Google platforms, ten times more than the Congress. On Facebook, the BJP officially spent Rs 1.32 crore (176,000 USD) between early February and April 20. While this is higher than any other party's expenditure, the figure still conceals other publicity initiatives. Unofficial BJP Facebook pages, such as "Bharat ke Mann ki Baat," "Nation with NaMo," and "My First Vote for Modi" cumulatively spent Rs 4.50 crores (600,000 USD) in the same period.[110] These figures were made public by the Huffington Post in a remarkable piece of investigative journalism that revealed that the organization behind these Facebook pages was a shadowy firm called the Association of Billion Minds, a political consultancy firm that worked exclusively with and for the BJP.[111]

In addition to these, Modi took advantage of government advertising, running up a bill of Rs 5,000 crores (0.67 billion USD) in four and a half years—as much as the Manmohan Singh government spent in ten years on advertising in the print media (Rs 2,136.39 crore [284.852 million USD]) and electronic media (Rs 2,211.11 [294,819 million USD]).[112]

The Weakening of the Election Commission of India

During the 2019 election campaign, BJP leaders were able to exploit the controversial themes mentioned above and use the kind of means elaborated earlier because the ECI did very little to implement its own Model Code of Conduct, one more sign of the weakening of the Commission that had begun a few years before.

While the ECI has always been one of India's most prestigious institutions, its integrity came into question in the first half of Narendra
Modi's first term. Some appointees have tried to resist the most blatant
abuses of power. Indicating that the ECI was well aware of the "creeping
'new normal' of political morality" revealed by the way elections were
contested, Election Commissioner O. P. Rawat declared in his 2017 key-
note address to the Consultation on Electoral and Political Reforms
organized by the Association for Democratic Reforms (ADR):

> Democracy thrives when elections are free, fair and transparent.
> However, it appears to a cynical common man that we have been
> scripting a narrative that places maximum premium on winning at all
> costs—to the exclusion of ethical considerations. . . . In this narra-
> tive, poaching of legislators is extolled as smart political manage-
> ment; strategic introduction of money for allurement, tough-minded
> use of state machinery for intimidation etc. are all commended as
> resourcefulness. . . . The winner can commit no sin; a defector cross-
> ing over to the ruling camp stands cleansed of all the guilt as also
> possible criminality. It is this creeping "new normal" of political mo-
> rality that should be the target for exemplary action by all political
> parties, politicians, media, civil society organisations, constitutional
> authorities and all those having faith in democratic polity for better
> election, a better tomorrow.[113]

Reacting to the large number of income-tax raids (investigations) affecting opposition leaders at election time (these will be examined in
the context of the 2019 elections below), the ECI "strongly advised"
Central Board Direct Taxes (CBDT) officials that "any action by its
enforcement agencies during election time should be 'neutral' and 'non-
discriminatory.'"[114] The ECI has also tried, in vain, to garner more
power to cancel elections locally in the event that voters of a constituency appeared to have been bribed by political parties.[115]

In reaction, the government of India followed a strategy consisting
of "limiting the EC's authority from within by appointing pliant election
commissioners,"[116] a tactic that has also affected other institutions, as
shown in the previous chapter. In July 2017, the appointment of A. K.

Joti as chief election commissioner (CEC), a former principal secretary to Narendra Modi when he was Gujarat chief minister, is a case in point. The ECI's policy changed soon after. In 2017, it went against its own convention when it announced dates for elections in Himachal Pradesh and not in Gujarat, despite the fact that these two states had been following the same electoral calendars since 1998 and often voted at the same time. This stratagem, as Milan Vaishnav points out, delayed the implementation of the Model Code of Conduct and therefore enabled Narendra Modi "to announce populist schemes designed to woo voters."[117] Similarly, the ECI changed the dates of important by-elections in Karnataka after the Supreme Court gave the dates of its own hearings regarding the disqualification of Congress defectors that the BJP was to renominate in 2019. Rajdeep Sardesai then asked in a Tweet, "Will Centre decide by-poll dates or EC?"[118]

This trend was to reach its culmination in 2019–2020. During the 2019 election campaign, in spite of the first article of this code—"No party or candidate shall include in any activity which may aggravate existing differences or create mutual hatred or cause tension between different castes and communities, religious or linguistic"—the ECI did not penalize BJP leaders who indulged in communally divisive discourse. The commission cleared Shah in two cases, including his Nagpur speech in which he likened Rahul Gandhi's second constituency, Wayanad, to Pakistan, and Modi in three cases, including his Nanded speech when he declared that in this constituency the "country's majority was in a minority."[119]

The ECI also cleared the prime minister even though his opponents brought to its notice the fact that he had canvassed in Gujarat on the first day of polling in violation of its regulations. The Congress then pointed out that NaMo TV[120] had no broadcast license and accused the BJP of sending the Income Tax Department to conduct raids against political opponents.[121] In the space of one month after the election schedule was announced, eighty-four places were raided, "all linked to opposition parties," including leaders from the Telugu Desam Party, the Janata Dal (Secular), the Dravid Munnetra Kazhagam, and, of course, the Congress. In Madhya Pradesh alone, for instance, "more than 300

IT officials have been conducting searches at more than 52 premises linked to aides of Chief Minister Kamal Nath, Praveen Kakkar and Rajendra Kumar."[122]

For weeks, the ECI did not act on any of these breaches, and it then cleared the prime minister and Amit Shah in eleven complaints lodged against them.[123] However, it was swift to condemn an opposition leader, Mayawati, for a divisive speech, banning her from campaigning for forty-eight hours. The ECI slapped a similar sanction on Yogi Adityanath for one of the three notices it had sent him for communally charged statements.[124] The Uttar Pradesh chief minister dismissed the sanction as inconsequential and retorted, "The election dais is not for singing *bhajans* [devotional songs], it's for attacking the opposition." He then proceeded to call the opposition "Babur ki aulad" (offspring of Babur).[125]

Not only did the ECI fail to deal with breaches of the Model Code of Conduct with a firm hand, but it also showed inconsistency when it did take cognizance of them. For instance, it did not take strong action against the union minister for women and child development, Maneka Gandhi, who, during one of her constituency rallies, said: "I am going to win for sure. If Muslims won't vote for me and then come to ask for work, I will have to think, what's the use of giving them jobs."[126] Though she was temporarily suspended from campaigning by the ECI, she immediately stated that in her new constituency (Sultanpur) she would replicate a system she had implemented in her old seat (Pilibhit): dividing the villages of the constituency into A, B, C, and D categories according to the number of votes the people of the different villages had given her and treat them accordingly. The ECI condemned the statement, which showed that the ballot was no longer secret,[127] but let her off with a mere warning.[128] Similarly, the ECI did not follow any consistent policy regarding canceling elections in constituencies where malpractice (including the role of money) was blatant: in two seats, repolling was ordered, but not in others.[129]

On May 7, the former chief election commissioner (CEC) S. Y. Quraishi took the rare step of criticizing his successors and enjoined them to "act tough." He expressed his deep dismay at the incumbent CEC's admission of powerlessness before the Supreme Court, declaring that the ECI was "toothless" in the face of Model Code of Conduct violations.[130]

It eventually transpired that the commissioners' decisions absolving Modi and Shah were not all unanimous, though. In three cases implicating them, one of the three election commissioners, Ashok Lavasa, dissented.[131] But as his note of dissent remained unrecorded, he finally stopped attending the ECI commissioners' meetings on violations of the Model Code of Conduct.[132] The ECI subsequently resisted demands to release Lavasa's dissenting notes after the election, stating that doing so could "endanger life or physical safety of an individual,"[133] a rather peculiar argument. Soon after, in August 2019, the government sent a letter to eleven Public Sector Undertakings to verify their records for any exercise of "undue influence" by Lavasa in favor of one of the companies owned by his wife during his tenure in the Power Ministry from 2009 to 2013. At the same time, his wife was served income tax notices on charges of alleged tax evasion.[134] Before his turn to become CEC came around—which should have been in April 2021, owing to his seniority—Lavasa resigned and was appointed vice president of the Asian Development Bank in August 2020.

During the 2019 election campaign, sixty-six retired bureaucrats, including Julio Ribeiro and Shiv Shankar Menon, had sent a letter to India's president about the decline of the ECI. They wrote:

> We are deeply concerned about the weak-kneed conduct of the ECI, which has reduced the credibility of this constitutional body to an all-time low. . . . The ECI's independence, fairness, impartiality and efficiency are perceived to be compromised today, thereby endangering the integrity of the electoral process, which is the very foundation of Indian democracy. We are distressed to note the misuse, abuse and blatant disregard of the Model Code of Conduct by the ruling party at the Centre, and the ECI's pusillanimity in coming down with a heavy hand on these violations.[135]

The declining independence of the Election Commission of India that affected the electoral process in 2019 contributed to the emergence of the Indian version of electoral authoritarianism.

Modi's BJP: The Elitist Hegemon
A Second Hindutva Wave

The seventeenth Indian general elections confirmed the BJP's hegemonic status in very similar terms to those of the previous election, which had already seen a record turnout that was exceeded by 1 percentage point, reaching 67 percent in 2019. In 2014, the party had won 282 seats out of 543, with 31 percent of the vote, fully benefiting from the inherent distortions of the single-round majority-based voting system. In 2019, it won 303 seats with 37.5 percent of the vote, which once again handed it an absolute majority, set at 272 seats—and exempted it from its dependence on its allies in the National Democratic Alliance, which won 353 seats (with 45 percent of the vote). Its rival, the Congress Party, scarcely gained any votes—from 44 to 52 seats with 19.5 percent of the vote (the same percentage as in 2014). And the coalition it led, the United Progressive Alliance, went from 60 seats (with 23 percent of the vote) to 91 (with 26 percent).

Regional parties not affiliated with either the NDA or the UPA were the main collateral victims of this election, despite the BSP's return to parliament, winning 10 seats in Uttar Pradesh. This was nevertheless a disappointing score because the BSP was relying heavily on its alliance with the Samajwadi Party in Uttar Pradesh to become once again the third-largest party in India. The defeat was bitterer still for the SP, which only won 5 seats—as few as it had garnered in 2014. If there was a certain erosion of regional parties, it was due to the remarkable headway the BJP made in some of their strongholds, even if the voting geography was very similar to that in 2014: the BJP took all the seats in Gujarat, Haryana, Delhi, Himachal Pradesh, and Rajasthan; all but one in Madhya Pradesh and Assam; and all but two in Karnataka. What was new were the strong inroads made by the BJP in eastern and northeastern India. The party took 9 of the 14 seats in Assam. In West Bengal, a state where it had never won more than 2 seats, it won 18, leaving only 22 to Mamata Banerjee's Trinamool Congress. By the same token, in Odisha, the BJP made a spectacular breakthrough, taking seats from Naveen Patnaik's

Biju Janata Dal, which held on to only 12 seats, compared to 20 in 2014. The only regional party outside the NDA to have met with outright success was the Dravida Munnetra Kazhagam (DMK), which triumphed in Tamil Nadu with 23 seats. As for the Congress, the only two states where it made significant progress were Punjab and Kerala, where it ousted the Communists, reduced on the national level to 5 seats out of 542, 3 for the CPI(M) and 2 for the CPI—the worst score in their history.

While the "saffron wave," so called for the color of Hindu nationalism, did not sweep evenly over India, the South and the East still resisting the BJP (except for Karnataka and Assam), in places where it did roll out, it crushed social distinctions even more than in 2014. The BJP's appeal among the lower castes has already been seen to be linked to its choice of candidates and the paradoxes of positive discrimination, as well as to vishwas politics. But the key factor in its victory once again resided in Modi's popularity. Therein lies the strength of a national-populist who manages to embody an entire people—not a people comprising all citizens, of course, but the dominant ethnic group forming a majority made up of "sons of the soil"—beyond social cleavages. Indeed, Oliver Heath shows that the most useful variable in predicting a BJP vote remains communal affiliation. Heath therefore considers that "a new communal cleavage, based on Hindu majoritarianism now structures political conflict, replacing the more internally differentiated caste cleavages that structured electoral competition during the multi-party era."[136] He finds a clear correlation between the percentage of Hindus and BJP votes: the more numerous Hindus are in a constituency, the larger the BJP vote—and the presence of Scheduled Castes no longer affects this trend:

> All other things being equal, in 2009 the size of the SC community used to have a significant and negative impact on the BJP's vote, indicating that the BJP performed worse in places where there were more SCs. In 2014, the size of the SC population was still significant and negative, though it perhaps didn't matter quite as much as it did in 2009 ($b = -0.205$ vs -0.269). However, in 2019 we can see that all

other things being equal the BJP no longer performs significantly worse in places with sizeable SC communities. Taken together these findings imply that the Hindu vote has become more consolidated behind the BJP and less internally divided.[137]

Similarly, the urban/rural divide no longer makes a significant difference: "The BJP still tends to be more popular in urban areas, but the relationship is not particularly strong." The only influential variable is the sex ratio: "Support for the BJP is also stronger in communities with patriarchal gender cultures, where the sex ratio is worse,"[138] a clear indication that the BJP's appeal is more pronounced in areas where a conservative brand of Hinduism prevails. This is consistent with the social profile of the party's leadership.

Plebeians' Revenge or Elite Revenge?

The social profile of the Seventeenth Lok Sabha suggests that 2019 marked the culminating point of the reaction to the Mandal Commission that the BJP had tried to orchestrate since the 1990s. The main beneficiaries of the Mandal moment, the dominant OBCs of the Hindi belt, appeared, indeed, as the collateral casualties of these elections. The Yadavs are a case in point, but they are not the only ones: for the first time, the share of the nondominant OBCs has been larger than the share of the dominant OBCs among the Lok Sabha MPs of the Hindi belt, as evident from figure 9.2.

Similarly, dominant Dalit jatis have lost their erstwhile preeminence. Here, the Jatavs are a case in point: out of the thirty-nine SC MPs of the Hindi belt, only five came from this caste group. The decline of the Yadavs and the Jatavs, who have traditionally supported the SP and BSP, reflects the BJP's tactic mentioned above: the party nominated candidates from the nondominant SC and OBC jatis to capitalize on their resentment—and it got their votes. In a way, therefore, the 2019 elections marked the revenge of the plebeians.

But it marked even more clearly the second act—after that of 2014—of the revenge of the upper-caste elite, which had already rallied behind

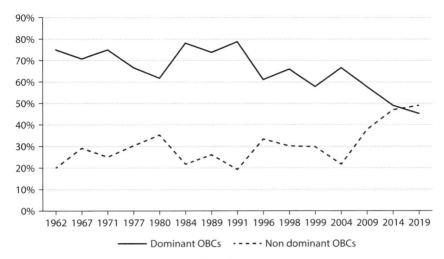

FIGURE 9.2. Dominant and nondominant OBC groups among
Hindi belt Lok Sabha MPs (1962–2019)
Source: C. Jaffrelot and G. Verniers, "The Reconfiguration of India's Political Elite:
Profiling the 17th Lok Sabha," *Contemporary South Asia* 28, no. 2 (May 18, 2020), 246,
https://doi.org/10.1080/09584935.2020.1765984

the BJP against the Dalits' and OBCs' assertiveness. As in 2014, upper-caste representation among BJP Lok Sabha MPs was significantly higher (at 36.3 percent, more than 7 percentage points above the average) than for its opponents (23.1 percent for Congress and 19.3 percent for regional parties), as evident from table 9.4.

The overrepresentation of upper-caste MPs on the BJP side reflects its ticket distribution. Across the country, the BJP nominated 146 upper-caste candidates (out of 414 candidates). Among these tickets, 109 went to Brahmins (71) and Thakurs (38) alone.[139] This overrepresentation of upper castes largely stemmed from the Hindi belt states, the BJP's stronghold. In these ten states,[140] 90 out of the BJP's 198 candidates belonged to the upper castes, and 81 of them got elected. If one removes SC and ST candidates from the picture, 62 percent of all general category candidates of the BJP and MPs were upper castes, against 37 percent for all other parties' candidates combined.

But the overrepresentation of upper-caste politicians among the BJP MPs is nothing compared to the situation prevailing among the BJP

TABLE 9.4. Caste group and community representation in the Lok Sabha among the BJP, Congress, and regional parties (2019)(%)

	BJP	Congress	Regional Parties
UC	36.3	23.1	19.3
IC	15.5	7.7	14.8
OBC	18.8	25	28.4
SC	16.2	11.5	17.6
ST	12.2	7.7	5.1
Muslims	0	5.8	10.8
Sikhs	1.62	7.7	1.7
Christians	0	11.5	0.6
Buddhists	0.3	0	0
Unidentified	0.0	0	1.7
Total	100	100	100
	N = 303	N = 52	N = 176

Source: SPINPER project—The Social Profile of the Indian National and Provincial Elected Representatives, a CNRS-supported international virtual lab associated with Ashoka University and Sciences Po.

ministers in the government that Narendra Modi formed after the 2019 elections. Out of fifty-five government members, 47 percent were from the upper castes (including 18 percent Brahmins), 13 percent were from intermediate castes (including Jats, Patels, Reddys, etc.), 20 percent were OBCs, 11 percent were from the Scheduled Castes, and 7 percent from the Scheduled Tribes. The rest—two people—were from the minorities, one Muslim and one Sikh.[141]

In 2019 as in 2014, the national-populist repertoire of Narendra Modi had submerged caste identities by using religion as the most effective unifying factor of the Hindus—beyond caste and class—to enable the upper castes to rule.

Like in 2014, the BJP's success in 2019 resulted mostly from the personal appeal of Narendra Modi, whose popularity was largely based on his national-populist style. This repertoire, however, did not only rely on his personal quality as a so-called poor Hindu son of the soil fighting against the cosmopolitan Nehru/Gandhi-dominated establishment, as it also emphasized the national-security dimension in the context of the Pulwama jihadi attacks. Modi's hyperpersonalized campaign also projected such providential qualities as protector of the poor through welfare schemes bearing the prime minister's stamp. The relative impact of this aspect (despite deepening social inequalities) showed that Modi, like other populist leaders, could generate trust among the poor even when he did not deliver—as if he was, now, beyond accountability. As the ultimate Chowkidar, he was, for many, the protector of the Hindus—be they poor or rich, Dalits or upper castes—against the threatening Other, the Muslim next door or the Islamic Republic of Pakistan.

As a result, the BJP victory in 2019 relied on Modi, like in 2014, despite the fact that as prime minister of India, he had not fulfilled his promises, largely because he had "detached politics from economics."[142] As Yogendra Yadav pointed out, his charisma and his identity cum security politics made him almost unaccountable. The very special relation that he had created with a large number of voters—and that the media called "Modi magic"—was rooted in the exceptional nature of his style. For instance, the Balakot strikes—something no Indian government had dared attempt since Indira Gandhi—endowed him with a particular legitimacy and authority (to use Max Weber's words). Such bold moves helped Indians to recover their self-esteem in the context of a strident brand of nationalism cultivated by the media. He relied on a similar politics of dignity vis-à-vis the poor. The need for national self-respect was such in 2019 that a small-time businessman told a NewsClick reporter: "Even assuming the strikes were false and never took place, they still prove what India is capable of."[143] In other words, Modi may lie, but it matters little, as the population wants to *believe* in India's power.

However, besides Modi's populist repertoire, the BJP's victory also stemmed from a well-oiled electoral machine rooted in the huge Sangh Parivar network. In contrast to other populist leaders who rely only on the power structure they have built, Modi used existing ones—including the RSS and the BJP apparatus—more than in 2014. Such a change is easily understandable: whereas in 2014 Modi had not fully trusted the Sangh Parivar cadres, in 2019, with Amit Shah as party president for five years, he had complete control over it. This old network was, however, supplemented by another vast system, one made of digital activists and trolls—vote mobilizers who paid allegiance to Modi.

These people, however, also seemed to have been more closely integrated into the BJP IT cells than in 2014. The main architect of this lo-
gistic, indeed, was none other than the party president, Amit Shah, who
also played a major role in selecting the party candidates. In doing so,
he played another traditional game: the old card of caste politics, by
giving tickets to politicians from nondominant SC and OBC jatis, who
resented the way some of their peers—including Jatavs and Yadavs—
cornered most of the quotas offered in the reservations system.

This tactic explains why plebeian SCs and OBCs were elected in
larger numbers than members of dominant SC and OBC jatis. But the
winners of the 2019 elections mostly came from the upper castes again,
as evident from the social profile of the Seventeenth Lok Sabha. Like in
2014, the populist repertoire has enabled elite groups that had been
partly dislodged from power in the wake of the Mandal moment to regain their hegemony.

In contrast to 2014, Modi's BJP was also able to win the Lok Sabha
elections because the political scene had become a clearly uneven playing field. In some respects, the difference was only of degree. The media,
for instance, were already biased in favor of the BJP in 2014—in quantitative as well as qualitative terms. Similarly, the BJP's financial resources were already larger than those of other parties. But not only
have these two factors of unfair elections worsened—as evident from
the way Modi's BJP monopolized the public scene—but a third, institutional one has emerged: the Election Commission of India has lost
some of its independence, and intimidation practices (including
income-tax raids against political opponents) have gained momentum.
These developments have laid the groundwork for a transition to a more
authoritarian regime that would almost officially be the hallmark of
Modi's second term.

10

The Making of an Authoritarian Vigilante State

SEVERAL POLITICAL SCIENTISTS analyzing the 2019 election results concluded that, by confirming the 2014 outcome, they heralded the crystallization of a new party system.[1] Gilles Verniers and I, instead, have argued that they accelerated the crystallization of a new *political* system characterized by the rise of a special kind of authoritarianism.[2]

While the 2019 elections, and the situation that had prevailed during Narendra Modi's first term, had already shown signs of this de-democratization process, the discourse and the attitude of the BJP leaders reconfirmed this trend immediately after Narendra Modi's second term began. The new home minister, Amit Shah, himself set the tone. Speaking at the 46th National Management Convention of the All India Management Association in New Delhi on September 17, he declared: "After 70 years of independence, there was a question in the minds of people . . . whether the multi-party democratic system had failed to fulfill the aspirations of the citizens of the country."[3] This "question" echoed the objective that Modi's BJP pursued explicitly and vocally: "Congress-free India," a country from where the main opposition party would be eradicated. This rejection of a multiparty democratic system flowed directly from the core ideology of Modi's national populism, an ideology where there is room for only one political force, the Hindu

nationalists, who embody the nation. Majoritarianism, therefore, is conducive not only to ethnic democracy but also to what is known as *illiberal democracy*.

Amit Shah also criticized, obliquely, the liberal values supporting
democracy when he revisited the genealogy of human rights. Speaking
at the 26th Foundation Day of the National Human Rights Commission
on October 12, 2019, he declared: "It is wrong to only look [at human
rights] through the international prism. . . . Every households [*sic*] in
towns and villages have their own ways to ensure that rights of not even
a single individual are violated. Protecting human rights is in our tradition. There's an inclusive system in our society and people have been
working in this regard. . . . The rights of children, women, the poor and
the underprivileged sections are inbuilt in the society, within our
family, without any intrusion from law."[4] The speech echoes, this time,
the modus operandi that Hindu nationalists have applied during Modi's first term: instead of using the state as an emancipatory force for
each and every citizen, they have tried to neutralize it in order to let
vigilantes and other offshoots of the Sangh Parivar impose societal
norms inherited from Hindu traditions—a conservative worldview
that was more prevalent in the Hindi belt, also known as the "cow belt,"
where BJP did well in 2019.

Narendra Modi's second term, however, has marked a transition from
this society-oriented approach to a more statist perspective. Certainly,
this strategy was already at work during his first term, when the state
apparatus was somewhat neutralized, as chapter 8 has shown. But in
2019, that was no longer sufficient: the state had to be used to its full
extent. First, conquering the state required dominating all the political
power centers—including state governments—at any cost. Second,
the BJP, given its increasingly dominant position, decided to change
the laws of the country and even the Constitution at the expense of
federalism and the minorities. Last but not least, the authoritarian rulers found it increasingly necessary to combat dissent—starting with
the basic freedom of expression—as their methods generated more
opposition.

Fighting Political Opponents by Other Means—
in and out of Parliament

In *How Democracies Die*, Steven Levitsky and Daniel Ziblatt argue that two mainstays of the democratic culture of a political class—which reinforce each other—are "mutual toleration and institutional forbearance." They argue that "politicians are more likely to be forbearing when they accept one another as legitimate rivals, and politicians who do not view their rivals as subversive will be less tempted to resort to norm breaking to keep them out of power."[5] Correlatively, they consider one of the "key indicators of authoritarian behavior" to be the fact that politicians "claim that their rivals constitute an existential threat, either to national security or to the prevailing way of life," or "describe their partisan rivals as criminals" or as "foreign agents."[6]

In Modi's India, the ruling party has routinely denied the legitimacy of political opponents, including the Congress, as evident from the explicit objective of a "Congress-free India." This facet of India's brand of authoritarianism was inherent in the BJP's national-populism, as mentioned above. During Modi's first term, it found expression in discourses and in some practices, such as the Speaker's refusal to recognize the Congress chief's status of Leader of the Opposition in the Lok Sabha. During Modi's second term, it has resulted in many more decisions. Not only has the BJP repeatedly tried to dislodge the Congress Party from power at the state level when it won elections, but in parliament, the BJP has refused to engage in debates with the opposition and has contravened some of the well-established parliamentary norms.

Losing Elections—but Not Power

Since 2014, the BJP has excelled at inciting cadres of other parties to defect and join its ranks before elections.[7] "Poaching" strong candidates from rival parties has helped the BJP to win in several states.[8] This tactic continued after the 2019 Lok Sabha election, as evident from the preelectoral scene in Maharashtra in the summer of 2019, where, as Suhas Palshikar observed, the BJP was "busy crushing competition, threatening its opponents and coercing non-BJP politicians into deploying their political energies in favor of the BJP."[9] In the Maharashtra state elections, the BJP and Shiv Sena fielded twenty and twenty-one turncoat candidates, respectively, mostly from Congress and its ally, the National Congress Party.[10] But this modus operandi took on greater proportions when the defections were intended to bring down Congress governments so as to "rule in every state from Panchayat [village councils] to parliament," as Amit Shah once said.[11]

During Modi's first term, to gain power in some of the Congress-ruled states, the BJP had attempted to resort to president's rule, but this tactic backfired in Uttarakhand and Arunachal Pradesh in 2016. In Uttarakhand, the union government opted for president's rule after the Congress chief minister, T. R. Rawat, failed to get a bill passed due to the revolt of certain party MLAs. Arun Jaitley, then finance minister, concluded that the Rawat government was "unconstitutional and immoral,"[12] but the Supreme Court restored it and arraigned the central government for its attitude: It "should be impartial [but] was acting like a 'private party,'" said the judge.[13] In Arunachal Pradesh, the Congress lost its majority after twenty-one of its MLAs defected to the BJP. The Modi government subsequently imposed president's rule. But soon after, the BJP MLAs supported one of the defectors, Kalikho Pul, who formed a government with the help of other defectors. This move was possible only because the governor—acting in a partisan manner at the behest of the central government—had advanced the assembly session by a month, something the Supreme Court deemed illegal. And for the first time in Indian history, a government that had been ousted under president's rule and replaced by another was restored.[14]

During Modi's second term, the BJP relied on other methods, combining incentives and intimidation to engineer defections and come to power without imposing president's rule. The BJP has thus managed to retain (or regain) power on several occasions, even when it has lost an election. Such a "strategy of cannibalization of its adversaries,"[15] to use Gilles Verniers's words, was first used in Karnataka.[16] Here, the chief minister and JD(S) leader, H. D. Kumaraswamy, alleged that the BJP had offered Rs 10 crores (about 1,333,330 USD) to some of his party's

MLAs.[17] These allegations have remained unsubstantiated, but one of these turncoats, M. T. B. Nagaraj, did purchase a Rolls-Royce soon after he shifted to the BJP.[18] The Congress and JD(S) defectors were taken to a hotel in Mumbai—where Congress leader D. K. Shivakumar tried to meet them, unsuccessfully, as the police of Maharashtra (a then BJP-ruled state) did not let him enter.[19] Eventually, the Speaker of the Karnataka assembly disqualified the sixteen defectors and disallowed them from contesting further elections to the Karnataka assembly. They turned to the Supreme Court, which upheld their disqualification but allowed them to contest in the following by-elections, missing a clear opportunity to dissuade MLAs from defecting to other parties.[20] Thirteen of them contested these by-elections as BJP nominees and won their seats again, allowing the party to retain power in Karnataka.

The second state on the BJP list was Madhya Pradesh, where the scenario was very similar. In early March 2020, former Madhya Pradesh chief minister Digvijay Singh claimed that the BJP was trying to topple the Congress state government by offering potential defectors Rs 25 to 35 crore (3 to 4 million USD).[21] Soon after, Jyotiraditya Scindia, who had lost his Lok Sabha seat and was not given the post of Madhya Pradesh Congress Committee president he coveted, resigned from Congress. The BJP immediately nominated him as one of its Rajya Sabha candidates.[22] He then took twenty-one other Congress-deserting MLAs of his faction to a hotel in Bangalore, where the police refused entry to Digvijay Singh when he came to talk to them—in fact, he was arrested by the Karnataka police.[23] The Madhya Pradesh governor—acting in a partisan manner again—immediately asked the Speaker to hold a floor test, something that the law does not permit and that the Congress did not want to do before the twenty-two MLAs went back to Bhopal.[24] The Congress chief minister Kamal Nath resigned a few days later, enabling the BJP to stage a comeback. In this incident, the BJP managed to exploit factional fighting within Congress as well as the lack of ideological commitment of Congress MLAs. In fact, in most of the opposition parties (including the Congress and state parties), substantial numbers of MLAs and MPs seem to be "for sale" (to paraphrase

Kalikho Pul's expression cited in chapter 8). But luring opponents was not the only technique the ruling party used to gain power: it also resorted to big-stick politics.

Politics of Intimidation

During the Emergency, Indira Gandhi and her son Sanjay often made use of income-tax raids to intimidate opponents or send them to jail. In 2019 the Modi government began using the same technique more systematically than in the previous four years (as the analysis of the Lok Sabha election has already suggested). In September 2019, during the campaigning for state elections in Maharashtra, the Enforcement Directorate (ED), the law enforcement agency under the Department of Revenue, Ministry of Finance, in charge of combating economic crime in India, registered cases against NCP leaders, including Praful Patel,[25] Sharad Pawar, and Ajit Pawar. Similarly, D. K. Shivakumar, a popular Congress leader of Karnataka, was arrested in another income-tax-related case as the BJP attempted to regain power in Karnataka. In 2020, when the Congress government was shaken by factional tensions between Ashok Gehlot and Sachin Pilot, not only did the BJP try to attract potentially dissident Congress MLAs by all sorts of means, but the ED summoned Gehlot's brother in an alleged fertilizer scam case that dated back to 2007. As Rajdeep Sardesai pointed out, "That a decade-old case is revived in the midst of political turmoil in Rajasthan is no coincidence."[26]

Besides income-tax-related and scam-related cases, the government did not hesitate to put opposition leaders under house arrest to prevent them from canvassing or taking part in protest movements. Former chief minister Chandrababu Naidu, the Telugu Desam Party (TDP) leader, and his son, Nara Lokesh, are cases in point from 2019,[27] as were P. Chidambaram, former home and finance minister from the Congress Party, who spent 106 days in jail under corruption charges. These are not isolated cases, as less prominent politicians have met the same fate, including Samajwadi Party MLAs, who were taken into preventive custody ahead of a public meeting held by Yogi Adityanath, the Uttar Pradesh chief minister, in Kanpur in September 2019. In 2020, the Uttar

Pradesh Congress chief was put under house arrest while he was on his way to protest against the manner in which the state government was covering up the gang rape and murder of a Dalit girl in Hathras.[28] Rahul Gandhi himself was stopped by the UP police—and then allowed to go—while on his way to Hatras. Politicians were not the only targets: a Magsaysay award-winning social activist, Sandeep Pandey, was put under house arrest while he intended to take part in a protest against the abolition of article 370 of the Constitution (see below).[29]

Charges against these opposition leaders vanished the moment they agreed to join the BJP. The TDP minister Y. S. Chowdhary is an example: the CBI, the ED, and the Income Tax Department conducted raids against him during the 2019 Lok Sabha election campaign, but all cases were suspended the moment he joined the BJP.[30] Similarly, Ajit Pawar, nephew of NCP president Sharad Pawar, was given a clean chit by the Maharashtra authorities when the BJP was courting his support so as to be able to form the state government after its ally, the Shiv Sena, withdrew from the NDA: nine cases against him were closed by the Anti-Corruption Bureau in forty-eight hours.[31] This attempt eventually failed, as the NCP refused to side with the BJP and instead formed a coalition government with the Shiv Sena and the Congress.

The "Conquest" of the Rajya Sabha

The BJP did not engineer defections of MLAs only in opposition-ruled states where it was eager to regain power. It used this method more systematically even in BJP-ruled states to win more seats in the Rajya Sabha, the upper house of parliament whose members are elected indirectly, mostly by MLAs.

During Narendra Modi's first term, the fact that the BJP was far from the majority was a serious handicap for the prime minister, as he could not fulfill some of the BJP election manifesto promises, given the fact that the Rajya Sabha and the Lok Sabha have almost equal footing in legislation.[32] But with the conquest of new states, the BJP's position gradually improved in the Rajya Sabha, an assembly where one-third of the 233 seats are up for election every two years. These gains can also be attributed to the party's use of various techniques of persuasion and intimidation to secure the support of non-BJP MLAs for BJP candidates. In Gujarat, for instance, where defections had already reduced the number of Congress MLAs from 99 in 2017 to 73 in 2020, 8 more were lured by the BJP, reducing the number of Congress MLAs to 65—who were taken to a resort (once again) to contain the hemorrhage. The Income Tax Department "searched 60 premises linked to the Karnataka Energy Minister, D. K. Shivakumar who was overseeing the stay of these MLAs."[33] Finally, the Congress could win only 1 Rajya Sabha seat in the state instead of 2, and the BJP took the 3 others.[34] Cross-voting had helped the BJP on several occasions to win more seats than it should have, given its initial strength in the assemblies.

In the Rajya Sabha, the BJP overtook Congress for the first time, by 1 seat—58 against 57—and became the largest party in the Rajya Sabha for the first time in the history of India in August 2017. But the NDA, with 80 seats, was 123 seats away from the majority. It continued to grow and reached the 69 mark in 2018. In 2019, with almost 100 seats (including 80 on the BJP side from June 2020 onward), the NDA was in a position to win its duels with the opposition in the upper house because it could rely on the support of non-NDA parties that would be prepared to support bills introduced by the Modi government, either because they truly favored them or because they got something in return. Commenting on the Muslim Women (Protection of Rights on Marriage) Bill, P. Chidambaram points out and explains the inconsistencies of several state parties:

> The AIADMK, JD(U), TRS and PDP which have spoken against the Bill vanished at the time of voting! Divide, cajole, intimidate, threaten or close "deals," the BJP has used every trick in its bag to pass laws that will reduce states to municipal administrations and add one more dimension to the sinister idea of Oneness—One Government for everything.[35]

Such tricks, and the bill in question, will be discussed further below and in chapter 11. Suffice it to say for the moment that the conquest of the Rajya Sabha (or, at least, its neutralization) has helped the BJP to establish a form of hegemony over parliament. This hegemony, however, was not complete, and on several occasions the BJP had to transgress certain norms of parliamentarism, a regime Narendra Modi tried in any event to circumvent.

The Decline of Parliament

In any democracy, parliaments are the institutions where the two mainstays of democratic culture that Levitsky and Ziblatt mention in their book—"mutual toleration and institutional forbearance"—are supposed to flourish, for the simple reason that the opposition is also represented in these aptly named representative assemblies. But such values can only materialize if parliament remains an important institution whose rules are respected by the executive.

In Modi's India, parliament has experienced a decline.[36] This evolution is paradoxical, because when he entered the Indian parliament for the first time in 2014 as prime minister designate, Narendra Modi bowed his forehead to the stairs to express his deep respect for what he called the "temple of democracy."[37] Retrospectively, this episode looks like another of his theatrical displays, as never before has an Indian prime minister neglected parliament so constantly. On average, he has spoken 3.6 times a year in parliament: 22 times in 2014–2019[38] (fewer times even than H. D. Deve Gowda,[39] who was prime minister for only two years). In contrast, A. B. Vajpayee made 16.7 speeches a year in parliament, 77 in six years.[40] And Manmohan Singh stands in the middle, having spoken 48 times in ten years in parliament.[41] In 2018, Narendra Modi spent fourteen hours in the Lok Sabha and ten hours in the Rajya Sabha, in contrast to Manmohan Singh, who did not speak much but who came and listened.[42]

To circumvent the parliament, Narendra Modi has issued a record number of ordinances. While ordinances are usually resorted to by minority governments or coalition governments, the Modi government has used them more than any of its predecessors, despite the fact that the BJP enjoys an absolute majority in the Lok Sabha. The number of ordinances jumped from six per year under Manmohan Singh to eleven per year under Modi.[43]

The Lok Sabha and the Rajya Sabha are gradually ceasing to be places for debate. First, the number of bills that have been referred to parliamentary committees—the deliberative core of parliamentary work—has shrunk dramatically, from sixty-eight (71 percent of the total) in the Fifteenth Lok Sabha to twenty-four (25 percent) in the Sixteenth Lok Sabha—and two out of the nineteen bills passed in the last 2020 session.[44] This is one reason bills are so poorly drafted: committees of scrutiny and oversight, traditionally not divided along party lines, used to amend bills very effectively and trained parliamentarians in the art of lawmaking. No recent major piece of legislation (including the bill revoking article 370 and carving two union territories out of the states of Jammu and Kashmir) has been processed by a house committee. Maansi Verma points out that "standing committees are routinely bypassed and if the government agrees to refer a Bill to a Committee for study, it is projected as an act of executive magnanimity. The executive also selectively approves recommendations made by a Standing Committee, many of which are ignored, and amendments to Bills proposed by MPs during a debate are defeated without even the pretense of a discussion on the same."[45]

Second, several key pieces of legislation have been passed as money bills even though they did not at all fit this category. Money bills are supposed to solely concern taxation or government spending. But several bills that had little to do with this definition have been passed as money bills under Narendra Modi simply because the upper house—where the BJP is still in a minority—cannot amend money bills. The Aadhaar bill is a case in point. The Speaker of the Lok Sabha certified that it was a money bill, and all the amendments proposed by the Rajya Sabha were rejected.

Third, ordinary bills are not often discussed, either because the drafts are handed over to the MPs at the last minute or because there is no time for debate. When they are discussed, opposition amendments are usually rejected to retain the originally introduced bill. If debate does occur, it is primarily for show, as a formality. In 2018, even the budget was not seriously discussed in parliament. In the Monsoon [summer] session of 2019 (considering both houses), four out of forty bills were passed on the same day they were introduced, and in summer 2020, two out of twenty-five bills were passed on the same day, and several bills were passed one day after their introduction, in violation of the Rules of Procedure, which provide for a two-day time lag between introduction and consideration of a bill.[46] As a result, opposition parliamentarians have lost interest even in attending parliamentary sessions.[47]

Fourth, the process of norm- and rule-breaking reached a peak in parliament during the summer session of 2020. Among the bills passed soon after being introduced was the Farmers' Produce Trade and Commerce (Promotion and Facilitation) Bill, 2020, which was vehemently opposed by Congress MPs and others in both assemblies. In the Rajya Sabha, "the government was not sure of its number and wanted to prevent division on the Bills or on the motion to send Bills to Select Committee, which the Opposition MPs were protesting about."[48] The Rajya Sabha Speaker did not allow more time for debate and did not even accede to the demand for a division,[49] whereas he is obliged to grant one even at the request of a single MP. The "farmers Bills" became laws in these unprecedented conditions. Opposition MPs protested in such a way that eight of them were suspended. Several opposition parties decided to boycott the rest of the session, and after this boycott, the members of the ruling party in the Rajya Sabha passed fifteen bills single-handedly, including far-reaching pieces of legislation regarding labor reform.[50] In the same session, allegedly because of the pandemic, question hours were canceled, suppressing one of the very few opportunities for two-way communication with the government. Subsequently, the winter session of parliament was canceled for the same reason in late 2020, and the Standing Committees ceased functioning as well—whereas in many countries, parliamentary work has been on line. Instead, the Modi government promulgated eleven ordinances.[51]

The decline of parliament is a problem for democracy in itself, for the reasons Levitsky and Ziblatt emphasize, but in India it has been instrumental, making it easier for the Modi government to amend the Constitution and to pass new laws.

The Making of a Majoritarian State Fighting Dissent

The hegemonic position that the BJP has gradually achieved since 2019, due, in particular, to the psychological boost resulting from Modi's landslide reelection, its dominant role in the Rajya Sabha, and the control the central government now exerts over key institutions of the Indian republic, has enabled the ruling party to reshape the Indian state during Modi's second term. If the first term saw the new assertiveness of Hindu nationalists in (and over) society, through, for instance, the growing influence of vigilante groups, during the second term, the state has played a larger part, and the officialization of majoritarianism, therefore, has found expression in new laws—whereas in 2014–2019, the legislative activity of the Modi government had been rather limited, partly because the BJP was challenged by strong opposition in the upper house.[52]

Among the legislative transformations that have made a huge impact on the Indian republic, the abrogation of article 370 of the Constitution that had given Jammu and Kashmir enhanced autonomy—at least on paper—and the Citizenship (Amendment) Act (CAA) deserve to be studied in detail, not only in themselves but also because of their implications. In both cases, Muslims were targeted and reacted. Their mobilization against the CAA, on constitutional grounds, was a milestone due to its magnitude, but it also showed that the state was now the key player in the majoritarian game, as evident from the brutality of police repression. In Uttar Pradesh, for instance, demonstrators were pitted against the police. This configuration was reconfirmed during the Delhi riots, which overlapped with anti-CAA agitation in February 2020, in which policemen were among the assailants.

Toward a Unitary Ethnostate: The End of the Jammu and Kashmir Exception

The ideology of Hindutva did not only aim to promote a Hindu Rashtra based on Hindu majoritarianism; it also wanted to build a unitary state at the expense of the Indian brand of federalism that reflected the old "Unity in Diversity" motto.[53] The Modi government particularly targeted the special status of Jammu and Kashmir, a state that had enjoyed more autonomy than others, on paper at least, since the 1950s. Article 370 of the Indian Constitution stated that the jurisdiction of the parliament of India and the union government extended over limited matters with respect to Jammu and Kashmir. For the rest, the state assembly exerted its jurisdiction on the basis of a separate constitution. Jammu and Kashmir also had a separate flag. This status was codified in the Constitution (Application to Jammu and Kashmir) Order, 1954 which made clear that only some provisions of the Indian Constitution applied to Jammu and Kashmir. One of the implications of this special status was enshrined in article 35A, according to which only locals could buy land and be eligible for public-sector jobs.

For the Sangh Parivar, the autonomy that the Kashmiris enjoyed was the root cause for separatism, whereas for the mainstream regional parties in the state, including the National Conference (NC) and the People's Democratic Party (PDP), separatism was fostered by the attitude of the central government, which, for decades, has de facto deprived the locals of their autonomy. Abolition of article 370 had been one of the mainstays of the BJP program (and before that of the Jana Sangh) for decades, but no BJP-led government had tried to implement it until 2019. The fact that the Modi government did so a few months after the Lok Sabha election is a clear indication that its perspective had changed and was now more state oriented: not only did the nation have to be reshaped according to its ideology, but the institutional framework too, including the federal structure, had to be recast.

The Revocation of Article 370 was steered through parliament by Amit Shah, the new home minister, who had immediately become the strongman of "Modi II." On August 5, 2019, he announced in the Rajya Sabha that the president of India had issued the Constitution (Application to Jammu and Kashmir) Order, 2019, superseding the 1954 order and removing the restriction that it had introduced. This in effect meant that the Jammu and Kashmir constitution was abrogated. Amit Shah also moved a resolution recommending to the president of the republic that he issue another order rendering all the clauses of article 370 inoperative. The resolution was adopted by both houses of parliament. On August 5, Amit Shah also introduced the Jammu and Kashmir Reorganisation Bill, 2019 in the Rajya Sabha to transform Jammu and Kashmir into a union territory and to split it into two union territories, one still called Jammu and Kashmir and the other consisting of Ladakh. The bill was passed with 125 votes in favor and 61 against. The following day, it was passed with 370 votes in favor and 70 against in the Lok Sabha. In addition to most of the parties of the NDA (the JD[U] excepted), the Bahujan Samaj Party, Aam Aadmi Party, Y.S.Reddy Congress, Biju Janata Dal, Telugu Desam Party, and All India Anna Dravida Munnetra Kazhagam voted with the BJP.[54] Several Congress party members, including Jyotiraditya Scindia, supported the BJP in parliament, despite the party's official line, in the name of "national integration."[55] These votes showed that the BJP was now in a position to have its bills passed in parliament not only owing to its newfound strength in the Rajya Sabha, where it could persuade state parties to follow suit by all kinds of means, but also because some of its political views were shared by prima facie opponents, including its definition of "national integration." This question will be revisited in the conclusion of the book.

Amit Shah and Narendra Modi justified the abrogation of article 370 in the name not only of national integration but also of development. In a televised speech Modi made on August 8, he claimed that article 370 prevented the inhabitants of Jammu and Kashmir from benefiting from the kind of development that the rest of India enjoyed and that the state had been deprived of so far[56]—a factually inaccurate argument, as Jean Drèze has shown.[57] The prime minister argued that, now, investors would make the region prosperous. On August 15, in his Independence Day speech, Modi claimed that the country had finally achieved its dream of "One Nation, One Constitution":

The abrogation of Article 370 and 35A has been carried out in both Rajya Sabha and Lok Sabha by two-thirds majority. This means that everyone wanted this decision, but perhaps they were waiting for somebody to initiate the same and carry it forward. I have come to accomplish the task assigned to me by my countrymen. I work selflessly. . . .

The system that prevailed over the past seventy years had aggravated separatism and given birth to terrorism. It had encouraged dynastic rule[58] and in a way strengthened the foundations of corruption and discrimination. We have to make efforts so that the women of Jammu & Kashmir and Ladakh get their rights. We have to make ef-

forts so that my dalit brothers and sisters living there get the rights
which they have been deprived of so far. The rights enjoyed by the
tribal people of India must also be available to my tribal brothers and
sisters of Jammu & Kashmir and Ladakh. . . .

My dear countrymen, peace and prosperity of Jammu & Kashmir
and Ladakh can be an inspiration for India. They can greatly contrib-
ute to India's development. We need to make efforts to bring back
their glorious past. The new system that has come into being after the
recent step will create facilities that will directly benefit the people of
the State. . . .

Today, as I address the nation from the Red Fort, I can proudly say
that every Indian today can speak of One Nation, One Constitution.[59]

The abrogation of article 370 was used repeatedly by Modi and Shah
during the state elections campaigns of 2019. The latter said that article
370 was "the gateway of terrorism in Jammu and Kashmir"[60] and, in
Jharkhand, that "by removing Article 370, Modiji has shown Pakistan
its place and shown it to the world that Kashmir is an inalienable part
of India. No one can raise an eye on Kashmir now."[61] Shah politicized
the issue by targeting the Congress, and in particular Jawaharlal Nehru,
who, he said, was responsible for the "'non-integration' of Kashmir with
India."[62] Modi emphasized the need for national integration too, with
different words, during his election tours. In Maharashtra, he said,
"Earlier, the slogan used to be *Kashmir hamara hai* [Kashmir is ours].
This must now change to *Naya Kashmir banana hai* [We must make a
new Kashmir]. We have to once again build a paradise [in Kashmir] . . .
hug each Kashmiri."[63] Despite the affectionate overtones of this speech,
it reflected a key Hindu nationalist idea: Kashmir was now theirs, something other BJP leaders expressed much more crudely in relation to
Kashmiri girls. M. L. Khattar, the chief minister of Haryana (a state
where the sex ratio is one of the most imbalanced), declared for instance
that his collaborators used to say, "We will bring girls from Bihar. Now
they say Kashmir is open, we can bring girls from there."[64] In an even
crasser style, the BJP MLA from Muzaffarnagar echoed, in a video clip,

the fact that his party "workers are very excited and those who are bach-
elors, they can get married there. There is no issue now. Earlier, there
was lot of atrocities on women. If a woman from there [Kashmir] got
married to a man from Uttar Pradesh, her citizenship would be revoked.
There was different citizenship for India and Kashmir."[65] He also said,
"Muslim party workers should rejoice in the new provisions. They can
now marry the white-skinned women of Kashmir."[66] The fact that
Jammu and Kashmir was, at last, under the domination of the central
government was evident from the situation that prevailed in the new
union territory after August 5.

STATE REPRESSION AND HUMILIATION

As the Modi government feared popular protests to the abrogation of
article 370,[67] weeks before August 5, 175,000 additional personnel were
deployed to one of the most militarized territories in the world. On
August 5, educational institutions and offices were ordered to be closed,
transports ceased to function, and, last but not least, there was a complete communication blackout as landlines and mobile phones were
blocked. In this context, Amit Shah declared, "Kashmir is moving
towards normalcy,"[68] and insisted that "not a single bullet has been fired
and not a single person has died."[69] In fact, the locals decided to enact
a "people's *hartal*" (mass strike) to show the world that it was not business as usual in the province: commercial establishments closed voluntarily except for two hours in the morning and in the evening. In parallel, large-scale protests took place,[70] prompting the government to
intensify repressive measures, which were already on the rise. While
journalists did not have easy access to the region, those who reached it
reported that shots had indeed been fired and that at least four people
had died immediately after the abolition of article 370, while others were
injured in brutal crackdowns on demonstrations: tear gas shells accounted for some casualties, and the use of pellet guns left some protesters blind in the Srinagar Valley.[71] A fact-finding mission comprising
advocates, trade unionists, human rights activists from the People's
Union for Civil Liberties, and a psychiatrist went to Jammu and Kash-

mir in late September / early October and submitted one of the first rather comprehensive reports on the post–August 5 situation in the province. They wrote,

> Since August 5, 2019, armed forces have been conducting raids on villages and localities in the city almost every night, and most definitely if there is any protest or incident of dissent on the part of the people. We heard that villagers were rendered sleepless because of the nightly raids, harassment, humiliation and torture. . . . People said that the forces barge into the village while screaming abuses and throwing stones at the houses breaking window panes. . . . There are cases of torture by the armed forces. In some instances, the torture is carried out with loudspeakers on, for the surrounding community to hear the victim scream as he is being brutalised.[72]

Cases of torture were publicized by some media outlets,[73] although most of the New Delhi–based TV channels took little interest in them, and the government exerted control over journalists as well as newspapers in Jammu and Kashmir. The new media policy released by the Jammu and Kashmir administration in 2020 was encapsulated in a fifty-three-page document that allowed the authorities to decide what news was "anti-social and anti-national"—and therefore illegal, this in the name of regulating reporting.[74]

In reaction to the "brutalization" of Kashmiris, 132 alumni, teachers, and students of the Indian Institutes of Technology wrote to the Modi government in October 2019.[75]

The situation remained far from normal because many aspects of daily life were disrupted and remained so: the economy was badly affected by the disruption of communication, marketplaces, and means of transportation (hitting the apple trade, for instance). While some landlines were restored and, subsequently, some mobile services too, social media and high-speed internet were not, for security reasons.[76] This lack of connectivity has had devastating effects on the economy, health, and education, especially during the COVID-19 lockdown.[77] But a member of the NITI Ayog, the institution that had replaced the Planning Commission in New Delhi in 2015, asked casually: "What difference does it make if there's no Internet there? What do you watch on Internet there? What e-tailing is happening there? Besides watching dirty films, you do nothing there."[78]

Such characterization of Kashmiri society reflected the contemptuous view of the province that some members of the Delhi-based ruling elite cultivated. While the repression described above is not terribly different from what happened in the past under Congress governments, this perception of the Other was particularly humiliating. Humiliation is one of the sentiments the Kashmiris interviewed by fact-finding missions or journalists mention the most frequently.[79] It existed before, but it was certainly exacerbated by remarks such as those mentioned above and by the way Kashmiris were also harassed out of Jammu and Kashmir.[80] Those who felt the most humiliated were probably the leaders of mainstream regional parties. Gowhar Geelani, a Lucknow-based journalist points out, "Politicians who believed that a democratic solution to the political question of Kashmir was possible within the ambit of the Indian Constitution are either in a state of shock or in mourning. With Jammu and Kashmir's constitutional guarantees gone with the wind, regional players like the National Conference (NC) and the People's Democratic Party (PDP) are feeling humiliated, insulted and betrayed. In private, they concede they are at the precipice of irrelevance."[81]

Indeed, the way the Modi government has dealt with Jammu and Kashmir shows that, in contrast to previous union governments— including the Vajpayee government—it aimed at polarizing the political scene of the region, besides modifying its governance, and changing its demography.

THE MAKING OF POLITICAL PRISONERS—AND POLARIZATION

The Modi government has turned its back on the Kashmir policy of all its predecessors, including the Vajpayee government, concerning the way they relate to local political forces. As Happymon Jacob points out,

"Traditionally, New Delhi used moderate pro-independence parties such as the Hurriyat Conference to reach out to the disaffected Kashmiri populace. Since August 2019, New Delhi has stopped considering the moderate separatists as stabilizing forces, and Kashmiris now look suspiciously at moderate politics of any kind. In short, the moderate separatists have been sidelined."[82] Not only that, but even the pro-India parties have been sidelined. Political leaders of the NC, PDP, Congress, and other opposition parties—including three former chief ministers, one former union minister, seven former state ministers, the mayor and deputy mayor of Srinagar, and a number of MLAs—were arrested, along with lawyers, businessmen, and NGO activists.[83] A total of 4,000 people were arrested, according to Amit Shah.[84] In fact, this number takes into account only those who had been arrested under the Public Safety Act (PSA),[85] a draconian preventive detention law under which a person can be arrested to prevent him or her from acting against "the security of the state or the maintenance of the public order" and kept in jail for two years before his or her trial. The total number of arrests was around 13,000 according to the People's Union for Civil Liberties (PUCL) fact-finding mission.[86] Some of the prisoners were sent to jails in Uttar Pradesh, Rajasthan, Bihar, and so on,[87] as those of Jammu and Kashmir were full. Other prisoners were in custody in the Centaur Hotel of Srinagar[88] or under house arrest, like the three ex–chief ministers Farooq Abdullah, Omar Abdullah, and Mehmooba Mufti. The authorities had to release many prisoners after six months (as per the law), and some of them could regain their freedom if they agreed to sign a bond saying that they would neither comment on the abrogation of article 370 nor hold rallies against this decision,[89] a practice that had already enabled many political prisoners to leave jail during the Emergency.[90] In order to maintain hundreds of people—unofficially 532,[91] including the 3 ex-chief ministers, in detention beyond the six-month period, the authorities invoked the PSA.[92]

The charges against these political prisoners were, as Radha Kumar points out, often "clearly absurd."[93] In many cases the accused were said to have participated in activities "highly prejudicial to the maintenance of public order" because they could convince people to vote even when separatists urged them to boycott the elections and "get a large number of people to protest against decisions taken by the government of India,"[94] which meant, as Kumar emphasizes, that the "Modi administration ha[d] now labelled dissent as sedition."

Omar Abdullah, who refused freedom in exchange for silence,[95] was accused of "using politics as a cover for his radical ideology and for planning activities against the Union government."[96] But not even one statement or one concrete incident was mentioned in the dossier, which read: "Despite the fact that the subject has been a mainstream politician, he has been planning his activities against the Union of India under the guise of politics. And while enjoying the support of gullible masses, he has been successful in execution of such activities." He was charged under the PSA in February and accused of "resorting to dirty politics, adopting a radical methodology by way of instigating general masses against the policies of the Central government" after the abrogation of article 370 by the BJP-led central government on August 5. Such an accusation sounds surrealistic, as Omar Abdullah was a prisoner of the Indian state without almost any contact with the outside world. Mehbooba Mufti was accused of similar "activities" and of something more. According to her PSA dossier: "She has been promoting separatism as corroborated by several confidential reports filed by [intelligence] agencies. . . . The subject is referred, for her dangerous and insidious machinations and usurping profile and nature, by the masses as 'Daddy's girl' and 'Kota Rani', based on the profile of a medieval queen of Kashmir, who rose to power by virtue of undertaking intrigues ranging from poisoning of her opponents to ponyardings [sic]."[97] Such a charge sheet relied more on speculation regarding the psychological features of the accused than on facts. Farooq Abdhullah and Omar Abdullah were released in March 2020, and Mehbooba Mufti, in October 2020, but their long detention reflected the will of the Modi government to gain control of Jammu and Kashmir by any means and to polarize the political scene in the region as well as nationally. Indeed, by targeting the leaders of parties that had constantly tried to work with the central government and even the BJP (the NC had been part of the NDA in the late 1990s and early 2000s when Omar was part of Vajpayee's government and the PDP ruled Jammu and Kashmir in a coalition with the BJP in 2015–2018), the Modi government has radically undermined the "pro-India" political forces of Jammu and Kashmir and mechanically promoted the anti-India ones. This strategy was bound to sideline the parties that could claim power again—and which were in favor of article 370. More generally speaking, with the moderate opposition to BJP marginalized, the Modi government could tell the rest of India that the separatists were the only significant players in Jammu and Kashmir and that this threat, connected to Pakistan, had to be dealt with. This would fit well in the security-oriented repertoire that had already gained momentum during the 2019 elections.

A NEW ASSIMILATION POLICY:
FROM GOVERNANCE TO DEMOGRAPHY

Another pillar of the Modi government's post-article 370 abrogation strategy pertained to the governance of Jammu and Kashmir. After the province became a union territory, its police now reported directly to the central government in the person of Amit Shah, and its strongman— under the president's rule that had been imposed in 2018—was the lieutenant governor appointed by New Delhi, G. C. Murmu, both close associates of Narendra Modi. G. C. Murmu was named lieutenant governor on October 31, 2019, the day the state was converted into a union territory. Murmu, a Gujarat cadre IAS officer, had been a close aide of Modi's and Shah's in Gujarat, where he had served as principal secretary to Narendra Modi when he was chief minister. In 2004, as joint secretary of the Home Department, he had assisted him in post-pogrom cases in such a way that, according to the witness R. B. Sreekumar (a 1971-cadre IPS officer), he appeared to be, "entrusted with the task of tutoring and briefing government officials deposing before the Nanavati Commission [that investigated the pogrom] by the highest authorities of the government and Home Department."[98] He was also cited in relation to the Ishrat Jahan fake encounter case in which Amit Shah was also named. Not only was the lieutenant governor close to the Modi government, but his team included only one Kashmiri Muslim, Farooq Khan. Some locals in the Valley of Srinagar "feared a government and administration that did not represent the Kashmiri Muslim majority of the region,"[99] given the fact that in civil bureaucracy, the police and judiciary, and even the Jammu and Kashmir Bank, Kashmiris have been sidelined.[100]

For them, this was reminiscent of the Dogra rule that prevailed under the Hindu dynasty reigning over the province before 1947. At that time, Kashmiri Muslims were often tilling the land of Hindu landowners. They got access to land in the context of postindependence land reform. The fear of the "comeback of Dogra rule"[101] not only concerned land but also the demographic balance. Under article 35A, the assembly of Jammu and Kashmir was empowered to define "permanent residents" of the state and to reserve for them certain rights, including the right to own land in the state and to have access to government jobs. Article 35A was one of the laws repealed after the abrogation of article 370. In March 2020, the Modi government replaced permanent residents with domiciles in Jammu and Kashmir by a new provision: the children of officers, soldiers, and members of the paramilitaries station in Jammu and Kashmir as well as anyone who had lived in the region for fifteen years, studied there for seven years, or written school board examinations was eligible to own land and hold government jobs. Interestingly, this new domicile law did not apply to the other newly created union territory, Ladakh, but only to Jammu and Kashmir. Omar Abdullah explained this difference by the fact that the central government "fear[ed] the reaction from the Buddhist population of Ladakh, whereas [they] are not bothered about how the population of J&K reacts."[102] This double standard suggests that the abolition of article 370 not only reflected the Modi government's craze for centralization but also aimed to show the only Muslim-majority state of the union its place.

Among Kashmiris, the fear of losing one's land was stoked by the fact that land had already started to be reserved for outside investors and the armed forces: 70 percent of the new mining contracts have gone to non-locals[103] and two laws (the Control of Building Operations Act, 1988, and the Jammu and Kashmir Development Act, 1970) were amended in July 2020 to introduce a "special dispensation for carrying out construction activities in Strategic Areas"—in other words, land could be easily acquired and transferred to the army for its own use, a process that has started already.[104] Furthermore, in July 2020 as well, the government decided that army and paramilitary forces would not require a No Objection Certificate from its home department "for acquisition or requisition of land in favour of the Army, B[order] S[ecurity] F[orce], CRPF and other similar organizations."[105]

But when "demographic change" is mentioned—with the case of Palestine often in the back of Kashmiris' minds when they speak about "a settler-colonialism project"[106]—they also think about the redrawing of electoral boundaries that has already begun. For them, this process was initiated in order to give the Jammu region and its Hindu majority "an edge over Kashmir in legislative numbers and so make sure the top elected representative of the new union territory will come from Jammu, whenever elections take place."[107] Significant change may occur, indeed, if domicile certificates are granted to people applying in the ten districts of Jammu: 32,000 people had already applied there in June 2020.[108] If the population of Jammu continues to increase, its number of constituencies will have to be adjusted accordingly.

While the changing status of Jammu and Kashmir affected "only" one province of India, the changing citizenship laws in 2019 were seen by all the secular-minded Indians and Muslims as a massive attack on the Indian Constitution.

Redefining Citizenship on an Ethnoreligious Basis

THE CITIZENSHIP (AMENDMENT) BILL/ACT

The Citizenship (Amendment) Act passed in December 2019 by the Indian parliament marked a shift toward an ethnoreligious definition of citizenship, a trend that had already been initiated many years ago by the first BJP-led government.

Initially, post-1947 India adopted a conception of citizenship that was universalistic and based on place of birth.[109] But this jus soli–oriented definition of who could be an Indian has gradually moved toward certain principles of the jus sanguinis doctrine. This change was largely due to developments that took place in Assam, which have already been alluded to. In this state, the rejection of Bengali-speaking (mostly Muslim) migrants culminated in the Nellie massacre in 1983, in the wake of which the 1985 accord signed by Rajiv Gandhi with those who claim that they represented the sons of the soil created three categories of migrants: those who had settled in Assam before 1966 were declared citizens, those who had come between 1966 and 1971 could apply for citizenship, and those who had arrived after 1971 (when Bangladesh was created) were considered illegal migrants. This new notion of "illegal migrants" came to the fore in the following years. In 2004, the BJP-led government of A. B. Vajpayee amended the Citizenship Act: now, even if a child was born on the Indian territory (jus soli), he or she was not eligible to citizenship by birth if one of his or her parents was an illegal migrant. One of the rules under the act was also amended substantially: "minority Hindus with Pakistani citizenship" could not be classified as illegal migrants. For the first time, religion was introduced as a criterion for eligibility to citizenship.[110]

The second NDA government, under Modi, further promoted this ethnoreligious characterization of citizenship. The BJP, as chapter 9 has shown, targeted illegal migrants during the 2019 Lok Sabha elections, promising to deport these "infiltrators." Before that, in July 2016, the BJP had tabled a Citizen (Amendment) Bill, which was referred to a joint parliamentary committee (JPC) one month later. But this committee did not submit its report until January 7, 2019. The bill passed immediately in the Lok Sabha, but it was not discussed in the Rajya Sabha on time. As a result, the issue of "illegal migrants" was still on the table at the time of the 2019 elections. The BJP started to adopt a shrill note on this question in September 2018 when its National Executive declared that the "Modi-led Indian government will not allow India to be used as a safe haven by illegal infiltrators. Each infiltrator will be identified, stripped of citizenship and deported."[111] During the election campaign, Narendra Modi used this plank less than Amit Shah did, who referred to it repeatedly, as mentioned in the previous chapter, in particular while he was touring West Bengal, one of the states the BJP wanted most to conquer. After the Modi II government was formed, Amit Shah played an even larger part in security-related issues as the new home minister. In this capacity, as mentioned in chapter 8, he amended the Foreigners (Tribunals) Order, 1964. While foreigners' tribunals had been limited to Assam until then, this amendment allowed state governments, union territories, and even district magistrates to create these tribunals anywhere in the country.

Amit Shah continued to campaign in favor of the Citizenship (Amendment) Bill (CAB) just before it was introduced in the Lok Sabha. In Calcutta, in October, he said: "I am assuring you that each and every infiltrator in India will be shown the door." And: "[But] I today want to assure Hindu, Sikh, Jain, Buddhist and Christian refugees, you will not be forced to leave India by the Centre."[112]

Amit Shah was also in charge of defending the CAB in parliament in December 2019. The bill aimed not only at welcoming Hindus, Sikhs, Buddhists, Jains, and Christians who were victims of religious persecution in Pakistan, Bangladesh, and Afghanistan and had found refuge in India prior to 2014 but also created a new path to Indian citizenship for them. These refugees would only have to prove six years of residence in India to apply for citizenship status rather than the twelve years that the law previously required.[113] Muslims were excluded from this track to citizenship, allegedly because Islam was the dominant religion in the three countries in question. As a result, Hazaras, Shias, and Ahmadis, even if they were persecuted in their own country, were not eligible for Indian citizenship if they had entered India as illegal migrants.

In the Lok Sabha, on December 10, 2019, Amit Shah introduced the bill by saying that it was intended to provide refuge to the "persecuted minorities of Pakistan, Bangladesh and Afghanistan. . . . It's a humanitarian issue, beyond political ideologies. . . . The Muslims in India have nothing to fear, they will continue to live peacefully. . . ."[114]

The CAB was passed with 311 votes for and 80 against. Amit Shah also introduced the bill in Rajya Sabha, where the BJP once again needed support from some non-NDA parties to get it passed (like a few months before when abolishing article 370), and it got it. The AIADMK, the

BJD, the YSR-Congress, and the TDP supported the bill, which was passed with 125 votes in favor and 105 against.[115] Many of these votes were purely tactical. The support of the YSR-Congress's leader, Jagan Reddy, for instance, was interpreted in transactional terms: "Jagan is in a bind—he needs to remain friendly with the Centre to ensure the hassle-free flow of funds to rebuild his state [from which Telangana had been carved out in 2014]."[116] The TDP—the YSR-Congress's arch opponent in the state Jagan Reddy was ruling, Andhra Pradesh—supported the CAB for nonideological reasons too: as four of its Rajya Sabha members had already defected to the BJP, it chose to defuse tensions.

Narendra Modi expressed himself on the CAB (which was renamed the Citizenship (Amendment) Act [CAA]) soon after to say in a tweet: "A landmark day for India and our nation's ethos of compassion and brotherhood! Glad that the #CAB2019 has been passed in the #RajyaSabha. Gratitude to all the MPs who voted in favour of the Bill. This Bill will alleviate the suffering of many who faced persecution for years."[117]

The CAA contravened article 14 of the Indian Constitution, which says, "The State shall not deny to *any person* equality before the law or the equal protection of the laws within the territory of India."[118] But, once again, the Supreme Court refrained for more than a year from looking into the issue—it has not yet done so at the time of this writing.

At the same time the CAA was passed, the Modi government used another legislative draft, again one dating back to the Vajpayee government: the National Register of Citizens (NRC), which had been established in 2003 to create a register of all Indian citizens. The NRC originally targeted undocumented migrants in Assam, where in August 2019 the administration declared 1.9 million people to be irregular immigrants. The Modi government decided to extend the NRC to the whole of India around the same time. Certainly, it replaced the NRC with the National Population Register (NPR) after some time, but in substance, that hardly made any difference: the combination of the two, the CAA and NPR, was bound to have consequences because Muslims with an illegal status, unlike other undocumented migrants, would not be eligible for refugee status or citizenship for that matter. As illegal migrants, they could be deported or end up in camps that the government recently asked Indian states to build. Niraja Gopal Jayal shows how high the stakes were:

> The NRC and the CAB are manifestly conjoined in their objectives. The first paves the way to statelessness and detention centres for many poor and vulnerable people, and most unjustly for those whose genuine nationality is repudiated *only on the basis of their faith.* The second offers a smooth path to citizenship for groups of migrants who are deemed acceptable *only on grounds of their faith.* In other words, faith is set to become the exclusive criterion for determining who is an Indian citizen and who is not, for inclusion as well as for exclusion. Together, the NRC and the CAB have the potential of transforming India into a majoritarian polity with gradations of citizenship rights that undermine the constitutional principle of universal equal citizenship; with privileges of inclusion being attached to some categories of citizens while others suffer the disabilities of exclusion.
>
> Though the Citizenship Amendment Bill ostensibly relates only to migrants seeking the legal status of citizenship, this is not just about migrants. The threat, rhetorical or otherwise, of a nationwide NRC shows that the fig leaf of illegal immigration is being used to bring the citizenship of *all* Muslim citizens into question. Migrants—beginning with those in Assam—are fast becoming a pretext to fabricate and advance a much more ambitious and nationwide project of "othering."[119]

The fact that the CAA and NRC worked in tandem was made clear by Amit Shah himself when he said during a press conference in West Bengal—the video of which was then posted on the BJP's YouTube page in April 2019: "Understand the chronology. . . . First the Citizenship (Amendment) Bill will come, all the refugees will be given citizenship, and after that the NRC will be prepared."[120] This meant that the non-Muslim undocumented migrants would gain access to some sort of naturalization procedure before the NRC was put in place. This NRC could only affect Muslims. Moreover, in September 2019, the RSS chief

Mohan Bhagwat made it clear that "no Hindu will have to leave over NRC."[121]

Militant Hindu WhatsApp groups gradually translated this message into their own idiom: the combination of the CAA and the NRC was a tool to "kick Muslims out of India." A journalist who had infiltrated these groups explains that "one major theme that a majority of the messages echo is that bringing the CAA and, then, the NRC, will automatically imply that India's Muslim population will be reduced. . . . They list a 'four-step' process for India becoming a Hindu nation—starting with the CAB, followed by the NRC, then a law to control population, ultimately followed by a Uniform Civil Code. The language employed in these posts is blatantly Islamophobic—the NRC is captioned as a 'Check and Throw,' while the law for population control is captioned 'No pig breeding.'"[122] Not only unofficial actors like the vigilantes and trolls of these WhatsApp groups stirred fear among Muslims, but the state itself behaved according to the same logic. In January 2020, Uttar Pradesh minister Shrikant Sharma declared that the state government had started the process of identifying refugees to implement the CAA and that 32,000 refugees had already been identified.[123] This statement came as a surprise as the enumeration process, following the NPR pattern, was not supposed to begin before spring.

Indian Muslims living outside of Assam were also disturbed by what they knew about the way the NRC had been applied there. The minister of state of home affairs, Nityanand Rai, had informed the Lok Sabha on November 19, 2019, that 1,025 Bangladeshis and 18 Myanmarese (probably Rohingyas) were in the detention camps of Assam.[124] At that time, 28 had died there.[125] Certainly, one may argue that they were illegal migrants living in dire conditions. But there were others, neither Bangladeshis nor Rohingyas, whom Nityanand Rai did not mention, as the total number of detained was above 3,000.[126] Among them, the case of a former army officer, Mohammad Sanaullah, who had also been sent to a camp because he was undocumented, made headlines:[127] it showed that well-established Indian Muslims could be detained. This decorated veteran of the Kargil War was freed on bail after eleven days thanks to the High Court.

Narendra Modi tried to alleviate Muslims' fears in a speech he delivered on December 22 in Delhi, where he claimed, "I want to tell the 130 crore [1.3 billion] citizens of India that since 2014 when my government came to power, there has been no discussion on NRC anywhere. . . . Those Muslims who were born on Indian soil, whose ancestors are children of Maa Bharti [Mother India], they have got nothing to do with CAA and NRC. They are not being sent to the detention centres. Nor does India have any."[128] This strategy of denial did not dissuade demonstrators from mobilizing against the CAB and then the CAA.

THE ANTI-CAA PROTEST

Three streams in the anti-CAA movement have been identified.[129] The smallest was made of the indigenous people of the Northeast, who saw the CAA as legitimizing the presence of non-Muslim foreigners in their ancestral area. Then came the "Citizen Opposition of 'Liberal', 'Left' and Others," to use H. Srikanth's terminology. Among them, students, social activists, and members of human rights movements and NGOs were in large numbers, but there were all kinds of activists, including Chandrashekhar Azad, the Dalit leader of the Bhim Army;[130] Siraj Bisaralli, a poet from Karnataka who was arrested because he recited a poem against the CAA;[131] and Sandeep Pandey, a Lucknow-based Magsaysay awardee who was also arrested for distributing pamphlets against the CAA.[132] There were thousands of such individual cases. Third, Muslims, of course, were especially mobilized—along with other minorities members, Sikhs and Christians in particular.[133] On the Muslim side, the massive presence of women, young and old, was a remarkable feature of this agitation.

The two last categories of protestors fought together across India. Their modus operandi was specific from two points of view: they wanted the CAA to be rolled back in the name of the Constitution of India (demonstrators often had a copy in hand), and their protest was based on the nonviolent principles of civil disobedience, or passive resistance. Sit-ins, therefore, were standard practice. In January 2020, forty of them took place around India, "often led by women like the best-known of them, at Shaheen Bagh in South East Delhi."[134] This sit-in started on December 14, 2019, and was dispersed on March 24, 2020, 101 days later, in the context of the COVID-19-related lockdown. Not only did the Shaheen Bagh demonstrators claim that they were defend-ing the Constitution, but they showed their patriotism by singing the national anthem on December 31, 2019, at midnight. On January 26, 2020, more than 100,000 people gathered together at Shaheen Bagh to celebrate the seventy-first Republic Day, and on February 14, 2020, the Shaheen Bagh demonstrators paid homage to the Indian soldiers who had been killed in Pulwama exactly one year before. In addition to the Dalit leaders mentioned above, Congress leaders (including Mani Shan-kar Aiyar and Shashi Tharoor) and artists (including the filmmaker Anurag Kashyap) visited Shaheen Bagh. In fact, protest art expressed the demonstrators' message of resistance, either via visuals (including paintings on walls or on the street) or poetry.[135] In addition, sacred texts of all the religions were read during public lectures.

Shaheen Bagh-like protests took place in Calcutta (Park Circus), Bangalore (Bilal Bagh), Mumbai (Nagpada and Agripada), Chennai (Old Washermanpeet), Pune (Konark Mall), Luknow (Clock Tower), Patna (Sabzibagh), Kanpur (Chaman Ganj), Malekotla (Anaj Mandi), Ranchi (Haj House), Deoband (Idgah ground), Allahabad (Mansoor Ali Park), Gaya (Shanti Bagh), and so on. On January 20, 2020, Rohan Venkataramakrishnan aptly observed that this mobilization represented "the first, sustained on-ground protests against Modi over the last six years."[136] The crackdown was equally unprecedented—and indicative of the shift mentioned above: violence against liberals and Muslims was not perpetrated primarily by vigilante groups but by the state.

Repression began immediately after the CAA was passed by the Rajya Sabha. Delhi was the first epicenter. On December 13, Jamia Millia students decided to march on parliament to protest against the CAA, but the police blocked the procession and dispersed the demonstrators with tear gas. Two days later, the police forcefully entered the university campus, without administrative authorization,[137] and assaulted stu-dents, even in the reading room, where tear gas was fired and equipment was ransacked—as shown on CCTV footage. Many students—both male and female—were molested and beaten up. At least eighty of them were hospitalized with serious injuries—including fractures and two with bullet wounds.[138] It is important to recall that while Delhi is a state of the Indian union, it does not enjoy the same autonomy as full-fledged states, and, in particular, the police report directly to the central government's Home Ministry.

Uttar Pradesh was the other state that saw the police unleashing violence. The first target was the campus of another Muslim university, Aligarh Muslim University (AMU), where a protest had gained momentum. On December 15—like in the case of Jamia Millia—the police and members of the Rapid Action Force (RAF) forcefully entered the university campus, breaking the iron gate at 10:00 P.M., and assaulted students.[139] On December 19, a fact-finding team consisting of human rights activists, academics, lawyers, and artists went to AMU. Their report, based on interviews of about 100 members of faculty, students, doctors, and several members of the university administration, states:

> The police persons and soldiers chased the terrified students everywhere, including into hostels and guest houses, firing teargas shells, stun grenades and reportedly bullets. They ran where they could. Some went into the university Guest House, others into hostels. Some even hid in terror for three hours behind the curtains of the mosque. We visited the heritage Morrison Boys' Hostel, where soldiers beat up guards and fired teargas into the rooms of the students to smoke them out. The room caught fire, which was doused on time by the students. Doctors from the university medical college rushed more than ten ambulances to pick up the injured students, but the soldiers refused to allow them to rescue the students, and even broke the bones of one ambulance driver.
>
> The team was shocked to find that a serving police officer on deputation from the UP cadre is appointed as Registrar of the university, and his attitude seemed that of a trigger-happy police person rather than a custodian of the students. He justified the police action as both necessary and restrained, and even spoke casually of the forces

using stun grenades. These are devices to temporarily blind and deafen the enemy, known sometimes to cause injury and burst into flames. It is likely that this caused the student to lose his hand when he picked up a device which he thought was a teargas shell; and also, possibly the fire in the hostel rooms.

Stun grenades are used only in war situations, or militarised police action such as against dangerous terrorists, never to quell student protests. Their use does not form part of the SOPs of normal law and order disturbances. And even during war, ambulances are permitted to rescue the injured. Students spoke of soldiers and police persons raising chilling slogans like Jai Shri Ram (popular with rioters and lynch mobs) while attacking the students and setting ablaze their scooters and vehicles. In the melee, exact figures are hard to verify, but the teachers and doctors we met estimate that around 100 students were picked up by the police, and another 100 were injured, 20 seriously. . . .

Video footage and on ground report show policemen destroying motorbikes and scooters parked within the university campus. Several vehicles are currently reported missing. . . .

One ambulance driver and his ambulance were beaten up by the police near the guest house. Despite explaining to the policemen that he was only an ambulance driver here to tend to the wounded, they beat him up, confiscated the ambulance's keys and vandalised the vehicle. The driver had to then return to the hospital with a broken hand, in the ambulance that was behind him. The destroyed ambulance was lying at the Staff Club until next morning. Due to threats of violence from the police and RAF, several ambulances that went to the site had to return midway, without picking up any injured student. . . .

Around 3 A.M. on the December 16, the nearly 60 students admitted in the trauma centre were asked to leave (not by the hospital) under fears that the police may pick them up from the hospital. Doctors report that police and RAF vans were stationed on the other end of the hospital, but they did not come in. . . .

While the police were attacking students, they used religiously charged terms such as "katua" (slur for circumcised), "haraamse paida hue (born out of sin)" and "aatankvaadi (terrorist)," alongside calls of violence such as "saamne se maaro (beat from the front)" and "maaro saalon ko (beat them up)." When the RAF entered Morrison Court hostel and when they were destroying vehicles on campus, they were heard shouting slogans such as "Bharat Mata ki Jai" and "Jai Shri Ram."[140]

The totally disproportionate use of force by the police and the RAF, and their sheer numbers—1,200 to 1,300 personnel intervened on the campus that night—matched the language they used. This language reflected a communal prejudice that was already obvious in the case of vigilantes who lynched and tortured Muslims, but this time, the main protagonists were state actors. Other campuses were affected to a lesser extent, including Nadwa College and the Indian Institute of Technology of Kanpur.

The repression against street demonstrators was also extreme in Uttar Pradesh. The police simply opened fire on them, as can be seen in videos.[141] On December 20, 6 people were killed (including 3 in Meerut).[142] On the following day, 10 more were killed and 218 people were arrested in Lucknow alone.[143] After a phase of denial, the police admitted to firing at anti-CAA protestors,[144] and many photographs,[145] as well as videos broadcast by NDTV and other TV channels, reconfirmed this fact.[146] In parallel, a record number of 21,500 people were charged in fifteen FIRs for violent incidents in Kanpur, as the police claimed that officers had bullet wounds.[147] By late December, already 1,113 persons had been arrested and 5,558 had been preventively detained in Uttar Pradesh.[148]

The police also targeted property owned by Muslims. Many videos showed policemen destroying CCTV before vandalizing shops or smashing cars.[149] Several CCTV videos were released to the public in Muzaffarnagar that showed police personnel vandalizing property and damaging cars and shops, even though the government blamed the protesters for the damage.[150] Not only did the police destroy a great deal of property outside Muslim homes, but they also entered their houses, terrorized them, stole jewelry, and ransacked interiors.[151] This repression reconfirmed the presence of nonuniformed men working with the police on the ground. These civilians, known as "police *mitr*" (the police's friends), suggest that the osmosis between the men in uniform and vigilante groups had deepened.[152]

Exposed by the media, the BJP government claimed that the police had first been attacked by demonstrators, who were also presented as looters and held responsible for the destruction of shops and the vandalization of public buildings.[153] Moreover, on December 22, the Uttar Pradesh government created a panel to assess property damage and recover the losses by seizing the property of the alleged protesters. That was in continuation of the Uttar Pradesh government's attempt at weakening the Muslims economically, a game plan that had started with the ban on slaughterhouses.

In Uttar Pradesh, the toll of the repression was twenty-three dead, officially. Similar forms of police action also occurred in Bihar[154] and in the Congress-governed state of Madhya Pradesh.[155] But Uttar Pradesh was the worst-affected state.

The trauma Indian Muslims experienced in the winter of 2019–2020 was also due to the treatment thousands of those arrested received at the hands of the police. The same pattern repeats itself in all the testimonies of those who dared to speak out afterward, a combination of physical and psychological violence. The AMU students who were taken into custody, for instance, were beaten up and humiliated: "Their phones were snatched and destroyed immediately. They were beaten on the way and eventually taken to the Akrabad Police Station, 25 kilometers away from the Bab-e-Syed gate. At the police station, they were stripped naked and asked to lie down on a dari [carpet] on the floor, face down. They were then beaten with leather belts."[156] Women were not spared. Sadaf Jafar, a Lucknow-based Congress activist, an ex-teacher, and an actress by profession, who demonstrated against the CAA, described her days in police custody and in jail in revealing terms:

[At the police station] male and female constables repeatedly slapped me and thrashed me with batons. The marks are still on my body. . . . Every time, the policemen passed by, they would ask my name and call me a "Pakistani." They kept abusing me and said that "I eat here, but loyalties are there." It was horrible. They always addressed me as "*tum log*" [collective "you people"]. More than the thrashing, it was the word "*tum log*" that pained me. I come from a family of freedom fighters. At the police station, one female constable pulled my hair, slapped me and scratched my face. None of the police officers, from constable to seniors, wore badges on their uniform. . . . At 11 P.M., a female constable took me to an officer's room who, she said, is the Inspector General of Police. Even before entering the room, he started abusing me. He said, "Why are you doing all this, even when the government is doing so much for you?"

Then he asked the female constable to put me in jail under section 307. He asked her to slap me. Then he got up and pulled my hair, kicked me in my stomach and knee. I knew then that my nightmare had begun. I was feeling very sick, shaken and abused. . . . I found out later that the male cop was not the I[nspector] G[eneral], but a senior officer. . . .

Nobody, including my sister, knew where I was. Around 11 A.M. the next day, my friend Kabir came to the station looking for me. He was beaten up and was stripped in front of me. I felt dehumanized, humiliated, hungry and was bleeding. When we reached jail, I saw young boys with injuries and stitches. And they were stripped in front of me. . . .

My Muslim identity is the only reason that such treatment was meted out to me. I am a social activist, poet and theatre activist. All these years, my identity never mattered to me. But that my religion defines me as a person now is disturbing. Those 19 days I spent in jail were less harrowing than one night in police custody. I got to see my children only after 11 days. For two days, my family was in the dark about my whereabouts.[157]

The dehumanization syndrome finds expression in Jafar's feeling of being "like Jew in Hitler's Germany," a sentiment arising from the way she was beaten and humiliated and also shown naked men as if Muslims were all animals with no sense of modesty. They are not seen as part of human civilization. This radical otherization also operated via the usual equating Muslim with Pakistani and therefore enemy.

Even children were victims of police repression. In three Uttar Pradesh districts (Bijnor, Muzaffarnagar, and Firozabad), a total of forty-one children were detained in December 2019 in the context of the crackdown on the anti-CAA movement. Some of them were arrested in a Muzaffarnagar madrassa. These minors were beaten up and deprived of sleep while in custody.[158]

According to the official toll, thirty-one people died during the anti-CAA movement, more than two-thirds of them in Uttar Pradesh.[159] The state chief minister, Yogi Adityanath, instead of expressing regret, first denied that the police had opened fire—arguing that those who had died had been killed by the "bullets of the rioters"[160]—and then justified the way the police behaved.[161]

The same pattern can be seen in the role of the police during the Delhi riots in early 2020 as well.

The Delhi Riots: Militants and Police vs. Muslims

The communal riots that took place in February 2020 in North East Delhi—a very densely populated district where, according to the 2011 census, Muslims represented more than 29 percent of the population and Hindus, about 68 percent—were primarily due to the BJP's reaction to the anti-CAA movement in the context of the state elections. During the election campaign, BJP leaders targeted protesters against the CAA in Delhi—not only in Shaheen Bagh but elsewhere in the city, including in North East Delhi, where many sit-ins were held—in order to polarize voters along communal lines. Amit Shah himself, during a meeting on January 27, declared: "When you press the button [of electronic voting machines] on February 8, do so with such anger that its current [poll result] is felt at Shaheen Bagh. . . . Your vote to BJP candidate will make Delhi and the country safe and prevent thousands of incidents like Shaheen Bagh."[162] Another member of the Modi government, Anurag Thakur, one week before, according to the fact-finding mission appointed by the Minorities Commission after the riots, had raised a slogan in an election rally in Delhi "where he incited the public present to repeat: 'Desh ke ghaddaron ko, goli maaron saalon ko' (Shoot down the rascals/the traitors to the country). Captured widely in print and electronic media, it is clearly shown and heard how he shouted the first part of the slogan, and directed the listening crowd to respond with the second half."[163]

A local BJP MP, Parvesh Verma, in another election meeting in Delhi, made an equally aggressive speech: "If in Delhi, BJP come, then after 11th [of February, when the election results would be released] give me one month, how many ever masjids have been built on government land in my Lok Sabha constituency, I won't leave even one of them standing."[164] On January 29, 2020, Tarun Chug, the BJP national secretary, tweeted the following: "We will not let Delhi become Syria and allow them to run an ISIS-like module here, where women and kids are used. They are trying to create fear in the minds of people of Delhi by blocking the main route [with the Shaheen Bagh sit-in]. We will not let this happen."[165] On the following day, one of the BJP candidates, Tajinder Bagga, comparing Shaheen Bagh to Pakistan, concluded an election speech with equally threatening words: "Shaheen Bagh has become a hub of anti-nationals. And on 11th February, after the results, a surgical strike will be done on this adda [den]."[166] Three days later, Yogi Adityanath, who had come from UP as a star campaigner, pointed out that "where 'boli' (words) don't work, 'goli' (bullet) does."[167]

This sample shows that the BJP election campaign had for weeks relied on its old repertoire of fear of the Other and anger in a systematically aggressive manner. As usual, this campaign used social media, including WhatsApp and Facebook.[168] According to the police, the "bulk of WhatsApp groups were created between February 23 and 24." They showed violent incidents that had nothing to do with Delhi "to inflame passion."[169] They were also used to give real-time information on where to gather and which shops and homes to target.

On February 11, 2020, the BJP faced a rude shock as only eight of its candidates, out of seventy, won a seat, against sixty-two for Arvind Kejriwal's Aam Aadmi Party (AAP). This defeat fostered factional tensions within the party and made the party cadres and activists extremely bitter. Some of them wanted to take revenge.[170] Their postelection meetings were as aggressive as the preelection ones. On February 23, 2020, Kapil Mishra, a former local AAP MLA and minister in Kejriwal's government who had joined the BJP in 2019 and lost the election in February 2020, led a provocative rally in North East Delhi, one kilometer away from an anti-CAA Muslim women sit-in in Jafrabad. Arguing that the demonstrators were inviting violence, he said, "This is what they wanted. This is why they blocked the roads. That's why a riot-like situation has been created. From our side not a single stone has been pelted. D[eputy] C[ommissioner of] P[olice] is standing beside us. On behalf of all of you, I am saying that till the time [U.S. president] Trump goes back [from India], we are going to go forward peacefully. But after that, we will not listen to the Police if roads are not cleared after three days."[171] In the context of the present discussion—aside from the systematic targeting of the Muslims during the BJP campaign and the use of social media that Mark Zuckerberg himself denounced in the case of Mishra's speech[172]—the most important point was the fact that Mishra addressed the gathering in the presence of the deputy commissioner of police for North East District, Ved Prakash Surya, who was standing right next to him *in full riot gear*. It projected an unparalleled visual by associating an expert in communal provocation and a custodian of law and order. Some BJP leaders criticized the inflammatory character of Mishra's speech,[173] which was to preface the beginning of the riot.

Indeed, local BJP leaders did not wait until after the U.S. president's visit but instead started to show their strength immediately, attacking Muslims in North East Delhi. They created WhatsApp groups to ensure coordination, and mass violence was unleashed from February 25 onward.[174] One of the sitting MLAs of East Delhi, Abhay Verma, took a procession across his constituency, chanting: "desh ke gaddaron ko, goli maaro saalon ko" (Shoot down the rascals/the traitors to the country).[175] Physical attacks took place at the same time in Shiv Vihar, one of the North East Delhi localities, as evident from the testimonies collected by the Delhi Minorities Commission (DMC) fact-finding committee:

On 25.02.2020 at around 4 P.M., several people came in Gypsy cars and stopped near the puliya [small bridge] on the nala [drain] connecting Johripur. They were wearing helmets and had a cloth mask to cover their faces. Then they started throwing petrol bombs in the gali [lane] dominated by Muslims. Thereafter, another group came from across the Nala Abadi side (Johripur area, which is a non-Muslim locality). They had a Santro Car with a gas cylinder inside it. At around 5 P.M., they let the car roll down a slope towards the residential area of Shiv Vihar. The car was on fire as it hit the puliya and it caused a huge blast. After that everyone got scared. The residents were crying in panic. But the mob kept throwing cylinders, gas golas [bombs] and bottles towards the residential areas.[176]

For four days, until curfew was imposed, North East Delhi saw a scenario unfold that had been observed before elsewhere, including in Gujarat in 2002—but on a smaller scale.[177] Thousands of assailants, led by Hindu nationalist cadres, including BJP former or sitting MLAs and municipal councilors,[178] came from outside the locality to help the local activists. They forcibly entered houses to attack men and women;[179] 600 houses were burned[180] and shops looted with a remarkably accurate selectivity, as adjacent houses and shops were spared when they belonged to Hindus;[181] markets were razed as well;[182] mosques were systematically targeted—they were looted, desecrated, and burned.[183] Sometimes those praying inside were attacked. Madrassas and cemeteries were damaged as well.[184] Most of the time, the attackers were chanting "Jai Shri Ram" and tried to force Muslims, including imams, to chant it too.[185] The other slogans they kept repeating were "Har Har Modi," "Modiji, kaat do in Mullon ko" (Modiji, cut these Muslims into pieces), "Aaj tumhe Azadi denge" (Today we will give you freedom),[186] and "Hindustan Hamaara hai, ek bhee Musalmaan nahi rahega yahaan" (India is ours, not even one Muslim will stay here!).[187] Kapil Mishra's slogans were similar: "Desh ke gaddaron ko, goli maaro saalo ko" (Shoot the traitors of this nation), "Jai Shri Ram" (Hail Lord Ram), and "Kattue Murdabad" (Down with the circumcised [a very derogatory expression to designate Muslims]).[188] Visual and oral aspects of the riots were widely known to the public because both witnesses and assailants alike made videos: the former to testify, the latter to boast of their deeds to the world and terrorize their victims.[189]

After four days, the official toll was fifty-five dead, including thirteen persons with non-Muslim names.[190] According to a police affidavit still full of loopholes, 13 mosques and 6 Hindu temples had been damaged; out of 185 damaged properties, 50 were identified as Muslim and 14 as Hindu, and out of 468 damaged shops, the breakdown was 173 and 42, respectively (among those whose owners' religion had been identified).[191] Thousands of people fled and found refuge in relief camps, but many preferred to stay with relatives and friends or returned to their ancestral places—they were therefore not counted as refugees.[192] Few returned after the riots. On the contrary, the hostile attitude of the local Hindus persuaded many Muslims who could still live in their house to sell them below market price for safety, following the usual post-riots ghettoization process.[193]

The fact that the state was involved in the Delhi riots was evidenced by the way the government interfered with the judiciary. Justice Muralidhar, in the Delhi High Court, was known for his pronouncements against communal violence. He delivered the verdict convicting members of the Uttar Pradesh police for the 1986 killing of Muslims in Hashimpura, and he convicted the former Congress MP Sajjan Kumar in a case related to the 1984 anti-Sikh pogrom. On February 25, 2020, he heard the petition filed by Harsh Mander to register an FIR against BJP leaders (including Kapil Mishra, Parvesh Verma, and Anurag Thakur) whose inflammatory speeches had contributed to the unleashing of violence. During the hearings he castigated the Delhi police for the way it failed to maintain law and order and protect citizens. "Hours after the proceedings were completed, the Ministry of Law and Justice issued a notification for Justice Muralidhar's transfer from the Delhi High Court to the Punjab & Haryana High Court."[194] This transfer had been recommended by the Collegium. The Delhi High Court Bar Association condemned it, considering it "detrimental to our noble Institution."[195]

While Hindu nationalists initiated the riots, the police played an important role in them. First, the police gave rioters "free reign to target Muslims." A twenty-two-year-old who took part in the Delhi riots after being given a rod by a Bajrang Dal member told the *Caravan* that the police "told us to go and attack inside, in the Muslim areas, that they won't come there. . . . They said, 'Show us that you're Hindu.'" The young man added that a police official had said to him, "When we get a message from above, I will stop you. But until then, do what you want."[196] The twenty-two-year-old also said that Kapil Mishra had "taken the public along with him, he has given many suggestions [to the rioters]."[197] Not only did the police give the rioters free reign, but they did not come to the rescue of Muslims, like in Gujarat in 2002. Many riot victims told the Delhi Minorities Commission fact-finding committee and journalists that they had called the police in vain and, when they saw them in the street, asked them to intervene. But they either did not respond or said that they had no order to rescue them.[198] In Ram Rahim Chowk, "Police did not help the victims in any way; it rather threatened them by saying that they might shoot them (the victims)."[199] In Shiv Vihar, "on 24 February 2020, a Police gypsy car was patrolling. On complaints by Muslims about the mob, the Police personnel said that they will not do anything to prevent it as they did not have order from higher-ups to prevent them."[200] When some police forces came to intervene, they were hailed by the attackers. An eyewitness told the DMC fact-finding committee that this happened on Karawal Nagar Road:

Mobs from both communities reached the main Karawal Nagar road and started stone pelting at each other. They did not stop at stones, but petrol bombs were also being thrown. There were no security forces to contain the violence. Almost half an hour after this, a Delhi Police vehicle arrived. Seeing the vehicle, the Hindu mob shouting "Jai Shree Ram" and "Bharat Mata ki Jai" started walking forward and at that moment a Delhi Police officer threw tear gas towards the group of Muslim residents. This prompted the Hindu group to start shouting "Delhi Police Zindabad [Long live Delhi Police]." It was an odd sight to see that Delhi Police was taking clear sides in these riots. It was only around 5 P.M. that I saw the Delhi Police trying to control both sides, at which they failed. The stone-pelters did not stop and Delhi Police had to retreat.[201]

The police were pelting the Muslim mob with stones, along with Hindu rioters, in several places.[202] They attacked women too, in the first place those who were taking part in the Chand Bagh sit-in.[203] In the complaints filed subsequently, victims declare that the police also incited the activists to attack them.[204] Like other rioters, some police officers took part in the looting and destruction of mosques, sometimes while chanting "Jai Shri Ram,"[205] usually after destroying the CCTV cameras.[206] In the case of Masjid Farooqia, "the perpetrators were police in uniform who attacked them while shouting 'Jai Shri Ram.' On 26 February at around 6:30–7 A.M., the mob broke the locks and entered the mosque. They destroyed the CCTVs and LLDs first."[207]

Possibly in reaction to the attitude of the police, two security personnel were killed during the riot: Ankit Sharma, an Intelligence Bureau staff member,[208] and Police Constable Ratan Lal.[209] Seemingly as a result, the police directly assaulted Muslims even more brutally. One of these attacks, on February 24, 2020, was filmed, and the videos went viral on the social media. The background story was narrated to the DMC fact-finding committee by one of the victims who had gone to Kardam Puri Pulia area in search of his son:

There he was surrounded by 6–7 policemen who beat him with their boots and sticks on his head, legs and whole body. Thereafter, the police dragged him to Mohalla Clinic on the main road. Three young men who were severely injured were already lying there and bleeding. The policemen threw him at that place. After some time, police brought one more person and threw him near them. Policemen kept beating all five of them with sticks and boots. Police told them to sing "Jana Gana Mana" (national anthem) and directed one Kausar to say "Bharat Mata Ki Jai" (Long Live Mother India). While beating them, the policemen were saying, "You want Azadi? Take this Azadi!" One policeman told them that even if they died, nothing will happen to the police officers. The policemen present there kept abusing them. Later, a policeman asked the other officers not to beat them. After some time, a police car came and took them to GTB Hospital. The doctor performed an X-ray of the complainant. He stated that the doctor told him that his X-ray will be available after two hours because he was a Muslim.[210]

Faizan, one of the five men who were beaten by the police in the Kardam Puri Pulia area and made to chant the national anthem while being filmed, died.[211]

Although there were instances in which policemen protected the victims—and took risks while doing so[212]—the role of the police during the Delhi riots was similar, to some extent, to the behavior they displayed during the crackdown on the anti-CAA movement. As a rule, after the violent episodes described above, whether in Jamia Milia, in AMU, in UP, or in North East Delhi, the police betrayed the rule of law by making it very difficult for the victims to file a complaint.[213] Those who filed complaints against the police and BJP leaders for their attitude during the Delhi riots were under huge pressure to withdraw their statements—and many complaints were buried anyway.[214] In the case of AMU, the fact-finding team wrote in their report: "Many students told us that they had been warned by the university authorities that if any student filed a complaint, they would be expelled from the university and criminal charges, even under the dreaded National Security Act, would be lodged against them."[215] Naturally, AMU has filed no complaints, and it seems "that the University officials signed the papers inviting the RAF into the campus after they had entered, in order to legitimise and legalise their entry."[216] In Muzaffarnagar, release of the children who had been arrested from the Saadat Madrassa was only obtained after the principal agreed to "sign affidavits asserting that none of their students had been beaten or tortured."[217] Some complaints were filed anyway, including one by the Jamia Alumni Association regarding the police action of December 15, 2019, during which university property worth Rs 2.66 crore (354,667 USD) was damaged, including Rs 4.75 lakh (6,330 USD) for 235 broken CCTV cameras.

While some CCTV footage could still be used, the police argued that they appeared "to be edited."[218]

Not only could the victims not file a complaint, but they were accused of being responsible for the violence itself[219]—whereas no FIR has been registered against Hindu activists who took part in the riots, BJP leaders who made provocative speeches, or policemen who were seen attacking Muslims on videos.[220] Citing an unnamed superintendent of police, the *New York Times*, after investigating the case, said that the police was under political pressure not to arrest Kapil Mishra or other "warriors of the government."[221] The detailed report filed by the fact-finding committee set up on March 9, 2020, by the Minorities Commission of the state of Delhi and from which much of the information above was drawn was not even used by the authorities. Not only that, but the chairman of the DMC, Zafarul-Islam Khan, was accused of sedition in April 2020 because of a Facebook post.[222] As a result, of the 1,153 accused against whom the police completed their investigation, 582 were Muslim and 571 were Hindu.[223]

Instead of punishing the real culprits, the narrative promoted by the police and the BJP government—both representing two sides of the same coin, that is, the state—consisted in attributing the responsibility of the Delhi riots to the Muslims.

AN ERA OF CONSPIRACY THEORIES: TURNING VICTIMS INTO CULPRITS—AND VICE VERSA

On March 10, Amit Shah, the home minister to whom the Delhi police reports directly, congratulated himself that the police succeeded in controlling the riots "within 36 hours," "not allowing the riots to spiral."[224] He also said that the situation improved after Ajit Doval visited the riot-affected areas[225] and that video footage would now help the police to identify the culprits—2,647 people, according to him, had already been arrested, a process human rights activists called a witch hunt and which targeted students[226] as much as young Muslims of North East Delhi.[227] Shah concluded that these "riots were 'pre-planned' conspiracy" and that it "will be a lesson for the country on what befalls those who indulge in rioting."[228] While opposition MPs demanded his resignation, a BJP MP, Meenakshi Lekhi, pointed out in parliament that Ankit Sharma, the Intelligence Bureau staffer, had been killed by "hatred": "400 wounds were found in his body," she claimed.[229]

While two Malayalam channels were banned by the Information and Broadcasting Ministry because of their "antinational" coverage of the Delhi riots,[230] the BJP's conspiracy theory and the strategy of Hindu victimization were propagated by *The Organiser*. The RSS mouthpiece first published an interview of Kapil Mishra that was prefaced in a style reminiscent of the post-Godhra incident, in which Hindu nationalists claimed that Muslims had started the violence: "The Delhi anti-Hindu riots have seen the worst of everything. Perhaps the biggest victim of manipulated narrative is BJP leader Kapil Mishra who is projected as the instigator of violence not just by the so-called anti-CAA protesters and their intellectual messiahs but also by the international media lobbyists."[231] In this interview, Mishra—who was raising funds for the Hindu victims of the Delhi riots[232]—argues that the anti-CAA demonstrators were responsible for the Delhi riots:

> The reality is violence has been going on in Delhi since December 16. The buses were set ablaze in Jamia; an Assistant Commissioner of police was hit with stones in Seemapuri, and an attempt was made to spread riot at Turkman Gate in Delhi. At the same time, railway stations in Bihar and Bengal were burnt, and public properties were set on fire in different parts of Uttar Pradesh and in rest of the country. All this has been happening for last 100 days in the name of CAA. Anti-CAA people were preparing for major violence in Delhi for a long time. . . . These so-called protesters were preparing for the riots for the last three months. They were making petrol bombs, storing stones, buying acid bottles for since long.[233]

This version of the facts is revealing of a classic Hindu nationalist tactic: finding excuses to legitimize their violent reactions (never action). As Mishra cannot allege any concrete threat (beyond stone pelting and car burning), he indulges in a conspiracy theory, claiming that Muslims were "preparing" for major violence. In March, this "theory" resulted in the drafting of an FIR, the famous "FIR 59" (from its complete name, FIR 59/2020) that accused the former JNU student Umar Khalid—who was to be arrested soon after[234]—of having planned the violence with associates, who had "collected arms and ammunition, while staging protests with women and children."[235] According to the police, the masterminds of the conspiracy, including Khalid, the AAP councilor Tahir Hussain, and businessman-turned-human-rights-activist Khalid Saifi (the founder of the NGO United Against Hate) had met on January 8 in order to foment a "big blast" during Donald Trump's visit "to defame the country in the international arena." A major hole in this narrative lies in the fact that the Trump visit was announced on January 13.[236]

The Organiser elaborated on this FIR to flesh out its conspiracy theory:

> These hated crimes by a particular community against Hindus was pre-planned and pre-determined. It has been established with the FIR's and then charge-sheet has been filed against the AAP counselor Tahir Hussain and 14 others in Karakardooma court of Delhi. This charge-sheet was in co-relation with the riots that took place in the Chand Bagh area of North-east Delhi on 24th and 25th February of this year. Delhi Police further enunciated in the said charge-sheet that on January 8th almost a month before February, North-east Delhi riots, Tahir Hussain met with Former JNU student Umer Khalid and Khalid Saifi and united against Hate at Shaheen Bagh Anti-CCA protest, and Umer asked Tahir "to be prepared for something big/ riots at the time of TRUMP's visit." He and other PFI members will help (Hussain financially). Then the chief mastermind who organised the violence in the region for which Tahir Hussain has received Rs. 1.30 crores [173,330 USD], his brother and 15 others also have been named as accused.

> Police further elaborated in charge-sheet that Tahir Hussain got his pistol released from Khajuri Khas police station, just before the riots started and didn't give any satisfactory reply for the same. He has to answer where are his live 14 cartridges also. Chand Bagh was the worst hit area where IB staffer Ankit Sharma was also found mur-

dered in a drain. Here in Jaffrabad riots case also the Delhi Police filled charge-sheet on June 2nd. Natasha Narwal and Devan Gana Kalita of "Pinjara Tod" group have been accused and arrested. They both were also a part of longer conspiracy and were found to be hand in glove with the "India Against Hate Group" as Umer Khalid. It was a targeted attack on Hindu community. The Hindu community was totally unaware about the attack while the attackers belonging to the Muslim community pre-planned not only the man power and other resources but also the timing as well. Whereas the culture of Bharat clearly gives us direction by way of Bhrtrihari's Niti Shatak which as follows:

अयंनिजःपरोवेतगिणनालघुचेतसाम् |
उदारचरितानांतुवसुधैवकुटुम्बकम् |

Meaning

The person with narrow-minded outlook thinks that he is mine, he is my enemy, But a person with a golden heart thinks . . . everyone on the earth is his brother.

The said factual information have been shared by the various independent social workers and other organisations like "GIA—Group of Intellectuals and Academicians" and "Call For Justice" another group of intellectuals.

As per the report of GIA there is not an iota of doubt that this riot is a tragic outcome of a planned and systemic radicalisation of minorities with a left Urban Naxal network operating in universities of the capital. The very presence of Jihadi organisations, like PFI (Popular Front of India) at Dharna sites have been established by the fact finding team of GIA. The recommendation observed by various independent fact-finding teams, thereby corroborating the same factual matrix in the charge-sheet filed by Delhi-Police on June 1st and 2nd. The needles of the clock are interlinked with each other, one moves with a greater speed then the other needle which moves slowly. The modus of operandi in these anti Hindu riots has the same pattern, as Tahir Hussain, Abdul Khalid, Gul Fisha, Shifa Ur Rehman etc. Have executed the riots on the ground level in conspiracy with bigger fishes having remote with International Jehadi and Urban naxal support like, Harsh Mander, Rajdeep Sardesai, Yogender Yadav[237] etc.

The various Stringent steps have to be taken by the Central Government to handle these dangerous Anti-National acts so that the majoritarian society who is very peaceful, progressive, educated and civilised should not be penalised for no wrong. . . .

The Bharatiya point of view in this context is squarely matching with four corners of this present situation, as said:

"कृण्वन्तोवश्विवंआर्यं"

Means every man on the Earth has the right to be educated and live healthy.

And

"अहसिापरमो धर्मः"

Meaning Non-violence is the ultimate duty.[238]

This long citation is useful to capture the mindset of the Sangh Parivar after the Delhi riots: Muslims and "urban Naxals" had been conspiring for a long time, and they took by surprise innocent Hindus, who could not in any case be responsible for the violence due to their sense of civilization. No evidence is needed here because the cultural and ideological differences are proof in themselves.

In April, the FIR 59 referred to many more sections of Indian law, including terrorism, rioting, possession of arms, attempt to murder, incitement of violence, sedition, murder, and promoting enmity between different groups on grounds of religion. Four of these sections were under the stringent antiterror law, the Unlawful Activities (Prevention) Amendment Act, 2019 (UAPA), which made crimes nonbailable. Finally, fourteen people were accused in this "plot," including the former Aam Aadmi Party councilor Tahir Hussain, presented by the police as the mastermind of the "conspiracy" along with Umar Khalid,[239] and accused of the murder of IB staffer Ankit Sharma, the president of the Jamia Millia Islamia Alumni Association, a lawyer and former Congress Party councilor, a social activist cum businessman,[240] an MBA graduate, and six students, two from JNU and four from Jamia, including Safoora Zargar[241] and Asif Iqbal Tanha.[242]

The accused's lawyers considered it "one of the most visible examples of how the Delhi Police, which reports to Home Minister Amit Shah, was using the riots as a pretext to place some of the Modi regime's most charismatic and outspoken critics under indefinite incarceration."[243] Indeed, the UAPA is one of the most draconian antiterror laws. It allows police up to six months to file charges against the accused—as compared to three months under regular criminal law—and the accused can be detained without trial for two years.[244]

Besides the FIR 59 accused, others have been arrested for sedition under the UAPA for other reasons, including for instigating the "Jamia riots" of December 15, 2019—before the police entered the campus forcibly. Sharjeel Imam, a JNU student who had taken part in the anti-CAA movement, is a case in point. He was arrested on January 28, 2020, by Delhi Police, who alleged that his speech promoted enmity among people, which led to riots. In April, a supplementary charge sheet was added to the first one, in which an imam was also accused of sedition.[245] He was accused of being a "highly bigoted person who completely lacks faith in the Constitution," partly because he read books on "collective violence" for his PhD on Partition (including those authored by political scientist Paul Brass) that contributed to making him "highly radicalized and religious bigoted."[246] Assessing the radicalization or religious bigotry of an individual on the basis of his bookshelves is a clear instance of cultural policing by the state.

The increasingly systematic accusation of sedition against demonstrators reflected the government's will to minimize any opposition in the street. In the case of the Jamia Millia "incident," the National Human Rights Commission (NHRC) to which the students had turned bought into the police's narrative of their protest being violent and justified their action on the campus. For the NHRC, since the students who had demonstrated violently were back at Jamia Millia, "police also entered inside the campus to contain the violent/unruly mob and to remove them from campus. However, these protesters entered inside the libraries and blocked their way as to prevent the police. As to remove them, police broke open the doors of the libraries." The commission concluded that the way the police beat up dozens of students "could have been avoided" but did not recommend prosecution of the guilty policemen, whose violent action was recorded by the CCTV.[247] It did not conclude that the police action had been disproportionate either.

In Uttar Pradesh, not only were victims held responsible for the violence that affected them, but they were also forced to pay for the damage to property that the riots and the face-to-face conflict with the police had led to. On December 19, Yogi Adityanath had declared that his government would "make those who damaged property pay for it."[248] And three days later, the UP government started to seize properties of those it accused of being responsible for the violence.[249] In February 2020, more than two months after the December anti-CAA demonstrations in Lucknow, the additional district magistrate issued an order for recovery of Rs 63 lakh (84,000 USD) as damage to property from forty-six people (including two men who were under house arrest at that time—and could not have damaged any property).[250] This procedure was possible more than two months after the demonstrations because, in the meantime, the UP government had introduced a new "commissionerate system,"[251] under which the police had magisterial power and reported directly to the state government—not to the district magistrate—to recover the money, by attaching property if need be. This change harked back to the apprehensions of the UP government regarding interference from the judiciary. It is also one of the reasons why the portraits of the forty-six people who were supposed to pay for the damage were widely publicized:[252] the UP government put up billboards in intersections in Lucknow, with names, addresses, and photos of some of the accused of violence during anti-CAA protests in Lucknow in December 2019, the same people who had been asked to pay compensation for damage to public property. One of the explanations for this "naming and shaming" technique was that the judiciary had started to release these people on bail and might exonerate them for lack of evidence: if the High Court continued with that kind of attitude, at least they would remain guilty in the eyes of the people's court.

This attempt at replacing judges by popular judgment was also evident from the way the BJP encouraged Indians to denounce their fellow citizens. The Mumbai BJP chief, for instance, bestowed the Alert Citizen Award on an Uber driver "for informing police about a passenger who was plotting an anti-national protest against the Citizenship Amendment Act and handing him over to the police."[253] Five days before, the Bombay High Court had set aside an order of the Aurangabad District additional district magistrate against allowing CAA protests. The judge said that the demonstrators could "not be called traitors, anti-nationals only because they want to oppose one law," and then he added:

> When we are considering a proceeding like the present one, we must keep in mind that we are a democratic republic country and our Constitution has given us rule of law and not rule of majority. When such an Act is made, some people, maybe of a particular religion like Muslims, may feel that it is against their interest and such Act needs to be opposed. It is a matter of their perception and belief and the Court cannot go into the merits of that perception or belief. . . . India got freedom due to agitations which were non-violent and this path of non-violence is followed by the people of this country till this date. We are fortunate that most of the people of this country still believe in non-violence. In the present matter also, the petitioners and companions want to agitate peacefully to show their protest.[254]

Two visions of justice were clearly in competition in Mumbai in February 2020.

The repression of the anti-CAA movement targeted not only Muslims but also secularists and liberals—who were increasingly stigmatized as "urban Naxals." The attitude of the government vis-à-vis this new category, as well as its growing use of conspiracy theories, indeed fits in with the increasingly authoritarian policy of the post-2019 BJP government and must, therefore, be examined closely.

Policemen as Vigilantes and "Urban Naxals" as Political Prisoners

The way urban Naxals have been harassed and arrested in India before and after 2019 shows that police forces reporting to BJP ministers have emulated the Hindu nationalist vigilantes to some extent and translated into action the increasingly authoritarian strategy of the government, a trend that also manifested in the decline of freedom of expression studied in chapter 8.

The Indian state has acquired additional features of a police state under the post-2019 BJP-led NDA government, primarily because of the way it amended the laws of the republic and used them. Immediately after Modi II was formed, Amit Shah introduced in parliament an amendment to the Unlawful Activities (Prevention) Amendment Act, a law that had been passed in 1963 in order to restrict freedom of expression and the right to assemble as well as to form association in the interest of the sovereignty and integrity of India. While the UAPA was already draconian for the reasons mentioned above, the amendment introduced by Shah and passed by the Indian parliament during the summer of 2019 empowered the state to designate individuals as terrorists. Previously, that was the case only for organizations.

This law was used, in particular, against a group of human rights activists, unionists, and intellectuals in the context of the Bhima Koregaon case, named after the village in Pune District (Maharashtra) where, in 1818, Dalit soldiers of the British army trounced the troops of the local ruler—a Brahmin, Peshwa Bajirao II. On January 1, 2018, like every year, Dalits of Maharashtra, mostly Mahars, gathered to commemorate this event in the form of an Elgaar Parishad (lit., congress for speaking aloud), organized by two retired lawyers, including an ex-Supreme Court justice. During their meeting, they contested the BJP's "homogenizing Hindutva"[255] that rejected divisions among Hindus and criticized the Modi government.[256] They were attacked by upper-caste Hindu nationalists and one of the latter died.[257] A Dalit activist filed a complaint against two men—Sambhaji Bhide, an activist "close to Prime Minister Narendra Modi"[258] who had been associated with the

RSS, and Milind Ekbote, a former BJP corporator who had gone to jail several times—for, among other things, participating in a communal riot.[259] The latter went to jail briefly, but the police, despite the report it had prepared that showed that both men were guilty of "a well-planed [*sic*] conspiracy,"[260] looked for other accused after a disciple of Bhide, Tushar Damgude, filed a complaint. This shift took place while the notion of a "Maoist conspiracy" was waved by a Pune-based RSS-affiliated think tank, the Forum for Integrated National Security.[261] Soon after, the police arrested new accused who were presented as "urban Naxals."

The expression *urban Naxals* is used to differentiate urban Maoists from the Maoists active in rural India (and in the tribal areas in particular) who supposedly follow the same Indian version of Maoism, or Naxalism—a movement named after the revolt of the peasants of Naxalbari in 1967. This contemporary expression was coined by Arun Jaitley in 2014 to describe activists of the Aam Aadmi Party, in spite of the fact that it was a regular political party.[262] But it was popularized by a Bollywood film director, Vivek Agnihotri, who defines an urban Naxal "as an intellectual, influencer or activist who is an invisible enemy of India."[263] The idea of such a conspiracy was propagated, however, by the Hindu nationalist movement. A 2019 booklet attributed to the Sangh Parivar and to which Agnihotri contributed, argued that urban Naxals had not only been "infiltrating into police, armed forces, bureaucracy, civil services, etc." but had also mounted a "campaign to overthrow the Indian government" and that "all left leaning professors and journalists [we]re Naxal supporters and even support[ed] violence by Naxal groups."[264] In September 2018, then home minister Rajnath Singh warned people that Naxalites had "come to the cities and are trying to influence people."[265] Narendra Modi himself told students in 2019 to wonder whether "urban Naxals, some people who consider themselves intellectuals, are not trying to gain political mileage by putting a gun over your shoulders. . . . You will have to find out if this is not a conspiracy by them to destroy your life. They cannot think of anything else but hatred for Modi."[266]

In June 2018, the police of Maharashtra—a state ruled by the BJP at the time—in the course of its investigation in the Bhima Koregaon case, arrested five "urban Naxals," who were accused not only of instigating violence in this particular case (despite the fact that only two of them took part in the Elgaar Parishad) but also of plotting a "Rajiv Gandhi style" assassination of Narendra Modi.[267] Their profile matched that described by Agnihotri: Surendra Gadling was a lawyer, Shoma Sen was a retired English professor, Sudhir Dhawale was a poet and publisher, and Mahesh Raut and Rona Wilson were human rights activists. Two months later, the police also arrested, in the same case, the "poet-activist" Varavara Rao,[268] the lawyer and trade unionist Sudha Bharad-waj,[269] and the human rights activists cum authors and columnists Arun Ferreira and Vernon Gonsalves. Two more "urban Naxals" were arrested in April 2020: first, Anand Teltumbde (a former business executive, regular contributor to the *Economic and Political Weekly*, and professor at the Goa Institute of Management),[270] who has authored many books including *Republic of Caste*, and second, Gautam Navlakha, an ex–editorial consultant with the *Economic and Political Weekly* and a member of the People's Union for Democratic Rights. Then, Hany Babu, an associate professor of Delhi University, was arrested as a "co-conspirator" for prop-agating Maoist ideology.[271] Finally, an eighty-three-year-old Jesuit priest who has worked all his life among the tribals of Jharkhand was ar-rested because of alleged Maoist ties.[272] They were all accused of con-spiracy aiming at overthrowing the government and assassinating the prime minister on the basis of letters recovered from the computers of two of the arrestees. Amnesty Tech (Amnesty International's digital-security team) subsequently discovered that one of these com-puters contained malware allowing remote access and alleged that the letters could have been planted.[273] The idea that the letters had been manufactured was supported by the fact that Naxals' communication is heavily coded.

While searching the houses of the accused, the police of Maharashtra indulged in cultural policing, listing books that were not banned as evi-dence against them[274] and commenting on their political ideas and so-cial attitudes. The policemen who searched the house of Varavara Rao's daughter and son-in-law, who heads the Department of Cultural Studies at the English and Foreign Languages University of Hyderabad, asked them, "Why are you reading books on Mao and Marx? Why do you have books published in China? . . . Why are there photos of Phule and Ambedkar in your house, but no photos of gods?"[275] To Rao's daughter, they said, "Your husband is a Dalit, so he does not follow any tradition. But you are a Brahmin, so why are you not wearing any jewellery or sindoor? Why are you not dressed like a traditional wife? Does the daughter have to be like the father too?"[276] These policemen echo here the discourse of Hindu nationalist vigilantes when they try to make people comply with the high tradition of their religion associated with upper castes and specific norms as well as forms of worship and reject leftist ideologies in a typically anti-intellectual manner.

The internationally renowned historian Romila Thapar and other scholars filed a petition in August 2018 against these arrests. But two of the three judges of the bench refused to release the accused on bail. Retired Justice Shah commented upon this decision in revealing terms. For him, "abuse of the UAPA and constant rejection of bail applications of accused as a means of silencing opposing voices can be seen most in the Bhima Koregaon cases, where mere *thought* has been elevated to a *crime*. In this matter, involving the arrests of many individuals, the so-called evidence was a typed, unsigned, undated document already in the public domain, which was taken from the devices of Varavara Rao and Gautam Navlakha, and attributed to them."[277]

The dissenting judge, Justice Chandrachud, observed that a "clear cut distinction has to be made between opposition to government and attempts to overthrow government by rising up in arms."[278] For him, the Bhima Koregaon case was "an attempt by the state to muzzle dissent. . . . Each of them is prosecuted for being a defender of persons subjected to human rights violations."[279] In other words, the accused of the Bhima Koregaon were victims of judicial authoritarianism and were political prisoners.

The political dimension of the Bhima-Koregaon case was evident from the fact that a day after the Shiv Sena-NCP-Congress government—which had just replaced the BJP-led government after the September 2019 elections—decided to review the charge sheet against the accused, the Union Ministry of Home Affairs handed over the investigation to the NIA to make sure that the procedure against them would continue.

During Modi's second term, the government of India has transitioned from a predominantly Hindu nationalist vigilantism-based agenda to a more Hindu statist authoritarianism-oriented one. Certainly, both repertoires overlap, but a clear shift has occurred. Before 2019, the key players were Hindu nationalist vigilante groups, including the Bajrang Dalis and the gau rakshak, who were responsible for cultural policing in the framework of opposing love jihad, the Ghar Wapsi movement, cow protection, and so on. Vigilantes were thus the main actors of anti-Muslim violence, including lynchings, whereas the police often remained passive spectators. During this phase, which coincides with Narendra Modi's first term, the state apparatus did not display an overt anti-Muslim attitude. Certainly, the police did not rescue Muslims targeted by vigilantes, but it did not often overtly attack them either.

During the first two years of Narendra Modi's second term, these vigilante groups remained active, but the anti-Muslim bias of key institutions of the Indian republic became more pronounced. First, the central government, owing to its electoral successes, became more assertive in parliament (including in the Rajya Sabha, where an increasingly large number of so-called opposition MPs fell in line) and, therefore, amended important laws and even the Constitution of India, as the abolition of article 370 regarding Jammu and Kashmir testifies. Second, the police in BJP-ruled states directly attacked Muslims in the context of repressive measures or riots.

Vigilantes were still active in 2019–2020. During the Delhi riots, for instance, they patrolled East Delhi to assault Muslims and keep journalists in check.[280] But in 2019–2020, the police formed a quasi-joint venture with them: policemen actively suppressed Muslims in reaction to the anti-CAA movement and then in the context of the Delhi riots and cracked down even more on student demonstrations and other collective protests, especially in Uttar Pradesh.

Muslims were not the only victims of this authoritarian use of state institutions. Political opponents were also at the receiving end. The parties that were not part of the NDA and that resisted the government, including the Congress, were not considered legitimate adversaries but instead enemies to be eliminated. As a result, parliament ceased to be a place for debate, and its rules were even broken on many occasions. All these changes are indicators of a dying democracy, to paraphrase Levitsky and Ziblatt. Besides the opposition represented in parliament, the opposition fighting the political system in the name of leftist ideas was targeted as not only illegitimate but also illegal. As a result, academics, human rights activists, and trade unionists, designated as "urban Naxals," were arrested by the police. Interestingly, the police repressed them not only because of their ideas—therefore making them political prisoners—but also on account of their lifestyle, which betrayed the Hindu orthopraxy, including the caste system. In that sense, the state was now doing the job of the vigilantes, inventing a form of state vigilantism.

The decline of democracy in India has been well documented, year after year, by countless surveys. The 2018 report released by the Varieties of Democracy Institute described India as an "electoral democracy" (and not as a "liberal democracy")[281] because of an "autocratization-process" that found expression in "a partial closing of the space for civil society," including NGOs and the media, and in a decline in political transparency.[282] Two years later, the annual report of the same institute pointed out that "India has continued on a path of steep decline, to the extent it has almost lost its status as a democracy."[283] The Democracy Index of the Economist Intelligence Unit showed that India had slipped ten places in the 2019 global ranking, to fifty-first place, behind South Africa, Malaysia, Colombia, and Argentina. In this index, India was now part of the "flawed democracies" because of "an erosion of civil liberties in the country"[284]—including in Jammu and Kashmir. In 2020, India ranked 110 out of 162 countries in terms of personal freedom.[285] The same year, Freedom House pointed out that India earned "the largest score decline among the world's 25 most populous democracies" in its yearly report.[286] As a result, India has now been placed by the organization among "countries in the spotlight," along with Haiti, Iran, Nigeria, Sudan, Tunisia, Turkey, Hong Kong, and Ukraine.[287]

11

Indian Muslims

FROM SOCIAL MARGINALIZATION TO INSTITUTIONAL EXCLUSION AND JUDICIAL OBLITERATION

THE POLICE, discussed extensively in the previous chapter, is not the only institution of the Indian state alienating Indian Muslims. This chapter will take stock of the impact of the Modi years in terms of the institutional exclusion of this religious minority beyond the police.[1] To assess this impact, it is necessary to go beyond the rhetoric. Modi, like most BJP leaders, very rarely expresses any anti-Muslim feeling in public. On the contrary, since his Gujarat years and his Sadbhavana Mission, he has made a point to apply his 2014 motto, "Sabka sath, sabka vikas" (With everybody, development for all), and even to appear compassionate vis-à-vis Indian Muslims. He invited Indian citizens to "hug" Kashmiris after the abrogation of article 370, and he systematically insisted on his open-minded approach to all communities. When the Modi government decided to reform Muslim customs, it was always in the name of modern, universalistic values. The abolition of the "triple *talaq*" (a custom enabling men to divorce their wives instantly) is a case in point. In June 2019, just after the Lok Sabha election, the Modi government had the Muslim Women (Protection of Rights on Marriage) Act passed in parliament to make triple talaq illegal and punishable by "imprisonment for a term which may extend to three years." While the law had a clearly emancipatory potential in favor of Muslim women, it introduced an equally clear asymmetry as "wife-abandonment . . . is not a crime for followers of any other faith in India."[2] But Modi presented it, very convincingly, in his Independence Day speech on August 15, 2019, as an extension to Muslims of the progressive reforms that Hindus enjoyed already:

> You would have seen how our Muslim daughters and sisters used to live in fear with the sword of Triple Talaq dangling over their heads. Even if they were not victims of Triple Talaq, they were constantly haunted by the fear that they could be subjected to it anytime. Many Islamic countries abolished this evil practice long time back. But for some reason we were hesitant to give our Muslim mothers and sisters their due rights. If we can abolish Sati Pratha, if we can enact laws to end female foeticide, if we can raise our voice against child marriage, if we can take strong steps against dowry system in this country, then why can't we raise our voice against Triple Talaq? We have taken this important decision in the spirit of India's democracy and constitution, to respect the thinking of Baba Saheb Ambedkar so that our Muslim sisters get equal rights; so that new confidence is generated in them; so that they also become active participants in the India's development journey. Such decisions are not for political gains.[3]

This discourse is well in tune with the way Hindu nationalism propagates an irenic view of society as minimizing conflicts. In 2020, while demonstrations by students and Muslims were being brutally quashed by the police and Hindu nationalist vigilantes, Narendra Modi delivered a lecture in which he presented India as the country of "peace, unity and brotherhood," a country where "one finds peace and harmony" because "the Indian way of conflict avoidance is not by brute force but by the power of dialogue."[4]

The key word here is *harmony*, a word that is used repeatedly in the few books Modi has authored[5] and that he often uses in his *Mann Ki Baat* program (see chapter 4). In his writings, he attributes his quest for unity and harmony to the RSS, whose mission, since its inception, has been "to unite the society through individual building in the service of Motherland" and whose principles have always been "renunciation, penance, devotion, loyalty and commitment": "I have been fortunate to acquire these traits while living in this tradition in the capacity of Sway-amsevak of the Rashtriya Swayamsevak Sangh."[6] Modi has tried to emu-late "this bright tradition of sacrificing life without expecting anything in return," "for the happiness of everybody." But this holistic worldview relies on a hierarchy that subalterns are urged to accept—be they from the lower castes or Muslims, the new second-class citizens.[7]

To measure the decline of Indian Muslims in terms of citizenship, their presence in some of the most important institutions over the long term is now analyzed. This approach shows that Muslims were never well represented in the Indian state apparatus. But under Modi, they have lost even more ground in power centers where they used to matter, including in elected assemblies. While this decline is primarily due to the BJP's accession to power, other parties are partly responsible for it too. The judiciary has also become less dependable than it once was. In fact, the attitude of the Supreme Court in 2019–2020 sealed the fate of Indian secularism and heralded the officialization of the Hindu Raj, a process to which new laws also contributed in 2020–2021.

Invisible in the Republic: Long-Standing but Aggravated Institutional Marginality

After Partition, Muslims' social marginalization was precipitated by the migration of elite groups (which left the community decapitated), socioeconomic backwardness, and lack of education.[8] More recently, the condition of Muslims has been affected by social processes men-tioned in part II, including forced ghettoization and economic stigma-tization in the context of cow protection movements. This section tries to show that the rise of the BJP has also affected Muslims in terms of access to some of the state's most important institutions—in which they had never been well represented anyway.

Muslims have remained on the sidelines of some of India's institu-tions since 1947, which has led Gurharpal Singh to conclude that India has been an ethnic democracy from its inception.[9] The situation prevail-ing in the police, the bureaucracy, and the army substantiates this view.

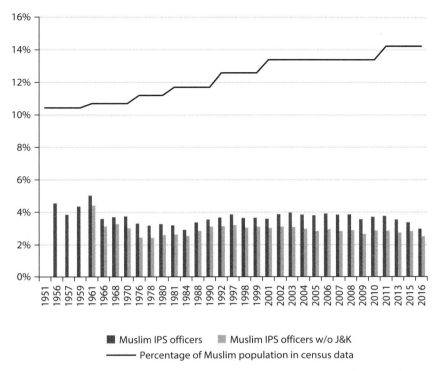

FIGURE 11.1. Muslims in the Indian population and among IPS officers (1951–2016)
Source: Christophe Jaffrelot, "A *De Facto* Ethnic Democracy? Obliterating and Targeting the
Other: Hindu Vigilantes and the Ethno-State," in *Majoritarian State: How Hindu Nationalism
Is Changing India,* ed. Angana Chatterji, Thomas Blom Hansen, and Christophe Jaffrelot
(London: Hurst, 2019), 44

Regarding police officers, the database I compiled with the help of
Shweta Bhutada shows that in the 1950s, the percentage of officers in the
Indian Police Service (IPS)—the elite leadership body for national
policing—was already lower than 5 percent, less than half the proportion
of Muslims in Indian society according to the 1951 census.[10] While the
share of Muslims in the population subsequently rose, reaching
14.25 percent in 2011, the proportion of Muslims in the IPS dwindled, falling beneath the 3 percent mark in 2016, and even as low as 2.5 percent of
the whole service if Jammu and Kashmir (the only dominantly Muslim
state—now a union territory—in India where Muslim police officers are

naturally a majority) is excluded from the calculation.[11] Never had the gap between the share of Muslims in the population and their proportion in the IPS been so wide—but it had always been considerable.[12]

The situation is less unfavorable to Muslims if the analysis is broadened to include police officers at the lower echelons. In 2013—the last year for which these data were compiled[13]—Muslims made up 6.27 percent of police officers in India. But their strength was on the wane. In 2004 they still composed 7.1 percent, then 7.5 percent in 2005, 9.1 percent in 2008 (a year for which statistics are skewed due to a lack of reporting by Madhya Pradesh), and 6.5 percent in 2011.[14]

The remarkable investigative work that appears in the *Status of Policing in India Report 2018* led to the creation of an indicator of sociocultural diversity within the Indian police forces. It shows that between 2006 and 2013, Muslims were particularly underrepresented in law enforcement agencies. While the average index was 0.31 (compared to 0.50 for women), it varied between 0.08 in Assam and 0.69 in Andhra Pradesh, with only 0.09 in Rajasthan and 0.18 in Uttar Pradesh.[15] More recent data have been released concerning Delhi. They showed that in 2017 the proportion of Muslims in the Delhi police was at an all time low at 1.7 percent (whereas Muslims represent about 13 percent of the state population).[16]

The situation is even more critical in the armed forces, and this has been true since 1947. That year, Partition led to the departure of virtually all Muslim officers to Pakistan.[17] Nehru himself expressed concern over the situation in 1953, the year in which his defense minister informed him that the percentage of Muslims in the Indian army had gone from 32 percent in 1947 to 2 percent: "In our Defence Services, there are hardly any Muslims left. . . . What concerns me most is that there is no effort being made to improve this situation, which is likely to grow worse unless checked."[18]

In fact, Muslims no longer made up more than 1 percent of higher-ranking officers (colonels and above) in 1981 according to Steven Wilkinson's reckoning.[19] This figure was confirmed in 1999 by former defense minister Mulayam Singh Yadav.[20] The man who succeeded him in this post under the Vajpayee government, George Fernandes, bluntly explained the situation: "The Muslim is not wanted in the Armed Forces because he is always suspect—whether we want to admit it or not, most Indians consider Muslims a fifth column for Pakistan."[21] These remarks date from 1985. That year an opinion poll showed that the majority of Hindus interviewed believed that Muslims should not be allowed to join the armed services.[22] These data were recently updated by Ali Ahmed's study on officers trained at the Indian Military Academy (IMA). From 2005 to 2011, 2 percent of them were Muslims, a figure still below the 2.62 percent found by the Sachar Committee for the previous period.[23]

Training the focus now on the elite corps of the bureaucracy, the Indian Administrative Service (IAS)—admission to which is through the same exam as the IPS—figure 11.2 shows that while the proportion of Muslims in the IAS rose slightly between 2006 and 2016, going from 3 to 3.3 percent,[24] this increase is minimal when compared to the Muslim population in India, which is also on the rise. Moreover, the share of Muslims entering via the parallel track (enabling state civil servants to enter the IAS) partly explains these results: in 2016, only 2.7 percent of Muslims in the IAS entered by passing the Union Public Service Commission (UPSC) exam for civil service jobs. In 2017, the situation had improved somewhat, with the share of Muslims among the candidates who passed the UPSC exam for jobs in the administration rising to 5.1 percent. But this figure fell to 4.5 percent in 2018.[25] It just so happens that that year, over half of the successful Muslim candidates had been trained by the Zakat Foundation of India, an NGO founded in 1997 that had gradually decided to emphasize activities that might give the community as a whole an elite once again.[26] Underrepresentation is partly due to the fact that many Muslims do not sit for the civil service exam. According to Amitabh Kundu's estimate, they make up only 8 percent of the candidates on average.[27]

At the level of the states, each with its own civil service, the situation is somewhat variable. In Maharashtra, for instance, although Muslims make up 11 percent of the population, only 5 passed the Maharashtra Civil Services exam out of 435 (or 1.14 percent) in 2015.[28] Despite this, in 2015, the new coalition government formed by the BJP and Shiv Sena decided not to defend in court the previous Congress government's plan to reserve 5 percent of the regional civil service for Muslims by

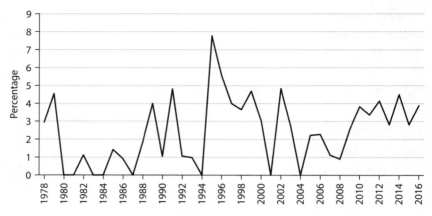

FIGURE 11.2. Percentage of Muslims in the IAS (1978–2017)
Source: Ministry of Home Affairs (Government of India), *The Civil List of Indian
Administrative Service*, New Delhi, 1978 to 2017

decree,[29] which brought the sum total of quotas over the 49 percent mark
that the courts set as a limit not to be exceeded.[30] Only some states in the
South continue to implement positive discrimination for Muslims. Aside
from Kerala and Karnataka, where the policy is long-standing,[31] Telangana, the youngest state in the Indian union—created in 2014 when
Andhra Pradesh was divided in two—is also striving to bring the quota for
Muslims in the civil service up to 12 percent, despite BJP opposition.[32]

While the proportion of Muslims in the civil service has never been
very high but is, at least, no longer dropping, their underrepresentation
in the judiciary apparatus was not as manifest. Since 2010, with the exception of the High Courts of Hyderabad (the capital of Andhra
Pradesh until 2014) and Jammu and Kashmir, the proportion of Muslims among High Court justices (regional courts operating at the state
level) is significantly lower than their percentage of the population in
states for which data are available. In West Bengal, their proportion was
8 percent in 2011 (whereas the percentage of Muslims in the population
was 27 percent). In Karnataka, it was 2.9 percent in 2011 (whereas their
share of the population was 12.9 percent). The proportion of Muslims
in the Jabalpur High Court (Madhya Pradesh) plummeted to 2.9 percent
(while their share of the state population increased to 6.6 percent). The

same goes for the court in Patna (Bihar), where Muslims made up 5.4 percent of the judges in 2011 (whereas their share in Bihar's population had risen from 12.45 to 16.9 percent).[33]

The Supreme Court has experienced a similar situation, as Gilles Verniers writes:

> In the 1950s, among the 24 judges appointed to the SC, only four were Muslims (16.6 per cent). No Muslims were appointed during the 1960s (out of 16 nominations). Only two Muslims were appointed in the 1970s (out of 26), four in the 1980s (out of 33), that is 12 per cent. The ratio of Muslim SC judges decreases after the 1980s at the same time as the number of nominations increases: three out of 40 in the 1990s, two out of 49 in the 2000s and three out of 40 since 2010, Justices MY Ekbal and FM Ibrahim Kalifulla in 2012 and Justice S Abdul Nazeer in 2017. In total, 18 Muslim judges were appointed in the SC, out of 229 (before 2018), that is slightly less than 8 per cent, for a demographic segment that represent 14.2 per cent of the total population [in 2011].[34]

While Muslims have traditionally been underrepresented in the state institutions reviewed above, for many years they were able to assert their numbers to win seats in various assemblies throughout India—including in the lower house of parliament, the Lok Sabha—in areas where their demographic weight was greater.[35]

But from 1980 to 2014, the number of Muslim MPs in the lower house of the Indian parliament—and hence their percentage—decreased by more than half (see table 11.1). This evolution is all the more significant as the share of Muslims in the Indian population rose during the same period (from 11.1 to 14.2 percent). As a result, the gap between the share of Muslims in the Indian population and their share in the Lok Sabha (which dropped from 9 to 4.2 percent) increased fivefold, jumping from 2 to 10 percentage points between 1980 and 2014. Responsibility for this trend lies primarily with the BJP, which has never endorsed more than a few Muslim candidates, and this in constituencies where the party had a slim chance of winning, even as its group in parliament continued to increase in numbers.

TABLE 11.1. Muslim MPs in the Lok Sabha

Year	% of Muslims according to the 10-year census	Total number of seats	Number of Muslim MPs	% of Muslim MPs
1980	11.4 (1981)	542	49	9
1984	11.4 (1981)	542	46	8.4
1989	11.4 (1981)	543	33	6
1991	12.6 (1991)	543	28	5.1
1996	12.6 (1991)	543	28	5.1
1998	12.6 (1991)	543	28	5.1
1999	12.6 (1991)	543	32	5.8
2004	13.4 (2001)	543	35	6.4
2009	13.4 (2001)	543	29	5.3
2014	14.2 (2011)	543	23	4.2
2019	14.2 (2011)	543	25	4.4

Sources: Christophe Jaffrelot and Gilles Verniers, "The Reconfiguration of India's Political Elite: Profiling the 17th Lok Sabha, *Contemporary South Asia* 28, no. 2 (May 18, 2020), https://doi.org/10.1080/09584935.2020.1765984, an article drawing its data from the SPINPER—The Social Profile of the Indian National and Provincial Elected Representatives, a CNRS-supported international research project associating Ashoka University and Sciences Po.

In 2009, the BJP fielded four Muslim candidates, or 0.48 percent of the total, only one of whom got elected. In 2014 and 2019, it fielded respectively seven and six Muslim candidates out of 428 and 436 (or less than 2 and 1.4 percent), and none were elected. For the first time in India's history, the winning party in the general elections had no Muslims in its parliamentary group, and therefore, states such as Maharashtra had no Muslim MP in the Lok Sabha—which was already the case in 2009.

The BJP's decision not to field many Muslim candidates aimed to liberate the party entirely from the "Muslim vote"[36] and, beyond that, minorities in general—following the strategy of Donald Trump, who appears to be a model for Hindu nationalists in this regard. One of them told Prashant Jha during the 2017 campaign in Uttar Pradesh: "Everyone was wooing the Muslims. We told the Hindus—they will unite, will we always remain divided? Trump in the US showed that it is not blacks and Hispanics and Muslims who will decide who becomes US president. It is whites. Here too, it is not Muslims who will decide who rules UP. It is all other Hindus. They want to defeat us. We want to defeat them and their parties. It is a battle."[37] It is difficult to find a clearer expression of political majoritarianism or ethnic democracy, which involves making the ethnic majority coincide with an electoral majority, thereby relegating minorities to the margins. All the more as the formation of a Hindu vote bank by the BJP, which in particular aimed to sideline minorities in the political arena, prompted other parties as well to cease nominating Muslim candidates, except in areas with a high Muslim majority. This tactic was especially clear in the Congress's case, which the BJP accused of cultivating a Muslim vote bank by showing concern for their social and economic condition (a false claim, moreover)[38] and sought to reassure the Hindu majority by turning away from Muslims. In 2009, the Congress, unwilling to embrace its traditional secularism, only endorsed 31 Muslim candidates (or 3.7 percent of the total), of whom only 11 won seats. That year, the parties that fielded the most Muslim candidates and got them elected were regional parties, starting with the Bahujan Samaj Party.[39] Five years later, the Congress fielded 27 Muslim candidates out of 462 (less than 6 percent of the total). Interestingly, in 2019, the party nominated 8 more Muslim candidates (8.6 percent of the total). Among non-Muslim parties, only the Rashtriya Janata Dal, the Samajwadi Party, the Trinamool Congress, and the CPI(M) fielded a percentage of Muslim candidates significantly higher than the share of Muslims in the population—at an all-India level, not necessarily in their state (see table 11.2). But in many cases, the candidates in question were in constituencies distant from the areas where these parties were strongest, and few of these candidates were returned.[40]

Not only did parties of all political stripes field fewer than 10 percent of Muslim candidates for the Lok Sabha in 2014 and even fewer, 8.6 percent, in 2019, but above all, hardly any were elected. Muslim MPs ultimately made up about 4.2–4.5 percent of elected representatives in the lower house. This underrepresentation, linked to the boom in Hindu majoritarianism, was reflected at the government level by an unprecedented situation. Only two members in the first Modi government—or less than 3 percent—were Muslims in 2014. Both had come from the Rajya Sabha (the upper house), given that there were none among the

TABLE 11.2. Muslim candidates in the 2014 and 2019 Lok Sabha elections, by party

Party	Muslim candidates		Total number of candidates		%	
	2014	2019	2014	2019	2014	2019
AAP	41	1	427	35	9.6	2.9
AGP	1	1	12	3	0.8	33.3
AIADMK	5	0	40	21	0.1	0
AIFB	5	3	39	35	12.8	8.6
AITC	21	12	131	62	16	19.4
AUDF	10	N/A	18	N/A	55.5	N/A
BJD	0	0	21	21	0	0
BJP	7	6	428	436	1.6	1.4
BSP	48	38	501	383	9.6	9.9
CPI	2	4	68	49	2.9	8.1
CPM	14	8	93	69	15	11.6
DMDK	0	0	14	4	0	0
DMK	2	0	35	23	5.7	0
INC	27	35	462	421	5.6	8.3
INLD	1	0	10	10	10	0
IUML	22	7	25	9	88	77.8
JD(S)	2	0	33	9	6	0
JD(U)	8	3	93	25	8.6	12
JKNC	3	3	3	3	100	100
JMM	2	1	22	13	9	7.7
LJP	1	1	7	6	14	16.7
MDMK	0	N/A	6	N/A	0	N/A
MNS	0	N/A	10	N/A	0	N/A
NCP	3	3	35	34	8.6	8.8
PMK	0	0	9	7	0	0
Peace Party	24	N/A	51	N/A	47	N/A
RJD	6	5	29	21	20.7	23.8
RLD	0	0	10	3	0	0
SAD	0	0	10	10	0	0
SHS	1	2	58	98	1.7	2
SP	36	8	195	49	18.4	16.3
TDP	2	0	30	25	6.7	0
TRS	1	0	17	17	5.9	0
Others	23	N/A	305	N/A	7.5	N/A
Total	320	396	3 245	4584	9.9	8.6

Source: SPINPER—The Social Profile of the Indian National and Provincial Elected Representatives, a CNRS-supported international virtual lab associated with Ashoka University and Sciences Po.

BJP MPs in the Lok Sabha and that only MPs can be appointed as government ministers in India. Still, the party in power wanted to include a token Muslim or two in its cabinet. In July 2016, the minister of minority affairs, Najma Heptulla, resigned but was replaced by another Muslim minister in this position, Mukhtar Abbas Naqvi (minister of state prior to that).[41] A second Muslim minister was then appointed to the cabinet, M. J. Akbar, who became minister of state for external affairs but who also resigned in 2018. Inventorying the loci of power in the Indian republic, the veteran journalist Shekhar Gupta concluded, "India's minorities have never been so out of the power structure. They are justified in having a sense of unease about it."[42] Since 2018, Naqvi is the only Muslim face in Modi's government.

However, an examination at the level of the states of the Indian union is necessary to make a full appraisal of the situation. Aside from the fact that there is no longer a single Muslim chief minister, the presence of Muslim representatives in state assemblies (as MLAs) and governments (as ministers or ministers of state) is on the wane. In December 2020, in ten states of India representing 80 percent of Indian Muslims (Uttar Pradesh, West Bengal, Bihar, Maharashtra, Assam, Kerala, Karnataka, Rajasthan, Gujarat, and Jharkhand), out of 281 government members, only 16 (that is 5.7 percent) were Muslim. This state of affairs was partly due to the rise to power of the BJP. The only BJP-ruled state that had a Muslim in its government was Uttar Pradesh. There were none in Gujarat, Karnataka, Assam, or Bihar (where the BJP has formed a coalition with the JD[U]). In 2014, before the victory of BJP in Uttar Pradesh and Assam, there were 34 Muslim ministers.[43] This situation was also a reflection of the MLAs' sociological profile.

According to the SPINPER data set, in the fourteen large states that renewed their assemblies between 2014 and 2018, Muslims only made up 9.3 percent of the candidates and 7.1 percent of those elected. These figures reflect primarily the BJP's performance in several states. In January 2018, out of 1,418 BJP elected representatives in these assemblies, only four were Muslim, and only two members of the BJP state governments (coalition governments are not taken into account here) were Muslim.[44] This situation holds true as much in states where the BJP has been governing for a long time (such as Gujarat, where the party has not endorsed a single Muslim candidate since 2007[45]) as for those recently conquered, such as Assam (34 percent Muslim), where, out of 61 MLAs (enabling it to win the elections in 2017), it has only one Muslim elected representative.[46]

In general, when the BJP conquers a new state previously ruled by a regional party, the number of Muslim MLAs drops (see table 11.3). The most spectacular example is found in Uttar Pradesh, where, in 2017, their proportion went from 17 to 6 percent. While the figure of 17 percent, achieved in 2012 mainly thanks to the success of the Samajwadi Party,[47] had brought the share of Muslim MLAs closer to their share of the population in Uttar Pradesh—that is, according to the 2011 census, 18.5 percent—the figure of 6 percent, associated with the BJP landslide victory, reflects an underrepresentation comparable to that of 1991, when the party had already taken control of the state.[48] In Bihar as well, correlatively to the rise of BJP in the 2020 election, the number of Muslim MLAs has dropped from 24 to 19 (out of 243).[49] For the first time since Independence, the state had a ruling coalition without a single Muslim elected representative.[50]

A similar diminution in the number of Muslim representatives was not noted when power changed hands from the Congress to the BJP, simply because the Congress never fielded very many Muslim candidates. In many states, the Congress no longer dares to nominate a large number of Muslim candidates out of fear of alienating the majority community by seeming to show favoritism toward a stigmatized minority. In Maharashtra, whatever the winning party, the proportion of Muslims among the MLAs has never exceeded 5 percent (i.e., half the proportion of Muslims in the state), including when the Congress won, because it never endorsed more than 7 percent of Muslim candidates. In Gujarat, Muslim assembly members already made up no more than 1 percent of the assembly in 1990, prior to when the BJP came to power—and they have remained at this level, as the Congress never fields more than a half dozen Muslim candidates in the elections. The situation is comparable in Madhya Pradesh and in Karnataka. In Rajasthan, by contrast, the Congress has always fielded the same number of Muslim candidates since

TABLE 11.3. Muslim candidates and MLAs in a selected number of state assemblies (%)

State	1962	1967–1969	1969–1971	1972–1978	1980–1983	1985–1987	1989–1991	1993–1996	1996–2001	2002–2006	2007–2011	2012–2016	2017–2019
Gujarat	**2.9**	**1.6**	**3.3**	**4.5**	**4.1**	**4.1**	**5.7**	**6.7**	**4.6**	**4.5**	**6.6**	**9**	**6.7**
	5.1	*2.3*	*1.8*	*2.2*	*6*	*4.9*	*1*	*0.5*	*2.7*	*1.6*	*2.7*	*1*	*1.6*
	8.1	8.1	8.1	8.4	8.5	8.5	8.5	8.7	8.7	9	9	9.7	9.7
Karnataka	N/A	N/A	N/A	**7.5**	**6.7**	**6.5**	**5.7**	**5.8**	**6.6**	**5.8**	**6.8**	**6.8**	**9.5**
				7.1	*1.3*	*4*	*4.9*	*2.7*	*5.3*	*1.8*	*2.7*	*2.7*	*3.1*
				10.6	11	11	11	11.6	11.6	12.2	12.2	12.9	12.9
Madhya Pradesh	**1.5**	**1.9**	**2.5**	**2.8**	**3.5**	**4.6**	**5.4**	**4.7**	**3.1**	**4**	**4.1**	**4.9**	**5.56**
	2.4	*1*	*2.7*	*0.9*	*2.1*	*1.5*	*0.9*	*0*	*1.8*	*0.9*	*0.4*	*0.4*	*0.87*
	4	4	4	4.4	4.8	4.8	4.8	5	5	6.4	6.4	6.6	6.6
Maharashtra	**3.8**	**2.2**	**4.6**	**4.7**	**4.9**	**7**	**8.9**	**7.6**	**7.8**	**8.7**	**10.3**	**9**	**12**
	4.2	*2.6*	*5.2*	*3.8*	*5.2*	*9*	*2*	*2.4*	*4.9*	*3.5*	*3.8*	*3.1*	*3.5*
	7.7	7.7	7.7	8.4	9.2	9.2	9.2	9.7	9.7	10.6	10.6	11.5	11.5
Odisha	NA	**0.6**	**0.5**	**0.7/1.6**	**0.9**	**1.2**	**0.8**	**1.2**	**1.1**	**1.5**	**1**	**1.2**	N/A
		0	*0.7*	*1.4/0.7*	*2*	*2.7*	*1.4*	*1.4*	*0.7*	*2*	*0*	*0.7*	
		1.2	1.2	1.5	1.6	1.6	1.6	1.8	1.8	2	2	2.2	
Rajasthan	**3.6**	**2.9**	**5**	**5.3**	**6.4**	**7.8**	**7.2**	**8.9**	**5.8**	**6.4**	**6.2**	**7.2**	**7.48**
	1.7	*3.2*	*3.2*	*4.5*	*5*	*4*	*4*	*2*	*6.5*	*2.5*	*6*	*1*	*4*
	6.5	6.5	6.5	6.9	7.3	7.3	7.3	8	8	8.5	8.5	9.1	9.1
Uttar Pradesh	**7.7**	**9.1**	**9.7**	**10/12**	**10.8**	**10.2**	**12.7/10.7**	**10.6**	**8.7**	**10.6**	**11.3**	**12.8**	**10.3**
	6.7	*6.8*	*8.2*	*9.7/11.5*	*11.7*	*12.2*	*9.6/5.5*	*7.5*	*11.7*	*11.7*	*13.9*	*16.9*	*5.6*
	14.6	14.6	14.6	15.5	15.9	15.9	15.9	17.5	17.5	18.5	18.5	19.3	19.3
West Bengal	**10.4**	**7.4**	**11.6/11.1**	**11**	**11.6**	**11.3**	**11**	**10.6**	**11.4**	**12**	**11.2**	**10.7**	**19.3**
	11.1	*13.6*	*13.6/13.6*	*14.7*	*14.6*	*12.9*	*14.6*	*15*	*14.3*	*14*	*20*	*20*	N/A
	20	20	20	20.5	21.5	21.5	21.5	23.6	23.6	25.3	25.3	27	N/A

Source: SPINPER—The Social Profile of the Indian National and Provincial Elected Representatives, a CNRS-supported international virtual lab associated with Ashoka University and Sciences Po.

Notes: The figures in boldface type are the percentages of Muslim candidates fielded by the two or three main parties; the figures in italics are the percentages of Muslims among MLAs; the figures underlined are the percentages of Muslims in the state in question according to the census of the decade under consideration.

Two figures occur in some squares when two elections took place in the period concerned. For a more comprehensive overview, including many more states, see Christophe Jaffrelot, "The Fate of Secularism in India," in *The BJP in Power: Indian Democracy and Religious Nationalism,* ed. Milan Vaishnav (Washington, DC: Carnegie Endowment for International Peace, 2019), 57, accessed September 9, 2020, https://carnegieendowment.org/files/BJP_In_Power_final.pdf.

the 1990s, despite the rise of Hindu nationalism. More interesting still, this number—between thirteen and fourteen, or at least 8 percent of the candidates, a proportion close to the share of Muslims in the population, 9 percent in 2011—is higher than it was in the 1960s to 1980s, a trend found, moreover, in Maharashtra.[51]

Today, the only state where the percentage of Muslims is on the rise among MLAs is none other than West Bengal, on account of the strategy of the Trinamool Congress (TMC), the majority party.

While adherents of the theory of substantive representation maintain that the identity of elected representatives matters little, as each member of an elected assembly advocates for the common interest, those who support the descriptive representation theory consider that social groups—be they linguistic, racial, or founded on gender, cultural, socioeconomic, or other features—should be represented as such to be defended in debates and through legislation.[52] A considerable body of research in the United States has shown that in the 1970s, the cause of minorities and women was primarily defended in Congress by representatives from their own ranks.[53] Similarly, in a groundbreaking study based on thousands of questions to the government by MPs in the Lok Sabha, Saloni Bhogale has shown that Muslim MPs, although they were a mere handful, asked a substantial and growing number of questions to the government about their community, whether on the subject of education, jobs, the use of Urdu, pilgrimage to Mecca, security, and so on. Even if the share of Muslim MPs went from 5.8 percent in 1999 to 4.2 percent in 2014, the percentage of questions pertaining to Muslims asked by them each year went from 18 percent to 25 percent between the legislatures voted in, in 1999 and 2014, a sign that non-Muslim MPs were less concerned about issues regarding the Muslim minority.[54]

All in all, while Muslims have never been represented commensurate with their demographic weight in Indian state institutions, their political influence has traditionally been fairly significant in some assemblies. This last refuge has shrunk since 2014 due to the BJP's electoral gains at both the national level and in some states such as Uttar Pradesh. This eviction from institutions, symptomatic of an ethnic democracy, has serious consequences for the political interests of the Muslim minority, especially in parliament. But its most significant effects are perceptible particularly from the standpoint of the safety and security of people and property.

Muslims in Dealings with the Police and the Courts

Muslim underrepresentation in Indian state institutions increases their vulnerability toward law enforcement, forces that come under direct government authority, whereas the courts have a greater degree of independence. While the situation is not recent, it has been exacerbated since the BJP came to power.

Ethnoreligious Bias in the Indian Police

The 2018 Common Cause / CSDS survey detailed in its *Status of Policing in India Report 2018* reflects this state of affairs, as 21 percent of respondents and 26 percent of Muslim respondents say the Indian police discriminate on the basis of religion. The percentage of Muslims sharing this opinion is as much as 50 percent in Maharashtra, 55 percent in Rajasthan, and 56 percent in Bihar.[55] Correlatively, 54 percent of Muslims are fearful of the police, as opposed to 24 percent of Hindus (though opinions vary considerably by caste).[56] Muslims who are the most fearful of the police are those who say they believe that the police falsely implicate Muslims in terror-related cases or they know of such incidents. (The question was worded as follows: "Police often implicates Muslims in false terrorism charges. Do you agree or disagree?").[57] While the bias of police officers on the ground discussed previously has been amply documented, in the early 2000s, and even more after 2014, India has witnessed certain elements of the Indian police *elite* exhibit anti-Muslim bias. In this regard, counterterrorism agencies warrant special attention.[58]

The aftermath of the bomb blasts at the Hamidiya mosque in Malegaon, which killed thirty-one people in 2006, offers an apt illustration of this scenario. The Mumbai Anti-Terrorism Squad (ATS) at first ascribed the attack to Muslim organized crime but then believed it saw

signs of the Student Islamic Movement of India (SIMI), thereby justifying recourse to the Maharashtra Control of Organised Crime Act
(MCOCA), the state emergency law used in the fight against terrorism.
The Muslims who were arrested allegedly targeted a mosque, according
to the judge who would reconstruct the ATS reasoning ten years later,
"to infuriate the Muslim Community to commit communal riots,"[59] in
order to radicalize the Muslim youth and mobilize them against the
Hindus. A dozen suspects were arrested, but as the inquiry dragged on,
it ended up being transferred to the Central Bureau of Investigation
(CBI) in 2007. After years of fruitless investigation, in 2010, the CBI finally had to take into account the confessions of a Hindu nationalist,
Swami Aseemanand, who had been arrested in another case but who
had acknowledged the responsibility of his movement, Abhinav Bharat,
in the Malegaon blasts—as well as in many others that had been attributed to Islamists.[60] The Manmohan Singh government handed the
Malegaon case over to the National Investigation Agency (NIA). The
NIA admitted that the confessions serving to indict the accused had
been obtained by the ATS under torture, and when the trial was finally
held in 2016, the judge concluded, "The ATS has fabricated false evidence against all the accused to scot-free the real culprits"[61] and that in
the case of nine of the accused, as they had "criminal antecedent, they
become scape-goat [sic] at the hands of ATS."[62] All were acquitted and
released after having spent ten years in prison for no reason.

Such a scenario is not entirely exceptional. In the same year, 2016, in
appeal, the Bombay High Court lifted all terror charges that the Mumbai
ATS had leveled against a young Muslim falsely accused of the German
Bakery bombing in 2010 (17 dead) in Pune. The trial court that had handed
down the first judgment had recommended the death penalty in 2013.[63]

Maharashtra police had been guilty of "mistakes" more than once. In
2015, the courts ordered the release of Abdul Wahid Shaikh after a trial
for seven bomb attacks in 2006 in several Mumbai trains that claimed
209 lives. After having spent nine years in prison (seven of them in isolation), Wahid Shaikh, a schoolteacher, published a book recounting how
he was arrested by the ATS in Mumbai along with twelve other accused
who had supposedly harbored Pakistani terrorists in Mumbai. Subject

to what he calls "third degree torture" (electric shocks to the genitals, *suryaprakash* oil put in the anus, and water boarding), all of the accused signed a confession, except him. He resisted owing to the help of one of the police officers, Vinod Bhatt, who was convinced of his innocence.[64] In the case of another train bombing—in 2003 in the station of the Mumbai suburb of Mulund—one of the accused remained in prison for ten years before a court recognized his innocence in 2017.[65]

But the Maharashtra police are not the only party guilty of such wrongdoing. The Gujarat police (as well as the state judiciary) have been publicly discredited in several similar cases. The Detection of Crime Branch of the Gujarat police was for instance ridiculed by the Supreme Court when an appeal was brought before it in the attack on the Akshardham Temple of Gandhinagar. On September 24, 2002, two gunmen penetrated this immense complex belonging to the Swaminarayan sect with AK-56 rifles and grenades, killing twenty-eight persons, including three law enforcement officers. A National Security Guard commando finally shot them dead the following day. The notes found in the pockets of the two men allegedly read: "This is a gift to Modi and Advani."[66] The Gujarat police immediately declared that the terrorists had been backed by Pakistan. Three of the accused were sentenced to death in 2010 after a highly controversial investigation[67] concluded that they had ties with Lashkar-e-Taiba and Jaish-e-Muhammad.[68] But the accused appealed the verdict, and the Supreme Court quashed the judgment of the special POTA (Prevention of Terrorism Act) court and the Gujarat High Court, two courts that had deliberated on the basis of evidence provided by the Gujarat police investigation: six of the accused who had been convicted of this attack were acquitted eleven years after being jailed, after the Supreme Court justices who examined the case file found it to be empty.[69]

The Madhya Pradesh police were also disavowed by a state court, which found that the charges leveled against three members of SIMI in the framework of the Unlawful Activities (Prevention) Act (UAPA) were baseless.[70] But they were unable to profit from this judgment because they were among the eight Muslims who were shot down as they were allegedly attempting to escape from prison, according to the police.[71] In Rajasthan, the police had a twenty-year-old pharmacy student sentenced for attacks that took place in 1993, aboard several trains, on the first anniversary of the Babri Masjid demolition, on the basis of his confession alone—such proof being considered sufficient in the framework of the TADA, Terrorist and Disruptive Activities (Prevention) Act. The Supreme Court cleared him twenty-three years later.[72]

The Delhi police nevertheless remain the force that has accumulated the largest number of similar cases, to the point that the Jamia Teachers Solidarity Association, an arm of the faculty at Jamia Millia Islamiya published a report on twenty-four comparable cases in 2016, with one difference: Muslims wrongly accused by the Delhi Police Special Cell (dedicated to antiterrorist investigations) were often Kashmiris.[73] Sometimes charges were lifted when the case was handed over to the CBI or the NIA;[74] sometimes the accused had to await trial. The case concerning the 2005 Delhi attacks that killed eighty people warrants particular attention. The Delhi Police Special Cell arrested five Muslims accused of acting for the Pakistani movement Lashkar-e-Taiba. The police acquitted two of them, both from Srinagar, in 2017—after they had spent twelve years in prison.[75] They, too, had been subject to torture by the police seeking to extract confessions from them.[76] Pratap Bhanu Mehta drew a more general lesson from their case, saying that, at the time, they were "the latest in a line of dozens of youths who turned out to have been accused without plausible evidence, and whose lives have been devastated by our justice system. . . . But it is worth asking why there is so little political discussion of these matters. There is discomfort raising possible issues of bias in policing."[77] The scale of anti-Muslim bias is even more obvious when attacks on mosques are blamed on Islamists and result in roundups of young Muslims.[78]

When the Judicial System
Comes to Muslims' Aid—or Does Not

On account of police bias, the percentage of Muslims awaiting trial in prison is traditionally high: 21 percent in 2016.[79] In some states this proportion is even double the percentage of Muslims in the population, as in Gujarat and Maharashtra, where the figures are 10 and 22 percent and 11.5 and 30 percent, respectively. The number of Muslims sentenced—15.8 percent—is, however, nearly proportional to their population, a sign that many of those arrested by the police are cleared by the courts once they go to trial.[80] But delays lengthen due to the backlog of cases in the courts: some Muslims have spent many years behind bars before being declared innocent.[81] In 2016 and 2017, the annual report of the National Crime Records Bureau did not give any information regarding the caste and religion of prison inmates. In 2018, new prison statistics were released. They reconfirmed the overrepresentation of Muslims in jail (18.8 percent), especially in UP (31.3 percent of the total number of Muslim prisoners), and the gap between undertrials (21.4 percent) and convicted (17.3 percent, a percentage on the rise).[82]

Not only does the judiciary take an inordinate amount of time to deliver its verdicts, but some verdicts also tend to reflect anti-Muslim bias, as evident from several revealing verdicts since the 1990s, after the demolition of the Babri Masjid—a turning point in this regard as well. After the mosque was demolished, the government of India outlawed the RSS, the VHP, and Bajrang Dal. But on June 4, 1993, the Delhi High Court canceled the ban order on the three organizations, finding that their leaders had no intention of causing harm to the Babri Masjid. The Bajrang Dal once again benefited from a favorable judgment in the case of Dara Singh, the man who murdered the missionary Graham Staines and his sons. The commission of inquiry appointed by Vajpayee—a one-man show made up of a single Supreme Court justice, D. P. Wadhwa—cleared the organization of all suspicion.[83] The VHP, the Bajrang Dal's parent organization, was treated the same way. In 2006, the Hindu Jagaran Manch (Forum for Hindu Awakening), a branch of the Sangh Parivar affiliated with the VHP, lodged a complaint in Haridwar—one of the Hindu holy cities—against M. F. Husain for "promoting ill will among religious groups, selling obscenities and perturbing national harmony." The court in Haridwar issued a warrant for the artist's arrest—he was ninety-one years old at the time—and ordered the seizure of his properties. His lawyer obtained referral of the case to the Supreme Court. On May 9, it stayed the Haridwar court decision. Husain moved to Qatar in 2003 but publicly apologized for a canvas representing India in the form of a naked goddess in 2006. He offered to give it to the Mumbai police force to be put up for auction, the proceeds of which would go to the families of police officers who were victims of the July 2006 attacks that had left nearly 200 dead. M. F. Husain died in exile in 2011.[84]

The lenient attitude of the judiciary vis-à-vis the Bajrang Dal and the VHP prepared the ground for the rise to power of an aggressive version of Hindu nationalism and reflected pro-Hindutva and anti-Muslim bias among judges. For these judges, such tendencies have become commonplace, and tongues have loosened—a sign that jurists do not live behind closed doors in the courtroom but in a society whose ideological center of gravity has slowly but surely been sliding toward Hindu nationalism for a quarter century. The trial of Shaikh Mohsin's murderers is a textbook case. Sometime after Modi's victory in 2014, Mohsin, a twenty-four-year-old computer engineer, was on his way home from the mosque when he was lynched in downtown Pune by twenty-three individuals, some of whom had just attended a Hindu Rashtra Sena (Army of the Hindu Nation) rally against derogatory images of Shivaji and Bal Thackeray uploaded on social media. Mohsin's beard seems to have prompted the attack that cost him his life. The court concluded that Mohsin was attacked "because he looked like a Muslim." His twenty-three assailants were arrested and charged with murder, but the High Court of Bombay granted them release on parole on the grounds that Mohsin's religion was a provocation: "The applicants/accused otherwise had no other motive such as any personal enmity against the innocent deceased Mohsin. The fault of the deceased was only that he belonged to another religion. I consider this factor in favour of the applicants/accused. Moreover, the applicants/accused do not have criminal record and it appears that in the name of the religion, they were provoked and have committed the murder."[85] That a difference in religion reflected in the young man's physical appearance was enough to justify a crime could only prompt the family to file an appeal. The Supreme Court, which overturned the judgment, stated, "The fact that the deceased [Mohsin] belonged to a certain community cannot be a justification for any assault much less a murder." It moreover invited the lower courts to be "fully conscious of the plural composition of the country while called upon to deal with rights of various communities." That it required an appeal to the highest court of the land to drive home such an obvious fact shows the degree of communal bias harbored by certain judges.

The Supreme Court has defended Muslims against the High Courts in several other cases. The Allahabad High Court in Uttar Pradesh, which had already handed down a very controversial judgment in the Ayodhya case in 2010,[86] thus decided in February 2018 to reclaim Waqf properties (mortmain properties bequeathed by Muslim notables to their community) in the state that did not meet zoning or architectural guidelines—both subjective notions. The Supreme Court stayed the decision before the BJP government could implement it.[87]

While judges—at least those on the Supreme Court—are often committed to mitigating the anti-Muslim bias of police officers, they do not always have the opportunity to do so, because perpetrators fail to be prosecuted. For instance, at the time of writing, only one case of lynching—among all those discussed in chapter 6, some of which date back many years—has landed in court. In many cases, no charges are brought, as police officers refuse to register victims' complaints or have not interrogated suspects. The case of Pehlu Khan is sadly typical. Although Khan had time to give the police the names of six of his assailants before he died, they were never troubled by the law. On the other hand, the police accused two of the people accompanying Pehlu Khan of having taken part in transporting cows for slaughter, whereas they were bringing them back from the cattle fair for their dairy.[88] Such role reversal, turning victims into criminals, is not rare according to Harsh Mander, a former senior civil servant who left the bureaucracy to found an NGO after the pogrom in Gujarat, the state where he was based. Following the repeated lynchings, Mander traveled through India to meet with victims' families, and this "caravan of love" defied threats of violence on several occasions.[89]

The only lynching case related to the cow protection movement ever brought to trial came in the context of an operation initiated by the High Court of Jharkhand to speed up proceedings in an effort to ease a huge trial backlog (where 76,071 cases were pending for five years or more). In March 2018, a fast-track court thus sentenced to life imprisonment eleven people charged with killing Alimuddin Ansari, a Muslim suspected of trading in beef, in June 2017.[90] The accused were nevertheless released on bail thanks in part to legal aid provided by a member of the Modi government, Jayant Sinha, who even greeted them with garlands around their necks upon their release.

To sum up, not only did Indian Muslims disappear from institutions of the Indian republic (where they had never been well represented anyway) and in particular from the Lok Sabha and state assemblies after the rise to power of the BJP, but they were affected by the communal bias of some of these institutions, including the police. While the judiciary remained the most neutral power center, with ups and downs, it too started to indulge in Hindu majoritarianism, as evident from two Supreme Court verdicts on the Ayodhya case in 2019–2020.

Judicial Majoritarianism: Preparing the Ground for a Ram Temple in Ayodhya

The way the Ayodhya case has been dealt with by the Indian judiciary over the last thirty years shows that some judges have gradually shifted away from secularism. After the demolition of the Babri Masjid, while sadhus had begun a fast in Ayodhya to protest the refusal of the authorities to permit *darshan* of Ram and Sita at the makeshift temple built by kar sevak there, the Lucknow bench of the Allahabad High Court ruled that darshan should be permitted on the grounds that Ram was a "constitutional entity and a reality of our national culture and fabric."[91] Large numbers of devotees immediately converged on Ayodhya. This decision made it more difficult to rebuild the Babri Masjid—as then prime minister Narasimha Rao had promised—given that a makeshift temple had been allowed to function on the site.

But on December 11, 1992, the Allahabad High Court gave its long-awaited decision concerning the 2.77 acres of land adjoining the Babri Masjid / Ramjanmabhoomi, the acquisition of which by the BJP government of Kalyan Singh in 1991 had been challenged by Muslim associations. The acquisition was canceled on several grounds, the principal one being that, since the notified area belonged to the Sunni Central Waqf Board and included a Muslim graveyard, such properties could not be acquired under the Land Acquisition Act.

On December 27, the central government issued an ordinance for the acquisition of all the disputed areas in Ayodhya. The presidential ordinance, issued on January 7, 1993, was confirmed on March 24, by the passing of a bill. The central government thereby acquired 67.7 acres and provided that the land would be made available to two trusts, which would construct, respectively, a Ram temple and a mosque. On December 27, 1992, the government had also requested the president to seek, under article 143(1), the opinion of the Supreme Court on the question of "whether a Hindu temple or any Hindu religious structure existed prior to the construction of the Ram-Janma Bhumi-Babri Masjid (including the premises of the inner and outer courtyards of such structure) in the area on which the structure stood."[92]

On October 24, 1994, the Supreme Court replied that the reference made under article 143(1) of the Constitution was "superfluous and unnecessary and d[id] not require to be answered."[93] In a dissenting note, the minority bench—two of the five judges—propounded a more fundamental reason for rejecting the presidential reference: it considered that the wording favored the Hindu community and was therefore opposed to secularism and thus unconstitutional. Second, the majority judgment upheld the sections of the act dealing with the acquisition of the disputed 67 acres of land in Ayodhya, empowering the government to delegate a trust to manage the property and enabling Hindus to worship in the makeshift temple. This decision was based on the concept of "comparative user," the Muslims being described as praying less often than Hindus in the disputed structure before its demolition. This argument was open to question because, as Rajeev Dhavan has pointed out, "If the Muslims had not prayed there since 1949, it was because they were prohibited from doing so by interlocutory restraint orders." The minority judges, moreover, wanted to strike down the act, concluding that to "condone the acquisition of a place of worship under these circumstances [was . . .] to efface the principles of secularism from the

Constitution." But the majority struck down as "unconstitutional" section 4(3) of the act, which abated any pending "suit, appeal or other proceeding." Thus, the proceedings pending in the Allahabad High Court were revived, and the question of whether Muslims had the right to worship in the disputed area had now to be decided on the completion of these pending suits. The Supreme Court thus thwarted the Hindu Trust's plan to start building a temple in Ayodhya before the completion of the judicial process. In addition, the court held that Kalyan Singh, by allowing a concrete platform to be built, was guilty of violating his assurance that no permanent structure would be erected on the disputed 2.77 acres on the Babri Masjid / Ramjanmabhoomi site. The former chief minister was sentenced to one day's imprisonment and fined Rs 2,000 (26.67 USD).

At around the same time, in the S. R. Bommai case (1994), a nine-judge bench judgment of the Supreme Court emphasized that secularism was essential to Indian democracy: "State is neither pro-particular religion nor anti-particular religion. It stands aloof, in other words maintains neutrality in matters of religion and provides equal protection to all religions."[94] For many years after that, the Supreme Court abstained from interfering with the work of the Allahabad High Court, except to refuse any attempt to modify the status quo before the final judgment.

The Allahabad High Court handed down a decision in 2010. It relied only moderately on a 2003 report of the Archeological Survey of India (ASI) arguing that the Babri Masjid had probably been built on the remnants of a Hindu temple,[95] but it concluded that the Babri Masjid had "ceased to be a mosque since 1934 when during a riot the same was substantially damaged and that thereafter no Muslim offered prayer/ namaz in the said premises," except on Friday.[96] The judgment also emphasized that "since the construction of the mosque, Hindus started treating/believing the site thereof as the exact birth place of Lord Ram."[97] As no party, in the eyes of the judges, could prove that the land where the Babri Masjid had been built belonged to Muslims or Hindus, they concluded that it was a case of "joint possession"[98]—Lord Ram being the original owner on the Hindu side as "an idol is a deity capable of holding property."[99] Finally, the court ordered that the land should be divided into thirds: one-third would go to the Nirmohi Akhara (one of the two Hindu plaintiffs), one-third to the Muslim party (the Sunni Central Waqf Board, UP), and one-third to the Sri Bhagwan Ram Viraj-man (the trust that represented the Hindu nationalists), the latter being "the portion below the central dome where at present the idol is kept in makeshift temple."[100]

Moreover, the judges lectured the Muslims of India:

> Muslims must also ponder that at present the entire world wants to know the exact teaching of Islam in respect of relationship of Muslims with others. Hostility—peace—friendship—tolerance—opportunity to impress others with the Message—opportunity to strike wherever and whenever possible—or what? In this regard Muslims in India enjoy a unique position. They have been rulers here, they have been ruled and now they are sharers in power (of course junior partners). They are not in majority but they are also not negligible minority (Maximum number of Muslims in any country after Indonesia is in India.) In other countries either the Muslims are in huge majority which makes them indifferent to the problem in question or in negligible minority which makes them redundant. Indian Muslims have also inherited huge legacy of religious learning and knowledge. They are therefore in the best position to tell the world the correct position. Let them start with their role in the resolution of the conflict at hand.[101]

The court, in other words, fitting in with the ethnic democracy narrative, invited the Muslims, as "junior partners," to make two major concessions: the site where the Babri Masjid stood would be used to build a Hindu temple, and two-thirds of the land would go to the Hindu parties. Both parties, Muslims as well as Hindus, appealed against a decision that they considered adverse (the latter because they wanted all of the land). It took ten years for the Supreme Court to revisit the issue before delivering its verdict—through a unanimous five-judge bench. This verdict was different from the Allahabad High Court's decision as the entire piece of land went to the Hindus, with the Muslims being given five acres of land in a "suitable, prominent place in Ayodhya" to build a mosque elsewhere. How did the judges come to this conclusion in September 2020?

They argued that the probability that the Hindus may have been originally in possession of all the land was higher. But they contradicted themselves on several occasions while making this point.

First, they submitted that "it cannot be said that the Muslims have been able to establish their possessory title to the disputed site as a composite whole."[102] But if it was a "composite whole"—a formula repeated four times in the judgment and close to the notion of joint possession—the Hindus should have also been asked to prove their possessory title. They were not. The judges assumed that "the Hindus have established a clear case of a possessory title to the outside courtyard by virtue of long, continued and unimpeded worship at the Ramchabutra [which is located in the outer courtyard, not in the mosque] and other objects of religious significance [sic]."[103] Here, the "proof" that Hindus worshipped on the premises of the mosque in the eighteenth century comes from vague testimonies of European travelers.

Second, the Muslims are presented as unable to show exclusive possession of the site *only* between 1528 and 1857, when British documents show that the site was disputed. But why would the Mughals and, subsequently, the Nawab of Oudh have let Hindus worship in the mosque before 1857? This simple question is not even asked.

Third, the judges did not claim to know where Lord Ram was born, but the Hindus' belief is for them sufficient to conclude that the Ramjanmabhoomi was *inside* the mosque. Despite the fact that Hindus, after the building of the Babri Masjid, worshipped in the outer courtyard, "there can be no manner of doubt that this was in furtherance of their belief that the birthplace of Lord Ram was within the precincts of and under the central dome of the mosque."[104] In that case, belief is as good as evidence—it seemed. And if Hindus believed that the Ramjanmabhoomi was below the central dome of the erstwhile Babri Masjid, this is where the Ram Mandir had to be built: "The continued faith and belief of the Hindu devotees in the existence of the Janmasthan below the three domed structure is evidenced by the activities of the Nirmohis, individual devotees such as Nihang Singh and the endless stream of Hindu devotees over the years who visited the disputed site. This is testament to the long-held belief in the sanctity of the disputed site as a place of worship for the Hindu religion."[105] It bears reiterating that the judges' idea that Hindus never stopped worshipping Ram in the premises of the Babri Masjid is based on the testimonies of European travelers in the eighteenth century—Joseph Tieffenthaler in particular. Hence, one more contradiction, as Tieffenthaler explains that the devotees believed that Ram's birthplace was marked by a small platform *outside* of the mosque.[106]

Like the Allahabad High Court in 2010, the Supreme Court acknowledged Hindu beliefs as evidence in 2020. This is obvious in the strange equivalence it established on the first page of its verdict: "The Hindu community claims it as the birthplace of Lord Ram, an incarnation of Lord Vishnu. The Muslim community claims it as the site of the historic Babri Masjid built by the first Mughal Emperor, Babur."[107] The Babri Masjid was not a claim but a building.

Certainly, judges were still interested in factual evidence. They referred to the 2003 ASI report in great detail, for instance. But they had to admit that the report failed to prove that the Babri Masjid had been built in the place of a temple, as its critics have argued for years. Instead of dismissing the report, however, they concluded that "ultimately, it lies within the jurisdiction of the court to decide whether the findings that are contained in the report of the ASI sub-serve the cause of truth and justice on the basis of relevance and preponderance of probabilities. Common sense ought to guide the exercise of judicial discretion, here as in other branches of the law."[108] Moreover, in the verdict, it is written that there was an "underlying structure" beneath the Babri Masjid that was "at least of equal, if not larger dimensions than the disputed structure" and "not of an Islamic origin"[109] because of the floral and human motives on the sculptures found during excavation—something that, according to the critics of the ASI report, could have come from recycled building material, not necessarily from a preexisting structure.

The verdict was also biased in favor of the majority community because it did not attempt to redress two illegal events, the criminal nature of which had nevertheless been acknowledged by the judges themselves. First, they admitted that "the exclusion of the Muslims from worship and possession took place on the intervening night between December 22/23, 1949 when the mosque was desecrated by the installation of Hindu idols. The ouster of the Muslims on that occasion was not through any lawful authority but through an act which was calculated to deprive them of their place of worship."[110] Instead of factoring in this crime, the judges saw it as one more proof that the Hindus looked at the Babri Masjid as Ram's birthplace and that "Muslims did not have exclusive possession over the inner court-yard."[111] Similarly, the demolition of the Babri Masjid on December 6, 1992, occurred "in violation of the status quo orders of this Court"[112] and "was an egregious violation of the rule of law."[113] But this did not need to be redressed either. Commenting on this contradiction, Tushar Gandhi said that if Godse was tried today, he would have been "murderer and patriot."[114]

Last but not least, the Supreme Court's bias was evidenced by the way it rejected the Allahabad High Court's proposal to share the land between Hindus and Muslims. The reason it gives in its verdict in this regard is very revealing: "Even as a matter of maintaining public peace and tranquility, the solution which commended itself to the High Court is not feasible. The disputed site admeasures all of 1500 square yards. Dividing the land will not subserve the interest of either of the parties or secure a lasting sense of peace and tranquility."[115] These words suggest that the Supreme Court's decision was not guided by the quest for justice only (or even mostly) but was overdetermined by the fear of tension and disorder. In the second part of the present book, it was observed that vigilante groups were in a position to impose their will on the police. They were here doing the same vis-à-vis the judiciary. In November 2018, the RSS itself had shown that it was prepared to flex its muscles to be allowed to build a temple on the site of the Babri Masjid. The organization was then disappointed by the way the Supreme Court kept postponing the moment when it would hear appeals filed against the Allahabad High Court judgment. The RSS's spokesperson, Bhai-yyaji Joshi, then declared: "We were expecting good news before this

Diwali. But the Supreme Court refused to give a verdict. . . . The court said its priorities are different. Because of this, Hindus feel insulted. It is surprising that the feelings of crores of Hindus are not a priority for the court." More importantly, he warned that the RSS would take up an agitation similar to the one in 1992 "if needed" to ensure the construction of a Ram temple in Ayodhya.[116]

The Supreme Court finally allotted five acres to the Muslim party to build a mosque elsewhere, invoking article 142 of the Indian Constitution, "to ensure that a wrong committed must be remedied"[117] because it was "necessary to provide restitution to the Muslim community for the unlawful destruction of their place of worship." But the court followed "the compensation route rather than restitution by invoking article 142,"[118] officializing the demotion of Muslims to the status of second-class citizens.[119] Indeed, the recognition of the Hindus' religious sentiment as the main reason why the court permitted the construction of a Ram temple on the remnants of the Babri Masjid prepared the ground for majoritarian justice. As Suhas Palshikar points out, "The Hindus have scored over Muslims—the belief that a deity was born at a certain place has been upheld. This will bring a new respect for the idea of Hindutva, it will also bring new power to that idea. The respect it will have earned will mean that Hindutva will now march as the ideology of India and the power it has acquired will mean less space for dissent."[120] In other words, the Ayodhya verdict embodies the antidemocratic character of majoritarianism. It stands at the interface of national populism and authoritarianism, the Hindu Rashtra and the Hindu Raj, as the judiciary has given legal sanction to the religious sentiments of the larger community and dismissed its opponents as antinationals who can only be second-class citizens—and repressed. This is typical of the judicial majoritarianism syndrome that C. M. Dorf has studied in the United States.[121]

In India, despite its communal bias, the Supreme Court claimed that it remained the custodian of the state's "constitutional obligations to uphold the equality of all religions and secularism which is a part of the basic features of the Constitution."[122] But the growing communalization of the judiciary also found expression in the fact that some lawyers

chanted "Jai Sri Ram" on the premises of the Supreme Court after the
Ayodhya verdict was announced.[123] Similarly, Hindu nationalists re-
joiced, but Narendra Modi made a point, in truly Orwellian fashion, of
promoting national harmony and congratulating himself on the effectiveness of India's democracy in a very revealing impromptu televised address he gave immediately after the verdict was announced:

> Friends, the entire world believes that India is the world's largest de-
> mocracy. Today, the world has also come to know that India's democ-
> racy is so alive and strong. After the verdict was out, the manner in
> which every group, people of every community, the entire country
> accepted it with an open heart symbolises India's ancient culture,
> traditions, and brotherhood. Brothers and sisters, the reason India is
> known for and we talk about it with pride is Unity in diversity. Unity
> in diversity—this mantra is today seen totally. I feel proud. Even after
> thousands of years, someone has to understand the main principle
> of India—unity in diversity. And he will definitely recall today's his-
> toric day and today's event. And this event is not taken from history.
> Crores of Indians are today themselves creating a new history. They
> are adding a new golden page to the history books. . . .
>
> Friends, today is a golden chapter in the history of India's judiciary.
> On this matter, during the hearing, the Supreme Court listened to
> everyone. It listened to them very patiently. And it is good news for
> the entire country that the verdict was unanimous. As a citizen, we
> all know that even if we have to solve a problem within the family,
> there is so much difficulty. This is not an easy task. Supreme Court
> has showcased great determination via this verdict. That's why the
> country's judges, courts and our judicial system today deserve to be
> specially congratulated. . . . The message of today is to connect, to get
> connected and to live together. Today is the occasion to wash away
> the ill-feelings in anyone's mind regarding all these things. In new
> India, there is no place for fear, ill-will, and negativity. . . .
>
> Welcome to a new start. Let us make a New India. We have to
> determine our trust and development taking into account whether
> someone has not been left behind. We have to take everyone to-

gether, ensuring the development of everyone, ensuring the confidence of everyone, we have to continue moving forward. Friends,
Supreme Court has given a verdict for the construction of Ram Mandir. . . . Our harmony, unity, peace, and love is very important for the
development of the country. We have to look towards the future. And
we have to keep working for India.[124]

Even though Narendra Modi claims that his mantra remains "unity in
diversity," his discourse, in fact, reflects a shift from this motto to a form
of "unity in hierarchy" that has clear affinities with the organic view of
society that Hindu nationalists have always cultivated. Indeed, in the
quotation above—representing two-thirds of the full speech—diversity
appears as a word only: the "construction of Ram Mandir" is hailed, not
that of a mosque, and not a word is to be found for the Muslims who
were defeated. This erasure of the Other is well in tune with a hierarchical approach in which minorities are tolerated only as second-class,
invisible citizens. The emphasis on duties rather than rights is also consistent with this worldview.

Muslims resigned themselves to the Supreme Court's verdict. They
did not file a review petition as they apprehended "further damage,"[125]
a fear that harks back to the judges' observations regarding "peace and
tranquility."

The officialization of Hindu hegemony over the Indian state under Narendra Modi reached its culmination in the Ayodhya affair. First, the
Supreme Court, in its unanimous verdict, not only handed over to the
Hindus the site where the Babri Masjid was located, but it directed
the central government to create a trust that would be in charge of "the
construction of a temple."[126] Why, in a secular state, should the central
government be in charge of the construction of the temple and not, also,
of the mosque for which the Supreme Court has also reserved space?
The dominant character of the Hindus was moreover reflected in the size
of the land allotted to them to build the Ram temple: sixty-seven acres,
against five acres for the Muslims. Second, the central government started
work on the construction project at the highest level. On February 5,

2020, Narendra Modi announced the formation of the Ram Janmab-hoomi Teertha Kshetra Trust in parliament. Nripendra Misra, who had been Modi's principal secretary between 2014 and 2019, was appointed the head of the temple construction committee of the trust on February 18, 2020, whereas a VHP old-timer, Mahant Nritya Gopal Das, became president of the trust. More importantly, the prime minister himself acted as the grand priest of the Bhoomi Pujan (groundbreaking ceremony for the construction of a grand temple). This event was paradoxical, not only because the *shilanyas* (the foundation-stone-laying ceremony) had already taken place in 1989[127] but also because, in contrast to Modi's call to unity, (1) the date of the ceremony, August 5, 2020, marked the first anniversary of the abolition of article 370, which reflected a specific conception of unity; and (2) many Hindu dignitaries, including Shankaracharyas, who had already been excluded from the trust,[128] were not invited to a ceremony[129] that, eventually, became a Sangh Parivar event starring the prime minister himself. As soon as it became clear that Narendra Modi would attend the Bhoomi Pujan, hundreds of secularists signed—in vain—an open letter, stating, "The Prime Minister going to Ayodhya to lay the foundation of the temple undermines our secular framework, and clearly endorses the majoritarian Hindutva agenda, despite his claims of building an inclusive India. It implies the negation of the Constitutional values."[130]

It was not sufficient that Narendra Modi merely attend the Bhoomi Pujan: during this daylong ceremony broadcast live on television, he was "not only the chief guest but also the master of ceremonies and the official *yajmaan* [patron of a religious ritual]."[131] On stage with Narendra Modi, who was performing the rituals, were rather unknown priests, as none of the Shankaracharyas had been invited, and none of the local Mahants were asked to officiate. This modus operandi is typical of the VHP, an organization that has systematically sidelined well-established Hindu religious figures and promoted "modern gurus"[132] who were more than happy to be offered a grandstand—and who often shared the Hindu nationalists' ideology. As a result, the Bhoomi Pujan rituals gave Mohan Bhagwat and Yogi Adityanath an opportunity to give speeches but did not comply with religious norms. For instance, according to

some senior clerics, the date chosen was not auspicious (but it was selected for other reasons, as mentioned above), and no ceremony of this
kind is complete without *havan* (a ritual burning of offerings such as
grains and ghee), *avahan* (invoking the gods), *sankalp* (making an oath)
in the beginning, and *prasad* (offering to God) at the end.[133] If one goes
by the *The Organiser*'s account, the fact that the Bhoomi Pujan—despite
the name of this ceremony—did not comply with ritual rules was not a
problem because "the entire struggle for the liberation of the Ram Janmabhoomi was not a religious one. Whether the continuous efforts on
the ground or the legal battle that took place since 1949, it was all about
the restoration of the national pride."[134] And this quest continued to
emulate foreign models, as evident from one of Ram Madhav's op-eds:
"Every nation has its sacred spaces and every religion its sacred places"—
like Mecca, which "is sacred as the birthplace of the Prophet" for Muslims.[135] India did not have such a place. Now it will get one.

The Bhoomi Pujan of August 5, 2020, will remain a milestone in Indian history. Suhas Palshikar described it as "the officialization of the
status of Hindu religion as the basis of the new republic."[136] For the first
time in the context of the republic of India, the head of the executive
performed religious functions associated with one creed, the creed of
the majority community. By merging temporal power with spiritual authority in the name of the Hindus, Narendra Modi has endowed the
state not only with a majoritarian identity but also with an ethnoreligious and even theocratic ideology.

This shift away from secularism was achieved owing to the Supreme
Court under the aegis of Chief Justice Rajan Gogoi. But it has been
reconfirmed by the CBI Special Court, which, a couple of months after
the Bhoomi Pujan, acquitted all the accused—BJP leaders (including
L. K. Advani and M. M. Joshi)—in the other Ayodhya case. An FIR had
been filed after the demolition of the Babri Masjid in 1992 accusing
them and forty-two other Hindu nationalist cadres of being responsible
for it. Contradicting the Liberhan Commission Report that had indicted top BJP leaders (including the two persons mentioned above)
and forty-six others—sixteen of whom had died—as being deeply involved in the planning of the demolition of the mosque, the CBI Special

Court concluded that there was no "conclusive proof" against them and that the Babri Masjid had been razed "spontaneously" by "anti-national elements." Surprisingly, the court did not accept videos of the event as evidence.[137]

While Muslims had never been well represented in Indian institutions, the rise to power of the BJP further marginalized them in elected assemblies—including the Lok Sabha. Gradually, this minority, which was already the prime target of Hindu vigilantes in the street, was excluded from the state as well. The disempowerment of Muslims reached its peak—to date—in the Supreme Court's decision granting the site where the Babri Masjid once stood to a Hindu trust that would build a temple in its place. This decision physically obliterated a phase of Indian history and a facet of India's identity.

The years 2019–2020, therefore, marked a transition from the making of a Hindu Rashtra at the societal level to an official Hindu Raj, all the more so as, at the same time, the state was actively involved in the repression of Kashmiris as well as anti-CAA demonstrators and in the Delhi riots. There is an element of continuity in this trajectory: the abiding objective of obliterating Muslims from the public eye, of making them disappear—either from mixed neighborhoods (see the campaign against land jihad) or from parliament. But there is also a significant difference: the brand of authoritarianism that gained momentum after the 2019 elections found particular expression in the attitude of the state vis-à-vis minorities, and, in parallel, Hindu majoritarianism was not de facto only but de jure.

Until 2019, few laws having an adverse impact on Muslims had been passed. In addition to those related to cow protection described in chapter 5, the only important piece of legislation that can be mentioned here is the Enemy Property Amendment Act (2017), through which Muslim citizens of India who had inherited property from an ancestor who had migrated to Pakistan or who had purchased property from a person who had migrated to Pakistan lost any legal claim to it.[138] After 2019, many more pieces of legislation were initiated by the central government and BJP state governments. Apart from the amendment to article 370, the

Muslim Women (Protection of Rights on Marriage) Act and the Citizenship (Amendment) Act, which were all passed by parliament, the Uttar Pradesh Prohibition of Unlawful Conversion of Religion Ordinance (2020) was particularly important. This ordinance, promulgated on November 27, 2020, prohibits any conversion for marriage, except when prior sanction was obtained from the state. Indeed, the person seeking to convert before marrying someone now has to apply to the District Magistrate, who must ask the police to check the "real intention," "purpose," and "cause of the proposed religious conversion."[139] If the conversion is attributable to "any gift," "gratification," "better lifestyle," or fear of "divine displeasure," then criminal action can be initiated against the person who "caused" the conversion.[140] This ordinance is similar to the anti-conversion law passed by the Uttarakhand assembly in 2018,[141] but what made a difference was the role of the police force, which had "full freedom to act on its own."[142] Such an ordinance was a clear attempt at legalizing the fight against "love jihad" that Yogi Adityanath's vigilante group was cultivating before he became chief minister. As chief minister, he continued to speak as a vigilante when he announced the new legislation: "We will bring an effective law—those who hide their name and identity and play with the honour of daughters and sisters, I am warning them in advance: if they don't stop, their funeral processions will be taken out."[143] Immediately after the promulgation of Yogi Adityanath's ordinance, a twenty-one-year-old Muslim man was arrested after his wife's family filed a case "under pressure from the police" alleging that the wife had not converted to Islam voluntarily.[144] Many other FIRs were registered against interfaith marriages, creating some psychosis among mixed couples,[145] so much so that after Yogi Adityanath's statement, the Allahabad High Court had to direct the police to protect couples "who were facing threat to life and liberty from relatives on account of their marriage outside caste/religion."[146] The fact that caste and religion were bracketed together here is very revealing. Like the vigilante groups studied in chapter 7, the state of Uttar Pradesh was trying to preserve the social order, which meant the caste system as much as the separation between Hindus and Muslims. This form of state vigilantism is a case of authoritarian orthopraxy (or orthopraxistic authoritarianism), in which the state is sanctioning and enforcing social—largely patriarchal—norms at the expense of individual freedom. Moreover, Satish Poonia, the Rajasthan BJP chief, justified the UP ordinance by arguing that "in our culture, marriage isn't just an individual choice, it also encompasses approval of religion & society."[147] The UP ordinance said that aside from "the aggrieved person," "his/her parents, brother, sister, or any other person who is related to him/her by blood, marriage or adoption may lodge a First Information Report [with the police] of such conversion,"[148] potentially strengthening family control over women.[149]

The UP ordinance has been very convincingly interpreted as an attempt "to carry the social exclusion of Muslims to its logical conclusion where, for all practical purposes, they are driven out of the social ecosystem altogether."[150] This trend was further amplified by the COVID-19 crisis. To begin with, Muslims were accused of spreading the virus. The main culprits, allegedly, were members of the Tabligh-e-Jama'at (a reformist Islamic movement), whose members were taking part in an international congregation, in Delhi, from March 13 to 15. There was nothing illegal about this congregation as Narendra Modi did not announce the lockdown until March 22, but BJP leaders, including Yogi Adityanath, nevertheless blamed the Tablighis through May,[151] and TV anchors, including Arnab Goswami on Republic TV and Rahul Kanwal on India Today TV, went berserk. This hysteria resulted in hundreds of arrests. The prisoners—who came from a dozen different countries—had to wait for months, in jail, for the courts' decisions, which acquitted them systematically.[152] Quashing three FIRs against thirty-five petitioners (twenty-nine of them foreigners), the Bombay High Court, looking at the way the pandemic had evolved after the Tablighis dispersed, said: "A political government tries to find the scapegoat when there is pandemic or calamity and the circumstances show that there is probability that these foreigners were chosen to make them scapegoats. . . . The aforesaid circumstances and the latest figures of infection in India show that such action against present petitioners should not have been taken."[153] In December 2020, nine months after the Tablighis were arrested, the Allahabad High Court told UP police officers that charging a person with attempt to murder for attending Tabligh-e-Jama'at congregation in New Delhi "reflects an abuse of the power of law."[154]

Besides the Tablighis, ordinary Muslims were targeted routinely during the pandemic, accelerating the process of exclusion described above.[155] Anti-Muslim campaigns became viral on the social media, with the hashtag "#Coronajihad,"[156] but harassment was not only virtual. Local leaders prevented Muslims from entering "Hindu areas" because they were suspected of spreading the virus. Rumors that they were spitting on purpose in Hindu areas resulted in riots and even lynching on at least one occasion.[157] Some Muslims were not accepted in hospitals[158]— whether they had come because they showed symptoms of infection or for any other reason[159]—or, when they were admitted, they were placed in wards separate from Hindus.[160] In Uttar Pradesh, where Muslims had already been affected economically by the closure of slaughterhouses, Hindu nationalists boycotted Muslim vendors or prevented them from working under the pretext that they were spreading the disease.[161]

The pandemic has exacerbated existing prejudice, making the exclusion of Muslims even more systematic. Hindu nationalists are aiming not only to make this community disappear from the public space because of its bothersome culture (from its namaz to its nonvegetarian diet). They are also striving to separate it completely and hermetically from the rest of society due to its perceived viral toxicity. This rejection of physical contact is reminiscent of the caste system and, in fact, comes as a confirmation that Muslims today may well be India's new Untouchables.

But this exclusion process has gone beyond the physical dimension, as evident from the way *any* attempt to build bridges between Hindus and Muslims has been resulting in majoritarian protests. The jeweler Tanishq, a brand of the Tata group, withdrew an advertisement featuring an interfaith couple after a massive campaign was initiated by Hindu nationalists on social media. A BJP leader had asked, "Why are you showing a Hindu 'daughter-in-law' to a Muslim family and glorifying it?" while "#BoycottTanishq" topped Twitter trends.[162] Another campaign targeted Netflix after a scene of the television series *A Suitable Boy*

showed a kiss between a Hindu girl and a Muslim boy.[163] These vi-
gnettes illustrate the societal impact of the cultural policing that vigilante groups began undertaking many years ago, as shown in part II of
the book.

In part III, a new development has been studied: the role of the state
in the officialization of this exclusion, a process particularly obvious in
Uttar Pradesh—where, for instance, the government did not even
spend 10 percent of the money released by the central government in
the framework of a scheme designed for improving the living conditions
and infrastructure in minority-concentrated areas.

While Uttar Pradesh is the new laboratory of Muslim exclusion—
and oppression[164]—the Allahabad High court occasionally continues
to take sides against the Hindu nationalist doxa. For instance, in 2020
the court directed the UP government to release Dr. Kafeel Khan, a
Gorakhpur-based doctor who was harassed for years and who had been
booked under the draconian National Security Act over his alleged anti-
CAA speech.[165] Khan immediately left UP with his family and settled
in the Congress-ruled state of Rajasthan. The Allahabad High Court
also dismissed a petition against a Muslim man that had been filed by
the parents of his wife, who had converted to Islam to marry him. The
judges said that the court was "enjoined to uphold the life and liberty of
an individual guaranteed under Article 21 of the Constitution of
India."[166] Finally, the Allahabad High Court accused the government
and its police of misusing the Uttar Pradesh Prevention of Cow Slaughter Act: "The Act is being misused against innocent persons. Whenever
any meat is recovered, it is normally shown as cow meat (beef) without
getting it examined or analyzed by the forensic laboratory. In most of
the cases, meat is not sent for analysis. Accused persons continue to
remain in jail for an offence that may not have been committed at all."[167]
Such instances show that there are still some forms of resistance to the
communalization of the Indian state, even though most of the trends
examined in this chapter and the previous ones point toward the making of a Hindu Raj.

Conclusion

THIS BOOK HAS TRIED TO MAKE SENSE of the political trajectory of India from populism to ethnic democracy and authoritarianism under Narendra Modi, a journey of less than ten years.

Its starting point lies in Hindu nationalism, an ideology based on a sense of vulnerability and prejudice vis-à-vis so-called threatening Others, including the Muslims, that the architects of Hindutva stigmatized and emulated. This movement crystallized 100 years ago, along with its key organization, the RSS, but its political party—the Jana Sangh and then the BJP—was unable to assume power until 2014, as it had failed until then to attract mass support. Over the first two decades of the twenty-first century, Hindu nationalism became coupled with a form of national populism represented by Narendra Modi, ensuring its success at the polls, first in Gujarat and then in India at large. The process was a cumulative one. The ideological foundation of Hindutva has remained intact, but it now incorporated a new aspect: a populist political style. This repertoire, which is Modi's hallmark, enabled the BJP to cross a new threshold, 30 percent of the vote, which the party had previously been unable to attain on account of its elitist profile.

It was, in fact, a case of *national* populism. Not only did Modi finally manage to seduce a substantial number of lower-caste citizens, most of them from the neo-middle class aspiring to the better days (*achhe din*)[1] that Modi—a self-made man from a poor background—had promised them, but he was able to broaden the party's social base by polarizing the electorate along an ethnoreligious dividing line: inheriting the legacy of the 2002 pogrom, which had transformed him into a Hindu Hriday Samrat (Emperor of Hindu Hearts), Modi projected himself as the protector of the Hindus vis-à-vis the Muslim Other and Pakistan. Both facets of this national populism found expression in a highly personalized political style, with Modi relating directly to the voters via all possible channels of communication (from social media to holograms) to saturate the public space. These new techniques have supplemented the RSS's tried-and-true activism resources, such as door-to-door campaigning by the extensive Sangh Parivar network. Under Modi, the government moved India toward a new form of democracy, an ethnic democracy as defined by Sammy Smooha, or majoritarianism. In this new political system, the majoritarian community is assumed to be one and the same as the nation, thereby relegating minorities to second-class citizens. In Israel, Smooha's model, this majoritarianism is enshrined in the law, as constitutional amendments establish the supremacy of the Jews. In Modi's India, during his first term, it was a de facto ethnic democracy, as amendments to the laws of the country remained minimal. The promotion of Hindu nationalism at the expense of secularism took the form of attacks against liberals (including NGOs, intellectuals, and universities like JNU) and the Saffronization of education. At the same time, minorities were subjected to both physical and symbolic violence by Hindu vigilante groups, which exerted a new form of cultural policing. These groups, usually under the umbrella of the Sangh Parivar, started to form a parallel state—with the tacit approval of the official state—as they launched one campaign after another, such as their fight against love jihad and land jihad, their attempts at reconverting those whose forefathers had embraced Islam or Christianity, and their attacks against people accused of slaughtering cows—a very emotional issue that was the root cause of a series of lynchings. Vigilantes were active not only in the street but also online, as evident from the psychological violence exerted by trolls—again with the blessings of the country's rulers.

India's trajectory from national populism to ethnic democracy suggests three general conclusions.

First, in twenty-first-century India, the moderation thesis seems less relevant than the polarization thesis. A number of political scientists have postulated that extremist parties tend to dilute their ideology once they begin to participate in the democratic process of electoral politics. The moderation thesis in particular holds that electoral competition prompts extremist parties to adopt a less exclusivist program with each successive election in order to cast a wider net. In fact, electoral competition has reinforced the radical version of Hindutva at the expense of more moderate BJP leaders who wanted, for instance, to actively pursue a politics of coalition. For the BJP under Modi, waving a largely exaggerated Islamic threat and orchestrating communal violence were viewed as the best way to mobilize a "Hindu vote" whenever the situation was conducive to such agitation. And in the early 2000s, the spate of Islamist attacks—some of which were planned by Indian Muslims retaliating against Hindu nationalists' atrocities—revived the majority's feeling of vulnerability that the Sangh Parivar could easily exploit.

The key role played by the RSS also shows that, contrary to the moderation thesis, political parties playing by the rules of party politics cannot turn their backs on the radical movements that spawned them. In this case, such emancipation from extremist elements was all the more difficult to achieve given that practically all the party's leaders and cadres received their training in the RSS.

All things considered, the BJP as it stood in 2014 had lost none of its original ideology and, on the contrary, wielded its Hindu nationalism to win an absolute majority that would release it from the compulsions of coalition politics. Once in power, it pursued the same path to win one regional election after another, playing on the same politics of fear that targeted both Muslims and the alleged Pakistani threat.

Second, Modi's policies have confirmed the hypothesis stated in the introduction, which postulated that the Sangh Parivar's recourse to large-scale national-populist mobilization was a response to the rise of lower castes in the years 1990–2000. National populism was a reaction to the risk of a loss in status facing the upper-caste middle class—BJP's core electorate—and the risk of division that caste politics posed to Hindu society. By mobilizing Hindus against Muslims, the Sangh Parivar prompted large swaths of the masses to no longer put their caste identity forward but instead their membership in the majority community that was destined to rule over India. This approach was especially effective with the angry young men of the neo-middle class.

This strategy worked to perfection in that during the five years of Modi's first term as prime minister the upper castes recovered their dominant position. They became powerful once again not only in parliament but also in assemblies of the states conquered by the BJP and in the BJP-dominated governments, where they had been steadily losing ground since 1989 vis-à-vis the main beneficiaries of the post-Mandal "silent revolution": dominant OBCs (including Yadavs) and dominant Dalits (including Jatavs). In fact, more than the return of the upper castes (who were already making a comeback under the UPA), it is the decline of these groups that were on the rise that mattered to the BJP and its upper-caste supporters who felt threatened by them. In the electoral arena, the BJP nominated candidates who did not belong to dominant Dalit or OBC jati but who instead resented the way these groups had risen to power and cornered reservations. In a way, the BJP reconstituted a coalition of extremes that was intended not only to mobilize against the Other (the Muslim) but also to sandwich common enemies of the elite and resentful plebeians.

Furthermore, public policies in favor of the populace were often reversed, whether it was positive discrimination for Scheduled Castes (which was diluted) or major programs to combat poverty started by the Manmohan Singh government (such as the Mahatma Gandhi National Rural Employment Guarantee Act). As it were, peasants were to some extent sacrificed for the interests of city dwellers, the BJP's primary electoral base. The very low prices set by the government for basic commodities—the price at which the state buys produce from farmers so as to spare urban dwellers any increase in food prices—attest to this.

Instead of developing redistribution policies and strengthening a welfare state, the Modi government invested in a politics of dignity aiming at endowing the poor with self-esteem and improving their well-being. Flagship schemes such as the Swachh Bharat Mission contributed to this strategy: like most of the centrally sponsored schemes, it was marketed—backed by a huge advertising budget—as a gift of Narendra Modi to the poor, whom he started to address every month in the *Mann Ki Baat* radio program from 2014 onward. It was well in tune with the populist repertoire, a repertoire in which the leader relates emotionally to the poor, claiming that they are his priority, while, in fact, he does not combat inequalities.

This strategy failed indeed to contain the rise of inequalities; in fact, mass poverty increased even before the Covid-19 pandemic, and the rural/urban divide continued to be more and more pronounced. These developments resulted from the ideological assumption that instead of assisting the poor and creating a culture of dependence, the middle class, the rich, and business interests should be liberated from state constraints. This supply-side policy found expression in the decline of direct taxes and the rise of indirect taxation. Correlatively, the superrich amassed an increasingly large share of the national wealth. This trend was not primarily due to Modi's faith in neoliberalism, however. In fact, his relationship with some of India's big businesses constituted a prime example of crony capitalism, which his close contacts were the first to benefit from. This connection enabled the BJP to raise funds for his election campaigns.

Third, the Indian variant of ethnic democracy needed to be qualified: in contrast to the Israeli "model," during Modi's first term India invented a de facto ethnic democracy in which the Constitution and most laws remained unchanged and in which the government remained in the background—mostly silent. Certainly, the state promoted the Hindu nationalist version of Hindu identity, Indian history, and the role of minorities in society and history. But it left most coercive actions to nonstate actors, such as to vigilante groups that exerted cultural policing in the street or to trolls doing the same on social media.

This division of labor reflected not only the strategy of the Modi government but also the evolution of the Sangh Parivar. Since the 1980s, this movement had developed subsidiaries intended to reach out to Dalits, OBCs, and upper-caste youth from the lower middle class. The

Bajrang Dal was especially good at attracting jobless plebeians, who improved their self-esteem and even acquired a new identity, by fighting the enemies of Hinduism. Emulating elite groups associated with the Hindu high tradition, which were more than happy to co-opt them and subcontract their dirty work to them, these lumpen elements epitomized a new version of Sanskritization.

Bajrang Dalis and gau rakshak were the foot soldiers of the de facto ethnic democracy that India became after 2014. They had no official connection to the state (except that the police let them operate freely in BJP-ruled states) but reported to a parallel power structure made up of RSS cadres. Some of them were part of the parastatal dimension of BJP governments, which had the appearance of a Janus-like figure with an official side and an unofficial one. The former embodied legality, but the latter was superior as it enjoyed legitimacy. This legitimacy came not only from the sacred nature of their fight for Hinduism and its symbols, including the cow, but also from their defense of a social order: their fight against love jihad was well in tune with the orthopraxy of the caste system, for instance. As a result, their brutal, illegal actions were not punished, and the impunity of their patrolling of society was acknowledged not only by the majority community but, nolens volens, by many of their victims, who no longer dared to turn to the state for help. In a de facto ethnic democracy, the motto "might is right" works in favor of majorities.

But the government's use of vigilante groups enables the official rulers to claim that they have nothing to do with what is systematically presented as the spontaneous defense of one's culture. This helps the Modi government to cultivate the traditional quietist repertoire of the RSS, while emphasizing the need for unity—a pillar of Narendra Modi's repertoire, as he claims, as populists always do, to speak for all the people; hence, his reference to his 1.3 billion "brothers and sisters." This is consistent with the Hindu nationalist attempt at developing unity among Hindus beyond caste (and class) divisions. Hindu nationalism indeed propagates an irenic view of society by minimizing social hierarchies and making them more acceptable. Its key word is *harmony*. This repertoire has found expression in *Mann Ki Baat*, a radio program whose overtones contrast dramatically with Modi's aggressive electoral speeches. It is a contrast that illustrates the complexity of populism: on one hand, populist leaders need to polarize; on the other, they need to unite to appear as true representatives of the nation. The task is easier for national-populists: even if they claim to embody the whole nation, they represent the majority community only and mobilize it against the Others.

Indeed, the atmosphere created by Sangh Parivar vigilante groups and BJP IT cell trolls has been largely responsible not only for the lynchings of Muslims but also for attacks on "liberals," including intellectuals and journalists. The guilty parties, in these cases, often belonged to the other Hindutva school of thought, inherited from Savarkar and made up of activists who explicitly legitimize violence. These groups, including the Sanatan Sanstha, work to dehumanize the Other, the Muslim, through a deeper process than the demonization orchestrated by Sangh Parivar ideologues, because their aim goes beyond weaponizing the fear of the Other to turn it into anger. Their goal is to eliminate the Other outright in a move from fear to hatred, from riots to targeted killings. While the former tactics are part of the Sangh Parivar's mobilization strategy, the latter has been used by outside elements in the Savarkarite tradition. Yet the frontier between these so-called fringe elements and the Sangh Parivar has become very porous.

Ethnic democracies flourish only under certain conditions.

First, ethnic democracies, according to Samy Smooha, can only survive if they are not subjected to outside pressure—and their consolidation is even a function of the external support they receive, as evidenced by the relationship between Israel and the United States. In the case of India, pressure has been rather limited. It is true that international sanctions were imposed on Narendra Modi when he was chief minister of Gujarat in reaction to the 2002 pogrom. In 2005, he was denied a diplomatic visa to enter the United States, and his existing tourist/business visa was revoked under Section 212 of the Immigration and Nationality Act, which makes any foreign government official who was responsible for or "directly carried out, at any time, particularly severe violations of religious freedom" ineligible for a visa.[2] But this boycott ended when he became prime minister. Since then, international criticism has come mostly from Muslim countries and the United Nations. Scholars of Gulf countries have protested against what they called India's Islamophobia.[3] The Organization of Islamic Cooperation has also protested officially— as have some states, including Iran and Turkey—against the way Muslims are treated in India in the context of the abolition of article 370, the anti-CAA movement, and the 2020 Delhi riots.[4] The United Nations has been more systematic. As early as 2018, in her report on contemporary forms of racism, racial discrimination, xenophobia, and related intolerance, E. Tendayi Achiume, the special rapporteur appointed by the United Nations Human Rights Council, said that "the election of the Hindu nationalist Bharatiya Janata Party (BJP) has been linked to incidents of violence against members of Dalit, Muslim, tribal and Christian communities. Reports document the use of inflammatory remarks by BJP leaders against minority groups, and the rise of vigilantism targeting Muslims and Dalits."[5] Subsequently, UN officials were concerned about the fate of human rights activists, journalists,[6] demonstrators who had been arrested after protesting against the CAA,[7] and the stateless people that the NRC is likely to create.[8] Michele Bachelet, the United Nations High Commissioner for Human Rights, pointed out that the CAA was "fundamentally discriminatory in nature" and invited India to "consider carefully the compatibility of the law with India's international human rights obligations."[9] In 2020, Bachelet went further. She "urge[d] the Government [of India] to ensure that no one else is detained for exercising their rights to freedom of expression and peaceful assembly—and to do its utmost, in law and policy, to protect India's robust civil society. I also urge the authorities to carefully review the FCRA for its compliance with international human rights standards and to release people charged under the Unlawful Activities Prevention Act for simply exercising basic human rights that India is obligated to protect."[10] The Indian government systematically ignored or rejected the UN reports, including the ones on the situation in Jammu and Kashmir.[11]

The European Union Parliament also showed some desire to act. Five EU Parliamentary groups, representing 559 members out of 751, initiated a strongly worded resolution condemning the CAA in early 2020,[12] but India successfully ramped up efforts to counter this move[13]—which remained a dead letter[14] as most of the country members, including France, chose to look at this law as an internal matter.[15] A few months before, twenty MEPs had written to three Indian ministers to protest the "crackdown" against rights activists.[16] Similarly, members of the U.S. Congress raised the issue of the CAA after the hearing of witnesses from Amnesty International and other NGOs. More importantly, the U.S. Commission on International Religious Freedom kept downgrading India in its yearly reports[17] and alerting India almost every time minorities were under attack (such as during the Delhi riots).[18] Donald Trump, however, never mentioned human rights or religious freedom as an India problem. On the contrary, in the speech he made during his February 2020 visit (when the Delhi riots were starting), he declared that India "has always been admired around the Earth as the place where millions upon millions of Hindus and Muslims and Sikhs and Jains, Buddhists, Christians, and Jews worship side by side in harmony."[19] In 2019, the United Kingdom and Canada jointly organized a conference on media freedom in London. The minister of information and broadcasting immediately wrote a letter to the High Commissioner of both countries against the "unwarranted remarks" that Vinod Jose, the executive editor of *The Caravan*, had expressed on this occasion.[20]

Western countries are not just reluctant to interfere in India's domestic affairs due to the very strong reactions of the Modi government when its democratic credentials are questioned. Their attitude also has much to do with the rise of China. First, the United States and several European countries consider that India can help balance out Chinese expansionism in Asia in the framework of their Indo-Pacific strategy. Second, compared to China, the Indian brand of authoritarianism naturally is much less liberticidal and systematic. The fact that India imports arms from these countries and represents a huge potential market for their multinationals should be factored in as well. Whatever the reason for this differential treatment, one of Smooha's criteria for defining an ethnic democracy—the absence of an adverse international context—is clearly fulfilled, and India continues to enjoy robust soft power, as most people outside the country generally view it as the world's largest democracy.

An ethnic democracy like India is also bound to stabilize if opposition parties remain weak and tend to converge with the dominant idiom of national politics. India's opposition parties, including Congress, have declined because of the unequal competition they were subjected to—as evident from the financial imbalance and the media bias mentioned in preceding chapters. But they were also victims of their own weaknesses. Not only have they suffered from factionalism—a problem that has been very obvious on the Congress side, where it has been aggravated by the BJP's strategy of co-option and horse trading—but opposition parties have appeared as ideologically confused.[21]

While the BJP articulated an increasingly aggressive ethnoreligious brand of nationalism, the Congress and state parties that used to pay allegiance to secularism have failed to give voice to an alternative narrative: the Sangh Parivar has turned secularism into a dirty word.[22] Not only have BJP opponents proven unable to defend the principle, but many of them have fallen in line, as evident from the voting patterns of Lok Sabha and Rajya Sabha MPs on article 370 and the CAA. Hindutva has gradually become a hegemonic discourse[23] in the sense that it is now the only legitimate political repertoire (to use Pierre Bourdieu's term)[24] and, as Fred Bayley said in another context, one of the normative rules of the political game, which "express ultimate and publicly acceptable values" and "set broad limits to possible action."[25] This trend is well illustrated by the "soft Hindutva" of Congressmen—or the not-so-soft Hindutva of Congressmen shifting to the BJP, such as J. Scindia, who, after leaving Congress, visited Hedgewar's home because it "gives inspiration on dedication to nation."[26] However, Congress leaders remained committed to secularism even at the state level, as mentioned in chapter 11. In Rajasthan, for instance, after the accused in the Pehlu Khan lynching case were acquitted, the Gehlot government simultaneously appointed a special investigation team and introduced a bill "criminalizing mob lynching."[27] The Aam Aadmi Party, while it claimed to be secular, indulged in an even more explicit saffronization, as Kejriwal himself emulated Narendra Modi in some ways and eulogized the Sangh Parivar, with whom he had joined hands during the Anna Hazare movement.[28] The AAP government remained remarkably silent during the Delhi riots, and afterward.[29] Congress and AAP—not to mention other state parties—tend to speak in multiple voices so as not to betray their secular image or to appear too close to the minorities.[30] Such an evolution is typical of the making of a stable ethnic democracy. In Israel, the Labor Party, which once offered an alternative to the Likud hardliners, has gradually subscribed to the Likud's vision of the nation or has preferred to remain silent—sealing the fate of the party.

National populism has not only made India an ethnic democracy; it has also prepared the ground for authoritarianism. Affinities between these two isms are obvious. Authoritarianism is inherent in national populism first because the national-populist leader personalizes politics in such a way that, once in office, he continues to concentrate power at the expense even of his party (which needs him more than he needs it). Second, this strong-man who claims to epitomize the nation is against political pluralism by definition (hence Modi's objective of a "Congress Mukt Bharat" and the fight against dissenting intellectuals, universities, independent journalists, NGOs, and so on). Third, his legitimacy supposedly prevails over all institutions as none of them are sanctified by popular mandate, not even the parliament since "his" MPs were elected thanks to him alone.

There is also a continuum between ethnic democracy and authoritarianism. After all, the former is a contradiction in terms as it does not recognize equal status for all citizens and even considers some minorities as posing a threat to the majoritarian nation—and its collective security. These minorities are easily stigmatized as antinational or simply ignored and/or excluded by/from the institutional framework of "their" country. While Muslims had always been underrepresented in the police, the army, the judiciary, and the bureaucracy, they were also, after 2014, practically obliterated from elected assemblies and governments. Ultimately, in the de facto ethnic democracy that India became in 2014, some of them feel like foreigners in their own country.

Since 2019, the government's growing authoritarianism has implied a certain officialization of this marginalization or even exclusion of Muslims. While under Modi I, nonstate actors were responsible for their oppression, under Modi II, the state and its institutions directly targeted them, largely because the 2019 elections had enhanced the government's authority—in the upper house in particular. In six months, a whole series of legal changes took place, ranging from the abrogation of article 370 to the Citizenship Amendment Act, two major decisions reflecting the will of Modi II to transform India into a more unitary state with a majoritarian overtone. At the state level, the UP ordinance against "love jihad" has also transferred some cultural policing from vigilante groups to the police.

Furthermore, beyond legislative changes, the BJP's authoritarianism vis-à-vis Muslims is reflected in the way opponents are quashed: hundreds of political prisoners were detained under draconian laws in Jammu and Kashmir, and anti-CAA demonstrators were also targeted by the police and jailed in large numbers. The police—which until then had allowed vigilantes to operate instead of systematically showing their antiminority bias—turned against Muslims even more openly during the Delhi riots of February 2020. The judiciary is another key institution of the state that has betrayed its commitment to the secular values of the Constitution on several occasions in recent years. Until now, Muslims who had been unfairly treated by the police had often been rescued by the judiciary. That has remained somewhat true, but with caveats. While judges have released many people who have been arrested by the police without good reason, the Supreme Court itself has stopped confronting the government. This change may be attributed to ideological affinities or the blackmailing of justices (including chief justices) by the executive. Whatever the reason, this evolution found expression in the Ayodhya verdict that allowed Narendra Modi to launch construction of a Ram temple, the symbol of the de jure ethnic democracy in the making.

Minorities are not the only casualties of the government's growing authoritarianism. The way the government has weakened and/or intensified its control over key institutions has mechanically worked toward establishing a national-authoritarian regime. If authoritarianism can be defined by the limits it places on pluralism, the Indian trajectory fulfills several key criteria. First, the decline of checks and balances resulted from successful attempts to weaken all the institutions that were in a position to balance the government's power. While the decline of the judiciary has been emphasized in previous chapters owing to the fact that it is the institution that could have most effectively resisted the government, other institutions have been emasculated or controlled by the executive. Parliament is a case in point, as are several key institutions of the state apparatus. The bureaucrats in charge of these alternative power centers—the Election Commission of India, the Lokpal, the Central Information Commission, the Central Bureau of Investigation, the National Investigation Agency, the Central Vigilance Commission, and so on—have all been selected meticulously. Those who took a stand against the rulers have been transferred. In parallel, the media's independence has been seriously curbed by restrictions on freedom of expression that affect internet access as well. In contrast, TV channels and newspapers that support the government have flourished.

India's brand of authoritarianism, however, needs to be qualified. It is a case of competitive authoritarianism, an ism that makes some room for the people's voice—as required by populism. Since the populists' legitimacy stems from popular support, they need the voters' support. But they make every endeavor to win elections by creating an uneven playing field. Such distortions are typical of electoral authoritarianism, a political system in which the rulers maximize their probability of winning by reducing the presence of their rivals in the media and by spending far more money than their opponents during the election campaign. In India, these distortions were made possible by electoral bonds, the intimidation of adversaries, the control exerted by the government over media outlets, and the weakening of the ECI.

Electoral authoritarianism, however, is only one facet of Modi's regime. There is also a social component. As mentioned above, Modi's populism appeared to India's elite as an antidote to caste politics, which, since Mandal, had resulted in the rise to power of plebeian groups. In that sense, it was a sort of counterrevolution. This conservative revolution has an authoritarian dimension as well. After all, democratization means two things: less concentration of power in few hands and more equality. Symmetrically, de-democratization does not refer only to the comeback staged by formerly dominant groups in the power structure; it also means less redistribution of resources. Charles Tilly pointed out that elite groups "have much greater means and incentives than ordinary people to escape or subvert democratic compacts when those compacts turn to their disadvantage"[31]—and this is what they did in India in the 2000s, when they started to be disillusioned with democracy and did not even vote as much as the poor.[32] The elite's eagerness to maintain the sociopolitical status quo, therefore, is not only the subtext of populism—it also overdetermines elite support for authoritarianism.

The elitist dimension of the present brand of Indian authoritarianism has two facets. First, inequalities in socioeconomic terms are again on the rise as the rich become richer and the poor (especially in the rural part of the country) do not benefit from redistribution programs and economic growth as much as they once did. Second, the state protects elite domination in terms of status. The rise to power of Modi's BJP has not only enabled upper-caste MLAs, MPs, and ministers to control power again, it has also allowed them to legitimize status-based hierarchy (as evident from the way Brahmins are publicly eulogized) and to promote their lifestyle. Laws regulating cow slaughter and marriage are meant to promote vegetarianism and to control personal relations. This is well in tune with Hindu nationalist ideology, where social norms prevail over individual choices. Criticizing the idea of fundamental rights, Deendayal Upadhyaya pointed out that "these rights are given to the individual in order that he may perform his social duties"[33]—preferably in the framework of the caste system that Upadhyaya defended by referring to the varna vyavastha. While this emphasis on Hindu orthopraxy found expression primarily in cultural policing by vigilante groups during Narendra Modi's first term, the state took over for them to a large extent after 2019, through new laws and new roles assumed by the police. Those who were declared urban Naxals were targeted in the name of both illegal and illegitimate actions. Indeed, the police have taken over the role of vigilante groups by denouncing the books the urban

Naxals read and the intercaste marriages they have made. The Indian variant of authoritarianism, therefore, implies a kind of anti-individualistic, state-enforced orthopraxy.

This brings us to the last qualification of the Indian version of this type of regime. In his typology of forms of authoritarianism, Juan Linz, elaborating on Max Weber's notion of sultanism, analyses "neo-sultanism" in a very heuristic manner. He defines it as a form of "personal rulership" based on "a mixture of fear and rewards."[34] Among such a ruler's "collaborators" are "members of his family, friends, cronies, business associates, and men directly involved in the use of violence to sustain the regime."[35] The political economy of this patrimonial-like form of authoritarianism is threefold: the rulers "demand gifts and payoffs from business for which no public accounting is given," they "establish profit-oriented monopolies," and "the economy [be it public or private] is subject to considerable governmental interference but not for the purposes of planning but of extracting resources."[36]

The notion of sultanism highlights a dimension of Modi's India that is difficult to explore—and that appears too discreetly in this book, partly due to the secretive political economy of the regime. On the basis of what little information is publicly available, one can assume that Narendra Modi has helped a limited number of industrial firms to grow— as he had done in Gujarat in 2002–2014—and, conversely, has imposed strict control over others. The former, the winners, are gradually acquiring a quasi-hegemonic position, like oligarchs.[37] A dozen companies are indeed on the rise at the time of this writing. In 2019, according to a study by Marcellus Investment Managers, a Mumbai-based firm, twenty companies "accounted for nearly 70% of India Inc's total earnings, up from 14% three decades ago,"[38] and up from less than 40 percent in 2014—when the process had already started under Manmohan Singh's second term. *The Economist* adds, "In a growing number of product categories . . . monopolies or duopolies skim off 80% of profits."[39] Among these twenty companies, one-third are well-run service-sector enterprises, one-third are rent-seeking public companies, and one-third "are huge private companies with mediocre returns but a knack for navigating both India's labyrinthine bureaucracy and its corridors of power."[40] While the second group is shrinking, the last one is growing in the context of a specific brand of crony capitalism. By contrast, entrepreneurs who are not close to the ruling clique and who do not have to pay (back) or cannot do so are submitted to all kinds of control, including tax raids—sometimes in the form of extortion.[41] The sultanist dimension of the regime relies on a form of osmosis between the political rulers and their cronies, a relationship based on all manner of "give and take," including electoral bonds and industrial licenses.

Why is authoritarianism not resisted more vigorously in India? Before closing, four explanations are ventured, which are not mutually exclusive.

The first reason has to do with the fact that populists-turned-authoritarians do nothing illegal at the start, and they adopt an incremental modus operandi. As Levitsky and Ziblatt have shown, "This is how democracies now die. Blatant dictatorship—in the form of fascism, communism, or military rule—has disappeared across the world. Military coups and other violent seizures of power are rare. Most countries hold regular elections. Democracies still die, but by different means. Since the end of the Cold War, most democratic breakdowns have been caused not by generals and soldiers but by elected governments themselves."[42] As they point out, "Often the assault on democracy begins slowly. For many citizens, it may, at first, be imperceptible. After all, elections continue to be held. Opposition politicians still sit in congress. Independent newspapers still circulate. The erosion of democracy takes place piecemeal, often in baby steps. Each individual step seems minor—none appear to truly threaten democracy. Indeed, government moves to subvert democracy frequently enjoy a veneer of legality: They are approved by parliament or ruled constitutional by the supreme court."[43] In the initial phase of authoritarianism, only minorities are affected, be they religious minorities or activists (liberals, human rights activists, and so on). The majority is safe, and in India it often indulges in Hindu majoritarianism: most citizens have no reason to complain, as their lives have not changed at all.

The second explanation may be that democracy, in today's India, has lost its importance, compared to security—a phenomenon that other countries have experienced before, including Pakistan, whose political background was similar to India's but which, fearing its big neighbor, became a security state in the 1950s.[44] Democracy has lost some of its prestige. In 2017, the CSDS report titled *The State of Democracy in South Asia* showed that the percentage of respondents who supported democracy had dropped from 70 to 63 percent between 2005 and 2017[45] and that the percentage of those who were satisfied with democracy had declined even more, from 79 to 55 percent. Among college graduates and above, 47 percent of shared this opinion.[46] While they remained attached to a representative form of government, the kind of governance they approved of relied on "strong men" and "experts": 52 percent of the respondents agreed with the statement "We should get rid of parliament and elections and have a strong leader to decide things." (42 percent of graduates and 46 percent of "25 years and below" approved); similarly, 54 percent agreed with the statement "We should get rid of elections and parliaments and have experts make decisions on behalf of the people."[47]

A 2017 Pew report reconfirmed the trend: 55 percent of the respondents backed "a governing system in which a strong leader can make decisions without interference from parliament or the courts," while 53 percent support military rule. Commenting on this result, the Pew team added, "Support for autocratic rule is higher in India than in any other nation surveyed," and India is "one of only four nations where half or more of the public supports governing by the military." An even larger proportion—two-thirds—say, "A good way to govern the country would be experts, not elected officials, making decisions according to what they think is best for the nation." Interestingly, BJP supporters and urban dwellers were overrepresented in the three groups—of those who support personal rule, military governance, and a technocratic regime.[48]

The demand for a strong leader is related to an acute feeling of vulnerability. According to the Pew survey, while "crime takes the top spot on the list, with 84% of Indians seeing it as a *very* big problem," "terrorism" comes immediately next to it for 76 percent of the respondents (before corruption and unemployment).[49] This is well in tune with the idea that ISIS appeared as the main threat to India for 66 percent of the respondents, ahead of every other threat.[50] The need for a strong state further arises from the drive to stifle unresolved issues and conflicts, as evident from the fact that a "63% majority believes the government should be using more military force" in Kashmir.[51]

The third explanation harks back to the political culture of India and the traditional submission to hierarchy and acceptance of authority, that of a charismatic leader in particular. In his closing speech to the Constituent Assembly in 1949, B. R. Ambedkar highlighted a cultural explanation of the submission to authority that seemed to him so commonplace in India:

> There is nothing wrong in being grateful to great men who have rendered life-long services to the country. But there are limits to gratefulness. As has been well said by the Irish Patriot Daniel O'Connel [sic], "no man can be grateful at the cost of his honour, no woman can be grateful at the cost of her chastity and no nation can be grateful at the cost of its liberty." This caution is far more necessary in the case of India than in the case of any other country, for in India, Bhakti or what may be called the path of devotion or hero-worship, plays a part in its politics unequalled in magnitude by the part it plays in the politics of any other country in the world. Bhakti in religion may be a road to the salvation of the soul. But in politics, Bhakti or hero-worship is a sure road to degradation and to eventual dictatorship.[52]

The words that Modi's supporters (known as *bhakts* [devotees]) use to describe his power often belong, indeed, to the realm of supernatural forces. Certainly, this image has been constructed by the public relations agencies he has hired since his Gujarat years, but a large fraction of the Indian public has made it its own in a rather uncritical manner. Hence the notion of "vishvas politics" articulated by Neelanjan Sircar, which assumes that Narendra Modi not only is above accountability but that he cannot do anything wrong. This was particularly obvious during the COVID-19 pandemic, a crisis that was not handled well by the government but that Narendra Modi was not blamed for.[53] When public opinion is so inclined, one of the limits to power vanishes if any form of authority—including abusive ones—seems legitimate.

Narendra Modi has acquired charisma in the Weberian sense owing to the manner in which he has achieved "big things"—which were not necessarily perceived as good things, as evident from the way the 2002 pogrom was reported in the media. He has shown his strength through disruptive decisions affecting the life of all citizens, such as demonetization. He has demonstrated his taste for the spectacular, with the statue of Sardar Patel, the tallest in the world. He convinced the UN to recognize June 21 as International Yoga Day. He has dared to attack Pakistan militarily beyond the territory of disputed Kashmir in Balakot. And he has initiated policies no one has ever attempted, such as the abolition of article 370.

But Modi is seen as exceptional not only on account of his acts but also owing to his style. He appears to sacrifice his life for the people—like a fakir (a word he uses to refer to himself), a figure he came to epitomize even more in 2020 by growing a long white beard. This echoes the ideal of the selfless world renouncer, a highly prestigious figure in Indian culture—and which Mahatma Gandhi (the most remarkable Indian "brand" for Modi) exemplified. Ambedkar in fact had Gandhi in mind in his criticism of the personality cult that is so prevalent in India in the above citation, because he was aware, as the Rudolphs were to show, that while Gandhi's charisma had "traditional roots," it was power oriented: the Mahatma was keen to exercise dominant authority.[54] If Modi belongs to a school of thought that has always opposed the Mahatma, he has emulated his "saintly politics"[55] to persuade Indian voters that he devotes all his energy to the nation, and even to the poor, in actions devoid of all corruption.

Last but not least, Modi, due to his social background, appears as a man of the people who has suffered from class and caste hierarchies and who cultivates a sense of victimization that Indian plebeians cannot help but share. He also cultivates his proximity to the people through his monthly radio program, *Mann Ki Baat*.

To sum up, Modi is a pure populist à la Ostiguy because he combines these exceptional achievements and a sense of morality with a very humble background, which means that he is seen as "a man like us who managed to become a superman." This is the main reason why he is not punished by voters when he fails to deliver on the economic front. Even in terms of policy, people retain their trust in him—hence the "vishvas" feeling.

But Modi is more than a populist, he is a *national*-populist. His style is especially popular because he has restored people's pride and sense of dignity. Thanks to him, not only do the poor feel better respected in India, but Indians feel they have earned the world's respect. Modi has constantly traveled across the globe, and these trips have been systematically publicized in the media on purpose. He has made a point of hugging the leaders of the world in front of the cameras and sharing the dais in large rallies with the most powerful, including Donald Trump in Houston and then in Ahmedabad. This international recognition has had a particularly strong impact on a population suffering from a deep, historical sense of vulnerability: the syndrome of the effete and "dying" race affecting Hindus, since the British Raj has remained particularly strong among those who fear the Other, who are jobless, who feel useless and/or have undergone socioeconomic decline. Gandhi, as the Rudolphs have shown, gave Indians renewed self-esteem by creating a "new courage" based on nonviolence.[56] Modi has given them self-respect, a word he repeated many times on August 15, 2019, during his Independence Day speech.[57]

Citizens are more prepared to pay allegiance to a strong leader who is endowed with exceptional, superhuman qualities, who protects them and restores their self-esteem. As he can do no wrong, the people willingly suspend their critical thinking and readily renounce some of their freedoms. This process was exemplified by the way Indira Gandhi and Sanjay Gandhi were reelected in 1980, less than two years after the Emergency—as if they were not responsible for this phase of dictatorship. Why were they not punished not once but again two years later? The interviews that Emma Tarlo conducted in Delhi slums that had resulted from the government's "rehabilitation" policy showed that "none [among the interviewees] associated their sufferings with Indira Gandhi,"[58] who was still seen as "a great leader," a "world-famous leader"—like Sanjay. Charisma is above accountability, and Modi has grasped these dynamics.

The last reason why few people resist the regime's liberticidal inclination is fear, a sentiment that is paralyzing an increasingly large number of Indian citizens. This factor has been mentioned previously in relation to newsrooms, but the media are not the only targets, and other people than journalists have censored themselves because of fear. In 2018, a division bench of the Bombay High Court observed: "We are witnessing a tragic phase in the country today. Citizens already feel that they can't voice their concerns or opinions fearlessly."[59] Besides those who are afraid to leave their neighborhood because their physical appearance designates them as a minority member, any institution and any group may be targeted, including bureaucrats and judges—who may be transferred or even sued and jailed.[60] Even some businessmen live in fear of Income Tax Department, Enforcement Directorate, and CBI raids, as suggested in previous chapters. The scion of one of the most prestigious industrial families of India, Rahul Bajaj, told Amit Shah during an industry awards event in Mumbai: "Nobody from our industrialist friends will speak, I will say openly. . . . An environment will have to be created. . . . When UPA II was in power, we could criticise anyone. . . . You [the government] are doing good work, but despite that we don't have the confidence that you will appreciate if we criticise you openly."[61] He added, in relation to the wave of lynchings: "It creates an environment of intolerance and we are scared. We don't want to say certain things but we see that until now no one has been convicted." Amit Shah responded, "There is no need for anybody to fear." But the psychosis Bajaj was referring to has been exacerbated by certain state policies as well as official speeches.

India has acquired some attributes of a police state not only by resorting routinely to draconian antiterror laws like the UAPA and by charging journalists for sedition, as mentioned above, but also by developing a sophisticated surveillance system. As mentioned in chapter 10, the accused in the Bhima Koregaon case were booked on the basis of evidence retrieved from their phones and computers. Soon after, it appeared that these phones and computers had been infected by snooping software developed by an Israeli company—the NSO Group—which sells it only to government agencies. This software, called Pegasus, gives attackers control over the mobile device of the person targeted.[62] WhatsApp—the application used by the attackers to break into phones—has sued the NSO Group,[63] but the Indian government, which in the previous months and years had upgraded its collaboration with Israel in several technological domains, including artificial intelligence,[64] has not commented on this affair.

In parallel, the government of India has initiated a surveillance system by resorting increasingly to facial recognition. After the Delhi riots, Amit Shah declared, "Police have identified 1,100 people through the facial recognition technology. Nearly 300 people came from Uttar Pradesh. It was a planned conspiracy."[65] How could the police know? It seems that "the footage procured from CCTV, media persons and the public was matched with photographs stored in the database of Election Commission and e-Vahan, a pan-India database of vehicle registration maintained by Ministry of Road Transport and Highways."[66] Gautam Bhatia points out that "such 'dragnet' screening is a blatant violation of privacy rights, as it essentially treats every individual like a potential suspect, subject to an endless continuing investigation."[67] This technique is more and more systematically resorted to by the government, as the Indian parliament has yet to enact a personal-data-protection law[68] loose enough to allow the government to use Aadhaar for facial recognition as well.[69]

The Supreme Court forced the Ministry of Information and Broadcasting to withdraw its proposal for social media monitoring in 2018, considering that if such a proposal were implemented, India would be "moving towards a surveillance state."[70] But in 2021, the government is still eager to develop a tool that would monitor social media users to identify their "sentiments" and track trends relevant to "government related activities" that "may have adverse negative impact on socioeconomic fabric of society."[71] These words, which hark back to the authoritarian orthopraxy mentioned above, come from the expression of interest that the I&B ministry has floated to empanel an entity to create such a tool. Even before such a tool has seen the light of the day, the authorities have already arrested a large number of social media users, including journalists, for messages or videos they had posted on Facebook or WhatsApp, even posts that were sometimes several years old.[72]

*

In 2019, Suhas Palshikar concluded his contribution to *Majoritarian State* by considering that "electoral defeat alone can puncture the BJP's resolute march towards crafting a new hegemony,"[73] but electoral defeat may not make much of a difference, or, to be more precise, while it is a necessary condition, it may not be a sufficient one. First, as mentioned in part II, the Sangh Parivar is so deeply entrenched in the social fabric that it may continue to dictate its terms to the state on the ground—and to rule in the street.[74] Second, the "deep state" may remain in a position to influence policies and politics even if the BJP is voted out. In that sense, Hindu nationalism does not rely as much on one man to push its agenda as the BJP does to win elections.

NOTES

Introduction

1. Larry Diamond, "Thinking about Hybrid Regimes," *Journal of Democracy* 13, no. 2 (April 2002): 21–35; and Leah Gilbert and Payam Mohseni, "Beyond Authoritarianism: The Conceptualization of Hybrid Regimes," *Studies in Comparative International Development* 46 (2011): 270–97.

2. David Collier and Steve Levistky, "Democracy with Adjectives: Conceptual Innovation in Comparative Research," *World Politics* 49, no. 3 (April 1997): 430–51; Fareed Zakaria, "The Rise of Illiberal Democracy," *Foreign Affairs* 76, no. 6 (November–December 1997): 22–43; Andreas Schedler, ed., *Electoral Authoritarianism: The Dynamics of Unfree Competition* (Boulder, CO: Lynne Rienner, 2006); Peter Smith and Melissa Ziegler, "Liberal and Illiberal Democracy in Latin America," *Latin American Politics and Society* 50, no. 1 (2008): 31–57; Steven Levitsky and Lucan A. Way, *Competitive Authoritarianism: Hybrid Regimes after the Cold War* (Cambridge: Cambridge University Press, 2010); and Leonardo Morlino, "Are There Hybrid Regimes? Or Are They Just an Optical Illusion?," *European Political Science Review* 1, no. 2 (2009): 273–96.

3. I studied this contradiction in detail in the first three chapters of my book *India's Silent Revolution—the Rise of the Lower Castes in North India* (New York: Columbia University Press; London: Hurst; New Delhi: Permanent Black, 2003).

4. Jaffrelot, *India's Silent Revolution*, 239–84.

5. Christophe Jaffrelot and Pratinav Anil, *India's First Dictatorship: The Emergency, 1975–77* (London: Hurst, 2020).

6. Christophe Jaffrelot, "Introduction," in *Rise of the Plebeians? The Changing Face of Indian Legislative Assemblies*, ed. Christophe Jaffrelot and Sanjay Kumar (New Delhi: Routledge, 2009), 1–23.

7. The Hindi belt comprises the following states of the Indian Union: Uttar Pradesh, Bihar, Madhya Pradesh, Rajasthan, Chhattisgarh, Jhkarkhand, Himachal Pradesh, Haryana, Uttarakhand, and Delhi.

8. Jaffrelot, *India's Silent Revolution*.

9. In 2004, according to the CSDS Data Unit, the turnout of the "Rich" was more than 2 percentage points below that of the "Poor" (C. Jaffrelot, "'Why Should We Vote?'—The Indian Middle Class and the Functioning of the World's Largest Democracy," in *Patterns of Middle Class Consumption in India and China*, ed. Christophe Jaffrelot and Peter van der Veer (New Delhi: Sage, 2008), 35–54.

10. Michael Walzer, *The Paradox of Liberation: Secular Revolutions and Religious Counterrevolutions* (New Haven, CT: Yale University Press, 2015).

Part I

1. See Sunil Khilnani, *The Idea of India* (London: Hamish Hamilton, 1997).

2. Rajeev Bhargava, "Indian Secularism: An Alternative, Trans-Cultural Ideal," in *The Promise of India's Secular Democracy* (Delhi: Oxford University Press, 2010), 63–105.

3. Charles Taylor, "The Meaning of Secularism," *Hedgehog Review* 12, no. 3 (Fall 2010): 23.

4. Cited in Sarvepalli Gopal, ed., *Jawaharlal Nehru: An Anthology* (Delhi: Oxford University Press, 1980), 330.

5. Cited in Stanley J. Tambiah, "The Crisis of Secularism in India," in *Secularism and Its Critics*, ed. Rajeev Bhargava (Delhi: Oxford University Press, 1998), 422–23.

6. M. K. Gandhi, *Indian Home Rule*, 5th English-language ed. (Madras: Ganesh, 1922), 49.

7. An overview of this history can be found in part I of my book *The Pakistan Paradox* (London: Hurst, 2015).

Chapter 1

1. On this movement of Muslim mobilization, see Gail Minault, *The Khilafat Movement: Religious Symbolism and Political Mobilization in India* (New York: Columbia University Press, 1982).

2. On the genesis of this sentiment in Hindu circles, see Christophe Jaffrelot, *The Hindu Nationalist Movement and Indian Politics, 1925 to the 1990s* (London: C. Hurst, 1996), 19.

3. P. C. Bamford, *Histories of the Non-Cooperation and Khilafat Movements* (1925; repr., Delhi: Government of India Press, 1985), 111; P. Spear, *The Nabobs* (London: Oxford University Press, 1932), 198–201; and J. Roselli, "The Self-Image of Effeteness: Physical Education and Nationalism in Nineteenth Century Bengal," *Past and Present* 86 (1980): 121–148.

4. Indus, s.v. "Census India 1931: Religion," last modified July 27, 2016, 21:20, http://indpaedia.com/ind/index.php/Census_India_1931:_Religion.

5. As did a famous Arya Samajist, Swami Shraddhananda, *Hindu Sangathan: Savior of the Dying Race* (Delhi: Arjun Press, 1926).

6. For further detail, see Christophe Jaffrelot, "The Idea of the Hindu Race in the Writings of Hindu Nationalist Ideologues in the 1920s and 1930s: A Concept between Two Cultures," in *The Concept of Race in South Asia*, ed. P. Robb (Delhi: Oxford University Press, 1995), 327–54.

7. V. D. Savarkar, *Hindutva: Who Is a Hindu?* (Mumbai: Asia Publishing House, 1962), 85.

8. Christophe Jaffrelot, "From Holy Sites to Web Sites: Hindu Nationalism, from Sacred Territory to Diasporic Ethnicity," in *Religions, Nations, and Transnationalism in Multiple Modernities*, ed. Patrick Michel, Adam Possamai, and Bryan Turner (Basingstoke, UK: Palgrave, 2017), 153–74. Regarding the "sacred geography of India," see Diana L. Eck, *India: A Sacred Geography* (New York: Three Rivers, 2012).

9. Regarding the relationship that "chosen people" have with their sacred land and golden age, see Anthony D. Smith, *Chosen People: Sacred Sources of National Identity* (Oxford: Oxford University Press, 2003), 131–217.

10. Savarkar, *Hindutva*, 90. In 2019, studying Herzl and Savarkar in a comparative perspective, Subramanian Swamy, a BJP MP, and Gadi Taub from the Hebrew University of Jerusalem

agreed that Zionism and Hindutva were very similar. B. Pruthi, "Hinduism and Judaism Should Come Together," *The Hindu*, August 27, 2019, https://www.thehindu.com/news/cities/mumbai/hinduism-and-judaism-should-come-together/article29263943.ece.

11. Savarkar explains that "any convert of non-Hindu parentage to Hindutva can be a Hindu, if *bona fide*, he or she adopts our land as his or her country and marries a Hindu, thus coming to love our land as a real Fatherland, and adopts our culture and thus adores our land as the Punyabhu. The children of such a union as that would, other things being equal, be most emphatically Hindus." Savarkar, *Hindutva*, 130. The idea that the Hindus were a historical people like the descendants of Israel's tribes was evidenced by the fact that in 2019, 1,000 "descendants" of Lord Ram came from Madhya Pradesh and Rajasthan to Ayodhya to have a Ram temple (re)built on the site where he was born. "1,000 'Descendants' of Lord Ram Reach Ayodhya, Demand Temple at Disputed Site," *Indian Express*, September 9, 2019, https://indianexpress.com/article/india/1000-descendants-of-lord-ram-reach-ayodhya-demand-temple-at-disputed-site-5977994/.

12. For more detail on this founding moment, see the first chapter of Jaffrelot, *Hindu Nationalist Movement*.

13. M. S. Golwalkar, *We, or Our Nationhood Defined* (1938; repr., Nagpur: Bharat Prakashan, 1947).

14. Golwalkar, *We*, 59.

15. Golwalkar, 38.

16. Golwalkar, 56.

17. To borrow the title of a book by Walter Andersen and Shriddhar Damle, *The Brotherhood in Saffron: The Rashtriya Swayamsevak Sangh and Hindu Revivalism* (New Delhi: Vistaar, 1987).

18. Christophe Jaffrelot, "Hindu Nationalism: Strategic Syncretism in Ideology Building," *Indian Journal of Social Science* 5, no. 42 (August 1992): 594–617.

19. See Birth Centenary Celebration Committee, *Dharmaveer Dr. B. S. Moonje Commemoration Volume* (Nagpur: Birth Centenary Celebration Committee, 1972), 5–7. For further detail, see Christophe Jaffrelot, "Opposing Gandhi: Hindu Nationalism and Political Violence," in *Violence/Non-Violence: Some Hindu Perspectives*, ed. Denis Vidal, Gilles Tarabout, and Eric Meyer (Delhi: Manohar, 2003), 299–324.

20. This practice reflects a widespread physical inferiority complex. M. K. Gandhi related in his autobiography that as a child he secretly ate meat to compete with meat-eating friends in running, as advised by Hindu reformers who claimed that emulating the diet of the British was the best way to rival them. M. K. Gandhi, *Autobiography: The Story of My Experiments with Truth*, trans. Mahadev Desai (1927; repr., Ahmedabad: Navajivan Trust, 1995), 16–18.

21. Jean A. Curran, *Militant Hinduism in Indian Politics* (New York: Institute of Pacific Affairs, 1955), 14, 43.

22. For further detail, see Christophe Jaffrelot, "India: The Politics of (Re)conversion to Hinduism of Christian Aboriginals," in *Annual Review of the Sociology of Religion*, vol. 2, ed. Patrick Michel and Enzo Pace, (Leiden, Netherlands: Brill, 2011), 197–215.

23. For further detail, see Manjari Katju, *Vishva Hindu Parishad and Indian Politics* (Hyderabad: Orient Longman, 2003); and Christophe Jaffrelot, "The Vishva Hindu Parishad: A

Nationalist but Mimetic Attempt at Federating the Hindu Sects," in *Charisma and Canon. Essays on the Religious History of the Indian Subcontinent*, ed. V. Dalmia, A. Malinar, and M. Christof (Delhi: Oxford University Press, 2001), 388–411.

24. For further detail, see Christophe Jaffrelot, "Hindu Nationalism and the Social Welfare Strategy," in *Development, Civil Society and Faith-Based Organisations: Bridging the Sacred and the Secular*, ed. G. Clarke and M. Jennings (New York: Palgrave, 2008), 240–59.

25. Curran, *Militant Hinduism*, 11.

26. Christophe Jaffrelot, *The Sangh Parivar: A Reader* (New Delhi: Oxford University Press, 2005), 445.

27. Regarding the modus operandi of the Sangh Parivar and the central role played by the pracharak, see Walter Andersen and Shridhar Damle, *The RSS: A View to the Inside* (Delhi: Penguin, 2018).

28. His brother, Gopal Godse, claimed that Nathuram never left the RSS. Author interview with Gopal Godse, Delhi, November 10, 1990.

29. Jaffrelot, "Opposing Gandhi."

30. On the history of the Jana Sangh, see B. Graham, *Hindu Nationalism and Indian Politics: The Origin and Development of the Bharatiya Jana Sangh* (Cambridge: Cambridge University Press, 1990).

31. This concept introduced by Rajni Kothari in the 1960s refers to Congress's ability to dominate the Indian political sphere, relying on the legitimacy conferred on it by the independence movement, by finding (and renewing) its representatives among local notables and adjusting to trends in public opinion to the point that the party sometimes appeared to form its own opposition at the local level. Rajni Kothari, "The Congress 'System' in India," *Asian Survey* 4 no. 12 (December 1964): 1161–73.

32. By these terms, B. Graham refers to Congress members involved in associations promoting the use of Hindi, defense of the sacred cow, and revival of Ayurvedic medicine. B. Graham, "The Congress and Hindu Nationalism," in *The Indian National Congress—Centenary Hindsights*, ed. D. A. Low (Delhi: Oxford University Press, 1988), 174.

33. See Jaffrelot and Anil, *India's First Dictatorship: The Emergency, 1975–77* (London: Hurst, 2020).

34. Untitled, *Hindu Vishva* 14, no. 7–8 (March 1979): 92.

35. D. K. Jha and K. Jha, *Ayodhya: The Dark Night; the Secret History of Ram's Appearance in Babri Masjid* (New Delhi: HarperCollins, 2012).

36. S. Gopal, ed., *Anatomy of a Confrontation: The Babri Masjid—Ramjanmabhumi Issue* (New Delhi: Viking, 1990).

37. David Ludden, ed., *Making India Hindu: Religion, Community, and the Politics of Democracy in India*, (Delhi: Oxford University Press, 1996).

38. Christophe Jaffrelot, "The Hindu Nationalist Reinterpretation of Pilgrimage in India: The Limits of *Yatra* Politics," *Nations and Nationalism* 15, no. 1 (2009): 1–19.

39. "Report of the Liberhan Ayodhya Commission of Inquiry—Full Text," *The Hindu*, November 24, 2009, https://www.thehindu.com/news/Report-of-the-Liberhan-Ayodhya-Commission-of-Inquiry-Full-Text/article16894055.ece.

40. Interview with L. K. Advani in *Outlook*, October 25, 1999, 38.

41. Lal Krishna Advani, *Inaugural Address by Shri L. K. Advani, President Bharatiya Janata Party, National Executive Meeting, New Delhi: 11 & 12 April 1998* (New Delhi: BJP, 1998).

42. Space lacks for a full analysis of the BJP under the Vajpayee government. The interested reader can refer to Christophe Jaffrelot, "The Hindu Nationalists and Power," in *The Oxford Companion to Politics in India*, ed. N. G. Jayal and P. B. Mehta (Delhi: Oxford University Press, 2010), 205–18.

43. The primeval man whose sacrifice, according to the Rig Veda, gave birth to society in the form of the varna vyavastha.

44. D. Upadhyaya, *Integral Humanism* (New Delhi: Bharatiya Jana Sangh, 1965), 43.

45. Upadhyaya, *Integral Humanism*, 62.

46. Upper-caste Hindus have allegedly left India because quotas prevented them from joining medical colleges and other public institutions.

47. *The Organiser*, August 26, 1990, 15.

48. M.V. Kamath, "Is Shudra revolution in the offing?," *The Organiser*, May 1, 1994, 6.

49. Editorial, *The Organiser*, December 5, 1993, 7.

50. See the final chapter of Jaffrelot, *India's Silent Revolution*.

51. M. N. Srinivas, *Social Change in Modern India* (Hyderabad: Orient Longman, 2000), 6.

52. For further detail, see Jaffrelot, *Hindu Nationalist Movement*, 431. When a BJP Rajya Sabha member, J. K. Jain, decided to fast against V. P. Singh's decision, the party high command reprimanded him, and he had to terminate his hunger strike.

53. This emerges clearly from the BJP newsletter, *About Us* 7, no. 17 (September 3, 1990), 6–7, and interviews that some of its leaders gave the press. See L. K. Advani's interview in *Hindustan Times*, Sunday supplement, September 23, 1990, 2.

54. Interview in *Sunday*, January 26, 1997, 13. See Christophe Jaffrelot, "The Sangh Parivar between Sanskritization and Social Engineering," in *The BJP and the Compulsions of Politics in India Today*, ed. Thomas Blom Hansen and Christophe Jaffrelot (Delhi: Oxford University Press, 1998), 267–90.

55. For further detail and a regional analysis, see Jaffrelot, *India's Silent Revolution*, 532.

56. B.C. Dutta, "Extended Reservations Can Lead to Economic Destabilisation and Social Divide," *The Organiser*, June 18, 2006, 15, https://www.organiser.org/archives/dynamic/modulesc745.html?name=Content&pa=showpage&pid=135&page=29.

57. For more detail, see Jaffrelot, *India's Silent Revolution*.

58. See the analysis of German and Russian nationalisms in Liah Greenfeld, *Nationalism: Five Roads to Modernity* (Cambridge, MA: Harvard University Press, 1992).

59. Shah Bano had been the spouse, since 1932, of a lawyer from Indore who married for the second time in 1975 and separated from her according to Muslim customary law in 1978. Invoking section 125 of the Code of Criminal Procedure, she sued him and as a result established her right to alimony. When, in 1980, she demanded a review of her allowance, her former husband appealed to the Supreme Court, pleading that according to Shariat law, he was not obliged to continue payments to her after the *iddat* (a period of three months after the divorce). The Supreme Court dismissed the appeal on April 23, 1985, pointing out that section 125 of the Code of Criminal Procedure applied to people of all faiths and that the Quran itself required that a divorced wife should be paid an allowance.

Chapter 2

1. Pierre-André Taguieff, *L'Illusion populiste. Essai sur les démagogies de l'âge démocratique* (Paris: Flammarion, 2007), 9. While the trend of populism that has swept across Western countries is generally interpreted as a right-wing phenomenon because in both Europe and in the United States it feeds on xenophobia, Chantal Mouffe has analyzed Podemos and La France Insoumise as leftist populisms. See her interview, "Pour un populisme de gauche," *Le Monde*, April 20, 2016, http://www.lemonde.fr/idees/article/2016/04/20/chantal-mouffe-pour-un -populisme-de-gauche_4905460_3232.html#PP7jRtsWFjQqxuhd.99.

2. Ernesto Laclau, *On Populist Reason* (London: Verso, 2005), 18.

3. Laclau, *On Populist Reason*, 83. See also 96–98.

4. Partha Chatterjee, *I Am the People: Reflections on Popular Sovereignty Today* (New York: Columbia University Press, 2019).

5. Cas Mudde and Cristóbal Rovira Kaltwasser, *Populism: A Very Short Introduction* (New York: Oxford University Press, 2017), 6.

6. Edward Shils, *The Torment of Secrecy* (Melbourne: Heinemann, 1956), 98.

7. Margaret Canovan, *Populism* (New York: Harcourt Brace Jovanovich, 1981), 260.

8. Jan-Werner Müller, *What Is Populism?* (Philadelphia: University of Pennsylvania Press, 2016).

9. Pierre Ostiguy, "Populism: A Socio-Cultural Approach," in *The Oxford Handbook of Populism*, ed. Cristóbal Rovira Kaltwasser, Paul A. Taggart, Paulina Ochoa Espejo, and Pierre Ostiguy (Oxford: Oxford University Press, 2017), 74.

10. Ostiguy, "Populism," 74.

11. Gino Germani, *Authoritarianism, Fascism and National Populism* (New Brunswick, NJ: Transactions Books, 1978).

12. The political role of these two emotions, fear and anger, has recently been studied in detail: see Arjun Appadurai, *Fear of Small Numbers: An Essay on the Geography of Anger* (Durham, NC: Duke University Press, 2006; and Pankaj Mishra, *Age of Anger: A History of the Present* (London: Penguin, 2018). We will return to these idioms in detail below.

13. Christophe Jaffrelot and Louise Tillin, "Populism in India," in *The Oxford Handbook of Populism*, ed. Cristóbal Rovira Kaltwasser, Paul A. Taggart, Paulina Ochoa Espejo, and Pierre Ostiguy (Oxford: Oxford University Press, 2017), 179–94.

14. Nilanjan Mukhopadhyay, *Narendra Modi: The Man, the Times* (New Delhi: Tranquedar, 2013), 52.

15. M. V. Kamath and Kalindi Randeri, *Narendra Modi: The Architect of a Modern State* (New Delhi: Rupa, 2009), 17.

16. Cited in Mukhopadhyay, *Narendra Modi*, 102.

17. In the RSS a prant pracharak is in charge of a territory that covers an area at least as extensive as a state.

18. Kamath and Randeri, *Narendra Modi*, 22.

19. He published a biography of Inamdar in 2001 entitled *Jyoti Punj*.

20. Mukhopadhyay, *Narendra Modi*, 122; and Pravin Sheth, *Images of Transformation: Gujarat and Narendra Modi* (Ahmedabad: Team Spirit, 2007), 57.

21. Kamath and Randeri, *Narendra Modi*, 37.

22. Mukhopadhyay, *Narendra Modi*, 125.

23. Mukhopadhyay, 126.

24. Kamath and Randeri, *Narendra Modi*, 38.

25. K. Nag, *The NaMo Story: A Political Life* (New Delhi: Roli Books, 2013), 53.

26. Ornit Shani, *Communalism, Caste and Hindu Nationalism* (Cambridge: Cambridge University Press, 2007).

27. Cited in Shani, *Communalism, Caste and Hindu Nationalism*, 71.

28. Cited in Shani, 71–72.

29. Nag, *NaMo Story*, 60.

30. Mukhopadhyay, *Narendra Modi*, 147.

31. A. Yagnik and S. Sheth, *The Shaping of Modern Gujarat* (Delhi: Penguin, 2005), 266.

32. Mukhopadhyay, *Narendra Modi*, 202.

33. Mukhopadhyay, 202; and Nag, *NaMo Story*, 61.

34. Nag, *NaMo Story*, 62.

35. Sheth, *Images of Transformation*, 57.

36. Sheth, 64.

37. Sheth, 77–78.

38. Vinod Mehta, *Lucknow Boy: A Memoir* (New Delhi: Penguin, 2011), 209.

39. Cited in Kamath and Randeri, *Narendra Modi*, 82 (emphasis mine).

40. Cited in Kamath and Randeri, 83.

41. Only the human toll of the violence in Nellie, Assam, in 1983 is comparable in scale.

42. Regarding the 2002 Gujarat violence, one of the best sources remains the report by the Concerned Citizens Tribunal, published in 2002. This "tribunal" was composed of eight people, presided by none other than a retired chief justice of India's Supreme Court, Justice V. K. Krishna Iyer. Its members included Justice P. B. Sawant, a former Supreme Court justice; Justice Hosbet Suresh, a retired Mumbai High Court judge; K. G. Kannabiran, a lawyer and president of the People's Union for Civil Liberties; Aruna Roy, founder of the well-known NGO Mazdoor Kisan Shakti Sangathan; K. S. Subramanian, a retired senior police officer and former director general of police in Tripura; Ghanshyam Shah, professor of Jawaharlal Nehru University (JNU); and Tanika Sarkar, also a professor at JNU. The tribunal drafted its report on the basis of "2,094 oral and written testimonies, both individual and collective, from victim-survivors and also independent human rights groups, women's groups, NGOs and academics." Concerned Citizens Tribunal—Gujarat 2002, *Crime against Humanity*, vol. 2, *An Inquiry into the Carnage in Gujarat: Findings and Recommendations* (Mumbai: Citizens for Justice and Peace, 2002), 9, accessed May 12, 2020, http://www.sabrang.com/tribunal/tribunal2.pdf.

43. Concerned Citizens Tribunal—Gujarat 2002, *Crime against Humanity*, 12.

44. The reader interested in the violence of 2002 can refer to the following works: Siddarth Varadarajan, ed., *Gujarat: The Making of a Tragedy* (New Delhi: Penguin India, 2002); John Dayal, ed., *Gujarat 2002: Untold and Re-told Stories of the Hindutva Lab*, vol. 1 (New Delhi: Media House, 2003); Martha Nussbaum, *The Clash Within: Democracy, Religious Violence and India's Future* (Cambridge, MA: Harvard University Press, 2007); and Harsh Mander, *Cry, My Beloved Country: Reflections on the Gujarat Carnage 2002 and Its Aftermath* (Noida, India: Rainbow, 2004).

45. Parvis Ghassem-Fachandi, *Pogrom in Gujarat: Hindu Nationalism and Anti-Muslim Violence in India* (Princeton, NJ: Princeton University Press, 2012), 59. One month later, Narendra Modi reiterated this interpretation in a long interview with the *Times of India* in which he stated, "The attack on the Sabarmati Express" was "a deep-rooted conspiracy and a pre-planned, cold-blooded attack." S. Balakrishnan, "Peace Has Returned to Gujarat, Claims Modi," *Times of India*, March 29, 2002, http://timesofindia.indiatimes.com/city/ahmedabad/Peace-has-returned-to -Gujarat-claims-Modi/articleshow/5307572.cms. The idea that the attack was "pre-planned" has never been substantiated by the slightest piece of evidence.

46. Ghassem-Fachandi, *Pogrom in Gujarat,* 59.

47. "National Human Rights Commission, 'Suo motu case no 1150/6/2001–2002,' April 1, 2002," in *The Gujarat Carnage,* ed. A. A. Engineer (Hyderabad: Orient Longman, 2003), 258–93. See S. B. Lokhande, *New Delhi, Communal Violence, Forced Migration and the State: Gujarat since 2002* (Cambridge: Cambridge University Press, 2015).

48. Christophe Jaffrelot and Charlotte Thomas, "Facing Ghettoisation in 'Riot-City': Old Ahmedabad and Juhapura between Victimisation and Self-Help," in *Muslims in Indian Cities: Trajectories of Marginalization,* ed. L. Gayer and Christophe Jaffrelot (London: Hurst, 2012), 43–79.

49. Parvin Ghassem-Fachandi made these observations after walking through Ahmedabad on February 28. Ghassem-Fachandi, *Pogrom in Gujarat,* 37–41.

50. Concerned Citizens Tribunal—Gujarat 2002, *Crime against Humanity,* 26.

51. In his speech against Modi given in Rajkot during the campaign, Jafri "urged people not to vote for him because he was an RSS man, and to vote for the Congress instead." Concerned Citizens Tribunal—Gujarat 2002, *Crime against Humanity,* 32.

52. These figures were communicated in 2002 by the additional director general of police of Gujarat, R. B. Sreekumar, to the chief election commissioner, J. M. Lyngdoh, who concluded from them that 154 out of the state's 182 constituencies had experienced communal violence. Ashish Khetan, "The Truth about the Godhra SIT Report," *Tehelka,* February 12, 2011, 40.

53. Yagnik and Sheth, *Shaping of Modern Gujarat,* 282.

54. Among the NGOs involved, in addition to Citizens for Justice and Peace (founded in April 2002 by, among others, Testa Setalvad and Javed Anand), and by far the most active (see Sabrang, https://sabrangindia.in), Human Rights Watch also played an important role. See Human Rights Watch, *"We Have No Order to Save You": State Participation and Complicity in Communal Violence in Gujarat,* vol. 14, no. 3 (C) (April 2003), http://www.hrw.org/reports /2002/india/India0402-03.htm. See also Human Rights Watch, *Compounding Injustice. The Government's Failure to Redress Massacres in Gujarat,* vol. 15, no. 3 (C) (July 2003), http://www .hrw.org/reports/2003/india0703/India0703full.pdf.

55. "PM Assures Economic Revival Package for State," *Economic Times* (Ahmedabad ed.), April 5, 2002, 1.

56. Kamath and Randeri, *Narendra Modi,* 141–43.

57. Shankkar Aiyar, "How Vajpayee Ended Up as the Hindutva Choir Boy," *India Today,* April 19, 2002, https://www.indiatoday.in/magazine/cover-story/story/20020429-how -vajpayee-ended-up-as-the-hindutva-choir-boy-795607-2002-04-29.

58. Vinod K. Jose, "The Emperor Uncrowned," *The Caravan,* March 1, 2012, http:// caravanmagazine.in/reportage/emperor-uncrowned?page=0,9.

59. This mechanism explains the correlation that Steven Wilkinson has noted between the election calendar and the cycle of riots. Steven Wilkinson, *Votes and Violence: Electoral Competition and Ethnic Riots in India* (Cambridge: Cambridge University Press, 2004).

60. Ghanshyam Shah, "Contestation and Negotiations: Hindutva Sentiments and Temporal Interests in Gujarat Elections," *Economic and Political Weekly*, November 30, 2002, 4838–43.

61. Kamath and Randeri, *Narendra Modi*, 138.

62. "Modi Flies Flag of Gujarat Pride in Open Letter," *The Telegraph*, July 20, 2002, 8, https://www.telegraphindia.com/india/modi-flies-flag-of-gujarat-pride-in-open-letter/cid/884334.

63. See, for instance, Arafaat A. Valiani, *Militant Publics in India: Physical Culture and Violence in the Making of a Modern Polity* (New York: Palgrave/Macmillan, 2011), 183–84.

64. "Sena Refuses to Bestow Hindu Hriday Samrat Title to Modi," *Indian Express*, July 13, 2013, http://www.indianexpress.com/news/sena-refuses-to-bestow-hindu-hriday-samrat-title-on-modi/1141340/.

65. Sheela Bhatt, "Gujarat IB Officers Transferred for Putting Modi's Controversial Speech on Record," Rediff.com, September 18, 2002, http://www.rediff.com/news/2002/sep/18guj2.htm.

66. Sanjay Basak, "Modi to Reform Gujarat Madrasas," *Asian Age* (Ahmedabad ed.), June 14, 2002, 2.

67. "Pakistan Responsible for Gujarat Unrest: Modi," *Times of India* (Ahmedabad ed.), June 9, 2002, 4.

68. Darshan Desai, "That Missing Healing Touch," *Outlook*, October 14, 2002, https://www.outlookindia.com/magazine/story/that-missing-healing-touch/217544.

69. Cited in Ward Berenschot, *Riot Politics: Hindu-Muslim Violence and the Indian State* (London: Hurst, 2011), 158.

70. S. Kumar, "Gujarat Assembly Elections 2002: Analysing the Verdict," *Economic and Political Weekly*, January 25, 2003, 275.

71. Box 2 in this article: S. Dasgupta, "Opinion Poll: Conclusive Victory for BJP, Gujarat Chief Minister Narendra Modi," *India Today*, December 16, 2002, 27, https://www.indiatoday.in/magazine/nation/story/20021216-opinion-poll-conclusive-victory-for-bjp-gujarat-chief-minister-narendra-modi-793890-2002-12-16.

72. When one of his biographers—and probably the best—asked him where his new ideas came from, he replied, "It is probably a god-gifted ability." Mukhopadhyay, *Narendra Modi*, 359. Modi has also paid close attention to his dress since he was a young man. Mukhopadhyay, 31.

73. *Times of India* (Ahmedabad ed.), December 11, 2007.

74. "It's Business with Navratri Pleasure at Gujarat Business Meet," Siliconindia.com, September 22, 2003, https://www.siliconindia.com/shownews/Its_business_with_Navratri_pleasure_at_Gujarat_business_meet-nid-20849-cid-3.html.

75. Mahesh Langa, "Gujarat Vibrancy Costs Rs 25 Cr," *Tehelka*, October 1, 2005, http://archive.tehelka.com/story_main14.asp?filename=Ne100105Gujarats_vibrancy.asp.

76. "Modi: Sadbhavana Mission Will End Vote Bank Politics," YouTube video posted by NDTV, accessed November 21, 2013, http://www.youtube.com/watch?v=z5MT91Gckfo.

77. Narendra Modi, "Sadbhavana Mission: A Touching People's Movement," accessed November 21, 2013, http://www.narendramodi.in/sadbhavana-mission-a-touching-people's-movement.

78. See the quantitative analysis described in Christophe Jaffrelot and Jean-Thomas Martelli, "Reading PM Modi, through His Speeches," *Indian Express*, August 15, 2017, https:// indianexpress.com/article/explained/reading-pm-modi-through-his-speeches-independence -day-4796963/.

79. Kapil Dave, "Unsure of 3 D Effect Will Work, Modi to Hit the Road," *Times of India* (Ahmedabad ed.), November 25, 2012, 1, https://timesofindia.indiatimes.com/gujarat-assembly -elections/Unsure-3D-effect-will-work-Narendra-Modi-to-hit-the-road/articleshow/17356410 .cms. Avinash Nair, "And They Were 26: Modi Scripts His 'Victory Sequel' in 3D Now," *Indian Express* (Ahmedabad ed.), December 3, 2012, 1, http://archive.indianexpress.com/news/and -then-there-were-26-modi-scripts-his-gujarat—victory-sequel—in-3d-now/1039492/.

80. Mukhopadhyay, *Narendra Modi*, 281.

81. Mukhopadhyay, 282.

82. B. Prabhakar, "How an American Lobbying Company Apco Worldwide Markets Narendra Modi to the World," *Economic Times*, December 9, 2012, https://economictimes .indiatimes.com/news/company/corporate-trends/how-an-american-lobbying-company -apco-worldwide-markets-narendra-modi-to-the-world/articleshow/17537402.cms?utm _source=contentofinterest&utm_medium=text&utm_campaign=cpps; S. Gatade, "APCO to Kotler—The Artificial Glossing of Modi's Image," NewsClick, January 17, 2019, https://www .newsclick.in/apco-kotler-artificial-glossing-modis-image; and S. Kasli, "Mechanics of Narendra Modi's PR Agency: APCO Worldwide—Orchestrating Our Future," Beyond Headlines, June 26, 2013, https://beyondheadlines.in/2013/06/mechanics-of-narendra-modis-pr-agency -apco-worldwide-orchestrating-our-future/.

83. Aou Esthose Suresh, "The Modi Machine: Makeover Gurus," *Indian Express*, October 20, 2013, http://www.indianexpress.com/story-print/1184809/.

84. On the professionalization of political consultants in India and the pioneering role of Prashant Kishor in particular, see Amogh Sharma, "The Backstage of Democracy: Exploring the Professionalisation of Politics in India" (PhD diss., Oxford University, 2020), 244.

85. Harit Mehta, "New Team Modi," *Times of India* (Ahmedabad ed.), September 23, 2012, 1.

86. Kishor moreover went to Congress shortly thereafter, before going to work for another party in 2018, as befits an image maker.

87. Sunil Khilnani, "Finely Slicing the Electorate: With Clever Use of Technology, Narendra Modi Plans to Customise Messages to Voters," *Times of India*, May 24, 2013, http://articles .timesofindia.indiatimes.com/2013-05-24/edit-page/39476042_1_personal-data-campaigns -rajesh-jain.

88. The former intelligence officer B. Raman wrote in 2012, "The style of the online blitzkrieg adopted by his die-hard followers in India and abroad reminiscent of the methods of the Nazi stormtroopers, continues to add to the disquiet." B. Raman, "Mr. Modi's Problem," OutlookIndia .com, September 3, 2012, http://www.outlookindia.com/article.aspx?282128. Elsewhere, he criticized the psychological warfare: "PSYWAR Methods Used by These Pro-Namo Elements Whom I Have Been Referring to as the NaMo Brigade." B. Raman, "A Wake Up Call," OutlookIndia .com, June 4, 2012, http://www.outlookindia.com/article.aspx?281135.

89. "Modi Pits Rupala against Keshubhai for BJP Chief's Post," *Times of India* (Ahmedabad ed.), October 12, 2006, 4.

90. Mukhopadhyay, *Narendra Modi*, 305.

91. "Sangh Farmers' Body Says Modi Must Go," *Times of India* (Ahmedabad ed.), May 18, 2004, http://articles.timesofindia.indiatimes.com/2004-05-18/india/28339993_1_cm-narendra -modi-sangh-parivar-maganbhai-patel.

92. Cited in Mukhopadhyay, *Narendra Modi*, 303.

93. Mukhopadhyay, 307. Manmohan Vaidya is the son of a very senior RSS leader, M. G. Vaidya, who has been publicly critical of Narendra Modi. See Sanjay Singh, "Vaidya vs Vaidya: How the BJP Is Caught in a Bind," Firstpost.com, November 12, 2012, http://www.firstpost.com/politics/vaidya -vs-vaidya-how-the-bjp-is-caught-in-a-bind-522986.html?utm_source=ref_article.

94. Mukhopadhyay, *Narendra Modi*, 53.

95. P. Dave, "RSS Miffed over Rifts in Gujarat BJP," Rediff.com, October 23, 2007, https:// www.rediff.com/news/report/gujpoll/20071023.htm.

96. Pravin Maniar, "RSS to Keep Away from Poll Work," interview by Tina Parekh, *DNA* (Ahmedabad ed.), November 25, 2007, 1.

97. S. Singh, "Vaidya vs Vaidya."

98. On Modi's recourse to a wholesale propaganda apparatus in the 2009 elections, see Ghanshyam Shah, "Goebbel's Propaganda and Governance: The 2009 Lok Sabha Elections in Gujarat," in *India's 2009 Elections: Coalition Politics, Party Competition and Congress Continuity*, ed. Paul Wallace and Ramashray Roy (New Delhi: Sage, 2011), 167–91.

99. "'Techno-Savvy' Modi to Welcome Narmada-Sabarmati Sangam," *Asian Age*, August 28, 2002, 9.

100. Many of the press photographs taken in this context show Narendra Modi on stage with Bohras. See, for instance, "Now, Muslims 'in' Modi's Gujaratis," *DNA* (Ahmedabad ed.), September 18, 2011, 1, https://www.dnaindia.com/india/report-now-muslims-in-narendra-modi-s -gujaratis-1588520.

101. "Wary of Jinnah Fiasco, Modi Refuses Skull Cap," *Hindustan Times* (New Delhi), September 20, 2011, 11, https://www.hindustantimes.com/india/wary-of-jinnah-fiasco-modi -refuses-skull-cap/story-S4ZyD3xGPLxlcD28Ls6BRJ.html.

102. Ajay Umat, "Official Iftars in Gujarat an All-Veg Affair," *Times of India*, August 15, 2012, http://articles.timesofindia.indiatimes.com/2012-08-15/ahmedabad/33216269_1_iftar-jain -monk-vegetarian-outlet.

103. See, for instance, his speech at Fergusson College, "Hon. Chief Minister's Speech at Fergusson College, Pune," July 14, 2013, http://www.narendramodi.in/shri-narendra-modi -speech-at-fergusson-college-pune/.

104. In 2012, the Gujarati government made another move affecting certain linguistic and religious minorities: the column for Sindhi, Tamil, Marathi, and Urdu medium graduates was left out in the form for the Teacher Eligibility Test. As a result, these graduates who wanted to teach in these languages could not apply to the upper primary teacher posts. See "No Mention of Urdu, 3 Other Languages in Guj Application Form," *Indian Express* (Ahmedabad ed.), June 4, 2012, 5, http://archive.indianexpress.com/news/no-mention-of-urdu-3-other-languages-in-guj -application-form/957596/.

105. "Can't Give Aid to Religious Places Damaged in Riots," *DNA* (Ahmedabad ed.), January 25, 2011, 1.

106. Christophe Jaffrelot, "Narendra Modi between Hindutva and Subnationalism: The Gujarati *Asmita* of a Hindu Hriday Samrat," *India Review* 15, no. 2 (2016): 196–217.

107. A. M. Shah, Pravin J. Patel, and Lancy Lobo, "A Heady Mix: Gujarati and Hindu Pride," *Economic and Political Weekly*, February 23, 2008, 21.

108. Shah, Patel, and Lobo, "Heady Mix," 21.

109. "Gujarat: Sardar Patel Statue to Be Twice the Size of Statue of Liberty," CNN-IBN, October 30, 2010, http://m.ibnlive.com/news/gujarat-sardar-patel-statue-to-be-twice-the-size -of-statue-of-liberty/431317-3-238.html.

110. "The Statue of Unity Cost Rs 2,989 Crore: Here's What Else That Money Could Have Bought," The Wire, October 31, 2018, https://thewire.in/politics/statue-of-unity-cost-narendra -modi.

111. Narendra Modi probably played the victim all the more easily as the United States and the European Union had canceled his visa and denied a new one in the wake of the pogrom.

112. Ajay Singh, "Modi on Mahatma, Economy and Strengths of India," GovernanceNow .com, September 17, 2013, http://www.governancenow.com/news/regular-story/modi -mahatma-economy-and-strengths-india.

113. Cited in "Modi Mocks PM as 'Maun Mohan Singh,'" *Indian Express* (Ahmedabad ed.), October 30, 2012, 1, https://indianexpress.com/article/cities/ahmedabad/in-himachal-modi -mocks-pm-calls-him-maun-mohan/.

114. "Modi Addresses Farmers, Blames Centre for Delay in Narmada," *Indian Express*, May 6, 2013, 4, https://indianexpress.com/article/cities/ahmedabad/modi-addresses-farmers-blames -centre-for-delay-in-narmada-gates/. The 16-meter-tall gates that Narendra Modi wanted to install would increase the reservoir's capacity from 1.27 to 4.75 million acre-feet by taking the height of the dam from 121.92 to 138.62 meters.

115. Cited in "Modi Attacks Cong on 2G, Coalgate," *Times of India* (Ahmedabad ed.), September 12, 2012, 5, https://timesofindia.indiatimes.com/city/ahmedabad/Narendra-Modi -attacks-Cong-on-2G-Coalgate/articleshow/16360226.cms.

116. "'UPA Released More Funds to Gujarat than NDA Govt,'" *Indian Express* (Ahmedabad ed.), October 6, 2010, 5.

117. "Modi Slams Cong for Ad Goof-up," *Indian Express* (Ahmedabad ed.), November 30, 2012, 3, http://archive.indianexpress.com/news/in-another-3d-address-narendra-modi-slams -cong-for-ad-goofup/1038445/.

118. "In Another 3-D Address, Narendra Modi Slams Cong for Ad Goof-Up," *Indian Express*, November 30, 2012, http://archive.indianexpress.com/news/in-another-3d-address-narendra -modi-slams-cong-for-ad-goofup/1038445/.

119. "Modi Says It Loud and Clear: It's Congress vs CM," *Indian Express* (Ahmedabad ed.), December 2, 2012, 1, http://archive.indianexpress.com/news/modi-says-it-loud-and-clear-it-s -congress-vs-cm/1039261/.

120. Cited in Mukhopadhyay, *Narendra Modi*, 293.

121. "Modi Slams Malik for Babri Comments," *Ahmedabad Mirror*, December 16, 2012, 4, https://ahmedabadmirror.indiatimes.com/ahmedabad/cover-story/modi-slams-malik-for -babri-comments/articleshow/36063196.cms.

122. The transcript of this interview was reproduced in the *Indian Express* in 2013. "'The Riots Took Place When I Was in Power, So I Know I Can't Detach Myself from Them,'" *Indian Express*,

September 17, 2013, http://m.indianexpress.com/news/the-riots-took-place-when-i-was-in
-power-so-i-know-i-cant-detach-myself-from-them/1170181/.

123. Pravin Sheth devotes an appendix in his book to examples of Narendra Modi's offensive
language. Sheth, *Images of Transformation*, 249.

124. See "Narendra Modi Dares 'Delhi Sultanate' on Advertisement Issue," *DNA*, June 30,
2010, https://www.dnaindia.com/india/report-narendra-modi-dares-delhi-sultanate-on
-advertisement-issue-1403297.

125. I. Hirway, Neha Shah, and Rajeev Sharma, "Political Economy of Subsidies and Incentives to Industries in Gujarat," in *Growth or Development: Which Way Is Gujarat Going?*, ed.
I. Hirway, A. Shah, and G. Shah (New Delhi: Oxford University Press, 2014), 149.

126. Archana Dholakia and Ravindra Dholakia, "Policy Reform in Economic Sectors," in *The
Making of Miracles in Indian States: Andhra Pradesh, Bihar and Gujarat*, ed. A. Panagariya and
M. G. Rao (New Delhi: Oxford University Press, 2015), 251–52.

127. Bibek Debroy, *Gujarat: Governance for Growth and Development* (New Delhi: Academic
Foundation, 2012), 71.

128. Government of Gujarat, *Industrial Policy—2009*, January 2009, 3, http://www.ic.gujarat
.gov.in/pdf/industrial-policy-2009-at-a-glance.pdf.

129. Government of Gujarat, *Industrial Policy—2009*, 13; and Hirway, Shah, and Sharma,
"Political Economy of Subsidies," 161–63.

130. Hirway, Shah, and Sharma, 156.

131. Dholakia and Dholakia, "Policy Reform," 254. At that time, the government had already
allocated more than 8,000 hectares to twenty-seven SEZs. Manshi Asher, "Gujarat and Punjab:
The Entrepreneurs Paradise and the Land of the Farmer," in *Power, Policy, and Protest: The Politics of India's Special Economic Zones*, ed. R. Jenkins, L. Kennedy and P. Mukhopadhyay (Oxford:
Oxford University Press, 2014), 140.

132. For more details, see Christophe Jaffrelot, "Business-Friendly Gujarat under Narendra
Modi—the Implications of a New Political Economy," in *Business and Politics in India*, ed. Christophe Jaffrelot, Atul Kohli, and Kanta Murali (New York: Oxford University Press, 2019),
211–33.

133. Comptroller and Auditor General of India, "Report No. 2 of 2013 Government of
Gujarat—Report of the Comptroller and Auditor General of India on Revenue Receipts," ac-
cessed September 21, 2020, http://saiindia.gov.in/english/home/Our_Products/Audit_Report
/Government_Wise/state_audit/recent_reports/Gujarat/2012/Report_2/Overview.pdf.

134. "Investors Back Out, Vibrant Plans Go Awry," *Times of India*, March 4, 2008, 1.

135. Nirendra Dev, *Modi to Moditva* (New Delhi: Manas, 2012), 157.

136. ISED Small Enterprise Observatory, *Gujarat Micro, Small and Medium Enterprises Report 2013* (Cochin, India: Institute of Small Enterprise and Development, 2013), 39.

137. The document presenting Gujarat's 2009 industrial policy read: "Though the state has
been witnessing very high levels of industrial activity, employment generation activities have
not kept pace with the same." Government of Gujarat, *Industrial Policy—2009*, 10.

138. The government then officially acknowledged that Gujarat had "612,000 educated-
unemployed persons." Avinash Nair, "Over 13.95 Lakh New Jobs in Gujarat since July 2011," *Indian Express*, April 11, 2017. According to the All India Council for Technical Education, engineers made up a large portion of this group. H. Dave, "More than 80% Engineers Are without

Jobs," *Ahmedabad Mirror*, March 28, 2017, http://ahmedabadmirror.indiatimes.com /ahmedabad/cover-story/more-than-80-engineers-are-without-jobs/articleshow/57880536 .cms?prtpage=1.

139. For further detail and an analysis of the impact of the job problem on the Patel movement, see Christophe Jaffrelot, "Quota for Patels? The Neo-middleclass Syndrome and the (Partial) Return of Caste Politics in Gujarat," *Studies in Indian Politics* 4, no. 2 (2016): 1–15.

140. National Sample Survey Office, *Key Indicators of Employment and Unemployment in India*, National Sample Survey, 2011, 102, accessed September 21, 2020, http://www .indiaenvironmentportal.org.in/files/file/key%20indicators%20of%20employment%20 and%20unemployment%20India%202011-12.pdf.

141. Reserve Bank of India, *State Finances: A Study of Budgets*, accessed February 4, 2018, https://www.rbi.org.in/scripts/PublicationsView.aspx?id=14834.

142. Reserve Bank of India, *State Finances*.

143. For further detail, see Christophe Jaffrelot, "What Gujarat Model?—Growth without Development and with Socio-political Polarisation," *South Asia: Journal of South Asian Studies* 38, no. 4 (2015): 820–38.

144. Note that in 2005 Gurajat ranked just behind Delhi for "grand corruption" but ahead of all the other states (except Himachal Pradesh and Kerala) in terms of "petty corruption"— something voters (who were not aware of "grand corruption") greatly appreciated. Jennifer Bussell, *Corruption and Reform in India* (Cambridge: Cambridge University Press, 2013), 43, 107, 188.

145. On the use of emotions in Indian politics in a comparative and historical perspective, see A. Blom and S. Tawa Lama-Rewal, eds., *Emotions, Mobilisations and South Asian Politics* (London: Routledge, 2020).

146. This common assumption has been suggested by Suzanne and Lloyd Rudolph, in particular. The first line of the first chapter of their magnum opus, *In Pursuit of Lakshmi*, reads: "The most striking feature of Indian politics is its persistent centrism." L. Rudolph and S. Hoeber Rudolph, *In Pursuit of Lakshmi: The Political Economy of the Indian State* (Hyderabad: Orient Longman, 1987), 19.

147. Cited in E. San Juan Jr., "Orientations of Max Weber's Concept of Charisma," *Centennial Review* 11, no. 2 (Spring 1967): 270–85, https://www.jstor.org/stable/23738015.

148. Nalin Mehta, "Ashis Nandy vs. the State of Gujarat: Authoritarian Developmentalism, Democracy and the Politics of Narendra Modi," in *Gujarat beyond Gandhi: Identity, Society and Conflict*, ed. Nalin Mehta and Mona Mehta (London: Routledge, 2011), 122.

149. S. Prasannarajan, "Narendra Modi, Master Divider," *India Today*, January 6, 2003, 6, https://www.indiatoday.in/magazine/cover-story/story/20030106-newsmaker-2002-with -gujarat-riots-narendra-modi-storms-the-mind-and-heart-of-india-793638-2003-01-06.

150. Regarding how a similar situation played out in the United States, see David L. Altheide, *Creating Fear: News and the Construction of Crisis* (Hawthorne, NY: Aldine de Gruyter, 2002).

151. See the special issue titled "Fear: Its Political Use and Abuse," in *Social Research* 71, no. 4, http://www.jstor.org/stable/40971977. Regarding how victims of the phenomenon perceive it, see Haleh Afshar, "The Politics of Fear: What Does It Mean to Those Who Are Otherized and Feared?" *Ethnic and Racial Studies* 36, no. 1 (2013): 9–27.

152. Srinath Jagannathan, Rajnish Rai, and Christophe Jaffrelot, "Fear and Violence as Organizational Strategies: The Possibility of a Derridean Lens to Analyze Extra-judicial Police Violence," *Journal of Business Ethics* (October 2020), https://doi.org/10.1007/s10551-020-04655-6.

153. 223 "Kill-Modi Plot Falls Flat," *Times of India* (Ahmedabad ed.), July 24, 2009, 1.

154. Mukul Sinha, "Countless Encounters: Death in Uniform," *Elaan*, no. 3, October 2009, 1, http://elaanmonthly.blogspot.fr/2009_10_01_archive.html.

155. Satish Jha, "Sadiq Jamal Encounter: 7 Years on CBI yet to Complete Probe, Two Cops Seek Discharge," *Deccan Herald*, August 7, 2020, https://www.deccanherald.com/national/sadiq-jamal-encounter-7-years-on-cbi-yet-to-complete-probe-two-cops-seek-discharge-870734.html.

156. Manas Dasgupta, "Ishrat Jahan Killing also a Fake Encounter: Probe Report," *The Hindu*, September 8, 2009, http://www.hindu.com/2009/09/08/stories/2009090856670100.htm.

157. "DG Vanzara: All You Need to Know about Gujarat's Former 'Supercop,'" FirstPost.com, September 3, 2013, http://www.firstpost.com/politics/dg-vanzara-all-you-need-to-know-about-gujarats-former-supercop-1082183.html.

158. "The Journalist Who Cracked Gujarat Fake Encounter Case," Rediff.com, April 25, 2007, http://www.rediff.com/news/2007/apr/25spec.htm.

159. "SC Orders Probe into 21 'Fake' Encounters in Guj," *Times of India* (Ahmedabad ed.), January 26, 2012, 1.

160. S. Jagannathan and Rajnish K. Rai, "Organisational Wrongs, Moral Anger and the Temporality of Crisis," *Journal of Business Ethics* 141, no. 4 (2016): 709–30; and S. Jagannathan and Rajnish K. Rai, "Organizing Sovereign Power: Police and the Performance of Bare Bodies," *Organization* 22, no. 6 (2015): 810–83.

161. A. Yadav, "Gujarat's Shame," *Tehelka*, July 24, 2010, http://old.tehelka.com/gujarats-shame/.

162. By mentioning the names of Gandhi and Patel, Modi hijacked the Congress's classical references and, especially, cast himself as heir to the two most prestigious figures of Gujarat, the state he purports to stand for.

163. See Jaffrelot and Thomas, "Facing Ghettoisation."

164. "Modi Pats Himself," *Indian Express* (Ahmedabad ed.), October 9, 2012, 4.

165. Satish Jha, "Modi Calls Patel 'Ahmedmian,' Says His Denial Sounds Fishy," *Indian Express* (Ahmedabad ed.), December 3, 2012, 5, http://archive.indianexpress.com/news/narendra-modi-calls-patel—ahmedmian—says-his-denial-sounds—fishy-/1039443/.

166. Harinder Baweja, "Modi Selects His Side, Rejects Muslim Candidates," *Hindustan Times*, December 10, 2012, http://www.hindustantimes.com/StoryPage/Print/970716.aspx.

167. The Congress Party's disorganization also contributed, but examination of this aspect would take us too far off the topic.

168. Among them are such subgroups as the Ismailis and the Bohras, both very powerful in Gujarat, whose relationship with the Sunni majority is complicated and on the contrary shows affinities with the BJP.

169. Minna Saavala, *Middle-Class Moralities: Everyday Struggle over Belonging and Prestige in India* (Hyderabad: Orient BlackSwan, 2010), 156.

170. Sheth, *Images of Transformation*, 20.

171. "Poll-Bound Modi Banks on 'Neo-middle Class," *Times of India* (Ahmedabad ed.), December 4, 2012, 1, https://timesofindia.indiatimes.com/gujarat-assembly-elections/Poll-bound-Modi-banks-on-neo-middle-class/articleshow/17472268.cms.

172. Maulik Pathak and Sahil Makkar, "Narendra Modi Seeks Support of 'Neo-middle-class' Voters," *Mint* (Bangalore ed.), December 4, 2012, 3, https://www.livemint.com/Politics/9fxiMtc1YhSKsJtNnPVbRM/Narendra-Modi-seeks-support-of-neo-middleclass-voters.html.

173. Gayer and Jaffrelot, *Muslims in Indian Cities*.

174. Cited in Sheth, *Images of Transformation*, 203.

175. Swapan Dasgupta, "Modi, Inept Pragmatist," *Indian Express*, November 24, 2007, http://www.indianexpress.com/news/modi-inept-pragmatist/242902/. Nirendra Dev considers that "Modi functions like a modern day CEO laying emphasis on the outcome and often allegedly putting the rules and normal norms in the backburner." Dev, *Modi to Moditva*, 169.

176. Cass Mudde, "Populism: An Ideational Approach," in *The Oxford Handbook of Populism*, ed. R. Kaltwasser, P. Taggart, P. Ochoa Espejo, and P. Ostiguy (Oxford: Oxford University Press, 2017), 29.

177. Front-page articles of the *Times of India* (Ahmedabad ed.), November 24, 25, and 26, 2007. See R. Sharma, "Young Modi Wanted Crocodile as a Pet," *Times of India*, November 24, 2007, http://timesofindia.indiatimes.com/articleshow/2566261.cms?utm_source=contentofinterest&utm_medium=text&utm_campaign=cppst; and R. Sharma, "'I Can Digest All Kinds of Poison,'" *Times of India* (Ahmedabad ed.), November 25, 2007, 1.

178. Ostiguy, "Populism," 84.

179. The diversity of styles—including dress—that Modi tended to adopt is also remarkable. It has prompted Nalin Mehta to describe him at once as a "sex symbol" and "part folk-hero, part superstar." Mehta, "Ashis Nandy," 122.

180. Christophe Jaffrelot, "Quota for Patels? The Neo-middle class Syndrome and the (Partial) Return of Caste Politics in Gujarat," *Studies in Indian Politics* 4, no. 2 (2016): 1–15.

181. This paragraph draws from Christophe Jaffrelot, "Refining the Moderation Thesis: Two Religious Parties and Indian Democracy; the Jana Sangh and the BJP between Hindutva Radicalism and Coalition Politics," *Democratization* 20, no. 5 (2013): 876–94.

182. Jillian Schwedler, *Faith in Moderation: Islamist Parties in Jordan and Yemen* (Cambridge: Cambridge University Press, 2006).

183. Robert Michels, *A Sociological Study of the Oligarchical Tendencies of Modern Democracy* (1915; repr., New York: Free Press, 1962), 333–41; and Joseph Schumpeter, *Capitalism, Socialism, and Democracy* (1950; repr., New York: Harper Perennial, 1975), 283.

184. Janine Clark, "The Conditions of Islamist Moderation: Unpacking Cross-Ideological Cooperation in Jordan," *International Journal of Middle East Studies* 38, no. 4: 539–60.

185. Irfan Ahmed, *Islamism and Democracy in India: The Transformation of Jamaat-e-Islami* (New Delhi: Permanent Black, 2010).

186. Yagnik and Sheth, *Shaping of Modern Gujarat*, 40.

187. Yagnik and Sheth, 47.

188. Regarding this and the ambivalence of Gujarat's native son Mahatma Gandhi, in this regard, see Christophe Jaffrelot, "The Congress in Gujarat (1917–1969): Conservative Face of a Progressive Party," *Studies in Indian Politics* 5, no. 2 (November 2017): 248–61.

189. According to Parvis Ghassem-Fachandi, in Gujarat, "the national border with Pakistan is a barrier that generates psycho-geographical effects." Ghassem-Fachandi, *Pogrom in Gujarat*, 132.

190. Ganesh Devy points out that in Gujarat, "you do not become a bad man in Gujarat if you hate Muslims, you are normal. Decent people hate Muslims." Ganesh Devy, "Hating Muslims Is a Natural Thing in Gujarat," *Tehelka*, May 20, 2006, http://archive.tehelka.com/story _main18.asp?filename=Ne052006view_point_CS.asp.

191. Jaffrelot and Thomas, "Facing Ghettoisation."

Chapter 3

1. At a time when no BJP leader had yet openly embraced the "Hindu nationalist" label, in 2013, Narendra Modi gave an interview in which he said: "I am nationalist. I am patriotic. Nothing is wrong. I am born Hindu. Nothing is wrong. So I'm a Hindu nationalist." See Deepshika Ghosh, "Narendra Modi's 'Hindu Nationalist' Posters Should Be Banned, Says Samajwadi Party," NDTV.com, July 24, 2013, http://www.ndtv.com/article/india/narendra-modi-s-hindu -nationalist-posters-should-be-banned-says-samajwadi-party-396494.

2. A source familiar with the case considers that the account given is a web of lies, but what matters most here is the impact it had on public opinion.

3. Prerana Thakurdesai, "How the Case Was Cracked," *India Today*, October 16, 2006, 26, https://www.indiatoday.in/magazine/cover-story/story/20061016-how-2006-mumbai-serial -blast-case-was-cracked-782208-2006-10-16.

4. The police implicated Indian Muslims as well in the 2008 Mumbai attacks, but as individuals, not as members of an Islamic organization. Lata Jagtiani, *Mumbai Terror Attacks* (New Delhi: Rupa, 2009), 243, 246–51.

5. Cited in Yoginder Sikand, "Islamist Assertion in Contemporary India: The Case of the Students Islamic Movement of India," *Journal of Muslim Minority Affairs* 23, no. 2 (October 2003): 343. See also R. Upadhyay, "Students Islamic Movement of India (SIMI)," South Asia Analysis Group, Paper 825, October 30, 2003.

6. Animesh Roul, "Students Islamic Movement of India: A Profile," *Terrorism Monitor* 4, no. 7 (April 6, 2006): 101–20.

7. Irfan Ahmad points out—citing the SIMI's action plan of 1991—that by jihad, the group meant "killing the enemy." Irfan Ahmad, *Islamism and Democracy in India: The Transformation of Jamaat-e-Islami* (New Delhi: Permanent Black, 2010), 175.

8. Cited in Ahmad, *Islamism and Democracy*, 164.

9. See an excerpt of the message from the Indian Mujahideen claiming the 2008 Ahmedabad attack appended to my article "La dialectique des terrorismes en Inde depuis 2001: La 'main de l'étranger,' les islamistes et les nationalistes hindous," *Critique internationale* 2, no. 47 (2010): 93–110, https://www.cairn.info/revue-critique-internationale-2010-2-page-93.htm.

10. Bruce Stokes, Dorothy Manevich, and Hanyu Chwe, "Indians Satisfied with Country's Direction but Worry about Crime, Terrorism," Pew Research Center (website), November 15, 2017, http://www.pewglobal.org/2017/11/15/indians-satisfied-with-countrys-direction-but -worry-about-crime-terrorism/.

11. Stokes, Manevich, and Chwe, "Indians Satisfied."

12. Subramanian Swamy, *Hindus under Siege: The Way Out* (New Delhi: Har-Anand, 2006), 28 (emphasis in the original).

13. Swamy, *Hindus under Siege*, 37 (emphasis in the original).

14. Swamy, 36.

15. Arjun Appadurai, *Fear of Small Numbers: An Essay on the Geography of Anger* (Durham, NC: Duke University Press, 2006), 51–53.

16. Pankaj Mishra draws examples as much from the nineteenth century as from the present. Pankaj Mishra, *Age of Anger: A History of the Present* (London: Penguin, 2018).

17. On the use of anger to provoke communal riots during the British Raj, see Margrit Pernau, "Anger, Hurt and Enthusiasm: Mobilising for Violence, 1870–1920," in *Emotions, Mobilisations and South Asian Politics*, ed. A. Blom and S. Tawa Lama-Rewal (London: Routledge, 2020), 95–112.

18. On this point, see Christophe Jaffrelot, "Les modèles explicatifs de l'origine des nations et du nationalisme," in *Théories du nationalisme*, ed. Gilles Delannoi and Pierre-André Taguieff (Paris: Kimé, 1991), 139–77.

19. Anuradha Kapur, "Deity to Crusader: The Changing Iconography of Ram," in *Hindus and Others: The Question of Identity in India Today*, ed. Gyanendra Pandey (New Delhi: Viking, 1993), 74–109.

20. Mrinal Pande, "Angry Hanuman: This Viral Image that Won Modi's Praise Symbolises Today's Aggressive, Macho India," Scroll.in, May 26, 2018, https://scroll.in/article/879108 /angry-hanuman-this-viral-image-that-won-modis-praise-symbolises-todays-aggressive-macho -india; and N. Bhowmick, "Militant Hinduism and the Reincarnation of Hanuman, The Wire, April 4, 2018, https://thewire.in/communalism/noidas-thriving-militant-hinduism-and-the -resurrection-of-hanuman.

21. Lucas Chancel and Thomas Piketty show that, while the real per-adult income growth was below 2 percent for the bottom 50 percent of Indian society in 1980–2015, it was above 5 percent for the top 10 percent. Lucas Chancel and Thomas Piketty, "Indian Income Inequality, 1922–2015: From British Raj to Billionaire Raj?," WID.world Working Paper Series no. 2017/11, July 2017, accessed November 18, 2020, https://wid.world/document/chancelpiketty2017 widworld/.

22. On the "emotional politics of the angry young man" in another context—Telugu cinema—see I. Rajamani, "Mobilising Anger in Andhra Pradesh," in *Emotions, Mobilisations and South Asian Politics*, ed. A. Blom and S. Tawa Lama-Rewal (London: Routledge, 2020), 187–204.

23. Cited in Prashant Jha, *How the BJP Wins: Inside India's Greatest Election Machine* (Delhi: Juggernaut, 2017), 165–66.

24. Jha, *How the BJP Wins*, 166.

25. Sudha Pai and Sajjan Kumar, *Everyday Communalism: Riots in Contemporary Uttar Pradesh* (Delhi: Oxford University Press, 2018), ix–x.

26. Pai and Kumar, *Everyday Communalism*, 3.

27. Pai and Kumar, 27.

28. Pai and Kumar, 31.

29. On the stigma affecting Dalits in the RSS, see the personal testimony of Bhanwar Megha-wanshi, *I Could Not Be Hindu: The Story of a Dalit in the RSS* (New Delhi: Navayana, 2020).

30. Swamy, *Hindus under Siege*, 64.

31. Regarding this foundational episode, see the article by Peter van Der Veer, "'God Must Be Liberated!' A Hindu Liberation Movement in Ayodhya," *Modern Asian Studies* 21, no. 1 (1987): 283–301.

32. Interview with Acharya Giriraj Kishore (senior vice president of the VHP) in New Delhi, February 11, 1994.

33. Vinay Katyar, "It Is a War-Like Situation," interview published in *Frontline*, April 24, 1992, 9–12.

34. Manjari Katju, *Vishva Hindu Parishad and Indian Politics* (Hyderabad: Orient Blackswan, 2010).

35. Interview in Bhopal with a local Bajrang Dal leader, the son of a police officer, who spoke on condition of anonymity.

36. Interview with Vinay Katiyar cited in Smita Gupta and Christophe Jaffrelot, "The Bajrang Dal: The New Hindu Nationalist Brigade," in *Living with Secularism: The Destiny of India's Muslims*, ed. Mushirul Hasan (Delhi: Manohar, 2007), 202.

37. Interview with Acharya Giriraj Kishore in New Delhi, February 11, 1994.

38. Acharya Giriraj Kishore, preface to *Shikshak Margdarshaka*, by R. P. Sharma (Delhi: Bajrang Dal, 1993).

39. Snigdha Poonam, *Dreamers: How Young Indians are Changing the World* (London: Hurst, 2018), 118.

40. Cited in Poonam, *Dreamers*, 126.

41. Moyukh Chatterjee, "The Ordinary Life of Hindu Supremacy: In Conversation with a Bajrang Dal Activist," *Economic and Political Weekly* 53, no. 4 (January 27, 2018), https://www .epw.in/engage/article/ordinary-life-hindu-supremacy.

42. Concerning the "adulation" for Modi in the Sangh Parivar, see Walter Andersen and Shridhar Damle, *The RSS: A View to the Inside* (Gurgaon: Penguin Viking, 2018), 19.

43. "Birth of 2nd Republic under Modi: Sanjaya Baru," *Times of India*, July 27, 2014, http:// timesofindia.indiatimes.com/articleshow/39078542.cms?utm_source=contentofinterest&utm _medium=text&utm_campaign=cppst.

44. Even in 1998 and 1999, when Vajpayee had the leading role, other party veterans such as Advani and M. M. Joshi were featured on posters.

45. M. Vaishnav, D. Kapur, and N. Sircar, "Growth Is No. 1 Poll Issue for Voters, Survey Shows," Carnegie Endowment, March 16, 2014, http://carnegieendowment.org/2014/03/16 /growth-is-no.-1-poll-issue-for-voters-survey-shows/h4gh.

46. "'I Have Come Here to Share Your Sadness and Make Your Problems Mine': Narendra Modi Campaigns in Amethi," NarendraModi.in, May 5, 2014, http://www.narendramodi.in/i -have-come-here-to-share-your-sadness-and-make-your-problems-mine-narendra-modi -campaigns-in-amethi/.

47. Bharatiya Janata Party, *Ek Bharat Shreshtha Bharat: Sabka Sath, Sabka Vikas; Election Manifesto 2014* (New Delhi: Bharatiya Janata Party, 2014), accessed February 4, 2015, http:// www.bjp.org/images/pdf_2014/full_manifesto_english_07.04.2014.pdf.

48. "In 2014, Let Us Not Vote for Any Party or Person but Let Us VOTE FOR INDIA!," NarendraModi.in, December 22, 2013, http://www.narendramodi.in/in-2014-let-us-not-vote -for-any-party-or-person-but-let-us-vote-for-india/.

49. "Hang Me if I Have Committed a Crime," *Ahmedabad Mirror*, April 17, 2014, 1, https:// ahmedabadmirror.indiatimes.com/ahmedabad/cover-story/hang-me-if-i-have-committed -crime/articleshow/35643182.cms.

50. Narendra Modi also dismissed the role the Central Bureau of Investigation (CBI) was playing in investigations regarding former members of his government in Gujarat, including Amit Shah, by saying that it was an instrument in the hands of the ruling Congress. He even renamed it "Congress Bureau of Investigation." By the end of the election campaign, he was to make similar remarks vis-à-vis the Election Commission. "CBI Will Fight Upcoming Polls, Not Congress, Says Narendra Modi," *Indian Express*, September 26, 2013, 12, https://indianexpress .com/article/india/politics/cbi-will-fight-upcoming-polls-not-congress-says-narendra-modi/.

51. See Ravish Tiwari, "Narendra Modi as a 'Backward Leader,' Nitish Kumar as an Upper-caste 'Hero,'" *Indian Express*, April 16, 2013, http://www.indianexpress.com/news/narendra -modi-as-a-backward-leader-nitish-kumar-as-an-upper-caste-hero/1102578/; "Narendra Modi: From Tea Vendor to PM Candidate," *Times of India*, September 13, 2013, http://articles .timesofindia.indiatimes.com/2013-09-13/india/42040411.

52. "Throw Out Congress, Save the Nation: Modi," *The Hindu*, May 3, 2013, https://www .thehindu.com/todays-paper/tp-national/tp-karnataka/throw-out-congress-save-the-nation -modi/article4679005.ece.

53. "Narendra Modi: The Times Now Interview," Mid-day.com, May 8, 2014, http://www .mid-day.com/articles/full-text-of-narendra-modis-interview-the-bjp-leader-opens-up /15282184.

54. We will return to the role of the press in Modi's India in the last part of the book.

55. S. Palshikar and K. C. Suri, "India's 2014 Lok Sabha Elections," *Economic and Political Weekly* 45, no. 39 (2014): 43–48.

56. The Muslims who attended the Jaipur meeting of Modi in September 2013 were requested to wear sherwanis and skullcaps when they were males and burqas when they were females. According to observers of Rajasthan's politics, "The dress code idea has been put forward to 'polish' the BJP's pro-Muslim image in the state." "BJP's Jaipur Rally to Display Modi's 'Burqa of Secularism,'" *Business Standard*, September 10, 2013, https://www.business-standard.com /article/politics/bjp-s-jaipur-rally-to-display-modi-s-burqa-of-secularism-113091000201_1 .html.

57. "Modi Kicks-Off 'Bharat Vijay' Campaign from Jammu," *Jagran Post*, March 26, 2014, http://post.jagran.com/modikicksoff-bharat-vijay-campaign-from-jammu-1395818051.

58. Abantika Ghosh, "Saffron in the Atmosphere, Narendra Modi Praises Ramdev," *Indian Express*, March 24, 2014. For more details on these figures of the Sangh Parivar, see Christophe Jaffrelot, "Ramdev, Swami without Sampradaya," *The Caravan*, July 1, 2011, http://www .caravanmagazine.in/perspectives/ramdev-swami-without-sampradaya; Christophe Jaffrelot, "The Other Saffron," *Indian Express*, October 6, 2014, http://indianexpress.com/article /opinion/columns/the-other-saffron/; and the remarkable biography by Priyanka Pathak-Narain, *Godman to Tycoon: The Untold Story of Baba Ramdev* (New Delhi: Juggernaut, 2017).

59. Prashant Pandey, "Narendra Modi in Varanasi: I'm Here on the Call of Ganga Mata," *Indian Express*, April 25, 2014, https://indianexpress.com/article/india/politics/modi-in-varanasi-im-here-on-the-call-of-ganga-mata/.

60. Cited in L. Verma, "Hindutva Is Backdrop for Modi in UP," *Indian Express*, December 21, 2013, http://archive.indianexpress.com/news/hindutva-is-backdrop-for-modi-in-up/1210180/0.

61. Bharatiya Janata Party, *Ek Bharat Shreshtha Bharat*, 27.

62. "Modi Returns Fire, Calls Arvind Kejriwal Pakistan Agent 'AK-49,'" *Hindustan Times*, March 26, 2014, https://www.hindustantimes.com/india/modi-returns-fire-calls-arvind-kejriwal-pakistan-agent-ak-49/story0TrX1M43uYZFWRR70eDd0I.html.

63. "'Anti-Modi People Should Go to Pak,'" *Times of India*, April 20, 2014, 1, https://timesofindia.indiatimes.com/news/Those-opposed-to-Narendra-Modi-should-go-to-Pakistan-BJP-leader-Giriraj-Singh-says/articleshow/33971544.cms.

64. Hilal Ahmed, "Muzaffarnagar 2013: Meanings of Violence," *Economic and Political Weekly* 48, no. 40 (October 5, 2013): 10–12; and "No Respite for Muzaffarnagar," *The Hindu*, December 25, 2013, https://www.thehindu.com/opinion/editorial/no-respite-for-muzaffarnagar/article5497971.ece.

65. Ravish Tiwari, "UP BJP Wants Tickets for Four Riot-Accused MLAs," *Indian Express*, March 10, 2014, https://indianexpress.com/article/cities/lucknow/uttar-pradesh-bjp-wants-tickets-for-four-riot-accused-mlas/.

66. Two of them got elected, one of whom was given a ministerial portfolio in the Modi government.

67. Quoted from Marya Shakil, "Vote for BJP to Take Revenge, No Need to Use Swords, Arrows: Amit Shah," CNN-IBN, April 5, 2014, http://ibnlive.in.com/news/vote-for-bjp-to-takerevengeno-need-to-use-swords-arrows-amit-shah/462708-37.html.

68. "BJP Defends Narendra Modi's Aide Amit Shah's 'Badla' Remark, Says He 'Captured the Mood of the Nation,'" *Indian Express*, April 5, 2014, https://indianexpress.com/article/india/politics/bjp-defends-narendra-modisaide-amit-shahs-badla-remark-says-he-captured-the-mood-of-the-nation/.

69. "Modi Aide Amit Shah Stirs Controversy, Says Azamgarh 'Base of Terrorists,'" *Indian Express*, May 5, 2014, https://indianexpress.com/article/cities/lucknow/in-fresh-row-amit-shah-says-azamgarh-base-of-terrorists-2/.

70. Election campaigns led by other populist leaders have been called tsunamis as well, starting with Beppe Grillo's "Tsunami Tour" in 2013.

71. Amogh Sharma, "The Backstage of Democracy: Exploring the Professionalisation of Politics in India" (PhD diss., Oxford University, 2020), 103.

72. Narendramodi.in, May 15, 2014, cited in Sharma, *Backstage of Democracy*, 103.

73. Rajdeep Sardesai, *The Election that Changed India* (New Delhi: Penguin India, 2014), 313.

74. K. K. Sruthijit, "Meet the Nonprofit Whose Backroom Work Powered Modi to Victory," Scroll.in, June 18, 2014, http://scroll.in/article/667401/Meet-the-nonprofit-whosebackroom-work-powered-Modi-to-victory/.

75. Lalmani Verma, "The NaMo Rath: Playing Near Them, 54-Inch Narendra Modi," *Indian Express*, March 23, 2014, http://indianexpress.com/article/india/politics/playing-near-them-54-inch-modi/.

76. "Modi's 'Chai pe Charcha'? What's that All About?," Rediff.com, February 12, 2014, http://www.rediff.com/news/report/slide-show-1-modis-chai-pe-charcha-whats-that-all-about/20140212.htm#3.

77. Cited in Jha, *How the BJP Wins*, 41.

78. Pradeep K. Chhibber and Susan L. Ostermann, "The BJP's Fragile Mandate: Modi and Vote Mobilizers in the 2014 General Elections," *Studies in Indian Politics* 2, no. 2 (2014): 1–15.

79. Chhibber and Ostermann, "BJP's Fragile Mandate," 3.

80. Chhibber and Ostermann, 10.

81. Sharma, *Backstage of Democracy*, 247.

82. Sharma, 247.

83. Sharma, 249.

84. Sharma, 249.

85. Sruthijit, "Meet the Nonprofit."

86. Uday Mahurkar and Kunal Pradhan, "Meet the Men behind Modi's Audacious Election Campaign," *India Today*, p. 39. (http://indiatoday.intoday.in/story/narendra-modi-bjpprime-ministerial-candidate-campaign-social-media/1/343517.html Last accessed February 4, 2015).

87. Sheela Bhatt, "Sheela Says: Meet a Modi Fanatic," Rediff.com, May 8, 2014, http://www.rediff.com/news/column/ls-election-sheela-says-meet-a-modi-fanatic/20140508.htm.

88. Archna Shukla, "The Splash: What Keeps the Narendra Modi Marketing Machine Tickling?," *Indian Express*, May 1, 2014, http://indianexpress.com/article/india/politics/the-splash-what-keeps-the-modi-marketing-machine-ticking/.

89. Sharma, *Backstage of Democracy*, 212.

90. Sardesai, *Election that Changed India*, 240.

91. Mahurkar and Pradhan, "Meet the Men," 38.

92. Cited in Sardesai, *Election that Changed India*, 242.

93. Regarding this aspect of the campaign, see Rammanohar Reddy, "Media in Contemporary India: Journalism Transformed into a Commodity," in *Business and Politics in India*, ed. C. Jaffrelot, A. Kohli and K. Murali (New York: Oxford University Press, 2019), 183–210.

94. See S. Rukmini, "Modi Got Most Prime-Time Coverage: Study," *The Hindu*, May 8, 2014, http://www.thehindu.com/elections/loksabha2014/modi-got-most-primetime-coverage-study/article5986740.ece; CMS Media Lab Analysis, "It Is Modi Driven Television Coverage—2014 Poll Campaign," May 8, 2014, https://cmsindia.org/sites/default/files/2019-05/2014-Lok-Sabha-Election-media-coverage.pdf.

95. "Black Money Power," *The Economist*, May 4, 2014, https://www.economist.com/banyan/2014/05/04/black-money-power. Regarding the role of money in Indian election campaigns, see D. Kapur and M. Vaishnav, eds., *Costs of Democracy: Political Finance in India* (Delhi: Oxford University Press, 2018).

96. Nilanjana Bhowmick, "The 2014 Elections Are the Most Expensive Ever Held in India," *Time*, April 11, 2014, http://time.com/33062/india-elections-expenditure/.

97. See the interview Amit Shah gave Patrick French, "The 'Shah' of BJP's Game Plan Who Wants to Alter India's Political Culture," *Hindustan Times*, July 17, 2016, https://www.hindustantimes.com/india-news/amit-shah-the-strategist-of-bjp-s-india-game-plan/story-FrosSiYHtTwhVxKBsjapsI.html.

98. Vinod K. Jose, "The Emperor Uncrowned," *The Caravan*, March 1, 2012, http://caravanmagazine.in/reportage/emperor-uncrowned?page=0,9.

99. Sheela Bhatt, "What Amit Shah's Fall Really Means," Rediff.com, July 28, 2010, http://news.rediff.com/special/2010/jul/24/what-amit-shahs-fall-really-means.htm.

100. On the relationship between Amit Shah and Narendra Modi, see Rana Ayyub, "Breakthrough Exposé: So Why Is Narendra Modi Protecting Amit Shah?," *Tehelka* 7, no. 28 (July 17, 2010), http://old.tehelka.com/breakthrough-expose-so-why-is-narendra-modi-protecting-amit-shah/.

101. C. Jaffrelot, "The Modi-centric BJP 2014 Election Campaign: New Techniques and Old Tactics," *Contemporary South Asia* 23, no. 2 (June 2015): 151–66

102. Dinesh Narayanan, "RSS 3.0," *The Caravan*, May 1, 2014, 42.

103. "RSS Proud of 'Strong Leader' Modi's Swayamsevak Background," *The Hindu*, March 7, 2014, https://www.thehindu.com/news/national/rss-proud-of-strong-leader-modis-swayamsevak-background/article5760884.ece.

104. Shyamlal Yadav, "Bhagwat Cautions RSS Cadres against Crossing Limits for BJP, Says Can't Chant 'Namo Namo,'" *Indian Express*, March 11, 2014, https://indianexpress.com/article/india/politics/bhagwat-cautions-rss-cadres-against-crossing-limits-for-bjp-says-cant-chant-namo-namo/.

105. Smita Gupta, "Far from the Din, RSS Working Hard for Modi's Success," *The Hindu*, April 19, 2014, http://www.thehindu.com/elections/loksabha2014/far-from-the-din-rss-working-hard-for-modissuccess/article5927259.ece.

106. Sabyasachi Bandopadhyay, "RSS "Systematic Campaign" behind BJP Entry in Bengal," *Indian Express*, May 21, 2014, http://indianexpress.com/article/cities/kolkata/rss-systematiccampaign-behind-bjp-entry-in-bengal/.

107. Poornima Joshi, "The Organiser: Amit Shah Takes Charge," *The Caravan*, April 1, 2014, 76–87.

108. Cited in Jha, *How the BJP Wins*, 50.

109. Cited in Jha, 52.

110. See C. Jaffrelot, "The Congress in Gujarat (1917–1969): Conservative Face of a Progressive Party," in "Political Conservatism in India," ed. C. Jaffrelot, special issue, *Studies in Indian Politics* 5, no. 2 (November 2017): 248–61.

111. Gilles Verniers, "The Resistance of Regionalism: BJP's Limitations and the Resilience of State Parties," in *India's 2014 Elections: A Modi-Led BJP Sweep*, ed. Paul Wallace (New Delhi: Sage, 2015): 28–47.

112. Christophe Jaffrelot, "'Why Should We Vote?': The Indian Middle Class and the Functioning of the World's Largest Democracy," in *Patterns of Middle Class Consumption in India and China*, ed. C. Jaffrelot and P. van der Veer (New Delhi: Sage, 2008), 35–54.

113. Christophe Jaffrelot, "The Class Element in the 2014 Indian Election and the BJP's Success with Special Reference to the Hindi Belt," in "Understanding India's 2014 Elections," special issue, *Studies in Indian Politics* 3, no. 1 (June 2015): 19–38.

114. Bhatt, "Meet a Modi Fanatic."

115. New Delhi Television became Modi's bête noire in 2002 after uncompromising reports the channel aired about the pogrom. NDTV journalists were set upon and some of their

vehicles destroyed. See Arafaat A. Valiani, *Militant Publics in India: Physical Culture and Violence in the Making of a Modern Polity* (New York: Palgrave/Macmillan, 2011), 184.

116. This key moment can be seen on YouTube: "Narendra Modi's Interview by Karan Thapar," YouTube video posted by Aleem Frinzy, accessed November 18, 2020, https://www.youtube.com/watch?v=YWk8cZXs1bQ.

117. Poonam, *Dreamers*, 125.

118. It would take me too far afield to discuss the sexual frustrations of young men forced into celibacy due to a highly imbalanced male/female ratio that has arisen out of the selective abortion of female fetuses. But this factor could certainly also account for their anger and violence. Dozens of millions of young Indian men are believed to be condemned to celibacy.

119. J. Helliwell, R. Layard, and J. Sachs, *World Happiness Report* (New York: UN Sustainable Development Solutions Network, 2014), 24, accessed September 23, 2020, http://media1.intoday.in/indiatoday/WorldHappinessReport2013_online_2.pdf.

120. For instance, Modi used an Adani aircraft on at least one occasion.

121. Rupam Jain Nair and Frank Jack Daniel, "Special Report: Battling for India's Soul, State by State," Reuters, October 12, 2015, https://www.reuters.com/article/us-india-rss-specialreport/special-report-battling-for-indias-soul-stateby-state-idUSKCN0S700A20151013.

122. In Karnataka, the BJP came in first in the 2018 elections, but Congress and the Janata Dal (Secular) formed a majority coalition in the Bangalore assembly.

123. Cited in Jha, *How the BJP Wins*, 44.

Chapter 4

1. Laclau, *On Populist Reason*, 81.

2. This is an approximation achieved using World Bank measurement tools. Counting the poor is a delicate exercise in India. Depending on whether one uses Indian or international criteria, there is a risk of generating a serious threshold effect that can bring tens of millions of people under the poverty line.

3. In one of his election campaign speeches, he stated that while the Congress wanted only one thing, to get rid of Modi, the BJP wanted only another, to get rid of poverty. "Congress Hopes to Get Rid of PM Modi, BJP Only Wants Poverty Gone, Says Amit Shah," News18, November 19, 2018, https://www.news18.com/news/politics/congress-hopes-to-get-rid-of-pm-narendra-modi-bjp-only-wants-poverty-gone-says-amit-shah-1944097.html.

4. "Narendra Modi Delivers First Address to Lok Sabha, Talks about Centre's Commitment to Serve the Poorest of the Poor," NarendraModi.in, June 11, 2014, https://www.narendramodi.in/narendra-modi-delivers-first-address-to-lok-sabha-talks-about-centres-commitment-to-serve-the-poorest-of-the-poor-6296.

5. Narendra Modi, *Mann Ki Baat: A Social Revolution on Radio* (New Delhi: BlueKraft Digital Foundation, 2019), 5.

6. Modi, *Mann Ki Baat*, 5.

7. Modi, 12.

8. Modi, 14.

9. Cited in Modi, 53.

10. In the same vein, Modi launched in 2016 a platform called Rate My Government, where citizens were invited to give their assessment of his work and his ministers' work. See "Rate My Government," Government of India, accessed October 20, 2020, https://www.mygov.in/mygov-survey/rate-my-government/.

11. Cited in Modi, *Mann Ki Baat*, 64–65.

12. For more detail, see C. Jaffrelot and J.-T. Martelli, *Mann Ki Baat* (forthcoming).

13. "Narendra Modi's First Independence Day Speech: Full Text," *India Today*, August 15, 2014, https://www.indiatoday.in/india/story/narendra-modi-independence-day-speech-full-text-red-fort-204216-2014-08-15.

14. R. K. Narayan offers the most telling account of Gandhi's obsession with cleanliness in one of his novels, *Waiting for the Mahatma* (Chicago: University Of Chicago Press, 1981).

15. Suhas Palshikar, "Politics of India's Middle Class," in *Middle Class Values in India and Western Europe*, ed. Imtiaz Ahmad and Helmut Reifeld (New York: Routledge, 2018), 178.

16. Narendra Modi told Assa Doron and Robin Jeffrey that, as a Sangh Parivar cadre, he decided in particular to educate people "not only about personal hygiene but also about social hygiene," while he was just back from the United States, in 1994, during the plague epidemic affecting Surat. Swachh Bharat had been his "dream since [his] RSS Pracharak days," he said. Assa Doron and Robin Jeffrey, *Waste of a Nation: Garbage and Growth in India* (Cambridge MA: Harvard University Press, 2018).

17. John Elliott, "Has Modi's Swachh Bharat Campaign Been a Success?," *LSE*, May 16, 2019, https://blogs.lse.ac.uk/southasia/2019/05/16/has-modis-swachh-bharat-campaign-been-a-success/.

18. Sagar, "Down the Drain," *The Caravan*, May 1, 2017, https://caravanmagazine.in/reportage/swachh-bharat-mission-heading-failure.

19. D. R. Bandela, "Union Budget 2020–21: Constant Decline in Swachh Bharat Mission Allocation," *Down to Earth*, February 4, 2020, https://www.downtoearth.org.in/news/economy/union-budget-2020-21-constant-decline-in-swachh-bharat-mission-allocation-69156.

20. Namitha Sadanand, "The Swachh Bharat Mission Has Built Toilets, but Failed to Get People to Use Them," Scroll.in, October 2, 2019, https://scroll.in/article/939096/the-swachh-bharat-mission-has-built-toilets-but-failed-to-get-people-to-use-them; "Why Millions of Indians Don't Use the Toilets They Have," *Times of India*, February 12, 2020, https://timesofindia.indiatimes.com/india/why-millions-of-indians-dont-use-the-toilets-they-have/articleshow/71438942.cms.

21. Chetan Chauhan, "No Water in 60% Toilets Puts Question Mark over Modi Govt's Swachh Bharat Mission," *Hindustan Times*, May 14, 2017, https://www.hindustantimes.com/india-news/no-water-in-60-toilets-built-under-swachh-bharat-mission/story-3rdu1Hv1UZbabYQhb68OTP.html.

22. Aarefa Johari, "The Modi Years: How Successful Is the Swachh Bharat Mission or Clean India Campaign?," Scroll.in, February 4, 2019, https://scroll.in/article/910562/the-modi-years-how-successful-is-the-swachh-bharat-mission-or-clean-india-campaign.

23. Sadhika Tiwari, "Indian Government Has Built 95 Million Toilets, but Little Has Changed for Manual Scavengers," Scroll.in, December 14, 2019, https://scroll.in/article/946746/indian-government-has-built-95-million-toilets-but-little-has-changed-for-manual-scavengers.

24. Tiwari, "Indian Government."

25. "Swachh Bharat Mission: The Last Push," *Down to Earth*, September 28, 2019, https://www.downtoearth.org.in/news/rural-water-and-sanitation/swachh-bharat-mission-the-last-push-66975-.

26. "Narendra Modi's First Independence Day Speech."

27. Here, the Modi government was emulating the UPA government, which had also used the Aadhaar ID numbers that had been generated for every India from 2009 onward as the main avenue for giving access to PDS (public distribution system) shops to the poor. Just as the UPA had done with Aadhaar, moreover, the Modi government used carrots and sticks to make sure that Indians opened accounts. The carrots have been mentioned above—a card, insurance, and so on. The sticks were indirect: not only did the poor have to open bank accounts to receive their benefits, but demonetization in 2016 (see elsewhere in this chapter) made such accounts popular as higher-denomination notes suddenly lost all their value. According to an experienced financier, the impact of demonetization on Jan-Dhan accounts can be gauged from the fact that "the average deposits in such accounts operating through our banking kiosks stood at Rs 480 per account before demonetisation, which increased to Rs 1,095 per account after that." The number of account holders increased from 255,100,000 on November 9, 2016, the day demonetization came into effect, to 265,000,000 in early 2017 and 314,500,000 in April 2018. "Deposits in Jan Dhan accounts cross Rs 80,000 crore," *Economic Times*, April 23, 2018, https://economictimes.indiatimes.com/industry/banking/finance/banking/deposits-in-jan-dhan-accounts-cross-rs-80000-crore/articleshow/63865987.cms?from=mdr.

28. World Bank Group, *The Global Findex Database Measuring Financial Inclusion and the Fintech Revolution*, Washington, DC: World Bank Group, 2018), 65, accessed June 26, 2020, https://globalfindex.worldbank.org/index.php/#GF-ReportChapters.

29. Anand Adhikari, "Jan Dhan Yojana Data Shows Rural Area Residents Using Bank Accounts More Often," *Business Today*, November 20, 2019, https://www.businesstoday.in/sectors/banks/zero-balance-dormant-bank-accounts-under-jan-dhan-yojana-on-a-steady-decline/story/390664.html.

30. Owing to PMJDY, bank account penetration in rural areas increased from 52 percent in 2014 to 79 percent in 2017. World Bank Group, *Global Findex*, 32. According to the report, "In 2014 adults in the richest 60 percent of its households were 15 percentage points more likely than those in the poorest 40 percent to have an account. Since then, thanks in part to a government policy aimed at increasing financial inclusion, account ownership has risen among wealthier and poorer adults alike—narrowing the gap to 5 percentage points." World Bank Group, *Global Findex*, 28.

31. World Bank Group, 25.

32. World Bank Group, 25.

33. Cited in Rohit Azad and Dipa Sinha, "The Jan-Dhan Yojana, Four Years Later," *The Hindu*, May 29, 2018, https://www.thehindu.com/opinion/op-ed/the-jan-dhan-yojana-four-years-later/article24017333.ece.

34. "PM Narendra Modi Launches Pradhan Mantri Ujjwala Yojana Scheme in Ballia, Says Petroleum Sector Is for Poor," *Financial Express*, May 1, 2016, https://www.financialexpress.com/economy/live-pm-narendra-modi-launches-pradhan-mantri-ujjwala-yojana-in-ballia-speech-highlights-free-cooking-gas-scheme/246378/.

35. "My Mother Inhaled Smoke to Cook for Us: PM Modi Explains Why Ujjwala Yojana Is Govt's Priority," *DNA*, May 28, 2018, https://www.dnaindia.com/india/report-my-mother-inhaled-smoke-to-cook-for-us-pm-modi-explains-why-ujjwala-yojana-is-govt-s-priority-2619544.

36. "Claims vs Reality: Who Benefited from PM Ujjwala Yojana?" *International Development Economics Associates*, November 27, 2019, https://www.networkideas.org/news-analysis/2019/11/claims-versus-reality-who-benefited-from-pm-ujjwala-yojana/.

37. Kundan Pandey, "LPG Connections Not Only Success Metric: CAG on Ujjwala," *Down to Earth*, December 12, 2029, https://www.downtoearth.org.in/news/governance/lpg-connections-not-only-success-metric-cag-on-ujjwala-68387.

38. Anil Sasi, "Steady Decline in Ujjwala Refills Triggers Fresh Concerns," *Indian Express*, January 2, 2020, https://indianexpress.com/article/business/steady-decline-in-ujjwala-refills-triggers-fresh-concerns-6195399/.

39. These conclusions have been substantiated by field studies. See "PM Narendra Modi's Ujjwala Yojana Scheme Provided LPG Access, but Failed to Promote Its Use, Says Study," *Financial Express*, January 24, 2020, https://www.financialexpress.com/economy/pm-narendra-modis-ujjwala-yojana-scheme-provided-lpg-access-but-failed-to-promote-its-use-says-study/1833877/.

40. Pandey, "LPG Connections."

41. Sumant Sen, "How Effective Has the Pradhan Mantri Ujjwala Yojana Been?," *The Hindu*, December 18, 2019, https://www.thehindu.com/data/data-how-effective-has-the-pradhan-mantri-ujjwala-yojana-been/article30338388.ece.

42. Utpal Bhaskar, "Ujjawala Scheme: Indian Oil, Others Defer Loan Recovery up to 6 LPG Refills," *Mint*, March 25, 2018, https://www.livemint.com/Industry/Um9Z4gsgdGExYmKdrgDrdI/Ujjawala-scheme-Indian-Oil-others-defer-loan-recovery-up-t.html.

43. S. Mehra and S. Kaur, "Despite Budget 2020's Tall Claims, It Falls Short on Its Promise to Reduce the Gender Gap," Scroll.in, February 20, 2020, https://scroll.in/article/953576/despite-budget-2020s-tall-claims-it-falls-short-on-its-promise-to-reduce-the-gender-gap.

44. Cited in P. Jha, *How the BJP Wins: Inside India's Greatest Election Machine* (Delhi, Juggernaut, 2017), 30.

45. On demonetization, the best sources are Rammanohar Reddy, *Demonetisation and Black Money* (Hyderabad: Orient Blackswan, 2017); J. Ghosh, C. P. Chandrasekhar, and P. Patnaik, *Demonetisation Decoded: A Critique of India's Currency Experiment* (London: Routledge, 2017); and A. Lahiri, "The Great Indian Demonetization," *Journal of Economic Perspectives* 34, no. 1 (Winter 2020): 55–74.

46. In fact, the fruits of corruption had already been laundered, particularly through huge real estate deals—and black money did not disappear from the Indian economy after 2016. Demonetization mainly aimed to deplete the BSP and the SP war chests with the approach of elections in Uttar Pradesh—which it did, while the BJP, informed of the maneuver ahead of time, kept all its resources and managed to carry a significant victory.

47. "PM Modi at Parivartan Rally in New Moradabad, Uttar Pradesh," YouTube video posted by Narendra Modi, December 3, 2016, https://www.youtube.com/watch?v=kJQTBrwpkwc. The transcription and translation in English is available at "Archives de catégorie: Select

Speeches," Democratic Decline, November 19, 2018, https://newdemagogue.hypotheses.org/category/documents/select-speeches.

48. W. H. Morris-Jones, "India's Political Idioms," in *Politics and Society in India*, ed. C. H. Philips (London: George Allen and Unwin, 1963), 140.

49. C. Jaffrelot, "The Political Guru: The Guru as *Éminence Grise*," in *The Guru in South Asia: New Interdisciplinary Perspectives*, ed. J. Copeman and A. Ikegame (London: Routledge, 2013), 80–96.

50. Lloyd I. Rudolph and Susanne Hoeber Rudolph, *The Modernity of Tradition: Political Development in India* (Chicago: University of Chicago Press, 1967), 159.

51. Cited in Jha, *How the BJP Wins*, 20.

52. He readily speaks of himself in the third-person singular, as a representative of the 1.25 billion Indians. "Budget 2016 Is My Exam, 125 Crore People Will Test Me: PM Modi," *Indian Express*, February 28, 2016, https://indianexpress.com/article/business/budget/budget-2016-is-my-exam-125-crore-people-will-test-me-pm-modi/.

53. Gandhi's speeches were indeed studded with recommendations carrying a tone of admonition and covering all aspects of life, from discipline to cleanliness in family life, and so on.

54. "Mahatma Gandhi Was India's Biggest Brand Ambassador: Narendra Modi," Zee TV, September 30, 2013, http://zeenews.india.com/news/maharashtra/mahatama-gandhi-was-india-s-biggest-brand-ambassador-narendra-modi_880259.html.

55. Jha, *How the BJP Wins*, 18.

56. Cited in Jha, 30.

57. See R. Jenkins and J. Manor, *Politics and the Right to Work: India's National Rural Employment Guarantee Act* (London: Hurst, 2017).

58. In 2016, the minimum wage in question ranged from 167 rupees per day in Bihar to 259 in Haryana (or 2.40 to 3.70 USD). "Revised MGNREGA Wages Put States in a Quandary," *Indian Express*, April 3, 2016, https://indianexpress.com/article/india/india-news-india/mgnrega-wages-states-in-a-quandary-over-new/.

59. An analysis by Jean Drèze shows that the growth rate for agricultural wages for men increased to 2.7 percent per year and for women to 3.7 percent per year during 2005–2006 to 2010–2011 as compared to 0.1 percent per year for men and negative for women in the pre-MGNREGA period (2000–2001 to 2005–2006). See Neelakshi Mann and Jairam Ramesh, "Rising Farm Wages Will Lift All Boats, " *The Hindu*, May 14, 2013, http://www.thehindu.com/opinion/op-ed/rising-farm-wages-will-lift-all-boats/article4712302.ece; and Harish Damodaran Surabhi, "Rural Wage Growth Lowest in 10 Years, Signals Farm Distress, Falling Inflation," *Indian Express*, January 7, 2015, http://indianexpress.com/article/india/india-others/rural-wage-growth-lowest-in-10-years-signals-farm-distress-falling-inflation.

60. P. Deshpande, "NDA Destroying MGNREGA: Has Modi Forgotten 'Sabka Saath, Sabka Vikas'?," *Indian Express*, February 3, 2016, https://indianexpress.com/article/blogs/mgnrega-surprising-to-see-nda-so-determined-to-destroy-it/.

61. "MNREGA, A 'Monument to Failure of Congress Govts': Modi," *The Hindu*, February 27, 2015, https://www.thehindu.com/news/national/mnrega-monument-to-failure-of-congress-govts-modi/article10701735.ece.

62. This achievement was sometimes realized through a mere book transaction, making it possible to transfer funds from one budget item to another, as in 2016. M. Guruswamy, "Why the Government's Claim about a Farmer-Oriented Budget Is Rather Exaggerated," Scroll.in, March 2, 2016, https://scroll.in/article/804423/why-the-governments-claim-about-a-farmer-oriented-budget-is-rather-exaggerated.

63. S. Daniyal, "Jaitley Just Awarded Modi's 'Monument to Congress Failure' Its Highest Ever Outlay," Scroll.in, February 28, 2015, https://scroll.in/article/710324/mnrega-jaitley-just-awarded-modis-monument-to-congress-failure-its-highest-ever-outlay.

64. B. Karat, "Retaining MGNREGA's Core," *The Hindu*, September 9, 2016; A. Aggarwal, "How the World's Largest Govt Jobs Programme Is Slowly Dying," Fact Checker, September 12, 2017, https://factchecker.in/how-the-worlds-largest-govt-jobs-programme-is-slowly-dying/.

65. S. Nair, "Fund Crunch: 88% of NREGA Budget over, 6 Months Left," *Indian Express*, October 19, 2017. See also A. Gulati, "Adrift and Directionless: Can MGNREGA Move from Being a 'Living Monument of UPA's Failure' to a Development Scheme?," *Times of India*, February 24, 2017, https://timesofindia.indiatimes.com/blogs/toi-edit-page/adrift-and- . . . m-being-a-living-monument-of-upas-failure-to-a-development-scheme/.

66. Deshpande, "NDA destroying MGNREGA."

67. These figures show that the decline had begun before Modi took office. (The peak of 283.59 crore was reached in 2009–2010.) See H. Damodaran and S. Nair, "UPA Flagship Scheme MGNREGA Back on Track," *Indian Express*, January 6, 2016, https://indianexpress.com/article/india/india-news-india/mgnrega-back-on-track-job-numbers-hit-five-year-high/.

68. R. Tewari, "NREGA: Each Household Got Only 39 Job Days Last Year," *Indian Express*, April 6, 2015, https://indianexpress.com/article/india/india-others/nrega-each-household-got-only-39-job-days-last-year/.

69. Tewari, "NREGA."

70. R. Tewari, "More than 70% NREGA Wages Unpaid This Fiscal," *Indian Express*, January 30, 2015, https://indianexpress.com/article/india/india-others/more-than-70-nrega-wages-unpaid-this-fiscal/.

71. S. Mathur and N. Bolia, "The MGNREGA index," *The Hindu*, May 31, 2016, https://www.thehindu.com/opinion/op-ed/the-mgnrega-index/article8668701.ece.

72. L. Nayar, "Schrödinger's Wage," *Outlook*, December 4, 2017, 54.

73. J. Ghosh, "Withdrawing the Line," *Indian Express*, April 21, 2016; and N. Dey and A. Roy, "Starving MGNREGA," *Indian Express*, March 30, 2016, https://indianexpress.com/article/opinion/columns/mgnrega-poverty-india-unemployment-farmer-suicide-drought/.

74. Dey and Roy, "Starving MGNREGA."

75. A. Banerjee and I. Anand, "The NDA-II Regime and the Worsening Agrarian Crisis," in *A Quantum Leap in the Wrong Direction?*, ed. R. Azad, S. Chakraborty, S. Ramani, and D. Sinha (Hyderabad: Orient Blackswann, 2019), 66–88.

76. Himanshu, "A Union Budget for the Village," *Indian Express*, February 27, 2016, https://indianexpress.com/article/opinion/columns/a-union-budget-for-the-village-rural-economy/.

77. Himanshu, "India's Farm Crisis: Decades Old and with Deep Roots," *India Forum*, April 29, 2019, https://www.theindiaforum.in/article/farm-crisis-runs-deep-higher-msps-and-cash-handouts-are-not-enough.

78. Ajay Vir Jakhar, "Farm Policies for India," *Indian Express*, November 21, 2017, https:// indianexpress.com/article/opinion/columns/farm-policies-for-indian-agriculture-sector-pm -narendra-modi-4946854/.

79. Regarding scams detected in the framework of this program, see P. Sainath, "Reliance General Insurance Accused of Crop Insurance Scam," *Khabar Bar*, November 8, 2018, https:// www.khabarbar.com/politics/reliance-insurancescam/; and C. Gonsalves, "A Wilful Negligence," *Indian Express*, November 23, 2017, https://indianexpress.com/article/opinion /columns/farmer-suicide-agrarian-crisis-a-wilful-negligence-pm-modi-4950115/.

80. For an overview, see "Give Farmers a Fair Deal," *The Tribune*, June 6, 2019, https://www .tribuneindia.com/news/in-focus/give-farmers-a-fair-deal/751342.html.

81. A. Waghmare, "Farm Distress: Markets, Not MSP, the Key," *Business Standard*, February 5, 2018, https://www.business-standard.com/budget/article/farm-distress-markets-not -msp-is-the-budget-focus-118020300800_1.html.

82. On the case of wheat—one among many others!—see M. Bhardwaj and R. Jadhav, "India Scraps Wheat Import Duty, Purchases May Hit Decade High," *Reuters*, December 8, 2016, https://in.reuters.com/article/india-wheat-import-duty-idINKBN13X0GG.

83. R. Kishore, "Worst Price Slump in 18 Years Shows Scale Of Farm Crisis," *Hindustan Times*, January 15, 2019, https://www.hindustantimes.com/india-news/worst-price-slump-in -18-years-shows-scale-of-farm-crisis/story-P2niBeuqAcaxgms3HmFCTK.html.

84. A. Dey, "Behind the Farmer Unrest in Haryana There Is a History of Instability in Crop Prices," Scroll.in, June 17, 2017, https://scroll.in/article/840866/behind-the-farmer-unrest-in -haryana-there-is-a-history-of-instability-in-crop-prices; M. Chari, "Explained: Behind the Farmer Protests in 16 States Are Bumper Harvests and Low Prices," Scroll.in, June 18, 2017, https://scroll.in/article/840896/explained-behind-the-farmer-protests-in-16-states-are -bumper-harvests-and-low-prices; and M. Chari, "Two Charts Show Why Western Madhya Pradesh Became the Epicenter of Violent Farmer Protests," Scroll.in, June 14, 2017, https:// scroll.in/article/840482/two-charts-show-why-western-madhya-pradesh-became-the -epicentre-of-violent-farmer-protests.

85. A. Saldanha and P. Salve, "India Faces $49.1 Billion Farm-Loan Waivers. That's 16 Times 2017 Budget for Rural Roads," *Quint*, June 16, 2017, https://www.bloombergquint.com/politics /india-faces-dollar491-billion-farm-loan-waivers-thats-16-times-2017-budget-for-rural-roads.

86. N. Bajpai, "Uttar Pradesh Makes Mockery of Farm Loan Waiver; Reductions Given between Rs 10 and Rs 500," *Indian Express*, September 13, 2017, https://www.newindianexpress .com/nation/2017/sep/12/uttar-pradesh-makes-mockery-of-farm-loan-waiver-reductions -given-between-rs-10-to-rs-500-1656209.html.

87. S. Daniyal, "'Government Has Sacrificed the Farmer': Farm Leader Raju Shetti Explains India's Agrarian Crisis," Scroll.in, November 25, 2017, https://scroll.in/article/858924 /government-has-sacrificed-the-farmer-farm-leader-raju-shetti-explains-indias-agrarian-crisis.

88. C. Jaffrelot and Sanjay Kumar, "The Impact of Urbanization on the Electoral Results of the 2014 Indian Elections: With Special Reference to the BJP Vote," in "Understanding India's 2014 Elections," special issue, *Studies in Indian Politics* 3, no. 1 (June 2015): 39–49.

89. A. Gulati, "Dismayed Farmers, Defunct Policies," *Indian Express*, August 31, 2015, https:// indianexpress.com/article/opinion/columns/dismayed-farmers-defunct-policies/.

90. Somesh Jha, "Consumer Spending Sees First Fall in Over 40 Years on Back of Weak Rural Demand: Report," *Business Standard*, November 15, 2019, https://www.business-standard.com /article/economy-policy/consumer-spend-sees-first-fall-in-4-decades-on-weak-rural-demand -nso-data-119111401975_1.html.

91. Himanshu, "What Happened to Poverty during the First Term of Modi?," *Mint*, August 15, 2019, https://www.livemint.com/opinion/columns/opinion-what-happened-to -poverty-during-the-first-term-of-modi-1565886742501.html.

92. D. Maiorano, "Why the Modi Government Shouldn't Be So Quick to Dismiss World Bank's Human Capital Index," The Wire, October 11, 2018, https://thewire.in/government /narendra-modi-govt-world-bank-human-capital-index.

93. Global Hunger Index, "2018 Global Hunger Index Results—Global, Regional, and National Trends," Global Hunger Index, accessed December 24, 2020, https://www .globalhungerindex.org/pdf/en/2018.pdf.

94. P. Mohan, "Rural India Is Eating Less than It Did 40 Years Ago," Scroll.in, August 26, 2016, https://scroll.in/article/814886/rural-india-is-eating-less-than-it-did-40-years-ago.

95. T. S. R. Subramanian, "The Hungry Nation," *Indian Express*, November 24, 2017, https:// indianexpress.com/article/opinion/columns/global-hunger-index-india-ranking-the-hungry -nation-4951570/.

96. Modi's attempts at appropriating Ambedkar—who had been appointed law minister in his first government by Nehru—and using him against Congress are well illustrated by the speech he made in 2016, when he went to Ambedkar's birthplace to commemorate his 125th birth anniversary. He then declared that Ambedkar fought against injustice in society and that the Congress should "repent" for "undermining" Ambedkar's legacy for sixty years. "At Ambedkar's Birthplace, PM Modi Praises Dalit Icon, Says His Fight Was for Equality, Dignity," *India Today*, April 14, 2016, https://www.indiatoday.in/india/story/at-ambedkars-birthplace -pm-modi-praises-dalit-icon-says-his-fight-was-for-equality-dignity-318050-2016-04-14.

97. Bharatiya Janata Party, *Ek Bharat, Shreshtha Bharat: Sabka Saath Sabka Vikas; Election Manifesto 2014* (New Delhi: BJP, 2014), https://www.thehinducentre.com/multimedia/archive /01831/BJP_Manifesto_1831221a.pdf.

98. S. K. Thorat, "Dalits in Post-2014 India: Wide Gap between Promise and Action," in *Majoritarian State: What Hindu Nationalism Is Doing to India*, ed. A. Chatterji, T. Blom Hansen, and C. Jaffrelot (London: Hurst, 2019), 217–36.

99. S. Dhingra, "UPSC Recruitment Has Fallen 40% since 2014 While Govt Struggles to Fill IAS-IPS Vacancies," ThePrint, April 17, 2019, https://theprint.in/india/governance/upsc -recruitment-has-fallen-40-since-2014-while-govt-struggles-to-fill-ias-ips-vacancies/222023/.

100. The same words were repeated twice in the manifesto. "Full Text: BJP Manifesto for 2014 Lok Sabha Elections," News18, April 7, 2014, 18, 21, https://www.news18.com/news /politics/full-text-bjp-manifesto-for-2014-lok-sabha-elections-679304.html.

101. "Only 89 of over 6000 Candidates Short-Listed for Lateral Entry into Civil Services," News18, February 18, 2019, https://www.news18.com/news/india/only-89-of-over-6000 -candidates-short-listed-for-lateral-entry-into-civil-services-2040673.html.

102. A. Deshpande and R. Ramachandran, "The 10% Quota: Is Caste Still an Indicator of Backwardness?," *Economic and Political Weekly* 54, no. 13 (March 30, 2019): 27.

103. Deshpande and Ramachandran, "10% Quota," 30.

104. A. Ashraf and Vignesh Karthik, "UPSC: Why EWS Quota Denies SCs, STs and OBCs Their Due," NewsClick, August 12, 2020, https://www.newsclick.in/UPSC-EWS-Quota-Denies-SCs-STs-OBCs-Their-Due.

105. See Christophe Jaffrelot and Gilles Verniers, "The Representation Gap," *Indian Express*, July 24, 2015, https://indianexpress.com/article/opinion/columns/the-representation-gap-2/.

106. The resurgence of the upper castes, which brought the sociological profile of the Indian parliament back to the 1980s, is even more spectacular at the state level. In Uttar Pradesh, for instance, the proportion of upper-caste MLAs jumped by 12 percentage points, reaching over 44 percent (its 1980 level) owing to the BJP landslide. Among the party's MLAs, 48 percent are from upper castes (compared to 23 percent OBCs and no Muslims). The situation reflects the fact that the BJP has often endorsed upper-caste candidates. Gilles Verniers, "Upper Hand for Upper Castes in House," *Indian Express*, March 20, 2017, https://indianexpress.com/article/explained/bjp-narendra-modi-rajnath-singh-adityanath-devendra-fadnavis-upper-hand-for-upper-castes-in-house-4576599/.

107. K. Adeney and W. Swenden, "Power Sharing in the World's Largest Democracy: Informal Consociationalism in India (and Its Decline?)," *Swiss Political Science Review* 25, no. 4 (2019): 458.

108. Jha, *How the BJP Wins*, 66.

109. Jha, 107.

110. "Most Indian Nobel Winners Brahmins: Gujarat Speaker Rajendra Trivedi," *Indian Express*, January 4, 2020, https://indianexpress.com/article/cities/ahmedabad/most-indian-nobel-winners-brahmins-gujarat-speaker-rajendra-trivedi-6198741/.

111. H. Khan, "'Brahmins Are Held in High Regard by Virtue of Birth': Lok Sabha Speaker Om Birla," *Indian Express*, September 11, 2019, https://indianexpress.com/article/india/brahmins-are-superior-by-birth-says-lok-sabha-speaker-om-birla-5983575/.

112. "Purifying Rituals at UP CM Bungalow, New Home for Yogi Adityanath," *Times of India*, March 20, 2017, http://timesofindia.indiatimes.com/articleshow/57738560.cms?utm_source=contentofinterest&utm_medium=text&utm_campaign=cppst.

113. "'Purification' Ceremony Conducted in Udupi after Dalit Meeting: Report," *Indian Express*, October 27, 2016, https://indianexpress.com/article/india/india-news-india/purification-ceremony-conducted-in-udupi-after-dalit-meeting-report-3105041/.

114. S. Nair, "Refrain from Using Word Dalit, Stick to Scheduled Caste: I&B Ministry Tells Media," *Indian Express*, September 4, 2018, https://indianexpress.com/article/india/refrain-from-using-word-dalit-stick-to-scheduled-caste-ib-ministry-to-media-5338274/.

115. Aseema Sinha, "India's New Porous State: Blurred Boundaries and the Evolving Business-State Relationship," in *Business and Politics in India*, ed. Christophe Jaffrelot, Atul Kohli, and Kanta Murali (New York: Oxford University Press, 2019), 50–94.

116. Rohini Singh, "In Selling Firm to Piramal Group as Minister, Piyush Goyal Pushes Ethical Boundaries," The Wire, April 28, 2018, https://thewire.in/political-economy/in-selling-firm-to-piramal-group-as-minister-piyush-goyal-pushes-ethical-boundaries.

117. For further detail, see Christophe Jaffrelot, *Le capitalisme de connivence en Inde sous Narendra Modi*, Les Etude du CERI no. 237, September 2018, accessed September 27, 2020, https://www.sciencespo.fr/ceri/sites/sciencespo.fr.ceri/files/Etude_237_0.pdf-.

118. "Indian Billionaires' Fortunes Rose by Rs 2,200 Crore a Day in 2018: Report," *Hindustan Times*, January 21, 2019, https://www.hindustantimes.com/business-news/indian-billionaires-fortunes-rose-by-rs-2-200-crore-a-day-in-2018-report/story-Dwpk2DilbQQYXJtyoqaVlL.html.

119. Using probably the same source, Crédit Suisse—a Zurich-based financial services company that is outside the NGO sphere—came to the same conclusion, showing that the richest 1 percent of Indians owned 58.4 percent of the country's wealth in 2016, compared to 53 percent in 2015 and 49 percent in 2014. M. Chakravarty, "The Richest 1% of Indians Now Own 58.4% of Wealth," *Mint*, November 24, 2016, https://www.livemint.com/Money/MML9OZRwaACyEhLzUNImnO/The-richest-1-of-Indians-now-own-584-of-wealth.html.

120. S. Srivastava, "Mukesh Ambani: Racing ahead of Peers," *Forbes India*, November 15, 2018, http://www.forbesindia.com/article/india-rich-list-2018/mukesh-ambani-racing-ahead-of-peers/51785/1.

121. IIFL Wealth and Hurun Report, *IIFL Wealth Hurun India Rich List 2019*, September 25, 2019, https://www.hurunindia.net/hurun-india-rich-list-2019.

122. S. Subramanian, "Doing the Maths: Why India Should Introduce a Covid Wealth Tax on the Ultra Rich," Scroll.in, April 16, 2020, https://scroll.in/article/959314/doing-the-maths-why-india-should-introduce-a-covid-wealth-tax-on-the-ultra-rich.

123. Credit Suisse, "Global Wealth 2019," accessed July 1, 2020, https://www.credit-suisse.com/about-us/en/reports-research/global-wealth-report.html, 147.

124. Kavaljit Singh, "It's Time for a Solidarity Tax," The Wire, May 22, 2020, https://thewire.in/government/coronavirus-solidarity-tax-wealthy.

125. In 2020, officials of the Indian Revenue Service Association (IRSA) proposed reintroducing a wealth tax in the context of the COVID-19 crisis. Three of them were divested "of official responsibilities for going public with their personal views, on the pretext of violating conduct rules." K. Singh, "It's Time."

126. R. Venkataramakrishnan, "Another U-Turn: Arun Jaitley's Budget Offers a Vision of India with a Not-So-Minimum Government," Scroll.in, March 1, 2015, https://scroll.in/article/710318/Another-U-turn:-Arun-Jaitley's-budget-offers-a-vision-of-India-with-a-not-so-minimum-government.

127. T. Kundu, "How Modi Government's Budgets Have Differed from UPA's," *Mint*, December 25, 2019, https://www.livemint.com/Politics/TqorrXZsEOA6409I1Q5pgP/How-Modi-governments-budgets-have-differed-from-UPA.html.

128. "Jaitley Gave Rs 2 Lakh Crore Bonanza to Corporates: Chidambaram," *Business Standard*, March 1, 2015, http://scroll.in/article/710729/jaitley-gave-rs-2-lakh-crore-bonanza-to-corporations-says-chidambaram.

129. "Govt Stares at Tax Shortfall of Rs 2 Lakh Crore; Little Room for Income Tax Cut," *Economic Times*, January 27, 2020, https://economictimes.indiatimes.com/news/economy/finance/govt-stares-at-tax-shortfall-of-rs-2-lakh-crore-room-for-income-tax-cut-limited/articleshow/73628793.cms.

130. A. Jha, "Rs 6,000 is 6% of a Small Farmer's Annual Income, According to NSSO Data," *Hindustan Times*, February 6, 2019, https://www.hindustantimes.com/india-news/rs-6-000-is-6-of-a-small-farmer-s-annual-income-according-to-nsso-data/story-rddMwohk6cSbxjo7E1GyKK.html.

131. A. Gulati, "No Budget for Farmers," *Indian Express*, February 2, 2019, https://indianexpress.com/article/opinion/columns/no-budget-2019-for-indian-farmers-protest-agrarian-crisis-5565432/.

132. "Gross Direct Tax Mop Up Dips 4.92% to Rs 12.33 Lakh Crore in FY20," *Financial Express*, June 7, 2020, https://www.financialexpress.com/economy/gross-direct-tax-mop-up-dips-4-92-to-rs-12-33-lakh-crore-in-fy20/1984148/.

133. Roshan Kishore, "Corporate Tax Cut a Bad Gamble," *Hindustan Times*, June 1, 2020, https://www.hindustantimes.com/india-news/corporate-tax-cut-a-bad-gamble/story-mM1aiOUhEgB10SHcdzCEFI.html.

134. See P. Bhattacharya and T. Kundu, "How Are State Governments Spending on Education, Health, and Irrigation?," *Mint*, April 26, 2017, https://www.livemint.com/Politics/PGqjzobMYX3uF2rZcIFd7H/How-are-state-governments-spending-on-education-health-and.html; and Christophe Jaffrelot and S. Kalyankar, "Demographic Dividend or Demographic Burden? India's Education Challenge," Institut Montaigne, September 13, 2019, https://www.institutmontaigne.org/en/blog/demographic-dividend-or-demographic-burden-indias-education-challenge.

135. I studied these practices as they took place in Gujarat in part 2 of "Business-Friendly Gujarat under Narendra Modi—the Implications of a New Political Economy," in *Business and Politics in India*, ed. Christophe Jaffrelot, Atul Kohli, and Kanta Murali (New York: Oxford University Press, 2019), 211–33.

136. Christophe Jaffrelot, "From Slowdown to Lockdown: India's Economy and the COVID-19 Shock," Institut Montaigne, Paris, June 11, 2020, https://www.institutmontaigne.org/ressources/pdfs/blog/slowdown-lockdown-policy-brief.pdf.

137. Anjan Basu, "Are India's Public Sector Banks at Their Nadir?," The Wire, March 19, 2018, https://thewire.in/banking/are-indias-public-sector-banks-at-their-nadir.

138. S. Sen, "Who Robs India's Banks?," The Wire, March 17, 2018, https://thewire.in/banking/who-robs-indias-banks; and "Bad Loans Push State-Run Banks Losses to Highest-Ever in FY18: Report," NDTV, May 30, 2018, https://www.ndtv.com/business/state-run-banks-post-total-rs-85-370-crore-loss-in-fy18-report-1860099.

139. "Is the Endgame for NPAs in Sight?," *The Hindu*, February 25, 2018, http://www.thehindu.com/business/Economy/is-the-endgame-for-npas-insight/article22852144.ece?homepage=true.

140. This is not the only cause of the banking crisis. For a detailed analysis, see C. P. Chandrashekhar and J. Ghosh, "The Banking Conundrum: Non-Performing Assets and Neo-Liberal Reform," *Economic and Political Weekly* 53, no. 13 (March 31, 2018): 129–37.

141. Credit Suisse Securities Research and Analytics, *House of Debt*, Zurich, October 21, 2015.

142. Jayati Ghosh, "Can Banking Recover?," *The Hindu*, February 26, 2018, http://www.thehindu.com/opinion/lead/can-banking-recover/article22852646.ece.

143. Jaffrelot, *Business-Friendly Gujarat*.

144. Credit Suisse Securities Research and Analytics, *House of Debt*, 22.

145. S. Chandwani, "How IBC Has Failed to Achieve Its Objectives?," *Lexology*, June 16, 2020, https://www.lexology.com/library/detail.aspx?g=b55bf3a6-6d45-4913-b1d1-b245ab857a97.

Conclusion to Part I

1. S. Kumar, "The Youth Vote Made a Difference for the Victory of the BJP," *Research Journal Social Sciences* 22, no. 2 (2014): 45–57.

2. S. Kumar and P. Gupta, "Where Did the BJP Get Its Votes from in 2019?," *Mint*, June 3, 2019, https://www.livemint.com/politics/news/where-did-the-bjp-get-its-votes-from-in-2019 -1559547933995.html.

3. P. Suryanarayan, "When Do the Poor Vote for the Right Wing and Why: Status Hierarchy and Vote Choice in the Indian States," *Comparative Political Studies* 52, no. 2 (2019): 209–45.

4. Tariq Thachil, *Elite Parties, Poor Voters: How Social Services Win Votes in India* (Cambridge: Cambridge University Press, 2014).

5. Christophe Jaffrelot and Louise Tillin, "Populism in India," in *The Oxford Handbook of Populism*, ed. Paul Taggart, Cristobal Rovira Kaltwasser, Paulina Ochoa Espejo, and Pierre Ostiguy (Oxford: Oxford University Press, 2017), 179–94.

6. The total cost of the project is Rs 1 trillion, a huge amount that is bound to add to the Indian debt service, as 80 percent of this money is borrowed from the Japan International Cooperation Agency. "Ahmedabad-Mumbai Bullet Train: India's First High-Speed Rail Project on Track Despite COVID-19; Details," *Financial Express*, July 9, 2020, https://www.financialexpress .com/infrastructure/railways/ahmedabad-mumbai-bullet-train-indias-first-high-speed-rail -project-on-track-despite-covid-19-details/2018591/.

Part II

1. Sammy Smooha, "The Model of Ethnic Democracy: Israel as a Jewish and Democratic State," *Nations and Nationalism* 8, no. 4 (2002): 479.

2. Smooha, "Model of Ethnic Democracy," 479.

3. Smooha, 486.

4. Cited in Yoav Peled and Doron Navot, "Ethnic Democracy Revisited: On the State of Democracy in the Jewish State," *Israel Studies Forum* 20, no. 1 (Summer 2005): 17.

5. Cited in Sammy Smooha, "Ethnic Democracy: Israel as an Archetype," *Israel Studies* 2, no. 2 (1997): 206–7.

6. Cited in Smooha, "Ethnic Democracy," 207.

7. Smooha, 216.

8. Smooha, 219–20.

9. Smooha, 220.

10. Smooha, 233.

11. Smooha, "Model of Ethnic Democracy," 481.

12. The material I use in this introduction overlaps with the data produced by Katharine Adeney in an article that was published just when the manuscript of this book was completed: "How Can We Model Ethnic Democracy? An Application to Contemporary India," *Nations and Nationalism*, July 24, 2020, https://doi.org/10.1111/nana.12654.

Chapter 5

1. See the video "I'm Now a Son of Varanasi, Says Narendra Modi," *India Today* (website), May 17, 2014, https://www.indiatoday.in/elections/video/narendra-modi-varanasi-ganga-aarti -amit-shah-453010-2014-05-17.

2. In November 2014, another female faith leader, Niranjan Jyoti, joined Narendra Modi's government. Never had India's Council of Ministers included so many religious figures.

3. A. Kalra, "India Gets Minister for Yoga and Traditional Medicine," Reuters, November 11, 2014, https://www.reuters.com/article/us-india-health-yoga/india-gets-minister-for-yoga-and -traditional-medicine-idUSKCN0IV13M20141111. The creation of the ministry was possibly overdetermined by the influence of Baba Ramdev. R. F. Worth, "The Billionaire Yogi behind Modi's Rise," *New York Times Magazine*, July 26, 2018, https://www.nytimes.com/2018/07/26 /magazine/the-billionaire-yogi . . . ckage&version=highlights&contentPlacement=3&pgtype =sectionfront.

4. See, for instance, the remarkable "subalternist" piece by Gyan Pandey, "Rallying Round the Cow: Sectarian Strife in the Bhojpuri Region, c. 1888–1917," in *Subaltern Studies II*, ed. Ranajit Cuha (Delhi: Oxford University Press, 1983), 60–128.

5. He was referring, by analogy to the Green Revolution, to the boom in the meat industry, making indirect reference to animal blood in slaughterhouses.

6. Shoaib Daniyal, "Why Politicians Can't Resist the Urge to Manipulate Hindu Sentiments around Cow Slaughter," Scroll.in, October 9, 2014, https://scroll.in/article/682814/why -politicians-cant-resist-the-urge-to-manipulate-hindu-sentiments-around-cow-slaughter.

7. In 2013–2014, buffalo meat exports brought in nearly as much income to India as did basmati rice. S. Sharma, "Are India's Rising Meat Exports Providing a Cover for Money Laundering?," Scroll.in, June 30, 2014, https://scroll.in/article/668385/are-indias-rising-meat -exports-providing-a-cover-for-money-laundering.

8. It is worth noting that four out of six of the main meat exporters are Hindus. "Out of Six Largest Meat Suppliers in India Four Are Hindus," *Muslim Mirror*, December 4, 2014, http:// muslimmirror.com/eng/out-of-six-largest-meat-suppliers-in-india-four-are-hindus/; and in 2005, Sangeet Som, one of the BJP's most ardent champions of the sacred cow, cofounded with Moinuddin Qureshi—an industry magnate—one of the main halal meat exporting companies to the Middle East, Al-Dua Food Processing. J. Joseph and M. Ali, "Sangeet Som, BJP's Leading Anti-Beef Crusader, Owned a Meat Exporting Company," *The Hindu*, October 10, 2015, https:// www.thehindu.com/news/national/Sangeet-Som-BJP%E2%80%99s-leading-anti-beef -crusader-owned-a-meat-exporting-company/article10149486.ece.

9. D. Nelson, "Drinking Milk from Non-Indian Cows 'Could Make Children Turn to Crime'," *The Telegraph*, April 24, 2015, https://www.telegraph.co.uk/news/worldnews/asia/india/11561612 /Drinking-milk-from-non-Indian-cows-could-make-children-turn-to-crime.html.

10. "'Cow Is the Only Animal that Inhales and Exhales Oxygen,' Says Uttarakhand CM," Scroll.in, July 26, 2019, https://scroll.in/latest/931875/cow-is-the-only-animal-that-inhales-and -exhales-oxygen-says-uttarakhand-cm.

11. V. Pathak, "RSS Now Cites Scientific Reasons for Cow Protection," *The Hindu*, October 10, 2015, http://www.thehindu.com/news/national/rss-now-cites-scientific-reasons-for -cow-protection/article7744540.ece.

12. S. Daniyal, "Maharashtra's Beef Ban Shows How Politicians Manipulate Hindu Sentiments around Cow Slaughter," Scroll.in, March 3, 2015, https://scroll.in/article/711064/maharashtras-beef-ban-shows-how-politicians-manipulate-hindu-sentiments-around-cow-slaughter. Petitioned by several parties, the court in Maharashtra eased this law by decriminalizing the possession of beef as long as the animal had been slaughtered outside the state.

13. A. Saldanha, "More than 99% Indians Now Live in Areas under Cow Protection Laws, Gujarat Has Strictest Rules," *Hindustan Times*, April 29, 2017, https://www.hindustantimes.com/india-news/more-than-99-indians-now-live-in-areas-under-cow-protection-laws-gujarat-has-strictest-rules/story-Z8v4B9skYXyoW79vZ6KHBI.html.

14. Sagari R. Ramdas, "The Sordid Truth about the BJP's Drive against Meat in UP," The Wire, April 9, 2017, https://thewire.in/121901/up-illegal-meat-bjp/.

15. Regarding the anticonstitutional aspect of BJP policy toward bovine slaughter, see Madhav Khosla, "What's at Steak? The Constitutional Cost of Beef Ban," *Open*, June 16, 2017, http://www.openthemagazine.com/article/cover-story/what-s-at-steak-the-constitutional-cost-of-beef-ban.

16. Deya Bhattacharya, "Yogi Adityanath's Crackdown on Abattoirs: Religionising of Plates Must Be Countered by Constitutional Checks," Firstpost, April 10, 2017, http://www.firstpost.com/politics/yogi-adityanaths-crackdown-on-abattoirs-religionising-of-plates-must-be-countered-by-constitutional-checks-3376594.html.

17. "Cattle Slaughter Notification: Supreme Court Issues Notice to Centre," *The Hindu*, June 15, 2017, http://www.thehindu.com/news/national/cattle-slaughter-notification-supreme-court-issues-notice-to-centre/article19053422.ece.

18. Apurva Vishwanath, "Govt Tells SC Cattle Slaughter Ban Will Not Be Implemented Immediately," *Mint*, March 16, 2017, http://www.livemint.com/Politics/FAoPVJMR63vlxUua1Mxf3J/Cattle-slaughter-ban-Supreme-Court-asks-Centre-to-file-resp.html.

19. Regarding this conservative trend, see Christophe Jaffrelot, "The Roots and Varieties of Political Conservatism in India" and "The Congress in Gujarat (1917–1969): Conservative Face of a Progressive Party," in "Political Conservatism in India," special issue, *Studies in Indian Politics* 5, no. 2 (November 2017): 205–17 and 248–61.

20. Cited in Satyabrata Pal, "The Perils of Saffron Nationalism," The Wire, March 25, 2016, http://thewire.in/2016/03/25/the-perils-of-saffron-nationalism-25853/. On the constituent assembly debates regarding the identity of India, see C. Jaffrelot, "Composite Culture Is Not Multiculturalism: A Study of the Indian Constituent Assembly Debates," in *India and the Politics of Developing Countries: Essays in Memory of Myron Weiner*, ed. A. Varshney (New Delhi: Sage, 2004), 126–49.

21. Bankim Chandra Chatterji, *Anandmath* (1882; repr., Delhi: Orient Paperbacks, 1992).

22. S. Ramaswamy, *The Goddess and the Nation: Mapping Mother India* (New Delhi: Zubaan, 2011).

23. BJP, "Nationalism: Article of Faith," in "Political Resolution Passed in the BJP National Executive Meeting at the NDMC Convention Centre," press release, March 20, 2016, http://www.bjp.org/en/media-resources/press-releases/political-resolution-passed-in-bjp-national-executive-meeting-at-ndmc-convention-centre-new-delhi-20-03-2016.

24. "Why Mohan Bhagwat Wants the Whole World to Chant 'Bharat Mata Ki Jai,'" *Indian Express*, March 28, 2016, http://indianexpress.com/article/cities/kolkata/want-the-whole-world-to-chant-bharat-mata-ki-jai-mohan-bhagwat/99/print/.

25. "Those Refusing to Say 'Bharat Mata Ki Jai' Should Have No Right to Stay in India: Fadnavis," *Indian Express*, April 3, 2016, http://indianexpress.com/article/cities/mumbai/cm -fadnavis-joins-bharat-mata-ki-jai-chorus/99/print/.

26. "Nitin Gadkari Kicks Up Row, Says We Are a Government of 'Ram Bhakts,'" *Indian Express*, January 22, 2015, http://indianexpress.com/article/india/india-others/nitin-gadkari -kicks-up-row-says-we-are-a-government-of-ram-bhakts/.

27. Sushma Swaraj and M. L. Khattar were speaking before members of the Global Inspiration and Enlightenment Organization of Gita, commemorating the 5,151st anniversary of this holy text. Representatives of some twenty foreign embassies were present. "Sushma Pushes for Declaring Bhagavad Gita as National Scripture," *The Hindu*, December 7, 2014, http://www .thehindu.com/news/national/sushma-pushes-for-declaring-bhagwad-gita-as-national -scripture/article6670252.ece.

28. "Sushma Swaraj's Suggestion on Bhagwada Gita against Secularism, Say NCP & SP; Congress Remains Silent," *Indian Express*, December 8, 2014, http://indianexpress.com/article /india/politics/sushma-swarajs-suggestion-on-bhagwada-gita-against-secularism-ncp-sp/.

29. "Sushma Swaraj's Call for Making Gita 'National Scripture' an Effort to Make India a Hindu Nation: NDA Ally, Opposition," *Indian Express*, December 8, 2014, http://indianexpress .com/article/india/india-others/nda-ally-opposes-gita-as-rashtriya-granth/.

30. "Union Minister Anantkumar Hegde Kicks Up Row with Remarks on Secularism" *The Hindu*, December 24, 2017, http://www.thehindu.com/news/national/karnataka/hegde-kicks -up-a-fresh-row-with-remarks-on-secularism/article22271584.ece?homepage=true; and "Parliament Winter Session Live Updates: Opposition Demands Anantkumar Hegde's Resignation; Both Houses Adjourned," *Indian Express*, December 27, 2017, http://indianexpress.com/article /india/parliament-winter-session- . . . adjournment-motion-anantkumar-hegdes-constitution -remark-5000571/.

31. A Sangh Parivar ideologue who speaks more freely than members of the government, K. N. Govindacharya, moreover said in 2016 that revision of the Constitution was indeed on the Hindu nationalist agenda: "We believe that Indian society and its cultural reality should be included in the Constitution. . . . Our Constitution is so vague, non-specific and basically a continuation of western philosophies of Hobbes, Locke and Kant. It is individual-centric and focused on his physical wellbeing. Our civilisation goes back 4,000–5,000 years." "RSS Ideologue Govindacharya: 'We Will Rewrite the Constitution to Reflect Bharatiyata,'" interview by Vrinda Gopinath, The Wire, June 20, 2016, https://thewire.in/politics/rss-ideologue -govindacharya-we-will-rewrite-the-constitution-to-reflect-bharatiyata. Appointed by the Modi government to head the Indira Gandhi National Centre for Arts, Ram Bahadur Rai, a veteran RSS member, also recommended reforming the Constitution, which he viewed as a sign of India's continuing "enslavement." "Ambedkar's Role in the Constitution Is a Myth," *Outlook*, June 13, 2016, https://www.outlookindia.com/magazine/story/ambedkars-role-in-the -constitution-is-a-myth/297259. Regarding Hindu nationalist plans to revise the Constitution, see Kuldip Kumar, "RSS and the Constitution: Ram Bahadur Rai's Comments Come at an Inopportune Moment," The Wire, June 9, 2016, http://thewire.in/2016/06/09/rss-and-the -constitution-ram-bahadur-rais-comments-come-at-an-inopportune-moment-41657/.

32. Aarefa Johari, "Controversial MP Sakshi Maharaj Has a Trail of Rape and Murder Charges behind Him," Scroll.in, January 10, 2015, https://scroll.in/article/699597/controversial -mp-sakshi-maharaj-has-a-trail-of-rape-and-murder-charges-behind-him; and R. M. Chaturvedi, "A Look at BJP MP Sakshi Maharaj's Long List of Crimes," *Economic Times*, October 21, 2015, http://m.economictimes.com/news/politics-and-nation/a-look-at-bjp . . . -sakshi -maharajs-long-list-of-crimes/amp_articleshow/49474193.cms.

33. "What Do These Nathuram Godse Fans Have in Common? They Are All Followed by PM Modi on Twitter," Alt News, October 2, 2017, https://www.altnews.in/godse-fans-common -followed-pm-modi/.

34. "BJP Lawmaker Sakshi Maharaj Calls Gandhi Assassin Nathuram Godse a 'Patriot,' Then Retracts," NDTV, December 11, 2014, https://www.ndtv.com/india-news/bjp-lawmaker-sakshi -maharaj-calls-gandhi-assassin-nathuram-godse-a-patriot-then-retracts-711854.

35. The RSS could resist the rise to power of Narendra Modi even less effectively after his 2014 victory. When Modi supported the candidature of Amit Shah, his closest confidant, to the post of BJP president, after the incumbent, Rajnath Singh, had become minister, the RSS tried to contain this new offensive. An RSS official who requested anonymity told Dhirendra K. Jha, "Complete control over the government and the party by one person would not be in the interest of the Sangh Parivar. . . . In the entire Sangh Parivar in Gujarat, it is Modi's men who take all decisions, and the detractors simply have no place in it. The Sangh cannot allow that to happen in the rest of the country." Dhirendra K. Jha, "Is the RSS against Amit Shah Becoming BJP President?," Scroll.in, June 2, 2014, http://scroll.in/article/666023/Is-the-RSS-against-Amit -Shah-becoming-BJP-president/.

36. Pavan Dahat, "Don't Allow Govt. to Overshadow BJP: RSS," *The Hindu*, July 19, 2014, http://www.thehindu.com/news/national/dont-allow-govt-to-overshadow-bjp-rss /article6226682.ece. These recommendations did not only arise from apprehensions about Modi's modus operandi but also from the memories of the Vajpayee government. According to Dilip Deodhar, "Amit Shah definitely got instructions on Friday to make the BJP no less powerful than the government. Another trend witnessed during the previous NDA regime was the organisation of the BJP had followed the mantra of 'Delhi to Galli' (Delhi to street.'" Cited in Jha, "RSS against Amit Shah."

37. This was discussed by senior RSS leaders and BJP ministers at Modi's house in July 2014. "BJP, RSS Discuss Contentious Issues," *The Hindu*, July 24, 2014, http://www.thehindu.com /news/national/bjprss-leaders-meet/article6245802.ece.

38. "In Govt-RSS Tango, 5 Ministers Meet Sangh," *Indian Express*, October 29, 2014, https:// indianexpress.com/article/india/politics/in-govt-rss-tango-5-ministers-meet-sangh/.

39. Ashutosh Bhardwaj, "Banning RSS Members from Joining Govt Service Unjust: Manmohan Vaidya," *Indian Express*, June 11, 2016, http://indianexpress.com/article/india/india -news-india/banning-rss-members-from-joining-govt-service-unjust-manmohan-vaidya -2846534/.

40. "Bhaiyji Joshi Visits Tinbigha Corridor," *The Organiser*, October 12, 2014.

41. "Five BJP Veterans Appointed as New Governors," NDTV, July 14, 2014, https://www .ndtv.com/india-news/five-bjp-veterans-appointed-as-new-governors-588266.

42. Shubhangi Khapre, "RSS Chief on DD BJP Lashes Out at Congress, Asks Why Did You Block Broadcast till Now?" *Indian Express*, October 4, 2014, https://indianexpress.com/article/india/india-others/rss-chief-on-dd-bjp-lashes-out-at-congress-asks-why-did-you-block-broadcast-till-now/.

43. M. Ghatwai, "Everyone Living in India Is Hindu, Says RSS Chief Mohan Bhagwat," *Indian Express*, February 9, 2017, http://indianexpress.com/article/india/everyone-living-in-india-is-hindu-says-rss-chief-mohan-bhagwat/Page; and "RSS Chief Mohan Bhagwat Says All Hindustanis Are Hindus, Triggers Controversy," *Indian Express*, August 11, 2014, http://indianexpress.com/article/india/politics/rss-chief-mohan-bhagwat-says-all-hindustanis-are-hindus-triggers controversy/.

44. "RSS Chief Mohan Bhagwat Says All Hindustanis Are Hindus, Triggers Controversy," *Indian Express*, October 12, 2014, https://indianexpress.com/article/india/politics/rss-chief-mohan-bhagwat-says-all-hindustanis-are-hindus-triggers-controversy/.

45. "Anybody Living in India Is Hindu: RSS Chief Mohan Bhagwat," *Times of India*, December 18, 2017, https://timesofindia.indiatimes.com/india/anybody-living-in-india-is-hindu-rss-chief/articleshow/62107639.cms.

46. Madhuparna Das, "RSS Leader Mohan Bhagwat Justifies 'Ghar Wapsi,' Says Will Bring Back Our Brothers Who Have Lost Their Way," *Indian Express*, December 21, 2014, https://indianexpress.com/article/india/politics/bhagwat-dares-oppn-says-if-dont-like-conversion-bring-law-against-it/.

47. T. A. Johnson, "Days before SC Hearing, RSS Chief Mohan Bhagwat Rules: Only Ram Temple Will Be Built in Ayodhya," *Indian Express*, November 25, 2017, https://indianexpress.com/article/india/days-before-sc-hearing-rss-chief-mohan-bhagwat-rules-only-ram-temple-will-be-built-in-ayodhya-4953218/.

48. "Article 35A Must Go: Mohan Bhagwat in J-K," *Indian Express*, October 1, 2017, https://indianexpress.com/article/cities/jammu/article-35a-must-go-jammu-kashmir-rss-leader-4869153/.

49. The RSS English-language weekly, *The Organiser*, devotes one of its weekly columns to teaching the history of India to children. Prateek Paul, "Children and Ideology: Interrogating Hindu Nationalism in *The Organiser*," (master's thesis, Ambedkar University, Delhi, 2018).

50. *The Organiser* thus lamented in 2015 that "in the name of secularism we have excluded our youth from the rich legacy of our literature and scriptures. . . . It is time to talk of 'Indianisation' of Indian history. Let us build a nation with the youth strong enough to proclaim their pride across the spectrum of the globe." K. N. Rao, "Indianisation of Indian history," *The Organiser*, July 19, 2015.

51. Dhirendra K. Jha, "RSS Sets Up Panel to Supervise Saffronisation of Education," Scroll.in, August 2, 2014, https://scroll.in/article/672545/rss-sets-up-panel-to-supervise-saffronisation-of-education.

52. S. N. Vijetha, "Historians Protest as Delhi University Purges Ramayana Essay from Syllabus," *The Hindu*, October 15, 2011, https://www.thehindu.com/news/national/Historians-protest-as-Delhi-University-purges-Ramayana-essay-from-syllabus/article13372074.ece.

53. Aarefa Johari, "The Textbook Vigilante: Meet the Man Who Got Doniger's Book on Hinduism Withdrawn," Scroll.in, February 12, 2014, https://scroll.in/article/656157/the-textbook-vigilante-meet-the-man-who-got-donigers-book-on-hinduism-banned.

54. Regarding this issue, which bothers many Indians, even in the scientific community, see Rohan Venkataramakrishnan, "Aryan Migration: Everything You Need to Know about the New Study on Indian Genetics," Scroll.in, April 2, 2018, https://scroll.in/article/874102/aryan -migration-everything-you-need-to-know-about-the-new-study-on-indian-genetics; and Tony Joseph, "How Genetics Is Settling the Aryan Migration Debate," *The Hindu*, June 16, 2017, https://www.thehindu.com/sci-tech/science/how-genetics-is-settling-the-aryan-migration -debate/article19090301.ece.

55. Ravi Kumar, "Nalanda: 9 Million Books Burnt in 1193 by Bakhtiyar Khilji Nalanda," *My India My Glory*, accessed September 27, 2020, https://www.myindiamyglory.com/2017/09/11 /nalanda-9-million-books-burnt/.

56. *The Muslim Issue* blog went on and on about this topic. Its URL was very revealing: https://themuslimissue.wordpress.com/2015/08/31/islamic-invasion-of-india-the-greatest -genocide-in-history/. It has been suspended for violating WordPress's terms of service and is no longer available.

57. Shoaib Daniyal, "Five Things Hindutva Historians Are Obsessed With," Scroll.in, July 7, 2014, https://scroll.in/article/669435/five-things-hindutva-historians-are-obsessed-with.

58. "Interview of the Week: We Need to Indianise Historical Research—Prof. Y. Sudershan Rao," *The Organiser*, October 19, 2014.

59. Switching from history to geography, Rao explained on his blog: "We already have history in form of Puranas, Ithiasas and Kavyas. What we need is to identify our ancient historical events in their proper geographical locations. This would enable us to authenticate our history from Puranas." Alokparna Das, "On His Blog, How to Back History Up with Puranas," *Indian Express*, July 16, 2014, https://indianexpress.com/article/india/india-others/on-his-blog-how -to-back-history-up-with-puranas/. In July 2014, Rao also said, "The stories of the *Ramayan* and the *Mahabharat* cannot be termed a-historical just because there is not enough archaeological hard evidence." (B. K. Mohanty, "*Mahabharat* Historian Gets Research Reins," *The Telegraph*, July 3, 2014, https://www.telegraphindia.com/1140703/jsp/nation/story_18576515.jsp# .U7jcrfmSx5J. This lack of distinction between history and mythology is typical of Hindu nationalism. See S. P. Udaykumar, *"Presenting" the Past: Anxious History and Ancient Future in Hindutva India* (Westport, CT: Praeger, 2005). See also Daniyal, "Five Things Hindutva Historians"; and Harbans Mukhia, "Between History and Mythology," *The Hindu*, July 17, 2014, https://www .thehindu.com/opinion/op-ed/between-history-and-mythology/article6218099.ece.

60. Rupam Jain and Tom Lasseter, "By Rewriting History, Hindu Nationalists Aim to Assert Their Dominance over India," Reuters, March 6, 2018, https://www.reuters.com/investigates /special-report/india-modi-culture/?utm_source=Twitter&utm_medium=Social.

61. Cited in Jain and Lasseter, "By Rewriting History."

62. Jain and Lasseter.

63. Omar Rashid, "Saffronisation of Education Good for India, Says Minister," *The Hindu*, June 19, 2016, https://www.thehindu.com/news/national/Saffronisation-of-education-good -for-India-says-Minister/article14431919.ece?css=print.

64. M. Lall, "Indian Education Policy under the NDA Government," in *Coalition Politics and Hindu Nationalism*, ed. K. Adeney and L. Saez (London: Routledge, 2005), 153–68.

65. Sylvie Guichard, *The Construction of History and Nationalism in India: Textbooks, Controversies and Politics* (London: Routledge, 2010).

66. Lars Tore Flaten, "Spreading Hindutva through Education: Still a Priority for the BJP?," *India Review* 16, no. 4 (2017): 377–400.

67. Achin Vanaik, *The Rise of Hindu Authoritarianism: Secular Claims, Communal Realities* (London: Verso, 2017), 365.

68. Science textbooks underwent 573 modifications, and social science textbooks, 316. Ritika Chopra, "From Swachh Bharat, Noteban to Ganga and Digital India: Govt Schemes Enter NCERT Textbooks," *Indian Express*, June 1, 2018, https://indianexpress.com/article/education /from-modis-swachh-bharat-noteban-to-ganga-and-digital-india-govt-schemes-enter-ncert -textbooks-5199426/.

69. Hari Vasudevan, "Not by the Book," *Indian Express*, June 15, 2018, https://indianexpress .com/article/opinion/columns/ncert-cbse-text-book-development-committee-5217818/.

70. Ritika Chopra, "New Icons in NCERT Books: Bajirao to Maharana Pratap," *Indian Express*, June 1, 2018, https://indianexpress.com/article/education/new-icons-in-ncert-books -bajirao-to-maharana-pratap-5196491/?12345.

71. Disha Nawani, "Modifying School Textbooks," *Economic and Political Weekly* 53, no. 29 (July 21, 2018), https://www.epw.in/journal/2018/29/commentary/modifying-school -textbooks.html.

72. Aarefa Johari, "Blowing Birthday Candles Is against Indian Culture, Says Man Who Is Now on Gujarat School Library Reading Lists," Scroll.in, July 26, 2014, https://scroll.in/article/671677 /blowing-birthday-candles-is-against-indian-culture-says-man-who-is-now-in-gujarat-school -syllabus; and Ritika Chopra, "Dinanath Batra's Moral Science and Verse Will Enter Haryana Textbooks," *Indian Express*, September 28, 2015, http://indianexpress.com/article/india/india -others/dinanath-batras-moral-science-and-verse-will-enter-haryana-textbooks/?SocialMedia.

73. Chopra, "Dinanath Batra's Moral Science."

74. Chopra.

75. Sharat Kumar, "Rajasthan Rewrites History: Maharana Pratap, Not Akbar, Won Battle of Haldighati," *India Today*, July 25, 2015, https://www.indiatoday.in/india/story/maharana -pratap-not-akbar-won-battle-of-haldighati-rajasthan-history-book-1026240-2017-07-25.

76. C. Jaffrelot and Pradyumna Jairam, "BJP Has Been Effective in Transmitting Its Version of Indian History to Next Generation of Learners," *Indian Express*, November 16, 2019, https:// indianexpress.com/article/opinion/columns/education-ours-and-theirs-6121982/.

77. Mahim P. Singh, "Jawaharlal Nehru Erased from Rajasthan School Textbook," *Indian Express*, May 8, 2016, http://indianexpress.com/article/india/india-news-india/jawaharlal -nehru-erased-from-rajasthan-school-textbook-2789754/99/print/.

78. Sujata Anandan, "Rewriting History; More about Politics and Less about Education?," *National Herald*, August 16, 2017, https://www.nationalheraldindia.com/education/rewriting -history-more-about-politics-and-less-about-education.

79. Sneha Chowdhury, "After Maharashtra, UP Government Proposes to Remove the Mughals from History Textbooks," NewsClick, September 18, 2017, https://www.newsclick.in/after -maharashtra-government-proposes-remove-mughals-history-textbooks.

80. Madhur Sharma, "Silent Burial for Sher Shah Suri, Mughal Empire in DU New Syllabus," Newslaundry, May 16, 2018, https://www.newslaundry.com/2018/05/16/delhi-university -history-syllabus-she-shah-suri-mughal-empire.

81. P. K. Maitra, "RSS Role in 'Nation-Building' Now a Part of Maharashtra Varsity's Syllabus," *Hindustan Times*, July 9, 2019, https://www.hindustantimes.com/india-news/rss-role-in
-nation-building-now-a-part-of-maharashtra-varsity-s-syllabus/story-C6WbwoGyDmyjOw
iNZGKbgJ.html.

82. "BJP All Set to Test UP School Students on Hindutva Propaganda," The Wire, August 2,
2017, https://thewire.in/163836/bjp-distributes-booklets-to-up-students-on-modi-yogi
-government-schemes/.

83. R. Belur, "Karnataka Government Drops Chapter on Tipu Sultan from Class 7 Book,"
Deccan Herald, July 28, 2020, https://www.deccanherald.com/state/karnataka-government
-drops-chapter-on-tipu-sultan-from-class-7-book-866603.html.

84. "Units on Tipu Sultan, Constitution Reduced as Karnataka Govt Cuts School Syllabi,"
The Wire, July 28, 2020, https://thewire.in/education/units-on-tipu-sultan-constitution
-reduced-as-karnataka-govt-cuts-school-syllabi.

85. T. Sanghera, "Modi's Textbook Manipulations," *Foreign Policy*, August 6, 2020, https://
foreignpolicy.com/2020/08/06/textbooks-modi-remove-chapters-democracy-secularism
-citizenship/.

86. "In Lucknow University, Exam Paper Becomes Loyalty Test," The Wire, March 19, 2018,
https://thewire.in/uncategorised/lucknow-university-question-paper-narendra-modi-bjp/
?utm_source=twpage.

87. "In Lucknow University."

88. The minister for human resource development viewed the rewriting of school textbooks
as a means to teach India's "glorious past." Ritika Chopra, "More Space in Classes VI to X
NCERT Books for Ancient Indian Knowledge Systems, Tradition," *Indian Express*, June 1, 2018,
https://indianexpress.com/article/education/ncert-school-books-class-six-to-ten-indian
-knowledge-system-tradition-5195025/.

89. "Darwin Theory Wrong; No One Has Seen Ape Turning into Man, Says MoS Satyapal
Singh," *The Hindu*, January 20, 2018, https://www.thehindu.com/news/national/darwin-theory
-wrong-no-one-has-seen-ape-turning-into-man-says-mos-satyapal-singh/article22481927.ece
?homepage=true.

90. Vasudevan Mukunth, "Dear Minister: An Indian Did Try to Fly but He Definitely Didn't
Invent the Aeroplane," The Wire, September 20, 2017, https://thewire.in/179334/satya-pal
-singh-ancient-vimana-shivkar-talpade-research/.

91. "Sita's Birth from Earthen Pot Shows Test Tube Baby Concept Existed during Ramayana,
Says UP Deputy CM Dinesh Sharma," *Hindustan Times*, June 1, 2018, https://www
.hindustantimes.com/india-news/sita-s-birthfrom-eart . . . g-ramayana-says-dinesh-sharma
/story-MySwttLXluiNG7KBg5AhuI.html.

92. "Rajasthan Education Minister Believes Brahmagupta Discovered Gravity 1,000 Years
before Newton," Scroll.in, January 9, 2018, https://scroll.in/latest/864353/rajasthan-education
-minister-believes-brahmagupta-discovered-gravity-a-1000-years-before-newton.

93. "Cancer Is Divine Justice for Sins Committed: Assam Health Minister," The Wire, November 23, 2011, https://thewire.in/199137/cancer-divine-justice-sins-committed-assam-health
-minister/.

94. "Cow Is the Only Animal."

95. M. Rahman, "Indian Prime Minister Claims Genetic Science Existed in Ancient Times," *The Guardian*, October 28, 2014, https://www.theguardian.com/world/2014/oct/28/indian-prime-minister-genetic-science-existed-ancient-times.

96. Anosh Malekar, "Darkness at Dawn: The Murders of Narendra Dabholkar, Govind Pansare and MM Kalburgi," *The Caravan*, August, 2016, http://www.caravanmagazine.in/reportage/darkness-at-dawn.

97. Jean-Thomas Martelli and Baris Ari, "From One Participant Cohort to Another: Surveying Inter-generational Political Incubation in an Indian University," *India Review* 17, no. 3 (2018): 263–300.

98. Ashok Swain, "JNU VC Jagadesh Kumar Does Not Seem Fit for His Job," Daily O, July 26, 2017, https://www.dailyo.in/voices/jnu-vc-rss-tanks-patriotism-hypernationalism/story/1/18597.html.

99. F. Iftikhar, "JNU Spending on Security Up, Research Budget Down," *Hindustan Times*, October 5, 2020, https://www.hindustantimes.com/delhi-news/jnu-spending-on-security-up-research-budget-down/story-XYRxiddp16Ma24phZHuCPL.html.

100. "Fines Mar the Start of New Semester at JNU," *Indian Express*, July 23, 2018, https://indianexpress.com/article/cities/delhi/fines-mar-the-start-of-new-semester-at-jnu-5270467/.

101. "2017 JNU Admissions—Over 80% Seat Cut for Researchers," Sabrangindia, March 25, 2017, https://sabrangindia.in/article/2017-jnu-admissions-over-80-seat-cut-researchers; and Aranya Shankar, "UGC Tightens Purse Strings, JNU V-C Says Research Will Suffer," *Indian Express*, May 3, 2017, http://indianexpress.com/article/education/ugc-tightens-purse-strings-jnu-v-c-says-research-will-suffer-4638104/.

102. On the way, "the vice chancellor arrogated himself the power to finalise the panel of experts, as part of the recruitment process." See Hartosh Singh Bal, "The Takeover," *The Caravan*, April, 2019, https://caravanmagazine.in/reportage/how-rss-infiltrating-india-intellectual-spaces.

103. Ananya Shakar, "Faculty Selection in JNU: Cracks on Campus," *Indian Express*, June 25, 2018, https://indianexpress.com/article/education/faculty-selection-in-jnu-cracks-on-campus-5042818/.

104. Ajoy Ashirwad Mahaprashasta, "Allegations of Political Bias in Faculty Hiring the Latest Battleline in JNU," The Wire, January 18, 2018, https://thewire.in/education/allegations-political-bias-faculty-hiring-latest-battleline-jnu.

105. Ajoy Ashirwad Mahaprashasta, "New JNU Appointees Caught in Plagiarism Charges," The Wire, April 3, 2018, https://thewire.in/education/jnu-scholars-plagiarism-vc.

106. Express News Service, "ABVP Man, Witness in JNU Sedition Case, Appointed Asst Professor," *Indian Express*, December 7, 2019, https://indianexpress.com/article/cities/delhi/abvp-man-witness-in-jnu-sedition-case-appointed-asst-professor-6154588/; Renu Sain, "JNU Clears Appointment of Admin of WhatsApp Group Involved in Jan 5 Violence?," NewsClick, February 22, 2020, https://www.newsclick.in/jnu-clears-appointment-admin-whatsapp-group-involved-jan-5-violence.

107. U. Vishnu, "New Faultlines in JNU after Deep Cuts in Research Seats," *Indian Express*, April 11, 2017, https://indianexpress.com/article/india/new-faultlines-in-jnu-after-deep-cuts-in-research-seats-4608207/; "JNUSU Seeks Lok Sabha Help over 'Reservation Violation,'"

Indian Express, April 5, 2018, https://indianexpress.com/article/cities/delhi/jnusu-seeks-lok -sabha-help-over-reservation-violation-5123729/.

108. Ayesha Kidwai, "The Many Reasons Behind the Anger in JNU," *The Wire*, March 6, 2018, https://thewire.in/229713/jnu-hiring-attendance-students-admission/; and K. Nagarajan, "How JNU Flouted Procedure to Revise Admission Criteria, Ignoring and Aggravating Concerns of Caste Discrimination," *The Caravan*, January 29, 2017, http://www.caravanmagazine.in /vantage/jnu-admission-caste-discrimination.

109. I am grateful to Jean-Thomas Martelli for this information.

110. Jean-Thomas Martelli, "The Spillovers of Competition: Value-Based Activism and Political Cross-Fertilization in an Indian Campus," *SAMAJ: South Asia Multidisciplinary Academic Journal* 22 (2019), https://doi.org/10.4000/samaj.6501.

111. A. Kumar, "JNU VC Sends Notice to 48 Teachers, Union Calls It 'Vindictive Targeting,'" *The Wire*, August 1, 2019, https://thewire.in/education/jnu-vice-chancellor-teachers-notice.

112. Kumar, "JNU VC Sends Notice."

113. Sanjay Baru, "Don't Destroy My University," *Indian Express*, August 7, 2018, https:// indianexpress.com/article/opinion/columns/higher-studies-jawaharlal-nehru-university -indian-students-stduying-abroad-5294734/.

114. Arpan Rai, "JNUTA Referendum: 279 of 300 Profs Who Voted Feel VC Should Resign," *The Quint*, August 8, 2018, https://www.thequint.com/news/education/jawaharlal-nehru -university-teachers-referendum-against-vc-mamidala-jagadesh-kumar.

115. Afzal Guru was found guilty of taking part in the plot that led to the attack on the Indian parliament by an Islamist commando in December 2001. The Indian courts sentenced him to death in 2006, and he was hanged in 2012. See Arundhati Roy, *The Hanging of Afzal Guru and the Strange Case of the Attack on the Indian Parliament* (New Delhi: Penguin, 2013).

116. "ABVP Protests against Pro-Afzal Guru Event at Jawaharlal Nehru University," Scroll.in, February 10, 2016, https://scroll.in/latest/803342/abvp-protests-against-screening-of-pro-afzal -guru-film-at-jawaharlal-nehru-university.

117. Priyanka Dubey, "Student Days—The Age of ABVP," *The Caravan*, October, 2017, http://www.caravanmagazine.in/reportage/age-of-abvp.

118. Dubey, "Student Days."

119. Dubey.

120. "Anti-India Acts Won't Be Tolerated: Rajnath Singh on JNU Row," *Economic Times*, February 12, 2016, https://economictimes.indiatimes.com/news/politics-and-nation/anti -india-acts-wont-be-tolerated-rajnath-singh-on-jnu-row/articleshow/50957307.cms?utm _source=contentofinterest&utm_medium=text&utm_campaign=cppst.

121. The faculty and the student body demonstrated great solidarity during this ordeal, which did not prevent internal debates, in particular in the course of a public lecture series on the theme "What is the Indian nation?" The texts can be found in R. Azad, J. Nair, M. Singh, and M. Sinha Roy, eds., *What the Nation Really Needs to Know: The JNU Nationalism Lectures* (New Delhi: HarperCollins, 2016).

122. "At Patiala House Court, Group of Lawyers Turns Violent, Attack JNU Students, Media," *Indian Express*, February 15, 2015, http://indianexpress.com/article/india/india-news -india/jnu-kanhaiya-kumar-patiala-house-court-lawyers-media-attacked/99/print/. See also

Rohan Venkataramakrishnan, "'We'll Break Your Phones and Your Bones': Journalists and JNU Students Attacked in Court," Scroll.in, February 16, 2016, http://scroll.in/article/803619/well-break-your-phones-and-your-bones-journalists-attacked-at-jnu-trial-court.

123. Anjali Mody and Mayank Jain, "Propaganda War: Sangh Parivar Takes to the Streets to Paint JNU as a 'Den of Traitors,'" Scroll.in, February 16, 2016, http://scroll.in/article/803644/propaganda-war-sangh-parivar-takes-to-the-streets-to-paint-jnu-as-a-den-of-traitors.

124. The text of the petition, written in the form of an open letter, is available on the internet: "JNU Events Signal Culture of Authoritarian Menace," *The Hindu*, February 17, 2016, http://www.thehindu.com/news/national/jnu-events-signal-culture-of-authoritarian-menace/article8245492.ece?css=print.ar.

125. Sara Hafeez, "JNU Row: Now, Delhi Police Seek Zee's Camera, Chip for Afzal Guru Event Footage," *Indian Express*, February 21, 2016, http://indianexpress.com/article/india/india-news-india/jnu-protest-kanhaiya-kumar-arrest-afzal-guru-event/99/print/.

126. "Three out of Seven JNU Clips 'Doctored,'" *Indian Express*, March 1, 2016, http://indianexpress.com/article/india/india-news-india/three-out-of-seven-jnu-clips-doctored/99/print/; and M. Janwalkar, "Words like 'Gun' Inserted in Kanhaiya Speech Video: Report on JNU Row," *Indian Express*, March 3, 2016, http://indianexpress.com/article/india/india-news-india/words-like-gun-inserted-in-kanhaiya-speech-video-report-on-jnu-row/99/print/.

127. Vishwa Deepak, "Zee News Journalist Quits in Disgust over JNU Coverage, Tells All in Letter," The Wire, February 21, 2016, http://thewire.in/2016/02/22/zee-news-reporter-quits-in-disgust-over-jnu-coverage-tells-all-in-letter-22290.

128. Narwal in fact explained that he had suggested the ABVP burn the *Laws of Manu*, an ancient Sanskrit text that codified the caste system, to demonstrate the organization's progressive credentials, but he was alone in supporting the idea. Jahnavi Sen, "Beating Up People for the Flag Is Not Nationalist, Say Ex-ABVP JNU Unit Members," The Wire, February 20, 2016, http://thewire.in/2016/02/20/beating-up-people-for-the-flag-is-not-nationalist-say-ex-abvp-jnu-unit-members-22177/.

129. The government of Delhi, led by a Modi opponent, Arvind Kejriwal, filed suit against ZeeTV.

130. Quoted in "Do Not Disagree: JNU Arrests over Afzal Guru Event Are Ill-Judged, Threatens Basic Rights," *Indian Express*, February 13, 2016, https://indianexpress.com/article/opinion/editorials/afzal-guru-film-jnu-student-protest-do-not-disagree/.

131. Jean-Thomas Martelli and Khaliq Parkar, "Diversity, Democracy, and Dissent: A Study on Student Politics in JNU," *Economic and Political Weekly* 53, no. 11 (March 17, 2018), https://www.epw.in/engage/article/diversity-democracy-dissent-study-student-politics-JNU.

132. Cited in "Twitterati Can't Get Over BJP MLA's Condom Count at JNU," *Indian Express*, February 23, 2016, http://indianexpress.com/article/trending/trending-in-india/bjp-mla-drugs-sex-condoms-in-jnu/. The same BJP MLA added in May 2016 that "rapes happen daily in JNU. It is hub of criminal activities." "After Condom Remark, Rajasthan BJP MLA Now Says Rapes Happen Everyday in JNU," *Indian Express*, May 25, 2016, http://indianexpress.com/article/india/india-news-india/after-condo . . . -rajasthan-bjp-mla-now-says-rapes-happen-everyday-in-jnu/99/print/.

133. "JNU Students Ate Beef, Worshipped Mahishasur: Police Report," *The Hindu*, February 18, 2016, http://m.thehindu.com/news/national/jnu-students-ate-beef-worshipped-mahishasur-police-report/article8249694.ece.

134. "Smriti Irani Briefs RSS, ABVP Members on Rohith Vemula, JNU Issues," *Indian Express*, March 8, 2016, http://indianexpress.com/article/india/india-news-india/smriti-irani-briefs-rss-abvp-members-on-rohith-vemula-jnu-issues/99/print/.

135. Supriya Sharma and Rohan Venkataramakrishnan, "'Insidious Intimidation': Delhi Police Knock on the Doors of Journalists Covering the JNU Row," Scroll.in, February 22, 2016, http://scroll.in/article/803975/insidious-intimidation-delhi-police-visit-homes-of-journalists-covering-the-jnu-row.

136. "JNU Row: Court Extends Police Custody of Umar Khalid, Anirban Bhattacharya by 2 More Days," *Indian Express*, February 27, 2016, http://indianexpress.com/article/india/india-news-india/jnu-row-co . . . stody-of-umar-khalid-anirban-bhattacharya-by-2-more-days/99/print/.

137. "JNU Tense after Violence at Film Screening Sparks Protests," *Indian Express*, April 9, 2018, http://indianexpress.com/article/cities/delhi/jnu-tense-after-violenc . . . lm-screening-sparks-protests-5155530/lite/?_twitter_impression=true.

138. Regarding the crackdown on a peaceful march in March 2018, see S. Visvanathan, "Through a Glass Darkly: A Witness Account of the Aftermath of JNU's Protest March," *The Wire*, March 29, 2018, https://thewire.in/education/through-a-glass-darkly-a-witness-account-of-the-aftermath-of-jnus-protest-march.

139. "In Solidarity against JNU Administration's 'Witch-Hunt against Dissenting Voices,'" *The Wire*, March 29, 2018, https://thewire.in/education/in-solidarity-against-jnu-administrations-witch-hunt-against-dissenting-voices.

140. M. Singh Manral, "JNU January 5 Violence: Police Give Themselves a Clean Chit," *Indian Express*, November 19, 2020, https://indianexpress.com/article/cities/delhi/jnu-january-5-violence-police-give-themselves-a-clean-chit-7056658/.

141. Zainab Ahmed, "Najeeb Disappearance Case: Is ABVP Scared of Supporting a Fair Investigation?," InUth, December 22, 2016, https://www.inuth.com/india/campus-watch/najeeb-disappearance-case-is-abvp-scared-of-supporting-a-fair-investigation/; and "Considering Filing Closure Report in Missing JNU Student Najeeb Ahmed Case: CBI to Delhi HC," *Indian Express*, July 12, 2018, https://indianexpress.com/article/india/considering-filing-closure- . . . t-in-missing-jnu-student-najeeb-ahmed-case-cbi-to-delhi-hc-5257025/.

142. Prashant Pandey, "Ranchi Professor Suspended for Inviting 'Mentor of Anti-Nationals' from JNU," *Indian Express*, March 30, 2016, http://indianexpress.com/article/india/india-news-india/ranchi-profe . . . r-suspended-for-inviting-mentor-of-anti-nationals-from-jnu/99/print/.

143. U. Sarkar, "Jodhpur: University Professor Suspended for Inviting JNU's Nivedita Menon to a Conference," Scroll.in, February 16, 2017, https://scroll.in/latest/829577/jodhpur-university-professor-suspended-for-inviting-jnus-nivedita-menon-to-a-conference.

144. Umar Khalid narrowly escaped a murder attempt perpetrated by two Hindu nationalists militants who presented themselves as *gau rakshak* (cow protectors) in August 2018. "Delhi Police Nabs Two Men for Attempting to Murder Umar Khalid," *Edexlive*, August 20, 2018,

https://www.edexlive.com/news/2018/aug/20/delhi-police-nabs-two-men-for-attempting-to
-murder-umar-khalid-3704.html.

145. "Ramjas College Violence: A Timeline," *Times of India*, March 2, 2017, https://
timesofindia.indiatimes.com/city/delhi/ramjas-college-violence-a-timeline/articleshow
/57378475.cms.

146. The letter he left is accessible at "My Birth Is My Fatal Accident; Rohit Vemula's Searing
Indictment of Social Prejudices," The Wire, January 17, 2017, https://thewire.in/politics/rohith
-vemula-letter-a-powerful-indictment-of-social-prejudices.

147. Nandini Sundar, "Academic Freedom and Indian Universities," *Economic and Political
Weekly* 53, no. 24 (June 16, 2018), https://www.epw.in/journal/2018/24/special-articles
/academic-freedom-and-indian-universities.html.

148. Nandini Sundar with Gowhar Fazili, "Growing Restrictions on Academic Freedom,"
Indian Cultural Forum, September 1, 2020, https://indianculturalforum.in/2020/09/01
/growing-restrictions-on-academic-freedom/#1.

149. Snigdha Poonam, *Dreamers: How Young Indians are Changing the World* (London: Hurst,
2018), 151–188.

150. In addition to universities, the case of the Tata Institute of Social Sciences in Mumbai
and the Film Institute in Pune warrant special mention on account of their governing bodies'
attitudes. "Protests at Film Institute in Pune after Actor-BJP Member Gajendra Chauhan Is
Appointed Chief," NDTV, June 13, 2015, https://www.ndtv.com/india-news/protests-at-film
-institute-in-pune-after-actor-bjp-member-gajendra-chauhan-is-appointed-chief-771313.

151. Amitav Rajan, "Foreign-Aided NGOs Are Actively Stalling Development, IB Tells PMO
in a Report," *Indian Express*, June 7, 2014, https://indianexpress.com/article/india/india-others
/foreign-aided-ngos-are-actively-stalling-development-ib-tells-pmo-in-a-report/.

152. Rohini Mohan, "Narendra Modi's Crackdown on Civil Society in India," *New York
Times*, January 9, 2017, https://www.nytimes.com/2017/01/09/opinion/narendra-modis
-crackdown-on-civil-society-in-india.html.

153. "Rs 12,500 Cr from Abroad and Only 2% NGOs Report It: Home Ministry," *Indian
Express*, June 16, 2014, http://indianexpress.com/article/india/india-others/rs-12500-cr-from
-abroad-and-only-2-ngos-report-it-home-ministry/.

154. Himradri Ghosh, "Under Modi Government, Foreign Funding of NGOs Has Come
Down," Newslaundry, May 20, 2016, https://www.newslaundry.com/2016/05/20/under-modi
-government-foreign-funding-of-ngos-has-come-down.

155. "FCRA Licenses of 10,117 NGOs Cancelled, UP and AP Top the List," News Minute,
April 28, 2015, https://www.thenewsminute.com/article/fcra-licenses-10117-ngos-cancelled
-and-ap-top-list.

156. Mausami Singh, "FCRA Licence of 20,000—or More than 50 per cent—of India's
NGOs Cancelled," *India Today*, December 27, 2016, http://indiatoday.intoday.in/story/fcra
-licence-of-20-000-of-india-ngos-cancelled/1/843912.html; and "FCRA licences of 20,000
NGOs cancelled," *Indian Express*, December 27, 2017, http://indianexpress.com/article/india
/fcra-licences-of-20000-ngos-cancelled-4447423/. According to the Home Ministry, "over
40,000 NGOs were registered under FCRA till 2011 but the numbers have approximately halved
after government tightened norms in 2014." R. Tripathi, "MHA Cancels FCRA Licences of 1,300

NGOs," *Economic Times*, November 8, 2019, https://economictimes.indiatimes.com/news/politics-and-nation/mha-cancels-fcra-licences-of-1300-ngos/articleshow/71964523.cms?utm_source=contentofinterest&utm_medium=text&utm_campaign=cppst.

157. V. Singh, "Parliament Proceedings. Government Tables Bill to Amend Foreign Contribution (Regulation) Act," September 20, 2020, https://www.thehindu.com/news/national/parliament-proceedings-government-tables-bill-to-amend-foreign-contribution-regulation-act/article32652630.ece.

158. A. Behar, "Behind the New Rules for NGOs to Get Foreign Funds, a Clear Political Message—Fall in Line," Scroll.in, September 24, 2020, https://scroll.in/article/973909/behind-the-new-rules-for-ngos-to-get-foreign-funds-a-clear-political-message-fall-in-line.

159. A short list was compiled by Meenakshi Ganguly, "Targeting NGOs Hurt Those Most in Need," *Asian Age*, December 22, 2016, http://www.asianage.com/india/all-india/221216/targeting-ngos-hurt-those-most-in-need.html.

160. The ANHAD website to which I was about to refer the interested reader has been shut down. The domain name is for sale.

161. See the website this link leads to: http://www.lawyerscollective.org.

162. Rahul Tripathi, "FCRA Licence of Indira Jaising's NGO Lawyers Collective Cancelled," *Indian Express*, December 7, 2016, http://indianexpress.com/article/india/indira-jaising-ngos-fcra-licence-cancelled-4414280/.

163. A. Bhuyan, "Documenting Anand Grover, Indira Jaising's Fight for Human Rights over the Years," The Wire, June 20, 2019, https://thewire.in/law/documenting-anand-grover-india-jaisings-fight-for-human-rights-over-the-years.

164. "Crackdown on Lawyers Collective, State Targeting Activists Again!," Sabrang, July 1, 2019, https://sabrangindia.in/article/crackdown-lawyers-collective-state-targeting-activists-again.

165. See her autobiography, Teesta Setalvad, *Foot Soldier of the Constitution: A Memoir* (New Delhi: LeftWord Books, 2017).

166. For further detail, see Christophe Jaffrelot, "Gujarat 2002: What Justice for the Victims?," *Economic and Political Weekly* 47, no. 8 (February 25, 2012), https://www.epw.in/journal/2012/08/special-articles/gujarat-2002-what-justice-victims.html.

167. Those are the terms, paradoxical to say the least, of the criminal charges drawn up by the ad hoc Bari Committee (named for its chair, who was also vice-chancellor of the Central University of Gujarat), whom the minister of human resource development had tasked with investigating specific allegations: Setalvad's misappropriation of funds were raised to build a museum to commemorate victims of the pogrom. See Shyamlal Yadav, "HRD Sets Up Panel to Probe Allegations against Teesta NGO," *Indian Express*, March 6, 2015, http://indianexpress.com/article/india/india-others/hrd-sets-up-panel-to-probe-allegations-against-teesta-ngo/; and Apoorvanand, "The Surgical Strikes on Teesta Setalvad Continue with the Bari Report, and We Should All Be Ashamed," Scroll.in, October 24, 2016, https://scroll.in/article/819646/the-surgical-strikes-on-teesta-setalvad-continue-with-the-bari-report-and-we-should-all-be-ashamed.

168. "Ford Foundation Freezes Funding to India as Modi Sarkar Clamps Down on NGOs," Firstpost, July 14, 2015, https://www.firstpost.com/blogs/life-blogs/ford-foundation-freezes-funding-to-india-as-modi-sarkar-clamps-down-on-ngos-2342146.html.

169. Cited in Ganguly, "Targeting NGOs."

170. Tripathi, "MHA Cancels FCRA Licences."

171. R. Tripathi, "Govt Set to Amend FCRA; Aadhar to be Mandatory for Registration," *Economic Times*, September 22, 2020, https://economictimes.indiatimes.com/news/economy/policy/govt-set-to-amend-fcra-aadhar-to-be-mandatory-forregistration/articleshow/78216211.cms?utm_source=contentofinterest&utm_medium=text&utm_campaign=cppst.

172. "Amnesty Halts India Ops Due to Govt's 'Reprisal', Approaches HC," *The Quint*, September 29, 2020, https://www.thequint.com/news/india/amnesty-international-stops-operations-in-india.

173. S. Yasir and H. Kumar, "Amnesty International Shutters Offices in India, Citing Government Attacks," *New York Times*, September 29, 2020, https://www.nytimes.com/2020/09/29/world/asia/india-amnesty-international.html.

174. J. Puri, "Sculpting the Saffron Body: Yoga, Hindutva, and the International Marketplace," in *Majoritarian State: How Hindu Nationalism Is Changing India*, ed. A. Chatterji, T. B. Hansen, and C. Jaffrelot (Hurst, London, 2019), 317.

Chapter 6

1. Chapter 16, which lists "internal threats," discusses Muslims, Christians, and Communists—far more powerful at the time than they are today and eminently secularist—in that order. M. S. Golwalkar, *Bunch of Thoughts* (1966; repr. Bangalore: Jagarana Prakashana, 1980), 233–64.

2. Subramanian Swamy, *Hindus under Siege: The Way out* (New Delhi, Har-Anand, 2006), 29

3. Swamy, *Hindus under Siege*, 55.

4. Swamy, 72–75.

5. Swamy, 5.

6. Gujarat offers a good illustration of the first instance and Odisha of the second. See Christophe Jaffrelot, "The BJP at the Centre: A Central and Centrist Party?," in *The BJP and the Compulsions of Politics*, ed. Thomas Blom Hansen and Christophe Jaffrelot (Delhi: Oxford University Press, 2001), esp. the section entitled "Gujarat, a Laboratory for Hindu Nationalism," 356–63; and Angana Chatterji, *Violent Gods: Hindu Nationalism in India's Present; Narratives from Orissa* (Gurgaon, India: Three Essays, 2009).

7. The first Christian symbol the Modi government attacked was Christmas, which it suggested replacing with another celebration, "Good Governance Day," during which schools would remain open, a measure that Human Resource Development Minister Smriti Irani had to renege on following a turbulent session in parliament. "Uproar in Lok Sabha over 'Order' to Keep Schools Open on X'Mas Day," *Economic Times*, December 15, 2014, http://economictimes.indiatimes.com/articleshow/45522034.cms?utm_source=contentofinterest&utm_medium=text&utm_campaign=cppst.

8. In January 2018, hundreds of ABVP activists stormed St. Mary's College in Vidisha (Madhya Pradesh) to perform this ritual, prompting the Catholic School Association to petition the courts. "Catholic School Association Moves Madhya Pradesh HC, Seeks Protection from ABVP," The Wire, January 15, 2018, https://thewire.in/213861/catholic-school-association-moves-madhya-pradesh-hc-seeks-protection-abvp/.

9. Claire Lesegretain, "En Inde, les nationalistes exigent des prières hindoues dans les écoles catholiques," *La Croix*, January 6, 2018, https://www.la-croix.com/Religion/Catholicisme/Monde/En-Inde-nationalistes-exigent-prieres-hindoues-ecoles-catholiques-2018-01-06-1200903927.

10. Aarti Dhar, "Mother Teresa's Aim Was Conversion, Says Bhagwat," *The Hindu*, February 24, 2015, http://www.thehindu.com/news/national/mother-teresas-aim-was-conversion-says-bhagwat/article6926462.ece.

11. Christophe Jaffrelot, "Militant Hindus and the Conversion Issue (1885–1990): From Shuddhi to Dharm Parivartan; The Politization and the Diffusion of an 'Invention of Tradition,'" in *The Resources of History: Tradition and Narration in South Asia*, ed. Jackie Assayag (Paris: EFEO, 1999), 127–52.

12. "Mother Teresa Part of Conspiracy for 'Christianization' of India: BJP MP Yogi Adityanath," *Indian Express*, June 21, 2016, http://indianexpress.com/article/india/india-news-india/mother-teres . . . -christianisation-of-india-says-bjp-mp-adityanath-2866131/99/print/.

13. Cited in John Dayal, "Why the Christian Community Should Steer Clear of the RSS 'Hand of Friendship,'" Scroll.in, February 11, 2016, http://scroll.in/article/802921/why-the-christian-community-should-steer-clear-of-the-rss-hand-of-friendship.

14. "Compassion Has Ended Its Program in India," Compassion International, March 2017, accessed April 4, 2018, https://www.compassion.com/india-update.htm.

15. Sandeep Singh, "Compassion International Reached End of Road for Its Operation in India for Diverting Money to Non-FCRA Registered Organisations," *The Organiser*, March 19, 2017, http://organiser.org//Encyc/2017/3/14/Compassion-International—Not-above-Law.aspx.

16. Sarah Zylstra, "Compassion: 145,000 Children Could Lose Sponsorship by Christmas," *Christianity Today*, December 9, 2016, http://www.christianitytoday.com/news/2016/december/compassion-international-child-sponsorship-india-christmas.html.

17. Ellen Barry and Suhasini Raj, "Major Christian Charity Is Closing India Operations amid a Crackdown," *New York Times*, March 7, 2017, https://mobile.nytimes.com/2017/03/07/world/asia/compassion-interna . . . ristian-charity-closing-india.html?referer=https://t.co/tFbmNw3Jvx.

18. Sashank Bangali, "An Indian Charity Battled Caste-Based Discrimination for Three Decades. Then It Became a Target," *Los Angeles Times*, January 18, 2017, http://www.latimes.com/world/la-fg-india-charity-2017-story.html.

19. Suhasini Haider and Vijata Singh, "No 'Compassion' for NGO in India Leaves Kerry Worried," *The Hindu*, September 4, 2016, http://www.thehindu.com/news/national/No-'compassion'-for-NGO-in-India-leaves-Kerry-worried/article14623228.ece?css=print&homepage=true.

20. Varghese K. George, "US Hails India's Easing of Curbs on Compassion International," *The Hindu*, October 19, 2016, http://m.thehindu.com/news/international/us-will-continue-to-push-for-ngos/article9240838.ece.

21. Dayal, "Why the Christian Community."

22. In Delhi, five churches were vandalized in two months in 2015. "Another Delhi Church Vandalised," *The Hindu*, February 3, 2015, http://www.thehindu.com/news/cities/Delhi/south-delhi-church-vandalised/article6847721.ece.

23. "Church Vandalised in Haryana, Cross Replaced with Hanuman Idol," *The Hindu*, March 15, 2015, http://www.thehindu.com/news/national/other-states/church-vandalised-in-haryana-cross-replaced-with-hanuman-idol/article6996137.ece.

24. "Mob 'Chanting Jai Sri Ram' Vandalises Church in Chhattisgarh," Scroll.in, March 6, 2016, https://scroll.in/latest/804690/mob-chanting-jai-sri-ram-vandalises-church-in-chhattisgarh.

25. "Mangalore Church Vandalised Days after Modi's Call for Tolerance," *India Today*, February 25, 2015, https://www.indiatoday.in/india/north/story/mangalore-church-vandalised-modi-call-religious-tolerance-241889-2015-02-25.

26. "Church Vandalized in Jharkhand, USCIRF Raises Alarm," Clarion, June 26, 2020, https://clarionindia.net/church-vandalised-in-jharkhand-uscirf-raises-alarm/.

27. S. Thomas, "Pastor Whipped and Beaten by the Police in Uttar Pradesh," Counter Currents, September 3, 2020, https://countercurrents.org/2020/09/pastor-whipped-and-beaten-by-the-police-in-uttar-pradesh/.

28. A. Bari Masoud, "During Lockdown 135 Cases of Hate Crime and Violence against Christians in India: Evangelical Commission," *Muslim Mirror*, July 14, 2020, http://muslimmirror.com/eng/despite-lockdown-135-cases-of-hate-crime-and-violence-against-christians-in-india-evangelical-commission/.

29. "135 incidents against evangelicals reported in India in the first half of 2020," Evangelical Focus, July 14, 2020, https://evangelicalfocus.com/world/7048/135-incidents-against-evangelicals-reported-in-india-in-the-first-half-of-2020.

30. "Police Detain Carol-Singing Group in Madhya Pradesh's Satna," *The Hindu*, December 15, 2017, http://www.thehindu.com/news/national/other-states/police-detain-carol-singing-group-in-madhya-pradeshs-satna/article21716250.ece?homepage=true.

31. "Pastor Shot Dead outside Church in Ludhiana," NDTV, July 16, 2016, https://www.ndtv.com/ludhiana-news/pastor-shot-dead-outside-church-in-ludhiana-1725439.

32. Church in Chains, *Official India: On the Side of the Militants; An Analysis of the Persecution of Christians in India with the Tacit Approval of Police and Government Officials (July–December 2017)*, Dublin, February 2018, accessed, December 25, 2020, http://www.churchinchains.ie/wp/wpcontent/uploads/2018/01/India-Persecution-Report-Jul-Dec-2017-WEB.pdf.

33. Church in Chains, *Official India*.

34. "Ludhiana Pastor Murder: Three Months on, Cops Fail to Crack Case, 'Withdraw' Kin's Security," *Hindustan Times*, October 9, 2017, https://www.hindustantimes.com/punjab/ludhiana-pastor-murder-three-months-on-cops-fail-to-crack-case-withdraw-kin-s-security/story-tayKSolXiJEFLIQeC9DCRN.html.

35. "Christian Persecution Rising in India," Release International, March 20, 2020, https://releaseinternational.org/christian-persecution-rising-in-india/.

36. *Martyrs for Jesus Christ: January to June 2020*, Persecution Relief Half-Yearly Report, July 2020, https://cdn.countercurrents.org/wp-content/uploads/2020/07/Persecution-Relief-Half-Yearly-Report-2020.pdf.

37. Note that the defense of secularism by a Catholic cardinal illustrates our analysis of this ism not in terms of *laïcité* but of equal recognition of all creeds by the state.

38. Liz Mathew, "Country Being Divided, Losing Faith in Govt, Says Catholic Body," *Indian Express*, December 22, 2017, http://indianexpress.com/article/india/country-being-divided -losing-faith-in-govt-catholic-body-4993755/.

39. Julio Ribeiro, "As a Christian, Suddenly I Am a Stranger in My Own Country, Writes Julio Ribeiro," *Indian Express*, March 17, 2017, http://indianexpress.com/article/opinion /columns/i-feel-i-am-on-a-hit-list/.

40. Gary Azavedo, "Rising Communal Violence in India Most Dangerous of All Social Distrusts: Archbishop Ferrao," *Times of India*, April 5, 2018, https://timesofindia.indiatimes.com /india/rising-communal-violence-in-india-most-dangerous-of-all-social-distrusts-archbishop -ferrao/articleshow/63633384.cms?.

41. Liz Mathew, "Rajnath Singh, Amit Shah Delhi Archbishop for 2019 poll remark," *Indian Express*, May 23, 2018, https://indianexpress.com/article/india/call-for-prayers-before-2019 . . . rnment-delhi-archbishop-anil-couto-rajnath-singh-amit-shah-5187350/.

42. "Catholic Head Meets Rajnath," *The Hindu*, May 24, 2018, https://www.thehindu.com /news/national/catholic-head-meets-rajnath/article23980853.ece?homepage=true.

43. Julio Ribeiro, "A Prayer for Secularism: Hindu Rashtra, which Would Make My Country a Saffron Pakistan, Is Profoundly Anti-National," *Times of India*, May 28, 2018 https://blogs .timesofindia.indiatimes.com/toi-edit-page/a-prayer-for-secularism-hindu-rashtra-which -would-make-my-country-a-saffron-pakistan-is-profoundly-anti-national/.

44. Social media enables Hindu nationalist officials to diffuse their anti-Muslim comments widely. Tripura's governor, Tathagata Roy, for instance, relished in the violence perpetrated against the Rohingyas in Myanmar, viewing it as revenge for the massacre of Hindus in West Bengal during Partition in 1947. He tweeted, "A bit of historic justice. Buddhist retribution for Hindu and Chakma genocide in East Bengal. The wheel grinds slowly but surely." Tathagata Roy, September 4, 2017, https://twitter.com/tathagata2/status/904752428523954176.

45. See Saeed Naqvi's autobiographical account, *Being the Other: The Muslim in India* (New Delhi: Aleph, 2016).

46. Pragya Kaushika, "Muslims Don't Vote Us (BJP) since We Are Patriotic: MP Parvesh Verma," *Indian Express*, December 20, 2016, http://indianexpress.com/article/india/parvesh -verma-muslim-remark-bjp-muslims-dont-vote-us-bjp-4436206/.

47. C. Bell, "Indian Politician: 'Taj Mahal Built by Traitors,'" *BBC News*, October 16, 2017, http://www.bbc.com/news/world-asia-india-41635770.

48. "Another Stab at Taj Mahal's Heritage," *The Hindu*, October 16, 2017, http://www .thehindu.com/news/national/other-states/sangeet-som-terms-mughal-emperors-traitors -questions-taj-mahal-history/article19870060.ece. See also "Who Is Sangeet Som?," *Indian Express*, October 18, 2017, http://indianexpress.com/article/who-is/who-is-sangeet-som-taj -mahal-history-muslims-hindu-4893208/.

49. Yogi Adityanath, the chief minister of Uttar Pradesh, who had said a few months before that the Taj Mahal did not reflect Indian culture, was obliged to distance himself from Som, concluding that the monument warranted respect at least out of consideration for the Hindu workers who built it.

50. S. Pandey, "Yogi Rechristens Mughal Museum after Shivaji, BJP Leaders Want Taj Mahal to Be Declared 'Tejolay,'" *Deccan Herald*, September 15, 2020, https://www.deccanherald.com

/national/national-politics/yogi-rechristens-mughal-museum-after-shivaji-bjp-leaders-want
-taj-mahal-to-be-declared-tejolay-887923.html.

51. Hindu nationalist circles have long been practiced in the art of dissimulation. See the
introduction to Christophe Jaffrelot, ed., *The Sangh Parivar: A Reader* (New Delhi: Oxford
University Press, 2005). After the 1998 elections, K. N. Govindacharya, a senior BJP official,
stated that Vajpayee, the moderate, was only a "mask," the actual party leader being L. K. Advani.
"Govindacharya Calls Vajpayee 'Mask,' Lands BJP in Crisis," Rediff.com, accessed September 27, 2020, http://m.rediff.com/news/oct/16bjp.htm.

52. Lalmani Verma and T. A. Johnson, "Who Loves Love Jihad," *Indian Express*, September 7,
2014, http://indianexpress.com/article/india/india-others/who-loves-love-jihad/.

53. This is one reason why Muslim films stars in Bollywood have been the particular targets
of Hindu nationalists—the other explanation for this relentless persecution is their incredible
popularity. Regarding the attacks against two Muslim figures in Hindi films, see Swati
Chaturvedi, *I Am a Troll: Inside the Secret World of the BJP's Digital Army* (New Delhi: Juggernaut, 2016), 66–68.

54. Lalmani Verma, "As 12 Seats in UP Prepare to Vote, 2 RSS Magazines Discuss 'Love
Jihad,'" *Indian Express*, September 6, 2014, http://indianexpress.com/article/india/india-others
/as-12-seats-in-up-prepare-to-vote-2-rss-magazines-discuss-love-jihad/.

55. Cited in Verma, "12 seats in UP."

56. "Report: Hindus Need to Act Tough against 'Love Jihad,'" *The Organiser*, April 19, 2015,
http://organiser.org//Encyc/2015/5/2/Report—Hindus-need-to-act-tough-against-'Love
-Jihad'.aspx.

57. Shoaib Daniyal, "Five Charts that Puncture the Bogey of Muslim Population Growth,"
Scroll.in, June 11, 2018, https://qz.com/379773/five-charts-that-puncture-the-bogey-of-muslim
-population-growth/.

58. Verma and Johnson, "Who Loves Love Jihad." A specialist on the issue of interfaith marriages in India, Jyoti Punwani, points out that many of those she studied did not involve the
spouse's conversion. J. Punwani, "Myths and Prejudices about 'Love Jihad,'" *Economic and Political Weekly* 49, no. 42 (October 18, 2014): 12–15. But Hindu nationalists peddle the opposite
idea, as seen in their 2014–2015 campaign targeting of the actress Kareena Kapoor, married to
a Muslim, whom they Photoshopped to show her face half covered with a full veil, a garment
she does not wear as a Hindu.

59. Interfaith marriages were officially made possible by the Special Marriage Act of 1954.

60. The nexus between the Bajrang Dal and lawyers in the Uttar Pradesh courts is well documented by Mohammed Ali, "The Rise of a Hindu Vigilante in the Age of WhatsApp and Modi,"
Wired, April 14, 2020, https://www.wired.com/story/indias-frightening-descent-social-media
-terror/.

61. Abhishek Dey, "Court Informers and Mohalla Spies: How Hindutva Groups in North
India Stop Inter-Faith Marriages," Scroll.in, August 5, 2018, https://scroll.in/article/888931
/court-informers-and-mohalla-spies-how-hindutva-groups-in-north-india-stop-inter-faith
-marriages.

62. "Operation Juliet: Busting the Bogey of 'Love Jihad,'" Cobrapost, October 4, 2015,
http://cobrapost.com/blog/operation-juliet-busting-the-bogey-of-love-jihad-2/900.

63. "Operation Juliet."

64. "Operation Juliet."

65. This tactic sent ten Muslims from Meerut District to prison, where it was difficult to obtain their release, even after the woman who gave false testimony retracted her statement—bravely so given the pressure she was under from the VHP. Irena Akbar, "As 'Love Jihad' Charge Falls Flat, Families of Ten Accused Wait for End of Ordeal," *Indian Express*, October 19, 2014, http://indianexpress.com/article/india/uttar-pradesh/as-love-jihad-charge-falls-flat-families -of-ten-accused-wait-for-end-of-ordeal/; and S. Roychoudhury, "As Meerut 'Love Jihad' Victim Retracts Her Claim, VHP Claims Conspiracy by UP Government," Scroll.in, October 14, 2014, https://scroll.in/article/683544/as-meerut-love-jihad-victim-retracts-her-claim-vhp-claims -conspiracy-by-up-government.

66. "Operation Juliet."

67. "Operation Juliet."

68. "Operation Juliet."

69. Mohammad Ali, "Bajrang Dal Disrupts Interfaith Couple's Marriage in Meerut," *The Hindu*, September 28, 2017, http://www.thehindu.com/news/national/other-states/bajrang -dal-di . . . aith-couples-marriage-in-meerut/article19769190.ece?homepage=true; and "Uttar Pradesh: Muslim Man Attacked as He Goes to Marry Hindu Woman at Ghaziabad Court," Scroll.in, July 24, 2018, https://amp.scroll.in/latest/887797/uttar-pradesh-muslim-man-attac . . . to-marry-hindu-woman-at-ghaziabad-court?__twitter_impression=true.

70. Ali, "Rise of a Hindu Vigilante."

71. In Gujarat and Madhya Pradesh, many parents have appealed to the Bajrang Dal. Christophe Jaffrelot, "The Militias of Hindutva: Between Communal Violence, Terrorism and Cultural Policing," in *Armed Militias of South Asia: Fundamentalists, Maoists and Separatists*, ed. Laurent Gayer and Christophe Jaffrelot, trans. C. Schoch, G. Elliott, and R. Leverdier (London: Hurst, 2009), 199–235.

72. "Hindu-Muslim Couple Gets Married amid High Security in Karnataka," *Indian Express*, April 18, 2016, http://indianexpress.com/article/india/india-news-india/hindu-muslim-couple -gets-married-amid-high-security-in-karnataka-2758177/.

73. Milind Ghatwai, "Hindu Girl Marries Muslim Boy, Police Say Marriage Not Valid," *Indian Express*, December 29, 2014, http://indianexpress.com/article/india/india-others/hindu -girl-marries-muslim-boy-police-say-marriage-not-valid/.

74. Varghese K. George, "Top Cops Divided on 'Love Jihad,'" *The Hindu*, September 21, 2014, https://www.thehindu.com/news/national/top-cops-divided-on-love-jihad/article6430631.ece.

75. Milind Ghatwai, "Advocates, Right-Wing Activists Prevent Inter-Religious Marriage in Bhopal," *Indian Express*, October 14 2014, http://indianexpress.com/article/india/india-others /advocates-right-wing-activists-prevent-inter-religious-marriage-in-bhopal/.

76. The judges also explained their decision in these words: "A girl aged 24 years is weak and vulnerable, capable of being exploited in many ways. Her marriage being the most important decision in her life, can also be taken only with the active involvement of her parents." Julien Bouissou, "En Inde, le fantasme du 'love jihad' gagne du terrain," *Le Monde*, December 8, 2017, http://www.lemonde.fr/m-actu/article/2017/12/08/en-inde-le-fantasme-du-love-jihad-gagne -du-terrain_5226779_4497186.html#ccXsLOViorkgbPDP.99.

77. Regarding this case, see Vijaita Singh, "NIA to File Report on 'Love Jihad,'" *The Hindu*, October 29, 2017, http://www.thehindu.com/news/national/nia-to-file-report-on-love-jihad/article19945302.ece?homepage=true; "Supreme Court Orders NIA to Probe Conversion of Kerala Woman to Islam," The Wire, August 16, 2017, https://thewire.in/law/supreme-court-kerala-nia-conversion; A. Vishwanath, "Supreme Court Goes after 'Love Jihad,' Sparks Fears of Overreach," ThePrint, August 16, 2017, https://theprint.in/report/supreme-court-goes-after-love-jihad-sparks-fears-of-overreach/6678/.

78. Lalmani Verma, "'Love Jihad' on Official Agenda of BJP's UP Unit, Meet Today," *Indian Express*, August 24, 2014, http://indianexpress.com/article/india/politics/love-jihad-on-official-agenda-of-bjps-up-unit-meet-today/.

79. Lalmani Verma, "BJP Puts Uttar Pradesh Campaign into Gear, Asks, 'Does Religion Give Them Licence to Rape?,'" *Indian Express*, August 24, 2014, http://indianexpress.com/article/india/politics/bjp-puts-up-campaign-into-gear-asks-does-religion-give-them-licence-to-rape/.

80. Lalmani Verma, "Filing 6 Cases a Day over 9 Months, UP's Anti-Romeo Squad Keeps a BJP Promise," *Indian Express*, January 24, 2018, http://indianexpress.com/article/india/uttar-pradesh-anti-romeo-police-scorecard-1700-cases-six-a-day-bjp-yogi-adityanath-5036857/.

81. Deep Mukherjee, "Rajasthan Hacking: WhatsApp Group with BJP MP, MLA as Members Hail Killer," *Indian Express*, December 10, 2017, http://indianexpress.com/article/india/rajasthan-hacking-whatsapp-group-with-bjp-mp-mla-as-members-hail-killer-4975919/.

82. Kavita Srivastava, "Fourth Rajasthan Lynching Demonstrates Indoctrination of Hate," *Indian Express*, December 9, 2017, http://indianexpress.com/article/opinion/fourth-rajasthan-lynching-demonstrates-indoctrination-of-hate-4975098/.

83. "RSS Affiliate Plans to Marry 2,100 Muslim Women to Hindu Men from Next Week," Scroll.in, December 1, 2017, https://scroll.in/latest/859907/rss-affiliate-plans-to-marry-2100-muslim-women-to-hindu-men-from-next-week.

84. "Child Marriage Will Put an End to 'Love Jihad,' Says BJP MLA Gopal Parmar," *India Today*, May 6, 2018, https://www.indiatoday.in/india/story/child-marriage-will-put-an-end-to-love-jihad-says-bjp-mla-gopal-parmar-1227492-2018-05-06.

85. Shyamlal Yadav, "Agra a Blip, RSS to Step Up 'Ghar Wapsi,'" *Indian Express*, December 11, 2014, http://indianexpress.com/article/india/india-others/agra-a-blip-rss-to-step-up-ghar-wapsi/.

86. Milind Ghatwai, "Want to Protect Hindus Today and 1,000 Years from Now: Pravin Togadia," *Indian Express*, December 22, 2014, http://indianexpress.com/article/india/india-others/will-raise-hindu-population-of-country-to-100-says-togadia/.

87. Ghatwai, "Want to Protect Hindus Today."

88. Manjari Katju, "The Politics of Ghar Wapsi," *Economic and Political Weekly* 50, no. 1 (January 3, 2015): 23.

89. VHP leaders told journalists from *The Hindu* that "those Muslims or Christians who reconvert to Hinduism in such programmes would be allowed to choose a caste for themselves once the VHP has investigated the tradition, faith, and culture of the convert's ancestors." Suhrith Parthasarathy, "Conversion and Freedom of Religion," *The Hindu*, December 23, 2014, http://www.thehindu.com/opinion/lead/conversion-and-freedom-of-religion/article6716638.ece.

90. Cited in Santosh Singh, "Babri Demolition Was Show of Hindu Unity, Don't Stop Ghar Wapsi: Adityanath to Govt," *Indian Express*, December 15, 2014, http://indianexpress.com /article/india/india-others/babri-demolition-was-show-of-hindu-unity-dont-stop-ghar-wapsi -adityanath-to-govt/.

91. Cited in Singh, "Babri Demolition Was Show."

92. Madhuparna Das, "RSS Leader Mohan Bhagwat Justifies 'Ghar Wapsi,' Says Will Bring Back Our Brothers Who Have Lost Their Way," *Indian Express*, December 21, 2014, http:// indianexpress.com/article/india/politics/bhagwat-dares-oppn-says-if-dont-like-conversion -bring-law-against-it/.

93. The requested donation amounts were Rs 500,000 to convert a Muslim and 200,000 to convert a Christian. M. Ali, "Hindutva Group Seeks Donations for Aligarh 'Conversion Camp,'" *Indian Express*, December 12, 2014, http://www.thehindu.com/news/national/hindutva-group -seeks-donations-for-aligarh-conversion-camp/article6686093.ece.

94. Venkitesh Ramakrishnan and Divya Trivedi, "By Means Mostly Foul," *Frontline*, December 22, 2014, http://www.frontline.in/the-nation/by-means-mostly-foul/article6715484.ece.

95. S. Mishra, "Family Planning," *The Week*, January 18, 2015, 32.

96. Venkaiah Naidu, the BJP minister who brought the idea of an anticonversion law before parliament, deemed that "thousands of crores of rupees are being pumped into the country to convert people." Venkaiah Naidu, "Conversions Have Been Going on for 200 Years," interview by S. Mishra, *The Week*, January 18, 2015, 34.

97. Arun Sharma, "After Many Reconverted in 'Ghar Wapasi,' Christians Allege Boycott," *Indian Express*, March 22, 2018, https://indianexpress.com/article/india/after-many -reconverted-in-ghar-wapasi-christians-allege-boycott-5106529/.

98. Rohini Chatterji, "Shamli: Bajrang Dal Activist Force 'Ghar Wapsi' on Dalit Man Who Had Converted to Islam," *Huffington Post*, April 26, 2018, https://www.huffingtonpost.in/2018 /04/26/shamli-bajrang-dal-acti . . . -had-converted-to-islam_a_23420600/?ncid=tweetlnkinh pmg00000001.

99. "21 Year Old Aligarh Youth Converts to Islam, Arrested," *Muslim Mirror*, May 21, 2018, http://muslimmirror.com/eng/21-year-old-aligarh-youth-converts-to-islam-arrested/.

100. Christophe Jaffrelot and Charlotte Thomas, "Facing Ghettoisation in 'Riot-City': Old Ahmedabad and Juhapura between Victimisation and Self-Help," in *Muslims of Indian Cities: Trajectories of Marginalization*, ed. Laurent Gayer and Christophe Jaffrelot (London: Hurst, 2012), 43–79.

101. Concerning this rather technical aspect, see Christophe Jaffrelot and Sharik Lalivala, "The Segregated City," *Indian Express*, May 26, 2018, http://indianexpress.com/article/opinion /columns/muslims-in-india-hindus-jains-gujarat-love-jihad-5191304/.

102. Aditi Vatsa, "Muslim Family in Meerut Buys House in Hindu Area: 'Being Accused of Land Jihad,'" *Indian Express*, December 21, 2017, http://indianexpress.com/article/india /muslim-family-in-meerut-buys-house-in-hindu-area-being-accused-of-land-jihad-4992204/.

103. Anjali Mody, "Gurgaon Namaaz Disruption Brings Majoritarian Bullying in Plain Sight of Aspirational India," Scroll.in, May 6, 2018, https://amp.scroll.in/article/878040/with -gurgaon-namaaz-disruption- . . . s-to-the-plain-sight-of-aspirational-india?__twitter _impression=true.

104. A government minister in Haryana, Anil Vij, reinforced this idea. Darab Mansoor Ali, "Muslims Shouldn't Read Namaaz in Public Spaces: Haryana CM Khattar," The Quint, May 7, 2018, https://www.thequint.com/news/india/secular-india-friday-namaaz-stopped-by-hindu-groups-in-gurugram.

105. Sakshi Dayal, "Gurgaon Outfits Demand: Allow Namaz Only in Areas with over 50% Muslims," Indian Express, May 1, 2018, http://indianexpress.com/article/india/gurgaon-outfits-demand-allow-namaz-only-in-areas-with-over-50-muslims-5157790/.

106. "On Namaz Row Haryana Chief Minister Khattar Clarifies, 'Haven't Spoken about Stopping Anyone,'" NDTV, accessed June 1, 2018, https://www.ndtv.com/india-news/haryana-chief-minister-ml-khattar-says-namaz-should-be-read-in-mosques-not-public-spaces-1847926.

107. However, the impact on rural society of Hindu nationalist activities, including cow protection, and riots, such as the one that took place in the villages of Muzaffarnagar district in 2013, has also been significant. See N. Verma, "'Gau Raksha' Has Made Me a Stranger in My Own Village," The Wire, July 6, 2019, https://thewire.in/religion/gau-raksha-bihar-ramnavami.

108. Apurva and Aditi Vatsa, "BJP Leader's Son among 15 Named in Dadri Lynching Chargesheet," Indian Express, December 24, 2015, http://indianexpress.com/article/india/india-news-india/bjp-leaders-son-among-15-named-in-dadri-lynching-chargesheet/99/print/.

109. Harsh Mander, "A Country for the Cow: The Chronicle of a Visit to Cow Vigilante Victim Pehlu Khan's Village," Scroll.in, April 25, 2017, https://scroll.in/article/print/835315/; Harsh Mander, "Pehlu Khan, One Year Later," Indian Express, April 21, 2018, http://indianexpress.com/article/opinion/columns/pehlu-khan-rajasthan-cow-lynching-5145631/.

110. "Rajasthan: Muslim Man Ferrying Cows Dead in Alwar, Police Probe Vigilantes," Indian Express, November 13, 2017, http://indianexpress.com/article/india/rajasthan-muslim-man-allegedly-killed-by-cow-vigilantes-in-alwar-investigation-on-4934166/.

111. "Muslim Men Lynched in West Bengal over Cow Theft Suspicions," The Wire, August 28, 2017, https://thewire.in/171413/west-bengal-cow-lynching/.

112. "Two Muslim Men, Suspected of Stealing Cows, Lynched in Assam," The Quint, April 18, 2017, http://www.huffingtonpost.in/2017/04/17/two-muslim-men-suspe . . . GVfaW QiOjEwMzMsImRhdGEiOnRydWV9&ncid=tweetlnkinhpmg00000001.

113. "3 Arrested for Beating Up Men Near Delhi for Allegedly Carrying Beef," NDTV, October 15, 2017, https://www.ndtv.com/cities/would-have-burnt-me-alive-disabled-man-attacked-on-beef-charges-recalls-horror-1763077.

114. M. Singh Sengar, "Man Accused of Carrying Beef Attacked with Hammer in Gurgaon, Cops Watch," NDTV, August 2, 2020, https://www.ndtv.com/gurgaon-news/gurgaon-man-bashed-with-hammer-by-cow-vigilantes-as-cops-watch-2272290.

115. The website Lynchings Acres India has identified most cases of lynching on an interactive map: https://uploads.knightlab.com/storymapjs/3880ebf0c4ae695337dae06e048988a9/lynchings-acres-india/draft.html (accessed March 26, 2018).

116. Ranjan, "Muslim Killed over Suspicion of Cow Slaughter in Madhya Pradesh," Hindustan Times, May 20, 2018, https://www.hindustantimes.com/india-news/muslim-assaulted-ove . . . ghter-in-madhya-pradesh-dies/story-edU6ykm1Fd30aKnay4cvkM.html.

117. "Jai Shri Ram: The Hindu Chant That Became a Murder Cry," BBC, July 10, 2019, https://www.bbc.com/news/world-asia-india-48882053.

118. M. Das, "How the Flip-Flops in Tabrez Ansari Lynching Make It a Textbook Case of Bungled Probe," ThePrint, September 27, 2019, https://theprint.in/india/how-the-flip-flops-in -tabrez-ansari-lynching-make-it-a-textbook-case-of-bungled-probe/296781/.

119. Regarding this "normalization" process, see S. Halarnkar, "This Photograph of Two Murdered Teens Should Disturb an India that Has Normalised Hate," Scroll.in, September 10, 2017, https://scroll.in/article/print/849804.

120. "Database on Bovine-Related Violence (from January 2010 to September 2, 2017," IndiaSpend.org, accessed March 26, 2018, https://docs.google.com/spreadsheets/d /13REUhD4fW6olOy_SjobWQRA1qQg3VY1pp87XMRJwJW4/pubhtml. This online publication set up another website dedicated to lynching victims in connection with sacred cows called Hate Crime: Cow-Related Violence in India (http://lynch.factchecker.in).

121. Delna Abraham and Ojaswi Rao, "86% Killed in Cow-Related Violence since 2010 Are Muslim, 97% Attacks after Modi Govt Came to Power," *Hindustan Times*, July 16, 2017, https:// www.hindustantimes.com/india-news/86-killed-in-cow-relat . . . after-modi-govt-came-to -power/story-w9CYOksvgk9joGSSaXgpLO.html.

122. "Mobocracy Can't Be the New Normal, Get a Law to Punish Lynching: SC to Govt," *Indian Express*, July 3, 2018, https://indianexpress.com/article/india/cji-condemns-lynchings -across-country-asks-parliament-to-make-new-law/.

123. Raheel Dhattiwala, "'Blame It on the Mob'—How Governments Shun the Responsibility of Judicial Redress," The Wire, August 17, 2018, https://thewire.in/communalism/mob -violence-lynching-government-legal-process.

124. See Randall Collins, *Violence: A Micro-Sociological Theory* (Princeton, NJ: Princeton University Press, 2009).

125. Muslims were not the only ones to suffer from cow protection laws and regulations. All peasants, no matter what their religion, were affected, especially after May 2017, when the Modi government amended the Prevention of Cruelty to Animals (Regulation of Livestock Market) Rules to prevent cows from being taken to cattle markets. The economic effect of this measure was catastrophic: for one, breeders no longer dared sell their cows, out of fear of being accused of wanting to see them end up in the slaughterhouse. Furthermore, being unable to dispose of old livestock, they let the animals wander and end up in the fields of vegetable producers. This prompted the government to relax the provisions of the Prevention of Cruelty to Animals Act of May 23, 2017, which regulated the cattle trade. Sowmiya Ashok, "Govt to Roll Back Move to Ban Sale of Cattle for Slaughter," *Indian Express*, November 30, 2017, http://indianexpress.com /article/india/govt-to-roll-back-move-to-ban-sale-of-cattle-for-slaughter-4961219/; and "End to Cattle Curbs: On Withdrawal of Sale Ban," The Hindu, April 12, 2018, https://www.thehindu .com/opinion/editorial/end-to-cattle-curbs/article23505866.ece. See also M. Chari, "Beef Ban: In Marathwada, Everyone Wants to Sell Cattle—but Nobody Can Buy," Scroll.in, April 6, 2016, https://scroll.in/article/806026/beef-ban-in-marathwada-everyone-wants-to-sell-cattle-but -nobody-can-buy. Buffalo meat exports, which suffered collaterally from the cow protection laws, although they had progressed from 3.2 to 4.78 billion USD between 2012–2013 and 2014– 2015, sank to 3.91 in 2016–2017 before rising back up to 4.04 after the new provisions. A. Gowen, "Cows Are Sacred to India's Hindu Majority: For Muslims Who Trade Cattle, That Means Growing Trouble," *Washington Post*, July 16, 2018, https://www.washingtonpost.com/world

/asia_pacific/cows-are-sacred-to-indias-hindu-majority-for-muslims-who-trade-cattle-that
-means-growing-trouble/2018/07/15/9e4d7a50–591a-11e8-9889-07bcc1327f4b_story.html?utm
_term=.8cebd9abc7fb.

126. Nelanshu Shukla, "Muslim Community Should Abstain from Touching Cows, Provoking Hindus: BJP Leader on Alwar Lynching," *India Today*, July 23, 2018, https://www.indiatoday
.in/india/story/muslim-community-should-abs . . . provoking-hindus-bjp-leader-on-alwar
-lynching-1294041-2018-07-23.

127. Sudha Pai and Sajjan Kumar, *Everyday Communalism: Riots in Contemporary Uttar
Pradesh* (Delhi: Oxford University Press), 2018.

128. Sakshi Dayal and Sukhbir Siwach, "Mob Assaults Two for 'Carrying Beef' in Faridabad,
Three Who Came to Their Aid," *Indian Express*, October 15, 2017, http://indianexpress.com/article
/india/mob-assaults-two-for-carrying-beef-in-faridabad-three-who-came-to-their-aid-4890872/.

129. That the choice of victims for assault had less to do with cow protection than with
underlying hostility toward Muslims is clear in the way Hindu cow breeders and transporters
were spared—like Pehlu Khan's truck driver who got away with merely being slapped, whereas
the others, all Muslims, were beaten (one of them to death) for the same "crime." See Mander,
"Country for the Cow."

130. A procession can be turned into a riot for instance when Hindu nationalists chant slogans against Islam as they go by a mosque during prayers, thus provoking a reaction from Muslims that served as a pretense to inflame a whole mob. Christophe Jaffrelot, "The Politics of
Processions and Hindu-Muslim Riots," in *Community Conflicts and the State in India*, ed. A.
Kohli and A. Basu (Delhi: Oxford University Press, 1998), 58–92.

Chapter 7

1. Gilles Favarel-Garrigues and Laurent Gayer, "Violer la loi pour maintenir l'ordre. Le vigilantisme en débat," *Politix* 115, no. 29 (2016): 9.

2. One of the first "vigilance committees" was established in 1856 by WASPs in San Francisco
to watch and discipline the Irish, who were supposedly criminally inclined.

3. For a detailed analysis of the complementarity of RSS and Bajrang Dal modus operandi,
see Christophe Jaffrelot, "The Militias of Hindutva: Between Communal Violence, Terrorism
and Cultural Policing," in *Armed Militias of South Asia. Fundamentalists, Maoists and Separatists*,
ed. Laurent Gayer and Christophe Jaffrelot, trans. C. Schoch, G. Elliott, and R. Leverdier (London: Hurst, 2009), 199–235.

4. Interview cited in Smita Gupta and Christophe Jaffrelot, "The Bajrang Dal: The New
Hindu Nationalist Brigade," in *Living with Secularism: The Destiny of India's Muslims*, ed. Mushirul Hasan (Delhi: Manohar, 2007), 204.

5. Cited in Dione Bunsha, "At a Hindutva Factory," *Frontline*, June 7–20, 2003, https://www
.frontline.in/static/html/fl2012/stories/20030620003210000.htm.

6. Cited in Smita Gupta, "Desi Mossad Is Getting Ready at Bajrang Dal's Ayodhya Camp,"
Indian Express, June 30, 2000, http://riots2002.blogspot.com/2012/06/desimossad-is-getting
-ready-at-bajrang.html.

7. Hubert Vaz, "Empowering Women: The VHP Way," *Indian Express*, May 21, 2003, https://www.countercurrents.org/comm-vaz210503.htm.

8. A. Jaiswal, "Bajrang Dal Camps a Hit with Youth," *Times of India*, May 28, 2017, https://timesofindia.indiatimes.com/city/agra/bajrang-dal-camps-a-hit-with-youth/articleshow/58883998.cms.

9. Interview with Surendra Jain, former BD president, by Smita Gupta, cited in Gupta and Jaffrelot, "Bajrang Dal."

10. In Odisha, the BD activist Dara Singh murdered the Australian missionary Graham Staines and his sons, burning them alive in their vehicle in January 1999.

11. For a systematic analysis, see Malvika Maheshwari, *Art Attacks: Violence and Offence-Taking in India* (Delhi: Oxford University Press, 2019), 207–70.

12. Pravin Swami, "Predatory Pursuit of Power," *Frontline*, May 23, 1998, https://www.frontline.in/static/html/fl1511/15110990.htm.

13. See "BJP—The Saffron Years," Sabrang Alternate News Network, accessed September 30, 2020, http://www.countercurrents.org/comm-sann290603:htm; and K. S. Narayanan, "When Might Is Right," *Deccan Herald*, July 1, 2001.

14. Cited in "No 'Water' Shooting in India: Singhal," *The Hindu*, February 5, 2000, https://www.thehindu.com/todays-paper/tp-miscellaneous/tp-others/no-water-shooting-in-india-singhal/article28000121.ece.

15. J. S. Bandukwala, "Why Gujarat 'Banned' Parzania," *Outlook*, February 19, 2007, https://magazine.outlookindia.com/story/why-gujarat-banned-parzania/233909.

16. Acharya mentioned "in his complaint that Bajrangi seems to be running a parallel government in the state." "Case against Bajrang Dal Leader over Screening of 'Parzania,'" *Zeenews*, February 7, 2007, https://zeenews.india.com/home/case-against-bajrang-dal-leader-over-screening-of-parzania_352686.html.

17. See the *Indian Express* (Ahmedabad ed.), March 22, 2007.

18. In this case, BD activists speaking this way apparently had nothing to fear from the police. One of them even admitted, "Earlier, there was a fear that the government would arrest us, but now with the Yogi government, we don't have any fear. . . . Even if a smuggler is killed during a fight, we don't have to worry about it. . . . All these BJP leaders, they've said: 'Do what you want to do about cow protection. Don't worry. If there is any problem, we are there for you.'" A. Gowen, "'We Don't Have Any Fear': India's Angry Young Men and Its Lynch Mob Crisis," *Washington Post*, September 3, 2018, https://www.washingtonpost.com/world/asia_pacific/we-dont-have- . . . -a0aa-11e8-a3dd-2a1991f075d5_story.html?utm_term=.6a0084f604cd.

19. Examples of Muslims being attacked by Hindu nationalists in front of the police are too numerous to cite them all. A typical case, which occurred in Alwar (Rajasthan), attests to vigilante impunity. D. Bhardwaj, "Muslims 'Attacked' by Hindu Outfits in Alwar," *Hindustan Times*, September 17, 2016, http://www.hindustantimes.com/jaipur/muslims-attacked-by-hindu-outfits-in-alwar/story-E2uWMKR004KK2V7hUxA9VJ.html.

20. In 2013, vigilantes professing to protect cows lynched three Muslims as the police watched in Haryana, for instance. See N. Dixit, "Justice Denied: A Road Accident that Wasn't, a Lynching that Was," *The Wire*, April 12, 2018, https://thewire.in/rights/justice-denied-a-road-accident-that-wasnt-a-lynching-that-was.

21. The terms of the debate are presented clearly in Favarel-Garrigues and Gayer, "Violer la loi pour maintenir l'ordre," 15.

22. Les Johnston, "What Is Vigilantism?" *British Journal of Criminology* 36, no. 2 (March 1, 1996): 220–36, https://doi.org/10.1093/oxfordjournals.bjc.a014083.

23. R. M. Brown, *Strain of Violence: Historical Studies of American Violence and Vigilantism* (New York: Oxford University Press, 1975).

24. Ray Abrahams, *Vigilant Citizens: Vigilantism and the State* (Cambridge, MA: Polity, 1998).

25. In Alwar, before he died, Pehlu Khan did not accuse a faceless mob but rather gave the names of the BD and VHP activists who attacked him. Zeba Siddiqui, Krishna N. Das, Tommy Wilkes, and Tom Lasseter, "Cow Politics," Reuters, November 6, 2017, https://www.reuters.com/investigates/special-report/india-politics-religion-cows/.

26. "'They Killed Cows, I Killed Them,' Lynching Accused Brags: NDTV Expose," NDTV, August 7, 2018, https://www.ndtv.com/india-news/ndtv-expose-when-key-accused-in-lynching-cases-admit-to-their-crimes-1896161.

27. Its predecessor, the Gau Raksha Samiti (Cow Protection Committee), was founded in 1998.

28. Ishan Marvel, "In the Name of the Mother: How the State Nurtures the Gau Rakshaks of Haryana," *The Caravan*, September 1, 2016, http://www.caravanmagazine.in/reportage/in-the-name-of-the-mother.

29. Marvel, "Name of the Mother."

30. Marvel.

31. Cited in Marvel.

32. The kind of osmosis prevailing in Haryana has also been observed in Punjab. Pragya Singh, "Four Stomachs to Fill," *Outlook*, August 15, 2016, https://www.outlookindia.com/magazine/story/four-stomachs-to-fill/297662.

33. Marvel, "Name of the Mother."

34. "Interview of Sh. Bhaniram Mangla, Chairman Haryana Gau Sewa Aayog," HinduPost, September 27, 2016, https://www.hindupost.in/politics/interview-sh-bhaniram-mangla-chairman-haryana-gau-sewa-aayog/. One national RSS leader uses cow dung to protect himself from the waves put out by his mobile phone. I. Mishra, "Cellphones Suck Energy, Just Put Some Cow Dung: RSS Ideologue," *Indian Express*, August 7, 2016, https://indianexpress.com/article/india/india-news-india/cellphones-suck-energy-just-put-some-cow-dung-rss-ideologue-2958597/.

35. Arora justifies the fight against cow slaughter by explaining that the money earned from it is used toward terrorism. N. Mohan, "Money Earned from Cow Slaughtering in Haryana Being Used for Terrorism: IPS Officer," *Hindustan Times*, August 30, 2016, https://www.hindustantimes.com/india-news/money-earned-from-cow . . . sed-for-terrorism-ips-officer/story-uT8bSEYwan4JY1YRhhBxtK.html. Two years later, the home minister ordered an investigation of Arora due to accusations of harassment by one of her subordinates. S. Yadav, "Centre Seeks Action Report on Plea against IPS Officer," *Times of India*, February 7, 2018, https://timesofindia.indiatimes.com/city/gurgaon/centre-seeks-action-report-on-plea-against-ips-officer/articleshow/62811981.cms.

36. Interview of Mangla, chairman of the Haryana Gau Sewa Aayog.

37. Marvel, "Name of the Mother."

38. Not only was the Gau Seva Aayog budget raised from Rs 18.5 million in 2014–2015 to Rs 37 million in 2016–2017. Siddiqui et al., "Cow Politics." But also the police were tasked with tasting *biryani* (a rice-based dish) to ensure it did not contain beef. "Haryana Cops Have a New Job: Sampling Biryanis," Rediff.com, September 9, 2016, http://www.rediff.com/news/report/haryana-cops-have-a-new-job-sampling-biryanis/20160909.htm. Rajasthan earmarked Rs 2.3 billion for cow protection in 2016–2017. Siddiqui et al., "Cow politics."

39. Navneet Sharma, "Hindutva Hotbed: RSS Imprint on Khattar Government Runs Deep in Haryana," *Hindustan Times*, November 7, 2016, https://www.hindustantimes.com/india-news/rss-imprint-on-khattar-g . . . sangh-parivar-men-at-all-levels/story-6X2VZR5xlDrin KthrtA68I.html.

40. Partha S. Biswas, "Maharashtra Govt Appoints Officers to Implement Beef Ban," *Indian Express*, June 3, 2016, http://indianexpress.com/article/cities/mumbai/maharashtra-state-govt-appoints-officers-to-implement-beef-ban-2831536/99/print/.

41. Smita Nair, "Refrain in Sangh Turf: Cards Will Give Us Power," *Indian Express*, August 23, 2016, http://indianexpress.com/article/india/india-news-india/maharasht . . . n-gau-rakshak-id-cards-animal-husbandry-modi-sangh-turf-2991489/.

42. Only the upper castes refrain strictly from eating beef and buffalo in India, and only Brahmins are strict vegetarians in a society where, according to a CSDS survey in 2006, 60 percent are not vegetarians. Rukmini S. "The Meat of the Matter," *The Hindu*, July 10, 2014, http://www.thehindu.com/opinion/blogs/blog-datadelve/article6195921.ece. Still, this observation requires qualification on a regional basis. In West Bengal, for instance, those who worship the goddess Kali, including Brahmins, eat meat. G. Chatterjee, "'In My Religion, Meat Is Ma Kali's Prasad': A Shakto Hindu Objects to Enforced Vegetarianism," Scroll.in, September 17, 2015, https://scroll.in/article/755412/in-my-religion-meat-is-ma-kalis-prasad-a-shakto-hindu-objects-to-enforced-vegetarianism.

43. P. Singh, "Four Stomachs to Fill."

44. In May 2018, the bribe rates applied by Uttar Pradesh police officers involved in this racketeering was made public by mistake over a WhatsApp account. "Huge Embarrassment for Yogi Adityanath! WhatsApp Message Exposes UP Police's 'Bribe Rate Card,'" Times Now, May 18, 2018, https://www.timesnownews.com/india/article/huge-embarrassment-for-yogi-adityanath-whatsapp-message-exposes-up-polices-bribe-rate-card/229448.

45. Siddartha Rai, "Mewat: Police Taking Bribes from Vendors to Allow Sale of Beef Biryani," *India Today*, September 10, 2016, https://www.indiatoday.in/mail-today/story/beef-biryani-mewat-sample-testing-police-bribe-340263-2016-09-10.

46. Annie Gowen, "Cows Are Sacred to India's Hindu Majority. For Muslims Who Trade Cattle, That Means Growing Trouble," *Washington Post*, July 16, 2018, https://www.washingtonpost.com/world/asia_pacific/cows-are-sacred-to-indias-hindu-majority-for-muslims-who-trade-cattle-that-means-growing-trouble/2018/07/15/9e4d7a50–591a-11e8-9889-07bcc1327f4b_story.html?utm_term=.8cebd9abc7fb; and D. K. Jha, "This Bandit-Turned-Cow Vigilante Feels Gau Rakshaks Are Worse than the Thugs of Chambal," Sabrang, August 30, 2016, https://sabrangindia.in/article/bandit-turned-cow-vigilante-feels-gau-rakshaks-are-worse-thugs-chambal.

47. P. Singh, "Four Stomachs to Fill."

48. Ankit Panda, "Speaking Out: Modi Condemns Cow Vigilantism in India," *The Diplomat*, August 8, 2016, https://thediplomat.com/2016/08/speaking-out-modi-condemns-cow -vigilantism-in-india/. Shortly prior to that, he had tweeted, "The sacred practice of cow worship & the compassion of Gau Seva can't be misused by some miscreants posing as Gau Rakshaks." P. Singh, "Four Stomachs to Fill."

49. "Punjab: Gau Raksha Dal Chief Satish Kumar Arrested," *Indian Express*, October 21, 2016, http://indianexpress.com/article/india/india-news-india/punjab-gau-raksha-dal-chief-satish -kumar-arrested-2988508/.

50. In Haryana, Mangla insisted that background checks had to be made to ensure that licensed gau rakshak had never been involved in criminal activities. "Haryana, Uttarakhand to Have Licensed Gau Rakshaks, Govt-Accredited Commission for Protection of Cows," FirstPost, August 9, 2017, https://www.firstpost.com/india/haryana-uttarakhand-to-have-licensed-gau -rakshaks-govt-accredited-commission-for-protection-of-cows-3904541.html.

51. Cited in Marvel, "Name of the Mother."

52. V. Deshpande, "PM Narendra Modi's Remark that 80 per cent Gau Rakshaks Are Fake Should Have Been Avoided: RSS," *Indian Express*, August 9, 2016, http://indianexpress.com /article/india/india-news-india/narendra-modi-fake-gau-rakshak-rss-beef-ban-cow-slaughter -gujarat-dalit-thrashing-2962750/.

53. Pavan Dahat, "RSS Chief Backs Gau Rakshaks, Lauds Army," *The Hindu*, October 11, 2016, http://www.thehindu.com/news/national/RSS-chief-backs-gau-rakshaks-lauds-Army /article15479013.ece.

54. S. Chaturvedi, D. Gellner, and S. K. Pandey, "Politics in Gorakhpur since the 1920s: The Making of a Safe 'Hindu' Constituency," *Contemporary South Asia* 27, no. 1 (2019), https://doi .org/10.1080/09584935.2018.1521785.

55. Christophe Jaffrelot, "The Other Saffron," *Indian Express*, October 6, 2014, http:// indianexpress.com/article/opinion/columns/the-other-saffron/.

56. Dhirendra K. Jha, *Shadow Armies: Fringe Organizations and Foot Soldiers of Hindutva* (New Delhi: Juggernaut, 2017), 36.

57. Shantanu Gupta, *The Monk Who Became Chief Minister: The Definitive Biography of Yogi Adityanath* (New Delhi: Bloomsbury, 2017), 72.

58. D. Jha, *Shadow Armies*, 45.

59. The development of HYV was particularly due to the fact that it filled the void created by the death of Rajput gangster V. P. Shahi, who had been killed by Sri Prakash Shukla's rival (Brahmin) gang. Thus deprived of a protector, the Rajputs turned to Yogi Adityanath, a caste fellow (D. Jha, 47).

60. Supriya Sharma, "They Paid a Price for Adityanath's Hate Speech—and Now Have Fallen Silent," Scroll.in, April 29, 2017, https://scroll.in/article/835416/they-paid-a-price-for -adityanaths-hate-speech-and-now-have-fallen-silent.

61. D. Jha, *Shadow Armies*, 49.

62. Violette Graff and Juliette Galonnier, "Hindu-Muslim Communal Riots in India II (1986– 2011)," *Encyclopeadia of Mass Violence*, August 20, 2013, https://www.sciencespo.fr/mass-violence -war-massacre-resistance/fr/document/hindu-muslim-communal-riots-india-ii-1986-2011.

63. D. Jha, *Shadow Armies*, 50.

64. Cited in D. Jha, 53.

65. "Will Install Gauri-Ganesh in Every Mosque, Says Yogi Adityanath," Zee News, February 10, 2015, http://zeenews.india.com/news/india/will-install-gauri-ganesh-in-every-mosque-says-yogi-adityanath_1543681.html.

66. "Hindu Yuva Vahini Membership Form," Hindu Yuva Vahini, accessed on January 23, 2019, http://biggboss11audition.in/hindu-yuva-vahini-membership-form/ (website no longer active).

67. Gupta, *Monk Who Became Chief*, 96–97.

68. Dhirendra K. Jha, "A Tug-of-War between the BJP and Yogi Adityanath Has Delayed the Cabinet Reshuffle," Scroll.in, June 30, 2016, http://scroll.in/article/print/810945; and Dhirendra K. Jha, "It's Clear the BJP Wants to Cut Yogi Adityanath to Size before the UP Elections," Scroll.in, June 2, 2016, https://scroll.in/article/809123/its-clear-the-bjp-wants-to-cut-yogi-adityanath-to-size-before-the-up-elections.

69. D. K. Jha, "The Rebellion of Adityanath's Outfit Could Hurt Not Just the BJP—but Its Firebrand Leader Too," Scroll.in, January 30, 2017, https://scroll.in/article/828022/the-rebellion-of-adiyanaths-outfit-could-hurt-not-just-the-bjp-but-their-firebrand-leader-too. However, Yogi Adityanath's militia continued to function after he became chief minister (A. Dey, "How Hindu Yuva Vahini's Name Got Linked with the Murder of a Muslim Man in Bulandshahr," Scroll.in, May 4, 2017, https://scroll.in/article/836528/how-hindu-yuva-vahinis-name-got-linked-with-the-murder-of-a-muslim-man-in-bulandshahr).

70. "ABP News-CSDS Lokniti—Uttar Pradesh Postpoll 2017 Survey Findings," CSDS, accessed September 30, 2020, http://www.lokniti.org/pol-pdf/ABP-News-CSDS-Lokniti-Uttar-Pradesh-Postpoll-2017-Survey-Findings-Final.pdf.

71. R. Singh, "Deputy CM-Designate Keshav Prasad Maurya: BJP's OBC Face with 10 Criminal Cases Was Associated with VHP," *Indian Express*, March 19, 2017, https://indianexpress.com/article/india/deputy-cm-designate-keshav-prasad-maurya-bjps-obc-face-with-10-criminal-cases-was-associated-with-vhp-4575440/; and O. Rashid, "Maurya, Dinesh and the Sangh," *The Hindu*, March 19, 2017, https://www.thehindu.com/news/national/other-states/maurya-dinesh-and-the-sangh/article17532776.ece.

72. O. Rashid, "Development Is My Priority: U. P. CM," *The Hindu*, March 19, 2017, https://www.thehindu.com/news/national/all-promises-will-be-fulfilled-yogi-adityanath/article17532195.ece.

73. Ellen Barry and Suhasini Raj, "Firebrand Hindu Cleric Ascends India's Political Ladder," *New York Times*, July 14, 2017, 1.

74. Barry and Raj, *Firebrand Hindu Cleric*, 1.

75. Barry and Raj, 1.

76. "Hindu Yuva Vahini Goons Climb atop Place of Worship in Bulandshahr to Hoist Tricolour, Chant Vande Matram," Janta Ka Reporter, August 26, 2017, http://www.jantakareporter.com/india/hindu-yuva-vahini-mosque-bulandshahr/145249/.

77. Kabir Agarwal, "Subverting the Rule of Law, Adityanath Style," The Wire, April 13, 2018, https://thewire.in/rights/subverting-the-rule-of-law-adityanath-style.

78. S. Mohan, "Hindu Yuva Vahini, Yogi Adityanath's Hindutva Army, Seeks to Rebrand Itself without CM's Support," Two Circles, May 29, 2018, https://twocircles.net/2018may29/423445.html.

79. Damayanti Datta, "Oye Romeo!," *India Today*, March 31, 2017, https://www.indiatoday.in/magazine/cover-story/story/20170410-anti-romeo-squads-yogi-adityanath-uttar-pradesh-986105-2017-03-31.

80. Regarding the effects of resorting to the NSA, see Neha Dixit's remarkable investigation, "1 Year, 160 Arrests: In Run Up to 2019, NSA Is the Latest Weapon against Muslims in UP," The Wire, September 10, 2018, https://thewire.in/rights/in-adityanaths-up-the-national-security-act-is-latest-weapon-against-muslims.

81. Interviews with victims' families and their lawyers in Lucknow, January 2018.

82. Dixit, "1 Year, 160 Arrests."

83. Qazi Faraz Ahmad, "1142 Encounters in 10 Months: Yogi Adityanath Government's Record against Crime," News18, February 5, 2018, https://www.news18.com/news/india/1142-encounter-in-10-months-yogi-adityanath-governments-record-against-crime-1651283.html.

84. Maulshree Seth, "Police Encounters Will Not Be Stopped, Says Yogi Adityanath," *Indian Express*, February 16, 2018, https://indianexpress.com/article/cities/lucknow/encounters-will-not-be-stopped-says-yogi-adityanath-5065806/.

85. Cherry Agarwal, "50 'Encounter' Deaths since Yogi Took Over, Victims' Kin Approach NHRC," Newslaundry, May 9, 2018, https://www.newslaundry.com/2018/05/09/uttar-pradesh-encounters-police-nhrc-yogi-adityanath-medias-role.

86. Akanksha Jain, "Extra-Judicial Killings in UP: NHRC Orders Fact-Finding Inquiry into 17 Cases," LiveLaw.in, May 17, 2018, https://www.livelaw.in/extra-judicial-killings-in-up-nhrc-orders-fact-finding-inquiry-into-17-cases/.

87. There are only two possible explanations, which are not mutually exclusive, for the fact that so many complaints had been held up for so long: either Yogi Adityanath's opponents were keeping this card in their hand to pull it out at an opportune moment, or they were hoping to thus neutralize similar complaints lodged against them in the event the BJP came to power. Regarding the slowness of such proceedings, see Ajit Sahi, "The UP Government's Colossal Cover-Up Attempt to Protect Adityanath," The Wire, July 27, 2017, https://thewire.in/communalism/adityanath-anti-muslim-cover-up.

88. "Adityanath Government Orders Withdrawal of Case against Adityanath," The Wire, December 27, 2017, https://thewire.in/208455/bjp-uttar-pradesh-adityanath/.

89. "Muzaffarnagar Riots: UP Government to Drop Cases against Prachi, and 5 BJP MLAs and MPs, Says Report," Scroll.in, April 26, 2018, https://scroll.in/latest/876973/muzaffarnagar-riots-up-government-to-drop-cases-against-prachi-and-5-bjp-mlas-and-mps-says-report.

90. Manish Sahu, "Yogi Govt Moves to Withdraw Hate-Speech Cases against Sadhvi Prachi, Sanjeev Balyan," *Indian Express*, April 26, 2018, http://indianexpress.com/article/india/up-govt-moves-to-withdraw-hate-speechcases-against-sadhvi-prachi-and-sanjeev-balyan-5152077/.

91. "Supreme Court Seeks Response from UP Government on Encounter Killings," The Wire, July 3, 2018, https://www.thewire.in/law/supreme-court-seeks-response-from-up-government-on-encounter-killings.

92. "Yogi Adityanath Hate Speech Case: Supreme Court Sends Notice to UP Govt," *Indian Express*, August 21, 2018, https://indianexpress.com/article/india/yogi-adityanath-hate-speech-case-supreme-court-sends-notice-to-up-govt-5316334/.

93. He has moreover done his best to weaken the judiciary in his state by not filling vacant positions. See Shruthi Naik, "As Judicial Vacancies Soar, Lawlessness in UP May No Longer Be Just a Metaphor," The Wire, September 6, 2018, https://thewire.in/law/as-judicial-vacancies -soar-lawlessness-in-up-may-no-longer-be-just-a-metaphor.

94. A. Ashirwad Mahaprashasta, "Parvez Parwaz, Petitioner in Adityanath Hate Speech Case, Sentenced to Life Imprisonment," The Wire, July 30, 2020, https://thewire.in/law/parvez -parwaz-rape-case-life-imprisonment-adityanath-gorakhpur-hate-speech-case.

95. "UP Government Asks Officials to Ensure Animals Are Not Sacrificed in the Open on Bakrid: Reports," Scroll.in, August 21, 2018, https://scroll.in/latest/891281/up-government-asks -officials-to-ensure-animals-are-not-sacrificed-in-the-open-on-bakrid-reports.

96. Several amateur videos showing how goats should be sacrificed for the Bakr Eid cele-bration in August 2018 were confiscated by the police. See, for instance, https://www.youtube .com/watch?v=vx6J6C5ozoY, accessed September 30, 2020 (video no longer active).

97. In a village of Bijnor District, Muslims do not celebrate Eid al-Adha because the police will not allow them to sacrifice a buffalo as they have been doing for fifty years. "Police Did Not Allow Muslims in UP Village to Sacrifice Buffaloes, Camels," Caravan News, August 24, 2018, http://caravandaily.com/portal/police-did-not-allow-muslims-in-up-village-to-sacrifice -buffaloes-camels/.

98. Sandipan Sharma, "Yogi Adityanath Govt in Uttar Pradesh Ignoring Taj Mahal Betrays Its Myopic View of History," FirstPost, September 13, 2018, https://www.firstpost.com/india /yogi-adiyanath-govt-in-uttar-pradesh-ignoring-taj-mahal-betrays-its-myopic-view-of-history -4105095.html; O. Rashid, "Taj Mahal Missing in U.P. Govt. Brochure," The Hindu, October 2, 2017, http://www.thehindu.com/news/national/taj-mahal-missing-in-up-govt-brochure /article19786586.ece.

99. "Adityanath: Foreign Dignitaries Are Now Being Gifted the Gita and not 'Un-Indian' Taj Mahal Replicas," Scroll.in, June 16, 2017, https://scroll.in/latest/840809/adityanath-foreign -dignitaries-are-now-being-gifted-the-gita-and-not-un-indian-taj-mahal-replicas.

100. "Museum's Name Changed, Agra Officials Hunt for Shivaji Links," Indian Express, Sep-tember 17, 2020, https://indianexpress.com/article/cities/lucknow/museums-name-changed -agra-officials-hunt-for-shivaji-links-6599120/.

101. A. Joshi, "A Thana Coloured Saffron," Indian Express, August 19, 2017, http:// indianexpress.com/article/opinion/columns/a-thana-coloured-s . . . ment-of-religious -displays-in-police-stations-is-troubling-4803148/.

102. Lalmani Verma, "Yogi Adityanath's Double Role: Chief Minister and Mahant," Indian Express, September 29, 2017, http://indianexpress.com/article/india/yogi-adityanath-double -role-chief-minister-mahant-navarati-priest-puja-4867508/.

103. Arjun Sidarth, "Video of ANI Reporter Touching Yogi Adityanath's Feet Raises Eye-brows," AltNews, December 28, 2017, https://www.altnews.in/video-ani-reporter-touching -yogi-adityanaths-feet-raises-eyebrows/.

104. For further detail, see Jaffrelot, "The BJP at the Centre: A Central and Centrist Party?," in The BJP and the Compulsions of Politics in India, 2ndEd., ed. T. B. Hansen and C. Jaffrelot (Delhi: Oxford University Press, 2001), 315–69 (see the section entitled "Gujarat, a Laboratory for Hindu Nationalism," 356–63).

105. A senior police officer explained that the district commanders of the Home Guards began to change as soon as the BJP came to power in Gujarat. Interview with a former police officer in Ahmedabad on condition of anonymity.

106. Interview with Digvijay Singh, April 7, 2007, in New Delhi.

107. Moyukh Chatterjee, "The Ordinary Life of Hindu Supremacy: In Conversation with a Bajrang Dal Activist," *Economic and Political Weekly: Engage* 53, no. 4 (January 27, 2018), https://www.epw.in/engage/article/ordinary-life-hindu-supremacy.

108. Interview with Jayant Sinha by Prashant Jha, "It's a Matter of Justice, Not Lynching: Jayant Sinha," *Hindustan Times*, July 23, 2018, https://www.hindustantimes.com/india-news/regret-garlanding-ramg . . . lynching-convicts-jayant-sinha/story-JYadtspAUurWZ8vRLaCcwI.html.

109. Vakasha Sachdev, "It's Free Speech: Gadkari Defends Garlanding Lynching Convicts," *The Quint*, August 14, 2018, https://www.thequint.com/news/politics/singhvi-book-launch-pranab-mukherjee-nitin-gadkari-jayant-sinha-jharkhand-lynching.

110. "Mob Lynching: Centre Forms High-Level Panel to Suggest Ways to Curb Violence," Scroll.in, July 23, 2018, https://scroll.in/latest/887675/mob-lynching-centre-forms-high-level-panel-to-suggest-ways-to-curb-violence.

111. "Lynching Won't Stop till Cow Gets Status of Rashtra Mata: Hyderabad BJP MLA," *Hindustan Times*, July 24, 2018, https://www.hindustantimes.com/india-news/lynching-won-t-stop-till-cow-gets-status-of-rashtra-mata-hyderabad-bjp-mla/story-9vVeVZRhcJ8SgbdLD7LHvM.html.

112. "Lynchings Are Increasing Because of Muslim Population Growth: BJP MP," *The Wire*, July 24, 2018, https://thewire.in/communalism/lynchings-are-increasing-because-of-muslim-population-growth-bjp-mp.

113. "Lynchings Will Stop if People Don't Eat Beef, Says RSS Leader Indresh Kumar," *Indian Express*, July 24, 2018, https://indianexpress.com/article/india/lynchings-will-stop-if-people-dont-eat-beef-says-rss-leader-indresh-kumar-5272422/.

114. "People's Frustration Due to Unemployment Is Leading to Lynchings: Vasundhara Raje," *The Wire*, July 31, 2018, https://thewire.in/politics/lynching-not-specific-to-rajasthan-vasundhara-raje.

115. I am grateful to Gilles Verniers for having confirmed this hypothesis, which I formulated during my fieldwork in Gujarat, in the case of Uttar Pradesh.

116. "Operation Juliet: Busting the Bogey of 'Love Jihad,'" *Cobrapost*, October 4, 2015, http://cobrapost.com/blog/operation-juliet-busting-the-bogey-of-love-jihad-2/900.

117. Chatterjee, "Ordinary Life."

118. Ward Berenschot, *Riot Politics: Hindu-Muslim Violence and the Indian State* (London: Hurst, 2011), 191.

119. Bruce Berman and John Lonsdale, *Unhappy Valley: Conflict in Kenya and Africa*, 2 vols. (London: James Currey; Nairobi: Heinemann Kenya; Athens: Ohio University Press, 1992).

120. Berman and Lonsdale, *Unhappy Valley*, 1:36–38.

121. Cited in B. V. Deshpande and S. R. Ramaswamy, *DR. Hedgewar, the Epoch-Maker: A Biography* (Bangalore: Sahitya Sindhu, 1981), 185–86.

122. "Vijayadashami Speech: Vigilant Society Is the Key, Govt Can Just Facilitate—Sarsanghchalak Mohan Bhagwat," *The Organiser*, October 5, 2014.

123. Siddiqui et al., "Cow Politics."

124. "Operation Juliet."

125. Sunil Singh, the director of a fiction film on the Ayodhya affair, also received death threats, after one ABVP leader promised a 100,000-rupee reward for anyone who would cut off both his hands. "Hindutva Activists Vandalise 'Game of Ayodhya' Director's House, Threaten to Kill Him," The Wire, December 4, 2017, https://thewire.in/201762/hindutva-activists -vandalise-game-ayodhya-directors-house-threaten-kill/.

126. Ashutosh Sharma, "Disagreements with RSS Ideologue Brings Income Tax Notice to Harsh Mander's Door," National Herald, September 22, 2017, https://www.nationalheraldindia .com/national/disagreements-with-rss-ideologue-brings-income-tax-notice-to-harsh-manders -door.

127. I explored this issue and the correlative "cyber shakha" in Christophe Jaffrelot, "From Holy Sites to Web Sites: Hindu Nationalism, from Sacred Territory to Diasporic Ethnicity," in Religions, Nations, and Transnationalism in Multiple Modernities, ed. Patrick Michel, Adam Possamai, and Bryan Turner (Basingstoke, UK: Palgrave, 2017), 153–74.

128. He even went so far as to assert, "This is the most interesting arm of the RSS, the IT arm." Cited in Swati Chaturvedi, I Am a Troll: Inside the Secret World of the BJP's Digital Army (New Delhi: Juggernaut, 2016), 135.

129. Chaturvedi, I Am a Troll, 125.

130. On the use of social media by the Sangh Parivar, see R. Chopra, The Virtual Hindu Rashtra (Delhi: HarperCollins, 2020); and on the BJP IT cell's disinformation activities, see P. Chaudhuri, "Amit Malviya's Fake News Fountain: 16 Pieces of Misinformation Spread by the BJP IT Cell Chief," Scroll.in, February 10, 2020, https://scroll.in/article/952731/amit-malviyas -fake-news-fountain-16-pieces-of-misinformation-spread-by-the-bjp-it-cell-chief.

131. Chaturvedi, I Am a Troll, 5.

132. Chaturvedi, 62

133. Chaturvedi, 56.

134. Shah Rukh Khan was a particular target because he expressed concern about the rise of intolerance in India. In the face of a campaign to boycott his latest film, he apologized for his statements in 2015. Chaturvedi, 67.

135. Chaturvedi, 72.

136. Chaturvedi, 83.

137. Chaturvedi, 84.

138. Chaturvedi, 85.

139. Chaturvedi, 89.

140. N. C. Asthana, "Inside the Minds of Internet Trolls: A Psychological Analysis," The Wire, April 28, 2020, https://thewire.in/communalism/internet-trolls-psychology.

141. Rituparna Chatterjee, "'I Couldn't Talk or Sleep for Three Days': Journalist Rana Ayyub's Horrific Social Media Ordeal over Fake Tweet," Daily O, April 26, 2018, https://www .dailyo.in/variety/rana-ayyub-trolling-fake-tweet-social-media-harassment-hindutva/story/1 /23733.html.

142. "'I Was Told Not to Do Journalism till 2019': Watch Barkha Dutt Speak about Bids to Intimidate Her," Scroll.in, June 8, 2018, https://scroll.in/video/881970/i-was-told-not-to-do

-journalism-till-2019-watch-barkha-dutt-speak-about-bids-to-intimidate-her; and "Barkha Dutt Alleges Threats from Some Govt. Quarters," *The Hindu*, June 7, 2018, https://www.thehindu .com/news/national/barkha-dutt-accuses-govt-of-intimidating-her/article24102748.ece.

143. Priyanka Jha, "Journalist Ravish Kumar Relentlessly Targeted on Social Media via Fake News," AltNews, May 9, 2018, https://www.altnews.in/journalist-ravish-kumar-relentlessly -targeted-on-social-media-via-fake-news/.

144. Ravish Kumar, *The Free Voice: On Democracy, Culture and the Nation* (New Delhi: Speaking Tiger, 2018), 8.

145. Kumar, *Free Voice*, 18, 27.

146. Cited in Kumar, 62.

147. See A. Sidharth, "Hindu khatre mein hai? How the Fake News Ecosystem Targets Minorities to Create a Fear Psychosis," AltNews, July 8, 2018, https://www.altnews.in/hindu -khatre-mein-hai-how-the-fake-news-ecosystem-targets-minorities-to-create-a-fear -psychosis/.

148. Chaturvedi, *I Am a Troll*, 16.

149. Chaturvedi, 17.

150. Cited in Chaturvedi, 26.

151. "What Do These Nathuram Godse Fans Have in Common? They Are All Followed by PM Modi on Twitter," AltNews, October 2, 2017, https://www.altnews.in/godse-fans-common -followed-pm-modi/.

152. Modi in particular followed the Twitter account of Nikhil Dadhich, who welcomed Gauri Lankesh's murder with these words: "Now that a bitch has died a dog's death, all the puppies are mewling in one voice." Cited in Kumar, *Free Voice*, 74.

153. "As I&T Minister Slams Trolls for Lauding Gauri Lankesh's Killing, PM Modi Draws Flak for Following Them on Twitter," *Indian Express*, September 7, 2017, http://indianexpress .com/article/india/gauri-lankesh-murder-express . . . s-on-killing-shameful-ravi-shankar -prasad-to-online-trolls-4831801/.

154. Cited in Chaturvedi, *I Am a Troll*, 43.

155. A sample of the messages the minister received is given in "Sushma Swaraj Shares Abuse She Faced Online for Helping Lucknow Interfaith Couple in Passport Row," News18, June 24, 2018, https://www.news18.com/news/india/sushma-swaraj-shares-abuse-she-faced-online-for -helping-lucknow-interfaith-couple-in-passport-row-1788883.html.

156. As mentioned in chapter 1, his brother, Gopal Godse, claimed that Nathuram never left the RSS. D. K. Jha makes the same argument in a very well-researched article: D. K. Jha, "The Apostle of Hate," *The Caravan*, January 1, 2020, https://caravanmagazine.in/reportage /historical-record-expose-lie-godse-left-rss.

157. Sujata Anandan, *Hindu Hriday Samrat* (Noida, India: HarperCollins, 2014).

158. Mohammad Ali, "Mahasabha Performs 'Bhumi Pujan' for Godse Temple in Meerut," *The Hindu*, December 25, 2014, https://www.thehindu.com/news/national/other-states /bhumi-pujan-for-godses-temple-performed-in-meerut/article6725057.ece.

159. S. Yasir, "Gandhi's Killer Evokes Admiration as Never Before," *New York Times*, February 4, 2020, https://www.nytimes.com/2020/02/04/world/asia/india-gandhi-nathuram -godse.html.

160. V. Kumar, "If Not Godse, I Would Have Killed Gandhi, Says Judge of Self-Styled Hindu Court," *India Today*, August 23, 2018, https://www.indiatoday.in/india/story/if-not-godse-i -would-have-killed-gandhi-says-judge-of-self-styled-hindu-court-1321657-2018-08-23.

161. For instance, the BJP MLA Raja Singh from Hyderabad—who has forty-three police cases against him—announced the creation of a "vigilante army" to "take care of the anti-nationals." P. Pavan, "BJP MLA Raja Singh Announces Forming Vigilante Groups to Send Internal Traitors out of India or to Hell," *Bangalore Mirror*, September 18, 2019, https:// bangaloremirror.indiatimes.com/news/india/watch-bjp-mla-raja-singh-announces-forming -vigilante-groups-to-send-internal-traitors-out-of-india-or-to-hell/articleshow/71188054.cms ?utm_source=contentofinterest&utm_medium=text&utm_campaign=cppst.

162. "Two Haryana Youth—Both Cow Vigilantes—Claim Responsibility of Attempting to End Khalid's Life," Newslaundry, August 16, 2018, https://www.newslaundry.com/2018/08/16 /two-haryana-youth-both-cow-vigilantes-claim-responsibility-of-attempting-to-end-khalids -life.

163. Prashant Pandey, "Meet the Men Who Beat Up Swami Agnivesh: BJP, RSS, Bajrang Dal," *Indian Express*, July 24, 2018, https://indianexpress.com/article/india/meet-the-men-who -beat-up-swami-agnivesh-bjp-rss-bajrang-dal-5272452/; and V. Pathak, "Jharkhand Govt. Abetted Attack: Agnivesh," *The Hindu*, July 28, 2018, https://www.thehindu.com/news/national /jharkhand-govt-abetted-attack/article24542624.ece.

164. "Swami Agnivesh Assaulted on Way to Pay Homage to Atal Bihari Vajpayee in New Delhi," *Indian Express*, August 17, 2018, https://indianexpress.com/article/india/swami -agnivesh-assault-ddu-marg-new-delhi-5311309/.

165. S. Prabal, "Sanatan Sanstha and Its Hindutva Designs," *Economic and Political Weekly* 33, no. 41 (October 13, 2018): 18.

166. A. Deshpande and G. S. Mengle, "For Sanatan Sanstha, All's Fair in the War for a Hindu Rashtra," *The Hindu*, September 1, 2018, https://www.thehindu.com/news/national/for -sanatan-sanstha-alls-fair-in-the-war-for-a-hindu-rashtra/article24843643.ece.

167. "Three Years after Dabholkar's Murder, CBI Arrests Sanatan Sanstha Member," *Deccan Chronicle*, June 11, 2016, https://www.deccanchronicle.com/nation/crime/110616/dabholkar -murder-case-cbi-makes-first-arrest-sanatan-sanstha-member-held.html; Rana Ayyub, "Deceptive Piety," *Tehelka*, October 31, 2009, http://www.tehelka.com/2009/10/deceptive-piety/; and A. Ghadyalpatil, "Inside the 'Hypnotic' World of Sanatan Sanstha," *Mint*, September 12, 2018, https://www.livemint.com/Politics/s9kuMJdW2dwqANcIlMQe1J/Inside-the-secret-world-of -Sanatan-Sanstha.html.

168. D. Jha, *Shadow Armies*, 13–14.

169. R. Rajput, "Ban on Sanatan Sanstha Difficult to Enforce, Says Maharashtra ATS," *Indian Express*, August 14, 2018, https://indianexpress.com/article/india/ban-on-sanatan-sanstha -difficult-to-enforce-says-maharashtra-ats-5305377/.

170. While the investigation is not yet complete, the police suspect that the Sanstha was behind most of these murders because the modus operandi was similar and the same pistol was used in two cases. T. A. Johnson, "Gauri Lankesh Murder: 'Man Held for Training Suspects in Guns also Trained Dabholkar Killers,'" *Indian Express*, August 24, 2018, https://indianexpress .com/article/india/gauri-lankesh-murder-man-held-for-training-suspects-in-guns-also-trained

-dabholkar-killers-5322075/; and S. Yogesh, "Hindutva Terror: Story of the Common Links between the Four Murders," NewsClick, August 20, 2018, https://www.newsclick.in/hindutva -terror-story-common-link-between-four-murders.

171. A. Malekar, "Darkness at Dawn: The Murders of Narendra Dabholkar, Govind Pansare and MM Kalburgi," *The Caravan*, August 1, 2016, http://www.caravanmagazine.in/reportage /darkness-at-dawn.

172. P. Sainath, "In Gauri Lankesh's Killing, the Murder Is the Message," The Wire, September 7, 2017, https://thewire.in/culture/gauri-lankesh-murder-rationalists.

173. Rana Ayyub, "Why Investigating Agencies Believe Sanatan Sanstha Is behind Dabholkar and Pansare's Murder," Daily O, March 11, 2015, https://www.dailyo.in/politics/sanatan-sanstha -narendra-dabholkar-govind-pansare-anti-superstition-hindutva-maharashtra/story/1/2492.html.

174. D. Jha, *Shadow Armies*, 25.

175. D. Jha, 27.

176. See the remarkable series of seventeen articles by Greeshma Khutar, "How Coastal Karnataka Was Saffronised: The Story of the Rise and Rise of Hindu Nationalism in Syncretic South Kanara," FirstPost, April 1, 2010, https://www.firstpost.com/india/how-coastal -karnataka-was-saffronised-the-story-of-the-rise-and-rise-of-hindu-nationalism-in-syncretic -south-kanara-6363461.html.

177. B. Valsan, "Gauri Lankesh Murder Case: 'Praveen Said Gauri Lankesh Was Anti-Hindu and Had to Be Killed . . . I Decided to Help'," *Bangalore Mirror*, June 6, 2018, https:// bangaloremirror.indiatimes.com/bangalore/cover-story/gauri-lankesh-murder-case-praveen -said-gauri-lankesh-was-anti-hindu-and-had-to-be-killed-i-decided-to-help/articleshow /64470641.cms.

178. T. A. Johnson, "What Was the Defamation Case against Slain Journalist Gauri Lankesh?," *Indian Express*, September 7, 2017, https://indianexpress.com/article/explained/what-was-the -defamation-case-against-slain-journalist-gauri-lankesh-4832061/.

179. R. Swamy, "Gauri Lankesh Would Have Been Alive if She Hadn't Written against RSS: BJP MLA Jeevaraj," *India Today*, September 8, 2017, https://www.indiatoday.in/india/story /gauri-lankesh-rss-bjp-mla-jeevaraj-1040239-2017-09-07.

180. Deshpande and Mengle, "For Sanatan Sanstha." See also "150 Pistols, 100 Bombs, 3000 Bullets Were on the Shopping List of Arrested Sanatan Sanstha, HJS Activists Raut and Gond-halekar," IndiaScoops.com, accessed September 30, 2020, http://scoops.indiascoops.com/150 -pistols-100-bombs-3000-bullets-were-on-the-shopping-list-of-arrested-sanatan-sanstha-hjs -activists-raut-and-gondhalekar/.

181. D. Balakrishnan, "36 Targets and 50 Shooters: Gauri Lankesh Murder Suspect's Diary Reveals Chilling Details," News18, June 30, 2018, https://www.news18.com/news/india/36-targets -and-50-shooters-gauri-lankesh-murder-suspects-diary-reveals-chilling-details-1796199.html.

182. Rajput, "Ban on Sanatan Sanstha"; and S. Daniyal, "As Terror Charges against Sanatan Sanstha Grow, Why Isn't the Government Banning It?," Scroll.in, June 21, 2016, https://scroll .in/article/810325/the-daily-fix-as-terror-charges-against-sanatan-sanstha-grow-why-isnt-the -government-banning-it.

183. See the Dhabolkar case in particular. "6 Years after Narendra Dhabolkar's Assassination, Masterminds Remain Free," NewsClick, August 18, 2019, https://www.newsclick.in/6-Years

-After-Narendra-Dhabolkar-Assassination-Masterminds-Free; and "Narendra Dabholkar Murder Case: Three Accused Get Bail as CBI Fails to File Chargesheet on Time," *Indian Express,* December 15, 2018, https://indianexpress.com/article/india/narendra-dabholkar-murder-case -three-accused-get-bail-as-cbi-fails-to-file-chargesheet-5493861/.

184. J. Patel, "Social Media Users Followed by PM Modi and BJP President Amit Shah Continue to Abuse Gauri Lankesh," AltNews, June 20, 2018, https://www.altnews.in/social-media -users-followed-by-pm-modi-and-bjp-president-amit-shah-continue-to-abuse-gauri-lankesh/.

185. "PM Modi Follows 4 Twitter Accounts that Trolled #GauriLankesh," AltNews, September 6, 2017, https://www.newslaundry.com/2017/09/06/modi-trolls-gauri-lankesh.

186. D. Jha, *Shadow Armies*, 92–93.

187. D. Jha, 94–95.

188. Cited in D. Jha, 99.

189. D. Jha, 88.

190. M. Ali, "The Rise of a Hindu Vigilante in the Age of WhatsApp and Modi," *Wired,* April 14, 2020, https://www.wired.com/story/indias-frightening-descent-social-media -terror/.

191. "NDA 2.0: Social Media 'Hero' Pratap Sarangi Faces Serious Criminal Cases," The Wire, June 1, 2019, https://thewire.in/politics/minister-of-state-pratap-sarangi-criminal-cases.

192. K. Chaudhuri, "Vandalism in Orissa," *Frontline,* March 30, 2002, https://frontline .thehindu.com/cover-story/article30244420.ece.

193. "'Do Those Who Don't Say Vande Mataram Have Right to Live in India?' Asks BJP MP," *Deccan Chronicle,* September 29, 2020, https://www.deccanchronicle.com/nation/current -affairs/250619/do-those-who-dont-say-vande-mataram-have-right-to-live-in-india.html.

Conclusion to Part II

1. As mentioned above, Hindu nationalist circles have long been practiced in the art of dissimulation. It bears repeating here what K. N. Govindacharya, then a highly influential BJP general secretary, said in 1997 in an interview: "Vajpayee is not the internal strength of the BJP, merely a mask. . . . You [the journalist] are talking to the RSS representative in the BJP. I am the sole individual who now communicates between the RSS and BJP." Cited in Saba Naqvi, *Shades of Saffron: From Vajpayee to Modi* (Chennai: Westland, 2018), 22.

2. Shoaib Daniyal, "The Age of Trolls: What the BJP's New Spokesperson Signifies for Indian Politics," Scroll.in, March 17, 2017, https://scroll.in/article/832012/the-age-of-trolls-what-the -bjps-new-spokesperson-signifies-for-indian-politics.

Part III

1. Steven Levitsky and Daniel Ziblatt, *How Democracies Die* (New York: Broadway Books, 2018), 65.

2. Juan Linz, *Totalitarian and Authoritarian Regimes* (Boulder, CO: Lynne Rienner, 2000), 161.

Chapter 8

1. Despite the fact that he had not appointed a Lokayukta for ten years in Gujarat.

2. "Narendra Modi's Open Letter to Anna Hazare," NarendraModi.in, April 11, 2011, http://www.narendramodi.in/narendra-modi's-open-letter-to-anna-hazare.

3. "Lokpal Panel: BJP Opposes PM Proposal to Make P.P. Rao Lok Pal Member," *Economic Times*, February 4, 2014, https://economictimes.indiatimes.com/news/politics-and-nation/lokpal-panel-bjp-opposes-pms-proposal-to-make-pp-rao-member/articleshow/29851135.cms.

4. In fact, the 10 percent threshold mattered for something different: "The speaker started the practice of recognising parliamentary parties as 'parties' and 'groups' for the limited purpose of allotting seats in the house, time for participating in the debates, rooms in Parliament House etc." P. D. T. Achary, "Leader of Opposition Is a Statutory Position, the '10% Rule' Is Not Founded in Law," The Wire, June 1, 2019, https://thewire.in/government/leader-of-opposition-parliament-lok-sabha.

5. Modi invoked section 12 of the Government of India (Transaction of Business) Rules, which gives the prime minister the power to have a decision approved ex post facto by the government.

6. A. Bhardwaj and A. Johri, "Waiting for the Lokpal," *The Hindu*, April 21, 2017, https://www.thehindu.com/opinion/op-ed/waiting-for-the-lokpal/article18186362.ece.

7. "Lokpal Law and Shelving of Kin Assets' Clause: Why, What Now," *Indian Express*, July 29, 2019, https://indianexpress.com/article/explained/lokpal-bill-narendra-modi-lok-sabha-pm-narendra-modi-govt-lokpal-and-lokayuktas-act-ngo-2941254/.

8. Bhardwaj and A. Johri, "Waiting for the Lokpal."

9. On the Modi government's attempt to weaken the anticorruption mechanisms by amending the PCA, see Yogendra Yadav's excellent analysis. Y. Yadav, "Time to Blow the Whistle," *The Hindu*, December 12, 2016, https://www.thehindu.com/opinion/lead/Time-to-blow-the-whistle/article16793830.ece.

10. "Anna Hazare Writes to PM, Says He's 'Mulling' Launching Agitation on Lokpal," Janta Ka Reporter, March 29, 2017, http://www.jantakareporter.com/india/anna-hazare-lokpal/111103/. Anna Hazare reiterated his threat in October 2017. "Anna Hazare Slams Modi Govt over Failure to Appoint Lokpal," *Business Standard*, October 3, 2017, https://www.business-standard.com/article/economy-policy/anna-hazare-slams-modi-govt-over-failure-to-appoint-lokpal-117100200784_1.html.

11. Bhadra Sinha, "'What's Stopping You?' SC Criticises Govt for Delay in Appointing Lokpal," *Hindustan Times*, November 23, 2016, https://www.hindustantimes.com/india-news/what-s-stopping-you-sc-criticises-govt-for-delay-in-appointing-lokpal/story-67P8nOJYe7qx5ZHpdnSbBL.html.

12. U. Anand, "Apex Court Reserves Order on Lokpal Appointment," *Indian Express*, March 29, 2017, https://indianexpress.com/article/india/supreme-court-apex-court-reserves-order-on-lokpal-appointment-4590056/.

13. "No Justification to Suspend Operation of Lokpal Act: Supreme Court," *Indian Express*, April 27, 2017, https://indianexpress.com/article/india/no-justification-to-suspend-operation-of-lokpal-act-supreme-court-4631029/.

14. G. V. Bhatnagar, "No Lokpal Appointed, Act Not Implemented Despite SC Relaxing Norms: Activists Write to Modi," The Wire, January 5, 2018, https://thewire.in/government/no-lokpal-appointed-act-not-implemented-despite-sc-relaxing-norms-activists-write-to-modi.

15. G. V. Bhatnagar, "After Misleading SC on Lokpal, Modi's Inclusion of Congress Leader in Panel Seen as 'Ploy,'" The Wire, February 26, 2018, https://thewire.in/economy/lokpal-selection-panel-whats-behind-making-congress-leader-kharge-a-special-invitee.

16. "India's First Lokpal Appointed: Justice Pinaki Chandra Ghose as Chief, 8 Members," The Wire, March 20, 2019, https://thewire.in/government/indias-first-lokpal-appointed-justice-pinaki-chandra-ghose-as-chief-8-members.

17. G. V. Bhatnagar, "Lokpal Is All Ready to Attack Corruption, but Lacks Teeth to Bite," The Wire, June 7, 2019, https://thewire.in/government/lokpal-corruption-format.

18. Bhardwaj and Johri, "Waiting for the Lokpal."

19. C. Jaffrelot, "Gujarat's Law unto Itself," Indian Express, September 30, 2013, https://indianexpress.com/article/opinion/columns/gujarats-law-unto-itself/.

20. G. V. Bhatnagar, "'Modi Government Is Making RTI Dysfunctional,'" The Wire, May 11, 2015, https://thewire.in/law/modi-government-is-making-rti-dysfunctional.

21. G. V. Bhatnagar, "With Four More Information Commissioners Set to Retire Centre's Deliberate Delay Continues," The Wire, September 9, 2018, https://thewire.in/government/with-four-more-information-commissioners-set-to-retire-centres-deliberate-delay-continues.

22. G. V. Bhatnagar, "RTI 'Report Card' Laments Pending Cases, Vacancies in Information Commissions," The Wire, October 12, 2019, https://thewire.in/government/rti-information-commissions-vacancies-pending-cases.

23. Between 2014 and 2020, not a single commissioner of the CIC "has been appointed without citizens having to approach the courts." A. Bhardwaj, "Our Institutions: Pillars of Society, Not Democracy," National Herald, August 15, 2020, https://www.nationalheraldindia.com/opinion/our-institutions-pillars-of-society-not-democracy.

24. D. Mishra, "Over 30,000 RTI Appeals and Complaints Are Pending before the Information Commission," The Wire, July 26, 2019, https://thewire.in/government/30000-appeals-complaints-information-commission-rti-amendment-bill.

25. In its annual report for 2015–2016, the CIC mentions that 43 percent of the rejections were due to reasons falling outside of recognized categories.

26. R. Bhattacharya, "The Home Ministry Has Perfected the Art of Flip-Flopping on RTI Applications," The Wire, August 19, 2016, https://thewire.in/government/mhas-rti-applications.

27. S. Ninan, "Defanging RTI, Step by Step," India Forum, August 23, 2019, https://www.theindiaforum.in/article/defanging-rti-step-step.

28. A. Srivastava, "In Response to RTI, RBI Says Sharing Details of Demonetisation Process May Hurt Country's Economic Interests," Outlook, May 10, 2017, https://www.outlookindia.com/newswire/story/in-response-to-rti-rbi-says-sharing-details-of-demonetisation-process-may-hurt-countrys-economic-interests/969108.

29. P. K. Dutta, "What Makes RTI Amendment Bill So Controversial?" India Today, July 23, 2019, https://www.indiatoday.in/news-analysis/story/what-makes-rti-amendment-bill-so-controversial-1572596-2019-07-23.

30. S. Misra, "Amended RTI Act: What Is at Stake?" Observer Research Foundation (website), July 29, 2020, https://www.orfonline.org/expert-speak/amended-rti-act-what-at-stake-53573/. Previously the state chief information commissioners and information commissioners were selected by a three-member panel consisting of the chief minister, the state's Leader of the Opposition or leader of the largest opposition party in the state assembly, and a state cabinet minister nominated by the chief minister.

31. A. Dev, "His Master's Voice," *The Caravan*, October 1, 2020, https://caravanmagazine.in/law/tushar-mehta-holds-court.

32. N. Sharma, "Amendment to Whistleblower Protection Law Sparks Outrage among Civil Society Activists," *Economic Times*, May 16, 2015, https://economictimes.indiatimes.com/news/economy/policy/amendment-to-whistleblower-protection-law-sparks-outrage-among-civil-society-activists/articleshow/47303193.cms?from=mdr.

33. R. Sridharan, "Institutions of Internal Accountability," in *Rethinking Public Institutions in India*, ed. D. Kapur, P. B. Mehta, and M. Vaishnav (Delhi: Oxford University Press, 2017), 291.

34. Arvind Verma, "The Police in India: Design, Performance and Adaptability," in *Public Institutions in India: Performance and Design*, ed. D. Kapur and P. B. Mehta (Delhi: Oxford University Press, 2005), 209–11.

35. S. K. Das, "Institutions of Internal Accountability," in *Public Institutions in India: Performance and Design*, ed. D. Kapur and P. B. Mehta (Delhi: Oxford University Press, 2005), 128–57.

36. C. Jaffrelot, "Indian Democracy: The Rule of Law on Trial," *India Review* 1, no. 1 (January 2002): 77–121.

37. "Narendra Modi Accuses CBI of Working for Political Masters in Delhi," *Economic Times*, June 24, 2013, https://economictimes.indiatimes.com/news/politics-and-nation/narendra-modi-accuses-cbi-of-working-for-political-masters-indelhi/articleshow/20744006.cms?utm_source=contentofinterest&utm_medium=text&utm_campaign=cppst.

38. "Congress Will Not Fight Elections, Will Field CBI Instead: Modi," *Times of India*, September 25, 2013, https://timesofindia.indiatimes.com/india/Congress-will-not-fight-elections-will-field-CBI-instead-Modi/articleshow/23057533.cms.

39. J. Venkatesan, "Supreme Court Orders Probe into All Fake Encounters in Gujarat," *The Hindu*, January 25, 2012, https://www.thehindu.com/news/national/Supreme-Court-orders-probe-into-all-fake-encounters-in-Gujarat/article13381810.ece. For an overview of these fake encounters, see Amnesty International, India: A Pattern of Unlawful Killings by the Gujarat Police: Urgent Need for Effective Investigations," May 24, 2007, accessed December 4, 2013, http://www.amnesty.org/en/library/asset/ASA20/011/2007/en/1c189822-d393-11dd-a329-2f46302a8cc6/asa200112007en.pdf.

40. Manas Dasgupta, "Ishrat Jahan Killing Also a Fake Encounter: Probe Report," *The Hindu*, September 8, 2009, http://www.hindu.com/2009/09/08/stories/2009090856670100.htm.

41. "Kauser Bi Killed, Body Burnt; Gujarat Govt to SC," Rediff.com, April 30, 2007, http://www.rediff.com/news/2007/apr/30fake.htm; and Z. Qureshi and V. Zaia, "Arham Farmhouse Owner Held by CBI," *Ahmedabad Mirror*, July 28, 2010, http://www.ahmedabadmirror.com/article/3/201007282010072803482392353076389/Arham-farmhouse-owner-held-by-CBI.html.

42. "DG Vanzara: All You Need to Know about Gujarat's Former 'Supercop,'" FirstPost, September 3, 2013, http://www.firstpost.com/politics/dg-vanzara-all-you-need-to-know-about-gujarats-former-supercop-1082183.html.

43. Syed Khalique Ahmed, "'We Hope to Get Justice'," *Indian Express*, January 13, 2010, http://archive.indianexpress.com/news/-we-now-hope-to-get-justice-/566722/.

44. "The Journalist Who Cracked Gujarat Fake Encounter Case," Rediff.com, April 25, 2007, http://www.rediff.com/news/2007/apr/25spec.htm.

45. Ajay Umat emphasizes that "this decision to transfer Vanzara could not have been taken by Amit Shah as per the rules of the business and it was only the Chief Minister who could have finally passed the order." Ajay Umat, "CBI Encounters 'Modi Hand' in Triple-Murder," *Sunday Times of India* (Ahmedabad ed.), May 19, 2013, 1, https://timesofindia.indiatimes.com/india/CBI-encounters-Modi-hand-in-triple-murder/articleshow/20131246.cms.

46. "SC Slams Gujarat Police Probe," *Indian Express*, January 13, 2010, http://archive.indianexpress.com/news/sc-slams-gujarat-police-probe-hands-sohrabuddin-case-to-cbi/566798/2.

47. "Amit and Coterie Ran Extortion Racket," *Hindustan Times*, July 24, 2010, http://www.hindustantimes.com/India-news/Ahmedabad/Amit-amp-coterie-ran-extortion-racket/Article1-576856.aspx.

48. U. Sengupta, "Little Gujarat in CBI Headquarters," *Outlook*, July 27, 2015, https://magazine.outlookindia.com/story/little-gujarat-in-cbi-headquarters/294874.

49. Haren Pandya was killed on March 26, 2003, in a mysterious manner. In September 2013, D. G. Vanzara, the Gujarat police officer who had originally investigated the Pandya murder, indicated before the Central Bureau of Investigation a political conspiracy behind the killing of Pandya. See Roxy Gagdekar, "Was It Tulsiram Prajapati Who Killed Haren Pandya," *DNA* (Ahmedabad ed.), August 30, 2011, http://www.dnaindia.com/india/1581624/report-was-it-tulsiram-prajapati-who-killed-haren-pandya; "D.G. Vanzara Sings about Haren Pandya's Murder, Says It Was Political Conspiracy: CBI," *Times of India*, September 21, 2013, http://articles.timesofindia.indiatimes.com/2013-09-21/india/42271814_1_sadiq-jamal-encounter-case-tulsiram-prajapati. A few weeks before Vanzara's statement, the CBI "found that three men are common to cases pertaining to the assassination of BJP leader Haren Pandya and the encounters of Ishrat Jahan and Sadiq Jamal." Satish Jha, "CBI Finds Common Link in Pandya Murder, Ishrat, Sadiq Encounters," *Indian Express*, August 15, 2013, http://www.indianexpress.com/news/cbi-finds-common-link-in-pandya-murder-ishrat-sadiq-encounters/1155731/.

50. Cited in Vinod K. Jose, "The Emperor Uncrowned," *The Caravan*, March 1, 2012, http://caravanmagazine.in/reportage/emperor-uncrowned?page=0,9. See also "The Haren Pandya Judgement: Dissection of a Botched Investigation," *Economic and Political Weekly* 46, no. 38 (September 17, 2011), https://www.epw.in/journal/2011/38/commentary/haren-pandya-judgment-dissection-botched-investigation.html.

51. D. Jha, "Modi Wants CBI to Hand Over Sensitive Division to Officer with Controversial Past," Scroll.in, July 6, 2015, https://scroll.in/article/739017/modi-wants-cbi-to-hand-over-sensitive-division-to-officer-with-controversial-past.

52. P. Guha Thakurta, "All Eyes on SC Hearing Challenging Rakesh Asthana's Appointment as CBI Special Director," *The Wire*, November 11, 2017, https://thewire.in/law/eyes-sc-hearing-challenging-rakesh-asthanas-appointment-cbi-special-director.

53. "Supreme Court Wants Modi Govt to Explain Rakesh Asthana's Appointment as CBI Director," *Sabrang*, December 9, 2016, https://www.sabrangindia.in/article/supreme-court-wants-modi-govt-explain-rakesh-asthanas-appointment-cbi-director.

54. "Supreme Court Seeks Government Reply on Appointment of Interim CBI Director," *The Wire*, December 9, 2016, https://thewire.in/government/supreme-court-seeks -government-reply-appointment-interim-cbi-director.

55. V. Singh, "'Asthana Elevated Despite Dissent Note,'" *The Hindu*, October 27, 2017, https://www.thehindu.com/news/national/asthana-elevated-despite-dissent-note /article19927505.ece.

56. "SC Reserves Order on Plea Challenging Appointment of IPS Officer Asthana as CBI Special Director," *Indian Express*, November 24, 2017, https://indianexpress.com/article/india /sc-reserves-order-on-plea-challenging-appointment-of-ips-officer-asthana-as-cbi-special -director/.

57. "SC Dismisses Plea Challenging Rakesh Asthana's Appointment as CBI Special Direc- tor," *Indian Express*, November 28, 2017, https://indianexpress.com/article/india/supreme -court-rakesh-asthana-central-bureau-of-investigation-common-cause-4958206/.

58. See the FIR filed by the CBI against Asthana, the number 2 of the organization. "Full Text of FIR against CBI Special Director Rakesh Asthana for Bribery," *The Wire*, October 22, 2020, https://thewire.in/government/full-text-of-fir-against-cbi-special-director-rakesh -asthana-for-bribery.

59. "Modi Ousts CBI Chief Alok Verma as Asthana Case Reaches Breakpoint," *The Wire*, October 24, 2018, https://thewire.in/government/centre-intervenes-in-cbis-civil-war-director -alok-verma-sent-on-leave. The CBI director was allegedly eased out—on the recommendation of a secret CVC interim report—because he had met Prashant Bhushan, Arun Shourie, and Yashwant Sinha, the three public figures who had filed a complaint at that time, urging the CBI to investigate the Rafale deal on the grounds of suspected corruption. N. Sharma, "CBI Chief Meeting Arun Shourie, Prashant Bhushan on Rafale Upsets Centre," NDTV, October 10, 2020, https://www.ndtv.com/india-news/narendra-modi-government-upset-with-cbi-director-alok -verma-for-meeting-arun-shourie-and-prashant-bh-1929413.

60. A. Ashirvad Mahaprashasta, "M. Nageshwar Rao: CBI Interim Chief Has Always Been on Right Side of the BJP," *The Wire*, October 29, 2018, https://thewire.in/government/m -nageswara-rao-cbi-bjp-narendra-modi-controversy.

61. Cited in Mahaprashasta, "M. Nageshwar Rao."

62. Cited in V. Venugopal, "M Nageswara Rao: New CBI Boss a Champion of 'Hindu Causes,'" *Economic Times*, October 26, 2018, https://economictimes.indiatimes.com/news /politics-and-nation/m-nageswara-rao-new-cbi-boss-a-champion-of-hinducauses/articleshow /66371553.cms?utm_source=contentofinterest&utm_medium=text&utm_campaign=cppst.

63. In early 2020, after Rao had been appointed director-general of the Home Guards, Fire Service and Civil Defence, he wrote an article in the *Organiser* against "the dangers of foreign funding" of Indian NGOs. As the FCRA had too many loopholes, he said, "the only way to save the country from this serious menace, which is endangering its unity and integrity by causing civilisational osteoporosis, is by banning all sorts of foreign 'donations,' whatever may be their purpose." Cited in D. Tiwary, "CBI Ex-Acting Chief in RSS Journal: Ban Foreign Funding of Indian NGOs," *Indian Express*, January 29, 2020, https://indianexpress.com/article/india/cbi -ex-acting-chief-in-rss-journal-ban-foreign-funding-of-indian-ngos-6240224/.

64. The CVC considered Asthana's accusations valid, despite the fact that it acknowledged that the CBI's "concern on the integrity of its special director, Rakesh Asthana, turned out to

be true." "Supreme Court's Interim Order in CBI Matter Places CVC Role under Scrutiny," The Wire, October 26, 2018, https://thewire.in/law/supreme-court-cbi-cvc.

65. "Centre Denies RTI Requests for Info on CBI Director's Removal," The Hindu, January 5, 2019, https://www.thehindu.com/news/national/centre-denies-rti-requests-for-info-on-cbi-directors-removal/article25921264.ece.

66. "CBI feud: We Had to Step In, Says Centre," The Hindu, December 5, 2018, https://www.thehindu.com/news/national/cbi-feud-we-had-to-step-in-says-centre/article25674257.ece.

67. K. Rajagopal, "Supreme Court Reinstates Alok Verma as CBI Director," The Hindu, January 8, 2019, https://www.thehindu.com/news/national/supreme-court-reinstates-alok-verma-as-cbi-director/article25938117.ece.

68. "CJI Nominates Justice AK Sikri on Panel to Decide CBI Director Verma's Fate," India Today, January 9, 2019, https://www.indiatoday.in/india/story/cji-justice-ak-sigri-panel-cbi-director-alok-kumar-verma-sc-1427134-2019-01-09.

69. "Tried to Uphold CBI Integrity, Attempts Were Being Made to Destroy It: Alok Verma on Being Removed as Chief," India Today, January 11, 2019, https://www.indiatoday.in/india/story/tried-to-uphold-cbi-integrity-attempts-were-being-made-to-destroy-it-alok-verma-on-being-removed-as-chief-1428424-2019-01-11.

70. "Justice (Retd) Patnaik Not on Same Page as CVC, Claims Alok Verma, Ousted CBI Chief in His Resignation Letter," National Herald, January 11, 2019, https://www.nationalheraldindia.com/india/justice-retd-patnaik-not-on-same-page-as-cvc-claims-alok-verma-ousted-cbi-chief-in-his-resignation-letter.

71. S. Chisti, "No Evidence of Corruption, Decision of PM-Led Panel on Alok Verma Very Hasty: SC's Monitor," Indian Express, January 12, 2019, https://indianexpress.com/article/india/alok-verma-cvc-panel-narendra-modi-supreme-court-5534472/.

72. S. Chaturvedi, "Exclusive: Entire CBI Team Probing Rakesh Asthana's Alleged Corruption Has Now Been Purged," The Wire, September 28, 2019, https://thewire.in/government/cbi-rakesh-asthana-corruption-investigation; and J. Mazoomdaar, "CBI Officer Who Led Investigation in Rakesh Asthana Case Seeks Voluntary Retirement," Indian Express, September 26, 2019, https://indianexpress.com/article/india/cbi-officer-who-led-investigation-in-rakesh-asthana-case-seeks-voluntary-retirement-6029587/.

73. "CBI Gives Clean Chit to Rakesh Asthana," Economic Times, February 12, 2020, https://economictimes.indiatimes.com/news/politics-and-nation/cbi-gives-clean-chit-to-rakesh-asthana/articleshow/74092501.cms.

74. The phrase "caged parrots" in the section subhead refers to the nickname given to the CBI under the UPA government. See Shekhar Gupta, "How CBI Went from Being a Caged Parrot to a Wild Vulture," ThePrint, November 17, 2018, https://theprint.in/national-interest/how-cbi-went-from-being-a-caged-parrot-to-a-wild-vulture/150694/.

75. I have studied this material in a rather systematic manner in C. Jaffrelot, "Abhinav Bharat, the Malegaon Blast and Hindu Nationalism: Resisting and Emulating Islamist Terrorism," Economic and Political Weekly 45, no. 36 (September 4–10, 2010): 51–58. Excerpts of the transcripts of the Abhinav Bharat's meetings are available, in English and in Hindi, on the website of the Economic and Political Weekly. See also C. Jaffrelot, "Malegaon: Who Is above the Law?," Economic and Political Weekly 47, no. 29 (July 21, 2012): 17–18; and C. Jaffrelot and M. Maheshwari, "Paradigmatic Shifts by the RSS? Lessons from Aseemanand's Confession," Economic and

Political Weekly 46, no. 6 (February 11, 2011): 42–46. The unfootnoted paragraphs below draw from these three sources.

76. "Tagging Terror with RSS Is a Conspiracy: Bhagwat," *Indian Express*, November 10, 2010, http://archive.indianexpress.com/news/tagging-terror-with-rss-is-a-conspiracy-bhagwat/709201/.

77. "RSS's Indresh: 'New Govt Should Review (Our) Cases,'" *Indian Express*, May 24, 2014, https://indianexpress.com/article/india/politics/rsss-indresh-new-govt-should-review-our-cases/.

78. S. Mehta, "The Meaning Very Clearly Was, Don't Get Us Favourable Orders: Malegaon SPP Rohini Salian," *Indian Express*, October 13, 2015, https://indianexpress.com/article/india/india-others/the-meaning-very-clearly-was-dont-get-us-favourable-orders/.

79. U. Anand, "Rohini Salian Names NIA Officer Who Told Her to 'Go Soft' against Malegaon Blasts Accused," *Indian Express*, October 13, 2015, https://indianexpress.com/article/india/india-news-india/rohini-salian-names-nia-officer-who-told-her-to-go-soft/.

80. "I Am out (of All NAI Cases), It Is a Matter of Faith, Principle: Special Public Prosecutor Rohini Salian, the Day After," *Indian Express*, June 26, 2015, https://indianexpress.com/article/india/india-others/i-am-out-of-all-nia-cases-its-a-matter-of-faith-principle-special-public-prosecutor-rohini-salian-the-day-after/.

81. M. Rao, "2008 Malegaon Blasts: NIA under Fire from Former Prosecutor as It Seeks to Drop MCOCA Charges," Scroll.in, February 4, 2016, https://scroll.in/article/802937/2008-malegaon-blasts-nia-under-fire-from-former-prosecutor-as-it-seeks-to-drop-mcoca-charges.

82. "2008 Malegaon Blasts Case: When Five Witnesses Became Two and Gave New Versions," *Indian Express*, June 27, 2016, https://indianexpress.com/article/india/india-news-india/malegaon-blasts-2008-nia-probe-sadhvi-pragya-clean-chit-2877998/.

83. R. Tripathi, "'Strong Anti-Minority Feelings': What the NIA Probe in Six Bomb Blasts Found," *Indian Express*, April 18, 2018, https://indianexpress.com/article/explained/nia-malegaon-blasts-samjhauta-express-case-mecca-masjid-verdict-ajmer-dargah-blast-5141597/.

84. D. Tiwary, "Clean Chit to Sadhvi, MCOCA Dropped, Karkare Probe Was Fudged: NIA's New Malegaon script," *Indian Express*, May 13, 2016, https://indianexpress.com/article/india/india-news-india/malegaon-blasts-2008-nia-probe-sadhvi-pragya-singh-gets-clean-chit-2797995/.

85. "Is the NIA Actively Working to Keep Aseemanand Out of Jail?," The Wire, April 9, 2017, https://thewire.in/politics/nia-aseemanand-bail-sabotage.

86. Interestingly, in the Malegaon case, the NIA requested that the trial's proceedings be on camera. S. Yamunan, "The Daily Fix: NIA's Bid to Evade Public Scrutiny in Malegaon Blast Trial Challenges Media Freedom," Scroll.in, August 21, 2019, https://scroll.in/article/934623/the-daily-fix-nias-bid-to-evade-public-scrutiny-in-malegaon-blast-trial-challenges-media-freedom.

87. See Dilip Simeon's comprehensive blog post. "Sabotage of Indian Criminal Justice Continues Unchecked: Aseemanand's 'Disclosure' Missing from Court," Dilip Simeon (blog), March 14, 2018, https://dilipsimeon.blogspot.com/2018/03/sabotage-of-indian-criminal-justice.html.

88. "Mecca Masjid Blast Case: Five Including Aseemanand Acquitted, Judge Who Delivered Verdict Resigns," *Indian Express*, April 17, 2018, https://indianexpress.com/article/india/mecca

-masjid-case-special-nia-judge-who-delivered-verdict-resigns-ravindra-reddy-hyderabad
-5139720/.

89. S. Sharma, "Not Just Rohini Salian: Public Prosecutor in Ajmer Blast Case Is Unhappy with NIA," Scroll.in, August 14, 2015, https://scroll.in/article/747397/not-just-rohini-salian
-public-prosecutor-in-ajmer-blast-case-is-also-unhappy-with-nia.

90. Tiwary, "Clean Chit to Sadhvi."

91. S. Mehta, "Malegaon Blasts Case: Salian Speaks Up Again after NIA's U-turn," *Indian Express*, April 14, 2016, https://indianexpress.com/article/india/india-news-india/salian
-speaks-up-again-after-nias-malegaon-u-turn/.

92. For an overview of the judicial trajectory of the Sohrabuddin case, see Harsh Mander and Sarim Naved, "Opinion: Sohrabuddin Sheikh Judgement Betrays Every Principle of Justice and Legal Procedure," Scroll.in, December 29, 2018, https://scroll.in/article/907331
/opinion-sohrabuddin-sheikh-case-judgement-betrays-every-principle-of-justice-and-legal
-procedure.

93. Ashish Khetan, "CBI under Modi Ensures the Accused Are Free and the Investigator Is on Trial," The Wire, February 10, 2018, https://thewire.in/law/since-may-2014-key-investigating
-officer-sohrabuddin-fake-encounter-case-trial.

94. A. Dev, "Death of Judge Loya: Medical Documents Rule Out Heart Attack, Says Leading Forensic Expert," *The Caravan*, February 11, 2018, https://caravanmagazine.in/vantage/death
-judge-loya-medical-documents-rule-heart-attack-forensic-expert.

95. Niranjan Takle, "Chief Justice Mohit Shah Offered Rs 100 Crore to My Brother for a Favourable Judgment in the Sohrabuddin Case: Late Judge Loya's Sister," *The Caravan*, November 21, 2017, https://caravanmagazine.in/vantage/loya-chief-justice-mohit-shah-offer-100-crore
-favourable-judgment-sohrabuddin-case. See also N. Takle, "A Family Breaks Its Silence: Shocking Details Emerge in Death of Judge Presiding over Sohrabuddin trial," *The Caravan*, November 20, 2017, https://caravanmagazine.in/vantage/shocking-details-emerge-in-death-of-judge
-presiding-over-sohrabuddin-trial-family-breaks-silence.

96. A. Kumar, "Justice A.P. Shah Says 'Suspicious Death' of Sohrabuddin Case Judge Needs Probe," The Wire, November 23, 2017, https://thewire.in/law/watch-justice-shah-suspicious
-death-judge-loya.

97. Mander and Naved, "Opinion."

98. See the list in the interview of Justice Thipsay: "I Have Seen the Discharge Orders . . . HC Should Examine These Orders: Justice (Retd) Abhay M Thipsay on Sohrabuddin Case," February 14, 2018, https://indianexpress.com/article/india/sohrabuddin-encounter-case-bh
-loya-death-bombay-high-court-amit-shah-bjp-justice-abhay-m-thipsay-cbi-5062871/.

99. Mander and Naved, "Opinion."

100. "Sohrabuddin Shaikh 'Fake' Encounter: Former Gujarat DIG Vanzara, Five Others' Discharge Upheld by Bombay HC," Times Headline, September 10, 2018, https://timesheadline
.com/india/sohrabuddin-shaikh-fake-encounter-former-gujarat-dig-vanzara-five-others
-discharge-upheld-bombay-hc-23473.html. See also S. Modak, "In Sohrabuddin Shaikh Case, Bombay HC Upholds Discharge of Gujarat DIG Vanzara and Four Other Police Officers," *Indian Express*, September 11, 2018, https://indianexpress.com/article/india/sohrabuddin-shaikh
-fake-encounter-former-gujarat-dig-vanzara-five-others-discharged-by-bombay-hc-5348373/.

101. S. Modak, "Sohrabuddin 'Fake' Encounter Case: One More Prosecution Witness Turns Hostile, Takes Count to 45," *Indian Express*, April 3, 2018, https://indianexpress.com/article/india/sohrabuddin-alleged-fake-encounter-case-one-more-prosecution-witness-turns-hostile-takes-count-to-45-5121158/.

102. "Sixtieth Witness in Sohrabuddin Sheikh Fake Encounter Case Turns Hostile," Scroll.in, June 5, 2018, https://scroll.in/latest/881429/sixtieth-witness-in-sohrabuddin-sheikh-fake-encounter-case-turns-hostile. See also "Sohrabuddin Case: 3 More Prosecution Witnesses Turn Hostile," *Times of India*, June 12, 2018, http://timesofindia.indiatimes.com/articleshow/64563370.cms?utm_source=contentofinterest&utm_medium=text&utm_campaign=cppst.

103. "'What Are You Doing to Protect Sohrabuddin Case Witnesses?' HC Asks CBI," The Wire, February 13, 2018, https://thewire.in/law/protect-sohrabuddin-case-witnesses-hc-asks-cbi.

104. "HC Judge Who Pulled Up CBI in Sohrabuddin Case Reassigned in 'Routine' Shuffle," The Wire, February 25, 2018, https://thewire.in/law/new-bombay-high-court-judge-assigned-to-hear-sohrabuddin-encounter-case.

105. "Sohrabuddin Case Final Hearing Ends; CBI Says Hostile Witnesses Hampered Probe," The Wire, December 6, 2018, https://thewire.in/law/sohrabuddin-case-final-hearing-ends-cbi-says-hostile-witnesses-hampered-probe.

106. S. Shantha, "Delay in Accepting Brother as Witness Adds New Wrinkle to Sohrabuddin Case," The Wire, June 9, 2018, https://thewire.in/rights/sohrabuddins-brother-asks-court-to-make-him-a-witness-in-fake-encounters-case.

107. Shantha, "Delay in Accepting Brother."

108. While the latter is facing two cases that—he claimed—have been fabricated, the former has been suspended from service, after the government refused his application for early retirement.

109. "Court on Sohrabuddin Case: CBI Had Theory, Script to Implicate Politicians," *Indian Express*, December 29, 2018, https://indianexpress.com/article/india/court-on-sohrabuddin-case-cbi-had-theory-script-to-implicate-politicians-5514455/.

110. "List of All 22 Accused Acquitted in Sohrabuddin Sheikh Fake Encounter Case," *Mumbai Mirror*, December 21, 2018, https://mumbaimirror.indiatimes.com/mumbai/crime/list-of-all-22-accused-acquitted-in-sohrabuddin-sheikh-fake-encounter-case/articleshow/67194773.cms.

111. S. Naved, "Between the NIA Amendment and Now UAPA, the Squeeze on Human Rights Is on," The Wire, July 24, 2019, https://thewire.in/government/the-centre-wants-to-give-the-nia-more-powers-but-it-wont-explain-why.

112. In fact, a few weeks later, the government returned another Collegium's judge proposal. This time, it asked the Collegium to reconsider the appointment of a Karnataka High Court judge as chief justice of the Punjab and Haryana High Court. M. Chhibber, "Government Returns Another SC Collegium's Judge Proposal," *Indian Express*, July 15, 2014, https://indianexpress.com/article/india/india-others/government-returns-another-sc-collegiums-judge-proposal/.

113. U. Anand, "Rejected for Judgeship, Gopal Subramanium Hits Out at NDA Govt, Supreme Court," *Indian Express*, June 26, 2014, http://archive.indianexpress.com/news/rejected-for-judgeship-gopal-subramanium-hits-out-at-nda-govt-supreme-court/1264310/0.

114. K. Ganz, "Gopal Subramanium's Heartbreakingly Honest 9-Page Withdrawal Letter: Bows Out to Avoid Clouding Others' Appointments," Legally India, June 25, 2014, https://www .legallyindia.com/the-bench-and-the-bar/gopal-subramanium-withdraws-writes-judiciary -compromised-because-gov-t-feared-he-wouldn-t-toe-their-line-20140625-4821.

115. S. Hegde, "Borking Gopal Subramanium," The Hindu, June 26, 2014, https://www .thehindu.com/opinion/op-ed/borking-gopal-subramanium/article6148766.ece.

116. K. Rajagopal, "CBI Does a U-turn on Subramanium," The Hindu, July 19, 2014, https:// www.thehindu.com/news/national/cbi-does-a-uturn-on-subramanium/article6226155.ece.

117. U. Anand, "Rejected for Judgeship, Gopal Subramanium Hits out at NDA Govt, Supreme Court," Financial Express, June 26, 2014, https://www.financialexpress.com/archive /rejected-for-judgeship-gopal-subramanium-hits-out-at-nda-govt-supreme-court/1264310/.

118. Madhav Khosla and Ananth Padmanabhan, "The Supreme Court," in Rethinking Public Institutions in India, ed. D. Kapur, P. B. Mehta, and M. Vaishnav (New Delhi: Oxford University Press, 2017, 104–38.

119. "Elders Clear Bill to Set Up Judicial Appointments Commission," The Hindu, September 5, 2013, https://www.thehindu.com/news/national/elders-clear-bill-to-set-up-judicial -appointments-commission/article5096598.ece.

120. "On Day Govt Moves Bill, Chief Justice Speaks Up," Indian Express, August 12, 2014, https://indianexpress.com/article/india/india-others/on-day-govt-moves-bill-chief-justice -speaks-up/.

121. See, for instance, Rajindar Sachar, "Hanging in Balance: No Executive Interference Required," Indian Express, August 15, 2014, https://indianexpress.com/article/opinion/columns /no-executive-interference-required/; and K. T. Thomas, "In Defence of Collegium," Indian Express, August 13, 2014, https://indianexpress.com/article/opinion/columns/in-defence-of -the-collegium/.

122. The Supreme Court had not struck down a constitutional amendment in thirty-five years.

123. The verdict is accessible at "Supreme Court . . . vs Union of India on 16 October, 2015," Indian Kanoon, accessed December 1, 2020, https://indiankanoon.org/doc/66970168/?type =print.

124. The majority verdict considered that "primacy of judiciary and limited role of the Executive in appointment of judges is part of the basic structure of the Constitution," a viewpoint with which the dissenting judge, Justice Chelameswar, disagreed. U. Anand, "Supreme Court Strikes Down NJAC, Revives Collegium System," Indian Express, October 17, 2015, https:// indianexpress.com/article/india/india-news-india/sc-strikes-down-njac-revives-collegium -system-of-appointing-judges/.

125. Khosla and Padmanabhan, "Supreme Court," 113.

126. "Supreme Court . . . vs Union," 320–21. See also A. A. Choudhary, "Giving Politician a Say in Judges' Selection Would Bring 'Spoils System' within Judiciary: SC," Times of India, October 16, 2015, https://timesofindia.indiatimes.com/india/Giving-politician-a-say-in-judges -selection-would-bring-spoils-system-within-judiciarySC/articleshow/49418456.cms.

127. M. Chhibber, "Government Says No to Crucial Objections of Supreme Court Collegium," Indian Express, June 28, 2016, https://indianexpress.com/article/india/india-news-india /sc-collegium-sc-judges-appointment-ts-thakur-nda-govt-2880284/.

128. Sheela Bhatt, "Memorandum of Procedure: Behind the Scenes, Govt and SC in Tug of War over Appointments—and Turf," *Indian Express*, July 15, 2016, https://indianexpress.com /article/india/india-news-india/supreme-court-high-court-judge-appointment-procedure -criteria-collegium-government-judiciary-2914823/.

129. U. Anand, "Chief Justice TS Thakur Questions PM Narendra Modi's Silence on Appointment of Judges," *Indian Express*, August 16, 2016, https://indianexpress.com/article/india /india-news-india/cji-t-s-thakur-questions-pm-narendra-modis-silence-on-appointment-of -judges-2977285/.

130. M. Chhibber, "Three Months after CJs' Meeting, Govt and Judiciary Yet to Agree on Minutes," *Indian Express*, July 25, 2016, https://indianexpress.com/article/india/india-news -india/supreme-court-high-court-judge-appointment-procedure-criteria-collegium -government-judiciary-memorandum-of-procedure-2933697/.

131. "No New Judges Appointed to Higher Judiciary for 8 Months," *Indian Express*, August 5, 2016, https://www.hindustantimes.com/india-news/no-new-judges-appointed-to-higher -judiciary-for-8-months-govt/story-H3Gh25FIRwm9u68KMq2WeM.html.

132. "80% of Funds for Developing Judicial Infra Remain Unspent," *Times of India* (New Delhi ed.), January 10, 2015, 15, https://timesofindia.indiatimes.com/india/Large-funds-for -developing-judicial-infrastructure-remain-unspent/articleshow/45830586.cms.

133. A. K. Aditya, "Judiciary Watch: 426 Vacancies in High Courts, Pendency Grows to More than 15 Lakh," Bar and Bench, December 10, 2015, https://www.barandbench.com/columns /judiciary-watch-426-vacancies-in-high-courts-pendency-grows-to-more-than-15-lakh.

134. M. Reddy, "Vacancies in High Courts Touch 470 as Govt.-Judiciary Logjam Continues," *The Hindu*, July 5, 2016, https://www.thehindu.com/news/national/Vacancies-in-high-courts -touch-470-as-govt.-judiciary-logjam-continues/article14471093.ece.

135. U. Anand, "CJI to Government: Don't Blame Us for Delay, Look Within," *Indian Express*, July 23, 2014, https://indianexpress.com/article/india/india-others/cji-to-government-dont -blame-us-for-delay-look-within/. The vacancies in the High Court jumped from 470 to 478 between July and August. M. Krishnan, "Judiciary Watch: 478 Vacancies in High Courts across the Country," Bar and Bench, August 6, 2016, https://www.barandbench.com/news/judiciary -watch-478-vacancies-high-courts-across-country.

136. Narendra Modi tried to comfort him, saying that he was prepared "to set up a joint panel of representatives drawn from the judiciary and the executive to deal with the problem." S. Prakash, "Chief Justice Breaks Down before PM over Burden on Judiciary," *Hindustan Times*, April 24, 2016, https://www.hindustantimes.com/india/pm-assures-emotional-cji-of-govt -support-in-increasing-judge-strength/story-EgEh9e7DkCgwyBOS5nI2PN.html.

137. "We Require More than 70,000 Judges to Clear Pending Cases: CJI TS Thakur," *Economic Times*, May 8, 2016, https://economictimes.indiatimes.com/news/politics-and-nation /we-require-more-than-70000-judges-to-clear-pending-cases-cji-ts-thakur/articleshow /52176581.cms.

138. There were more than 4 million pending cases before the High Courts alone in 2019. "Over 3.5 Crore Cases Pending across Courts in India, Little Change in Numbers Since 2014," *The Wire*, November 27, 2019, https://thewire.in/law/pending-court-cases.

139. Anand, "Chief Justice TS Thakur."

140. "You Cannot Bring the Entire Institution to a Grinding Halt: SC Slams Modi Govt," *Sabrang*, October 28, 2016, https://sabrangindia.in/article/you-cannot-bring-entire-institution-grinding-halt-sc-slams-modi-govt.

141. U. Anand, "SC Slams Govt, Says Can't Let You Decimate the System," *Indian Express*, October 29, 2016, https://indianexpress.com/article/india/india-news-india/supreme-court-judges-appointment-njac-collegium-government-inaction-inefficiency-or-unwillingness-3727713/. According to another press report, the conversation was slightly different: "For nine months, the names the Collegium gave you have been languishing with you. . . . You have been sitting over the names. What are you waiting for? Some change in the system? Some revolution in the system?' . . .

"Mr. Rohatgi countered that the law provided for an MoP to be finalised before appointments are made.

"'The MoP is your red herring. The Law Minister and the government has repeatedly told us that the process of finalisation of MoP will not stall judicial appointments process. Now are you saying that there is a deadlock on the MoP and you want it cleared first before appointing judges?' Justice Thakur asked." K. Rajagopal, "Centre Is Trying to Decimate Judiciary: SC," *The Hindu*, October 28, 2016, https://www.thehindu.com/news/national/Centre-is-trying-to-decimate-judiciary-SC/article16084597.ece.

142. Anand, "SC Slams Govt."

143. Rajagopal, "Centre Is Trying."

144. "No Abnormal Increase in High Court Vacancies: Centre," *The Hindu*, October 29, 2016, https://www.thehindu.com/news/national/No-abnormal-increase-in-High-Court-vacancies-Centre/article16085288.ece.

145. "'Courts Lying Vacant without Judges': CJI TS Thakur Lambasts Centre," *Indian Express*, November 26, 2016, https://indianexpress.com/article/india/india-news-india/cji-thakur-lambasts-centre-says-courts-lying-vacant-without-judges-collegium-sysytem-4396198/.

146. "Supreme Court Collegium Rejects Govt's No to 43 Names for Judges in High Courts," *Indian Express*, November 19, 2016, https://indianexpress.com/article/india/india-news-india/sc-collegium-rejects-govts-no-to-43-names-for-judges-in-high-courts-4382958/.

147. "Appointment of Judges Function of Executive, Says Parliamentary Committee," *Indian Express*, December 8, 2016, https://indianexpress.com/article/india/supreme-court-judges-appointment-collegium-parliamentary-committee-4417496/.

148. S. Rautray, "Justice TS Thakur Was Unable to Fill Judicial Posts," *Economic Times*, January 2, 2017, https://economictimes.indiatimes.com/news/politics-and-nation/justice-ts-thakur-was-unable-to-fill-judicial-posts/articleshow/56281544.cms?utm_source=contentofinterest&utm_medium=text&utm_campaign=cppst.

149. A. Dev, "In Sua Causa: What the Judiciary Has Done to Itself," *The Caravan*, July 1, 2019, https://caravanmagazine.in/magazine/2019/07.

150. Cited in A. Dev, "'Operation Successful; Patient Dead': A Troubling New Clause Allows the Government to Reject a Judge's Appointment on the Grounds of National Security," *The Caravan*, March 17, 2017, https://caravanmagazine.in/vantage/operation-successful-patient-deada-troubling-new-clause-allows-government-reject-judges-appointment-grounds-national-security.

151. In July 2017, the differences that remained were listed in a letter that the Law Ministry wrote to the Supreme Court: First, "the government wanted to keep the reasons for rejecting a candidate's selection on the grounds of 'national security and overriding public interest' confidential and share it only with the CJI." Second, "the Supreme Court was against creating a secretariat for vetting and clearing names of judges and forming a committee of judges, who were not part of the collegium to screen complaints against sitting judges." Third, it "was also not in favor of having search and evaluation committees for selecting candidates." M. Krishnan, "Disagreements Stall Rules on Appointment of Judges," *Hindustan Times*, January 6, 2020, https://www.hindustantimes.com/india-news/disagreements-stall-rules-on-appointment-of-judges/story-FilVn4bFayBzQU0H7j7B9H.html.

152. In fact, the Supreme Court showed some leniency even before Justice Khehar became India's chief justice, as evident from the verdict of the bench he headed after hearing a petition filed by the NGO Common Cause to set aside the appointment of K. V. Chowdary as the central vigilance commissioner because, as head of the income-tax department, "he had not probed documents found during a search of the offices of Hindalco Industries, owned by the Aditya Birla Group, and a raid at the Delhi and Noida offices of the Sahara India group." A. Dev, "Balancing Act," *The Caravan*, June 1, 2017, https://caravanmagazine.in/reportage/chief-justice-khehar-executive-judiciary. See above details about this case.

153. "SC Refuses Plea on Alleged Dilution of Whistleblower Law," *The Hindu*, January 13, 2017, https://www.thehindu.com/news/national/SC-refuses-plea-on-alleged-dilution-of-whistleblower-law/article17030428.ece.

154. Dev, "Balancing Act."

155. In the Westminster type of parliamentary system, a money bill does not imply changes in public laws but concerns solely taxation and government spending. That is why it does not need to be examined by the upper house of parliament.

156. Aadhaar is the name of a biometric identification system that was initiated by the Manmohan Singh government in 2009. It had been conceived at the time as a way of giving every Indian a unique identification number, without making it mandatory. In particular it was meant to secure access of the poor to their food ration and to prevent fraud. See Christophe Jaffrelot and Nicolas Belorgey, "L'identification biométrique de 1,3 milliard d'Indiens: Milieux d'affaires, Etat et société civile," *Les Etudes du CERI*, no. 251, September 2018, https://www.sciencespo.fr/ceri/fr/papier/etude.

157. Out of the five judges, four wrote the majority verdict. Judge D. Y. Chandrachud, in his minority opinion, penned a scathing and remarkably well argued indictment against it, prompting him to declare Aadhaar unconstitutional. This judgment has been cited by the Jamaican Supreme Court to justify its invalidation of a scheme comparable to Aadhaar.

158. Interview with Karuna Nundy, New Delhi, January 2020.

159. "Loya Case Judge Is Close to BJP: Dave," *Times of India*, January 14, 2018, http://timesofindia.indiatimes.com/articleshow/62492769.cms?utm_source=contentofinterest&utm_medium=text&utm_campaign=cppst.

160. Atul Dev, "The Darkest Hour," *The Caravan*, July 1, 2018, 35.

161. Cited in D. Mahapatra, "We Felt Then-CJI Was Being Remote-Controlled: Justice Kurian Joseph," *Times of India*, December 3, 2018, http://timesofindia.indiatimes.com/articleshow/66912798.cms?utm_source=contentofinterest&utm_medium=text&utm_campaign=cppst.

162. "Supreme Court to Hear Plea Seeking Probe into Judge Loya's Death," *Indian Express*, January 11, 2018, https://indianexpress.com/article/india/supreme-court-to-hear-plea-seeking-probe-into-judge-loyas-death-5020157/.

163. G. Bhatia, "Loya Case: Supreme Court Has Delivered a Trial Court Judgement—without Actually Holding a Trial," *Indian Express*, April 24, 2018, https://scroll.in/article/876707/loya-case-supreme-court-has-delivered-a-trial-court-judgement-without-actually-holding-a-trial.

164. S. Chisthti, "Govt Has Struck at the Very Heart of Judicial Freedom: Former CJI R.M. Lodha," *Indian Express*, April 27, 2018, https://indianexpress.com/article/india/govt-has-struck-at-the-very-heart-of-judicial-freedom-former-cji-rm-lodha-5153513.

165. M. Chhibber, "Modi Govt Takes on SC Again, Appoints Indu Malhotra but Doesn't Clear K.M. Joseph," ThePrint, April 25, 2018, https://theprint.in/india/governance/modi-govt-takes-on-sc-again-appoints-indu-malhotra-but-doesnt-clear-k-m-joseph/52757/.

166. A. Mandhani, "Justice Chelameswar Calls for Full Court Discussion on Govt. Interference in Judicial Appointments [Read Letter]," LiveLaw.in, March 29, 2018, https://www.livelaw.in/justice-chelameswar-calls-full-court-discussion-govt-interference-judicial-appointments/.

167. "Ok for Centre to Reject Justice Joseph, Says Chief Justice: 10 Points," NDTV, April 26, 2018, https://www.ndtv.com/india-news/is-government-above-the-law-congress-attack-over-judge-km-josephs-appointment-1843100.

168. "Supreme Court Collegium Meets but Defers Decision on Justice Joseph's Elevation," *Indian Express*, May 3, 2018, https://indianexpress.com/article/india/supreme-court-collegium-meeting-cji-dipak-misra-justice-k-m-joseph-elevation-deffered-5160846/. See also A. P. Kumar, "It's Clear Dipak Misra Is Unwilling or Unable to Defend the Supreme Court's Best Interests," Scroll.in, May 5, 2018, https://scroll.in/article/877840/opinion-its-clear-dipak-misra-is-unwilling-or-unable-to-defend-the-supreme-courts-best-interests.

169. Cited in Chhibber, "Modi Govt Takes."

170. M. Chhibber, "In a First, Modi Govt Changes Collegium's Recommendation on HC Judge's Appointment," ThePrint, April 23, 2018, https://theprint.in/india/governance/modi-govt-changes-collegiums-recommendation-hc-judges-appointment/51742/.

171. M. Chhibber, "Appointment of These 4 as Judges Has Been Stuck for 2 Yrs & Modi Govt Hasn't Given Reasons," ThePrint, May 31, 2018, https://theprint.in/india/governance/appointment-of-these-4-as-judges-has-been-stuck-for-2-yrs-modi-govt-hasnt-given-reasons/64625/.

172. "Centre Returns 2 Names for Appointment to Allahabad HC the Second Time in 2 Years," Law Gupshup, June 25, 2018, https://lawgupshup.com/2018/06/centre-returns-2-names-for-appointment-to-allahabad-hc-the-second-time-in-2-years/.

173. On other occasions, the government refused to appoint a judge to one High Court but agreed to appoint him to another—and the Collegium obliged them. See the case Justice Aniruddha Bose explained in M. Chhibber, "Modi Govt Rejects Judge's Name as Delhi High Court Chief Justice, Cites Lack of Experience," ThePrint, July 19, 2018, https://theprint.in/india/governance/modi-govt-rejects-judges-name-as-delhi-hc-chief-justice-cites-lack-of-experience/85105/.

174. Rajeev Dhavan, "View: Why HC Judges Can't Be Transferred According to Whim & Fancy," *Economic Times*, September 29, 2017, https://economictimes.indiatimes.com/news/politics-and-nation/view-why-government-cannot-transfer-hc-judges-according-to-whim-fancy/articleshow/60876393.cms?from=mdr.

175. S. Yamunan, "Supreme Court Collegium Should Explain Why Justice Jayant Patel's Transfer Was in Public Interest," Scroll.in, accessed August 17, 2020, https://scroll.in/article /852239/supreme-court-collegium-should-explain-how-justice-jayant-patels-transfer-was-in -public-interest.

176. M. Sebastian, "Centre's Scramble For One-Upmanship Over Judicial Appointments," Live Law.in, August 5, 2018, https://www.livelaw.in/centres-scramble-for-one-upmanship-over -judicial-appointments/.

177. "Chelameswar Letter Text: 'Bonhomie between Judiciary, Government Sounds Death Knell to Democracy,'" Scroll.in, March 29, 2018, https://scroll.in/article/873787/full-text -bonhomie-between-judiciary-and-government-sounds-the-death-knell-to-democracy.

178. "CJI Impeachment Motion: Full text of the Statement Issued by Congress and Six Other Opposition Parties," FirstPost, April 20, 2018, https://www.firstpost.com/india/cji -impeachment-motion-full-text-of-the-statement-issued-by-congress-and-six-other-opposition -parties-4439531.html.

179. Rohan Venkataramakrishnan, "So, What Did the Congress Achieve by Trying to Im- peach Chief Justice Dipak Misra?," Scroll.in, May 13, 2018, https://scroll.in/article/878695/so -what-did-the-congress-achieve-by-trying-to-impeach-chief-justice-dipak-misra.

180. Amit Choudhary, "Electoral Bonds Retrograde Step, against Transparency of Political Funding: EC to SC," *Times of India*, March 27, 2019, https://www.newsrain.in/news/68601455 /Electoral-bonds-retrograde-step,-against-transparency-of-political-funding:-EC-to-SC.

181. V. Sachdev, "Why the SC's Electoral Bonds Order Leaves a Lot to Be Desired," The Quint, accessed August 20, 2020, https://www.thequint.com/voices/opinion/why-supreme -court-electoral-bonds-interim-order-ineffective.

182. M. Chhibber, "How Modi Govt Tried to Stall Akil Kureshi's Appointment as MP High Court Chief Justice," ThePrint, September 23, 2019, https://theprint.in/judiciary/how-modi -govt-tried-to-stall-akil-kureshis-appointment-as-mp-high-court-chief-justice/295290/.

183. "Centre Blocking Elevation of Justice Kureshi, Who Once Sent Amit Shah to Custody," The Wire, June 21, 2019, https://thewire.in/law/centres-refusal-to-elevate-justice-kureshi-raises -troubling-questions.

184. Other transfers could be mentioned to illustrate the way judges have been punished in the recent past, including those of Justice Vijaya Tahilramani, who had convicted eleven people in the Bilkis Bano gang-rape case (the gang rape had taken place during the Gujarat pogrom) as acting chief justice of Bombay High Court; Justice Abhay Thipsay, of Bombay High Court, who had sentenced to life imprisonment nine of the twenty-one accused in the Best Bakery case (also related to the Gujarat pogrom); and Justice Rajiv Shakdher, who had lifted the travel ban on Priya Pillai, a Greenpeace activist who had been offloaded from a plane in 2015 because she was about to testify before British parliamentarians about the environmental implications of India's intention to mine coal in a Madhya Pradesh forest.

185. M. B. Lokur, "Collegium's Actions Show that the NJAC which Was Struck Down Four Years Ago Is Back, with a Vengeance," *Indian Express*, October 16, 2019, https://indianexpress.com /article/opinion/columns/govt-calling-the-supreme-court-shots-narendra-modi-6070659/.

186. The episodes mentioned in this paragraph, ranging from the conquest of the BJP in Gujarat and Modi's postpogrom judicial problems are elaborated on in my forthcoming book, *Saffron Modernity: Narendra Modi's Experiments with Gujarat.*

187. R. Jagannathan, "NJAC: Singhvi, Jaitley Hold Mirror to Supreme Court, and the Picture Isn't Pretty," FirstPost, October 19, 2015, https://www.firstpost.com/politics/njac-singhvi -jaitley-hold-mirror-to-supreme-court-and-the-picture-isnt-pretty-2473508.html.

188. These words were used against the order of a Supreme Court bench directing the government to establish a National Disaster Mitigation Fund within three months to help the rural population that was badly affected by a severe drought. The court was responding to a public interest writ petition filed by Swaraj Abhiyan because the parliament—whose sovereignty Jaitley was defending—had not established the fund that was supposed to result from the Disaster Management Act that it had passed in 2005. H. Mander, "Asking the Centre to Fulfill Its Obligations under Laws It Passed Is Not Judicial Overreach," Scroll.in, June 10, 2016, https://scroll.in /article/809651/asking-the-centre-to-fulfill-its-obligations-under-laws-it-passed-is-not-judicial -overreach.

189. Jaffrelot, "Indian Democracy."

190. Akhil Bharatiya Adhivakta Parishad, homepage, accessed December 1, 2020, http:// www.adhivaktaparishad.org/index.php.

191. Dev, "In Sua Causa." The dilution of the Prevention of Atrocities Act gave rise to such an uproar that the Modi government moved a review petition that resulted in a partial recall of its previous order: there was no longer any need for a preliminary inquiry before registering an FIR; nor were prior sanctions any longer necessary before arrests of public servants or private persons could be made. But such petitions were not moved when the Supreme Court upheld a 2017 order of the Allahabad High Court ordering the universities to implement reservations at the department level, a change that was bound to reduce the number of posts available.

192. R. Balaji, "Top Court Berth Eludes Judge," *The Telegraph*, September 1, 2013, https:// www.telegraphindia.com/india/top-court-berth-eludes-judge/cid/260067.

193. V. Simja, "The Zero Case Deadly Implications of the Birla-Sahara Judgment," *Economic and Political Weekly* 52, no. 10 (March 11, 2017), https://www.epw.in/journal/2017/10/insight /zero-case.html.

194. Simja, "Zero Case Deadly Implications." To assign the Birla-Sahara papers case to the bench headed by Justice Mishra contravened the code of conduct for judges in India where it is written: "A judge shall not hear and decide a matter in which a member of his family, a close relation or a friend is concerned."

195. For a comprehensive study of the role of Arun Mishra in the Supreme Court, see V. Venkatesan, "How Justice Arun Mishra Rose to Become the Most Influential Judge in the Supreme Court," The Wire, September 1, 2020, https://thewire.in/law/justice-arun-mishra -judgments-analysis.

196. V. Venkatesan, "As Judge, Arun Mishra Was Almost Predictable When the State Was before Him," The Wire, September 3, 2020, https://thewire.in/law/justice-arun-mishra -predictable-legacy.

197. "PM Modi a Versatile Genius Who Thinks Globally and Acts Locally: Justice Arun Mishra," *Economic Times*, February 22, 2020, https://economictimes.indiatimes.com/news /politics-and-nation/pm-modi-a-versatile-genius-who-thinks-globally-and-acts-locally-justice -arun-mishra/articleshow/74255056.cms. Previously, only High Court judges had eulogized Narendra Modi with such zeal. For instance, the Patna High Court chief justice had described Modi as a "model and a hero" (R. Jain, "PM Modi Is a Model & a Hero, Says Patna High Court

Chief Justice M. R. Shah," ThePrint, August 18, 2018, https://theprint.in/india/governance/pm
-modi-is-a-model-a-hero-says-patna-high-court-chief-justice-m-r-shah/100960/.)

198. On the ideological affinities between Justice Mishra and the Hindu nationalists, in addition to the two articles by V. Venkatesan mentioned above, see the two other parts of his series: "Justice Arun Mishra's Disregard for Precedent Led to Charge of Judicial Indiscipline," The
Wire, September 4, 2020, https://thewire.in/law/arun-mishra-judicial-indiscipline-supreme
-court; and "Justice Arun Mishra's Social Conservatism a Key Factor in His Neglect of Judicial
Precedents," The Wire, September 2, 2020, https://thewire.in/law/justice-arun-mishra-judicial
-precedent.

199. Akhil Bharatiya Adhivakta Parishad, "Executive Body," accessed December 1, 2020,
http://www.adhivaktaparishad.org/executivebody.php.

200. S. Philip, "After Constitution, Army, RSS Keeps Indians Safe: Former Supreme Court
Judge," Indian Express, January 4, 2018, https://indianexpress.com/article/india/after
-constitution-army-rss-keeps-indians-safe-supreme-court-ex-judge-5010704/.

201. On two occasions, in 2015 and 2019, the Supreme Court also regretted that no attempt
had been made, despite judicial exhortations, to frame a uniform civil code in India, an article
of faith of the BJP for decades. "No Attempts Made to Frame Uniform Civil Code in India, Rues
SC," The Quint, September 14, 2019, https://www.thequint.com/news/law/supreme-court-on
-uniform-civil-code.

202. Regarding secularism, Supreme Court Justice A. R. Dave declared, in the course of a
conference organized by the Gujarat Law Society in August 2014: "Had I been the dictator of
India, I would have introduced Gita and Mahabharata in Class I. That is the way you learn how
to live life. I am sorry if somebody says I am secular or I am not secular. . . . Our old tradition
such as 'guru-shishya parampara' is lost, if it had been there, we would not have had all these
problems (violence and terrorism) in our country." "If I Were a Dictator, I Would Introduce Gita
in Class I: Supreme Court Judge," Times of India, August 2, 2014, https://timesofindia.indiatimes
.com/india/If-I-were-a-dictator-I-would-introduce-Gita-in-Class-I-Supreme-Court-judge
/articleshow/39481111.cms?utm_source=contentofinterest&utm_medium=text&utm
_campaign=cppst.

203. Arshu John, "Rajan Gogoi's Gift to the Government," The Caravan, February 1, 2020,
https://caravanmagazine.in/reportage/ranjan-gogoi-gifts-government.

204. M. Jain, "'Out of 4600 Declared Foreigners Only 4 Have Been Deported? Is It Not Your
Constitutional Duty?' CJI Pulls Up Assam Chief Secy," Live Law.in, April 9, 2019, https://www
.livelaw.in/top-stories/assam-detention-centre-cji-sc-foreigners—144172?infinitescroll=1.

205. John, "Rajan Gogoi's Gift."

206. John.

207. John. On the role of Chief Justice Gogoi in the "NRC process" in Assam, see Shekhar
Gupta, "Why the Root of Delhi's Hindu-Muslim Riots Is a Malevolent Creeper Planted by
Supreme Court," ThePrint, March 1, 2020, https://theprint.in/national-interest/why-the-root
-of-delhis-hindu-muslim-riots-is-a-malevolent-creeper-planted-by-supreme-court/373115/.

208. Simja, "Zero Case Deadly Implications," 39. Dipak Misra does not have a brother named
Aditya. According to one of Misra's relatives, Pul had mistaken his brother for his brother-in-law
Aditya Mahapatra. Dev, "Darkest Hour," 40.

209. The case was not fully investigated, despite Pul's widow's efforts. Dev, "Darkest Hour," 46–47.

210. In this case, which pertained again to attempts by litigants to blackmail judges with money, the manner in which Chief Justice Misra constituted the bench was also questioned. Dev, 47–50. See also A. Dev, "Corruption Allegations and Courtroom Drama: What Happened in the Chief Justice's Court Yesterday," *The Caravan*, November 11, 2017, https://caravanmagazine .in/vantage/corruption-allegations-courtroom-drama-the-chief-justices-court.

211. Dev, "Darkest Hour," 30.

212. On the way Chief Justice Gogoi ignored the rule "no one should be a judge in his own cause," see M. Chhibber, "Recusal Has Become a Selective Call of Morality for Supreme Court Judges," ThePrint, October 14, 2019, https://theprint.in/opinion/recusal-supreme-court -judges-gautam-navlakha-kashmir-cji-gogoi/303036/.

213. Dev, "In Sua Causa."

214. Dev.

215. Dev.

216. Chief Justice Kehar applied it when he was approached by Pul's widow, Chief Justice Misra applied it in the Prasad Education Trust case, and Chief Justice Gogoi applied it in the sexual harassment case mentioned above.

217. Madan B. Lokur, "Judicial Independence: Three Developments that Tell Us Fair Is Foul and Foul Is Fair," The Wire, March 23, 2020, https://thewire.in/law/judicial-independence -three-developments-that-tell-us-fair-is-foul-and-foul-is-fair.

218. S. Mishra, "Govt Is Blackmailing CJI Misra, Says Prashant Bhushan," *The Week*, January 28, 2018, https://www.theweek.in/theweek/cover/government-is-blackmailing-dipak -misra.html.

219. The idea that the Modi government could "manage" the Supreme Court emerged from statements of the BJP chief minister of Karnataka himself after he had engineered defections of Congress MLAs and had to have them elected again—something the Supreme Court has objected to but did not prevent. "'Modi and Shah Can Manage Supreme Court Judges': Yeddyurappa Allegedly Claims in Tapes Released by Kumaraswamy," NewsCentral24x7, February 8, 2019, https://newscentral24x7.com/karnataka-yeddyurappa-audio-clip-modi-shah-can -manage-supreme-court-judges-kumaraswamy-operation-kamala/.

220. "In Unprecedented Move, Modi Government Sends Former CJI Ranjan Gogoi to Rajya Sabha," The Wire, March 16, 2020, https://thewire.in/law/cji-ranjan-gogoi-rajya-sabha -nomination.

221. "BJP for 'Cooling Period' before Judges Head Tribunals," *Outlook*, September 30, 2012, https://www.outlookindia.com/newswire/story/bjp-for-cooling-period-before-judges-head -tribunals/776850.

222. Ajaz Ashraf, "How to Ensure Independence of Judiciary: Pay Full Salary to Judges till Death," Scroll.in, April 11, 2015, https://scroll.in/article/719495/how-to-ensure-independence -of-judiciary-pay-full-salary-to-judges-till-death.

223. There were many others. For instance, in 2018, after retiring from the Supreme Court, A. K. Goel—who was already close to the Sangh Parivar anyway—was appointed head of the National Green Tribunal.

224. Lokur, "Judicial Independence."

225. "A Bar Silenced under Threat of Contempt Will Undermine Court's Independence: Lawyers Express Dismay over SC Verdict in Prashant Bhushan Case," Bar and Bench, August 27, 2020, https://www.barandbench.com/news/lawyers-express-dismay-over-sc-verdict-in-prashant-bhushan-case.

226. P. B. Mehta, "SC Was Never Perfect, but the Signs Are That It Is Slipping into Judicial Barbarism," *Indian Express*, November 18, 2020, https://indianexpress.com/article/opinion/columns/supreme-court-arnab-goswami-bail-article-32-pratap-bhanu-mehta-7055067/.

227. According to Atul Dev, this expression refers to the way the "judiciary helped the rise of Nazi Germany by granting much mercy to the right and no quarter to the left, heedless of the principle of equality before the law." A. Dev, "Now as Farce," *The Caravan*, November 30, 2020, https://caravanmagazine.in/media/supreme-court-media-end-silence-courts.

228. L. Henderson, "Authoritarianism and the Rule of Law," UNLV School of Law, Scholarly Works, 1991, paper no. 867, p. 380, accessed October 4, 2020, http://scholars.law.unlv.edu/facpub/867.

229. Ninan, "India's Media Landscape Changed."

230. Elaborating on the notion of "one-way communication," Suhas Palshikar argues that Modi "is a leader who does not like to enter into dialogue, doesn't want an exchange with the media. He won't brook hard questioning." S. Palshikar, "Modi Has Brought into Practice a Style of One-Way Communication: Giving Out Messages," *Indian Express*, May 21, 2019, https://indianexpress.com/article/opinion/columns/lok-sabha-elections-narendra-modia-amit-shah-political-interview-media-friendly-press-conference-5739260/.

231. "Javadekar Asks Media to Maintain 'Lakshman Rekha,'" *The Hindu*, November 16, 2014, https://www.thehindu.com/news/national/national-press-day-javadekar-asks-media-to-maintain-lakshman-rekha/article6605323.ece.

232. Aliya Ram, "India's Jaitley Calls for Limits on Free Speech," *Financial Times*, February 26, 2017, https://www.ft.com/content/e2a44a08-fc05-11e6-96f8-3700c5664d30.

233. For instance, in 2016, the editor of The Wire, Siddharth Vadarajan, was prevented from entering the campus of Allahabad University by ABVP members who called him "antinational." "Threats to Journalist an Attack on Freedom of Expression: Editors Guild," *Indian Express*, January 24, 2016, https://indianexpress.com/article/cities/delhi/threats-to-journalist-an-attack-on-freedom-of-expression-editors-guild/.

234. D. Ghoshal, "Modi Government Freezes Ads Placed in Three Indian Newspaper Groups," Reuters, June 28, 2019, https://www.reuters.com/article/us-india-media/modi-government-freezes-ads-placed-in-three-indian-newspaper-groups-idUSKCN1TT1RG.

235. Adam Withnall, "How Modi Government Uses Ad Spending to 'Reward or Punish' Indian Media," *The Independent*, July 20, 2019, https://www.independent.co.uk/news/world/asia/india-modi-government-media-ad-spending-newspapers-press-freedom-a8990451.html.

236. "Fali S Nariman too Agrees with Janta Ka Reporter, Links Sambit Patra Episode to CBI Raids," Janta Ka Reporter, June 9, 2017, http://www.jantakareporter.com/india/fali-s-nariman-janta-ka-reporter/129585/.

237. "Tax Raid on Raghav Bahl: Editors Guild Says Motivated Searches Will Undermine Media Freedom," ThePrint, October 11, 2018, https://theprint.in/india/governance/tax-raid

-on-raghav-bahl-editors-guild-says-motivated-searches-will-undermine-media-freedom/132899/.

238. K. Kaushik, "Centre Bans Two Malayalam TV Channels for Delhi Riots Coverage," *Indian Express*, March 7, 2020, https://indianexpress.com/article/india/delhi-violence-two-malayalam-news-channels-banned-ministry-of-information-and-broadcasting-6303175/.

239. "Ban Recalls Emergency: Withdraw It: Editors Guild on NDTV India," *Indian Express*, November 5, 2016, https://indianexpress.com/article/india/india-news-india/ban-on-ndtv-india-reminiscent-of-emergency-editors-guild-3737687/.

240. "Exclusive: Punya Prasun Bajpai Reveals the Story behind His Exit from ABP News," *The Wire*, August 6, 2018, https://thewire.in/media/punya-prasun-bajpai-abp-news-narendra-modi.

241. "The Foundation for Media Professionals Issues a Statement on ABP News," Newslaundry, August 7, 2018, https://www.newslaundry.com/2018/08/07/the-foundation-for-media-professionals-issues-a-statement-on-abp-news.

242. According to a detailed piece of investigation journalism published at The Wire, Ghosh's exit took place after Narendra Modi himself met the owner of the newspaper. A. Srivas, "Hindustan Times Editor's Exit Preceded by Meeting Between Modi, Newspaper Owner," The Wire, September 25, 2017, https://thewire.in/media/hindustan-times-bobby-ghosh-narendra-modi-shobhana-bhartia.

243. U. R. Yadav, "FIR against Aakar Patel over His Twitter Post," *Deccan Herald*, June 5, 2020, https://www.deccanherald.com/city/bengaluru-crime/fir-against-aakar-patel-over-his-twitter-post-845838.html.

244. "Sedition Case: SC Grants Interim Relief from Arrest to Journalist Vinod Dua, Refuses to Stay Probe," *Indian Express*, June 14, 2020, https://indianexpress.com/article/india/vinod-dua-sedition-case-6458027/.

245. "UP Police Registers FIR against Journalist Supriya Sharma for Report on PM's Adopted Village," The Wire, June 18, 2020, https://thewire.in/media/up-police-fir-supriya-sharma-journalist-domari.

246. "India: Media's Crackdown during COVID-19 Lockdown," Rights and Risks Analysis Group, New Delhi, June 15, 2020, p. 4, accessed September 16, 2020, http://www.rightsrisks.org/wp-content/uploads/2020/06/MediaCrackdown.pdf.

247. Some of their stories are found in A. Kumar and M. Singh, "Missing from Headlines: How the Adityanath Regime Is Going After Local Journalists," Newslaundry, July 7, 2020, https://www.newslaundry.com/2020/07/07/missing-from-headlines-how-the-adityanath-regime-is-going-after-local-journalists.

248. "Journalist Prashant Kanojia Arrested by UP Police for Allegedly Sharing Morphed Post on Ram Temple," Scroll.in, August 18, 2020, https://scroll.in/latest/970703/journalist-prashant-kanojia-arrested-by-up-police-in-connection-with-some-tweets-reports.

249. A.A. Jafri, "UP: FIR against Scribe for Allegedly 'Maligning' Government," NewsClick, August 8, 2020, https://www.newsclick.in/UP-FIR-scribe-allegedly-maligning-government.

250. I. Ara, "DM, Public Provide Food after Hungry Kids Seen Eating 'Grass' in Modi's Constituency," The Wire, March 26, 2020, https://thewire.in/rights/varanasi-hunger-national-lockdown.

251. S. Philip and M. Sahu, "SC Plea Today, Journalist Siddique Kappan's Family Asks: Aren't We Citizens?," *Indian Express*, November 16, 2020, https://indianexpress.com/article/india /siddique-kappan-journalist-jail-up-supreme-court-7052829/.

252. "Criminal Charges against News Editor in India Must Be Dismissed," Pen America, April 13, 2020, https://pen.org/press-release/criminal-charges-against-news-editor-in-india -must-be-dismissed/.

253. See "Chhattisgarh: Journalist Charged with Sedition for Sharing Cartoon on SC Verdict in Loya Case," Scroll.in, May 1, 2018, https://scroll.in/latest/877453/chhattisgarh-journalist -charged-with-sedition-for-sharing-cartoon-on-sc-verdict-in-loya-case; and "After Spending 17 Months in Jail, SC Grants Bail to Chhattisgarh Journalist Santosh Yadav," *Indian Express*, February 27, 2017, https://indianexpress.com/article/india/after-spending-17-months-in-jail -chhattisgarh-journalist-santosh-yadav-granted-bail-4546569/.

254. See "Emergency? Here Are 9 Cases Where BJP Leaders Didn't Jump to Arrested Journalists' Defence," The Wire, November 4, 2020, https://thewire.in/media/journalist-arrest -arnab-goswami-bjp-defence.

255. "Exclusive: Indian Journalism Is Facing an Unprecedented Crisis: Josy Joseph," Sabrang, September 18, 2018, https://sabrangindia.in/interview/exclusive-indian-journalism-facing -unprecedented-crisis-josy-joseph.

256. K. Kohli, "'We Cannot Get a Call from Amit Shah': Media Group Caught in Self-Censorship Vice," The Wire, March 28, 2018, https://thewire.in/media/vice-india-amit-shah -times-bridge-group.

257. P. B. Mehta, "State and Capital," *Indian Express*, July 28, 2018, https://indianexpress.com /article/opinion/columns/state-and-capital-5280117/.

258. A. Tiwari, "How Republic TV and Zee Media 'Illegally' Reached Millions of Viewers," Newslaundry, December 11, 2020, https://www.newslaundry.com/2020/12/11/how-republic-tv -and-zee-group-illegally-reached-millions-of-viewers.

259. Goswami's complacency was on display for everyone to see as early as 2016 when Modi gave him his first one-on-one interview on a private channel. N. Chaturvedi, "Full Text of Narendra Modi's Interview with Arnab Goswami," Huffington Post, June 27, 2016, https://www .huffingtonpost.in/2016/06/28/narendra-modi-interview_n_10697454.html.

260. "Complaints Lodged against Republic TV Anchor Arnab Goswami in Chhattisgarh," Newsd, April 22, 2020, https://newsd.in/complaints-lodged-against-republic-tv-arnab -goswami-in-chhattisgarh-sonia-gandhi/; F. Tandel, "Mumbai Police Files FIR against Arnab Goswami, Accuses Him of Spreading Hatred," *Hindustan Times*, May 4, 2020, https://www .hindustantimes.com/india-news/mumbai-police-file-fir-against-arnab-goswami-accuses -him-of-spreading-hatred/story-8tfFHRTG7xImSCrgpS1PWI.html; and P. Goyal, "'High Time to Stop Such Hate-Spreaders': Complaint Filed against Republic, Arnab Goswami under Cable Act," Newslaundry, June 6, 2020, https://www.newslaundry.com/2020/06/06 /high-time-to-stop-such-hate-spreaders-complaint-filed-against-republic-arnab-goswami -under-cable-act.

261. Christophe Jaffrelot and Vihang Jumle, "One-Man Show," *The Caravan*, December 15, 2020, https://caravanmagazine.in/media/republic-debates-study-shows-channel-promotoes -modi-ndtv.

262. Tavleen Singh, "Media Has Been Managed So Well by Modi Government that for Ministers to Dare Speak of 'Press Freedom' Is Offensive," *Indian Express*, November 8, 2020, https://indianexpress.com/article/opinion/columns/arnab-goswami-arrest-narendra-modi-tavleen-singh-7001283/.

263. "SC Bar Association Head Says Instant Listing of Arnab Goswami's Bail Plea 'Deeply Disturbing,'" ThePrint, November 10, 2020, https://theprint.in/judiciary/sc-bar-association-head-says-instant-listing-of-arnab-goswamis-bail-plea-deeply-disturbing/541655/.

264. "Arnab Goswami Programme Leads to £20,000 Fine for UK Licensee," *Times of India*, December 23, 2020, http://timesofindia.indiatimes.com/articleshow/79904365.cms?utm_source=contentofinterest&utm_medium=text&utm_campaign=cppst.

265. S. Barooah-Pisharoty, "Well-Known Poet-Scientist Gauhar Raza on Being Labelled an 'Anti-National,'" The Wire, March 11, 2016, https://thewire.in/politics/well-known-poet-scientist-gauhar-raza-on-being-labelled-an-anti-national.

266. "Full Text: Arnab Goswami Violates Norms of Professionalism and Fairness, Say Activists in Open Letter," Scroll.in, February 26, 2015, https://scroll.in/article/709880/full-text-arnab-goswami-violates-norms-of-professionalism-and-fairness-say-activists-in-open-letter.

267. Sayed Shahnawaz Hussain (@ShahnawazBJP), "The case by Kerala Govt against senior journalist @sudhirchaudhary is an attack on Press Freedom & is aimed at silencing the Media. What is the Communist Party afraid of? The Truth??," Twitter, May 7, 2020, 8:13 a.m., https://twitter.com/shahnawazbjp/status/1258369387880484864.

268. Safoora, "Rajat Sharma Gives Communal Color to Bandra Gathering," *Siasat Daily*, April 18, 2020, https://www.siasat.com/rajat-sharma-gives-communal-color-bandra-gathering-1875027/.

269. "More Trouble for Arnab Goswami as Powerful Demand Grows to Ban 'Preachers of Hate, Including Republic TV, Zee News, India TV, Aaj Tak, ABP and Times Now' in UAE," Janata Ka Reporter, May 7, 2020, http://www.jantakareporter.com/entertainment/more-trouble-for-arnab-goswami-as-powerful-demand-grows-to-ban-preachers-of-hate-including-republic-tv-zee-news-india-tv-aaj-tak-abp-and-times-now/289827/.

270. Interestingly, when the Supreme Court suspended an openly Islamophobic series by Sudarshan News that accused Muslims of infiltrating the Indian bureaucracy, the Information and Broadcasting Ministry objected that such decisions jeopardized freedom of expression ("Sudarshan TV Case: Centre Tells SC Not to Lay Down 'Any Further Guidelines' for Rest of Mainstream Media," *Indian Express*, January 5, 2020, https://indianexpress.com/article/india/sudarshan-tv-supreme-court-media-guidelines-centre-affidavit-6599313/.) On Sudarshan News, see Meghnad S., "Bloodlust TV: Bigotry on Suresh Chavhanke's Sudarshan News, Sponsored by the Taxpayer," Newslaundry, October 28, 2019, https://www.newslaundry.com/2019/10/28/bloodlust-tv-bigotry-on-suresh-chavhankes-sudarshan-news-sponsored-by-the-taxpayer.

271. Ravish Kumar, "'Those Who Throw Ink Have Become Party Spokesmen, Those Who Use Ink Are Propagandists,'" The Wire, March 20, 2018, https://thewire.in/politics/ravish-kumar-speech-journalism-kuldip-nayyar-award.

272. "Operation 136: Part 1 Intro," Cobrapost, March 26, 2018, https://www.cobrapost.com/blog/Operation-136:-Part-1/1009. See also "Cobrapost Sting: Big Media Houses Say Yes to

Hindutva, Black Money, Paid News," The Wire, May 26, 2018, https://thewire.in/media/cobrapost-sting-big-media-houses-say-yes-to-hindutva-black-money-paid-news.

273. See "Operation-136 II, The Times Group- Part 3 of 3," YouTube video posted by Cobrapost, May 25, 2018, accessed September 17, 2020, https://www.youtube.com/watch?v=kr4GNJyNfkc&index=45&t=0s&list=PLtIitJsHQm66Z2Vk7Us-YE_Bhyo_eYG_.

274. "Large Media Houses Accused of Striking Deals for Paid News to Promote Hindutva Agenda," The Wire, March 27, 2018, https://thewire.in/media/large-media-houses-seen-striking-deals-for-paid-news-to-promote-hindutva-agenda.

275. Reporters sans frontiers, "Modi Tightens His Grip on the Media," 2020 World Press Freedom Index, accessed September 16, 2020, https://rsf.org/en/india.

276. Bloomberg, the American media house, has been unable to get a license. See V. Goel and J. Gettleman, "Under Modi, India's Press Is Not So Free Anymore," New York Times, April 2, 2020, https://www.nytimes.com/2020/04/02/world/asia/modi-india-press-media.html.

277. Freedom House, "India," Freedom in the World, accessed September 16, 2020, https://freedomhouse.org/country/india/freedom-world/2020.

278. S. Jash, "India Is Leading the World in Internet Shutdowns," Slate, April 17, 2019, https://slate.com/technology/2019/04/india-internet-shutdowns-digital-authoritarianism-democracies.html.

279. S. Faleiro, "How India Became the World's Leader in Internet Shutdowns," MIT Technology Review, August 19, 2020, https://www.technologyreview.com/2020/08/19/1006359/india-internet-shutdowns-blackouts-pandemic-kashmir/.

280. Software Freedom Law Center, "Internet Shutdowns," https://internetshutdowns.in, accessed December 28, 2020.

281. R. Bhatia, "'Exceptional' Cases of Internet Shutdown More Common since 2014," The Quint, September 2017, https://www.thequint.com/tech-and-auto/tech-news/difficulty-as-india-restricts-use-of-internet.

282. S. Nazmi, "Why India Shuts Down the Internet More than Any Other Democracy," BBC News, December 19, 2019, https://www.bbc.com/news/world-asia-india-50819905.

283. D. Dutt Roy, "Farmers' Protest Facebook, Instagram Pages Blocked, Restored after 3 Hours," NDTV, December 21, 2020, https://www.ndtv.com/india-news/protesting-farmers-allege-their-facebook-instagram-accounts-blocked-after-live-event-today-2341279.

284. Ipsita Chakravarty, "The BJP Is Afraid of Saffron Terror Probes because They Point to the RSS," Scroll.in, June 26, 2015, https://scroll.in/article/736886/the-main-reason-the-bjp-is-afraid-of-saffron-terror-probes-they-seem-to-point-to-the-rss.

285. Among the many critical assessments of the Supreme Court's decline, see K. Rajagopal, "Yes, the Supreme Court Has Been Floundering, Says Indira Jaising," The Hindu, March 3, 2018, https://www.thehindu.com/society/yes-the-supreme-court-has-been-floundering-indira-jaising/article22907531.ece.

286. S. Shantha, "I Am Waiting for the Right Moment to Strike. I Will Speak Up: Rohini Salian," The Wire, April 23, 2018, https://thewire.in/law/i-am-waiting-for-the-right-moment-to-strike-i-will-speak-up-rohini-salian.

287. S. Sharma, "Not Just Rohini Salian."

288. P. Donthi, "Undercover: Ajit Doval in Theory and Practice," The Caravan, September 1, 2017, https://caravanmagazine.in/reportage/ajit-doval-theory-practice.

289. Cited in Donthi, "Undercover."

290. Cited in Donthi.

291. For more details, see Bilal A. Baloch, "Crisis, Credibility and Corruption: How Ideas and Institutions Shape Government Behaviour in India" (PhD diss., Oxford University, 2017), 151.

292. Cited in Donthi, "Undercover."

293. If the institution of the governors was already politicized, the Ministry of External Affairs is now experiencing the same process to a lesser extent. S. Vadarajan, "MEA's Latest: BJP the 'Only Alternative,' Only Hindus Are 'Spiritual,'" The Wire, September 30, 2017, https://thewire.in/diplomacy/mea-bjp-propaganda-hindutva-deendayal-upadhyaya-integral-humanism.

294. The weakening of other institutions—including the Indian Parliament, which will be dealt with in chapter 10—could be mentioned here. The comptroller and auditor general whose "Audit Reports on Union Government (Finance Accounts)" are no longer finalized ahead of budget sessions, and whose activity has significantly declined, is a case in point. H. Upadhyaya, "Delayed Audit Reports, Lower Output Marked Last Two Years of CAG's Functioning," The Wire, July 24, 2020, https://thewire.in/political-economy/cag-delayed-audit-reports-lower-output-defence-services.

295. This "parliament" was organized by civil society organizations in reaction to the trend described in this chapter.

296. "Justice A.P. Shah: Powerful Executive Has Sidelined All Institutions, This Is How Democracy Dies," The Wire, August 18, 2020, https://thewire.in/government/justice-a-p-shah-powerful-executive-has-sidelined-all-institutions-this-is-how-democracy-dies.

Chapter 9

1. Andreas Schedler, "The Logic of Electoral Authoritarianism," in *Electoral Authoritarianism. The Dynamics of Unfree Competition*, ed. A. Schedler (Boulder, CO: Lynne Rienner, 2006), 8.

2. Schedler, "Logic of Electoral Authoritarianism," 9.

3. "Mood of the Nation: NDA Loses Sheen, but Narendra Modi Shines Bright," *India Today*, August 20, 2018, https://www.indiatoday.in/india/story/mood-of-the-nation-nda-loses-sheen-but-narendra-modi-shines-bright-1319332-2018-08-20.

4. Modi was projected by the BJP as not only the strongman India needed but also as the only leader who could guarantee political stability, compared to the coalitions that the opposition would have to resort to if the BJP did not win a clear-cut majority. N. Hebbar, "'If It Is Not Modi, It Will Be Instability, Corruption, Nepotism', Says Ram Madhav," *The Hindu*, March 11, 2019, https://www.thehindu.com/elections/lok-sabha-2019/if-it-is-not-modi-it-will-be-instability-corruption-nepotism-says-ram-madhav/article26502451.ece.

5. The following pages draw from C. Jaffrelot and Gilles Verniers, "The BJP's 2019 Election Campaign: Not Business as Usual," *Contemporary South Asia* 28, no. 2 (May 18, 2020): 155–77, https://doi.org/10.1080/09584935.2020.1765985.

6. "Prime Minister Narendra Modi Interview to Indian Express: 'Khan Market Gang Hasn't Created My Image, 45 Years of Tapasya Has . . . You Cannot Dismantle It,'" *Indian Express*,

May 13, 2019, https://indianexpress.com/elections/pm-narendra-modi-interview-to-indian
-express-live-lok-sabha-elections-2019-bjp-5723186/.

7. O. Rashid, "Modi Hits Back on 'Fake OBC' Jibes, Says He Is 'Most Backward,'" *The Hindu*,
April 27, 2019, https://www.thehindu.com/elections/lok-sabha-2019/modi-hits-back-on-fake
-obc-jibes-says-he-is-most-backward/article26964347.ece.

8. "Congress People Hate Me So Much that They Dream of Killing Me: PM Modi," *Economic
Times*, May 1, 2019, https://economictimes.indiatimes.com/articleshow/69132192.cms?from
=mdr&utm_source=contentofinterest&utm_medium=text&utm_campaign=cppst.

9. "Your Father's Life Ended as Bhrashtachari No 1: PM Modi to Rahul Gandhi," *India Today*,
May 5, 2019, https://www.indiatoday.in/elections/lok-sabha-2019/story/father-bhrashtachari
-pm-modi-rahul-gandhi-rajiv-1517385-2019-05-05.

10. See the first appendix of Jaffrelot and Verniers, "BJP's 2019 Election Campaign."

11. See the second appendix of Jaffrelot and Verniers, "BJP's 2019 Election Campaign."

12. W. H. Morris-Jones, "India's Political Idioms," in *Politics and Society in India*, ed. C. H.
Philips (London:
George Allen and Unwin, 1963), 140; and Lloyd I. Rudolph and Susanne Hoeber Rudolph,
The Modernity of Tradition: Political Development in India (Chicago: University of Chicago Press,
1967), 159.

13. For more details, including photographs, see Jaffrelot and Verniers, "BJP's 2019 Election
Campaign."

14. "IAF Missile Brought Down Mi-17 Helicopter in Budgam, Says Probe," *Deccan Chronicle*,
August 24, 2019, https://www.deccanchronicle.com/nation/current-affairs/240819/iaf-missile
-brought-down-mi-17-helicopter-in-budgam-says-probe.html.

15. "PM Narendra Modi: Guided by Modi Hate, Opposition Hating India," *Indian Express*,
March 2, 2019, https://indianexpress.com/elections/pm-narendra-modi-guided-by-modi-hate
-opposition-hating-india-5607565/.

16. A. S. T. Das, "Congress Demoralizing Jawans by Asking for Air Strike Proof," *Indian
Express*, March 2, 2019, https://www.newindianexpress.com/nation/2019/mar/03/congress
-demoralizing-jawans-by-asking-for-air-strike-proof-pm-modi-at-patna-rally-1946140.html.

17. A. Deshpande, "I-T Raids Have Exposed the Real Chor, Narendra Modi Tells in Maharashtra's Latur," *The Hindu*, April 9, 2019, https://www.thehindu.com/elections/lok-sabha-2019
/i-t-raids-have-exposed-the-real-chor-narendra-modi-tells-in-maharashtras-latur
/article26779958.ece.

18. "Watch: Delhi BJP chief Manoj Tiwari Campaigns for Votes Dressed in Army Fatigues,"
Scroll.in, March 3, 2019, https://scroll.in/video/915265/watch-delhi-bjp-chief-manoj-tiwari
-campaigns-for-votes-dressed-in-army-fatigues.

19. "Air Strike Will Help BJP Win More than 22 Lok Sabha Seats in Karnataka: B S Yeddyurappa," *New Indian Express*, February 27, 2019, https://www.newindianexpress.com/states
/karnataka/2019/feb/27/airstrike-will-help-bjp-win-more-than-22-seats-in-state-b-s
-yeddyurappa-1944515.html.

20. "Narendra Modi Adds Chowkidar to His Twitter Handle Name," *The Hindu*, March 17,
2019, https://www.thehindu.com/elections/lok-sabha-2019/narendra-modi-adds-chowkidar
-to-his-twitter-handle-name/article26561703.ece.

21. On Modi's 2014 campaign, see C. Jaffrelot, "The Modi-Centric BJP 2014 Election Campaign: New Techniques and Old Tactics," *Contemporary South Asia* 23, no. 2 (June 2015): 151–66.

22. R. Mishra, "Congress Contesting LS Polls to Give Free Hand to Terrorists, Says PM Modi," *Hindustan Times*, April 6, 2019, https://www.hindustantimes.com/lok-sabha-elections /congress-contesting-ls-polls-to-give-free-hand-to-terrorists-says-pm-modi/story -plKzfy6Xl4mtAVAZHTjBxK.html.

23. M. Ghatwai, "Madhya Pradesh: You Vote for Lotus, You Are Pressing Trigger to Kill Terrorists, Says PM Modi," *Indian Express*, May 18, 2019, https://indianexpress.com/elections /madhya-pradesh-you-vote-for-lotus-you-are-pressing-trigger-to-kill-terrorists-says-pm-modi -5734452/.

24. "This 'Chowkidar' Will Complete What Remains to Be Done: Modi," *The Hindu*, April 2, 2019, http://www.thehindu.com/elections/lok-sabha-2019/a-contaminated-alliance-narendra -modi/article26714346.ece.

25. I. Chakravarti, "The Daily Fix: In the BJP's 2019 Manifesto, Development Plays Second Fiddle to Politics of Fear; Focusing on National Security, It Conjures Up a Country under Siege," Scroll.in, April 9, 2019, https://scroll.in/article/919383/the-daily-fix-in-the-bjps-2019 -manifesto-development-plays-second-fiddle-to-politics-of-fear.

26. A. Shankar, "BJP Member Gets EC Notice over Ad Featuring Army," March 28, 2019, https://indianexpress.com/elections/bjp-member-gets-ec-notice-over-ad-featuring-army -5646159/.

27. In the beginning of the election campaign, as India decided to stop the flow of water of three rivers into Pakistan, union water resources minister Nitin Gadkari directed his department to prepare a report on how to block "other water resources" from flowing into the neighboring country. "We do not want even a single drop of water to reach Pakistan," he said. "'Don't Want Single Drop to Reach Pakistan': Nitin Gadkari Seeks Report on Stopping Flow of 'Other Water Resources' into Country," FirstPost, February 22, 2019, https://www.firstpost.com/india/dont -want-single-drop-to-reach-pakistan-nitin-gadkari-seeks-report-on-stopping-flow-of-other -water-resources-into-country-6134561.html.

28. BJP, *Sankalpit Bharat, Sashakt Bharat: Sankalp Patra; Lok Sabha 2019*, April 8, 2019, accessed December 3, 2020, https://assets.documentcloud.org/documents/5798075/Bjp -Election-2019-Manifesto-English.pdf. Interestingly, this version of the BJP manifesto consulted on February 3, 2020, still omitted Parsis and Christians, in spite of the fact that party leaders had said that this discrepancy with the text of the Citizenship (Amendment) Bill was a mistake. L. Mathew, "Citizenship Bill: BJP Manifesto Drops Parsis and Christians, then Rewritten," *Indian Express*, April 10, 2019, https://indianexpress.com/elections/citizenship-bjp-manifesto-drops -parsis-and-christians-rewritten-elections-5667717/.

29. S. Sahay Singh, "Amit Shah Promises a National Register of Citizens for West Bengal," *The Hindu*, March 29, 2019, https://www.thehindu.com/elections/lok-sabha-2019/amit-shah -promises-a-national-register-of-citizens-for-west-bengal/article26680349.ece.

30. During another meeting in West Bengal, Amit Shah declared, "Infiltrators are like termites in the soil of Bengal. . . . A Bharatiya Janata Party government will pick up infiltrators one by one and throw them into the Bay of Bengal." D. Ghoshal, "Amit Shah Vows to Throw Illegal

Immigrants into Bay of Bengal," Reuters, April 12, 2019, https://www.reuters.com/article/india
-election-speech/amit-shah-vows-to-throw-illegal-immigrants-into-bay-of-bengal
-idUSKCN1RO1YD.

31. During the 2019 election campaign, Narendra Modi often called the opposition and its
"Mahagatbandan alliance" (Grand alliance) "Mahamilavati" in order to disqualify it.

32. Cited in L. Verma and K. Upadhyay, "Modi in West UP: Remember Atrocities against
Daughters," *Indian Express*, April 6, 2019, https://indianexpress.com/elections/modi-in-west
-up-remember-atrocities-against-daughters-lok-sabha-elections-2019-5661360/.

33. Thakur had been arrested for her participation in Abhinav Bharat (Young India), a Hindu
nationalist movement suspected of having perpetrated four anti-Muslim attacks that claimed
dozens of lives in 2008. C. Jaffrelot, "Abhinav Bharat, the Malegaon Blast and Hindu Nationalism: Resisting and Emulating Islamist Terrorism," *Economic and Political Weekly* 45, no. 36 (September 4–10, 2010): 51–58.

34. "Congress Works to Build Narrative, They Pick Something, Build False Script for Propaganda: PM on Sadhvi Pragya," Times Now, April 19, 2019, https://www.timesnownews.com
/elections/article/congress-works-to-build-narrative-they-pick-something-build-false-script
-for-propaganda-pm-on-sadhvi-pragya/403383.

35. "Modi's Appeal in the Name of Voters' Religion Makes Wardha Speech a Corrupt Practice," The Wire, April 2, 2019, https://thewire.in/law/modi-appeal-religion-wardha-speech
-corrupt-practice.

36. V. Deshpande, "Amit Shah on Rahul's Wayanad Show: Is It in India or Pakistan?," MSN,
April 10, 2019, https://www.msn.com/en-in/news/maharashtra/amit-shah-on-rahuls-wayanad
-show-is-it-in-india-or-pakistan/ar-BBVMlVg.

37. "Rahul Gandhi Was Born to a Muslim and Christian, How Did He Become a Brahmin?'
Asks Union Minister," Scroll.in, March 12, 2019, https://scroll.in/latest/916237/rahul-gandhi
-born-to-a-muslim-and-a-christian-claims-union-minister-anantkumar-hegde.

38. "Congress Suffering from 'Muslim League Virus', Says Yogi Adityanath," *The Hindu*,
April 5, 2019, https://www.thehindu.com/elections/lok-sabha-2019/congress-suffering-from
-muslim-league-virus-says-yogi-adityanath/article26746162.ece; and "'They Gave Terrorists
Biryani, We Fed Them Bombs': Yogi Adityanath Draws Parallel between Cong, BJP," News18,
March 24, 2019, https://www.news18.com/news/politics/they-gave-terrorists-biryani-we-fed
-them-bombs-yogi-adityanath-draws-parallel-between-congress-and-bjp-2076305.html.

39. A. Srivas and J. Sen, "Statistical Commission Experts Resign in Protest over Jobs Data,
Govt Attitude," The Wire, January 30, 2019, https://thewire.in/government/two-members-of
-indias-national-statistical-commission-quit-over-bodys-ineffectiveness.

40. Centre for Monitoring Indian Economy, *Unemployment in India: A Statistical Profile*,
September–December 2019, 13, accessed October 1, 2020, https://unemploymentinindia.cmie
.com/kommon/bin/sr.php?kall=wstatmore.

41. S. Varma, "Unemployment at Nearly 10%, among Youth It's 28%," NewsClick, September 19, 2019, https://www.newsclick.in/unemployment-nearly-10-among-youth-its-28.

42. For a detailed assessment, see C. Jaffrelot, "From Slowdown to Lockdown: India's Economy and the COVID-19 Shock," Institut Montaigne, Paris, June 11, 2020, https://www
.institutmontaigne.org/ressources/pdfs/blog/slowdown-lockdown-policy-brief.pdf.

43. V. Attri and A. Jain, "Post-Poll Survey: When Schemes Translate into Votes," *The Hindu*, May 27, 2019, https://www.thehindu.com/elections/lok-sabha-2019/when-schemes-translate -into-votes/article27256139.ece.

44. Y. Aiyar, "Leveraging Welfare Politics," *Journal of Democracy* 30, no. 4 (October 2019): 84.

45. R. Deshpande, L. Tillin, and K. K. Kailash, "The BJP's Welfare Schemes: Did They Make a Difference in the 2019 Elections?," *Studies in Indian Politics* 7, no. 2 (2019): 224.

46. N. Sircar, "The Politics of Vishwas: Political Mobilization in the 2019 National Election," *Contemporary South Asia* 28, no. 2 (2020), https://doi.org/10.1080/09584935.2020.1765988.

47. A. S. Mishra, "How People Gave a Thumbs Up to Modi's Politics of Performance," *Mint*, May 24, 2019, https://www.livemint.com/elections/lok-sabha-elections/how-people-gave-a -thumbs-up-to-modi-s-politics-of-performance-1558638883492.html.

48. H. Damodaran, "LPG, Toilet, House: BJP Built Solid Rural Assets but Income Didn't Rise," *Indian Express*, December 12, 2018, https://indianexpress.com/article/explained/lpg -toilet-house-bjp-built-solid-rural-assets-but-income-didnt-rise-5489311/.

49. "India Spent Nearly 4000 Crore on Swachh Bharat Info, Education in 5 Years," *India Today*, September 16, 2019, https://www.indiatoday.in/education-today/news/story/india -spent-nearly-4kcr-on-swachh-bharat-info-education-in-five-years-1599732-2019-09-16. This trend was not new: it was noticed as early as 2016. M. Balachandran, "The Modi Government Spent $52 Million on Just Publicising Its Flagship Schemes Last Year," Quartz India, May 9, 2016, https://qz.com/india/678585/the-modi-government-spent-52-million-on-just-publicising-its -flagship-schemes-last-year/.

50. A. Jha, "Rs 6,000 Is 6% of a Small Farmer's Annual Income, according to NSSO Data," *Hindustan Times*, February 6, 2019, https://www.hindustantimes.com/india-news/rs-6-000-is-6 -of-a-small-farmer-s-annual-income-according-to-nsso-data/story-rddMw0hk6cSbxj07 E1GyKK.html. See also A. Gulati, "No Budget for Farmers," *Indian Express*, February 2, 2019, https://indianexpress.com/article/opinion/columns/no-budget-2019-for-indian-farmers -protest-agrarian-crisis-5565432/.

51. For more detail on Modi and the variants of populism, see Partha Chatterjee, "Populism Plus," India Forum, June 3, 2019, https://www.theindiaforum.in/article/populism-plus.

52. For instance, during the campaign, Nirmala Sitharam, the then defense minister, de-clared: "I am going to say this in every place that I go to, where BJP candidates are contesting. The people have to vote for Modi, not the candidate. When you choose the 'lotus' (BJP's poll symbol), it is your direct vote to elect Modi. Cited in Adita Raja and Aishwarya Mohanty, "Vote for PM Modi, Not BJP Candidate: Nirmala Sitharaman to Voters." *Indian Express*, April 7, 2019, https://indianexpress.com/elections/dont-vote-for-candidate-vote-for-modi-sitharaman-lok -sabha-elections-2019-5662908/.

53. This proportion falls below 30 percent in the Hindi belt states that form the BJP's strong-holds: Uttar Pradesh, Madhya Pradesh, Rajasthan, Jharkhand, Chhattisgarh, Uttarakhand, and Himachal Pradesh. S. Shastri, "The Modi Factor in the 2019 Lok Sabha Election: How Critical Was It to the BJP's Victory?," *Studies in Indian Politics* 7, no. 2 (2019): 214.

54. Interview with Digvijay Singh in Bhopal on April 25, 2019; and "How RSS Turned the Wind in Favour of BJP Four Months After Losing MP Assembly Polls," The Wire, May 25, 2019, https://thewire.in/politics/rss-bjp-madhya-pradesh-win.

55. Sircar, "Politics of Vishwas."

56. S. Vyas, "BJP's 92,000 Booth Monitoring Teams to Increase Voter Turnout," *The Hindu*, March 26, 2019, https://www.thehindu.com/elections/lok-sabha-2019/bjps-92000-booth-monitoring-teams-to-increase-voter-turnout/article26638062.ece.

57. R. Singh, "How Modi Is Restructuring the BJP," *The Caravan*, June 30, 2019, https://caravanmagazine.in/politics/how-modi-restructuring-bjp.

58. Vandita Mishra, "Lok Sabha Elections 2019: Arid Chitrakoot Fertile for 'Superman, Saviour,'" *Indian Express*, May 7, 2019, https://indianexpress.com/elections/chitrakoot-bundelkhand-elections-2019-modi-bjp-bsp-5711871.

59. D. Narayan and V. Ananth, "How the Mobile Phone Is Shaping to Be BJP's Most Important Weapon in Elections," *Economic Times*, August 23, 2018, https://economictimes.indiatimes.com/news/politics-and-nation/how-the-mobile-phone-is-shaping-to-be-bjps-most-important-weapon-in-elections/articleshow/65508743.cms.

60. P. Chhibber and S. Ostermann, "The BJP's Fragile Mandate: Modi and Vote Mobilizers in the 2014 General Elections," *Studies in Indian Politics* 2, no. 2 (2014): 137–51.

61. K. Uttam, "For PM Modi's 2019 Campaign, BJP Readies Its WhatsApp Plan," *Hindustan Times*, September 29, 2018, https://www.hindustantimes.com/india-news/bjp-plans-a-whatsapp-campaign-for-2019-lok-sabha-election/story-lHQBYbxwXHaChc7Akk6hcI.html.

62. Uttam, "WhatsApp Plan."

63. This is what some BJP officers refer to as the "three *k*'s": *karyalay* (office), *karyakarta* (activists), and *kosh* (money).

64. R. Bhattacharya, "In Cooch Behar, BJP's Social Media Boss Is 36-Year-Old Shop Owner Who Juggles 1,114 WhatsApp Groups," *Indian Express*, April 12, 2019, https://indianexpress.com/elections/in-cooch-behar-bjps-social-media-boss-is-36-yr-old-shop-owner-who-juggles-1114-whatsapp-groups-5669638/.

65. S. Shankar Singh, *How to Win an Indian Election: What Political Parties Don't Want You to Know* (New Delhi: Penguin, 2019).

66. "PM Modi to Interact with Those Who've Taken 'Main Bhi Chowkidar' Pledge: At 500 Places, on March 31," *Indian Express*, March 19, 2019, https://indianexpress.com/elections/pm-modi-to-interact-with-people-who-pledged-for-mai-bhi-chowkidar-campaign-on-march-31-rs-prasad-5633692/.

67. "India's Election Campaign Is Being Fought in Voters' Pockets," *The Economist*, April 11, 2019, https://www.economist.com/asia/2019/04/13/indias-election-campaign-is-being-fought-in-voters-pockets; and "India: The WhatsApp Election," *Financial Times*, accessed October 1, 2020, https://www.ft.com/content/9fe88fba-6c0d-11e9-a9a5-351eeaef6d84.

68. In 2018, 500 million Indians were on the internet (a 65 percent increase over 2016), partly because of the launch of Jio by Reliance, whose inaugural offer (4G service free for six months) racked up 100 million subscribers in 170 days—the number could almost instantly be activated if the subscriber's identity could be verified with an Aadhaar number. The face of Modi was on the offer, epitomizing the complementarity between him and Mukesh Ambani: the latter benefited from the popularity of the former, and the former was to benefit from the new channels of communication developed by the latter—not to mention the incentive to enroll with Aadhaar. Narayan and Ananth, *How the Mobile Phone*; and S. Ninan, "How India's Media Landscape

Changed over Five Years," India Forum, June 28, 2019, https://www.theindiaforum.in/article
/how-indias-media-landscape-changed-over-five-years.

69. M. Krishnan, "Social Media in India Fans Fake News," The Interpreter, May 2, 2019,
https://www.lowyinstitute.org/the-interpreter/social-media-india-fans-fake-news.

70. Shreyya Rajgopal, "Who's Texting? It's the Elections. Impact of Social Media on Electoral Politics in India: A Study of the 2018 Madhya Pradesh State Elections" (Master's thesis,
Paris School of International Affairs, 2019).

71. N. Gleicher, "Removing Coordinated Inauthentic Behavior and Spam from India and
Pakistan," Facebook, April 1, 2019, https://newsroom.fb.com/news/2019/04/cib-and-spam
-from-india-pakistan/.

72. P. Chaudhuri, "Facebook Purge: Hundreds of BJP-Related Pages Were Taken Down—
but Not Mentioned in Firm's Release, Scroll.in, April 7, 2019, https://scroll.in/article/919208
/facebook-purge-hundreds-of-bjp-related-pages-were-taken-down-but-not-mentioned-in
-firms-release.

73. See P. Chaudhuri, "Alt News Exposé: Fake News Peddling FB Page 'The India Eye' and
Its Gujarat Connection," AltNews, September 22, 2018, https://www.altnews.in/alt-news
-expose-fake-news-peddling-fb-page-the-india-eye-and-its-gujarat-connnection/; and P. Sinha,
"BJP IT Cell Head Amit Malviya Tries to Malign Ravish Kumar by Sharing a Mischievously
Edited Video Clip," AltNews, September 11, 2019, https://www.altnews.in/bjp-cell-head-amit
-malviya-tries-malign-ravish-kumar-sharing-mischievously-edited-video-clip/.

74. Shivam Shankar Singh, "Former BJP Data Analyst on How the Party Wins Elections and
Influences People," The Caravan, January 29, 2019, https://caravanmagazine.in/politics/shivam
-shankar-singh-as-told-to-bjp-data.

75. N. Purnell and J. Horwitz, "Facebook's Hate-Speech Rules Collide With Indian Politics,"
Wall Street Journal, August 14, 2020, https://www.wsj.com/articles/facebook-hate-speech-india
-politics-muslim-hindu-modi-zuckerberg-11597423346.

76. "No, This Photo of Rajiv Gandhi and Narasimha Rao Was Not Taken at Indira Gandhi's
Funeral," Boom, February 1, 2019, https://www.boomlive.in/no-this-photo-of-rajiv-gandhi-and
-narasimha-rao-was-not-taken-at-indira-gandhis-funeral/. The text of the original post said: "At
Indira Gandhi's funeral—why is son Rajeev Gandhi offering prayers in Islamic mode? Nearby
PV Narasimha Rao is doing it the Hindu way."

77. A. Sidharth, "Did Rahul Gandhi Suggest a 5000 Crore Loan for Pakistan? Fake Screenshot of ABP News Viral," AltNews, December 3, 2018, https://www.altnews.in/did-rahul
-gandhi-suggest-a-5000-crore-loan-for-pakistan-fake-screenshot-of-abp-news-viral/.

78. A. Sidharth and S. Bhatt, "Photoshopped Image of Priyanka Gandhi Wearing a Cross
Now Viral as a Meme," AltNews, April 2, 2019, https://www.altnews.in/photoshopped-image
-of-priyanka-gandhi-wearing-a-cross-now-viral-as-a-meme/.

79. J. Patel, "No, Ashok Gehlot Was Not Waving Pakistan's Flag as Claimed on Social Media,"
Alt News, Nov. 29, 2019 (https://www.altnews.in/no-ashok-gehlot-was-not-waving-pakistans
-flag-as-claimed-on-social-media/ Last accessed October 1, 2020).

80. P. Chaudhuri, "Old Video Resurfaces to Falsely Claim Congress Workers Raised 'Pakistan Zindabad' Slogans," AltNews, April 2, 2019, https://www.altnews.in/old-video-resurfaces
-to-falsely-claim-congress-workers-raised-pakistan-zindabad-slogans/. There were other posts

of the same kind. P. Chaudhuri, "Multiple Videos Falsely Claim Congress Workers Thrashed by Police for Chanting 'Pakistan Zindabad," Alt News, February 11, 2019, https://www.altnews .in/multiple-videos-falsely-claim-congress-workers-thrashed-by-police-for-chanting-pakistan -zindabad/.

81. "Fake News to Spread BJP Message: Amit Shah," Brut India Facebook post, September 22, 2018, https://www.facebook.com/brutindia/videos/557431361375964/. See also "Real or Fake, We Can Make Any Message Go Viral: Amit Shah to BJP Social Media Volunteers," The Wire, September 26, 2018, https://thewire.in/politics/amit-shah-bjp-fake-social-media -messages.

82. I have scrutinized these forms of horizontal clientelism in *India's Silent Revolution*.

83. C. Jaffrelot, "Class and Caste in the 2019 Indian Election—Why Have So Many Poor Started Voting for Modi?," *Studies in Indian Politics* 7, no. 2 (November 2019): 1–12.

84. C. Jaffrelot and A. Kalaiyasaran, "Quota and Bad Faith," *Indian Express*, January 14, 2019, https://indianexpress.com/article/opinion/columns/yogi-adityanath-quota-reservation-bjp -uttar-pradesh-5536651/.

85. G. Verniers, "Breaking Down the Uttar Pradesh Verdict: In Biggest Bout, Knockout," *Indian Express*, May 28, 2019, https://indianexpress.com/article/explained/lok-sabha-elections -uttar-pradesh-bjp-modi-amit-shah-yogi-5751375/.

86. M. A. Beg, S. Pandey, and S. Kare, "Post-Poll Survey: Why Uttar Pradesh's Mahagathbandhan Failed," *The Hindu*, May 26, 2019, https://www.thehindu.com/elections/lok-sabha -2019/post-poll-survey-why-uttar-pradeshs-mahagathbandhan-failed/article27249310.ece.

87. C. Jaffrelot and A. Kalaiyarasan, "Quota, Old plus New," *Indian Express*, March 2, 2019, https://indianexpress.com/article/opinion/columns/general-category-quota-dalit-sc-st -reservation-old-plus-new-5607504/.

88. Verniers, "Breaking Down the Uttar Pradesh Verdict."

89. As Shoaib Daniyal points out, "While social media might help, the core of politics remains the ground organisation of parties"—a conclusion he draws from the fact that 64 percent of the voters interviewed by the CSDS-Lokniti for its National Election Survey do not use social media at all. This was, indeed, evident from the fact that BJP could use social media only because its foot soldiers had collected phone numbers on the ground. S. Daniyal, "In Charts: Was The Influence of Social Media on the 2019 Lok Sabha Election Exaggerated?," Scroll.in, June 27, 2019, https://scroll.in/article/927651/in-charts-was-the-influence-of-social-media-on-the-2019-lok -sabha-election-exaggerated.

90. On the role of the media in fostering militarism, see the investigative pieces by Salil Tripathi, "How the Fog of War Has Blinded Journalists to Their Roles," *The Caravan*, March 2, 2019, https://caravanmagazine.in/media/question-journalists-support-for-armed-forces.

91. Rammanohar Reddy convincingly explains the pro-regime bias of the Indian media by the ownership pattern and the business model at large: as most of the newspapers and TV channels belong to industrialists who cannot afford to alienate the government and need the government's ads, the journalists who dare to oppose the regime are asked to fall in line. R. Reddy, "Media in Contemporary India: Journalism Transformed into a Commodity," in *Business and Politics in India*, ed. C. Jaffrelot, Atul Kohli, and Kanta Murali (New York, Oxford University Press, 2019), 183–209.

92. R. Chopra, "Why Election Commission Frowned on DD Coverage: BJP Got 160 Hours in a Month, Congress 80," *Indian Express*, April 15, 2019, https://indianexpress.com/elections /why-ec-frowned-on-dd-coverage-bjp-got-160-hrs-in-a-month-congress-80-5675641/.

93. "Top Hindi Channels Gave Modi-Shah 2.5x More Airtime than Rahul-Priyanka," The Wire, May 14, 2019, https://thewire.in/media/narendra-modi-amit-shah-rahul-priyanka -gandhi-hindi-tv.

94. S. Rukmini, "How India Votes: The News Media Is Helping BJP Win Elections—and the Public Does Not Mind," Scroll.in, January 14, 2019, https://scroll.in/article/909195/how -india-votes-the-news-media-is-helping-bjp-win-elections-and-the-public-does-not-mind.

95. "BARC week 46: Uptick in English News Channel Viewership," Indiantelevision.com, November 22, 2019, https://www.indiantelevision.com/television/tv-channels/viewership /barc-week-46-uptick-in-english-news-channel-viewership-191122.

96. For more detail, see Christophe Jaffrelot and Vihang Jumle, "One-Man Show," *The Caravan*, December 15, 2020 (https://caravanmagazine.in/media/republic-debates-study-shows -channel-promotoes-modi-ndtv).

97. I am grateful to Vihang Jumle for compiling these data.

98. "About $6.5 billion was spent during the US presidential and congressional races in 2016, according to OpenSecrets.org, which tracks money in American politics." B. Pradhan and S. Kumaresan, "Indian Elections become World's Most Expensive: This Is How Much They Cost," *Business Standard*, June 4, 2019, https://www.business-standard.com/article/elections/lok -sabha-elections-2019-become-world-s-most-expensive-leave-us-behind-119060301330_1.html.

99. Centre for Media Studies, "Poll Expenditure: The 2019 Elections," New Delhi, 2019, accessed October 1, 2020, http://cmsindia.org/cms-poll/Poll-Expenditure-the-2019-elections -cms-report.pdf.

100. A. Mohan, "Cash, Goods Worth Rs 3,400 Crore Seized during Lok Sabha Elections 2019: EC," *Business Standard*, May 20, 2019, https://www.business-standard.com/article /elections/cash-goods-worth-rs-3-400-crore-seized-during-lok-sabha-elections-2019-ec -119052000047_1.html.

101. "In 2019, Is BJP Riding a Modi Wave or a Money Wave?," The Wire, May 6, 2019, https:// thewire.in/politics/bjp-modi-political-funding-money.

102. "Analysis of Sources of Funding of National Parties of India, FY 2017–18," Association for Democratic Reforms, January 23, 2019, https://adrindia.org/content/analysis-sources -funding-national-parties-india-fy-2017-18.

103. A. Kumar, "Political Funding from Unknown Source Still Rampant: ADR Report," *Hindustan Times*, October 6, 2020, https://www.hindustantimes.com/india-news/political -funding-from-unknown-source-still-rampant-adr-report/story-8WGmh6dwWRNFs TaoleVmSP.html.

104. Association for Democratic Reforms, "Analysis of Sources."

105. A. Rashid, "Electoral Bonds Have Legalised Crony Capitalism: Ex-Chief Election Commissioner SY Quraishi," *Outlook*, April 7, 2019, https://www.outlookindia.com/website/story /india-news-electoral-bonds-have-legalised-crony-capitalism-ex-chief-election-commissioner -sy-quraishi/328299.

106. "Modi Wave or a Money Wave?"

107. "Political Advertising for India," cited in "In 2019, Is BJP Riding a Modi Wave or a Money Wave?," The Wire, May 6, 2019, https://thewire.in/politics/bjp-modi-political-funding-money.

108. P. Chaudhuri, "Pro-BJP Pages Account for 70% of Ad Spending Made Public by Facebook, Analysis Shows," Scroll.in, March 10, 2019, https://scroll.in/article/916044/pro-bjp-pages-account-for-70-of-ad-spending-made-public-by-facebook-analysis-shows.

109. A former data analyst with the BJP, Shivam Shankar Singh explains that to secure their huge number of followers, the pro-BJP Facebook pages had to "pay Facebook to boost [their] posts." S. Shankar Singh, "Former BJP Data Analyst on the Party Wins Elections and Influence people," The Caravan, January 29, 2019 - https://caravanmagazine.in/politics/shivam-shankar-singh-as-told-to-bjp-data.

110. Cited in Chaudhuri, "Pro-BJP Pages."

111. S. Bansal, G. Sathe, R. Khaira, and A. Sethi, "How Modi, Shah Turned a Women's NGO into a Secret Election Propaganda Machine," Huffington Post, April 5, 2019, https://www.huffingtonpost.in/entry/how-modi-shah-turned-a-women-s-rights-ngo-into-a-secret-election-propaganda-machine_in_5ca5962ce4b05acba4dc1819.

112. D. Mishra, "Modi Government Has Already Spent Double What the UPA Did on Publicity," The Wire, October 29, 2018, https://thewire.in/government/modi-bjp-government-publicity-advertisement.

113. R. Chopra, "Election Commissioner Speaks Out 'Winning at All Cost, without Ethics, Is New Normal in Politics,'" Indian Express, August 18, 2017, https://indianexpress.com/article/india/winning-at-all-cost-without-ethics-is-new-normal-in-politics-ec-speaks-out-gujarat-rajya-sabha-elections-4801871/.

114. "EC Summons CBDT Officials to Discuss IT Raids on Opposition Leaders," The Wire, April 9, 2019, https://thewire.in/government/election-commission-it-raids-bjp-congress.

115. See "Not against Electoral Bonds, but Opposed to 'Anonymity Attached to It': EC," Indian Express, April 10, 2019, https://indianexpress.com/article/india/not-against-electoral-bonds-but-opposed-to-anonymity-attached-to-it-ec-5669288/; and R. Chopra, "Election Commission Seeks More Power, Rejected," Indian Express, November 21, 2016, https://indianexpress.com/article/india/india-news-india/election-commission-ec-power-jurisdiction-voting-4386614/.

116. S. Ostermann and A. Ahuja, "Institutional Tug of War: The Election Commission in a Time of Executive Resurgence," Center for the Advanced Study of India, accessed August 24, 2020, https://casi.sas.upenn.edu/iit/ostermannahuja.

117. M. Vaishnav, "India's Elite Institutions Are Facing a Credibility Crisis," Mint, February 20, 2018, https://www.livemint.com/Opinion/vvPejHxB52AVzqQBRLoIWL/Indias-elite-institutions-are-facing-a-credibility-crisis.html.

118. Rajdeep Sardesai (@sardesairajdeep), "Election Commission first announces dates for Karnataka by polls. now, suddenly postpones the election. surely EC knew rebel MLAs case was before SC when dates were announced. what is going on here? Will Centre decide by-poll dates or EC?," Twitter, September 26, 2019, 8:40 A.M., https://twitter.com/sardesairajdeep/status/1177201342072467456.

119. R. Chopra, "Amit Shah's Wayanad-Pak Speech: EC Clears Him, One Member Dissenting," Indian Express, May 4, 2019, https://indianexpress.com/elections/lok-sabha-elections-2019-amit-shah-shah-wayanad-pak-speech-ec-clears-him-one-member-dissenting-5709821/;

and "Fourth Clean Chit: EC Lets Off PM Modi for 'Majority-Minority' Speech in Nanded," *Indian Express*, May 3, 2019, https://indianexpress.com/elections/fourth-clean-chit-ec-lets-off -pm-modi-for-majority-minority-speech-in-nanded-5709519/.

120. During the 2019 election campaign, Narendra Modi launched his own TV channel, NaMo TV, on March 31, which was aired free of charge by DTH operators (and which went off the air once the elections were over).

121. Even Shekhar Gupta had to recognize after the 2019 elections that these raids were part of an exceptional form of vendetta. S. Gupta, "Modi-Shah's BJP Has Taken India's Politics of Vendetta to a New Level," ThePrint, August 31, 2019, https://theprint.in/national-interest/modi -shahs-bjp-has-taken-indias-politics-of-vendetta-to-a-new-level/284807/.

122. "11 Raids in a Month on Opposition, Tax Department Says Can't Give Details," NDTV, April 10, 2019, https://www.ndtv.com/india-news/11-raids-in-a-month-on-opposition-tax -department-says-cant-give-details-2021070.

123. K. Rajagopal, "Supreme Court Asks ECI to Decide by May 6 Congress's Complaints against Modi, Amit Shah 'Hate' Speeches," *The Hindu*, May 2, 2019, https://www.thehindu.com /elections/lok-sabha-2019/supreme-court-asks-election-commission-to-decide-by-may-6 -congress-complaints-against-narendra-modi-amit-shah/article27011640.ece.

124. In one rally, Adityanath declared, "If the Congress, the Samajwadi Party and the BSP have faith in Ali, then we too have faith in Bajrang Bali." While Ali is revered by Muslims as the Prophet Muhammad's successor, Bajrang Bali is another name for Lord Hanuman.

125. S. Raghotham, "Unable to Tame PM, EC and SC Have Failed Us," *Deccan Herald*, May 11, 2019, https://www.deccanherald.com/lok-sabha-election-2019/opinion-unable-to-tame-pm -ec-and-sc-have-failed-732168.html.

126. "'Won't Work for You if You Don't Vote for Me': Maneka Gandhi Tells Muslim Voters," News Minute, April 12, 2019, https://www.thenewsminute.com/article/won-t-work-you-if-you -don-t-vote-me-maneka-gandhi-tells-muslim-voters-99915.

127. The electronic voting machines have made this decline of secret ballots possible as politicians (at least those of the ruling party) know the voting pattern at the booth level—that is, at the level of socially and communally homogenous localities.

128. A. Bhaumik, "EC Lets Off Maneka with Warning," *Deccan Herald*, April 29, 2019, https://www.deccanherald.com/national/ec-lets-off-maneka-with-warning-731292.html.

129. Tamil Nadu is a case in point. See "Cash for Votes: EC's Selective Interference Brings Its Neutrality under a Cloud," The Wire, May 22, 2019, https://thewire.in/law/cash-for-votes -election-commission-selective-interference.

130. S. Y. Quraishi, "The Election Commission Must Act Tough," *The Hindu*, May 6, 2019, https://www.thehindu.com/opinion/op-ed/the-election-commission-must-act-tough /article27051618.ece.

131. S. Dhingra, "Big Split in Election Commission as EC Ashok Lavasa Stands Up against Clean Chits to Modi," ThePrint, May 5, 2019, https://theprint.in/india/campaign-controversies -split-election-commission-as-ec-lavasa-dissents-on-modi-clean-chits/231290/.

132. "Ashok Lavasa Opts Out of Election Commission Meets over Clean Chit, CEC Responds," *Economic Times*, May 18, 2019, https://economictimes.indiatimes.com/articleshow /69383788.cms?utm_source=contentofinterest&utm_medium=text&utm_campaign=cppst.

133. See "Disclosure of Ashok Lavasa's Dissent Note May Endanger Life or Physical Safety of Individual: EC," *India Today*, June 24, 2019, https://www.indiatoday.in/india/story/election -commission-disclosure-of-ashok-lavasa-dissent-note-pm-modi-speech-may-endanger-life-or -physical-safety-of-individual-1555235-2019-06-24.

134. R. Sarin, "Check if EC Ashok Lavasa Used Influence during Power Stint: Govt to PSUs," *Indian Express*, November 5, 2019, https://indianexpress.com/article/india/ashok-lavasa -election-commissioner-power-ministry-6103347/; and "Election Commissioner Ashok Lavasa's Wife Gets I-T Notices on Charges of Alleged Tax Evasion," Scroll.in, September 24, 2019, https://scroll.in/latest/938295/election-commissioner-ashok-lavasas-wife-gets-i-t-notices-on -charges-of-alleged-tax-evasion.

135. "EC Credibility Crisis: 66 Ex-Bureaucrats Write to Prez," *Deccan Herald*, April 9, 2019, https://www.deccanherald.com/national/national-politics/ec-credibility-crisis-66-ex -bureaucrats-write-to-prez-727737.html.

136. Oliver Heath, "Communal Realignment and Support for the BJP, 2009–2019," *Contemporary South Asia* 28, no. 2 (2020): 195–208, https://doi.org/10.1080/09584935.2020.1765986.

137. Heath, "Communal Realignment and Support," 205.

138. Heath, 197.

139. For a comparison of these data—which come from the Social Profile of Indian National and Provincial Elected Representatives (SPINPER) data set—with other parties, see C. Jaffrelot and G. Verniers, "The Reconfiguration of India's Political Elite," *Contemporary South Asia* 28, no. 2 (2020): 242–54.

140. Again: Bihar, Chhattisgarh, Delhi, Haryana, Himachal Pradesh, Jharkhand, Madhya Pradesh, Rajasthan, Uttarakhand, and Uttar Pradesh.

141. These data draw from the SPINPER data set.

142. Y. Yadav, "BJP Has Detached Politics from Economics," ThePrint, October 23, 2019, https://theprint.in/opinion/bjp-has-detached-politics-from-economics-it-will-haryana -maharashtra/309936/.

143. "Why Modi's Popularity Graph and Economic Hardships Don't Match," NewsClick, May 14, 2020, https://www.newsclick.in/Modi-Popularity-Graph-Economic-Hardships-Don't -Match-FDI.

Chapter 10

1. M. Vaishnav and J. Hintson, "India's Fourth Party System," Carnegie Endowment for International Peace, Washington DC, August 19, 2019, https://carnegieendowment.org/2019/08 /19/india-s-new-fourth-party-system-pub-79686; and P. Chhibber and R. Verma, "The rise of the Second Dominant Party System in India: BJP's New Social Coalition in 2019," *Studies in Indian Politics* 7, no. 2 (2019): 132.

2. Christophe Jaffrelot and Gilles Verniers, "A New Party System or a New Political System?," *Contemporary South Asia* 28, no. 2 (2020), https://doi.org/10.1080/09584935.2020.1765990.

3. Press Information Bureau, Government of India, "Union Home Minister Shri Amit Shah Chairs the 46th National Management Convention Held by All India Management Association

(AIMA)," press release, September 17, 2019, https://pib.gov.in/PressReleseDetailm.aspx?PRID
=1585302.

4. "Redefine Human Rights in Indian Context, Says Amit Shah, Wants Electricity, Food to
Be Added," *Mint*, October 13, 2019, https://www.livemint.com/news/india/redefine-human
-rights-in-indian-context-says-amit-shah-wants-electricity-food-to-be-added-11570934132285
.html.

5. S. Levitsky and D. Ziblatt, *How Democracies Die* (New York: Broadway Books, 2019), 111.

6. Levitsky and Ziblatt, *How Democracies Die*, 23.

7. "BJP, a Party of Political Turncoats: Increasing Trends since 2014," Sabrang, August 9, 2017,
https://www.sabrangindia.in/article/bjp-party-political-turncoats-increasing-trends-2014.

8. A. Katyal, "The Great BJP Poaching Plan: If You Can't Beat Them, Get Them to Join the
Party," Scroll.in, March 31, 20127, https://scroll.in/article/833250/the-great-bjp-poaching-plan
-if-you-cant-beat-them-get-them-to-join-the-party.

9. S. Palshikar, "In Maharashtra, BJP Works on Constructing All-India Politics While also
Appropriating the Regional Space," *Indian Express*, October 18, 2019, https://indianexpress.com
/article/opinion/columns/the-bjps-double-engine-maharashtra-assembly-polls-narendra
-modi-devendra-fadnavis-6074930/.

10. Alok Deshpande, "22 Maharashtra MLAs Switch Parties since 2014 Elections; NCP
Worst-Hit," *The Hindu*, September 16, 2019, https://www.thehindu.com/news/national/other
-states/22-mlas-switch-parties-since-2014-elections-ncp-worst-hit/article29426778.ece; and
Lyla Adam, "Maharashtra Assembly Election: Turncoats' Time," *Frontline*, October 25, 2019,
https://frontline.thehindu.com/politics/article29657615.ece.

11. "The big news: Amit Shah wants BJP to rule 'from Panchayat to Parliament,' and 9 other
top stories," Scroll.in, April 16, 2017, https://scroll.in/latest/834733/the-big-news-amit-shah
-wants-bjp-rule-from-panchayat-to-parliament-and-9-other-top-stories. This objective reflected
not only the BJP's ideological stand—according to which the party was the only legitimate ruler
in India—but also its leaders' desire to use the resources of the state, including its financial resources, to support the Sangh Parivar's projects.

12. "President's Rule in Uttarakhand; Congress Says 'Murder of Democracy,'" *The Hindu*,
March 27, 2016, https://www.thehindu.com/news/national/other-states/President's-rule-in
-Uttarakhand-Congress-says-'murder-of-democracy'/article14177982.ece.

13. "Uttarakhand HC Quashes President's Rule," *The Hindu*, April 21, 2016, https://www
.thehindu.com/news/national/other-states/uttarakhand-presidents-rule-high-court-pained-at
-centres-behaviour/article8503518.ece.

14. "Arunachal Political Crisis: A Timeline," *The Hindu*, December 30, 2016, https://www
.thehindu.com/news/national/other-states/Arunachal-political-crisis-A-timeline
/article14983750.ece.

15. "Karnataka & Goa Congress Defections: Political Opportunism or Did Ideology Never
Matter?," ThePrint, July 11, 2019, https://theprint.in/talk-point/karnataka-goa-congress
-defections-political-opportunism-or-did-ideology-never-matter/261701/.

16. In fact, the BJP engineered similar defections in Goa in 2017, but in contrast to what
happened in Karnataka, it was already in office in the state as part of the ruling coalition. In Goa,
in February 2017, the BJP played the defection card to prevent the Congress, which had the

largest number of MLAs, from forming the government. But in July 2019, to consolidate its strength in parliament and to discard its coalition partner, the Goa Forward Party, which was cobbled together in haste after the 2017 state election, the BJP "acquired" ten other MLAs from the Congress.

17. "BJP Offered Rs 10 Crore to JDS MLA, Says Karnataka CM Kumaraswamy," *Indian Express*, June 10, 2019. After losing the 2018 Karnataka election, the BJP had already tried to reach out to Congress and JD(S) MLAs, offering them inducements to leave their party. "Congress Releases More Tapes: Yeddyurappa, Son Allegedly Caught Luring Cong MLAs," News Minute, May 19, 2018, https://www.thenewsminute.com/article/congress-releases-more-tapes -yeddyurappa-son-allegedly-caught-luring-cong-mlas-81573.

18. "Disqualified Karnataka MLA Buys India's Most Expensive Car Worth Rs 11 Crore," News18, August 20, 2019, https://www.news18.com/news/auto/disqualified-karnataka-mla -buys-india-most-expensive-car-worth-rs-11-crore-2272641.html.

19. K. M. Rakesh, "Karnataka Ground Zero in Mumbai: D.K. Shivakumar's Bid to Meet MLAs & the Retaliation," *The Telegraph*, July 11, 2017, https://www.telegraphindia.com/india /karnataka-ground-zero-in-mumbai-d-k-shivakumar-s-bid-to-meet-mlas-the-retaliation/cid /1694246.

20. R. Gowda, "Did Our Judges Miss a Chance to Stem the Rot in the System?," *Deccan Chronicle*, November 14, 2019, https://www.deccanchronicle.com/nation/current-affairs /141119/did-our-judges-miss-a-chance-to-stem-the-rot-in-the-system.html. Whether the Supreme Court (whose attitude will be easier to understand by the end of this chapter) was fully applying the Constitution in this particular instance has been hotly discussed. S. Fernandes, "21st Century Aaya Rams and Gaya Rams," Bar and Bench, April 13, 2020, https://www .barandbench.com/columns/21st-century-aaya-rams-and-gaya-rams.

21. M. Ghatwai, "Bid to Topple MP Govt? Congress Says Its MLAs Confined in Gurugram Hotel, BJP Denies," *Indian Express*, March 4, 2020, https://indianexpress.com/article/india /madhya-pradesh-kamal-nath-congress-bjp-6297845/.

22. S. Mishra, "How Maharaj and Shivraj Toppled Kamal Nath Government," India Ahead, March 20, 2020, https://www.indiaaheadnews.com/nationwide/madhya-pradesh-how -maharaj-and-shivraj-toppled-kamal-nath-government-350291.

23. "Digvijaya Singh in Preventive Custody for Trying to Meet Rebel Congress MLAs in Bengaluru," ThePrint, March 18, 2020, https://theprint.in/india/digvijaya-singh-in-preventive -custody-for-trying-to-meet-rebel-congress-mlas-in-bengaluru/382879/.

24. "Explained: What Happened during Madhya Pradesh Assembly Session?," *Indian Express*, March 16, 2020, https://indianexpress.com/article/explained/what-happened-in-madhya -pradesh-assembly-session-6316590/.

25. The Patel case was related to a deal struck in 2007; it was revisited twelve years later in the middle of the state election campaign.

26. R. Sardesai, "In the Quest for Power, the Ethical Decline of the BJP," *Hindustan Times*, July 30, 2020, https://www.hindustantimes.com/columns/in-the-quest-for-power-the-ethical -decline-of-the-bjp/story-Yz5RdY5UNMMzqoAAHvDPKM.html.

27. "Andhra Pradesh: Ahead of 'Chalo Atmakur' Rally, Chandrababu Naidu, Son Put under House Arrest," *Financial Express*, September 11, 2019, https://www.financialexpress.com/india

-news/andhra-pradesh-ahead-of-chalo-atmakur-rally-chandrababu-naidu-son-put-under
-house-arrest/1702687/.

28. "UP Congress Chief Put under House Arrest ahead of Rahul Gandhi's Scheduled Visit to Hathras," *The Hindu*, October 3, 2020, https://www.thehindu.com/news/national/other
-states/up-congress-chief-put-under-house-arrest-ahead-of-rahul-gandhis-scheduled-visit-to
-hathras/article32758328.ece.

29. "Sandeep Pandey Put under House Arrest before Kashmir Protest Second Time in Week," *The Wire*, August 16, 2019, https://thewire.in/rights/sandeep-pandey-put-under-house
-arrest-over-kashmir-protest-second-time-in-week.

30. C. M. Ramesh, another TDP Rajya Sabha member, followed the same trajectory for the same reason. Both were industrialists "under the scanner of Income Tax, CBI and Enforcement Directorate." D. Tiwary, "TDP MPs Join BJP: Two MPs Face CBI, ED, I-T Probes, BJP Had Called Them 'Mallyas,'" *Indian Express*, June 21, 2019, https://indianexpress.com/article/india
/tdp-mps-joins-bjp-two-face-cbi-ed-it-probes-mallyas-5791624/.

31. "48 Hours after Ajit Pawar Ties Up with BJP, Nine Cases in Irrigation Scam Closed by Anti-Corruption Bureau," FirstPost, December 7, 2019, https://www.firstpost.com/india/48
-hours-after-ajit-pawar-ties-up-with-bjp-nine-cases-in-irrigation-scam-closed-by-anti
-corruption-bureau-7697761.html.

32. Money bills are one exception, as the Rajya Sabha cannot block the Lok Sabha's decision in such cases.

33. R. Chopra, "Election Commissioner Speaks Out," *Indian Express*, August 18, 2017, https://indianexpress.com/article/india/winning-at-all-cost-without-ethics-is-new-normal-in
-politics-ec-speaks-out-gujarat-rajya-sabha-elections-4801871/.

34. "Gujarat Rajya Sabha Election Result: Smooth Sailing for BJP, but Here Is What Has Left Congress Rattled," *Financial Express*, June 20, 2020, https://www.financialexpress.com
/india-news/gujarat-rajya-sabha-election-2020-result-candidates-bjp-congress/1997783/.

35. P. Chidambaram, "Across the Aisle: BJP Has Used Every Trick in Its Bag to Pass Laws in Rajya Sabha," *Indian Express*, August 4, 2019, https://indianexpress.com/article/opinion
/columns/across-the-aisle-coercive-federalism-parliament-monsoon-session-5875927/.

36. This section draws from Christophe Jaffrelot and Vihang Jumle, "Bypassing Parliament," *Indian Express*, October 15, 2020, https://indianexpress.com/article/opinion/columns
/narendra-modi-government-parliament-lok-sabha-rajya-sabha-6725428/.

37. "Modi Describes Parliament as 'Temple of Democracy,'" *Business Standard*, May 20, 2014, https://www.business-standard.com/article/politics/modi-describes-parliament-as-temple-of
-democracy-114052000994_1.html.

38. "Audio Speeches—Shri Narendra Modi, May 26, 2014 to May 25, 2019, May 30, 2019 Onwards," Parliament Library, Parliament of India, accessed October 7, 2020, http://164.100.47
.193/Audio_Speeches_PM/Shri_modi.htm.

39. "Audio Speeches—Shri H D Deve Gowda, 1 June 1996 to 21 April 1997," Parliament Library, Parliament of India, accessed October 7, 2020, http://164.100.47.193/Audio_Speeches
_PM/HD_Deve_Gowda.htm.

40. "Audio Speeches—Shri A B Vajpayee, October 13, 1999 to May 22, 2004, March 19, 1998 to October 13, 1999, May 16, 1996 to June 1, 1996," Parliament Library, Parliament of India, ac-

cessed October 7, 2020, http://164.100.47.193/Audio_Speeches_PM/Shri_Atal_Bihari
_Vajpayee.htm.

41. "Audio Speeches—Shri Manmohan Singh, 22 May 2004 to 26 May 2014," Parliament
Library, Parliament of India, accessed October 7, 2020, http://164.100.47.193/Audio_Speeches
_PM/Dr_Manmohan_Singh.htm.

42. P. B. Mehta, "Betrayal of Procedure in Parliament Is Not Just about Technicalities: Defer-
ence to Process Builds Trust," *Indian Express*, September 22, 2020, https://indianexpress.com
/article/opinion/columns/parliament-monsoon-session-farm-bills-modi-govt-railroading-the
-bill-6605281/.

43. "List of Ordinances Promulgated, Text of the Central Ordinances—Legislative References," Legislative Department, Ministry of Law and Justice, Government of India, accessed
October 7, 2020, http://legislative.gov.in/documents/legislative-references.

44. V. Rodrigues, "Parliamentary Scrutiny on the Back Burner," *The Hindu*, September 26,
2020, https://www.thehindu.com/opinion/lead/parliamentary-scrutiny-on-the-back-burner
/article32699224.ece; "Bills Referred to Committees" (for Fifteenth, Sixteenth, and Seventeenth
Lok Sabha under all committees), Lok Sabha, Parliament of India, accessed December 28, 2020,
http://loksabhaph.nic.in/Committee/Bill_Search.aspx. See also "Functioning of 16th Lok
Sabha (2014–2019)," PRS Legislative Research, https://www.prsindia.org/parliamenttrack/vital
-stats/functioning-16th-lok-sabha-2014-2019; and Maansi Verma, "Who Controls Parliament?
Instead of Building a Robust System, We Have Bled Its Vitality, Dignity and Efficacy," *Firstpost*,
September 22, 2020, https://www.firstpost.com/india/who-controls-parliament-instead-of
-building-a-robust-system-we-have-bled-its-vitality-dignity-and-efficacy-8840041.html.

45. Verma, "Who controls Parliament?"

46. "Bills List," Ministry of Parliamentary Affairs, Government of India, accessed October 7,
2020, https://mpa.gov.in/bills-list.

47. "Ghulam Nabi Azad Interview: 'Why Attend Parliament If Bills Rushed through without
Scrutiny," *The Indian Express*, July 25, 2019, https://indianexpress.com/article/india/ghulam-nabi
-azad-interview-why-attend-parliament-if-bills-rushed-through-without-scrutiny-5849448/.

48. Verma, "Who controls Parliament?"

49. Something that remained unreported because, apparently, the footage of Rajya Sabha TV
was doctored. K. T. S. Tulsi and T. Puri, "Were Crucial Minutes of TV Footage during Passage
of the Farm Bills, as well as the Rajya Sabha Rulebook, Muted?," *Times of India*, October 6, 2020.

50. "Opposition Absent, 15 Bills Passed in Rajya Sabha in Two Days," NDTV, September 23,
2020, https://www.ndtv.com/india-news/opposition-absent-15-bills-passed-in-rajya-sabha-in
-two-days-2300057.

51. Verma, "Who controls Parliament?"

52. Consequently, the Modi government made extensive use of ordinances.

53. See Y. Aiyar and L. Tillin, "'One Nation,' BJP, and the Future of Indian Federalism," *India
Review* 19, no. 2 (March–April 2020): 117–35.

54. "Article 370 Revoked: Which Political Parties Supported the Bill, Which Opposed It,"
India Today, August 6, 2019, https://www.indiatoday.in/india/story/jammu-and-kashmir
-article-370-revoked-political-parties-support-oppose-1577561-2019-08-05.

55. "Article 370: Jyotiraditya Scindia, Deepender Hooda, Janardan Dwivedi Go against Congress Stand," *The Hindu*, August 6, 2019, https://www.thehindu.com/news/national/article-370 -jyotiraditya-scindia-deepender-hooda-janardan-dwivedi-go-against-congress-stand /article28838142.ece.

56. "Modi Makes His Case on Kashmir," *Foreign Policy*, August 8, 2020, https://foreignpolicy .com/2019/08/08/modi-makes-his-case-on-kashmir/.

57. "Economist Jean Dreze: Article 370 Helped Reducing Poverty in Jammu and Kashmir," *National Herald*, August 9, 2019, https://www.nationalheraldindia.com/india/economist-jean -dreze-jandk-more-developed-than-gujarat-special-status-helped-reducing-poverty.

58. Here Modi refers to the fact that leaders of the National Conference and the PDP were the son (or grandson) and daughter of the parties' founders.

59. " Independence Day: Full Text of PM Modi's Address to Nation," *Business Today*, August 15, 2019, https://www.businesstoday.in/current/economy-politics/independence-day-pm -modi-address-nation-full-text-speech-15-august-red-fort/story/372903.html.

60. A. Chakraborty, "Amit Shah Says Articles 370, 35A Were 'Gateway of Terror,' PM Narendra Modi Shut Them," NDTV, October 31, 2019, https://www.ndtv.com/india-news/amit-shah -says-articles-370-35a-were-gateway-of-terror-pm-narendra-modi-shut-them-2124903.

61. "PM Modi Showed Pakistan Its Place by Diluting Article 370: Amit Shah," *Indian Express*, September 18, 2019, https://indianexpress.com/article/india/amit-shah-article-370-modi -pakistan-kashmir-issue-6006449/.

62. "Sardar Patel Should Have Handled Kashmir instead of Nehru: Amit Shah," *India Today*, September 22, 2019, https://www.indiatoday.in/india/story/amit-shah-kashmir-sardar-patel -jawaharlal-nehru-article-370-1601983-2019-09-22.

63. A. Mahale, "Hug Each Kashmiri, Build a New Paradise: Narendra Modi," *The Hindu*, September 19, 2019m https://www.thehindu.com/news/national/prime-minister-narendra -modi-addresses-a-huge-rally-in-nashik/article29457043.ece.

64. See the video posted on Twitter (https://twitter.com/manakgupta/status /1160083098253455360) and cited in Arundathi Roy, "The Silence Is the Loudest Sound," *New York Times*, August 15, 2019, https://www.nytimes.com/2019/08/15/opinion/sunday/kashmir -siege-modi.html.

65. The fairness of the girl's skin color is always valued in northern Indian matrimonials. A. Rehman, "Now Anyone Can Get Married to a Fair Kashmiri Girl: BJP MLA," *Indian Express*, August 7, 2019, https://indianexpress.com/article/india/now-anyone-can-get-married-to-a -fair-kashmiri-girl-bjp-mla-5884310/.

66. "Watch: 'Now Marry the White-Skinned Women of Kashmir,' UP MLA Vikram Saini Tells Party Workers," Scroll.in, August 7, 2019, https://scroll.in/video/933097/watch-now -marry-the-white-skinned-women-of-kashmir-up-mla-vikram-saini-tells-party-workers.

67. It was so keen to show to the world that Jammu and Kashmir were peaceful that a delegation of members of the European Parliament belonging to extreme rightist parties was invited to visit the region in October 2019. "22 of 27 EU Parliamentarians Visiting Kashmir Are from Right-Wing Parties," *The Telegraph*, October 28, 2019, https://www.telegraphindia.com/india /22-of-27-eu-parliamentarians-visiting-kashmir-are-from-right-wing-parties/cid/1714921.

68. "Omar and Mehbooba Detained under PSA . . . Had to Take Precautions: Amit Shah," *Indian Express*, October 15, 2019, https://indianexpress.com/article/india/omar-and -mehbooba-detained-under-psa-had-to-take-precautions-amit-shah-6069182/.

69. "Fact Check: 4 Kashmiris Died after Security Forces Action, yet Amit Shah Says 'No Deaths,'" The Wire, October 8, 2019, https://thewire.in/politics/jk-unionterritory-status-amit -shah.

70. PUCL, "Imprisoned Resistance—5th August and Its Aftermath," PUCL, November 12, 2019, 28, http://www.pucl.org/reports/imprisoned-resistance-5th-august-and-its-aftermath. Other reports with similar findings have been made: Fédération Internationale des Droits de l'Homme, "Update on Human Rights Violations in Indian-Administered Jammu & Kashmir since August 2019," FIDH, September 26, 2019, https://www.fidh.org/IMG/pdf/20190926 _india_j_k_bp_en.pdf; and the National Federation of Indian Women. J. Wallen, "Young Boys Tortured in Kashmir Clampdown as New Figures Show 13,000 Teenagers Arrested," *The Telegraph*, September 25, 2019, https://www.telegraph.co.uk/news/2019/09/25/young-boys -tortured-kashmir-clampdown-new-figures-show-13000/.

71. "Fact Check: 4 Kashmiris." See S. Zargar, "Meet the Amateur Pellet Doctors of Srinagar Who Treat Protestors Too Scared to Go to Hospital," Scroll.in, September 19, 2019, https:// scroll.in/article/937742/meet-the-amateur-pellet-doctors-of-srinagar-who-treat-protestors -too-scared-to-go-to-hospital. See also N. M. Haroon, "Blindness in Kashmir," *Scientific American*, November 19, 2019, https://blogs.scientificamerican.com/observations/blindness-in -kashmir/.

72. PUCL, "Imprisoned Resistance," 6–7. For detailed accounts, see Haroon, "Blindness in Kashmir," 32. The PUCL fact-finding mission also mentions the case of forced labor imposed on those who have been arrested and detained illegally: "Those picked up are illegally kept in the camps of the armed forces for one night or days on end as per the whims and fancies of the armed forces during which time they are subject to torture and humiliation. They are also com- pelled to do forced labour in the camp. After the armed forces are done with him, they are re- leased to the police who keep them in the police lockup for days on end. Once they reach the police station, it is the turn of the police to terrorize, intimidate and humiliate those detained. The police make monetary demands from the family members to release those arrested. These amounts range from Rs. 20,000/- and Rs. 30,000/-." Haroon, "Blindness in Kashmir," 34.

73. See Q. Rehbar and M. Zahra, "Accounts of Torture and Harassment by Indian Army in South Kashmir," *The Caravan*, October 26, 2019, https://caravanmagazine.in/conflict/accounts -torture-harassment-indian-army-south-kashmir; and A. Zargar, "Kashmir: Where Boys Are 'Being Rowed through Paradise on a River of Hell,'" NewsClick, September 16, 2019, https:// www.newsclick.in/Kashmir-Boys-Being-Rowed-Paradise-River-Hell.

74. S. Zargar, "Jammu and Kashmir's New Media Policy Is Aimed at Demolishing the Local Press, Editors Say," Scroll.in, June 24, 2020, https://scroll.in/article/964900/jammu-and -kashmirs-new-media-policy-is-aimed-at-demolishing-the-local-press-editors-say.

75. "IITians Write to Centre Against 'Brutalisation' of Kashmiris," The Wire, October 9, 2019, https://thewire.in/rights/iitians-write-to-centre-against-brutalisation-of-kashmiris.

76. "After 70 Days of Lockdown, BSNL Postpaid Mobile Services Restored in Kashmir; No Internet Yet," *Indian Express*, October 14, 2019, https://indianexpress.com/article/india/after

-70-days-of-lockdown-postpaid-services-restored-in-kashmir-on-bsnl-network-6068279/. See also A. Sharma, "J&K: Social Media Ban to Continue; 481 Websites on Whitelist," *Indian Express*, February 7, 2020, https://indianexpress.com/article/india/jk-internet-restoration-social -media-whitlisted-websites-6256586/.

77. S. Zargar, "A Year without High-Speed Internet Ravaged Health, Education, Entrepreneurship in Kashmir," Scroll.in, August 1, 2020, https://scroll.in/article/968719/a-year-without -high-speed-internet-ravaged-health-education-entrepreneurship-in-kashmir.

78. "People in J&K Use Internet Only to Watch Dirty Films, Says NITI Aayog Member," *The Hindu*, January 19, 2020, https://www.thehindu.com/news/national/people-in-jk-use-internet -only-to-watch-dirty-films-says-niti-aayog-member/article30599605.ece.

79. This notion is mentioned fifteen times in the fact-finding report "Imprisoned Resistance."

80. Students and Kashmiri tradesmen were assaulted across India. See "Rajasthan: Four Kashmiri Students Thrashed at Mewar University, Four Arrested," *Times of India*, November 24, 2019, http://timesofindia.indiatimes.com/articleshow/72204048.cms?utm_source =contentofinterest&utm_medium=text&utm_campaign=cppst.

81. G. Geelani, "Concertina in Our Souls," *The Telegraph*, August 2, 2020, https://www .telegraphindia.com/india/how-the-abrogation-of-article-370-has-radically-changed-kashmirs -political-landscape/cid/1787974.

82. Happymon Jacob, "Toward a Kashmir Endgame? How India and Pakistan Could Negotiate a Lasting Solution," United States Institute of Peace, special report no. 474, August 2020, accessed September 4, 2020, https://www.usip.org/publications/2020/08/toward-kashmir -endgame-how-india-and-pakistan-could-negotiate-lasting-solution.

83. B. Masood, "Detained in Jammu and Kashmir: Three Former CMs, Ex Ministers, MLAs, Mayor," *Indian Express*, August 19, 2019, https://indianexpress.com/article/india/detained-in -jk-ex-top-ministers-mlas-mayor-5915920/.

84. "Omar and Mehbooba Detained."

85. PUCL, "Imprisoned Resistance," 50.

86. PUCL, "Imprisoned Resistance," 7.

87. PUCL, "Imprisoned Resistance," 52. See the case of seventy-six-year-old Mian Abdul Qayoom, the vice president of the High Court's Bar Association of Srinagar, who was lodged in Agra jail. S. Parthasarathy, "Liberty at the Government's Whim," *The Hindu*, February 11, 2020 (https://www.thehindu.com/opinion/lead/liberty-at-the-governments-whim /article30785807.ece Last accessed September 3, 2020).

88. H. Ellis-Petersen, "'Humiliating to the Core': How India Turned a Kashmir Hotel into a Jail," *The Guardian*, February 21, 2020, https://www.theguardian.com/world/2020/feb/20 /how-india-turned-kashmir-centaur-hotel-into-a-jail-for-politicians.

89. A. Wani, "Freedom, Conditions Apply: Detained J K Leaders Can't Comment or Hold Rallies on Art 370 for a Year, Says Bond," *India Today*, October 21, 2019, https://www.indiatoday .in/india/story/jammu-kashmir-detained-political-leaders-bond-surety-article-370-1611538 -2019-10-21.

90. C. Jaffrelot and P. Anil, *India's First Dictatorship: The Emergency, 1975–77* (London, Hurst, 2020).

91. N. Iqbal, "J&K: Detained Leaders May Be Moved, Admin Bill over Rs 3 Crore," *Indian Express*, November 7, 2019, https://indianexpress.com/article/india/jk-detained-leaders-may -be-moved-admin-billed-over-rs-3-crore-6106966/.

92. N. Ganai, "Arrests under PSA Amount to 'Thought Crime,' Say Kashmir Lawyers as 100s Remain under Detention," *Outlook*, October 3, 2019, https://www.outlookindia.com/website /story/india-news-arrests-under-psa-amount-to-thought-crime-say-kashmir-lawyers-as-100s -remain-under-detention/339932. See also N. Masih, "India Detains Prominent Kashmiri Leader under Law Critics Call Draconian," *Washington Post*, September 16, 2019, https://www .washingtonpost.com/world/asia_pacific/india-detains-prominent-kashmiri-leader-under-law -critics-call-draconian/2019/09/16/941692cc-d869-11e9-adff-79254db7f766_story.html.

93. Radha Kumar, "Govt Sends a Chilling Message by Slapping the PSA on Omar Abdullah and Mehbooba Mufti," *Indian Express*, February 11, 2020, https://indianexpress.com/article /opinion/columns/jammu-kashmir-psa-detention-article-370-6261340/.

94. M. Ahmad, "J&K Leader's Ability to Convince People to Vote during Boycotts Cited as Reason for PSA Charge," The Wire, February 8, 2010, https://thewire.in/rights/ali-mohammed -sagar-jk-psa-2.

95. As in the mid-1970s during the Emergency, the authorities asked some opposition leaders who had been arrested to sign bonds through which they committed themselves to stay silent in exchange for their release. See the case of Omar Adbullah (S. Vadarajan, "Omar Abdullah: 'Govt Tried to Gag Me, Was Asked to Sign a Bond Forcing Me to Stay Silent," The Wire, July 30, 2020, https://thewire.in/politics/omar-abdullah-interview-bond-detention-political-future).

96. Peerzada Ashiq, "Omar Abdullah Used Politics to Cover His Radical Ideology: Public Safety Act Dossier," *The Hindu*, February 10, 2020, https://www.nytimes.com/2019/08/15 /opinion/sunday/kashmir-siege-modi.html.

97. U. Misra, "Explained: Who Was Kota Rani, Likened to Mehbooba Mufti in Her PSA Dossier?," *The Indian Express*, February 11, 2020, https://indianexpress.com/article/explained /kota-rani-kashmir-mehbooba-mufti-psa-6260940/.

98. "Who Is G.C. Murmu, Modi Aide and Now J&K's First Lt Governor?" *The Week*, October 25, 2019, https://www.theweek.in/news/india/2019/10/25/who-is-gc-murmu-modi-aide -and-now-jks-first-lt-governor.html.

99. S. Zargar, "One Year after Special Status Ended, Kashmiris Have Disappeared from Government in J&K," Scroll.in, July 31, 2020, https://scroll.in/article/968571/one-year-after-special -status-ended-kashmiris-have-disappeared-from-government-in-j-k.

100. "In Civil Bureaucracy, Police and Judiciary, Muslims in Kashmir Are Being Side Lined: G.H. Mir," *Kashmir Press*, July 7, 2020, https://thekashmirpress.com/2020/07/07/in-civil -bureaucracy-police-and-judiciary-muslims-in-kashmir-are-being-side-lined-g-h-mir/.

101. I. Chakravarty, "'Comeback of Dogra Rule': With Special Status Gone, Kashmiris Fear Losing Land Rights Once Again," Scroll.in, September 9, 2019, https://scroll.in/article/936652 /comeback-of-dogra-rule-with-special-status-gone-kashmiris-fear-losing-land-rights-once-again.

102. Vadarajan, "Omar Abdullah"

103. N. Sidiq, "Kashmir's Mineral Contracts Largely Handed to Non-locals," Anadolu Agency, July 27, 2020, https://www.aa.com.tr/en/asia-pacific/kashmir-s-mineral-contracts -largely-handed-to-non-locals/1923634.

104. S. Zargar, "A Year of Government Policies that Eroded Hard-Won Land Rights in Jammu and Kashmir," Scroll.in, August 4, 2020, https://scroll.in/article/969275/a-year-of-government-policies-that-eroded-hard-won-land-rights-in-jammu-and-kashmir.

105. N. Iqbal, "J&K: Army, CRPF, BSF Will No Longer Require NOC for Land Acquisition," Indian Express, July 28, 2020, https://indianexpress.com/article/india/jk-army-crpf-bsf-will-no-longer-require-noc-for-land-acquisition-6526708/.

106. P. Donthi, "Occupation Hazards," The Caravan, August 1, 2020, https://caravanmagazine.in/conflict/the-heavy-cost-of-revoking-article-370-in-kashmir.

107. Donthi, "Occupation Hazards."

108. "Kashmir Muslims Fear Demographic Shift as Thousands Get Residency," Al Jazeera, June 28, 2020, https://www.aljazeera.com/news/2020/06/kashmir-muslims-fear-demographic-shift-thousands-residency-200627103940283.html.

109. See C. Jaffrelot, "Composite Culture Is Not Multiculturalism: A Study of the Indian Constituent Assembly Debates," in India and the Politics of Developing Countries: Essays in Memory of Myron Weiner, ed. A. Varshney (New Delhi: Sage, 2004), 126–49.

110. A. Roy, "The Citizenship (Amendment) Bill, 2016 and the Aporia of Citizenship," Economic and Political Weekly 54, no. 49 (December 14, 2019): 28–34.

111. R. Tewari, "Modi Government Adopts Shrill Note on NRC, Says Similar Exercise for Rohingyas Underway," ThePrint, September 9, 2018, https://theprint.in/india/governance/modi-government-govt-adopts-shrill-note-on-nrc-says-similar-exercise-for-rohingyas-underway/114820/.

112. R. Venkataramakrishnan, "The Daily Fix: Make No Mistake, Amit Shah's NRC Plan Is Both Bigoted and Unconstitutional," Scroll.in, October 3, 2019, https://scroll.in/article/939279/the-daily-fix-make-no-mistake-amit-shahs-nrc-plan-is-both-bigoted-and-unconstitutional.

113. C. Jaffrelot, "Citizenship Law in India, a Populist Polarization?," Institut Montaigne, February 6, 2020, https://www.institutmontaigne.org/en/blog/citizenship-law-india-populist-polarization.

114. "Lok Sabha Passes Citizenship Amendment Bill 2019; Amit Shah: There Will Be NRC," Economic Times, December 10, 2019, https://economictimes.indiatimes.com/news/politics-and-nation/lok-sabha-passes-citizenship-amendment-bill-2019-amit-shah-there-will-be-nrc/articleshow/72449821.cms?utm_source=contentofinterest&utm_medium=text&utm_campaign=cppst.

115. "Rajya Sabha Passes Citizenship Amendment Bill," Times of India, December 11, 2019, https://timesofindia.indiatimes.com/india/rajya-sabha-passes-citizenship-amendment-bill/articleshow/72479562.cms.

116. G. Nagaraja, "Citizenship Amendment: Andhra, Telangana Parties Voted in Surprising Ways; Here's Why," The Wire, December 14, 2019, https://thewire.in/politics/andhra-pradesh-telangana-jagan-naidu-kcr-cab.

117. D. D. Roy, "'Landmark Day for India': PM Modi on Parliament Clearing Citizenship Bill," NDTV, December 11, 2019, https://www.ndtv.com/india-news/pm-narendra-modi-on-parliament-clearing-citizenship-bill-landmark-day-for-india-2147302.

118. Ministry of Law, Justice and Company Affairs, The Constitution of India, New Delhi, Government of India, 1983, 7 (italics added).

119. Niraja Gopal Jayal, "Faith-Based Citizenship: The Dangerous Path India Is Choosing," *India Forum*, November 13, 2019, https://www.theindiaforum.in/article/faith-criterion-citizenship. Italics in the original.

120. Cited in Arshu John, "Sealed and Delivered," *The Caravan*, February 1, 2020 https://caravanmagazine.in/reportage/ranjan-gogoi-gifts-government.

121. "'No Hindu Will Have to Leave over NRC,'" *The Telegraph*, September 22, 2019, https://www.telegraphindia.com/west-bengal/no-hindu-will-have-to-leave-over-nrc/cid/1706854.

122. K. Purohit, "Post CAA, BJP-Linked WhatsApp Groups Mount a Campaign to Foment Communalism," The Wire, December 18, 2019, https://thewire.in/media/cab-bjp-whatsapp-groups-muslims. This article is worth reading not only because of the information it contains but also because of the screenshots it shows.

123. "Over 32,000 Refugees Identified in 21 Districts for CAA: UP Minister," *India Today*, January 13, 2020, https://www.indiatoday.in/india/story/over-32000-refugees-identified-in-21-districts-for-caa-uttar-pradesh-minister-1636551-2020-01-13.

124. "Modi Says No Detention Camps, Minister Accepted 6 in Assam," *Outlook*, December 23, 2019, https://www.outlookindia.com/newsscroll/modi-says-no-detention-camps-minister-accepted-6-in-assam/1692393.

125. F. Ameen, "28 Deaths in Assam's Detention Camps, Minister Tells Rajya Sabha," *The Telegraph*, November 27, 2019, https://www.telegraphindia.com/india/28-deaths-in-assam-s-detention-camps-minister-tells-rajya-sabha/cid/1722471.

126. "Govt Lodged 3,331 People in Assam Detention Centres, 10 Died Last Year," *Business Standard*, March 17, 2020, https://www.business-standard.com/article/pti-stories/10-inmates-of-detention-centres-in-assam-died-in-last-one-year-govt-120031700816_1.html.

127. R. Karmakar, "Hell, Not Detention Centre: Assam 'Foreigner' after PM Remark," *The Hindu*, December 23, 2019, https://www.thehindu.com/news/national/hell-not-detention-centre-assam-foreigner-after-pm-remark/article30381296.ece.

128. A. Sharma, "What NRC, Detention Centres? When Prime Minister Modi Abandoned Truth at Ramleela Maidan," Asiaville, December 23 2019, https://www.asiavillenews.com/article/what-nrc-detention-centres-when-prime-minister-modi-abandoned-truth-at-ramleela-maidan-25130.

129. See H. Srikanth, "Three Streams in the Anti-CAA Movement," India Forum, January 21, 2020, https://www.theindiaforum.in/article/three-streams-anti-caa-movement.

130. A. Bose and E. Agha, "'The Hindu Who Went to Jail for Us': How Chandrashekhar Azad Went from Poster Boy to Hero at Shaheen Bagh," News18, January 23, 2020, https://www.news18.com/news/india/the-hindu-who-went-to-jail-for-us-how-chandrashekar-azad-went-from-poster-boy-to-hero-at-shaheen-bagh-2469505.html. Another Dalit leader, Jignesh Mevani, also delivered a speech at Shaheen Bagh.

131. D. Devaiah, "Karnataka: Poet, Editor Arrested in Koppal District over Anti-CAA Poem," *Indian Express*, February 20, 2020, https://indianexpress.com/article/india/karnataka-poet-journalist-arrested-in-koppal-caa-poem-6275793/.

132. "Lucknow: Magsaysay Winner Sandeep Pandey Arrested While Distributing Anti-CAA Pamphlets," Scroll.in, February 17, 2020, https://scroll.in/latest/953459/lucknow-magsaysay-winner-sandeep-pandey-arrested-while-distributing-anti-caa-pamphlets.

133. See M. Ghazali, "Top Sikh Body Akal Takht Extends Support to Anti-CAA Protests," NDTV, February 15, 2020, https://www.ndtv.com/india-news/top-sikh-body-akal-takht -extends-support-to-anti-caa-protests-2180483; and "Religion Should Never Be Criteria for Citizenship, Says Archbishop of Bengaluru," *The Hindu*, January 9, 2020, https://www.thehindu .com/news/cities/bangalore/religion-should-never-be-criteria-for-citizenship-says -archbishop-of-bengaluru/article30522147.ece.

134. R. Venkataramakrishnan, "The Political Fix: After a Month of Citizenship Act Protests in India, What Have We Learned?," Scroll.in, January 20, 2020, https://scroll.in/article/950351 /the-political-fix-after-a-month-of-citizenship-act-protests-in-india-what-have-we-learned. The map of the protest inserted in this article is worth examining: it evaluates the strength of the anti-CAA protest day by day between January 6 and 13.

135. From February 2 to 8, 2020, a musical and cultural event called Artists Against Communalism was held in solidarity with anti-CAA protests.

136. Venkataramakrishnan, "Political Fix."

137. Senior advocate Indira Jaising emphasized this point before the Delhi High Court, seeking an independent investigation into the police brutality at the campus. "Jamia Violence: Delhi Police Acted with 'Sheer Vindictiveness' against Students, Says Indira Jaising," Scroll.in, August 5, 2020, https://scroll.in/latest/969477/jamia-violence-delhi-police-acted-with-sheer -vindictiveness-against-students-says-indira-jaising.

138. On the police operation on the Jamia Millia campus, see "Protests Erupt across India over CAA, Police Action against Jamia Students," *Economic Times*, December 16, 2019, https:// economictimes.indiatimes.com/news/politics-and-nation/from-lucknow-to-hyderabad -protests-across-campuses-against-police-crackdown-in-jamia/articleshow/72743549.cms ?from=mdr; M. Singh, "80 Students Undergo Treatment at Delhi Hospital after Violence at Jamia," *India Today*, December 17, 2019, https://www.indiatoday.in/india/story/jamia-protests -anti-citizenship-amendment-act-caa-injured-hospital-1629100-2019-12-17; "'Cops Entered Bathrooms, Libraries and Beat Up Girls': Jamia Students Recount Sunday Night Horror," News18, December 16, 2019, https://www.news18.com/news/india/cops-entered-bathrooms -libraries-and-beat-up-girls-jamia-students-recount-sunday-night-horror-2425629.html; and "Jamia Protest: Two Men Admitted to Safdarjung Hospital with 'Gunshot Injury', Say Sources," *New India Express*, December 16, 2019, https://www.newindianexpress.com/cities/delhi/2019 /dec/16/jamia-protest-two-men-admitted-to-safdarjung-hospital-with-gunshot-injury-say -sources-2077001.html.

139. The Aligarh Muslim University claimed, retrospectively, that it had invited the police to intervene, but why, in that case, did they break the main gate? See "At Least 60 Injured in Police Crackdown at Aligarh Muslim University," *The Hindu*, December 15, 2019, https://www .thehindu.com/news/national/students-injured-in-police-crackdown-at-aligarh-muslim -university/article30313968.ece. One student's hand had to be amputated. P. Srivastava, "Bared: Police 'Brutality' on AMU Students," *The Telegraph*, December 18, 2019, https://www .telegraphindia.com/india/bared-police-brutality-on-amu-students/cid/1728324.

140. "The Siege of Aligarh Muslim University: A Fact Finding Report—How the UP Police Reduced a University to a Battleground on December 15, 2019," NewsClick, December 24, 2019, https://www.newsclick.in/Siege-Aligarh-Muslim-University-Fact-Finding-Report.

141. "CAA Protests: Video Shows Police Firing at Protesters, Contrary to UP DGP Claims," *Gulf News*, December 23, 2019, https://gulfnews.com/world/asia/india/caa-protests-video-shows-police-firing-at-protesters-contrary-to-up-dgp-claims-1.1577078324096.

142. "7 Killed as U.P. Protests against Citizenship Law Turn Violent," *The Hindu*, December 20, 2020, https://www.thehindu.com/news/national/6-killed-as-up-protests-against-citizenship-law-turn-violent/article30361932.ece.

143. "16 Killed, 263 Cops Injured in Uttar Pradesh in Protests against Citizenship Amendment Act," News18, December 21, 2019, https://www.news18.com/news/india/16-killed-263-cops-injured-in-uttar-pradesh-in-protests-against-citizenship-amendment-act-2432177.html.

144. S. Pandey, "UP Police Admit to Firing at Anti-CAA Protesters," *Deccan Herald*, December 24, 2019, https://www.deccanherald.com/national/national-politics/up-police-admit-to-firing-at-anti-caa-protesters-788388.html.

145. "UP: Postmortem Shows Anti-CAA Protester Killed in Police Firing Was Shot in Eye," *The Week*, January 7, 2020, https://www.theweek.in/news/india/2020/01/07/up-postmortem-shows-anti-caa-protester-killed-in-police-firing-was-shot-in-eye.html; "After Denials, Police Admit They Did Open Fire on December 15 during Anti-CAA Protests," *The Hindu*, January 6, 2020, https://www.thehindu.com/news/cities/Delhi/after-denials-police-admit-they-did-open-fire-on-december-15/article30489076.ece.

146. "Video Suggests UP Cop Opened Fire, Contrary to 'No Police Firing' Claim," YouTube video posted by NDTV, December 21, 2019, https://www.youtube.com/watch?v=2zaHHqyVmfY.

147. "21,500 Booked for Violence in Kanpur," *India Today*, December 24, 2019, https://www.indiatoday.in/amp/india/story/21-500-booked-for-violence-in-kanpur-1631048-2019-12-24.

148. "Anti-CAA Protests: 1,113 Arrests, 5,558 Preventive Detentions, 19 Dead in UP," *India Today*, December 27, 2019, https://www.indiatoday.in/india/story/anti-caa-protests-1-113-arrests-5-558-preventive-detentions-19-dead-in-up-1631814-2019-12-27.

149. See the case of Muzaffarnagar: "Watch: CCTV Captures Police Personnel Allegedly Destroying CCTV outside Mosque in UP's Muzaffarnagar," YouTube video posted by The Quint, December 22, 2019, https://www.youtube.com/watch?v=cV3RbVeCvNg.

150. "Shocking! UP Police Caught Vandalising Property in Muzaffarnagar during Anti-CAA Protests [WATCH]," Times Now, December 25, 2019, https://www.timesnownews.com/india/article/shocking-up-police-caught-vandalising-property-in-muzaffarnagar-during-anti-caa-protests-watch/531626; A. Pandey, "Video Shows Cops Vandalising Shops, Vehicles In UP's Kanpur Amid Protests," NDTV, December 25, 2019, https://www.ndtv.com/india-news/citizenship-amendment-act-video-shows-cops-vandalising-shops-vehicles-in-ups-kanpur-amid-protests-2154193.

151. U. Singh Rana, "Cops Barged into Our Homes at Night, Smashed Everything, Snatched Cash and Jewellery, Say Muzaffarnagar's Muslim Families," News18, December 25, 2019, https://www.news18.com/amp/news/india/cops-barged-into-our-homes-at-night-smashed-everything-snatched-cash-and-jewellery-say-muzaffarnagars-muslim-families-2435565.html.

152. Sagar, "Uttar Pradesh's Police Mitr: A Militia in the Guise of Community Policing?" *The Caravan*, January 25, 2020, https://caravanmagazine.in/politics/uttar-pradesh-police-mitr-spo-civilians.

153. A. Pandey, "UP Police Say 57 Cops Had Bullet Injuries in Clashes: We Found Only One," NDTV, January 4, 2020, https://www.ndtv.com/india-news/citizenship-amendment-act-up-police-say-57-cops-had-bullet-injuries-in-clashes-but-only-one-found-2158556.

154. M. N. Parth, "Watch: In Aftermath of Police Action during Anti-CAA Protests in Bihar's Aurangabad, Video Proof Emerges of Cops Wrecking Vehicles, Barging into Homes," FirstPost, January 3, 2020, https://www.firstpost.com/india/watch-in-aftermath-of-police-action-during-anti-caa-protests-in-bihars-aurangabad-video-proof-emerges-of-cops-wrecking-vehicles-barging-into-homes-7855681.html.

155. "Anti-CAA Stir: Video Shows Cops Smashing Windshields of Parked Vehicles in MP's Jabalpur," News18, December 26, 2019, https://www.news18.com/news/india/anti-caa-stir-video-shows-cops-smashing-windshields-of-parked-vehicles-in-mps-jabalpur-2436777.html.

156. "Siege of Aligarh Muslim University."

157. P. Nair, "'I Felt Like a Jew in Hitler's Germany': Sadaf Jafar on Police Detention," Outlook, January 15, 2020, https://www.outlookindia.com/website/story/india-news-i-felt-like-a-jew-in-hitlers-germany-sadaf-jafar-on-police-detention/345729.

158. N. Suresh and S. Ali, "UP Police Detained 41 Children during CAA Protests, Some Were Tortured, Says Citizens' Report," Scroll.in, February 13, 2020, https://scroll.in/article/952964/up-police-detained-41-children-during-caa-protests-some-were-tortured-says-citizens-report.

159. S. Sen and N. Singaravelu, "How Many People Died during Anti-CAA Protests?," The Hindu, January 6, 2020, https://www.thehindu.com/data/data-how-many-people-died-during-anti-caa-protests/article30494183.ece.

160. O. Rashid, "Not a Single Person Died by Police Bullet during Anti-CAA Protests: Adityanath," The Hindu, February 19, 2020, https://www.thehindu.com/news/national/not-a-single-person-died-of-police-bullet-during-anti-caa-protests-adityanath/article30860925.ece.

161. "'If Someone Is Coming to Die, How Can He Be Alive': Yogi on Deaths in Anti-CAA Violence," Indian Express, February 19, 2020, https://indianexpress.com/article/india/yogi-adityanath-anti-caa-protest-deaths-up-police-6276134/.

162. R. Chatterji, "Press Button with Such Anger that Shaheen Bagh Feels Current, Says Amit Shah," Huffington Post, January 27, 2020, https://www.huffingtonpost.in/entry/delhi-assembly-elections-2020-amit-shah-shaheen-bagh_in_5e2e62d9c5b67d8874b4f4d7.

163. Report of the DMC Fact-Finding Committee on North-East Delhi Riots of February 2020 (Delhi: Delhi Minorities Commission, Government of NCT of Delhi, 2020), 27, accessed August 31, 2020, https://ia601906.us.archive.org/11/items/dmc-delhi-riot-fact-report-2020/-Delhi-riots-Fact-Finding-2020.pdf.

164. "'Will Remove Shaheen Bagh Protesters, Mosques on State Land': West Delhi BJP MP Parvesh Verma's Poll Promise," FirstPost, January 28, 2020, https://www.firstpost.com/politics/will-remove-shaheen-bagh-protesters-mosques-on-state-land-west-delhi-bjp-mp-parvesh-vermas-poll-promise-7965961.html.

165. DMC Fact-Finding Committee, 28.

166. G. Radha-Udaykumar, "BJP's Tajinder Bagga Warns Shaheen Bagh of Surgical Strike on Feb 11," India Today, January 30, 2020, https://www.indiatoday.in/elections/delhi-assembly-polls-2020/story/tajinder-bagga-bjp-on-shaheen-bagh-1641578-2020-01-30.

167. "Shaheen Bagh, Biryani, Bullets, Pakistan—What Yogi Adityanath Said at Delhi Rallies," ThePrint, February 2, 2020, https://theprint.in/politics/shaheen-bagh-biryani-bullets-pakistan -what-yogi-adityanath-said-at-delhi-rallies/358759/.

168. For a sample of the "posts that call[ed] for violence against minorities and for the protection and making of a Hindu Rashtra," see P. Kavish, "Delhi Riots Carefully Orchestrated Using Social Media?," Sabrang, February 29, 2020, https://sabrangindia.in/decoding-hate /delhi-riots-carefully-orchestrated-using-social-media.

169. M. Singh Manral, "WhatsApp Groups Created to Spread Hate Just before Surge in Delhi Violence: Police Probe," Indian Express, March 4, 2020, https://indianexpress.com/article /cities/delhi/whatsapp-group-delhi-violence-police-probe-kapil-mishra-anti-caa-protest -6298099/.

170. V. Mubayi, "After Losing Delhi Election, BJP Wreaking Vengeance on City's Minorities," Alternatives International, February 29, 2020, https://www.alterinter.org/?After-Losing-Delhi -Election-BJP-Wreaking-Vengeance-On-City-s-Minorities.

171. DMC Fact-Finding Committee, 31.

172. B. Taskin, "Zuckerberg Uses Kapil Mishra's 'Delhi Riots Threat' to Outline Facebook's Hate Speech Policy" ThePrint, August 31, 2020, https://theprint.in/india/zuckerberg-uses -kapil-mishras-delhi-riots-threat-to-outline-facebooks-hate-speech-policy/435845/.

173. A BJP MP of Delhi, Gautam Gambhir considered Kapil Mishra's speech "not acceptable." D. Dutta Roy, "'Kapil Mishra's Speech Unacceptable': BJP's Gautam Gambhir on Delhi Violence," NDTV, February 25, 2020, https://www.ndtv.com/india-news/delhi-violence -gautam-gambhir-says-kapil-mishras-speech-unacceptable-2185318. A Bengal BJP leader, Subhadra Mukherjee, even resigned, saying that she could not be in the same party as Kapil Mishra and Anurag Thakur because of their "brand of politics." "Delhi Violence: Bengal BJP Leader Resigns, Says Can't Be in a Party with Anurag Thakur, Kapil Mishra," Scroll.in, March 1, 2020, https://scroll.in/latest/954793/delhi-violence-bengal-bjp-leader-resigns-says-cant-be-in-a -party-with-anurag-thakur-kapil-mishra.

174. After the riots, one of the police's charge sheets said: "As per the chat of [the Kattar Hindu Ekta] WhatsApp group, the accused persons . . . conspired to teach Muslims a lesson for attacking the Hindus. They equipped themselves with lathis, danda, sticks, swords, firearms, etc., and killed nine innocent Muslim persons including Hashim Ali and his brother Aamir Khan." A. Mohan, "Riot Accused Thought Themselves Saviours of Community: Chargesheet," Indian Express, October 7, 2020, https://indianexpress.com/article/cities/delhi/delhi-riot -accused-thought-themselves-saviours-of-community-chargesheet-6705963/.

175. "BJP MLA Abhay Verma Leads East Delhi March with 'Goli maaro saalo ko' as Mob Violence Continues," Scroll.in, February 26, 2020, https://scroll.in/video/954331/bjp-mla -abhay-verma-leads-east-delhi-march-with-goli-maaro-saalo-ko-as-mob-violence-continues.

176. DMC Fact-Finding Committee, 34. Acid was also thrown at the faces of men and women. Delhi Minorities Commission, 50.

177. Also in contrast to what happened in Gujarat, the assailants apparently belonged to upper castes. Sagar, a journalist working for The Caravan, reported: "Many men among them wore t-shirts that had 'Brahman,' 'Jat' and 'Jai Shri Ram' written on them and from my conversation with them I gleaned that many of them belonged to other upper castes such as Rajputs and

Baniyas." Sagar, "Hindu Supremacist Mobs Orchestrate Violence against Muslims Where BJP Won in Delhi Elections," *The Caravan*, February 25, 2020, https://caravanmagazine.in/religion /delhi-violence-north-east-maujpur-jaffrabad-babarpur-muslims-hindu. During the riots, Kapil Mishra and his supporters, in his speeches and in their slogans, arraigned the Dalits: "Beat the Dalits" was one of their mottos. And he said: "Those who clean the toilets of our homes, should we now place them on a pedestal?" Prabhijit Singh, "Dead and Buried," *The Caravan*, June 21, 2020, https://caravanmagazine.in/politics/delhi-police-ignored-complaints-against-kapil -mishra-bjp-leaders-leading-mobs-delhi-violence.

178. P. Singh, "Dead and Buried"; and A. Menon and A. S. Iyer, "Delhi Riots Exclusive: BJP Councillor Led Mob, Claims 'Eyewitness,'" *The Quint*, June 30, 2020, https://www.thequint .com/news/politics/delhi-riots-bjp-councillor-kanhaiya-lal-kapil-mishra-jagdish-pradhan -muslims.

179. Women were assaulted in many different ways. The DMC fact-finding committee devotes a full section of its report to this issue. *DMC Fact-Finding Committee*, 61–68.

180. Shams Ur Rehman Alavi, "Delhi Horror: Documenting the Organised Mob Violence and Killings in India's National Capital," NewsBits, March 4, 2020, http://www.newsbits.in/delhi -horror-documenting-the-organised-mob-violence-and-killings-in-indias-national-capital.

181. A businessman who happened to be a BJP cadre said that his factory had been burned because he had a "Muslim name," suggesting that, like in Gujarat in 2002, the rioters were using lists of residents—maybe the voters lists. "Factory Burnt, BJP Man Says Ignored by Party because 'I Have Muslim Name,'" *Indian Express*, March 5, 2020, https://indianexpress.com /article/cities/delhi/factory-burnt-bjp-man-says-ignored-by-party-6299749/.

182. In Tyre Market, the fire brigade that had rushed to the place was attacked physically. *DMC Fact-Finding Committee*, 48.

183. Anjali Mody, "In Photos: Fourteen Delhi Mosques and a Dargah that Were Burnt by Hindutva Vigilantes in Three Days," Scroll.in, March 12, 2020, https://scroll.in/article/955713 /in-photos-fifteen-muslim-shrines-in-delhi-that-were-burnt-by-hindutva-vigilantes-in-three -days.

184. See the list of the twenty-two mosques, madrassas, and cemeteries that have been destroyed: *DMC Fact-Finding Committee*, 124.

185. *DMC Fact-Finding Committee*, 47. Nine of the 40 Muslims who were killed during the Delhi riots were assaulted because they refused to chant "Jai Shri Ram." "List of Muslims Killed or Assaulted after Refused to Chant 'Jai Shri Ram,'" *Maktoob*, August 5, 2020, https:// maktoobmedia.com/2020/08/05/list-of-muslims-killed-or-assaulted-after-refused-to-chant-jai -shri-ram/.

186. Cited in *DMC Fact-Finding Committee*, 50.

187. Cited in *DMC Fact-Finding Committee*, 65.

188. P. Singh, "Dead and Buried."

189. The architects of the riots had asked the assailants "to make videos of two–four of them being burnt alive" according to one of the complainants who heard them saying these words. P. Singh, "Dead and Buried." See also "Delhi Violence: A Rioter Posted This Live Video during Mob Action This Week," Scroll.in, March 1, 2020, https://scroll.in/video/954741/delhi-violence -a-rioter-posted-this-live-video-during-mob-action-earlier-this-week.

190. See the list in *DMC Fact-Finding Committee*, 111–18.

191. S. Vadarajan, "Delhi Police Affidavit Shows Muslims Bore Brunt of Riots, Silent on Who Targeted Them and Why," The Wire, July 16, 2020, https://thewire.in/communalism/delhi-police-affidavit-shows-muslims-bore-brunt-of-riots-silent-on-who-targeted-them-and-why.

192. J. Sinha, "Delhi: Riot-Hit Families Line Up outside Eidgah in Mustafabad, Now a Relief Centre," *Indian Express*, March 4, 2020, https://indianexpress.com/article/cities/delhi/delhi-riot-hit-families-line-up-outside-eidgah-in-mustafabad-now-a-relief-centre-6298053/.

193. T. Aswani, "Muslims in Northeast Delhi Sell Homes below Market Rate to Escape 'Continuing Harassment,'" The Wire, October 30, 2020, https://thewire.in/communalism/muslims-northeast-delhi-sell-homes-harassment-riots.

194. V. Sachdev, "Justice Muralidhar Will Not Continue Hearing Hate Speech FIR Case," The Quint, February 26, 2020, https://www.thequint.com/news/law/justice-muralidhar-delhi-violence-fir-case-hate-speech-transferred-chief-justice-high-court.

195. Sachdev, "Justice Muralidhar Will Not Continue Hearing Hate Speech FIR Case."

196. A. Pandey and S. Tantray, "A Hindu Rioter Speaks: Delhi Violence Was 'Revenge' against Muslims, Police Gave Free reign," *The Caravan*, July 31, 2020, https://caravanmagazine.in/crime/delhi-rioter-testimony-hindu-revenge-muslims-police-free-reign.

197. Pandey and Tantray, "A Hindu Rioter Speaks."

198. After the riots, policemen told the *New York Times* that, when the riots started, "officers in the affected areas were ordered to deposit their guns at the station houses." Jeffrey Gettleman, Sameer Yasir, Suhasini Raj, and Hari Kumar, "How Delhi's Police Turned against Muslims," *New York Times*, March 12, 2020, https://www.nytimes.com/2020/03/12/world/asia/india-police-muslims.html.

199. *DMC Fact-Finding Committee*, 71.

200. *DMC Fact-Finding Committee*, 36.

201. Cited in *DMC Fact-Finding Committee*, 81.

202. *DMC Fact-Finding Committee*, 74.

203. *DMC Fact-Finding Committee*, 65.

204. P. Singh, "Dead and Buried."

205. K. Shroff, "Men in Uniform Torched Mustafabad's Farooqia Masjid, Assaulted People Inside: Locals," *The Caravan*, March 11, 2020, https://caravanmagazine.in/conflict/men-in-uniform-torched-mustafabads-farooqia-masjid-assaulted-people-inside-locals. See also K. Shroff, "Delhi Violence: Cops Shouted 'Jai Shri Ram' with Armed Hindu Mob, Charged at Muslims," *The Caravan*, February 25, 2020, https://caravanmagazine.in/conflict/delhi-violence-cops-shouted-jai-shri-ram-with-armed-hindu-mob-charged-at-muslims.

206. *DMC Fact-Finding Committee*, 40, 45.

207. *DMC Fact-Finding Committee*, 44.

208. "IB Staffer Ankit Sharma, Killed in Delhi Riots, Was Stabbed 12 Times & Had 33 Blunt Injuries," ThePrint, March 14, 2020, https://theprint.in/india/ib-staffer-ankit-sharma-killed-in-delhi-riots-was-stabbed-12-times-and-not-400-times/380720/.

209. The *New York Times*, whose journalists emphasize that "Delhi's police turned against Muslims," mentions the fact that not only one police officer was killed but that eighty others were injured, especially when Muslim protesters outnumbered the police. Gettleman et al., "Delhi's Police Turned."

210. Cited in *DMC Fact-Finding Committee*, 77.

211. A. Yadav, "Ground Report: Delhi Police Actions Caused Death of Man in Infamous National Anthem Video," Huffington Post, March 2, 2020, https://www.huffingtonpost.in /entry/delhi-riots-police-national-anthem-video-faizan_in_5e5bb8e1c5b6010221126276. See also "Delhi Violence: Video Showed Men Being Made to Sing Anthem, One Is Now Dead," *Indian Express*, February 29, 2020, https://indianexpress.com/article/cities/delhi/delhi -violence-video-national-anthem-6291881/.

212. See, for instance, "Delhi Riots: 'Hero Cop' Who Braved a Mob to Save Lives," BBC, February 28, 2020, https://www.bbc.com/news/world-asia-india-51670093.

213. "Delhi Police Is Ignoring Complaints and Scuttling Investigation in Communal Violence Cases," Scroll.in, March 11, 2020, https://scroll.in/article/955748/delhi-police-is-ignoring -complaints-and-scuttling-investigation-in-communal-violence-cases.

214. P. Singh, "Dead and Buried."

215. "Siege of Aligarh Muslim University."

216. "Siege of Aligarh Muslim University."

217. Suresh and Ali, "UP Police Detained."

218. "Police Action Damaged 25 CCTV Cameras on Campus, Jamia Tells MHRD," The Wire, February 19, 2020, https://thewire.in/rights/police-action-damaged-25-cctv-cameras-on -campus-jamia-tells-mhrd.

219. V. Lalwani, "In Delhi Violence Investigation, a Disturbing Pattern: Victims End Up Being Prosecuted by Police," Scroll.in, May 23, 2020, https://scroll.in/article/962526/in-delhi -violence-investigation-a-disturbing-pattern-victims-end-up-being-arrested-by-police.

220. For more detail, see P. Singh, "Dead and Buried."

221. S. Yasser and K. Schultz, "India Rounds Up Critics under Shadow of Virus Crisis, Activ- ists Say," *New York Times*, July 19, 2020, https://www.nytimes.com/2020/07/19/world/asia /india-activists-arrests-riots-coronavirus.html.

222. A. Bedi, "Delhi Minorities Commission Chief Charged with Sedition for 'Provocative' Social Media Post," ThePrint, May 2, 2020, https://theprint.in/india/delhi-minorities -commission-chief-charged-with-sedition-for-provocative-social-media-post/413112/.

223. S. Sharma, "Delhi Police, Your Bias Is Showing: Look at Your Own Data on the Riots Investigation," Scroll.in, September 18, 2020, https://scroll.in/article/973400/delhi-police-your -bias-is-showing-look-at-your-own-data-on-the-riots-investigation.

224. "In LS Debate on Delhi Riots, Amit Shah Lauds Police for 'Controlling Violence in 36 Hours,'" The Wire, March 11, 2020, https://thewire.in/communalism/lok-sabha-delhi-riots -amit-shah.

225. The deployment of the NSA in a riot-affected area remains a mysterious, unprecedented decision. See "Ajit Doval's Deployment to Quell Delhi Violence beyond NSA's Role; Here's Why Modi Had to Rely on His Man Friday to Clean Up MHA's Mess," FirstPost, February 28, 2020, https://www.firstpost.com/india/ajit-dovals-deployment-to-quell-delhi-violence -beyond-nsas-role-heres-why-modi-had-to-rely-on-his-man-friday-to-clean-up-mhas-mess -8098561.html.

226. "Artistes Release Statement against 'Witch-Hunt' of Students by Delhi Police," *New Indian Express*, April 19, 2020, https://www.newindianexpress.com/nation/2020/apr/19 /artistes-release-statement-against-witch-hunt-of-students-by-delhi-police-2132313.html.

227. Sagar, "Detentions, Arrests, Interrogations: Fear Reigns in Muslim Neighborhoods of Northeast Delhi," *The Caravan*, March 11, 2020, https://caravanmagazine.in/conflict/detentions -delhi-violence-northeast-muslim-arrests-riots-police-crime-branch.

228. "LS Debate on Delhi Riots."

229. Ankit Sharma had, in fact, been stabbed, twelve times. A. Bhardwaj, "IB Staffer Ankit Sharma, Killed in Delhi riots, was stabbed 12 times & had 33 blunt injuries," ThePrint, March 13, 2020, https://theprint.in/india/ib-staffer-ankit-sharma-killed-in-delhi-riots-was-stabbed-12 -times-and-not-400-times/380720/.

230. The police order cited by the *Organiser* accused one of these two channels. Media One simply reported that "violence took place mostly in Muslim dominated area of Chand Bagh, Delhi. While telecasting the news, the channel carried the news of stone pelting, arson and injured people being taken to hospital." In other words, the channel showed the reality. "Delhi Anti-Hindu Riots: I&B Ministry Bans Two Malayalam Channels for 48 Hours for 'Promoting Communal and Anti-National Attitude,'" *The Organiser*, March 6, 2020, https://www.organiser .org/Encyc/2020/3/6/Ministry-bans-two-Malayalam-channels-.html. At least a dozen of journalists were attacked while they were covering the Delhi riots and when they investigated subsequently (S. Basu, "Delhi: The Anatomy of a Riot," *The Diplomat*, February 27, 2020, https:// thediplomat.com/2020/02/delhi-the-anatomy-of-a-riot/).

231. N. K. Azad, "'I Am a Simple Karyakarta, and Their Problem Is I Dared to Stand against Their Might,'" *The Organiser*, March 6, 2020, https://www.organiser.org/Encyc/2020/3/6 /Kapil-Mishra-BJP-Interview-I-am-a-simple-Karyakarta.html.

232. "Kapil Mishra Raises More Than Rs 71 Lakh for Hindu Victims of Delhi Riots," The Wire, March 2, 2020, https://thewire.in/communalism/kapil-mishra-crowdfunding-campaign -hindu-victims-delhi-riots.

233. "Kapil Mishra Raises More."

234. "Delhi Police Books Umar Khalid & Jamia Students under UAPA for Northeast Delhi Violence," ThePrint, April 21, 2020, https://theprint.in/india/delhi-police-books-umar-khalid -jamia-students-under-uapa-for-northeast-delhi-violence/406259/.

235. B. Sharma, "Delhi Riots: How The Police Is Using FIR 59 to Imprison Students and Activists Indefinitely," Huffington Post, June 16, 2020, https://www.huffingtonpost.in/entry /delhi-police-riots-students-anti-caa-activists-arrest_in_5ee7ab99c5b651a404b0591a. See also S. Pasha, "The Delhi Violence FIRs Are Like Blank Cheques, to Be Encashed by the Police Any Time," The Wire, April 30, 2020, https://thewire.in/communalism/the-delhi-violence-firs-are -like-blank-cheques-to-be-encashed-by-the-police-any-time.

236. A. Iyer and A. Menon, "Delhi Riots: Is Trump Visit a Hole in Police's Conspiracy Theory?," The Quint, June 12, 2020, https://www.thequint.com/news/india/delhi-riots-trump-visit -police-conspiracy-theory-tahir-hussain-umar-khalid.

237. In a supplementary charge sheet that was filed in connection with the Delhi riots but only to do with the anti-CAA mobilization, it was alleged that Yogendra Yadav had "instructed" a JNU PhD student, Sharjeel Imam (who had been arrested), in mobilizing students of Jamia Millia Islamia, Aligarh University, and Delhi University. According to the charge sheet, the protest at Jamia was meant to "paralyse, destabilise and disintegrate Delhi by undertaking unlawful activity." B. Sinha, "Yogendra Yadav 'Instructed' Imam to Mobilise Students for Anti-

CAA Protests, Says Delhi Police," ThePrint, November 28, 2020, https://theprint.in/india/yogendra-yadav-instructed-imam-to-mobilise-students-for-anti-caa-protests-says-delhi-police/553745/.

238. Sanjeev Uniyal, "Anti-Hindu Delhi Riots," *The Organiser*, June 12, 2020, https://www.organiser.org/Encyc/2020/6/12/Fire-of-Hatred.html.

239. M. Singh Manral, "Tahir Hussain Chargesheet Claims Delhi Riots Planning Began in January," *Indian Express*, June 3, 2020, https://indianexpress.com/article/cities/delhi/tahir-chargesheet-claims-planning-began-in-jan-6439867/.

240. This man, Khalid Saifi, who has been tortured in jail, apparently, is considered by the police as "a go-between for Umar Khalid and Tahir Hussain. . . . The police also claim that Saifi met and received money from Zakir Naik, an Islamic preacher and fugitive wanted by the Indian government, and that he is a key conspirator who instigated the Delhi Riots that claimed 52 lives." B. Sharma, "I Don't Fear Investigation, but He Deserves Bail: Khalid Saifi's Wife as He Completes Four Months in Jail," Huffington Post, June 29, 2020, https://www.huffingtonpost.in/entry/khalid-saifi-bail-delhi-riots-delhi-police_in_5ef37957c5b615e5cd37e8fb.

241. V. Singh, "India: Charged with Anti-Terror Law, Pregnant Woman Sent to Jail," Al Jazeera, April 26, 2020, https://www.aljazeera.com/news/2020/04/india-charged-anti-terror-law-pregnant-woman-jail-200426100956360.html.

242. Asif Iqbal Tanha, a member of the Students Islamic Organisation (the student union of the Jama'at-e-Islami), took an active part in the Jamia Coordination Committee that mobilized students against the CAA. "Delhi Police Slaps UAPA against Jamia Student Asif Iqbal Tanha; Shaheen Bagh Resident 'Part of Conspiracy' behind February Riots, Say Cops," First-Post, May 21, 2020, https://www.firstpost.com/india/delhi-police-slaps-uapa-against-jamia-student-asif-iqbal-tanha-shaheen-bagh-resident-part-of-conspiracy-behind-february-riots-say-cops-8393691.html.

243. Sharma, "Delhi Riots."

244. Zargar was eventually granted bail, because she was in the second trimester of her first pregnancy. On the way, the pregnancy of Zargar—a twenty-seven-year-old married woman—was "explained" by a TV anchor. See M. Arif, "Actor Payal Rohatgi's Outburst against Safoora Zargar Typifies Right Wing Obsession with Muslim Sexuality," FirstPost, June 25, 2020, https://www.firstpost.com/india/actor-payal-rohatgis-outburst-against-safoora-zargar-typifies-right-wing-obsession-with-muslim-sexuality-8482581.html.

245. "Sharjeel Imam Chargesheeted in Seditious Speech Case," *Economic Times*, April 18, 2020, https://economictimes.indiatimes.com/news/politics-and-nation/sharjeel-imam-chargesheeted-in-seditious-speech-case/articleshow/75217894.cms?from=mdr.

246. B. Sinha, "Sharjeel 'Radicalised' by Books He Read for Thesis on Partition, Delhi Police Chargesheet Says," ThePrint, October 27, 2020, https://theprint.in/india/sharjeel-radicalised-by-books-he-read-for-thesis-on-partition-delhi-police-chargesheet-says/506598/.

247. S. Pacha, "NHRC Blames Jamia Students for Police Violence, Wants 'Real Motive' of Anti-CAA Protest Probed," The Wire, June 26, 2020, https://thewire.in/rights/nhrc-blames-jamia-students-for-police-violence-wants-real-motive-of-anti-caa-protest-probed.

248. "CAA Protests: Will Seize Properties of Those Who Indulge in Violence, Says Yogi Adityanath," *India Today*, December 19, 2019, https://www.indiatoday.in/india/story/caa

-protests-will-seize-properties-of-those-who-indulge-in-violence-says-yogi-adityanath-1629778
-2019-12-19.

249. K. Abhishek, "CAA Protests: UP Government Starts Process to Seize Property of Protesters Involved in Violence," *India Today*, December 22, 2019, https://www.indiatoday.in/india
/story/caa-protests-up-government-starts-process-seize-property-protesters-involved
-violence-1630471-2019-12-22.

250. "Anti-CAA Protests: Sadaf, Darapuri among 28 Told to Pay Rs 63 Lakh as Damage to Property," *Indian Express*, February 20, 2020, https://indianexpress.com/article/india/anti-caa
-protests-sadaf-darapuri-among-28-told-to-pay-rs-63-lakh-as-damage-to-property-6276661/.

251. D. Tiwary, "Explained: What Is a Police Commissionerate System?" *Indian Express*,
January 15, 2020, https://indianexpress.com/article/explained/explained-what-is-the
-commissionerate-system-recently-implemented-in-lucknow-noida-6214871/.

252. A. Pandey, "CAA Violence-Accused 'Named and Shamed' on Yogi Adityanath's Orders,"
NDTV, March 6, 2020, https://www.ndtv.com/india-news/in-lucknow-up-government-names
-and-shames-caa-violence-accused-with-hoardings-2190735.

253. "Mumbai BJP Chief Honours Uber Driver for Informing Cops about Man Who Discussed Anti-CAA Protest in His Cab," *India Today*, February 8, 2020, https://www.indiatoday
.in/india/story/mumbai-bjp-chief-honours-uber-driver-for-informing-cops-about-man-who
-discussed-anti-caa-protest-in-his-cab-1644485-2020-02-08.

254. S. Modak, "Can't Label Anti-CAA Protesters Traitors . . . Need to Protect Rights: Bombay High Court," *Indian Express*, February 15, 2020, https://indianexpress.com/article/india
/bombay-high-court-anti-caa-protesters-traitors-6268888/.

255. A. Ingole, "Movements as Politics: Bhima Koregaon in the Times of Hindutva," *Economic and Political Weekly* 53, no. 2 (January 13, 2018), https://www.epw.in/journal/2018/2
/commentary/movements-politics.html.

256. K. Iyer and S. Khapre, "Amid Second Round of Arrests and Maoist Link Claims, a Look at Why Elgaar Has Come to Matter," *Indian Express*, September 2, 2018, https://indianexpress
.com/article/india/why-elgaar-parishad-has-come-to-matter-december-31-2017-bhima
-koregaon-pune-police-5335510/.

257. A. Johari, A. Dey, M. Charian, and S. Satheesh, "From Pune to Paris: How a Police Investigation Turned a Dalit Meeting into a Maoist Plot," Scroll.in, September 2, 2018, https://
scroll.in/article/892850/from-pune-to-paris-how-a-police-investigation-turned-a-dalit
-meeting-into-a-maoist-plot.

258. "Many Friends of Sanbhaji Bhide: Bhima Koregaon Riots Accused Enjoys Massive Social Media Following, including Tushar Damgude," FirstPost, August 29, 2018, https://www
.firstpost.com/india/many-friends-of-sambhaji-bhide-bhima-koregoan-riots-accused-enjoys
-massive-social-media-following-including-tushar-damgude-5066761.html.

259. A. Dey, "Bhima Koregaon: Hindutva Leader Milind Ekbote Is Lying Low after Getting Bail," Scroll.in, September 5, 2018, https://scroll.in/article/893032/bhima-koregaon-hindutva
-leader-milind-ekbote-is-lying-low-after-getting-bail.

260. "Bhima Koregaon Exclusive: 'Secret' Official Report Blames Sambhaji Bhide and Milind Ekbote for the Violence," Times Now, September 1, 2018, https://www.timesnownews.com
/india/article/exclusive-bhima-koregaon-violence-secret-state-documents-pune-police
-maharashtra-government-accuse-sambhaji-bhide-milind-ekbote-for-clashes-hindutva/278017.

261. Johari et al., "From Pune to Paris."

262. Subsequently, Jaitley spoke of "half Maoists," describing them as "a serious threat to Indian democracy. Willingly or otherwise, they become over-ground face of the underground." Cited in G. Singh, "The State Is Using the 'Maoist' Label to Muzzle Liberal Criticism," The Wire, August 28, 2018, https://thewire.in/rights/the-state-is-using-the-maoist-label-to-muzzle-liberal-criticism.

263. Vivek Agnihotri, *Urban Naxals: The Making of Buddha in a Traffic Jam* (Gurugram, India: Garuda Prakashan, 2018).

264. D. Grey, "RSS Circulates Booklet Targeting 'Urban Naxals,'" Sabrang, July 22, 2019, https://sabrangindia.in/article/rss-circulates-booklet-targeting-urban-naxals.

265. "Naxalites Have Now Come to Cities, Are Trying to Influence People: Rajnath Singh," *Hindustan Times*, September 1, 2018, https://www.hindustantimes.com/india-news/naxalites-have-now-come-to-cities-are-trying-to-influence-people-rajnath-singh/story-fdHc6NmfOTvfn7ThzdWhEN.html.

266. "Citizenship Act Protests: 'Urban Naxals' Instigating Students for Their Politics, Claims PM Modi," Scroll.in, December 17, 2019, https://scroll.in/latest/947096/citizenship-act-protests-urban-naxals-instigating-students-for-their-politics-claims-pm-modi.

267. On the publicity orchestrated around attempts at killing Narendra Modi—which is part of the repertoire of victimization—see Tushar Dhara, "The Many Plots to Assassinate Narendra Modi," *The Caravan*, September 2, 2018, https://caravanmagazine.in/politics/many-plots-to-assassinate-narendra-modi.

268. See P. Chakrabarti, "Varava Rao: Understanding His Politics, Literary Work, and the Elgar Parishad Case," *Indian Express*, July 17, 2020, https://indianexpress.com/article/explained/varavara-rao-politics-jail-coronavirus-6510434/.

269. On the career of Sudha Bharadwaj, see M. Gupta, "'If You Try to Be Safe and in the Middle, You Will Never Succeed,'" The Wire, September 28, 2018, https://thewire.in/rights/a-woman-must-develop-her-own-identity-and-not-be-subsumed-by-the-collective.

270. See his open letter: "'I Can't Counter State Propaganda': Anand Teltumbde's Open Letter a Day before He Is to Be Arrested," Scroll.in, April 13, 2020, https://scroll.in/article/959082/i-cant-counter-state-propaganda-anand-teltumbes-open-letter-a-day-before-he-is-to-be-arrested.

271. N. Sharma, "Delhi Professor Arrested in Bhima Koregaon Case over 'Maoist ideology,'" NDTV, July 28, 2020, https://www.ndtv.com/india-news/du-professor-hany-babu-arrested-in-bhima-koregaon-case-over-maoist-ideology-2270381.

272. "Explained: Who Is Stan Swamy, the Latest to Be Arrested in the Elgar Parishad Case?," *Indian Express*, October 17, 2020, https://indianexpress.com/article/explained/who-is-stan-swamy-6717126/. See also Swamy's interview by C. Choudhary, "If you raise questions, you are anti-government, anti-national: Adivasi-rights activist Stan Swamy on the Bhima-Koregaon crackdown," *The Caravan*, September 3, 2018, https://caravanmagazine.in/government-policy/interview-adivasi-rights-activist-stan-swamy-bhima-koregaon-crackdown.

273. M. Kaushik and A. Sivan, "Bhima Koregaon Case: Prison-Rights Activist Rona Wilson's Hard Disk Contained Malware that Allowed Remote Access," *The Caravan*, March 12, 2020, https://caravanmagazine.in/politics/bhima-koregaon-case-rona-wilson-hard-disk-malware-remote-access.

274. P. Nair, "Bhima Koregaon Files: The Story Of Nine Activists Being Punished Without Trial," *Outlook*, September 23, 2019, https://magazine.outlookindia.com/story/india-news -bhima-koregaon-files-the-story-of-nine-innocent-activists-being-punished-without-trial /302119.

275. S. Janyala, "Elgaar Parishad Probe: Policemen Referred to My Caste, Asked Why No Sindoor, Says Arrested Activist Varavara Rao's Daughter," *Indian Express*, August 30, 2018, https://indianexpress.com/article/india/elgaar-parishad-probe-policemen-referred-to-my -caste-asked-why-no-sindoor-says-arrested-activist-varavara-raos-daughter-5331859/.

276. Janyala, "Elgaar Parishad Probe."

277. A.P. Shah, "The Only Institution Capable of Stopping the Death of Democracy Is Aiding It," The Wire, September 18, 2020, https://thewire.in/law/supreme-court-rights-uapa-bjp -nda-master-of-roster.

278. T. Anwar, "Bhima Koregaon: Differentiate between Dissent and Attempts to Overthrow Govt Using Arms, Says SC," NewsClick, September 19, 2018, https://www.newsclick.in/bhima -koregaon-differentiate-between-dissent-and-attempts-overthrow-govt-using-arms-says-sc.

279. R. Chandra, "Activists' Arrests: The Exceptional Has Been Made the New Normal," The Wire, November 1, 2018, https://thewire.in/rights/activists-arrests-the-exceptional-has-been -made-the-new-normal.

280. One was made to recite the Hanuman Chalisa and then to drop his pants to show that he was not a Muslim—a common occurrence during the riots. They then took his phone and handed him over to the police. P. L. Vincent, "Delhi Violence: Forced to Drop Pants, Says Journalist," *The Telegraph*, February 26, 2020, https://www.telegraphindia.com/india/delhi-violence -forced-to-drop-pants-says-journalist/cid/1749013.

281. *Democracy for All? V-Dem Annual Democracy Report 2018*, V-Dem Institute, University of Gothenburg, Sweden, 2019, 29, accessed September 15, 2020, https://www.v-dem.net/media /filer_public/68/51/685150f0-47e1-4d03-97bc-45609c3f158d/v-dem_annual_dem_report _2018.pdf.

282. *Democracy for All?*, 33. For more details, see Sten Widmalm, "Is India's Democracy Really in Decline?," The Wire, April 6, 2019, https://thewire.in/politics/is-indias-democracy -really-in-decline; and S. Widmalm, "Under Modi Govt, a Two-Pronged Attack on India's Democracy," The Wire, April 7, 2019, https://thewire.in/politics/india-democracy-modi -government.

283. *Autocratization Surges—Resistance Grows: Democracy Report 2020*, V-Dem Institute, Stockholm, March 2020, 4, accessed January 7, 2021, https://www.v-dem.net/media/filer _public/de/39/de39af54-0bc5-4421-89ae-fb20dcc53dba/democracy_report.pdf. According to the Institute's criteria, India was ranked 90 out of 179 countries (p. 34).

284. Economist Intelligence Unit, *Democracy Index 2019: A Year of Democratic Setbacks and Popular Protest*, 2020, 26–27, accessed September 15, 2020, https://www.eiu.com/topic /democracy-index.

285. I. Vasquez and F. McMahon, *The Human Freedom Index: A Global Measurement of Personal, Civil, and Economic Freedom* (Washington and Vancouver: CATO Institute and Fraser Institute, 2020), 22, https://www.cato.org/sites/cato.org/files/2020-12/human-freedom-index -2020.pdf.

286. Freedom House, *Freedom in the World 2020*, Washington, DC, 2020, 3, accessed September 16, 2020, https://freedomhouse.org/sites/default/files/2020-02/FIW_2020_REPORT _BOOKLET_Final.pdf.

287. A. Joshua, "India Crashes on Freedom Index," *Telegraph*, March 4, 2020, https://www .telegraphindia.com/india/india-crashes-on-freedom-index/cid/1751136.

Chapter 11

1. This chapter draws from my contribution to the Muslims in India in a Time of Hindu Majoritarianism project supported by the Henry Luce Foundation. I am very grateful to all the participants for their remarks on the previous versions of this text.

2. Nithya Subramanian and Shoaib Daniyal, "The Election Fix: Muslims Are Constantly Discussed but Seriously Underrepresented in Indian Politics," Scroll.in, April 21, 2019, https:// scroll.in/article/920747/the-election-fix-muslims-are-constantly-discussed-but-seriously -underrepresented-in-indian-politics; and F. Agnes, "Aggressive Hindu Nationalism: Contextualising the Triple Talaq Controversy," in *Majoritarian State: How Hindu Nationalism Is Changing India*, ed. Angana Chatterji, Thomas Blom Hansens, and Christophe Jaffrelot (London: Hurst, 2019), 335–52.

3. "Narendra Modi Independence Day 2019 Full Speech: PM Says New Approach Was Needed in J&K, $5 Trillion Economy Target Is Achievable," FirstPost, August 15, 2019, https:// www.firstpost.com/india/narendra-modi-independence-day-2019-full-speech-pm-says-new -approach-was-needed-in-jammu-and-kashmir-5-trillion-economy-target-is-achievable-7167511 .html.

4. "Indian Way of Conflict Avoidance Is by Dialogue, Not by Brute Force: PM Modi," NDTV, January 16, 2020, https://www.ndtv.com/india-news/prime-minister-narendra-modi -indian-way-of-conflict-avoidance-is-by-dialogue-not-by-brute-force-2165178; and "PM Narendra Modi: Indian Way of Life Offers the World Hope against Hate," *Indian Express*, January 17, 2020, https://indianexpress.com/article/india/indian-way-of-life-offers-the-world-hope -against-hate-pm-modi-6220358/.

5. See, for instance, Narendra Modi, *Social Harmony* (New Delhi: Prabhat Prakashan, 2015).

6. Modi, *Social Harmony*, 19–20.

7. See Bhanwar Meghawanshi, *I Could Not Be Hindu: The Story of a Dalit in the RSS* (New Delhi: Navayana, 2020).

8. C. Jaffrelot, "The Muslims of India," in *India since 1950: Society, Politics, Economy and Culture*, ed. C. Jaffrelot (New Delhi: Yatra Books, 2011), 564–80.

9. "India as an Ethnic Democracy," Sciences Po Archives, accessed October 3, 2020, https:// hal-sciencespo.archives-ouvertes.fr/medihal-01411920v1.

10. Christophe Jaffrelot and S. Bhutada, "The Uniform Code," *Indian Express*, July 13, 2018, https://indianexpress.com/article/opinion/columns/indian-police-service-muslim-police -officials-5257238/.

11. For a visual representation of this evolution, see the figure in Christophe Jaffrelot, "A *De Facto* Ethnic Democracy? Obliterating and Targeting the Other, Hindu Vigilantes and the

Ethno-state," in *Majoritarian State: How Hindu Nationalism Is Changing India*, ed. Angana Chatterji, Thomas Blom Hansens, and Christophe Jaffrelot (London: Hurst, 2019), 41–67.

12. For a long time, Muslims were able to take advantage of the parallel track offered at the state level, through which police officers recruited by the state administration could join the IPS (partly through seniority). But this recruitment channel has dried up: while Muslims made up 7 percent of the class of 2006, the number of fell to 3.8 percent in 2016. See Zeeshan Shaikh, "Ten Years since Sachar Report, Muslims Still 3 Percent in IAS, IPS," *Indian Express*, August 18, 2016, http://indianexpress.com/article/india/india-news-india/ten-years-since-sachar-report-muslims-still-3-in-ias-ips-2982199/.

13. In 2014, the Modi government decided to no longer make public the percentage of Muslims in the Indian police, which amounted to rescinding an innovation introduced by the Vajpayee government in 1999. Z. Sheikh, "Data on Muslims in Police Will No Longer Be Public," *Indian Express*, November 30, 2015, http://indianexpress.com/article/india/india-news-india/data-on-muslims-in-police-will-no-longer-be-public/.

14. The official sources used here, which are difficult to access and incomplete, are the annual reports by the National Crime Records Bureau, called *Crime in India*, in the chapter "Police Strength, Expenditure & Infrastructure." See the following links: http://scrbwb.gov.in/CII/CD-CII2004/cii-2004/CHAP17.pdf; http://ncrb.gov.in/StatPublications/CII/CII2005/cii-2005/CHAP17.pdf; http://ncrb.gov.in/StatPublications/CII/CII2008/cii-2008/Chapter%2017.pdf; http://home.up.nic.in/CII-ADSI%202011/Data/CD-CII2011/cii-2011/Chapter%2017.pdf.

15. Common Cause and CSDS, *Status of Policing in India Report 2018* (Delhi: Lokniti-CSDS and Common Cause, 2018), 193.

16. Ankur Otta, "Not of the People," *Indian Express*, November 14, 2017, https://indianexpress.com/article/opinion/columns/muslims-in-delhi-police-jobs-delhi-police-recruitment-crime-in-delhi-national-crime-records-bureau-4936111/.

17. S. Cohen, *The Pakistan Army* (Karachi: Oxford University Press, 2006), 59–60.

18. Cited in Omar Khalidi, *Khaki and the Ethnic Violence in India: Army, Police and Paramilitary Forces during Communal Riots* (New Delhi: Three Essays, 2003), 11.

19. Steven I. Wilkinson, *Army and Nation: The Military and Indian Democracy since Independence* (Cambridge, MA: Harvard University Press, 2015), 139.

20. Khalidi, *Khaki*, 24.

21. Cited in Khalidi, 23.

22. Khalidi, 23.

23. Ali Ahmed, "The Missing Muslim Army Officers," *Economic and Political Weekly* 53, no. 4 (January 27, 2018): 12.

24. Shaikh, "Ten Years."

25. For the list of the lucky few, see Abuzar Niyazi, "Muslim IAS Officers List 2019," Kulhaiya, July 8, 2019, http://www.kulhaiya.com/education/upsc-ias-hindi/muslim-ias-toppers.

26. See the Zakat Foundation of India, homepage, accessed May 14, 2018, http://www.zakatindia.org.

27. Shaikh, "Ten Years."

28. "Maharashtra Civil Sevices [*sic*]: Only 05 Muslims in List of 435 Successful Candidates," Ummid, April 7, 2015, http://www.ummid.com/news/2015/April/07.04.2015/maharashtra-mpsc-results-2015.html.

29. "Maharashtra Government Does Away with 5% Job Quota for Muslims," *Business Standard*, March 4, 2015, http://www.business-standard.com/article/pti-stories/maharashtra-government-does-away-with-5-job-quota-for-muslims-115030401498_1.html.

30. Regarding this jurisprudence, see C. Jaffrelot, *India's Silent Revolution—The Rise of the Lower Castes in North India* (New Delhi: Permanent Black, 2003).

31. Christophe Jaffrelot and A. Kalaiyasaran, "The Myth of Appeasement," *Indian Express*, April 20, 2018, https://indianexpress.com/article/opinion/columns/muslims-socio-economic-development-5144318/.

32. "Telangana Assembly Passes Bill to Increase Muslim Quota Despite BJP Protest," *Indian Express*, April 16, 2017, http://indianexpress.com/article/india/muslim-quota-reservation-tel . . . -passes-bill-to-increase-muslim-quota-despite-bjp-protest-4615466/. The only state in which total quotas exceed 49 percent is Tamil Nadu.

33. See Christophe Jaffrelot and Gilles Verniers, "Absence on the Bench," *Indian Express*, September 10, 2018, https://indianexpress.com/article/opinion/columns/muslims-in-prison-india-judiciary-supreme-court-5347728/.

34. Jaffrelot and Verniers, "Absence on the Bench."

35. Adnan Farooqi, "Political Representation of a Minority: Muslim Representation in Contemporary India," *India Review* 19, no. 2 (2020): 153–75.

36. On the notion of "Muslim vote" and its limits, especially regarding the idea that Muslims vote for Muslim candidates, see Oliver Heath, Gilles Verniers, and Sanjay Kumar, "Do Muslim Voters Prefer Muslim Candidates? Co-religiosity and Voting Behaviour in India," *Electoral Studies* 38 (June 2015): 10–18.

37. Cited in Prashant Jha, *How the BJP Wins: Inside India's Greatest Election Machine* (Delhi: Juggernaut, 2017), 174.

38. Jaffrelot and Kalaiyasaran, "Myth of Appeasement."

39. For further detail, see Christophe Jaffrelot, Virginie Dutoya, Radhika Kanchana, and Gayatri Rathore, "Understanding Muslim Voting Behaviour," *Seminar* 602 (2009): 43–48.

40. Christophe Jaffrelot and Gilles Verniers, "Invisible in the House," *Indian Express*, May 28, 2014, http://indianexpress.com/article/opinion/columns/invisible-in-the-house/.

41. The fact that he was a Shia is not necessarily incidental, given the affinities between this community and the BJP. Christophe Jaffrelot and H. A. Rizvi, "A Curious Friendship," *Indian Express*, May 9, 2018, http://indianexpress.com/article/opinion/columns/a-curious-friendship-uttar-pradesh-shia-leaders-yogi-adityanath-5168745/.

42. Smita Gupta, "Do Minorities Matter?," ThePrint, August 11, 2017, https://theprint.in/2017/08/11/do-minorities-matter/amp/.

43. Z. Shaikh, "Muslim Ministers: Numbers Lag Far behind Share in Population," *Indian Express*, November 27, 2020, https://indianexpress.com/article/explained/muslim-ministers-population-parliament-bjp-nda-7067496/.

44. This was Yunus Khan, in Rajasthan. S. Rukmini, "Just One Muslim among 151 Ministers in BJP-Ruled States," *The Hindu*, April 9, 2016, http://www.thehindu.com/news/national/just-one-muslim-among-151-ministers-in-bjpruled-states/article6564908.ece.

45. See Christophe Jaffrelot, "The Muslims of Gujarat during Narendra Modi's Chief Ministership," in *Indian Muslims. Struggling for Equality and Citizenship*, ed. Riaz Hasan (Melbourne: Melbourne University, 2016), 235–58; and "Gujarat Elections: The Sub-Text of Modi's

'Hattrick'—High Tech Populism and the 'Neo-Middle Class,'" *Studies in Indian Politics* 1, no. 1 (June 2013): 79–96.

46. N. Mannathukkaren, "The Fast Disappearing Muslim in the Indian Republic," *Indian Express*, January 22, 2018, http://indianexpress.com/article/opinion/the-fast-disappearing -muslim-in-the-indian-republic-bjp-mla-hindu-saffron-religion-5034205/.

47. Gilles Verniers, "The Rising Representation of Muslims in Uttar Pradesh," Hindu Centre for Politics and Public Policy, April 8, 2014, https://www.thehinducentre.com/verdict /commentary/article5886847.ece.

48. A. Saldanha, "Muslim Representation in UP Assembly Plummets with 2017 Elections," The Wire, March 14, 2017, https://thewire.in/culture/muslim-representation-up-plummets.

49. "Number of Muslim MLAs in Bihar down from 24 to 19," *Ummid*, November 11, 2020, https://ummid.com/news/2020/november/11.11.2020/list-of-muslim-mlas-in-bihar-assembly -2020.html.

50. "Bihar Alliance without a Single Elected Muslim," *Telegraph*, January 7, 2021, https:// www.telegraphindia.com/india/bihar-alliance-without-a-single-elected-muslim/cid/1797699.

51. For a more complete overview, see Christophe Jaffrelot and Gilles Verniers, "The Dwindling Minority," *Indian Express*, July 30, 2018, https://indianexpress.com/article/opinion /columns/muslims-politicians-in-india-bjp-narendra-modi-government-5282128/.

52. On this classic controversy in political science, see Hanna Pitkin, *The Concept of Representation* (Berkeley: University of California Press, 1972); and, more recently, Peter Allen, *The Political Class: Why It Matters Who Our Politicians Are* (Oxford: Oxford University Press, 2018).

53. Robert Weissberg, "Collective vs. Dyadic Representation in Congress," *American Political Science Review*, 72, no. 2 (1978): 535–47; Melissa J. Marschall and Anirudh V. S. Ruhil, "Substantive Symbols: The Attitudinal Dimension of Black Political Incorporation in Local Government," *American Journal of Political Science* 51, no. 1 (2017): 17–33; Lani Guinier, *The Tyranny of the Majority: Fundamental Fairness in Representative Democracy* (New York: Free Press, 1994); Phillip Paolino, "Group-Salient Issues and Group Representation: Support for Women Candidates in the 1992 Senate Elections," *American Journal of Political Science* 39, no. 2 (1995): 294–313; Sue Thomas, "The Impact of Women on State Legislative Policies," *Journal of Politics* 53, no. 4 (1991): 958–76.

54. Saloni Bhogale, "Querying the Indian Parliament: What Can the Question Hour Tell Us about Muslim Representation in India?" (working paper, Trivedi Centre for Political Data, Ashoka University, January 2018), 27.

55. Common Cause and CSDS, *Status of Policing*, 77.

56. Common Cause and CSDS, 93–95.

57. Common Cause and CSDS, 97.

58. For further detail, see Christophe Jaffrelot, "La dialectique des terrorismes en Inde depuis 2001: la 'main de l'étranger', les islamistes et les nationalistes hindous," *Critique internatonal* 47 (2010): 93–110.

59. Judgment of V. V. Patil, special judge, City Civil and Session Court, Mumbai, "In the special court under MCOC Act 1999 and NIA Act 2008 at Greater Mumbai," MCOC Special Case no. 23 of 2016, p. 6.

60. Regarding Abhinav Bharat and its actions, see Christophe Jaffrelot, "Abhinav Bharat, the Malegaon Blast and Hindu Nationalism: Resisting and Emulating Islamist Terrorism," *Economic*

and Political Weekly 45, no. 36 (September 4–10, 2010): 51–58; and Christophe Jaffrelot and Malvika Maheshwari, "Paradigm Shifts by the RSS? Lessons from Aseemanand's Confession," *Economic and Political Weekly* 46, no. 6 (February 5–11, 2011): 42–46.

61. Judgment of V. V. Patil, special judge, City Civil and Session Court, Mumbai, "In the special court under MCOC Act 1999 and NIA Act 2008 at Greater Mumbai," MCOC Special Case no. 23 of 2016, p. 14.

62. Judgment of V. V. Patil, special judge, City Civil and Session Court, Mumbai, "In the special court under MCOC Act 1999 and NIA Act 2008 at Greater Mumbai," p. 31.

63. Vijay Hiremath, "German Bakery Blast Acquittal: The ATS Owes Us an Explanation," Scroll.in, March 27, 2016, https://scroll.in/article/805640/german-bakery-blast-acquittal-the -ats-owes-us-an-explanation.

64. Subject to pressure from his hierarchy, Bhatt killed himself by throwing himself under a train near where one of the 2006 attacks had taken place. Zeeshan Shaikh, "2006 Mumbai Blasts Case: Acquitted after 9 Years, Wahid Says Has Lost Faith in the System," *Indian Express*, September 30, 2015, http://indianexpress.com/article/cities/mumbai/2006-mumbai-blasts-case -acquitted-after-9-yrs-wahid-says-has-lost-faith-in-the-system/; and A. A. Mahaprashasta, "Interview: Of Torture, Impunity and the False Charges on Abdul Wahid Shaikh," The Wire, May 20, 2017, https://thewire.in/137846/abdul-wahid-shaikh-acquitted-interview/.

65. Mateen Hafeez and Pradeep Gupta, "Mulund Train Bomb Blast Case: Saquib Nachan Released from Jail," *Times of India*, November 22, 2017, https://timesofindia.indiatimes.com /city/thane/mulund-train-bomb- . . . st-case-saquib-nachan-released-from-jail/articleshow /61753143.cms.

66. D. Buncha, "Akshardham Ups the Ante," *Frontline*, October 12–25, 2002, http:// dionnebunsha.com/akshardham-ups-the-ante/.

67. See Praveen Swami, "Akshardham: A Search for Truth," *Frontline*, October 24, 2003, 38.

68. Manas Dasguta, "Death Sentence for Akshardham Temple Attack Convicts Upheld," *The Hindu*, June 2, 2010, http://www.thehindu.com/news/national/death-sentence-for -akshardham-temple-attack-convicts-upheld/article443455.ece.

69. "Dham Attack Case: Three Years after SC Rejects Probe, New Arrest," *Indian Express*, November 5, 2017, http://indianexpress.com/article/india/akshardham-attack-case-three -years-after-sc-rejects-probe-new-arrest-4922689/.

70. Sheriff M. Kaunain, "Evidence Not Believable, Court Said in Case Linked to 3 of Killed SIMI Men," *Indian Express*, November 5, 2016, http://indianexpress.com/article/india/india-news-india /evidence-no . . . lievable-court-said-in-case-linked-to-3-of-killed-simi-men-3738020/.

71. Regarding the controversies surrounding this case, see K. Ambazsta, "Encounter vs Rule of Law," *Indian Express*, November 3, 2016, http://indianexpress.com/article/opinion/columns /bhopal-encounter-simi-activists-jailbreak-killed-3734268/.

72. Muzamil Jaleel, "After 23 Years in Jail, I Am Free but What You See Now Is a Living Corpse, Says Nisar," *Indian Express*, May 20, 2016, http://indianexpress.com/article/india/india-news -india/babri-masjid . . . urt-acquitted-in-babri-anniversary-train-blasts-case-nisar-2824883/.

73. Sumegha Gulati, "'Innocents Suffer with the Guilty': How Delhi Police Special Cell Ruined Young Kashmiri Lives," Scroll.in, October 26, 2015, https://scroll.in/article/763915 /innocents-suffer-with-the-guilty-how-delhi-police-special-cell-ruined-young-kashmiri-lives.

74. See the case of two young Biharis wrongly accused of being involved in two attacks (in 2008 and 2011) and ultimately cleared by the NIA in 2015. V. Singh, "NIA Drops Terror Charge against 2 Azamgarh Men," *The Hindu*, October 16, 2015, http://www.thehindu.com/news /national/nia-drops-terror-charge-against-2-azamgarh-men/article7766963.ece.

75. "3 Delhi Blasts Accused Walk Free," *The Hindu*, February 19, 2017, http://www.thehindu .com/news/national/2005-Delhi-serial-blasts-Delhi-Court-acquits-two-accused /article17312745.ece?homepage=true.

76. Bashaarat Masood, "2005 Delhi Serial Blasts: Forced Us to Eat Faeces, Made Us Sign Blank Papers, Says Fazili," *Indian Express*, February 22, 2017, http://indianexpress.com/article /india/2005-delhi-serial-blasts-forced-us-to-eat-faeces-made-us-sign-blank-papers-says-fazili -4537298/.

77. Pratap Bhanu Mehta, "Delhi Blast Acquittals: When Will Politics Go beyond My Favourite Innocent vs Yours?," *Indian Express*, February 22, 2017, http://indianexpress.com/article /opinion/columns/2005-delhi-blast-accused-acquitted-hussain-fazli-and-mohd-rafiq-shah -4536921/.

78. Such partiality also transpires through police officers' remarks. One of those who tortured a suspect in the Delhi blasts reportedly told him: "Agar tum threat nahi ho, potential threat to ho hi!" (You may not be a threat now, but you are definitely a potential threat). Cited in Majid Maqbool, "Framed, Tortured, Released after 12 Years: The Story of the Delhi Blasts 'Mastermind,'" *The Wire*, March 7, 2017, https://thewire.in/politics/framed-tortured-released-after-12 -years-the-story-of-2005-delhi-blasts-mastermind-tariq-ahmed-dar.

79. Deeptiman Tiwary, "Over 55 per cent of Undertrials Muslim, Dalit or Tribal," *Indian Express*, November 1, 2016, https://indianexpress.com/article/india/india-news-india/over-55 -per-cent-of-undertrials-muslim-dalit-or-tribal-ncrb-3731633/.

80. Deeptiman Tiwary, "Share of Muslims in Jail Bigger than in the Population, Show NCRB Data," *Indian Express*, November 3, 2016, https://indianexpress.com/article/explained /muslims-daliots-undertrials-in-prison-ncrb-3734362/.

81. Jyoti Punwani, "List of Innocents," *Indian Express*, April 2, 2018, http://indianexpress .com/article/opinion/columns/list-of-innocents-yogi-adityanath-bjp-congress-north-east -uttarakhand-5119821/.

82. S. Joy, "Majority Prisoners in Indian Jails Are Dalits, Muslims," *Deccan Herald*, January 1, 2020, https://www.deccanherald.com/national/north-and-central/majority-prisoners-in -indian-jails-are-dalits-muslims-790478.html.

83. His report consequently found its way to the VHP website, accessed November 23, 2000, http://www.vhp.org/wadhwa.htm (site no longer available).

84. Regarding M. F. Husain's troubles with the Indian courts, see Malvika Maheshwari, *Art Attacks: Violence and Offence-Taking in India* (Delhi: OUP, 2019), 207–70.

85. K. Rajagopal, "Cannot Justify Murder Saying Victim Belonged to a 'Certain Community': SC," *The Hindu*, February 15, 2018, http://www.thehindu.com/news/national/cannot -justify-murder-saying-victim-belonged-to-a-certain-community-sc/article22759193.ece.

86. See Christophe Jaffrelot, "The Ayodhya Verdict: One More Missed Opportunity?," *The Caravan*, October 1, 2010, http://www.caravanmagazine.in/perspectives/ayodhya-verdict-one -more-missed-opportunity.

87. "SC Bars UP Government for Interfering in Waqf Issues," *Muslim Mirror*, May 1, 2018, http://muslimmirror.com/eng/sc-bars-government-interfering-waqf-issues/.

88. Harsh Mander, "Pehlu Khan, One Year Later," *Indian Express*, April 21, 2018, http://indianexpress.com/article/opinion/columns/pehlu-khan-rajasthan-cow-lynching-5145631/.

89. "Harsh Mander: When Our Caravan of Love Defied Threats of Violence to Pay Tribute to Pehlu Khan," Scroll.in, September 16, 2017, https://scroll.in/article/850860/harsh-mander-when-our-caravan-of-love-defied-threats-of-violence-to-pay-tribute-to-pehlu-khan.

90. P. Pandey, "Jharkhand: Behind Lynching Convictions, High Court Drive Involving Police, Prosecutors," *Indian Express*, April 30, 2018, https://www.bing.com/search?q=Alimuddin%20Ansari&pc=cosp&ptag=G6C999N0765D010318A316A5D3C6E&form=CONBDF&conlogo=CT3210127.

91. This paragraph and the two following ones draw from Christophe Jaffrelot, *The Hindu Nationalist Movement and Indian Politics* (London: Hurst, 1996), chap. 13 and epilogue.

92. Supreme Court of India, "Special Reference No. 1 of 1993 vs Ram Janma Bhumi-Babri Masjid . . . on 27 January, 1993," Bench: M. N. Venkatachaliah, A. M. Ahmadi, J. S. Verma, G. N. Ray, and S. P. Bharucha, https://indiankanoon.org/doc/188962496/.

93. Supreme Court of India, "Dr. Ismail Faruqui Etc, vs Union of India and Others on 24 October 1994," AIR 1995 SC 605 A, https://indiankanoon.org/doc/37494799/. See also S. Padmavathi and D. G. Hari Prasath, *Supreme Court Judgement on Ayodhya Issue: Ram Janmabhoomi—Babri Masjid Land Title dispute. Part 2* (Chennai: Notion Press, 2019).

94. S. R. Bommai and Ors. vs. Union of India and Ors., March 11, 1994, Hello Counsel, accessed September 7, 2020, http://www.hellocounsel.com/wp-content/uploads/2018/01/S.R.-Bommai-Vs.-Union-Of-India-9JBSC-11.03.1994-1994-AIR-1918-1994-SCC-3-1.pdf.

95. "Judgment delivered on 30.09.2010. In the High Court of Judicature at Allahabad (Lucknow Bench). Other Original Suit (O.O.S.) No.1 of 1989," eLegalix, 130–31, accessed September 7, 2020, http://elegalix.allahabadhighcourt.in/elegalix/ayodhyafiles/honsukj.pdf.

96. "Judgment delivered on 30.09.2010," 201–2.

97. "Judgment delivered on 30.09.2010," 243.

98. "Judgment delivered on 30.09.2010," 251–55.

99. "Judgment delivered on 30.09.2010," 259.

100. "Judgment delivered on 30.09.2010," 284.

101. "Judgment delivered on 30.09.2010," 279.

102. "In the Supreme Court of India Civil Appellate Jurisdiction," Civil Appeal Nos. 10866–10867 of 2010, *The Hindu*, 892, accessed September 7, 2020, https://www.thehindu.com/news/national/article29929717.ece/Binary/JUD_2.pdf.

103. "In the Supreme Court of India Civil Appellate Jurisdiction," 915.

104. "In the Supreme Court of India Civil Appellate Jurisdiction," 885.

105. "In the Supreme Court of India Civil Appellate Jurisdiction," 165.

106. See G. Deleury, ed., *Les Indes florissantes. Anthologie des voyageurs français, 1750–1820* (Paris: Robert Laffont, 1991), 737. See also the addenda to the 2020 Supreme Court verdict, *The Hindu*, 81–82accessed December 9, 2020, https://www.thehindu.com/news/national/article29929717.ece/Binary/JUD_2.pdf.

107. "In the Supreme Court of India Civil Appellate Jurisdiction," 6.

108. "In the Supreme Court of India Civil Appellate Jurisdiction," 560.

109. "In the Supreme Court of India Civil Appellate Jurisdiction," 594–95.

110. "In the Supreme Court of India Civil Appellate Jurisdiction," 921–22.

111. "In the Supreme Court of India Civil Appellate Jurisdiction," 892.

112. "In the Supreme Court of India Civil Appellate Jurisdiction," 895.

113. "In the Supreme Court of India Civil Appellate Jurisdiction," 913.

114. "Tushar Gandhi on Ayodhya Verdict: If Godse Tried Today, He Would Have Been 'Murderer and Patriot,'" *Indian Express*, November 9, 2019, https://indianexpress.com/article /india/tushar-gandhi-on-ayodhya-verdict-if-godse-tried-today-he-would-have-been-murderer -and-patriot-6111521/.

115. Addenda to the 2020 Supreme Court verdict, 922.

116. K. D. Sutar, "Will Launch 1992-Like Agitation for Ram Mandir if Needed: RSS," *India Today*, November 2, 2018, https://www.indiatoday.in/india/story/rss-ram-mandir-ayodhya -1992-agitation-1380991-2018-11-02.

117. Sheriff M. Kaunain, "Explained: What Is Article 142, Invoked by SC to Give Land for a Mosque?," *Indian Express*, November 9, 2019, https://indianexpress.com/article/explained /ayodhya-ram-temple-babri-masjid-article-142-supreme-court-6111920/.

118. R. Dwivedi, "Ayodhya Verdict: Balancing While Condemning the 1992 Demolition," *Economic Times*, November 11, 2019, https://economictimes.indiatimes.com/news/politics-and -nation/ayodhya-verdict-balancing-while-condemning-the-1992-demolition/articleshow /72007260.cms?utm_source=contentofinterest&utm_medium=text&utm_campaign=cppst.

119. M. K. Venu, "Ayodhya Dispute: Was Public Peace Privileged over Justice?," The Wire, November 11, 2019, https://thewire.in/law/ayodhya-dispute-public-justice.

120. Suhas Palshikar, "Ayodhya Verdict Opens Door for Claims Based on Community Identity, Construction of Faith," *Indian Express*, November 11, 2019, https://indianexpress.com /article/opinion/columns/ayodhya-verdict-supreme-court-lord-ram-ramjanmabhoomi -temple-babri-6113594/.

121. C. M. Dorf, "The Majoritarian Difficulty and Theories of Constitutional Decision-Making," *Journal of Constitutional Law* 13, no. 2 (2010): 283–304. See also A. Barak, "A Judge on Judging: The Role of a Supreme Court in a Democracy," *Harvard Law Review* 116, no. 16 (2002–2003): 19–162.

122. Addenda to the 2020 Supreme Court verdict, 122.

123. "Watch: Supreme Court Lawyers Chant 'Jai Shri Ram' after Ayodhya Verdict," Scroll.in, November 9, 2019, https://scroll.in/video/943174/watch-following-ayodhya-verdict-lawyers -at-the-supreme-court-chant-jai-shri-ram.

124. A. Oka, "Ayodhya Verdict: Here Is Prime Minister Narendra Modi's Full Speech," Republic World, November 9, 2019, https://www.republicworld.com/india-news/general-news /ayodhya-verdict-here-is-prime-minister-narendra-modis-full-speech.html. See also "Ayodhya Verdict PM Speech Live: SC Verdict Has Brought a New Dawn for Us, Says Modi," *The Hindu*, November 9, 2019, https://www.thehindu.com/news/national/live-updates-ayodhya-verdict -prime-minister-narendra-modi-addresses-nation/article29931605.ece.

125. That was the conclusion of the resolution adopted by the working committee of the Jamiat Ulama-i-Hind, where it was also said: "The judgement is the darkest spot in the history

of free India. In such a situation we cannot expect any better award from the concerned judges." A. Ghosh, "Ayodhya Ruling Darkest Spot in History but Won't Go for Review: Jamiat," *Indian Express*, November 22, 2019, https://indianexpress.com/article/india/ayodhya-ram-mandir -supreme-court-babri-masjid-6131062/. See also M. Wajihuddin, "100+ Renowned Muslims Oppose Ayodhya Review," *Times of India*, November 26, 2019, https://timesofindia.indiatimes .com/india/100-renowned-muslims-oppose-ayodhya-review/articleshow/72232650.cms.

126. Addenda to the 2020 Supreme Court verdict, 926.

127. Jaffrelot, *Hindu Nationalist Movement*, 399.

128. C. L. Manoj, "Digvijaya Singh Questions Composition of Ram Mandir Trust," *Economic Times*, February 22, 2020, https://economictimes.indiatimes.com/news/politics-and-nation /digvijaya-singh-questions-composition-of-ram-mandir-trust/articleshow/74251179.cms?utm _source=contentofinterest&utm_medium=text&utm_campaign=cppst.

129. F. Khan, "Ram Temple Ceremony a BJP-RSS Event, Party Stealing Credit—Congress over Not Being Invited," ThePrint, September 8, 2020, https://theprint.in/india/ram-temple -ceremony-a-bjp-rss-event-party-stealing-credit-congress-over-not-being-invited/469967/.

130. Cited in "Bhoomi Pujan: Over 300 Concerned Citizens Make 'Last Appeal' to PM Modi to Not Attend," The Wire, August 4, 2020, https://thewire.in/communalism/ayodhya-bhoomi -pujan-modi-ram-temple-nfiw-last-appeal.

131. S. Pradhan, "At Ayodhya Bhoomi Pujan, Modi Became All-in-One; Proper Rituals Not Followed, Allege Pundits," The Wire, August 7, 2020, https://thewire.in/politics/ayodhya -bhoomi-pujan-narendra-modi-priests-pundits.

132. C. Jaffrelot, "The Vishva Hindu Parishad: Structures and Strategies," in *Religion, Globalization and Political Culture in the Third World*, ed. J. Haynes (London, Macmillan, 1999), 191–212; and C. Jaffrelot, "The Vishva Hindu Parishad: A Nationalist but Mimetic Attempt at Federating the Hindu Sects," in *Charisma and Canon: Essays on the Religious History of the Indian Subcontinent*, ed. V. Dalmia, A. Malinar, and M. Christof (Delhi: Oxford University Press, 2001), 388–411.

133. Pradhan, "Ayodhya Bhoomi Pujan."

134. P. Ketkar, "Reconstruction and Rejuvenation," *The Organiser*, July 28, 2020, https:// www.organiser.org/Encyc/2020/7/28/Reconstruction-for-Rejuvenation.html.

135. Ram Madhav, "Ayodhya Represents a Shared Sentiment of Sacredness," *Indian Express*, August 5, 2020, https://indianexpress.com/article/opinion/columns/ayodhya-ram-temple -hindus-jain-tirthankaras-ram-madhav-6539531/.

136. S. Palshikar, "At Ayoydhya, we will see dismantling of the old, and the bhoomi pujan of the new republic," *Indian Express*, August 4, 2020, https://indianexpress.com/article/opinion /ayodhya-ram-temple-bhoomi-pujan-pm-narendra-modi-6537822/.

137. "All 32 Acquitted in Babri Demolition Case Due to 'Lack of Proof'; Defence Claims Singhal, Advani Tried to Save Structure," FirstPost, September 30, 2020, https://www.firstpost .com/india/babri-masjid-verdict-all-32-accused-including-advani-joshi-acquitted-cbi-court -observes-incident-not-pre-planned-8865681.html.

138. On the way this bill was passed, see M. Verma, "How the Central Government Subverted Both Procedure and Good Faith in Passing the Enemy Property Amendment Bill," *The Caravan*, April 8, 2017, https://caravanmagazine.in/vantage/government-subverted-procedure -good-faith-passing-enemy-property-bill.

139. The Uttar Pradesh Prohibition of Unlawful Conversion of Religion Ordinance, 2020 (U.P. Ordinance n° 21 of 2020), https://www.scconline.com/blog/wp-content/uploads/2020/12/UP_Prohibition_of_Unlawful_Conversion_of_Religion_Ordinance_2020.pdf.

140. See *The Uttar Pradesh Prohibition of Unlawful Conversion of Religion Ordinance* and A. Vishwanath, "In Name of Conversion, UP 'Love Jihad' Law Targets Inter-Faith Unions," December 2, 2020, https://indianexpress.com/article/india/up-love-jihad-law-religious-conversion-7075981/.

141. "State Anti-conversion Laws in India," Washington, The Law Library of Congress, 2018, https://www.loc.gov/law/help/anti-conversion-laws/india-anti-conversion-laws.pdf.

142. Jyoti Punwani, "Why Only the UP Law on Inter-Faith Marriages Is Creating Turmoil," The India Forum, February 5, 2021, https://www.theindiaforum.in/letters/law-inter-faith-marraige.

143. "Raising 'Love Jihad' Bogey, Yogi Threatens Death for Men Who 'Hide Identity, Disrespect Sisters,'" The Wire, November 1, 2020, https://thewire.in/communalism/raising-love-jihad-bogey-yogi-threatens-death-for-men-who-hide-identity-disrespect-sisters.

144. A. Mishra, "Chorus in UP Village: Police Pro-active, Forced 'Love Jihad' Arrest," *Indian Express*, December 4, 2020, https://indianexpress.com/article/india/chorus-in-up-village-police-pro-active-forced-love-jihad-arrest-7089467/.

145. Omar Rashid, "Ground Zero: Love on the Razor's Edge in Uttar Pradesh," Latest News, December 12, 2020 https://ouruttarakhand.in/ground-zero-love-on-the-razors-edge-in-uttar-pradesh/.

146. "Upholding Love: In Last One Month, Allahabad High Court Grants Protection to over 125 Inter-Faith/Caste Couples," *Livelaw*, December 1, 2020, https://www.livelaw.in/top-stories/allahabad-high-court-grants-protection-to-over-125-inter-faithcaste-couples-166645.

147. Rohan Venkataramakrishnan, "'Love Jihad': As Pandemic Rages, BJP States Turn Focus to Laws Based on Hindutva Conspiracy Theory," Scroll.in, November 21, 2020, https://scroll.in/article/979015/love-jihad-as-pandemic-rages-bjp-states-turn-focus-to-laws-based-on-hindutva-conspiracy-theory.

148. The Uttar Pradesh Prohibition of Unlawful Conversion of Religion Ordinance.

149. On the patriarchal dimension of the Uttar Pradesh Prohibition of Unlawful Conversion of Religion Ordinance, see Charu Gupta, "Love Taboos: Controlling Hindu-Muslim Romances," The India Forum, February 5, 2021, https://www.theindiaforum.in/article/love-laws-making-hindu-muslim-romances-illegitimate.

150. N. C. Asthana, "Ulterior Motive of 'Love Jihad' Laws Is to Drive Muslims out of the Social Ecosystem," The Wire, November 9, 2020, https://thewire.in/communalism/love-jihad-laws-muslim-exclusion-ulterior-motive-hindutva.

151. "Yogi Adityanath Blames Islamic Sect for Spread of Coronavirus," NDTV, May 4, 2020, https://www.ndtv.com/india-news/yogi-adityanath-blames-islamic-sect-tablighi-jamaat-for-spread-of-coronavirus-2222426.

152. "Court Acquits 34 Tablighi Attendees Directing Them to Deposit Rs 6,000 in PM CARES," *Muslim Mirror*, August 20, 2020, http://muslimmirror.com/eng/court-acquits-34-tablighi-attendees-directing-them-to-deposit-rs-6000-in-pm-cares/.

153. "'Unjust and Unfair': What Three High Courts Said about the Arrests of Tablighi Jamaat Members," Scroll.in, August 24, 2020, https://scroll.in/article/971195/unjust-and-unfair-what -three-high-courts-said-about-the-arrests-of-tablighi-jamaat-members.

154. "Allahabad HC: UP Police Charge against Tablighi Reflects Abuse of Power of Law," *Indian Express*, December 9, 2020, https://indianexpress.com/article/india/allahabad-hc-up -police-charge-against-tablighi-reflects-abuse-of-power-of-law-7097238/.

155. L. Murthy, *The Contagion of Hate in India*, Association for Progressive Communication, 2020, https://www.apc.org/en/pubs/contagion-hate-india.

156. S. Desai and A. Amarasingam, *#Coronajihad. COVID-19, Misinformation, and Anti-Muslim Violence in India*, ISD/Strongcities Network, London, Washington, Beirut and Toronto, 2020, https://strongcitiesnetwork.org/en/coronajihad-covid-19-misinformation-and-anti -muslim-violence-in-india/.

157. A. Saikia, "The Other Virus: Hate Crimes against India's Muslims Are Spreading with Covid-19," Scroll.in, April 8, 2020, https://scroll.in/article/958543/the-other-virus-hate-crimes -against-indias-muslims-are-spreading-with-covid-19.

158. K. Agarwal, "UP Hospital Bars Muslim Patients Who Don't Come with Negative Test for COVID-19," The Wire, April 19, 2020, https://thewire.in/communalism/up-hospital-bars -muslim-patients-who-dont-come-with-negative-test-for-covid-19.

159. "Odisha HC Orders Probe in Death of a Muslim Who Was Denied Dialysis in Lock-down," *Hindustan Times*, April 30, 2020, https://www.hindustantimes.com/india-news/odisha -hc-orders-probe-in-death-of-a-muslim-who-was-denied-dialysis-in-lockdown/story -205siq8mIUWoSCaFbDETqI.html; A. Wadhawan, "Rajasthan: Doctor Refuses to Admit Preg-nant Woman because She's Muslim, Her Child Dies after Delivery," *India Today*, April 4, 2020, https://www.indiatoday.in/india/story/rajasthan-doctor-refuses-to-admit-pregnant-woman -because-she-s-muslim-her-child-dies-after-delivery-1663352-2020-04-04; and J. Wallen, "Indian Hospitals Refuse to Admit Muslims as Coronavirus Causes Islamophobia Surge," *The Telegraph*, April 19, 2020, https://www.telegraph.co.uk/news/2020/04/19/indian-hospitals-refuse-admit -muslims-coronavirus-causes-islamophobia/.

160. "Covid-19: Separate Wards for Hindu and Muslim Patients Made in Ahmedabad Hos-pital," Scroll.in, April 15, 2020, https://scroll.in/latest/959274/covid-19-separate-wards-for -hindu-and-muslim-patients-made-in-ahmedabad-hospital; and S. Jha, "Govt Hospital in Ahmedabad Allegedly Separates Hindu, Muslim Coronavirus Patients; Govt Denies," *Deccan Herald*, April 15, 2020, https://www.deccanherald.com/national/west/govt-hospital-in -ahmedabad-allegedly-separates-hindu-muslim-coronavirus-patients-govt-denies-825586.html.

161. "Covid-19: Muslim Vendors Stopped from Selling Vegetables in UP, Accused of Being Tablighi Members," Scroll.in, April 14, 2020, https://scroll.in/latest/959111/covid-19-muslim -vendors-stopped-from-selling-vegetables-in-up-accused-of-being-tablighi-members; and "Uttar Pradesh BJP MLA Harasses, Threatens Muslim Vegetable Vendor," The Wire, April 29, 2020, https://thewire.in/communalism/up-bjp-mla-anti-muslim.

162. "Jewelry Ad Featuring Interfaith Couple Sparks Outrage in India," *New York Times*, October 13, 2020, https://www.nytimes.com/2020/10/13/world/asia/india-ad-love-jihad -tanishq.html.

163. E. Schmall, "With a Kiss, Netflix Gets Tangled in India's Religious Tensions," *New York Times*, November 28, 2020, https://www.chicagotribune.com/consumer-reviews/sns-nyt-india -netflix-kiss-20201128-bjtf7qplancgvfnugo2n5wttru-story.html.

164. In late 2020, at the time of writing, Uttar Pradesh Muslims were still asked to pay for the damages related to the anti-CAA protest and its repression, for instance. V. Lalwani, "'We've Become like Beggars': UP Accused Pay Price for CAA Protests without Being Convicted in Court," Scroll.in, December 9, 2020, https://scroll.in/article/980187/weve-become-like -beggars-up-accused-pay-price-for-caa-protests-without-being-convicted-in-court.

165. "NSA Charges against Dr Kafeel Khan Dropped, Allahabad HC Directs Immediate Release," *India Today*, September 1, 2020, https://www.indiatoday.in/india/story/nsa -charges-against-dr-kafeel-khan-dropped-allahabad-hc-directs-immediate-release-1717309 -2020-09-01.

166. A. Pandey, "'We Don't See Priyanka, Salamat as Hindu-Muslim': Big Court Verdict in UP," NDTV, November 24, 2020, https://www.ndtv.com/india-news/allahabad-high-court -cancels-2019-fir-against-uttar-pradesh-man-we-dont-see-couple-as-hindu-muslim-2329352.

167. "UP's Anti-Cow Slaughter Law Is Being Misused: Allahabad High Court," October 26, 2020, https://thewire.in/law/uttar-pradesh-cow-slaughter-law-misuse-high-court.

Conclusion

1. The main slogan of Modi's BJP in the 2014 election campaign was "Acche din aane waale hain" (Good days are coming). Narendra Modi borrowed these words from Manmohan Singh (A. Deshmane, "PM Modi's Slogan 'Acche Din Aane Wale Hain' Was Stolen from Former PM Manmohan Singh's Statement," *Economic Times*, March 19, 2015, https://m.economictimes.com /news/politics-and-nation/pm-modis-slogan-acche-din-aane-wale-hain-was-stolen-from -former-pm-manmohan-singhs-statement/articleshow/46615980.cms.

2. "No Entry for Modi into US: Visa Denied," *Times of India*, March 18, 2005, http:// timesofindia.indiatimes.com/articleshow/1055543.cms?utm_source=contentofinterest&utm _medium=text&utm_campaign=cppst.

3. S. A. Siddiqui, "Arab Intellectuals Condemn the Rising Islamophobia in India, Call Inter-national Community to Take Action," *Milli Chronicle*, April 18, 2020, https://millichronicle.com /2020/04/arab-intellectuals-condemn-the-rising-islamophobia-in-india-call-international -community-to-take-actions/; and "Militant Hindus Spreading Hatred against Muslims Should Be Sent Back to India from Gulf: Saudi Scholar," *Muslim Mirror*, April 16, 2020, http:// muslimmirror.com/eng/militant-hindus-spreading-hatred-committing-crimes-against -muslims-should-be-sent-back-to-india-from-gulf-countries-saudi-scholar/.

4. For further detail, see Christophe Jaffrelot and Haider Abbas Rizvi, "Muslim Countries with which India Had Increasingly Good Relations Have Become Less Friendly," *Indian Express*, April 22, 2020, https://indianexpress.com/article/opinion/strap-muslim-countries-with -which-india-had-increasingly-good-relations-have-become-less-friendly-6373721/.

5. "Report by UNHRC Links Inflammatory Remarks by BJP Leaders to Rise in Vigilantism in India," *Outlook*, September 13, 2018, https://www.outlookindia.com/website/story/unhrc

-special-rapporteurs-report-links-inflammatory-remarks-by-bjp-leaders-to-rise-in-vigilantism
-in-india/316460.

6. D. Narayanan, "UN Body Asks Modi Govt to Protect Journalist Rana Ayyub," ThePrint,
accessed September 18, 2020, https://theprint.in/defence/un-body-asks-modi-govt-to-protect
-journalist-rana-ayyub/62354/.

7. "'Chilling Message to Civil Society': UN Experts Call on India to Release Anti-CAA
Activists," The Wire, June 26, 2020, https://thewire.in/diplomacy/united-nations-experts-india
-anti-caa-activists-arrests.

8. A. Narrain, "UN Human Rights Chief's CAA Plea Puts the Spotlight on India's International Law Obligations," Scroll.in, March 5, 2020, https://scroll.in/article/955177/un-human
-rights-chiefs-caa-plea-puts-the-spotlight-on-indias-international-law-obligations; and "Citizenship Amendment Act May Leave Muslims Stateless, says U.N. Secretary-General António
Guterres," The Hindu, February 19, 2020, https://www.thehindu.com/news/national
/citizenship-amendment-act-may-leave-muslims-stateless-says-un-secretary-general-antnio
-guterres/article30863390.ece.

9. "'Fundamentally Discriminatory': UN Human Rights Chief Expresses Concern on Citizenship Act," The Wire, December 13, 2019, https://thewire.in/rights/united-nations-high
-commissioner-for-human-rights-cab.

10. "Bachelet Dismayed at Restrictions on Human Rights NGOs and Arrests of Activists in
India," UN Human Rights Commission, October 20, 2020, https://www.ohchr.org/SP
/NewsEvents/Pages/DisplayNews.aspx?NewsID=26398&LangID=E.

11. In 2019, the Indian government lodged a diplomatic protest with the UN Human Rights
office whose report was described as "false and motivated." See "'False and Motivated Narrative': India Hits out at UN Body over Report on Kashmir," Indian Express, July 8, 2019, https://
indianexpress.com/article/india/un-rights-report-jammu-kashmir-pakistan-mea-5820922/.

12. "Joint Motion for a Resolution on India's Citizenship (Amendment) Act, 2019," European
Parliament, January 29, 2020, https://www.europarl.europa.eu/doceo/document/RC-9-2020
-0077_EN.html.

13. Indrani Bagchi, "India Ramps Up Efforts to Counter Anti-CAA Move in European,"
Times of India, January 28, 2020, http://timesofindia.indiatimes.com/articleshow/73679348
.cms?utm_source=contentofinterest&utm_medium=text&utm_campaign=cppst.

14. On the way Hindu nationalists celebrated this "huge diplomatic victory," see "Huge
Diplomatic Victory for India—EU Refuses to Sign on Draft Resolution against CAA as Pakistan's Effort Fails Miserably," The Organiser, January 30, 2020, https://www.organiser.org/Encyc
/2020/1/30/EU-refuses-to-sign-on-draft-resolution-against-CAA.html.

15. "For France, New Citizenship Law Internal Matter of India: French Govt Sources," Times
of India, January 27, 2020, https://timesofindia.indiatimes.com/india/for-france-new
-citizenship-law-internal-matter-of-india-french-govt-sources/articleshow/73667910.cms.

16. "Members of European Parliament Ask India to 'End Crackdown' on Rights Activists,"
The Wire, March 5, 2019, https://thewire.in/rights/members-of-european-parliament-ask-india
-to-end-crackdown-on-rights-activists.

17. L. Jha, "Religious Freedom in India on 'Negative Trajectory': USCIRF," Outlook, May 2,
2016, https://www.outlookindia.com/newswire/story/religious-freedom-in-india-on-negative

-trajectory-uscirf/938767; and "Cow Slaughter Ban to Dadri Lynching: What USCIRF Report on Religious Freedom Says about India," *Indian Express*, July 23, 2016, https://indianexpress .com/article/india/india-news-india/uscirf-religious-freedom-india-cow-slaughter-to-dadri -lynching-heres-what-the-uscirf-report-on-religious-freedom-says-about-india/.

18. USCIRF Condemns Violence in India's Capital City," United States Commission on International Religious Freedom, February 26, 2020, https://www.uscirf.gov/news-room/press -releases-statements/uscirf-condemns-violence-in-india-s-capital-city.

19. "Full Text of US President Donald Trump's Speech in India," NDTV, February 24, 2020, https://www.ndtv.com/india-news/full-text-of-us-president-donald-trumps-speech-in-india -2185045.

20. S. Ramachandran, "India Protests 'Unwarranted Remarks,'" *Hindustan Times*, August 2, 2019, https://www.pressreader.com/india/hindustan-times-st-mumbai/20190802 /281689731426828.

21. For instance, some chief ministers (including Naveen Patnaik and Nitish Kumar), whose parties had supported the CAB, declared that they opposed the NRC, whereas both these pieces of legislation were unanimously seen as two sides of the same coin. C. G. Manoj, "Another CM Opposes NRC: Naveen Patnaik Latest, after His Party Voted for CAB," *Indian Express*, December 19, 2019, https://indianexpress.com/article/india/another-cm-opposes-nrc-naveen-patnaik -latest-after-his-party-voted-for-citizenship-amendment-bill-6174035/. N. Verma, "Decoding Nitish Kumar's Curious Stand on NRC-CAA," The Wire, December 21, 2018, https://thewire .in/politics/nitish-kumar-caa-nr.

22. C. Jaffrelot, "The Fate of Secularism in India," in *The BJP in Power: Indian Democracy and Religious Nationalism*, ed. Milan Vaishnav (Washington, DC: Carnegie Endowment for International Peace, 2019), https://carnegieendowment.org/2019/04/04/fate-of-secularism-in -india-pub-78689.

23. S. Palshikar, "Towards Hegemony: The BJP beyond Electoral Dominance," in *Majoritarian State: How Hindu Nationalism is Changing India*, ed. A. Chatterji, T. Blom Hansen, and C. Jaffrelot (London: Hurst, 2019), 101–16.

24. P. Bourdieu, "La représentation politique—éléments pour une théorie du champ politique," *Actes de la recherche en sciences sociales* 36, no. 7 (February–March 1981): 3–24; and *La distinction. Critique sociale du jugement* (Paris: Minuit, 1979), 465.

25. F. G. Bailey, *Stratagems and Spoils: A Social Anthropology of Politics* (Oxford: Blackwell, 1969), 4.

26. V. Deshpande, "Scindia Visits RSS Founder's Home in Nagpur: 'Place Gives Inspiration on Dedication to Nation,'" *Indian Express*, August 25, 2020, https://indianexpress.com/article /india/scindia-visits-rss-founders-home-in-nagpur-place-gives-inspiration-on-dedication-to -nation-6569746/.

27. "Pehlu Khan Lynching Case Highlight: Rajasthan Govt to Appeal against Verdict in Higher Court," *Indian Express*, August 14, 2019, https://indianexpress.com/article/india/pehlu -khan-lynching-verdict-live-updates-rajasthan-5903575/; "Rajasthan Appoints SIT to Re-Investigate Pehlu Khan Case," *The Hindu*, August 17, 2019, https://www.thehindu.com/news /national/other-states/rajasthan-appoints-sit-in-pehlu-khan-case/article29117711.ece; and F. Ahmad and Anmolan, "Rajasthan's Effort to Criminalise Mob Lynching Is a Good Start," *The*

Hindu, August 5, 2019, https://www.thehindu.com/opinion/op-ed/rajasthans-effort-to
-criminalise-mob-lynching-is-a-good-start/article28816623.ece.

28. A. Iyer and A. Rozario, "Kejriwal Coming Out to Be a True Disciple of PM Modi': Delhi
RSS," The Quint, February 23, 2020, https://www.thequint.com/news/politics/aap-arvind
-kejriwal-hanuman-saurabh-bhardwaj-sunderkand-hindus-rss-sangh. Arvind Kejriwal (@cof-
feestains11) has apparently praised RSS on at least one occasion: "Do respond 1) Do u oppose
any complicity of Anna \ Kejriwal with RSS 2) Do u oppose prosecution of Kanhaiya under
sedition laws? 3) Do you expect Delhi Govt to pass resolution against NRC-NPR 4) Do u
welcome abrogation of 370 If ans to any one is yes, u need to resolve it," Twitter, May 1, 2020,
1:23 a.m., https://twitter.com/coffeestains11/status/1234001200967815170. On AAP's "soft Hindutva," see Nissim Mannathukkaren, "AAP: Soft Hindutva or a Bulwark without Illusions?,"
The Wire, February 18, 2020, https://thewire.in/politics/aap-soft-hindutva; and Suhas Palshikar, "By Ignoring Ideological Questions, AAP Remains within BJP's Framework," *Indian
Express*, February 12, 2020, https://indianexpress.com/article/opinion/columns/delhi
-election-results-aap-arvind-kejriwal-bjp-6263301/.

29. "Delhi Riots: 270 Eminent Citizens Write to CM Kejriwal Urging Probe by Retired
Judge," The Wire, July 28, 2020, https://thewire.in/communalism/delhi-riots-chief-minister
-arvind-kejriwal-police-probe.

30. A. Menon, "'B-Team' or 'Secular Alternative': Where Does AAP Really Stand?," The
Quint, July 25, 2020, https://www.thequint.com/news/politics/aap-arvind-kejriwal-aam
-aadmi-party-bjp-b-team-congress-alternative-galwan-covid#read-more.

31. Charles Tilly, *Democracy* (Cambridge: Cambridge University Press, 2007), 195.

32. Peter R. De Souza, Suhas Palshikar, and Yogendra Yadav, eds., *State of Democracy in South
Asia* (Delhi: Oxford University Press, 2008). On the illiberalism of the Indian middle class, see
Patrick Heller and Leela Fernandes, "Hegemonic Aspirations: New Middle Class Politics and
India's Democracy in Comparative Perspective," *Critical Asian Studies* 38, no. 4 (2006):
495–522.

33. Cited in S. Varadarajan, "The MEA Should Stay away from BJP Propaganda and Hindutva," The Wire, September 30, 2017, https://thewire.in/diplomacy/mea-bjp-propaganda
-hindutva-deendayal-upadhyaya-integral-humanism.

34. Juan Linz, *Totalitarian and Authoritarian Regimes* (Boulder, CO: Lynne Rienner, 2000), 151.

35. Linz, *Totalitarian and Authoritarian Regimes*, 152.

36. Linz, 152.

37. V. Rao, "The Rise of Monopolies in 'New India,'" *Deccan Herald*, November 19, 2020,
https://www.deccanherald.com/opinion/panorama/the-rise-of-monopolies-in-new-india
-917337.html.

38. "India Inc's Profits Increasingly Belong to a Tiny Clutch of Companies," *The Economist*,
May 21, 2020, https://www.economist.com/business/2020/05/21/india-incs-profits
-increasingly-belong-to-a-tiny-clutch-of-companies.

39. "India Inc's Profits."

40. "India Inc's Profits."

41. In 2019 the CEO of Biocon, Kiran Mazumdar-Shaw, said that a "government official" had
"told her not to speak about issues such as income tax harassment." K. M. Rakesh, "Yes, I Was

Told Not to Say Such Things: Kiran Mazumda-Shawn," *The Telegraph*, August 3, 2019, https://www.telegraphindia.com/india/yes-i-was-told-not-to-say-such-things-about-issues-like-income-tax-harassment-kiran-mazumdar-shaw/cid/1695811.

42. Steven Levitsky and Daniel Ziblatt, *How Democracies Die* (New York: Broadway Books, 2018), 4.

43. Levitsky and Ziblatt, *How Democracies Die*, 77.

44. See C. Jaffrelo, *The Pakistan Paradox: Instability and Resilience* (London: Hurst, 2015), chap. 5.

45. S. Shastri, S. Palshikar, and S. Kumar, eds., *State of Democracy in South Asia: Report II* (Jakkasandra, India: Jain University Press, 2017), 23.

46. Shastri, Palshikar, and Kumar, *State of Democracy*, 34.

47. Shastri, Palshikar, and Kumar, 27–29.

48. Bruce Stokes, Dorothy Manevich, and Hanyu Chwe, "The State of Indian Democracy," Pew Research Center, Global Attitudes and Trends, November 15, 2017, http://www.pewglobal.org/2017/11/15/the-state-of-indian-democracy/. To compare India to other countries, see Richard Wike, Katie Simmons, Bruce Stokes, and Janell Fetterolf, "Globally, Broad Support for Representative and Direct Democracy," Pew Research Center, Global Attitudes and Trends, October 16, 2017, http://www.pewglobal.org/2017/10/16/globally-broad-support-for-representative-and-direct-democracy/.

49. Bruce Stokes, Dorothy Manevich, and Hanyu Chwe, "Indians Satisfied with Country's Direction but Worry about Crime, Terrorism," Pew Research Center, Global Attitudes and Trends, November 15, 2017, http://www.pewglobal.org/2017/11/15/indians-satisfied-with-countrys-direction-but-worry-about-crime-terrorism/.

50. Bruce Stokes, Dorothy Manevich, and Hanyu Chwe, "India and the World," Pew Research Center, Global Attitudes and Trends, November 15, 2017, http://www.pewglobal.org/2017/11/15/india-and-the-world/.

51. Stokes, Manevich, and Chwe, "India and the World."

52. Cited in Christophe Jaffrelot and Narender Kumar, *Dr Ambedkar and Democracy. An Anthology* (New Delhi: Oxford University Press, 2018), 196.

53. In 2020, "Mood of the Nation" opinion polls showed that "even though 25 percent of the respondents believe that the Modi government's handling of the Covid-19 pandemic has been its single biggest failure, they do not blame the prime minister for it." Raj Chengappa, "The Modi Mantra," *India Today*, August 8, 2020, https://www.indiatoday.in/magazine/cover-story/story/20200817-the-modi-mantra-1708699-2020-08-08.

54. L. Rudolph and S. Hoeber Rudolph, *The Modernity of Tradition: Political Development in India* (Chicago: University of Chicago Press, 1967). See part 2, "The Traditional Roots of Charisma: Gandhi," and, in particular, the section called "Self-Control and Political Potency." On Gandhi's sense of authority, see also D. Dalton, "Gandhi: Ideology and Authority," *Modern Asian Studies* 3, no. 4 (1969): 377–93.

55. Rudolph and Rudolph, *Modernity of Tradition*.

56. Rudolph and Rudolph, 183.

57. In this speech, the words "self-respect," "self-confidence," and "self-esteem" recurred fourteen times. "Independence Day: Full Text of Narendra Modi's Red Fort Speech," News18, Au-

gust 16, 2019, https://www.news18.com/news/india/independence-day-full-text-of-narendra-modis-red-fort-speech-2271575.html.

58. E. Tarlo, *Unsettling Memories: Narratives of the Emergency in Delhi* (London: Hurst, 2003), 207.

59. A. Ganguly, "Tragic Phase of Fear: Court," *The Telegraph*, October 19, 2020, https://www.telegraphindia.com/india/tragic-phase-of-fear-court/cid/1353077. The atmosphere in Varanasi, Modi's constituency, offers a good illustration of this phenomenon because in this place more than elsewhere, "everyone is suspicious of everyone." A. Tewary, "Political Discussions Fall Silent as Fear Grips Varanasi," *The Hindu*, January 1, 2020, https://www.thehindu.com/news/national/other-states/political-discussions-fall-silent-as-fear-grips-varanasi/article30453511.ece.

60. In Gujarat, good illustrations of these practices that reflect the vindictiveness of leaders who never forget and forgive are evident from the systematic punishment inflicted on policemen (including Sanjeev Bhat) and lawyers who did their duty in Gujarat. On the condemnation of Sanjeev Bhatt in 2019 in a 1990 custodial death case, see Mahesh Langa, "Sacked IPS Officer Sanjiv Bhatt Gets Life Term in 1990 Custodial Death Case," *The Hindu*, June 20, 2019, https://www.thehindu.com/news/national/other-states/sanjiv-bhatt-sentenced-to-life-in-three-decade-old-custodial-death-case/article28084395.ece.

61. "The Fear Factor: Fact-Checking Amit Shah's Response to Industrialist Rahul Bajaj," The Wire, December 1, 2019, https://thewire.in/government/rahul-bajaj-amit-shah-dissent-pragya-thakur.

62. P. Dahat, G. Sathe, and A. Sethi, "Bhima Koregaon Lawyers Were Targeted in WhatsApp Spyware Scandal," Huffington Post, October 31, 2019, https://www.huffingtonpost.in/entry/whatsapp-hacking-bhima-koregaon-lawyers-targeted_in_5dba8e9ae4b066da552c5028; and S. Shantha, "Indian Activists, Lawyers Were 'Targeted' Using Israeli Spyware Pegasus," The Wire, October 31, 2019, https://thewire.in/tech/pegasus-spyware-bhima-koregaon-activists-warning-whatsapp.

63. R. Satter and E. Culliford, "WhatsApp Sues Israel's NSO for Allegedly Helping Spies Hack Phones around the World," Reuters, October 29, 2019, https://www.reuters.com/article/us-facebook-cyber-whatsapp-nsogroup-idUSKBN1X82BE.

64. "Prime Ministers Narendra Modi and Benjamin Netanyahu Welcome New Age of Collaboration for Israel and India," PRNewswire, January 29, 2018, https://www.prnewswire.com/news-releases/prime-ministers-narendra-modi-and-benjamin-netanyahu-welcome-new-age-of-collaboration-for-israel-and-india-300589299.html.

65. Vijaita Singh, "1,100 Rioters Identified Using Facial Recognition Technology: Amit Shah," *The Hindu*, March 12, 2020, https://www.thehindu.com/news/cities/Delhi/1100-rioters-identified-using-facial-recognition-technology-amit-shah/article31044548.ece.

66. V. Singh, "1,100 Rioters Identified."

67. G. Bhatia, "India's Growing Surveillance State," *Foreign Affairs*, February 19, 2020, https://www.foreignaffairs.com/articles/india/2020-02-19/indias-growing-surveillance-state.

68. For more detail, see Christophe Jaffrelot and Aditya Sharma, "Personal Data Protection Bill 2019 Needs to Be Debated Thoroughly," *Indian Express*, January 7, 2021, https://indianexpress.com/article/opinion/columns/personal-data-protection-bill-2019-privacy-laws-7135832/.

69. In October 2020, Vivek Raghavan, the chief product manager and biometric architect of the Unique Identification Authority of India (UIAI), declared that the UIAI was "developing face authentication system which will be available to all the Aadhaar holders." The UIAI had "allowed face recognition as an additional means of Aadhaar authentication" in 2018. "Aadhaar Authentication via Face Recognition from July: How It Will Work," NDTV, January 15, 2018, https://www.ndtv.com/business/aadhaar-authentication-via-face-recognition-from-july-how-it-will-work-1800194.

70. S. Barik, "The Government Wants to Surveil Social Media Users, and Track Their 'Sentiments,'" *Indian Express*, January 7, 2021, https://indianexpress.com/article/opinion/columns/personal-data-protection-bill-2019-privacy-laws-7135832/.

71. Barik, "The Government Wants to Surveil Social Media Users."

72. "Five New Ways in Which the Government Is Spying on You," Democratic Decline, January 13, 2021, https://newdemagogue.hypotheses.org/3905.

73. Palshikar, "Towards Hegemony," 11.

74. In 1996, in the last sentence of the conclusion of my first book on Hindu nationalism (when few academics and liberals took the Sangh Parivar seriously), I had already pointed out that the groundwork of the offshoots of the RSS "if sustained, will help the latter to crystallise a Hindu identity which in the long term could challenge the durability of India's multicultural society." C. Jaffrelot, *The Hindu Nationalist Movement and Indian Politics* (London: Hurst, 1996), 532.

SELECT BIBLIOGRAPHY

Books and PhD Theses

Ahmed, I. *Islamism and Democracy in India. The Transformation of Jamaat-e-Islami.* New Delhi: Permanent Black, 2010.

Anandan, S. *Hindu Hriday Samrat.* Noida, India: Harper Collins, 2014.

Andersen, W., and S. Damle. *The Brotherhood in Saffron. The Rashtriya Swayamsevak Sangh and Hindu Revivalism,* New Delhi: Vistaar Publication, 1987.

———. *The RSS: A View to the Inside.* Delhi: Penguin, 2018.

Bamford, P. C. *Histories of the Non-Cooperation and Khilafat Movements.* 1925. Reprint, Delhi: Government of India Press, 1985.

Berenschot, W. *Riot Politics: Hindu-Muslim Violence and the Indian State.* London: Hurst, 2011.

Chatterji, A. *Violent Gods: Hindu Nationalism in India's Present; Narratives from Orissa.* Gurgaon, India: Three Essays, 2009.

Chatterji, B. C. *Anandmath.* 1882. Reprint, Delhi: Orient Paperbacks, 1992.

Chaturvedi, S. *I Am a Troll: Inside the Secret World of the BJP's Digital Army.* New Delhi: Juggernaut, 2016.

Collins, R. *Violence: A Micro-Sociological Theory.* Princeton, NJ: Princeton University Press, 2009.

Curran, J. A. *Militant Hinduism in Indian Politics.* New York: Institute of Pacific Affairs, 1955.

Debroy, B. *Gujarat: Governance for Growth and Development.* New Delhi: Academic Foundation, 2012.

Dev, N. *Modi to Moditva.* New Delhi: Manas, 2012.

Eck, D. L. *India: A Sacred Geography.* New York: Three Rivers, 2012.

Gandhi, M. K. *Autobiography: The Story of My Experiments with Truth.* Translated by Mahadev Desai. 1927. Reprint, Ahmedabad: Navajivan Trust, 1995.

———. *Indian Home Rule.* 5th English ed. Madras: Ganesh, 1922.

Ghassem-Fachandi, P. *Pogrom in Gujarat: Hindu Nationalism and Anti-Muslim Violence in India.* Princeton, NJ: Princeton University Press, 2012.

Ghosh, J., C. P. Chandrasekhar, and P. Patnaik. *Demonetisation Decoded: A Critique of India's Currency Experiment.* London: Routledge, 2017.

Golwalkar, M. S. *Bunch of Thoughts.* 1966. Reprint, Bangalore: Jagarana Prakashana, 1980.

———. *We, or Our Nationhood Defined.* 1938. Reprint, Nagpur, India: Bharat Prakashan, 1947.

Graham, B. *Hindu Nationalism and Indian Politics: The Origin and Development of the Bharatiya Jana Sangh.* Cambridge: Cambridge University Press, 1990.

Guichard, S. *The Construction of History and Nationalism in India: Textbooks, Controversies and Politics*. London: Routledge, 2010.

Gupta, S. *The Monk Who Became Chief Minister: The Definitive Biography of Yogi Adityanath*. New Delhi: Bloomsbury, 2017.

Jaffrelot, C. *The Hindu Nationalist Movement and Indian Politics, 1925 to the 1990s*. London: C. Hurst, 1996.

———. *India's Silent Revolution—The Rise of the Lower Castes in North India*. New York: Columbia University Press; London: Hurst; New Delhi: Permanent Black, 2003.

Jaffrelot, C., and P. Anil. *India's First Dictatorship: The Emergency, 1975–77*. London: Hurst, 2020.

Jagtiani, L. *Mumbai Terror Attacks*. New Delhi: Rupa, 2009.

Jenkins, R., and J. Manor. *Politics and the Right to Work: India's National Rural Employment Guarantee Act*. London: Hurst, 2017.

Jha, D. K. *Shadow Armies: Fringe Organizations and Foot Soldiers of Hindutva*. New Delhi: Juggernaut, 2017.

Jha, D. K., and K. Jha. *Ayodhya: The Dark Night; The Secret History of Ram's Appearance in Babri Masjid*. New Delhi: Harper Collins, 2012.

Jha, P. *How the BJP Wins: Inside India's Greatest Election Machine*. Delhi: Juggernaut, 2017.

Kamath, M. V., and Kalindi Randeri. *Narendra Modi: The Architect of a Modern State*. New Delhi: Rupa, 2009.

Katju, M. *Vishva Hindu Parishad and Indian politics*. Hyderabad: Orient Longman, 2003.

Khilnani, S. *The Idea of India*. London: Hamish Hamilton, 1997.

Kumar, R. *The Free Voice: On Democracy, Culture and the Nation*. New Delhi: Speaking Tiger, 2018.

Lokhande, S. B. *New Delhi, Communal Violence, Forced Migration and the State: Gujarat since 2002*. New Delhi: Cambridge University Press, 2015.

Maheshwari, M. *Art Attacks. Violence and Offence-Taking in India*. Delhi: Oxford University Press, 2019.

Mander, H. *Cry, My Beloved Country: Reflections on the Gujarat Carnage 2002 and Its Aftermath*. Noida, India: Rainbow, 2004.

Meghawanshi, B. *I Could Not Be Hindu: The Story of a Dalit in the RSS*. New Delhi: Navayana, 2020.

Mehta, V. *Lucknow Boy: A Memoir*. New Delhi: Penguin, 2011.

Minault, G. *The Khilafat Movement—Religious Symbolism and Political Mobilization in India*. New York: Columbia University Press, 1982.

Modi, N. *Social Harmony*. New Delhi: Prabhat Prakashan, 2015.

Mukhopadhyay, N. *Narendra Modi: The Man, the Times*. New Delhi: Tranquedar, 2013.

Nag, K. *The NaMo Story: A Political Life*. New Delhi: Roli Books, 2013.

Naqvi, S. *Being the Other: The Muslim in India*. New Delhi: Aleph, 2016.

Nussbaum, M. *The Clash Within: Democracy, Religious Violence and India's Future*. Cambridge, MA: Harvard University Press, 2007.

Pai, S., and S. Kumar. *Everyday Communalism: Riots in Contemporary Uttar Pradesh*. Delhi: Oxford University Press, 2018.

Pathak-Narain, P. *Godman to Tycoon: The Untold Story of Baba Ramdev*. New Delhi: Juggernaut, 2017.

Poonam, S. *Dreamers. How Young Indians Are Changing the World*. London: Hurst, 2018.

Ramaswamy, S. *The Goddess and the Nation: Mapping Mother India*. New Delhi: Zubaan, 2011.

Rudolph, L., and S. H. Rudolph. *In Pursuit of Lakshmi: The Political Economy of the Indian State*. Hyderabad: Orient Longman, 1987.

———. *The Modernity of Tradition: Political Development in India*. Chicago: University of Chicago Press, 1967.

Saavala, M. *Middle-Class Moralities: Everyday Struggle over Belonging and Prestige in India*. Hyderabad: Orient BlackSwan, 2010.

Sardesai, R. *The Election that Changed India*. New Delhi: Penguin India, 2014.

Savarkar, V. D. *Hindutva: Who Is a Hindu?* Mumbai: Asia, 1962 [1923].

Setalvad, T. *Foot Soldier of the Constitution: A Memoir*. New Delhi: LeftWord Books, 2017.

Shani, O. *Communalism, Caste and Hindu Nationalism*. Cambridge: Cambridge University Press, 2007.

Sharma, A. *The Backstage of Democracy: Exploring the Professionalisation of Politics in India*. PhD thesis, Oxford University, 2020.

Shraddhananda, Swami. *Hindu Sangathan: Savior of the Dying Race*. Delhi: Arjun, 1926.

Singh, S. S. *How to Win an Indian Election: What Political Parties Don't Want You to Know*. New Delhi: Penguin, 2019.

Swamy, S. *Hindus under Siege: The Way Out*. New Delhi: Har-Anand, 2006.

Tarlo, E. *Unsettling Memories: Narratives of the Emergency in Delhi*. London: Hurst, 2003.

Thachil, T. *Elite Parties, Poor Voters: How Social Services Win Votes in India*. Cambridge: Cambridge University Press, 2014.

Udaykumar, S. P. *"Presenting" the Past: Anxious History and Ancient Future in Hindutva India*. Westport, CT: Praeger, 2005.

Upadhyaya, D. *Integral Humanism*. New Delhi: Bharatiya Jana Sangh, 1965.

Valiani, A. *Militant Publics in India: Physical Culture and Violence in the Making of a Modern Polity*. New York: Palgrave Macmillan, 2011.

Vanaik, A. *The Rise of Hindu Authoritarianism: Secular Claims, Communal Realities*. London: Verso, 2017.

Wilkinson, S. I. *Army and Nation: The Military and Indian Democracy since Independence*. Cambridge, MA: Harvard University Press, 2015.

Yagnik, A., and S. Sheth. *The Shaping of Modern Gujarat*. Delhi: Penguin, 2005.

Documents and Reports

Centre for Media Studies. *Poll Expenditure: The 2019 Elections*. New Delhi, 2019. https://cmsindia.org/sites/default/files/2019-05/Poll-Expenditure-the-2019-elections-cms-report.pdf.

Common Cause and CSDS. *Status of Policing in India Report 2018*. Delhi: Lokniti-CSDS and Common Cause, 2018.

Concerned Citizens Tribunal. *Gujarat 2002: Crime against Humanity*. Vol. 2, *An Inquiry into the Carnage in Gujarat: Findings and Recommendations*. Mumbai: Citizens for Justice and Peace, 2002.

Freedom House. *Freedom in the World 2020: A Leaderless Struggle for Democracy*. Washington DC: Freedom House, 2020. https://freedomhouse.org/sites/default/files/2020-02/FIW_2020_REPORT_BOOKLET_Final.pdf.

Human Rights Watch. "Compounding Injustice: The Government's Failure to Redress Massacres in Gujarat." *Human Rights Watch* 15, no. 3 (July 2003). https://www.refworld.org/docid/3f4f59546.html.

———. "'We Have No Order to Save You.' State Participation and Complicity in Communal Violence in Gujarat." *Human Rights Watch* 14, no. 3 (April 2003). https://www.hrw.org/report/2002/04/30/we-have-no-orders-save-you/state-participation-and-complicity-communal-violence.

Report of the DMC Fact-Finding Committee on North-East Delhi Riots of February 2020. Delhi: Delhi Minorities Commission, Government of NCT of Delhi, July 2020. https://ia601906.us.archive.org/11/items/dmc-delhi-riot-fact-report-2020/-Delhi-riots-Fact-Finding-2020.pdf.

"Report of the Liberhan Ayodhya Commission of Inquiry—Full Text." *The Hindu*, November 24, 2009. https://www.thehindu.com/news/Report-of-the-Liberhan-Ayodhya-Commission-of-Inquiry-Full-Text/article16894055.ece.

RSF (Reporters without Borders). "Modi Tightens His Grip on the Media." In 2020 World Press Freedom Index, 2020. https://rsf.org/en/india.

V-Dem Institute. *Democracy for All? V-Dem Annual Democracy Report 2018*. Sweden: V-Dem Institute, University of Gothenburg, 2019. https://www.v-dem.net/media/filer_public/68/51/685150f0-47e1-4d03-97bc-45609c3f158d/v-dem_annual_dem_report_2018.pdf.

Edited Volumes

Azad, R. Nair, J. and M. Singh, eds. *What the Nation Really Needs to Know: The JNU Nationalism Lectures*. New Delhi: Harper Collins, 2016.

Blom, A., and Tawa Lama-Rewal, eds. *Emotions, Mobilisations and South Asian Politics*. London: Routledge, 2020.

BlueKraft Digital Foundation. *Mann ki baat: A Social Revolution on Radio*. New Delhi: BlueKraft Digital Foundation, 2019.

Dayal, J., ed. *Gujarat 2002: Untold and Re-told Stories of the Hindutva Lab*. Vol. 1. New Delhi: Media House, 2003.

De Souza, P. R., S. Palshikar, and Y. Yadav, eds. *State of Democracy in South Asia*. Delhi: Oxford University Press, 2008.

Engineer, A. A., ed. *The Gujarat Carnage*. Hyderabad: Orient Longman, 2003.

Gayer, L., and C. Jaffrelot, eds. *Muslims of India's Cities: Trajectories of Marginalization*. London: Hurst; New York: Columbia University Press; New Delhi: HarperCollins, 2012.

Gopal, S., ed. *Anatomy of a Confrontation: The Babri Masjid—Ramjanmabhumi Issue*. New Delhi: Viking, 1990.

———, ed. *Jawaharlal Nehru: An Anthology*. Delhi: Oxford University Press, 1980.

Jaffrelot, C., ed. *The Sangh Parivar: A Reader*. New Delhi: Oxford University Press, 2005.

Kapur, D., and M. Vaishnav, eds. *Costs of Democracy: Political Finance in India*. Delhi: Oxford University Press, 2018.

Ludden, D., ed. *Making India Hindu: Religion, Community, and the Politics of Democracy in India*. Delhi: Oxford University Press, 1996.

Shastri, S., S. Palshikar, and S. Kumar, eds. *State of Democracy in South Asia: Report II*. Jakkasandra, India: Jain University Press, 2017.

Varadarajan, S., ed. *Gujarat: The Making of a Tragedy*. New Delhi: Penguin India, 2002.

Book Chapters

Agnes, F. "Aggressive Hindu Nationalism: Contextualising the Triple Talaq Controversy." In *Majoritarian State: How Hindu Nationalism Is Changing India*, edited by Angana P. Chatterji, Thomas Blom Hansen, and Christophe Jaffrelot, 335–52. London: Hurst, 2019.

Asher, M. "Gujarat and Punjab: The Entrepreneurs Paradise and the Land of the Farmer." In *Power, Policy, and Protest: The Politics of India's Special Economic Zones*, edited by R. Jenkins, L. Kennedy, and P. Mukhopadhyay, 137–69. Oxford: Oxford University Press, 2014.

Banerjee, A., and I. Anand. "The NDA-II Regime and the Worsening Agrarian Crisis." In *A Quantum Leap in the Wrong Direction?*, edited by R. Azad, S. Chakraborty, S. Ramani, and D. Sinha, 66–88. Hyderabad: Orient Blackswann, 2019.

Bhargava, R. "Indian Secularism: An Alternative, Trans-Cultural Ideal." In *The Promise of India's Secular Democracy*, 285–97. Delhi: Oxford University Press, 2010.

Das, S. K. "Institutions of Internal Accountability." In *Public Institutions in India*, edited by D. Kapur and P. B. Mehta, 128–57. Oxford: Oxford University Press, 2005.

Dholakia, A., and R. Dholakia. "Policy Reform in Economic Sectors." In *The Making of Miracles in Indian States: Andhra Pradesh, Bihar and Gujarat*, edited by A. Panagariya and M. G. Rao, 251–52. New Delhi: Oxford University Press, 2015.

Graham, B. D. "The Congress and Hindu Nationalism." In *The Indian National Congress—Centenary Hindsights*, edited by D. A. Low, 170–87. Delhi: Oxford University Press, 1988.

Gupta, S., and C. Jaffrelot. "The Bajrang Dal: The New Hindu Nationalist Brigade." In *Living with Secularism: The Destiny of India's Muslims*, edited by Mushirul Hasan, 197–222. Delhi: Manohar, 2007.

Hirway, I., N. Shah, and R. Sharma. "Political Economy of Subsidies and Incentives to Industries in Gujarat." In *Growth or Developmen: Which Way Is Gujarat Going?*, edited by I. Hirway, A. Shah, and G. Shah, 139–92. New Delhi: Oxford University Press, 2014.

Jaffrelot, C. "The Bajrang Dal: The New Hindu Nationalist Brigade." In *Living with Secularism: The Destiny of India's Muslims*, edited by Mushirul Hasan, 197–222. Delhi: Manohar, 2007.

———. "The BJP at the Centre: A Central and Centrist Party?" In *The BJP and the Compulsions of Politics*, edited by Thomas Blom Hansen and Christophe Jaffrelot, 356–63. Delhi: Oxford University Press, 2001.

———. "Business-Friendly Gujarat under Narendra Modi—the Implications of a New Political Economy." In *Business and Politics in India*, edited by Christophe Jaffrelot, Atul Kohli, and Kanta Murali, 211–33. New York: Oxford University Press, 2019.

———. "Composite Culture Is Not Multiculturalism: A Study of the Indian Constituent Assembly Debates." In *India and the Politics of Developing Countries, Essays in Memory of Myron Weiner*, edited by A. Varshney, 126–49. New Delhi: Sage, 2004.

———. "A *De Facto* Ethnic Democracy? Obliterating and Targeting the Other, Hindu Vigilantes and the Ethno-state." In *Majoritarian State: How Hindu Nationalism Is Changing India*, edited by Angana Chatterji, Thomas Blom Hansen, and Christophe Jaffrelot, 41–67. London: Hurst, 2019.

———. "From Holy Sites to Web Sites: Hindu Nationalism, from Sacred Territory to Diasporic Ethnicity." In *Religions, Nations, and Transnationalism in Multiple Modernities*, edited by Patrick Michel, Adam Possamai, and Bryan Turner, 153–74. Basingstoke, UK: Palgrave, 2017.

———. "Hindu Nationalism and the Social Welfare Strategy." In *Development, Civil Society and Faith-Based Organisations: Bridging the Sacred and the Secular*, edited by G. Clarke and M. Jennings, 240–59. New York: Palgrave, 2008.

———. "The Hindu Nationalists and Power." In *The Oxford Companion to Politics in India*, edited by N. G. Jayal and P. B. Mehta, 205–18. Delhi: Oxford University Press, 2010.

———. "The Idea of the Hindu Race in the Writings of Hindu Nationalist Ideologues in the 1920s and 1930s: A Concept between Two Cultures." In *The Concept of Race in South Asia*, edited by P. Robb, 327–54. Delhi: Oxford University Press, 1995.

———. "India: The Politics of (Re)conversion to Hinduism of Christian Aboriginals." In *Annual Review of the Sociology of Religion*, vol. 2, edited by Patrick Michel and Enzo Pace, 197–215. Leiden, Netherlands: Brill, 2011.

———. "Introduction." In *Rise of the Plebeians? The Changing Face of Indian Legislative Assemblies*, edited by Christophe Jaffrelot and S. Kumar, 1–23. New Delhi: Routledge, 2009.

———. "Militant Hindus and the Conversion Issue (1885–1990): From Shuddhi to Dharm Parivartan. The Politization and the Diffusion of an 'Invention of Tradition.'" In *The Resources of History: Tradition and Narration in South Asia*, edited by Jackie Assayag, 127–52. Paris: EFEO, 1999.

———. "The Militias of Hindutva: Between Communal Violence, Terrorism and Cultural Policing." In *Armed Militias of South Asia. Fundamentalists, Maoists and Separatists*, edited by Laurent Gayer and Christophe Jaffrelot, translated by C. Schoch, G. Elliott, and R. Leverdier, 199–235. London: Hurst, 2009.

———. "The Muslims of Gujarat during Narendra Modi's Chief Ministership." In *Indian Muslims: Struggling for Equality and Citizenship*, edited by Riaz Hasan, 235–58. Melbourne: Melbourne University Publishing, 2016.

———. "The Muslims of India." In *India since 1950: Society, Politics, Economy and Culture*, edited by C. Jaffrelot, 564–80. New Delhi: Yatra Books, 2011.

———. "Opposing Gandhi: Hindu Nationalism and Political Violence." In *Violence/Non-Violence: Some Hindu Perspectives*, edited by Denis Vidal, Gilles Tarabout, and Eric Meyer, 299–324. Delhi: Manohar, 2003.

———. "The Political Guru: The Guru as Éminence Grise." In *The Guru in South Asia: New Interdisciplinary Perspectives*, edited by J. Copeman and A. Ikegame, 80–96. London: Routledge, 2013.

———. "The Politics of Processions and Hindu-Muslim Riots." In *Community Conflicts and the State in India*, edited by A. Kohli and A. Basu, 58–92. Delhi: Oxford University Press, 1998.

———. "The Sangh Parivar between Sanskritization and Social Engineering." In *The BJP and the Compulsions of Politics in India Today*, edited by T. B. Hansen and Christophe Jaffrelot, 22–71 and 267–90. Delhi: Oxford University Press, 1998.

———. "The Vishva Hindu Parishad: A Nationalist but Mimetic Attempt at Federating the Hindu Sects." In *Charisma and Canon: Essays on the Religious History of the Indian Subcontinent*, edited by V. Dalmia, A. Malinar, and M. Christof, 388–411. Delhi: Oxford University Press, 2001.

———. "The Vishva Hindu Parishad: Structures and Strategies." In *Religion, Globalization and Political Culture in the Third World*, edited by J. Haynes, 191–212. London: Macmillan, 1999.

———. "'Why Should We Vote?' The Indian Middle Class and the Functioning of the World's Largest Democracy." In *Patterns of Middle Class Consumption in India and China*, edited by C. Jaffrelot and P. van der Veer, 35–54. New Delhi: Sage, 2008

Jaffrelot, C., and C. Thomas. "Facing Ghettoisation in 'Riot-City': Old Ahmedabad and Juhapura between Victimisation and Self-Help." In *Muslims of India's Cities. Trajectories of Marginalization*, edited by Laurent Gayer and Christophe Jaffrelot, 43–79. London: Hurst, 2012.

Jaffrelot, C., and L. Tillin. "Populism in India." In *The Oxford Handbook of Populism*, edited by Paul Taggart, Cristobal Rovira Kaltwasser, Paulina Ochoa Espejo, and Pierre Ostiguy, 179–94. Oxford: Oxford University Press, 2017.

Kapur, A. "Deity to Crusader: The Changing Iconography of Ram." In *Hindus and Others: The Question of Identity in India Today*, edited by Gyanendra Pandey, 74–109. New Delhi: Viking, 1993.

Khosla, M., and A. Padmanabhan. "The Supreme Court." In *Rethinking Public Institutions in India*, edited by D. Kapur, P. B. Mehta, and M. Vaishnav, 104–38. New Delhi: Oxford University Press, 2017.

Mehta, N. "Ashis Nandy vs. the State of Gujarat: Authoritarian Developmentalism, Democracy and the Politics of Narendra Modi." In *Gujarat beyond Gandhi: Identity, Society and Conflict*, edited by Nalin Mehta and Mona G. Mehta, 577–96. New Delhi: Routledge, 2010.

Morris-Jones, W. H. "India's Political Idioms." In *Politics and Society in India*, edited by C. H. Philips, 133–54. London: George Allen and Unwin, 1963.

Palshikar, S. "Politics of India's Middle Class." In *Middle Class Values in India and Western Europe*, edited by Imtiaz Ahmad and Helmut Reifeld, 171–93. New York: Routledge, 2018.

———. "Towards Hegemony: The BJP beyond Electoral Dominance." In *Majoritarian State: How Hindu Nationalism Is Changing India*, edited by Angana Chatterji, Thomas Blom Hansen, and Christophe Jaffrelot, 101–16. London: Hurst, 2019.

Pandey, G. "Rallying Round the Cow: Sectarian Strife in the Bhojpuri Region, c. 1888–1917." In *Subaltern Studies II*, edited by Ranajit Guha, 60–129. Delhi: Oxford University Press, 1983.

Puri, J. "Sculpting the Saffron Body: Yoga, Hindutva, and the International Marketplace." In *Majoritarian State: How Hindu Nationalism Is Changing India*, edited by Angana Chatterji, Thomas Blom Hansen, and Christophe Jaffrelot, 317. London: Hurst, 2019.

Rajamani, I. "Mobilising Anger in Andhra Pradesh." In *Emotions, Mobilisations and South Asian Politics*, edited by Amélie Blom and Tawa Lama-Rewal, 187–204. London: Routledge, 2019.

Reddy R. "Media in Contemporary India: Journalism Transformed into a Commodity." In *Business and Politics in India*, edited by C. Jaffrelot, A. Kohli, and K. Murali, 183–210. New York: Oxford University Press, 2019.

Shah, G. "Goebbel's Propaganda and Governance: The 2009 Lok Sabha Elections in Gujarat." In *India's 2009 Elections: Coalition Politics, Party Competition and Congress Continuity*, edited by Paul Wallace and Ramashray Roy, 167–91. New Delhi: Sage, 2011.

Sinha, A. "India's New Porous State: Blurred Boundaries and the Evolving Business-State Relationship." In *Business and Politics in India*, edited by Christophe Jaffrelot, Atul Kohli, and Kanta Murali, 50–94. New York: Oxford University Press, 2019.

Sridharan, R. "Institutions of Internal Accountability." In *Rethinking Public Institutions in India*, edited by D. Kapur, P. Mehta, and M. Vaishnav, 269–96. New Delhi: Oxford University Press, 2017.

Tambiah, S. J. "The Crisis of Secularism in India." In *Secularism and Its Critics*, edited by R. Bhargava, 422–23. Delhi: Oxford University Press, 1998.

Thorat, S. K. "Dalits in Post-2014 India: Wide Gap between Promise and Action." In *Majoritarian State: How Hindu Nationalism Is Changing India*, edited by Angana Chatterji, Thomas Blom Hansen, and Christophe Jaffrelot, 217–36. London: Hurst, 2019.

Verma, A. "The Police in India: Design, Performance and Adaptability." In *Public Institutions in India: Performance and Design*, edited by D. Kapur and P. B. Mehta, 209–11. Delhi: Oxford University Press, 2005.

Verniers, G. "The Resistance of Regionalism: BJP's Limitations and the Resilience of State Parties." In *India's 2014 Elections: A Modi-Led BJP Sweep*, edited by Paul Wallace, 28–47. New Delhi: Sage, 2015.

Journal Articles

Adeney, K., and W. Swenden. "Power Sharing in the World's Largest Democracy: Informal Consociationalism in India (and Its Decline?)." *Swiss Political Science Review* 25, no. 4 (2019): 450–75.

Ahmed, H. "Muzaffarnagar 2013: Meanings of Violence." *Economic and Political Weekly* 48, no. 40 (October 2013): 10–12.

Aiyar, Y. "Leveraging Welfare Politics." *Journal of Democracy* 30, no. 4 (October 2019): 78–88.

Aiyar, Y., and L. Tillin. "'One Nation,' BJP, and the Future of Indian Federalism." *India Review* 19, no. 2 (March–April 2020): 117–35.

Chandrashekhar, C. P., and J. Ghosh. "The Banking Conundrum: Non-Performing Assets and Neo-Liberal Reform." *Economic and Political Weekly* 53, no. 13 (March 31, 2018): 129–37.

Chatterjee, M. "The Ordinary Life of Hindu Supremacy: In Conversation with a Bajrang Dal Activist." *Economic and Political Weekly* 53, no. 4 (January 27, 2018): 1–8.

Chaturvedi, S., D. Gellner, and S. K. Pandey. "Politics in Gorakhpur since the 1920s: The Making of a Safe 'Hindu' Constituency." *Contemporary South Asia* 27, no. 1 (2019): 40–57.

Chhibber, P., and S. Ostermann. "The BJP's Fragile Mandate: Modi and Vote Mobilizers in the 2014 General Elections." *Studies in Indian Politics* 2, no. 2 (2014): 1–15.

Chhibber, P., and R. Verma. "The Rise of the Second Dominant Party System in India: BJP's New Social Coalition in 2019." *Studies in Indian Politics* 7, no. 2 (2019): 131–48.

Dalton, D. "Gandhi: Ideology and Authority." *Modern Asian Studies* 3, no. 4 (1969): 377–93.

Deshpande, A., and R. Ramachandran. "The 10% Quota: Is Caste Still an Indicator of Backward-ness?" *Economic and Political Weekly* 54, no. 13 (March 30, 2019): 27–32.

Deshpande, R., L. Tillin, and K. K. Kailash. "The BJP's Welfare Schemes: Did They Make a Difference in the 2019 Elections?" *Studies in Indian Politics* 7, no. 2 (2019): 219–33.

Farooqi, A. "Political Representation of a Minority: Muslim Representation in Contemporary India." *India Review* 19, no. 2 (2020): 153–75.

Favarel-Garrigues, G., and L. Gayer. "Violer la loi pour maintenir l'ordre: Le vigilantisme en débat." *Politix* 29, no. 115 (2016): 7–33.

Flaten, L. "Spreading Hindutva through Education: Still a Priority for the BJP?" *India Review* 16, no. 4 (2017): 377–400.

Graff, V., and J. Galonnier. "Hindu-Muslim Communal Riots in India II (1986–2011)." *Encyclopedia of Mass Violence*, August 20, 2013. https://www.sciencespo.fr/mass-violence-war-massacre-resistance/en/document/hindu-muslim-communal-riots-india-ii-1986-2011.html.

Heath, O. "Communal Realignment and Support for the BJP, 2009–2019." *Contemporary South Asia* 28, no. 2 (2020): 195–208.

Heath, O., G. Verniers, and S. Kumar. "Do Muslim Voters Prefer Muslim Candidates? Co-religiosity and Voting Behaviour in India." *Electoral Studies* 38 (June 2015): 10–18.

Heller, P., and L. Fernandes. "Hegemonic Aspirations: New Middle Class Politics and India's Democracy in Comparative Perspective." *Critical Asian Studies* 38, no. 4 (2006): 495–522.

Ingole, A. "Movements as Politics: Bhima Koregaon in the Times of Hindutva." *Economic and Political Weekly* 53, no. 2 (January 13, 2018): 12–14.

Jacob, H. *Toward a Kashmir Endgame? How India and Pakistan Could Negotiate a Lasting Solution.* United States Institute of Peace, special report no. 474, August 2020.

Jaffrelot, C. "Abhinav Bharat, the Malegaon blast and Hindu nationalism: Resisting and Emulating Islamist Terrorism." *Economic and Political Weekly* 45, no. 36 (September 4–10, 2010): 51–58.

———. "Class and Caste in the 2019 Indian Election—Why Have So Many Poor Started Voting for Modi?" *Studies in Indian Politics* 7, no. 2 (November 2019): 1–12.

———. "The Class Element in the 2014 Indian Election and the BJP's Success with Special Reference to the Hindi Belt." In "Understanding India's 2014 Elections," special issue, *Studies in Indian Politics* 3, no. 1 (June 2015): 19–38.

———. "The Congress in Gujarat (1917–1969): Conservative Face of a Progressive Party." In "Political Conservatism in India," special issue, *Studies in Indian Politics* 5, no. 2 (November 2017): 248–61.

———. "La dialectique des terrorismes en Inde depuis 2001: La 'main de l'étranger,' les islamistes et les nationalistes hindous." *Critique Internationale* 2, no. 47 (2010): 93–110.

———. "Gujarat 2002: What Justice for the Victims?" *Economic and Political Weekly* 47, no. 8 (February 25, 2012): 77–89.

———. "Gujarat Elections: The Sub-Text of Modi's 'Hattrick'—High Tech Populism and the 'Neo-Middle Class.'" *Studies in Indian Politics* 1, no. 1 (June 2013): 79–96.

———. "Hindu Nationalism: Strategic Syncretism in Ideology Building." *Indian Journal of Social Science* 5, no. 42 (August 1992): 594–617.

———. "The Hindu Nationalist Reinterpretation of Pilgrimage in India: The Limits of *Yatra* Politics." *Nations and Nationalism* 15, no. 1 (2009): 1–19.

———. "How Can We Model Ethnic Democracy? An Application to Contemporary India." *Nations and Nationalism*, July 24, 2020, 1–19.

———. "Indian Democracy: The Rule of Law on Trial." *India Review* 1, no. 1 (January 2002): 77–121.

———. "Malegaon: Who Is above the Law?" *Economic and Political Weekly* 47, no. 29 (July 21, 2012): 17–18.

———. "The Modi-centric BJP 2014 Election Campaign: New Techniques and Old Tactics." *Contemporary South Asia* 23, no. 2 (June 2015): 151–66.

———. "Narendra Modi between Hindutva and Subnationalism: The Gujarati *Asmita* of a Hindu Hriday Samrat." *India Review* 15, no. 2 (2016): 196–217.

———. "Quota for Patels? The Neo-middleclass Syndrome and the (Partial) Return of Caste Politics in Gujarat." *Studies in Indian Politics* 4, no. 2 (2016): 1–15.

———. "Refining the Moderation Thesis: Two Religious Parties and Indian Democracy; The Jana Sangh and the BJP between Hindutva Radicalism and Coalition Politics." *Democratization* 20, no. 5 (2013): 876–94.

———. "The Roots and Varieties of Political Conservatism in India." In "Political Conservatism in India," special issue, *Studies in Indian Politics* 5, no. 2 (November 2017): 205–17.

———. "What Gujarat Model? Growth without Development and with Socio-political Polarisation." *South Asia* 38, no. 4 (2015): 820–38.

Jaffrelot, C., V. Dutoya, R. Kanchana, and G. Rathore. "Understanding Muslim Voting Behaviour." *Seminar*, no. 602 (2009): 43–48.

Jaffrelot, C., and S. Kumar. "The Impact of Urbanization on the Electoral Results of the 2014 Indian Elections: With Special Reference to the BJP Vote." In "Understanding India's 2014 Elections," special issue, *Studies in Indian Politics* 3, no. 1 (June 2015): 39–49.

Jaffrelot, C., and M. Maheshwari. "Paradigmatic Shifts by the RSS? Lessons from Aseemanand's Confession." *Economic and Political Weekly* 46, no. 6 (February 5, 2011): 42–46.

Jaffrelot, C., and G. Verniers. "The BJP's 2019 Election Campaign: Not Business as Usual." *Contemporary South Asia* 28, no. 2 (2020): 155–77.

———. "A New Party System or a New Political System?" *Contemporary South Asia* 28, no. 2 (2020): 141–54.

Jagannathan, S., and R. K. Rai. "Organisational Wrongs, Moral Anger and the Temporality of Crisis." *Journal of Business Ethics* 141, no. 4 (2016): 709–30.

———. "Organizing Sovereign Power: Police and the Performance of Bare Bodies." *Organization* 22, no. 6 (2015): 810–83.

Kothari, R. "The Congress 'System' in India." *Asian Survey* 4, no. 12 (December 1964): 1161–73.

Lahiri, A. "The Great Indian Demonetization." *Journal of Economic Perspectives* 34, no. 1 (Winter 2020): 55–74.

Martelli, J. "The Spillovers of Competition: Value-Based Activism and Political Cross-Fertilization in an Indian Campus." *SAMAJ: South Asia Multidisciplinary Academic Journal* 22 (2020): https://journals.openedition.org/samaj/6501.

Martelli, J., and B. Ari. "From One Participant Cohort to Another: Surveying Inter-Generational Politicial Incubation in an Indian University." *India Review* 17, no. 3 (2018): 263–300.

Martelli, J., and K. Parkar. "Diversity, Democracy, and Dissent: A Study on Student Politics in JNU." *Economic and Political Weekly* 53, no. 11 (March 17, 2018): 1–30.

Nawani, Disha. "Modifying School Textbooks." *Economic and Political Weekly* 53, no. 29 (July 21, 2018): 12–15.

Palshikar, S., and K. C. Suri. "India's 2014 Lok Sabha Elections." *Economic and Political Weekly* 49, no. 39 (2014): 43–48.

Prabal, S. "Sanatan Sanstha and Its Hindutva Designs." *Economic and Political Weekly* 53, no. 41 (October 13, 2018): 17–20.

Punwani, J. "Myths and Prejudices about 'Love Jihad.'" *Economic and Political Weekly* 49, no. 42 (October 18, 2014): 12–15.

Roselli, J. "The Self-Image of Effeteness: Physical Education and Nationalism in Nineteenth Century Bengal." *Past and Present* 86 (1980): 121–48.

Roul, A. "Students Islamic Movement of India: A Profile." *Terrorism Monitor* 4, no. 7 (April 6, 2006): 9–10.

Roy, A. "The Citizenship (Amendment) Bill, 2016 and the Aporia of Citizenship." *Economic and Political Weekly* 54, no. 49 (December 14, 2019): 28–34.

Shah, A. M., P. J. Patel, and L. Lobo. "A Heady Mix: Gujarati and Hindu Pride." *Economic and Political Weekly* 43, no. 8 (February 23 2008): 19–22.

Shah, G. "Contestation and Negotiations: Hindutva Sentiments and Temporal Interests in Gujarat Elections." *Economic and Political Weekly* 37, no. 48 (November 30, 2002): 4838–43.

Shastri, S. "The Modi Factor in the 2019 Lok Sabha Election: How Critical Was It to the BJP's Victory?" *Studies in Indian Politics* 7, no. 2 (2019): 206–18.

Sikand, Y. "Islamist Assertion in Contemporary India: The Case of the Students Islamic Movement of India." *Journal of Muslim Minority Affairs* 23, no. 2 (October 2003): 335–45.

Sircar, N. "The Politics of Vishwas: Political Mobilization in the 2019 National Election." *Contemporary South Asia* 28, no. 2 (2020): 178–94.

Stokes, B., D. Manevich, and H. Chwe. "Indians Satisfied with Country's Direction but Worry about Crime, Terrorism." *Pew Research Center, Global Attitudes and Trends*, November 15, 2017, 1–45.

Sundar, N. "Academic Freedom and Indian Universities." *Economic and Political Weekly* 53, no. 24 (June 16, 2018): 48–57.

Suryanarayan, P. "When Do the Poor Vote for the Right Wing and Why? Status Hierarchy and Vote Choice in the Indian States." *Comparative Political Studies* 52, no. 2 (2019): 209–45.

Upadhyay, R. "Students Islamic Movement of India (SIMI)." South Asia Analysis Group Paper 825, October 30, 2003.

Van Der Veer, P. "'God Must Be Liberated!' A Hindu Liberation Movement in Ayodhya." *Modern Asian Studies* 21, no. 1 (1987): 283–301.

Verniers, G., and C. Jaffrelot. "The Reconfiguration of India's Political Elite: Profiling the 17th Lok Sabha." *Contemporary South Asia* 28, no. 2 (2020): 242–54.

INDEX